www.brookscole.com

www.brookscole.com is the World Wide Web site for Brooks/Cole and is your direct source to dozens of online resources.

At *www.brookscole.com* you can find out about supplements, demonstration software, and student resources. You can also send email to many of our authors and preview new publications and exciting new technologies.

www.brookscole.com
Changing the way the world learns®

Exploring the Digital Domain

An Introduction
to Digital Information Fluency

Second Edition

Ken Abernethy
Tom Allen

Furman University

THOMSON

™

BROOKS/COLE

Australia • Canada • Mexico • Singapore • Spain
United Kingdom • United States

THOMSON
BROOKS/COLE

Publisher: *Bill Stenquist*
Acquisitions Editor: *Kallie Swanson*
Editorial Assistant: *Aarti Jayaraman*
Technology Project Manager: *Burke Taft*
Executive Marketing Manager: *Tom Ziolkowski*
Marketing Assistant: *Jennifer Gee*
Advertising Project Manager: *Vicky Wan*

Print/Media Buyer: *Rebecca Cross*
Editorial Production Project Manager: *Kelsey McGee*
Permissions Editor: *Bob Kauser*
Interior Design: *Lisa Delgado*
Cover Image and Design: *Gopa & Ted2, Inc.*
Cover Printing, Printing and Binding: *Quebecor World-Dubuque*
Composition and Production: *Graphic World, Inc.*

Printed in the United States of America
1   2   3   4   5   6   7   07   06   05   04   03

For more information about our products, contact us at:
Thomson Learning Academic Resource Center
1-800-423-0563
For permission to use material from this text, contact us by:
Phone: 1-800-730-2214
Fax: 1-800-730-2215
Web: http://www.thomsonrights.com

Brooks/Cole–Thomson Learning
10 Davis Drive
Belmont, CA 94002
USA

Asia
Thomson Learning
5 Shenton Way #01-01
UIC Building
Singapore 068808

Australia/New Zealand
Thomson Learning
102 Dodds Street
Southbank, Victoria 3006
Australia

Canada
Nelson
1120 Birchmount Road
Toronto, Ontario M1K 5G4
Canada

Europe/Middle East/Africa
Thomson Learning
High Holborn House
50/51 Bedford Row
London WC1R 4LR
United Kingdom

Library of Congress Control Number: 2003113927

ISBN 0-534-40707-2

Dedication

To my grandchildren,
Kathleen, Nathan, Preston, and "Josephine."
—KCA

To my children,
John and Kara.
—JTA

Brief Contents

Contents

PART TWO   Text and Numbers

Chapter 7   Managing Information

PART THREE   Sights and Sounds

Chapter 8   Digital Images

Chapter 9   Making Pictures with Computers

Chapter 10   The Sound and the Fury—Digital Style

PART FOUR   Inside the Computer

PART FIVE   Running the Show—Software

Chapter 14   Developing Applications

Chapter 15   Operating Systems

PART SIX   Networks

Chapter 16   Data Communications

PART SEVEN   Putting Information to Work

Preface

Computer Literacy, Information Fluency, and the Digital Generation

In a few years, most of us have changed our opinions dramatically about computers and computing. The machines that once were "curiosities," "interesting," or even "intimidating" have become "necessities" and "must-haves" for our homes and offices. This remarkable change in attitudes is due to the equally remarkable adaptability of computer systems to perform myriad tasks quickly and easily. Even the most vocal antitechnologues have become addicted to the conveniences of electronic document preparation and electronic mail. Surprisingly, though, few computer users are able to exploit many of the newer capabilities that these machines offer. Most users are familiar with word processing, but only a few have the know-how to publish documents on the World Wide Web. The worlds of image processing, digital sound, intelligent agents, wireless computing, and blogs are as still undiscovered territory for many. Although most computer users would swear to the utility of their systems, the bottom line is that only a fraction of its riches have been mined by many of them. To be able to exploit these new and interesting capabilities, computer users must achieve a new standard of computer literacy. This book is our attempt to push the old boundaries of computer literacy into new ground.

Computer literacy is a slippery notion. The term functions much like the terms *democracy, freedom,* and *common sense.* Just about everyone knows precisely what he or she means, but no one seems to be able to agree on that meaning. And like democracy and freedom, we all agree that computer literacy is a good thing, even if we don't mean quite the same thing by it. If you are not convinced of these claims, examine the proliferation and variety of computer literacy courses on our college and university campuses. Today, most of these courses have evolved to include a wide assortment of topics and skills. They include a few apparent fundamentals: studying practical software such as word processing, spreadsheets, and (recently) Internet applications; some basic concepts about computer technology; and a consideration of social and ethical issues related to computing and information management. Many courses address a few other topics such as the history of computing, software development, perhaps some type of elementary programming experience. But the variety in which these topics are packaged and delivered is dizzying.

To complicate matters more, computer literacy today is a swiftly moving target. What skills should we choose to develop? In the area of applications, for example, software vendors are continually upgrading, revising, and replacing their products with new features and looks. You can be sure that as soon as you gain some level of comfort and familiarity with one product, it will be entirely replaced by some new version. If students acquire training on specific applications, these skills will depreciate as rapidly as the software versions on which they are based. Instead of training, students would profit more from a conceptual understanding of what these applications are about. Armed with this knowledge, they might better adapt to the changing environment.

Hardware platforms are changing rapidly as well. Nearly all desktop computer systems today have increased storage and performance capacities. These newer systems make it possible to perform meaningful work in such areas as sound, image, and video processing—work that would have been unthinkable a few years ago.

Several years ago it would also have been impractical to discuss computing applications without recognizing the great differences in their look, feel, and functionality on different hardware/software platforms. But today, due in some measure to market forces and to the influences of networking for desktop systems, there is a slow but evident convergence among software applications. In short time, Internet access has evolved from a curiosity to a mainstay for a large percentage of our population. The popularity of the World Wide Web is the chief reason for this explosive growth. The remarkable ease and utility of publishing on the Web has had a significant impact on the way that we organize and deliver information locally and abroad. (In fact, these changes are so rapid that they outpace any attempt to describe their status and significance with traditional printed media.) The impact on computing literacy is obvious. Several years ago, most people would have considered knowledge and familiarity with Internet tools to be interesting but strictly a frill or optional. Today, students demand this knowledge as part of the basic package.

Since our first two editions (beta and first), others have joined the movement for rethinking information technology education. The Association of Colleges and Research Libraries of the American Library Association (ACRL) has defined a broader standard of **information literacy.** Recently, the National Research Council (NRC) has raised the bar even higher in advocating a new standard, **information fluency.** (Our Web site has links to these and other organizations as well as the documents referenced here.)

Information literacy is "the set of skills needed to find, retrieve, analyze, and use information." The ACRL emphasizes that while technology can help us solve many of our problems in managing information, it has also created obstacles. The literate person today lives in a continual state of "data smog"—a glut of data—passing as information. Accordingly, the challenge today is separating the wheat from the chaff rather than finding the buried treasure.

The NRC has advocated information fluency because literacy "is too modest a goal in the presence of rapid change. . . . A better solution is for the individual to plan to adapt to the changes in technology." Besides basic skills, being fluent means understanding foundational concepts on which the technology is derived and developing higher-level intellectual capabilities for applying the technology. The NRC rightly emphasizes that information fluency is itself dynamic and a lifelong goal.

There is a third factor to consider, too. In recent years, we have noticed a significant change in the background and experiences of our students. Many of our students have literally grown up using computers; they are indeed the digital generation. In the past, students were intimidated and mystified with the technology. Today's generation of students treat computers no differently than other common household appliances. But greater experience does not necessarily imply greater knowledge. In fact, familiarity with the technology has bred a certain degree of indifference for many. The previous generation could be motivated by the novelty of the technology itself. For the current generation, this puts the cart before the horse. As the ACRL and NRC argue, we need to motivate our students to recognize the uses and benefits of digital information technology. In other words, our students should be directed to the object of that technology, managing information. Certainly digital information technology has always been about information; but sometimes we lose sight of that in teaching the technology.

On the other hand, some of our digital generation students are indeed knowledgeable about topics that would be considered advanced several years ago (e.g., Web hosting and publishing, household networks, imaging with digital cameras, etc.). Thus, we should also serve our (nonprofessional) students who seek a deeper understanding about special topics of interest and experience.

In short, our audience has differing needs with respect to breadth and depth. Even the elevated standard of information fluency depends more on context than legislation. For example, what constitutes information fluency for a graphic artist is very different from that of a medical health professional. Depth of understanding is required for both, but the skills and concepts are very different. Our target is not only a moving one, but one that is multifaceted.

We think that there are a number of important lessons to be learned from considering these issues. First, and obviously, the current continuum of computer literacy/information literacy/information fluency must take into account the changes in the computing environments of the workplace and home. They should incorporate more about digital media and networking. Moreover, whatever the baseline concept of computer literacy means, it probably should not be bound to particular systems, software versions, and so on. These are static goals, and our target is a moving one. For similar reasons, it is much more practical to study the applications by what they do rather than the idiosyncrasies of how they appear on a particular machine. All these point to a standard that is both more conceptual and more dynamic than past ones. We have wrestled with many of these issues on our own campus. This text is derived from our experiences offering a computer literacy course to a clientele that is capable, somewhat experienced, and inquisitive about the whys and wherefores as much as the hows and how-tos. We do not presume to have resolved the issue of what is computer literacy (or any of these other terms) once and for all. However, we believe that our approach has benefits and can be applied to other, similar situations.

This approach is both thematic and conceptual. The organizing theme for our book is that the computer system is not merely a tool but rather itself a medium for representing, storing, manipulating, and communicating different forms of information: text, numbers, graphics, images, sounds, and video. The common denominator for these differing forms of information is the fact that they must be digitized to be stored on and handled by our computers. Data within this digital domain can be studied, combined, transformed, and transmitted with an apparent ease that belies the true complexities of these tasks. But not all is golden—information converted to digital form must bear some costs: approximations, alterations, and limits. The digerati (a person literate in digital media) understands the nature of digital media—both their uses and limitations. Thus, this book focuses on information and its representation via digital media rather than the customary survey of applications software designed to process these media.

We have tried to adopt a conceptual approach to treating these topics as well. Our assumption is that if you explain why something behaves the way it does, a quick study can apply this knowledge to related instances. We believe that it is more useful, for example, to understand the basic functions of an operating system than to learn a specific set of commands to invoke these functions. In the same vein, what you learn about Word Whiz 7.32 will be yesterday's news; but what you learn about document preparation in general and such specific issues as character coding and file formats will survive. Of course, concepts without instances are vague. So, we have offered a number of concrete examples for these general ideas. This naturally includes specific operating systems and software products. However, these are illustrations, and we make no pretense to be treating any of these software systems completely.

We offer a somewhat deeper treatment of some topics than often found in typical computer literacy texts. Our approach, however, is incremental. We introduce basic concepts in plain language. These concepts are revisited later and developed further. For the inquisitive, we offer more technical background that may be optionally consulted. This so-called "spiraling" approach, we believe, is effective for meeting needs for different degrees of sophistication. The role of the instructor is integral for this text. There are many paths through this material, and the instructor should serve as a guide for both the class and individuals within it.

Text Organization and Features

The textbook contains seven units. Each unit has several chapters organized by a unifying theme. The first unit introduces the student to the digital domain: the world of digital information technology. The student is introduced to the concepts of information, information technology, digital information technology, and digital media. Chapters on the computing basics and networking provide an introduction to foundational concepts, which will be developed further in the rest of the text. The second unit features the traditional media of text and numbers as well as databases that often integrate them. Digital imaging, graphics, sound, music, and video are the focus of the third unit. The fourth unit extends the foundation laid for understanding how computers can accomplish these amazing feats. Conventional hardware topics are treated, but the perspective is dominated by the types of desktop systems that the student is likely to encounter in the lab, at work, and at home.

The fifth unit features chapters on programming and how operating systems manage our computers. The sixth unit contains chapters on data communications and networks—large and small. The final unit culminates with some larger issues that are best considered after achieving some maturity: data compression, data security, cryptography, and emerging digital technologies.

It is important to emphasize that this text exists in two separate dimensions: in print and online. A number of textbooks claim an accompanying Web site, but these are often add-ons or frills to the printed material. This text is very different. The printed book and Web site are integral. In some instances, the printed text acts as an interface to the online material. For example, a basic concept or issue is introduced in the printed text; development, examples, and applications are found on the Web site. These are designated as "*Discovery*" sections—i.e., "*Discovering More About* ____." The Web offers a richer medium for exploring these topics than found in print alone. These sections often incorporate discovery-based learning methods that are made possible by the interactive features available on the Web. In other instances, the Web site serves as an ancillary to the text. Specifically, the printed text offers pointers to the inquisitive student who seeks more information on related topics or issues. These are indicated as "*Focus*" sections—i.e., "*Focus On* _____." *Focus* sections serve as sidebars for introducing ideas that are interesting and useful, but optional. A printed text is static, but a Web site is a dynamic, evolving entity. We hope to augment the book and enhance its currency and relevance with the resources within these Web pages.

Courses in computing and information technology often incorporate a hands-on laboratory component. To assist instructors, we have also assembled a sizable compendium of tutorials, lab activities, and projects on our Web site. Some are designed for specific software applications; others are generic. We welcome your suggestions or links for additional materials that may supplement this resource.

The Web site contains a hyperlinked glossary of terms cited in the text. In addition, there is Web log (blog) that regularly posts information about new developments affecting topics or issues in the text. A discussion board permits readers to comment or offer suggestions on these topics. Chapter outlines offered as multimedia presentations (PowerPoint files) are there, too. Students may find them useful as study guides. Instructors may wish to use them for creating their own overheads or electronic presentations.

Each of the chapters concludes with a summary of central ideas, a list of the key terms, and some questions for reviewing important concepts. As mentioned, most of the chapters incorporate *Discovery* sections and *Focus* sidebars on the Web site. *Social Themes Essays* introduce the student to the moral, social, and political implications of computer use and information systems. We have greatly expanded the range of topics from previous editions. The Web site also offers additional materials that students may employ to quiz themselves on topics studied in each chapter.

An instructor's manual is available to text adopters on the Web site, too. It has PowerPoint outlines for each chapter; answers to the chapter exercises; answers or suggestions for implementing projects; and, of course, sample questions for composing tests on the material. There are also suggestions for organizing lectures with readings based on our experiences with using these materials for the past seven years.

New in the Second Edition

Readers of our beta and first editions will find a number of changes in this edition. The most significant is the reorganization of the chapters. To support the aforementioned spiral approach, many of the introductory chapters are new. A number of topics have been updated and expanded; some of these are presented online rather than in print. This will enable us to keep abreast with changes and new developments better.

We have expanded our treatment of researching information on the Web, including an introduction to keyword searching using Boolean and mathematical operators. Web publishing is incorporated in text and document preparation—where it fits more naturally. The development of the history of computing and computing machines has been extended (and posted online). There are now separate chapters on secondary memory and input/output devices. These incorporate updated and new material on a litany of acronyms such as CD-RW, DVD, LCD, USB, and Firewire. In the area of data communications and networks, we have added material on DSL, cable (CATV) modems, and wireless LAN technologies. We have also better integrated the TCP/IP protocol model with our treatment of client/server applications.

Missing are chapters on integrating multimedia and AI, but new chapters on data security and emerging technologies have been added. In the latter, we offer brief introductions that would serve as starting points, we think, for interesting and thought-provoking studies and discussions in your classes. Topics include bioinformatics, nanotechnology, and grid computing.

The most significant change, of course, is the organization of the text around the integration of print and online materials. We are convinced that both are important. The Web is undoubtedly an exciting and rich medium for presenting information. We can do many things there that would not be practical in print. But, even though the Information Age has indeed arrived, these new technologies have not yet entirely replaced the convenience and economy of the portable, handheld book. We believe that mixing media is the best approach for our goals. Thanks go to our publisher for supporting this approach.

Coordinating Coursework with This Text

A significant challenge for producing any textbook is to present sufficient coverage of topics to suit a variety of tastes and needs. The result is usually overkill: the breadth of coverage is often too great for most college courses. We have been quite conscious of this dilemma in the preparation of this text. With the exception of the first four, many of the chapters (and, thus, most of the units) have been written with few dependencies on earlier materials. This affords an instructor considerable flexibility in organizing and coordinating this text with his or her approach and course.

We offer several suggested treatments employing this text. These are based on different approaches as well as different schedules. At our university, for example, we have used the text in introductory computing for both general and specialized audiences. General audiences are served by a course that features computing applications with an emphasis on digital media and networking. We have also offered a course primarily for students in arts and communications on the use of computers for graphic design and publishing. Students in economics and business have taken a course that emphasizes information technology and systems. We have also used the text to support a course for pre–service education professionals. Likewise, we believe that this edition would be especially useful for schools and programs in information technology or informatics offering a general introductory course. In our field, many introductions to the discipline of computer science emphasize programming. We believe that this book would also be appropriate as an alternative approach for general audiences and a prelude to programming courses. The table provided on the Web page offers chapter coverage for these possible treatments—assuming different schedules.

CT   = emphasis on computing and computing technology
CA   = emphasis on computing and computing applications
ITS   = emphasis on information technology and information systems
GAP   = emphasis on computing and graphic arts and publishing
CS-0   = an alternative introduction to computer science for general education

Acknowledgments

We have class-tested this material and would like to thank our students who helped us to improve the text by their questions, comments, and reactions. Several of our colleagues also participated in class-testing versions of this text. We would like to thank Margaret Batchelor, Bryan Catron, Paula Gabbert, Paige Meeker, and Kevin Treu. Our thanks go to the reviewers of this edition, Jim Ball of Indiana State University, Stan Kwasny of Washington University, and Ron Schwartz of Florida Atlantic University, for their comments and general support of the project.

A Final Note

We encourage your reactions and comments on any portion of the text. Please feel free to contact our publisher or us. You may use the automated electronic mail or discussion links located on our Web site. If you have corrections, comments, or suggestions for links and additions to the Web site, we would greatly appreciate them. See you in the Digital Domain.

Ken Abernethy
Tom Allen
Department of Computer Science
Furman University

PART. One

Getting Started

Chapter 1

Introduction: Understanding Information Technology

OBJECTIVES

- The importance of information for a wide assortment of enterprises

- Understanding the roles of information technologies in shaping how we manage and preserve information

- How digital information technology subsumes and merges other information technologies

- How digital information technology is changing the quantity and quality of information affecting our lives, our work, and our world

Our lives are awash in information. From the moment we arise each morning, we are surrounded by a seemingly endless array of sources that produce, store, or dispense information. Our alarm clocks are tuned to any one of hundreds of radio broadcast stations that greet us with news, weather, and entertainment. Television offers an equally wide assortment of similar broadcast and cable transmissions. At the breakfast table, for example, we can dine while consulting a single screen for the latest international news, current weather for the United States, and stock market quotes from NASDAQ, Wall Street, or the foreign markets. Our telephones—wired or wireless—connect us to almost any point anywhere on the globe. Millions of conversations like ours flood the channels and airwaves. From our home

3

computers, we can pay our bills and balance our checkbooks, send and receive correspondence, purchase goods and services, and read online magazines and newspapers. Even the appliances in our home keep track of things; in fact, they can be organized to send radio transmissions to exchange information and coordinate their activities. Overhead, silent satellites gather data about the weather, population concentrations, and a host of other subjects.

Our own identities are traced by an electronic trail of school transcripts, credit histories, medical records, employment files, and so on. Should these records all disappear in an instant, we would have an unbelievably difficult time persuading others who we are. If you are not convinced of this, think about the annoyances of merely completing a credit transaction without proper identification.

Business is information and information is business, too. At most of our jobs, we spend a significant portion of the workday tending to communications, sifting through reports and records, deciding on what is important and what is not. At the end of the day, we have put in long hours, but very few of us have manufactured goods or products to show for it. What we produce is just as important, although more ephemeral. The financial world of banking is more about the electronic transfer of credits than moving money or gold. Commerce still offers goods and services, but its survival and well-being are no longer measured solely by these material goods and services. Every purchase we make at home or on the road is logged and stored in retail databases. Seasons, cycles, and trends are endlessly plotted and analyzed. Margins of profits and losses are no longer based on inventories, but less tangible things like supply chains. The stock market itself will more likely rise and fall due to reports, indicators, rumors, and predictions than traditional measures like company profits, capital investment, and debt. Everywhere information is the legal tender.

We are living in the Information Age. Our lives, work, and world are all about information. Computers and digital technology have contributed to this flood of information, and they are the best means by which we can cope with it. In this book, we offer insight and skills for managing information. The key is learning how information is captured, preserved, processed, and exchanged in the digital domain. And, although digital information technology has significant advantages and promise, it also has distinct limitations and liabilities. Mastering the digital domain also means balancing these costs and benefits.

The Nature of Information

This is indeed the Information Age, but information has had a central role in our existence since the beginning. Biologists tell us that one of the hallmarks of life is the ability of an organism to adapt to its surroundings. But, in order to adapt, it must first respond to the conditions of those surroundings. Thus, it is fundamental that all living things are sensitive to external stimuli. When a pin pricks your skin, a sharp pain results. The sudden appearance of a large object in your visual foreground produces the startle response—adrenalin surges in your body and your body prepares to respond to the potential threat. These are some simple examples of this essential characteristic of living things.

In a broader context, though, we can think of sensory responsiveness as a form of **communication**—that is, the conveyance of information. The sender transmits an encoded message that is interpreted by a receiver. The encoded message contains information that has meaning or significance for the receiver. Thus, organisms have evolved to interpret their natural environment as containing information. Visual perception, for instance, fits the communication model well. Human vision is tuned to a specific bandwidth of electromagnetic energies emanating from the environment—light. But, our receptors do not scan the full range of these frequencies; instead, they sample specific bands within this range (high, middle, and low). This is sufficient for the visual cortex to compose color information. Nor do we process all of the energies available in the visual environment. Instead, our perceptors are attuned to receive dramatic changes: sharp contrasts in the spatial field, and abrupt changes in the position of objects over time. Perception is not a passive process; it is attuned to a specific medium or channel and is highly selective in what it interprets (receives) as signals (encoded messages).

But the communication model is applicable in even broader contexts. Within the organism, its functioning at various levels involves the sending and receiving of encoded messages (information). Cells in an organism must communicate in order to regulate growth and development. Some forms of communication are local; others are long-distance. Consider local cell-to-cell communication first. All cells have a resting potential; that is, they maintain an electrical charge across the plasma membrane of the cell. Some cells, however, such as neurons, are excitable. They may be stimulated to create a tiny electrical current. Specifically, certain external conditions can reduce the charge across the membrane, causing depolarization. If the voltage reduces beyond its threshold value, an action potential or nerve impulse is generated. The effect of external stimuli is all-or-nothing. As long as the threshold is achieved, a full action potential is generated. This is how neurons transmit signals locally from one cell to the next. Other forms of communication travel longer distances. For example, hormones are secreted by cells that travel in the bloodstream to distant target cells. Insulin is a case in point. It regulates the flow of glucose in the blood by stimulating cells to take up and store glucose as well as inhibiting its production. At a higher level of organization, nerve signals cause muscle fibers to contract or expand. These are just a few examples of how organisms send and receive information at many different levels of organization.

Of course, organisms have evolved to use encoded signals within the species as well. Encoded signals can be interpreting natural signs or direct communication. Migrating birds, for instance, often respond to changes in seasonal weather and the positions of the sun and stars to commence annual long-distance treks. Anomalous animal behavior has often been observed with the onset of significant natural events such as earthquakes. Birds, fish, and mammals may be capable of interpreting environmental cues that have eluded us in recognizing such events. Some animals respond to the shortening days, reduced sunlight, and decreasing food supply as signs that induce hibernating behavior. Reversing these cues can bring the same species out of hibernation.

The dances of the European honeybee are often cited as an animal communication system. Scout bees returning to the hive indicate the location and extent of a food source using characteristic dances. Ants use chemical secretions called pheromones for communication. There may be as many as ten different secretions/message complexes in an ant's repertoire. Simple carbon dioxide, for example, promotes clustering for working on larger tasks. Each colony has a unique odor that identifies it and its members. This separates neighbors from intruders. Likewise, foraging ants secrete special pheromones along the trail when returning food to the colony. The density of these trails acts a strong recruiting agent for other ants to follow. High-density trails are more impelling than lower density. As the food supply wanes (i.e., fewer returning foragers), the number of ants recruited naturally dwindles. Birdcalls have been identified as signaling the presence of predators. The calls are different depending upon whether the threat is from below or above.

These and other examples convince us that information is fundamental for life in general. But what exactly is information? We have said a lot of things about it so far without explaining what it is. The problem is that the concept of information is a lot like those of gravity and energy. These concepts are so fundamental, they act as primitives in their domains—everything else is based on them. **Information** basically refers to knowledge, facts, significance, and

Figure 1.1
Claude Shannon, pioneer in information and communication sciences.

meaning—though none of these captures it entirely. Claude Shannon and Warren Weaver in their groundbreaking *A Mathematical Theory of Communication* (1949) described information as what is known beyond chance predictions. See Figure 1.1. Information decreases uncertainty and therefore aids decision-making. In their view, information is measured by the extent to which it is ordered or organized. By contrast, noise is random and disordered. At the other extreme, though, predictable order is monotonous and uninformative. Information lies somewhere between. To some extent, information is surprising, unexpected, or new, but it reduces our uncertainty about predicting states of the world.

Information in most instances is useless unless it is transmitted or communicated. As a species, we have developed natural forms of representing and communicating information: signals and natural languages. But, signs and speech are ephemeral; they are bound by the present. Perhaps the defining characteristic of our species is that we have developed technologies to extend these and other powers.

Technologies and Information Technology

Technologies are artificial instruments, processes, or systems that extend our natural capabilities. The wheel, for example, is an extension of the foot as a mode of transportation. Agriculture is an extension of our social institution for gathering food. The microscope and

Figure 1.2
The screw-type version of the Gutenberg Press is shown in this lithograph. Gutenberg advanced the technology of printing by developing movable type, which reduced the labor and time required to prepare pages for printing. The result was that printed products became more economical and more widely available. Likewise, the technology became more abundant.

Figure 1.3
Lions are depicted in this restored cave drawing from Chauvet-Pont-d'Arc, France. The discovery at Chauvet proves that over 31,000 years ago, our ancestors had developed sophisticated techniques for capturing and conveying information pictorially.

the electric light bulb extend our power of vision into unseen worlds. Technologies also alter and modify our environments. The influences of technologies on society and individuals are sometimes immense and obvious, but these changes can also be subtle and indirect. For example, the invention of the printing press had enormously significant and well-documented effects on the development of the modern world. See Figure 1.2. But, on the other hand, as technologist Marshall McLuhan argued, the invention of the lowly stirrup contributed indirectly to the rise of feudalism in Western Europe.[1]

Of all forms of technology, **information technologies** are perhaps the most important. From the beginning, humans have extended natural forms of representing and communicating information to incorporate artificial or external forms. See Figure 1.3. Writing, for example, is an artificial form of transmitting and storing the spoken word. As such, writing is a form of information technology. Writing preserves and stores the spoken word externally to the speaker. Thus, it can go beyond the presence of the speaker in both space and time. Indeed, written language can preserve our knowledge and experience beyond our mortality. Certainly, most of what we have achieved as a civilization would not have been possible without our inheritance of the knowledge of generations that have preceded us. This fact alone, perhaps, makes written language the most significant information technology developed by our species. Yet, information technologies can have shortcomings, liabilities, and even ill consequences. The written word, for example, loses some of the richness of meaning conveyed by the spoken word. (Think of the experience of listening to a talented storyteller.) The written word has saved many, but, unfortunately, also has helped condemn many men and women to their deaths unjustly. The bottom line is that technologies can yield both good and evil.

Digital Information Technology

Electronic **digital information technology** is the latest generation of information technologies, but, it represents a different brand of information technology. Previously, new information technologies have often competed with and replaced existing ones. The telephone replaced the telegraph for obvious reasons. Television has relegated radio to a subordinate niche. Digital information technology is different because it is a form of technology that extends other technologies. In short, digital information technology has the capability to imitate other technologies. Electronic printed documents mimic conventional typeset ones. Digital audio recordings reproduce sounds like their analog counterparts. To the listener, wireless digital telephony works like normal (wired) telephone service. But its imitation is not mere replication. Digital information technologies offer value-added features. Electronic documents, for example, can be automatically scaled for different media. The same content can be printed on paper, posted on the World Wide Web, and transmitted to handheld personal digital assistants (PDAs) or palmtops and cell phone screens with no extra formatting or fuss. Electronic databases, unlike conventional ones, can be searched and queried automatically, revealing facts that would be difficult to find otherwise. Finally, digital information technology can extend the technologies that it imitates by merging them in new and interesting ways. The Web, for example, merges text, numeric data, images, sounds, and video into a seamless medium for posting and sharing content-rich documents.

In support of what we are arguing, consider the rapid acceptance of digital information technologies in so many different arenas and enterprises. As a species, we are a conservative lot. Only a few of us are automatically attracted to new things just because of their novelty. Most of us feel more comfortable with the familiar. On the other hand, we will adapt to and adopt those things that we perceive as genuinely valuable. Digital information technology must be a case in point. Consider how quickly we have adopted it in so many forms. Would you be willing to give up the Web? E-mail?

---

[1] Marshall McLuhan and Quentin Fiore. *War and Peace in The Global Village.* New York: Bantam Books, 1968, 26–34.

Indeed, the world of information is going digital. The evolution to digital forms of information has influenced the workplace, the marketplace, our schools, and our homes. In some instances, the changes have been dramatic; in others they have been subtle—almost imperceptible. Considered together, these changes have been highly significant, helping to redefine the ways in which we think about and use information to communicate with each other. An important goal in this book is to guide your exploration of what we call the **digital domain.** For the time being, consider these examples of the inroads that digital information technology has made in a few short years.

Digital Documents

Typewriters have become relics of an age forgotten in favor of electronic digital word processing. You can now create, edit, and format documents with a flexibility and speed unthought of before computers. The typesetting of books like this one now depends more on digital methods than traditional, conventional techniques. In the past, publishing was the province of the professional; today even school children can produce a typeset book. In short, digital documents are easier to create, store, transmit, and manipulate. One consequence of digital document preparation is that we now create a lot more documents—notes, letters, reports, and books—than ever before.

Digital Numeric Processing

Since their first appearance more than 50 years ago, computers have assisted us in many tasks that involve numerical computation. The earliest computers supported national defense and other government functions. They calculated ballistic tables for artillery, performed computations for developing the first atomic bomb, processed census information, and even predicted presidential elections. Unfortunately, these early computers were expensive and required considerable skill and expertise to operate. Today, the accessibility of computers for numeric processing is widespread. Spreadsheets and statistical and mathematical software offer powerful tools for numerical computation and are easy to use. Most of these tools also have graphing and visualization features that convert large data sets and models to more convenient and accessible forms. Today anyone can command both processing power and productivity for "number crunching" from a desktop computer that far outstrips that of the early giant computers.

Digital Music

Most of the music that you listen to is recorded, stored, and played back using digital methods. Compared with phonograph and audiotape, compact disc digital audio offers much higher fidelity sound. Phonographs and tapes have inherent noise noticeable in playback; their media usually suffer from the wear and tear of constant replay as well. Not so for compact discs. CDs are less noisy and last longer, making digital recording a significantly better archive for important performances. Today we can only imagine how brilliant were the talents of performers such as Enrico Caruso, Toscaninni, and George Gershwin. Their surviving recordings are dim and fading replicas. On the other hand, today's artists can be preserved for all posterity. When you tell your grandchildren how they just don't make music like they used to, you'll be able to prove it by inflicting on them recordings of your favorites that sound just as new as they did the day you bought them.

Digital Photography

When the family is forcibly collected at the photography studio for a portrait, the photographer most likely uses digital methods to capture and process your likenesses. After the shooting, the photographer can use a computer system to display instantly the proofs that used to take days or weeks to process. Thus, you can be photographed and choose which shots you want almost instantly. At the same time, the photographer can show you samples of how these photos may be retouched or processed to make you look even better than you naturally do. Professional photography has made the move to digital methods. Journalistic photography today is often processed digitally; fewer "wet" darkrooms are left in the offices of newspaper and magazine publishers. Recently, consumer versions of digital cameras have become even more affordable. Armed with these and image processing software, you, too, can produce results that approach those of many professionals.

Digital Graphic Arts

Computer graphics (CG) is the artificial generation of images. The field has evolved from computing curiosity to the mainstream. Today, commercial artists employ computer graphics extensively to produce images for newspapers, magazines, and television.

Computer-generated animation is used to create or enhance commercials, television shows, and full-length feature films. Indeed, very few films are produced without the benefit of computer-generated effects. The contributions of CG effects to films like the *Harry Potter* sagas and *The Lord of the Rings Trilogy* are abundant and obvious.

Even more important, digital processes are making inroads into areas of filmmaking that were the traditional province of analog methods, and not so obvious. For example, the film *O Brother, Where Art Thou?* broke new ground by incorporating digital intermediate processing exclusively. Cinematographer Roger Deakins wanted this Depression-era version of Mark Twain–meets–Homer to have a distinctive look with washed and faded colors. He achieved this by shooting the film using conventional 35-mm stock. The film was then scanned and digitized. The digital version was processed to achieve the color and lighting effects that he desired. Afterwards it was converted back to film for theaters. If you see the film, notice that the sky is blue and that flesh tones are natural, yet the backgrounds are faded pastels. This would be impossible using conventional film and lighting effects. Although he did it to achieve special effects, Deakins recognized the general advantages of digital intermediate processing. It offers the cinematographer much greater control over the images of the film. Differences in lighting conditions and film stock can be minimized in postproduction. Likewise, the digital format is natural for archiving and other releases such as DVD. As the technology improves, we can expect its wider acceptance in the film industry. The day of the totally digital "film" is not far away.

Digital Television

Television is migrating to the digital domain as well. Today you can purchase a small, 18-inch diameter satellite dish and receiver for a hundred dollars. In spite of its size, it can receive hundreds of television channels beamed directly from satellites that are in fixed orbit around the earth. The picture that you receive is crisp, detailed video, and the audio is multichannel CD-quality stereo sound. All of this is possible because the transmission and processing are digital. Compared with conventional cable TV service, digital satellite television offers higher fidelity, greater choice, and fewer interruptions of service.

The future of television is undoubtedly digital. The U.S. standard for high-definition television (HDTV) is a digital one. HDTV offers tremendous gains in resolution that mean unparalleled realism in picture quality. Many of your favorite network programs today are simulcast in HDTV. The FCC has mandated that all broadcast television stations convert to these digital standards for all programming over the next several years.

Virtual Reality

Virtual reality (VR) is a new technology that immerses the user into the illusion of a three-dimensional world built from 3-D graphic models and sophisticated animation techniques. In contrast to a viewer merely watching conventional graphics that are projected onto a video display, the viewer dons special video goggles, headsets, and even gloves for manipulating objects in a specially designed model world. The objective is to create an artificial experience of new phenomena, with a natural look and feel to the conjured experience. Early versions of VR have created artificial rooms and buildings, projected users on journeys across the surface of Mars, and produced trips to virtual art galleries—complete with an extensive collection of art objects. These applications of VR technology have been largely experimental or exploratory. In the near future, as the technology develops, more serious commercial applications will appear. For instance, VR promises to be an invaluable training medium. See Figure 1.4. In medical applications, it can be used to train surgeons. Using ultrasound imaging, VR can also augment the surgeon during live operations as well as provide additional "visual" cues about the displacement and location of a patient's organs and tissues.

Digital Communications

Person-to-person telephone service is a fact that we all take for granted. Compared with realizing radio and television broadcasting, achieving such service is incredibly complex. A radio transmission can be broadcast across the airwaves. Listeners can receive it merely by purchasing a receiver and tuning in the signal. On the other hand, for conventional telephony, each user must be capable of reaching any other user at any time. The communication must be exclusive and two-way; simple broadcast methods will not do. Consider that there are billions of users worldwide and that sizable distances separate them. Under these circumstances, wired telephone service is amazing. Digital methods have helped to extend service to all points of the globe and have improved performance at the same time. Digitizing voice and data have made transmission faster. Digital techniques are used to combine and transmit thousands of conversations simultaneously on a single carrier. Digital switching systems process and route hundreds of thousands of calls per hour. As commercial communication carriers have converted to digital media and techniques, consumer services have expanded, but the costs have not. In the future, all-digital networks promise to add processing power and intelligence to our telephone service.

Digital methods have also enhanced our wireless communications technologies. Digital signaling methods have extended the range of our devices and permitted greater numbers of users over an already crowded bandwidth. The quality and reliability of the service have also improved in the digital domain.

The Internet

The explosive growth of long-distance networks and the creation of the global Internet are direct consequences of the digitization of commercial communication. Computer networks that were once restricted to a local area can now connect to thousands of other networks around the world. Dedicated network lines called *backbones* carry millions of individual packets of digital data. These packets hop from one network to another until they reach their intended

Figure 1.4

The University of Michigan Virtual Reality Laboratory has adapted its VR environment CAVE for athletic training. A football player learns to recognize the offensive tendencies of an opposing team by reading keys from formations and player movements. The CAVE is a room-sized cube composed of three walls and a floor on which computer-generated images are projected. The viewing glasses help to create a more realistic scene, for example, by removing the perception of corners.

destination. In this manner, you can send and receive electronic mail, transfer files of data and software, or browse through information on a computer system located thousands of miles away. All of this is possible almost instantly and from the convenience of your own desktop.

The World Wide Web

The use of the Internet has literally exploded over the past several years. A major force in this growth has been the **World Wide Web** (or **Web** for short) and the availability of user-friendly programs, called **Web browsers** (*Netscape Navigator* and *Microsoft Internet Explorer* are two of the most popular), for accessing its wealth of multimedia information. The World Wide Web is a confederation of computer systems that adhere to a common set of guidelines for storing and presenting information to users. These guidelines make it completely straightforward for computer users all over the world to publish multimedia information they have created or collected to all other Web users. Web browser programs exploit the Web's commonality to make all information on the Web accessible in an extremely easy-to-use graphical user interface. This ease of use has made the Web a universal success and phenomenon.

Collections of organized information stored and made available to Web users in a single location are referred to as **Web sites.** You will shortly learn about the Web site that accompanies this text. The individual computer files that comprise a Web site are called **Web pages.** You can always scroll to view all the information on a Web page (although it may extend over several screens). You use the mouse to click over connecting links that access one Web page from another. Most Web sites contain several (perhaps many) Web pages connected to each other for easy access.

These examples illustrate the ways in which digital information has improved or supplanted other conventional forms and how such information can be made available worldwide almost instantly. Of course, none of these capabilities would be possible without the technology of the electronic digital computer. How will this technology ultimately change our world and our lives? Will these changes be for the better or the worse? No one knows the complete answers to such questions. What is clear is that life in the 21st century will be inextricably intertwined with a changing communications paradigm, and the new paradigm will exhibit an increasing dependence on and exploitation of computers and computer networks. Preparation for life in this era will require, even demand, an understanding of the technologies underlying these fundamental changes. This book is intended as a guide to help you achieve this understanding.

Computing and Information Technology

A computer system is not merely a tool but rather a medium for representing, storing, manipulating, and communicating different forms of information: text, numbers, graphics, images, sounds, and video. The common denominator for these differing forms of information is that they all can be digitized for use by our computers. This data can be studied, combined, transformed, and transmitted with an apparent ease that belies the true complexities of these tasks. Digitized data and the systems that handle it constitute the digital domain.

We usually think of computers as tools. We use computers to do this and that. One of the goals of this book is to convince you that a computer system is a medium, not just a helper or instrument. A medium is a vehicle or agent for something. For example, air is the medium for sound; writing is a medium for words and thoughts. The computer is a medium for ideas and information. Computers can be used not only to express, but to communicate these ideas as well. They can store knowledge and facts. But more important, computer systems can store and manipulate information in many different forms.

Informational media include text, illustrations, photographs, animation, video, sounds, voice, and music. The modern computer is an all-purpose medium for informational media. Regardless of the media, the computer system represents, stores, and transmits all in its native digital form. That a computer converts text and graphics, for example, to a digital format means that it can process them in similar fashion and at the same time. Multimedia refers to the integration of various forms of information such as text, graphics, sound, and images.

The modern computer system is a multimedia machine; that is, it is capable of integrating two or more conventional forms of informational media in a single electronic document. Because we can express and combine various forms of information using a computer, we can interact, explore, and learn even more from that information. In this way, the computer becomes a vehicle for knowledge rather than just a tool that stores, distributes, and displays information.

This book describes how the computer can be used to create, express, and communicate ideas in various forms. Some of the ideas discussed in this book are new and evolving; others are as old as the advent of electronic digital computers more than 50 years ago. After all, modern computer systems are electronic digital machines; they have always had this capability for combining and transmitting informational media. However, desktop or personal computers have only recently had the power to exploit these capabilities for both multimedia and data communications over networks.

The remarkable advances in the price-to-performance ratio of computer hardware over the past few years, together with a new generation of computer software, are driving dramatic developments in this innovative computer use. In the early days of computing, it was recognized that the speed of computers was especially useful for processing large amounts of numeric and text information. Today, developments in software and hardware are creating opportunities to exploit the computer's capabilities for representing and processing different, richer forms of information that enhance our intellectual abilities. Thus, the traditional model of employing computation for numbers and text is being replaced by a new paradigm. At the heart of these developments is the emergence of two primary technologies: the ability of modern desktop computer systems to collect, store, retrieve, display, and generally manage information in a variety of media and the possibilities for cooperative work using fully interconnected computers and computer networks.

Computer networks are also playing a dominant role in integrating technology into our lives. Networks connect computers in our offices and labs; they also can link us to other computers across the nation and around the world. Using networks, computer systems can share resources and information. That many forms of information can be exchanged instantaneously over long distances has changed the way we work and play. For example, employees in many corporations and other organizations rely more on electronic mail than conventional mail for communication with coworkers.

Indeed, networks have created a new habitat, commonly called **cyberspace.** These new opportunities have a profound effect on ways we work and interact with one another. Not only is information more readily available, it is also richer and strikingly more dynamic. In cyberspace, you are immersed in and engaged by information rather than merely possessing it.

Communication technologies have existed for a long time. So, what is special about data communications over computer networks? First, the technology driving data communications offers far greater capacity and speed than any other previous form. For example, we now have the capability to store and send whole libraries of information much more quickly than sending a simple message by ordinary postal service. Because this data is represented digitally, we can combine and communicate various forms of information simultaneously, for example, text, audio, and images.

Connectivity means more than simply people communicating with other people. Computer networks also make it possible for individuals to communicate with other computers over long distances. For instance, from your home computer, you can easily borrow both software and processing power from a computer system far away. You can also ask the distant computer system to supply you with the latest stock market quotes, college basketball scores, or international news. When traveling, you can telephone your computer system at home or office to check for electronic mail or messages.

In the past, computers were isolated and largely incompatible. Today, networks support communication from computer to computer as well. Computer systems can request and receive services from other computers automatically and invisibly to the user. This offers a number of advantages. Borrowing processing from a remote system extends the capabilities of your own computer. It also means that computers of different scale and performance can exchange the results of processing almost seamlessly. Distributing the work of processing among cooperating computer systems is still in its infancy. We can expect that it will have a profound effect on computing in the future. Indeed, the idea of individual or autonomously functioning computer systems will very likely become archaic. Perhaps William Gibson's vision in *Neuromancer* of the worldwide network of cooperating computer systems called the *Matrix* holds more fact than fancy. (It was Gibson who coined the term *cyberspace* to denote this new dimension.)

Who Benefits from Digital Information Technology?

Digital information technology is important for at least three segments of society: information consumers, information providers, and informational workers. These three groups represent most of society; they touch nearly all walks of life and most forms of endeavor.

- An **information consumer** is anyone who either needs or stands to benefit from relevant information services. Consumers may employ that information for a variety of tasks associated with both work and leisure.

- **Information providers** are the vendors and distributors of information services. These include the enterprises of publishing, entertainment, education, and all others whose mission, at least in part, involves imparting information to consumers.

- An **information worker** is someone whose profession depends on the analysis, assessment, and manipulation of specific forms or classes of information. Information workers include a wide variety of professions: scientists, physicians, tax lawyers, journalists, professors, managers, graphic artists, and many others.

For example, suppose that you are planning a vacation to Scotland. As a potential tourist, you become an information consumer. Where should you go? When is the best time to go? How should you get there? Where should you stay? A travel agent is a relevant information provider for this undertaking. The agent can provide useful information on flights, accommodations, and itineraries. The pilot of your flight depends on information workers like the meteorologist who forecasts the atmospheric conditions over the Atlantic. How could information technology further enhance these activities? The travel agent could consult the World Wide Web for descriptions and photographs of hotels from which to choose. Possible itineraries could be plotted and maps automatically generated that show the travel routes. You, the information consumer, could examine these documents in the comfort of your own home after downloading the information using an Internet service provider who connects your home system to the Web. A meteorologist will likely use information technology to help forecast for your flight. Complex three-dimensional models representing atmospheric dynamics can be depicted graphically to model current conditions. Some of this information may even be supplied to the pilot by means of computerized displays and audio format. In these and many other ways, information technology can affect the manner in which we do our work and even choose our leisure time activities.

Digitization and the Information Consumer

The information consumer benefits from the digitization of information in a variety of ways. Here is a brief catalog of the kinds of services that are or will soon be available. In each instance, consider the advantages that these digital services have over comparable ones delivered using more conventional methods.

- **Research and Reference Materials.** Converting reference information to electronic form has immediate dividends. It can be stored more efficiently and accessed or transferred much more quickly than conventional forms. Add the multimedia factor to this, and the dividends are even greater. Information that combines text, graphics, images, video, and sound is richer, more engaging, and easier to absorb than traditional printed reference materials. Also, that it is electronic means that it can be distributed far and wide. To take advantage of a printed encyclopedia, for example, you must own it or have access to it. Electronic research and reference materials do not have to be physically present. You can access them remotely over networks. As an added benefit, information providers don't have to worry about damage to or loss of electronic information in the same way that libraries, for instance, must for their printed collections.

- **Education.** The purpose of institutional education is to prepare an individual to meet the challenges of living. In short, educators prepare students to spend a life educating themselves. Digital information technology will play an important role in this education for several reasons. First, technology itself will be significant in both workplace and the home. Students must understand and master it to succeed in the future. Just as important for the educator, computing technology will become a new partner in the process of general education. As a resource and a tool, computing technology has myriad applications in the classroom, lab, and library. Computers can bridge long distances, they can conjure up worlds and experiences, they can assist and monitor learners, and they can be repositories for a wealth of information in many forms.

- **Games and Entertainment.** Fantasy adventure computer games such as *Final Fantasy* and *Tomb Raider* have created intoxicating diversions with over-the-top action enhanced by realistic three-dimensional graphics, engrossing sound effects, and music. With their simple, natural interfaces for interaction, these games effectively integrate several informational media to create a more engaging, realistic experience.

  The digital dividend will be extended to other entertainment forms in the future. Interactive television promises to immerse the viewer in the performance or event being broadcast. For example, imagine controlling the camera shots at a World Series game directly from your remote control. You choose from a number of camera positions; at the same time, you can control the mix and sound levels of the players and the fans. Choose your own replays and slow motion, stop-action sequences. (This must be couch potato heaven!)

- **Telemarketing.** A lot of people scoffed when networks such as QVC launched 24-hour shopping channels. The success of such home shopping networks speaks to a simple fact about human nature: When a service is delivered in a form that is easily accessible, we embrace it. Electronic marketing via networks and home computers is another version of this simple idea, offering individuals the opportunity to choose from a wide variety of products. It can provide the consumer with demos, advertisements, and electronic catalogs. Using catalogs, individuals can order products even more quickly and easily than through shopping channels.

  Using computer networks as a market medium has a distinct advantage over television marketing. Television is a broadcast medium. Even cable transmissions depend on the economics of scale: Masses must receive these mass communications to justify the expense. Computer networks, however, communicate more like telephones; they support point-to-point communications. This means that information can afford to be highly specialized and tailored for each individual consumer. Computer telemarketing can thus create micromarkets. In the future, we might expect to find more specialized retailers that exploit the digital advantage and fewer mass retailers on the scale of the venerable Sears & Roebuck model.

Digitization and the Information Provider

The information service industry also benefits from the digital boon. Here is a sample of the ways in which information services have been and will be improved.

■ **Consumer and Retail Kiosks.** Kiosks are public facilities designed to make information available to many people. Kiosks are typically placed in locations that have high visibility and heavy consumer traffic. Computer kiosks replace traditional informational booths found on street corners and in malls, hospitals, office buildings, and the like. The advantages of a computer kiosk are its attractiveness, flexibility, and convenience for its consumers. Interactive displays permit consumers to search for relevant information in a self-directed manner and at a self-paced rate. These computer-based kiosks can also collect information about their own use, too. Such feedback may be very useful, even vital, for the information provider.

■ **Network Information Delivery.** The growth of data communication networks is staggering. Business and commerce could hardly be conducted today without electronic mail, file transfers, and remote logins. These applications permit us to share resources with other persons and systems—sometimes distantly. At the same time, individuals have benefited from the growth of commercial network access providers such as America Online. These services offer connectivity to users who wish to gather information or share ideas with others. The future promises even greater growth and opportunity. Increased load capacities (often called *bandwidth*) for existing networks will allow richer sources of information, such as video and audio, to be transmitted in real time. Wireless networking will extend connectivity beyond office and home to remote spots. In the not too distant future, computers, telephones, and televisions will merge into a seamless appliance for communication.

■ **Sales and Commercial Presentations.** An effective presentation is one that gains our attention and enables us to retain the information presented. How many sales talks or commercial presentations have you endured in which the speaker simply talked at the audience? Presentations that make effective uses of graphics or video for illustration are not only more interesting, they are usually more memorable. It is a fact that we can absorb and retain visual data at a rate over twice that of verbal or textual data. Multimedia presentations make the development and delivery of such multifaceted communication much easier.

■ **Simulations and Training.** Most companies and institutions need to train employees in a variety of subjects. Training is an expensive and difficult endeavor for a number of reasons. It is difficult to manage because its success depends on fitting a range of topics to a variety of individuals with different aptitudes and learning styles. Training also requires constant updating to be relevant. Computer-based training can help diminish some of these obstacles and their associated expense. Flight simulators are a good example of computer training modules that simulate activities for the trainee in a concrete, hands-on, and individualized manner. These training modules can be updated easily to reflect new conditions or objectives. In addition, because the computer is the vehicle for training, it can gather important information about the trainee's performance. Some training modules even have built-in intelligence to evaluate that performance and make decisions on how to enhance it with other activities. All of this is done automatically and economically.

■ **Electronic Publishing.** Electronic books offer several advantages that conventional printed texts do not. First, information can be enriched with appropriate multimedia content; speech, images, and video can enhance the message. Second, electronic information can be organized in different and innovative ways. A printed text is a linear document—you read one page after another from beginning to end. An electronic book, however, might be designed to be read in many different orders. As in a do-it-yourself tour, you are free to choose those paths that are most interesting. Finally, electronic documents can be edited and updated easily. New editions can be prepared and disseminated much more quickly and cheaply than those of conventional printed books.

Even print publishing can benefit from the conversion to the digital domain. Readers can pick and choose segments of texts for personalized editions—called *on-demand* or *just-in-time publishing*. For example, some companies today offer individually tailored versions of textbooks that contain only those units or chapters that fit the course's content or the instructor's teaching style. The review, selection, and preparation of these on-demand texts can be handled almost entirely electronically.

Digitization and the Information Worker

Information or knowledge workers can also expect the digitization of the workplace to produce palpable gains. Here are some of the most common areas of productivity.

- **Electronic Databases.** Electronic **databases** are collections of data stored on a computer and organized for convenient and easy retrievals. Databases help us conquer the problems of scale by automating the organization of large bodies of information. Using its analytical and retrieval tools, we can often learn more about our collected data than would be practical using conventional methods. In addition to the conventional text and numeric data, databases can store digital graphics, video, and audio samples that increase the value of the information set immensely.

- **Data Visualization.** Large amounts of data often overwhelm the individuals who attempt to analyze or assess it. Visual representations ranging from graphs and plots to complex dynamic models aid these endeavors. Computing enhances analysis by automating the visualization process.

- **Groupware or Cooperative Computing.** Most informational enterprises engage in tasks requiring the cooperative effort of workers. **Groupware** extends the idea of a team by supporting the team with various computing services. For example, suppose a team is working on a budget proposal. Perhaps the basic budget document originates with one team member but is passed electronically to others for their suggestions, corrections, and additions. After various team members have made their contributions, the entire team can review and approve the final proposal without the necessity of a face-to-face meeting. Networked computing enhances the productivity of teams by improving communication while automating records and document archives.

- **Personal Communications.** In addition to the existing technologies of voice telephony, electronic mail, and text-based network services, the digital dividend contributes enhanced forms of communication. Video-conferencing can link multiple sites rather than just point to point. Participants can see the other groups and themselves in separate windows on a computer screen. At the same time, the group can manipulate a common document in another window. Multimedia e-mail involves transmitting both voice and images along with or in place of conventional text files. In fact, speech recognition and synthesis can automate many normal mail and phone messaging tasks.

About This Book

In this chapter, we have tried to portray the excitement and effectiveness of the powerful new information and communication paradigms that are still evolving. The rest of the book delves into the world of digital information technology in more detail. Our goal, of course, is to provide you a deeper understanding of the advantages and limitations of creating and managing information in the digital domain. In addition to the "whys" and "wherefores," we offer some of the "know-how" needed to increase your information-handling skills.

To facilitate these ends, the book has two dimensions: the printed pages before you and an integrated Web site. Unlike other books with Web sites, ours is not intended as an add-on or extra frill. As you will soon discover, the text and Web site are often tightly coupled. In most instances, Web entries develop ideas and issues that could not be treated in print effectively. For example, the digital domain rapidly shifts and changes. Today's latest thing is tomorrow's old news. Web pages can be updated and posted in a timelier manner. Moreover, some topics are best illuminated using the advantages of the Web's multimedia and interactive facilities. Links to the Web site also provide greater detail and development on topics of interest. Readers can pick and choose among them according to their interests and needs. Finally, the Web site permits us to integrate better useful learning materials for hands-on activities and developing skills.

Each chapter includes links to associated pages on our Web site. These amplify or continue the line of thought presented there. In some instances, the printed text acts as an interface to the online material. For example, a basic concept or issue is introduced in the printed text of a chapter; development, examples, and applications are found on the Web site. These are designated as *Discovery* sections—that is, "*Discovering More About_____.*" These sections often incorporate discovery-based learning methods that are made possible by the interactive features available on the Web. In other instances, the Web site serves as an ancillary to the text. Specifically, most chapters offer pointers to the inquisitive student who seeks more information on related topics or issues discussed there. These are indicated as *Focus* sections, that is, "*Focus on _____.*" *Focus* sections serve as sidebars for introducing ideas that are interesting and useful, but optional. *Social Themes Essays* introduce the student to the moral, social, and political implications of computer use and information systems. In addition, each chapter has *Problems and Projects,* and *Test Your Knowledge* sections. These are intended to provide activities and exercises that reinforce what you have learned. Some chapters offer *Tutorials* for hands-on experience working with applications and methods discussed. The Web site also affords readers a chance to post questions and share information. In short, the Web site permits us to exemplify and exploit some of the interesting and useful advantages of the digital domain.

■ Summary

Information refers to knowledge, facts, and meaning. As such, it is an essential ingredient of most human enterprises. Human history is marked by the development of significant information technologies that extend our natural capabilities for representing, using, and exchanging information. Digital information technology is the most recent and distinctive of these technologies. Digital information technology can subsume and merge older technologies in new and interesting ways. The development of the electronic digital computer is central to the emergence of digital information technology.

Today's computer systems are far more than computational and text processing tools. They provide a new communication paradigm for representing and communicating information in a wide variety of media: text, numbers, graphics, images, sounds, and video. All these differing forms of information can be digitized, combined, transformed, and transmitted with relative ease employing worldwide computer networks. This world of digital information is what we have dubbed the *digital domain.*

The digital domain has had a pervasive and transforming influence on the workplace, the marketplace, our schools, and our homes, redefining the ways in which we think about and use information to communicate with each other. That many forms of information can be exchanged instantaneously over long distances will continue to change the way we work and play. Electronic mail has already become the norm for communication with coworkers in many organizations; the World Wide Web is the information resource of first choice for many people; and a school or workplace without networked computers is becoming hard to imagine.

■ Terms

communication
cyberspace
database(s)
digital domain
digital information technology
groupware

information
information consumer
information providers
information technologies
information worker
technologies

Web browsers
Web pages
Web sites
World Wide Web

■ Questions for Review

1. What is information?

2. How is information important for living things?

3. How does information affect our daily lives (both our work and leisure time)?

4. What is a technology? How do technologies affect individuals and society? Explain.

5. What is information technology? How does digital information technology resemble and differ from other information technologies? Explain.

6. Describe some of the ways in which digital information technology affects how you work.

7. Can you think of ways, in addition to those cited in the text, in which information consumers can benefit from digital information technology?

8. Can you think of ways, in addition to those cited in the text, in which information providers can exploit digital information technology?

9. What is an information worker? Give examples.

10. Can you think of ways, in addition to those cited in the text, in which information workers can employ digital information technology?

11. What is a Web site? A Web page?

12. What is a Web browser?

Chapter 2

The Digital Domain

OBJECTIVES

- The nature of the digital domain

- Distinguishing analog versus digital forms of information

- The advantages of electronic digital media

- The universal language of computers: binary encoding of data

- The basics of how information is converted to digital (binary) form

As mentioned in the last chapter, computers are the spearhead for the revolution in information technology today. This revolution is marked by the convergence or assimilation of many different technologies into one seamless platform. Ten years ago, computers, telephones, televisions, books, postal service, audio, and most other informational technologies were distinctive, alternative forms for representing, storing, and delivering thoughts, ideas, and expressions of feelings. Today the boundaries between these technologies are melting. In the future, distinguishing them may be impractical. What has fueled this revolution? As we alluded previously, the conversion of information technology to the digital domain is the single most important factor. But what is the digital domain? Why is it so important? What advantages does it offer over conventional information technologies? These and other related issues are the subjects of this chapter.

What Is the Digital Domain?

All forms of information, or **data,** in the modern electromagnetic computer are encoded by way of a finite discrete symbol system. Finite means that the number of available symbols is limited. **Discrete** means definite or distinct, so a discrete system is a set of interpretations, each of which is distinct, unambiguous, and precise. This means that any legitimate symbol sequence has a definite meaning that cannot be confused with that of any other symbol sequence.

For example, the letters of the alphabet compose a discrete symbol system. Each letter is distinct; no two letters can be confused. The same is true for combinations of such symbols. For instance, the words *torn* and *worn* are clearly different. Regardless of what these words might mean in a given language (English), the written words are quite distinct. The precision and clarity afforded by discrete symbols systems are very useful for many practical matters. To illustrate the point, consider these instructions: "Bring some chairs into the room" and "Bring three chairs into the room." Which instruction is easier to interpret? Obviously, the second one is precise and unambiguous. It is consistently repeatable as well; any two persons who carried it out would fetch the same number of chairs.

Just as words denote and express our thoughts and feelings, a computer represents and stores information in the symbols of a formal language. The formal language of a computer is based on a digital symbol system. **Digital** means a discrete system whose symbols are numbers. Using numbers for symbols has some advantages over other discrete symbol systems.

Digital symbol systems are easier to implement. Modern technologies can generate symbols based on numbering more reliably and economically than other types of symbols. Whether the medium is electronic or otherwise, creating, transmitting, and storing symbols that are numeric, that is, based on counting, is easier. (Remember that Paul Revere employed a digital messaging system for convenience, too: 1 = "by land," 2 = "by sea.")

Numbers have a natural ordering, too. We can exploit this ordering when devising coding systems to make our work easier. For example, suppose that we arranged each person in a group by height and assigned them a number in ascending order from shortest to tallest. It would be a simple matter to decide whether one person is taller or shorter than another by comparing their designated numbers. Person 3 is shorter than person 5, but taller than person 1. Such decisions could be made without any further measurements. The facts are embedded in our coding system.

The set of all numbers is infinite, but computers, like other machines, have limited resources. Consequently, all data or information processed by a computer system is necessarily encoded using a finite digital symbol system. When our subject—the information itself—is finite or limited, this poses no real problems. But, as we shall see later, there are cases in which our digital symbol system cannot fully capture our subject entirely. Although this is certainly a liability, the practical consequences are not always dire.

That all data is represented in computers as numbers means that a common underlying symbol system serves as the basis for all forms of expression. This is another significant feature. Think of how advantageous it would be if everyone used precisely the same alphabet the world over. Even if this alphabet were used to represent different languages, it would still mean that publishing (storing information) and communications (transmitting information) would be a great deal easier than it is now.

All computing is based on the fact that numbers are used to denote the things that interest us. Whether these numbers represent words, pictures, sounds, music, measurements, qualities, or whatever else we choose, they are all collections of numbers in the end. The collective set of numeric coding schemes used to represent the data that computers process constitutes what we call the digital domain. As you shall see, all computerized information is captured, stored, processed, and transmitted in the digital domain; this is the chief source of the great power and flexibility of modern computing. Understanding the scope and range of the digital domain reveals the true potential of the computer as an information and communications machine.

Analog Versus Digital Information

Even though modern information technologies are based on digital representations of data, many natural forms of representing information are analog. Strictly speaking, the terms *analog* and *digital* fit more comfortably in the discourse of signal processing, the realm of communications technologies. Considering these concepts in the context of how information may be represented in general, however, is useful. **Analog** representations are continuous over some dimension, such as time. Sound provides a good example for how information may be represented in analog form. Sounds are rapid vibrations that are transmitted as variations in air pressure. If you were to measure the intensity of a tone, for instance, it would be plotted as a continuously undulating line or wave, like the one depicted in Figure 2.1. Its amplitude or intensity would vary smoothly and continuously over time.

Continuity is an essential feature of analog information. At every instant, we can measure the amplitude of a sound, for example. Hence, the curve in Figure 2.1 plots an infinite amount of information because a continuous curve has an infinite number of points. Just about everything in nature is susceptible to an analog representation. Besides sound, light, water, electricity, wind, and so on are all measurable using analog methods.

In contrast, digital information is, of course, discrete and finite. A digital representation of sound, for example, would be a finite series of instantaneous pulses. The intensity of the pulse is measured at distinct intervals of time. Between these intervals no measurements are made. Figure 2.2 shows the same sound illustrated in Figure 2.1, but represented digitally. In contrast to analog forms, a digital representation contains a finite amount of information. Digital information sacrifices exactness for a precise, compact representation.

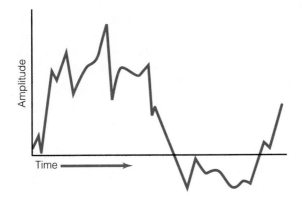

Figure 2.1
Sound can be plotted as a wave whose amplitude varies continuously over time. Here is a sample wave pattern.

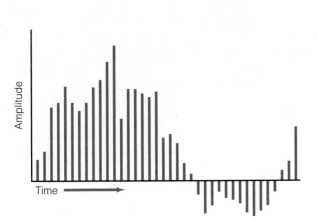

Figure 2.2
A sampled version of the sound wave in Figure 2.1 is shown here. The bars represent sampled amplitudes measured at regular intervals. These values can be used to reconstruct a facsimile of the original analog signal.

Even so, if the number of intervals over time is sufficient, a digital representation is a good facsimile of its analog counterpart. In fact, under the right conditions, digital and analog representations can be exchanged for one another with acceptable accuracy. Thus, analog representations of information based on sound, images, and the like can be digitized or converted to a digital representation. Conversely, the digital information stored and processed on a computer system can be converted to analog form for other uses. Compact discs, for instance, store music in digital form, but a CD player converts it back to analog form to drive your speakers.

Advantages of the Digital Domain

So far we have emphasized the digital or discrete character of computing. Keep in mind that computers are electronic machines, too. This is also a significant factor: The operation of a computer system is based on the flow, processing, and interchange of electronic signals. Electronic devices are very fast; the operating speeds of a modern computer system are measured in billionths of a second. Even its slowest devices, those hampered by mechanical components, operate at speeds that are blindingly fast to us. Digital electronic signals offer great flexibility, too. They may be amplified, combined, sorted out, filtered, and manipulated in various ways.

Because the digital domain is predominantly an electronic one, this marriage of electronic technology with digital data representation results in a number of distinct advantages over conventional information technologies based on analog forms. To appreciate the power and flexibility of digital forms of information, let's consider each of these factors briefly.

- **Precision.** As mentioned, the underlying language of digital media is numeric. Numbers are distinct and unambiguous; this means that digital representations can be manipulated precisely. For example, a conventional black-and-white photograph likely contains hundreds of shades of gray. A digitized photograph, however, assigns a distinct value for each separate shade of gray. See Figure 2.3. We could match two shades of gray in separate areas of a digitized image simply by comparing their numbers. If the numbers are the same, the shades are identical. Matching shades of gray in a conventional photograph would be subjective, more difficult, and therefore less reliable.

- **Ordinality.** Numbers express ordering, too; for example, 1 comes before 2, 2 before 3, and so on. This concept of ordering is called **ordinality.** The encoding of digital data can take advantage of this built-in ordinality. For example, we can arrange the shades of gray discernible in a black-and-white image from darkest black to the lightest white. We could then assign increasing values so that low numbers mean dark shades and high values light ones, as in Figure 2.4. This makes comparing two shades in a digital image a simple matter—the darker shade has a lower number. The ordering of values has a variety of important uses for nearly all forms of data.

- **Efficient Storage.** Digital media are physically represented and stored using electronic, electromagnetic, or optical technologies. All of these offer the basic advantage of compact storage. In other words, the amount of information stored per unit of measure is much greater than with any conventional media. For example, the single letter "e" on this page takes up as much width as roughly 300 copies of "e" when they are stored on a compact disc.

    If we assume that a typical page has 70 symbols per line (counting punctuation and spaces) and has 50 lines, then the average page stores about 3500 symbols. If a typical printed book numbered 300 pages, it would store more than 1 million symbols. Yet these totals are puny compared with the capacities of different forms of computer storage, as shown in Table 2.1. A single floppy disk could store the equivalent of almost one and one-third books. A typical CD-ROM could store almost 650 books. By contrast, if the hard drive of your system could store up to 34 billion symbols, it would take a printed book with more than 9.8 million pages to match this capacity.

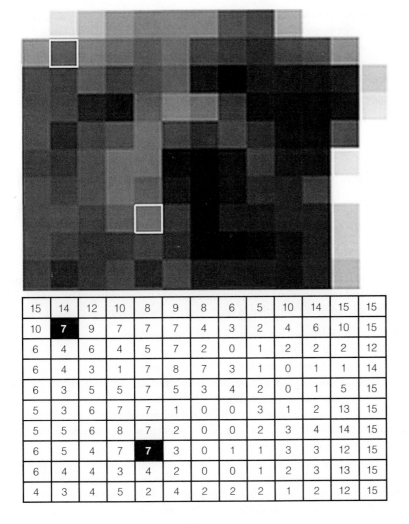

15	14	12	10	8	9	8	6	5	10	14	15	15
10	**7**	9	7	7	7	4	3	2	4	6	10	15
6	4	6	4	5	7	2	0	1	2	2	2	12
6	4	3	1	7	8	7	3	1	0	1	1	14
6	3	5	5	7	5	3	4	2	0	1	5	15
5	3	6	7	7	1	0	0	3	1	2	13	15
5	5	6	8	7	2	0	0	2	3	4	14	15
6	5	4	7	**7**	3	0	1	1	3	3	12	15
6	4	4	3	4	2	0	0	1	2	3	13	15
4	3	4	5	2	4	2	2	2	1	2	12	15

Figure 2.3
The blocks in the top half of the diagram show a close-up view of a digitized image composed of uniformly sized areas called pixels (for picture elements). The pixels denote shades of gray in a monotone (black and white) photo. Can you identify the pixels that have the same shades of gray by visual inspection? Note, for example, the two boxed pixels in the image. Are they the same shade of gray? Contrasts with the surrounding blocks often play tricks on the eye and make it difficult to determine. When shades of gray are represented by numbers (as in the bottom half of the diagram), it is easy to decide. Both the numbers are the same. This is how a computer compares digital data.

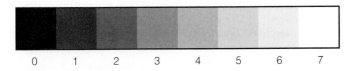

0   1   2   3   4   5   6   7

Figure 2.4
Eight shades of gray from darkest to lightest can be arranged in order and numbered from 0 to 7, respectively. Deciding whether an image is lighter or darker than another can be decided by comparing their number values. If a given value is lower than some other, it is darker. If it is higher, it is lighter.

■ **Fast Transfer.** The technologies supporting digital media can transport or transfer digital data rapidly compared with other forms. For example, an average typist can transcribe 40 to 60 words per minute. On the other hand, the slowest connector on a desktop computer can transfer data at a rate almost 1800 times as fast. Other types of connections are much faster.

■ **Absolute Replication.** If you photocopy a document or image, the resulting copy is not a perfect duplicate. Xerography, like photography, is an analog process; each time a duplicate is itself duplicated, a small but noticeable degradation of the image occurs. If we continued to photocopy each new copy, eventually the imperfections and noise inherent in the process would become clearly visible. On the other hand, when you duplicate a digital picture or document, the copy replicates the original. Not only is there no degrading of the signal, the copy is indistinguishable from the original. (After all, both are just lists of numbers.) This constitutes **absolute replication.** This is why a musical performance recorded to digital compact

Table 2.1 *Using a printed book as a standard measure, the capacities of different forms of computer storage are compared.*

COMPARING MEDIA	
Page	70 symbols × 50 lines
Book	300 pages
Floppy disk	1.33 books (1.4 million symbols)
CD-ROM	649.1 books (680 million symbols)
DVD-R	4,806 books (5 billion symbols)
Hard drive	30,678 books (34 billion symbols)

disc sounds the same time after time. The same is not true for analog phonograph records and tape; wear and tear ultimately corrupt the recording. The capability for unlimited, absolute replication is an important characteristic of digital media.

■ **Resolution Independence.** Roughly speaking, **resolution** defines the capacity for detail contained in a message or signal. For example, a television picture has a resolution that is based on and limited by the number of scan lines that constitute the screen. Audio signals also have limited capacities for representing the highs and lows of the original sound. Signals with greater resolution usually have higher fidelity. In an analog system, the sender and receiver of a signal must be perfectly matched. Specifically, the receiver must be capable of handling the resolution of the signal created by the sender.

Digital systems are not so limited. In fact, for digital systems, the quality of the received signal can be easily scaled to the characteristics of the receiver rather than those of the original source. Practically speaking, this means that computers with very different performance characteristics can transfer and portray the same data. For example, high-resolution images and high-fidelity sound can be processed and portrayed acceptably by systems that are not equipped to handle such resolution. The resolution of the digital data is independent of the machines processing it.

■ **Random and Selective Access.** Digital data can be organized to permit two distinct forms of access. Because discrete data consists of physically distinct chunks of symbols, we can organize it so. In other words, we can stuff digital data into bins or convenient pockets for later access. If we know exactly where each of these bins is located, then we can access that data directly. This is called **random access** because the amount of time it takes to find the item does not depend on the previous access. See Figure 2.5. By contrast, in analog systems, access is always sequential. Consider, for example, an audio cassette tape. To play a song stored in the middle of the tape, you must physically move past all the songs that precede it.

Digital data can be searched out selectively, too. **Selective access** means that the item is found based on analyzing its content for desired properties. For example, the locations of all the occurrences of a given word in a document can be found by searching through the text for sequences of letters that match it. See Figure 2.6.

■ **Compression.** Information is interesting to us because it is neither totally redundant nor completely random. An unmodulated droning sound contains little or no information for us. In fact, if it is not too loud, after a while we become inured to it and fail to notice it at all. On the other hand, when you view your television screen between channels, you see a snowy picture filled with random noise.

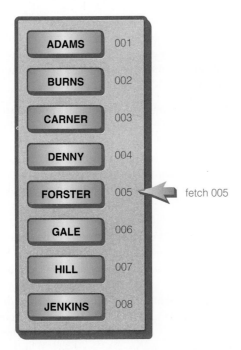

Figure 2.5
Digital data can be organized in standard units. These units can be numbered or addressed for convenient access. If we know the number of a particular item, we can fetch it directly. This is called **random access.** *Random access is a faster and more efficient means of locating digital data.*

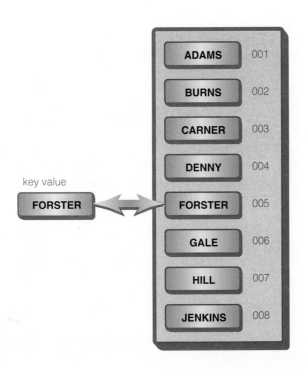

Figure 2.6
Digital data can also be searched based on content. For example, using the key, we can try to find a match with a list of names stored in the bins. This is called **selective access.** *We do, of course, need a search strategy to find our results. We might jump around randomly in the list until we find our match or run out of items to consult. A more orderly strategy would be to use a* **serial search.** *This means starting at either bin #001 or #008 and examining each in order until the search is done,*

Nothing is discernible about it, either. Information lies somewhere in between chaotic randomness (TV snow) and total redundancy (droning sound). Information has some redundancy or patterns, but it also has some novelty or disruption of redundancy.

When information is represented digitally—that is, numerically—we can exploit this propensity for patterns. In short, we can describe the extent to which information contains redundancy and novelty numerically. This is the heart and soul of **data compression** techniques—that is, methods used to combine binary data into more compact forms. Data compression replaces numeric sequences by other, more concise numeric sequences, yet the reverse process can reproduce the originals when needed. Compressed data requires less space for storage and is transmitted more quickly. As you shall see, data compression is a convenience for some and a necessity for other, richer forms of information. (You will find out more about data compression in Chapter 20.)

■ **Content Analysis and Synthesis.** Digital data is subject to processes that analyze and combine it in useful ways. This, of course, is the intent of computing. For example, a large collection of photographs stored conventionally (in albums, perhaps) can be unwieldy. The same collection stored as digitized images can be processed using selective techniques that look for specific structures or content. Thus, the images can be classified and sorted for quick access. At the same time, digital images can be abstracted and combined in new ways, offering even greater practical uses.

When you visit a favorite retail Web site, for example, the Web site may be configured to recognize whether you are new or a returning visitor. It can record the pages visited and examine these choices later to look for specific patterns. In this way, the data is analyzed to infer what sorts of interests you have and what products you might be willing to purchase. Each time you return to the site, more data is analyzed to create a newer, more accurate profile of you as a potential customer. Thus, a computer system can not only record and store information, its processing capabilities may be used to analyze and synthesize that information to produce even more useful forms of information.

Digital Basics: Binary Bits and Bytes

As mentioned earlier, digital representations of information involve numerically encoding it as data. The numerical coding scheme for all forms of digital data, however, is a binary one rather than the decimal one we are accustomed to. The **binary numbering system** is a base-2 positional numbering system. Let us elaborate in more detail.

A **positional notation** is one in which the order or position of each symbol conveys a special meaning. In a nonpositional notation, each occurrence of a given symbol has the same meaning as any other occurrence. For example, if we counted sheep using simple tick marks, four sheep might be represented in this manner.

Each tick means one sheep; the order of the ticks adds no special significance to the number. Decimal notation, on the other hand, is a positional scheme. The decimal numbers

$$346$$
$$463$$

both contain the same symbols, but they denote different numbers. In the first decimal number, the 3 denotes three hundreds (3×10^2), the 4 denotes four tens (4×10^1), and the 6 signifies six units (6×10^0). In a positional notation, both the numerals and their respective positions are significant for denoting the number.

As you can see, each digit position in the decimal notation represents some product of a power of 10. We can rewrite any number in the base-10 system as the sum of the products of its powers of 10:

$$(3 \times 10^2) \quad + \quad (4 \times 10^1) \quad + \quad (6 \times 10^0)$$
$$300 \quad + \quad 40 \quad + \quad 6 \quad = 346$$
$$[\text{hundreds} \quad + \quad \text{tens} \quad + \quad \text{units}]$$

In base-10, there are exactly ten different numerals available as symbols $\{0, 1, 2, \ldots, 9\}$.

We are so accustomed to using decimal notation that it seems both natural and intuitive. In spite of this fact, other base positional notations are available to represent numbers. **Octal** is base-8. Each symbol denotes a power of eight, and numerals are limited to the set $\{0, 1, 2, \ldots, 7\}$. The numerals 346 in an octal representation are as follows:

$$\begin{array}{ccccc} (3 \times 8^2) & + & (4 \times 8^1) & + & (6 \times 8^0) \\ 192 & + & 32 & + & 6 & = 230 \text{ (decimal)} \end{array}$$

Binary, of course, is a base-2 notation. This means that each symbol represents a power of 2, and there are two available numerals for representing numbers, specifically $\{0, 1\}$. Suppose that 110011 expresses a binary value. Its interpretation would be as follows:

$$\begin{array}{ccccccccccccc} (1 \times 2^5) & + & (1 \times 2^4) & + & (0 \times 2^3) & + & (0 \times 2^2) & + & (1 \times 2^1) & + & (1 \times 2^0) \\ 32 & + & 16 & + & 0 & + & 0 & + & 2 & + & 1 & = 51 \end{array}$$

Because binary is a positional notation, the order of symbols is still significant for determining the number denoted. But because binary is base-2, there are only two possible symbols, and each position is a power of 2. This means that quantities expressed in binary notation will likely require more symbols than decimal notation. For example, the decimal number 111 would be expressed in binary as 1101111.

$$\begin{array}{ccccccccccccc} (1 \times 2^6) & + & (1 \times 2^5) & + & (0 \times 2^4) & + & (1 \times 2^3) & + & (1 \times 2^2) & + & (1 \times 2^1) & + & (1 \times 2^0) \\ 64 & + & 32 & + & 0 & + & 8 & + & 4 & + & 2 & + & 1 & = 111 \end{array}$$

Binary notation is very simple because only one of two values is needed to express any binary digit. This is the main reason why binary numbering is preferred for encoding data in a computer system. Binary numbers are simply easier to store, transmit, and process electronically than is our conventional decimal notation. Consequently, all forms of digital data are represented fundamentally using some binary coding scheme. Whether the data denotes text, numbers, pictures, sounds, or whatever, it is encoded on a computer system as some sequence of binary digits.

Each *binary digit* is called a **bit.** A single bit, though, is not very expressive. At most, it can denote one of two values. Instead, bits are usually combined to form larger sequences or **strings.** A very common unit is a string of eight bits called a **byte.** A byte can denote $2 \times 2 \times 2 \times 2 \times 2 \times 2 \times 2 \times 2 = 2^8$ or 256 possible values, that is, from 0 (00000000) to 255 (11111111). One byte could be used to encode a single item of information potentially having as many as 256 interpretations, depending on its value.

For example, one byte is sufficient to denote both uppercase and lowercase alphabets, as well as other printed character symbols used to compose text. Suppose that we assigned uppercase 'A' the value of 00000000 (0), 'B' the value 00000001 (1), 'C' the value 00000010 (2), and so on. The lowercase letter 'a' could be encoded starting at 00011011 (27), 'b' the value 00011100 (28), through 'z' with the value 00011000 (48). This would still leave plenty of assignments for punctuation, numerals, special symbols, and the like. Similarly, we could denote 256 shades of gray or colors for some piece of a picture and store that picture element in a single byte, too. And, of course, we could use a single byte to denote a simple, unsigned integer value from 0 to 255, as well.

These are just some of the ways in which binary numbering can be used to encode data of various forms. It may be necessary to combine bits into larger strings or sequences, but the principle remains the same. All meaningful forms of information are represented by some collection and configuration of binary numbers.

In every computer system, each item of data is usually constrained to some maximum number of bits called its **precision.** For example, a text symbol may have a precision of 8 bits or a byte; integers may have a precision of 64 bits or 8 bytes. Whether it is a byte or larger, the precision is always finite. This, of course, implies that any digital symbol system used for computer storage is finite as well. Only so many meanings can be denoted when there is a finite limit on the number of different values used to represent them. This principle is called **finite precision.** As you will see in subsequent treatments, whether you are representing numbers, text, pictures, sounds, or whatever, finite precision will often have significant consequences for that coding scheme.

Working with Binary Numbers

Reading long strings of 1s and 0s can be both tedious and difficult. Computing professionals rarely deal with binary numbering directly, so there is little need for you to do so. Instead, binary strings can be represented more compactly and conveniently using hexadecimal numbering. If you can count to 15, you can use hexadecimal numbering to represent binary strings.

Hexadecimal is a base-16 notation. This means that any hexadecimal digit (called *hex,* for short) has the range of 0 to 15; and each hex digit position is a power of 16. An obvious problem, though, is how to represent hex digits that are 10 or greater (in decimal)? The answer is to invent new digits for the decimal equivalents of 10, 11, 12, 13, 14, and 15. In hex, these are assigned respectively the letters A, B, C, D, E, and F.

The convenience of hex numbering is this: A single hex digit represents the same value as four binary digits. To put it another way, a byte—8 binary digits—can be represented by a two-digit number in hexadecimal. (For details of how this works, see the online resource, "Discovering More About Binary Numbers.") Consult Table 2.2. Each 4-digit binary sequence has a unique equivalent hex digit value. Thus, we can represent any arbitrary binary number by substituting the appropriate hex digit for each four-digit sequence in binary.

Suppose, for example, that a byte held the binary value of 11111111. Divide the byte into two four-bit sequences, namely 1111 and 1111. We can see from Table 2.1 that our byte would be represented as FF in hexadecimal. (We saw earlier that 11111111 = 255 in decimal; $F \times 16^1 + F \times 16^0 = 15 \times 16 + 15 \times 1 = 255$.) Also previously we saw that 1101111 is equal to 111 in decimal. What would be the hex equivalent? Again, if we divide the original number into 4-bit sequences, we get 0110 and 1111. Notice that a leading zero was added to the most significant portion of the number to produce four-bit segments. This, of course, does not affect its value; but it is convenient for the hex conversion. After consulting the table, it is evident that the hex equivalent is 6F. (Compare: $6 \times 16^1 + F \times 16^0 = 96 + 15 = 111$.)

Table 2.2   *There are 15 different digit values in the base-16 or hexadecimal notation. The equivalent value for each hex digit is shown in both binary and decimal.*

Base 10		Base 2		Base 16
0	=	0000	=	0
1	=	0001	=	1
2	=	0010	=	2
3	=	0011	=	3
4	=	0100	=	4
5	=	0101	=	5
6	=	0110	=	6
7	=	0111	=	7
8	=	1000	=	8
9	=	1001	=	9
10	=	1010	=	A
11	=	1011	=	B
12	=	1100	=	C
13	=	1101	=	D
14	=	1110	=	E
15	=	1111	=	F

The conversion process works nicely in reverse as well. Suppose that a byte is numbered 2A in hex. What is the binary equivalent? The digit 2 = 0010 in binary and A = 1010; so 00101010 (or 101010) is the binary equivalent. (Do the conversions to decimal to convince yourself that it is correct.) With a little practice, you will be working in binary with the best of them.

Converting Information to Digital Form

Any piece of information that is stored, transmitted, or otherwise processed by computers must be represented in binary digital form. The process of converting information into a binary representation is called **digitization.** The nature of this process, however, depends on whether the original information is analog or discrete.

Digitizing Discrete Forms of Information

You will recall that discrete forms of information are those whose interpretations are distinct and unambiguous. Text and numbers represent information in a discrete form. To digitize a discrete form of information, all that is necessary is to agree on a mapping of the original symbol system to a binary numbering. Consider the following example.

Suppose we want to represent any decimal number using a binary scheme that encodes each digit of that number. This means that the original number is divided into individual digits and each digit is encoded distinctly as a symbol. The resulting string of binary codes would denote the original decimal number. A natural way of mapping each digit to a binary number is simply to represent it by its binary equivalent. Consequently, we could use the following table as a mapping of our symbol systems.

Base 10		Base 2
0	=	0000
1	=	0001
2	=	0010
3	=	0011
4	=	0100
5	=	0101
6	=	0110
7	=	0111
8	=	1000
9	=	1001

Digits 8 and 9 require a minimum of four bits to encode them, so we will adopt a uniform precision of four bits for each digit code. This makes it more convenient to both store and convert values back and forth. How then would we convert 346 to this digital form? By substituting each decimal numeral with the corresponding four-bit pattern, we get the sequence

0011	0100	0110
3	4	6

In fact, a method very similar to this one, called **binary coded decimal** (or **BCD**), is used by some computer systems to represent some forms of numeric information.

Even though this technique of representing numbers is acceptable, there are some trade-offs. First, digitized numbers using this scheme are variable-length codes. Specifically, the length of the code sequences depends on how many decimal digits were present in the original number. When converting back to decimal form, we have to account for how many four-bit sequences are needed to interpret the original number accurately. If a series of numbers was stored in this manner consecutively in a series of bytes, for example, we have to keep track of where one number ends and another starts. A second problem is performing arithmetic with numbers digitized in this manner. Multiplying 346 by 3 would require converting the numbers to some other form to complete the operation—and then converting it back using our binary-based code. (Can you see why this is necessary?) For these reasons, although it is perfectly suitable for some applications, BCD and our simplified version of it are not the favored methods used to digitize numeric information.

The moral of this story, though, is a simple one. Any coding scheme that you adopt will have some benefits and some trade-offs. In later chapters, we will examine in greater detail how various forms of information are normally digitized. In these treatments, we will consider both the strengths and weaknesses of these techniques. An appreciation of these factors is essential for managing digital information effectively.

Digitizing Analog Forms of Information

Most natural forms of information are analog. For instance, consider a shade of red. How red is it? There is no precise way to determine this. It is not difficult to compare it with other shades. We might even be able to order them or even match identical or resembling shades. Even so, we do not normally deal with colors using a discrete representation or measure.

On the other hand, a discrete representation is precisely what is required to digitize analog forms of information such as pictures, recorded sounds, and so on. For analog data, the process of digitization requires two steps: sampling the information and quantizing the sample. **Sampling**—as the name suggests—means choosing some discrete sample of the information as representative of the whole. Once this is done, the sample can be measured, or **quantized,** using a discrete scale that can be mapped to a binary encoding.

Admittedly, this all sounds pretty complicated, but the principle is not. In fact, you have probably employed this method when using an ordinary bathroom scale to weigh yourself. Such scales use a spring-loaded mechanism to measure weight as a function of the pressure exerted on that mechanism. The more you weigh, the more compression the springs register. Older models use an analog dial that reacts to the spring compression measured continuously as pounds over time.

Suppose that you step onto such a scale. How much do you weigh? Normally, when you first step on such a scale, the dial fluctuates greatly as the spring mechanism attempts to stabilize under the force of your body weight. If the mechanism is sensitive, it will react to even the slightest changes in pressure. The result is that the dial fluctuates continuously—even if only by small amounts. If you fidget or shift your weight, the scale will fluctuate appreciably. At some point, though, you will decide that the dial registers a representative measure of your current weight. When you decide to read the scale, you are sampling the information. In other

DISCOVERING MORE

Binary Numbers

Hexadecimal numbering is used in a variety of contexts to represent the underlying binary values used for representing information in the digital domain. From text codes to color numbers to memory addresses, hex is the lingua franca of the digitally fluent. To find out more about binary numbers and other positional notations, consult the online resource, "Discovering More About Binary Numbers."

words, even though the measure may fluctuate continuously over time, this instant's reading is an acceptable sample of its overall content.

But what does the dial read? The dial is usually marked conveniently with a sequence of hash marks and numbers that serve as a discrete scale for expressing your weight. Thus, the measuring scale has been quantified, so each reading can be assigned a discrete value that is both distinct and unambiguous. Suppose that the arrow sits between two hash marks on the scale. The normal thing to do is to round off the value to one of these numbers. Even though the scale may measure your weight exactly, you often have to compromise such analog measures to express them precisely. The process of quantizing an analog measure to a discrete scale almost always involves some estimation or rounding for the sake of precision.

Precision is a very useful attribute, usually worth some loss of accuracy. Besides being concise, precise measurements are unequivocal or repeatable. For example, if you tell someone that you weigh 150 pounds, he or she can understand that by repeating what it means. (Imagine filling a bag with sand until it weighs 150 pounds and then trying to lift and carry it. You would get an accurate idea of what 150 pounds means.) Accordingly, we are often willing to sacrifice some tolerance for exactness to achieve precision.

The process of sampling and quantization in the digital domain is similar, but it varies depending on the original form of information being digitized. Consider the case of converting a black-and-white photograph of a dog to digital form. See Figure 2.7a. The goal, of course, is to convert the photo to some sequence of binary numbers so that its important properties are captured with both acceptable accuracy and precision.

In this instance, because the original is a photo, the sampling would be done spatially rather than over time. It would involve breaking up the structure of the picture into smaller elements that faithfully represent its pictorial content. A convenient way to do this is to place a grid over the photo that divides it into separate, but equally sized areas. The areas should be small enough to capture meaningful detail. Each of the squares in the grid, like the one in Figure 2.7b, is called a **picture element** or **pixel.** Each pixel is a sample from the original picture taken from the spatial domain. In Figure 2.7b, the sample rate is 28×44 for a total of 1,232 pixels. If you examine the grids in the figure, you may note that some of them contain more than one shade. For example, at the boundaries, part of a grid may contain both dog and the white background. Digital information, however, must be unambiguous. Consequently, the process of sampling usually incorporates some technique whereby ambiguous information is rendered uniform. In Figure 2.7c, the pixels are averaged to produce uniform shades of gray within.

Quantizing this sampled photo means converting the shade of intensity within a given pixel to some precise quantity. Assume that we decide to adopt a scale of 16 different discernible shades from black to white. To quantize each pixel, we have to decide which shade value most accurately represents the pixel content. We could assign the values 0 through 15 to denote ascending intensities from darkest black to brightest white, as shown in Figure 2.7d.

Converting these 16 values to a binary representation is easy enough. We could use a straight binary encoding of the original values requiring a precision of 4 bits per pixel. Our sample image (1,232 pixels) could be stored as a series of 616 bytes (2 pixels per byte).

This is basically how images are digitized for processing using computers. As the example in Figure 2.8 attests, two very different sources of error are inherent to the process. First, the sampling rate may introduce some error. In Figure 2.8b, some of the pixels contain more than one shade of gray or intensity. These differences must be discounted in favor of a single interpretation. When the digitized image is converted back to a visible form, as in Figure 2.8c, some sampling error is evident. If the sampling rate is poorly matched to the content of the image, the details of the original may be irretrievably lost, as shown in Figure 2.8b. A second kind of error may be introduced during quantization. The measuring scale may be too coarse; specifically, it may not have a sufficient range of values to differentiate details appropriately. For example, in Figure 2.8c, the effect of using only four shades of gray results in false contours on the surface of the dog. This means differentiating areas sharply in the digital image that vary more smoothly in the original.

Figure 2.7

*Digitizing the photo of man's best friend involves two states: **sampling** and **quantizing**. The process of sampling is shown here in two steps. First the image (a) is subdivided into regular units called pixels, as shown in (b). The area enclosed by the pixel boundaries is averaged to produce a uniform shade of gray. This averaging is shown in (c). Some of the detail in the original image may be lost if the sampling resolution is too coarse. Quantizing converts the shade of each pixel to a discrete value or number on a uniform scale, as shown in (d). Shades are matched as closely as possible to those values permitted by the scale. These numbers are then stored in a format that can be converted back to an image for display. The scale should have enough range to capture differences in shades from the sampled image. If the range is too small, fidelity will be lost.*

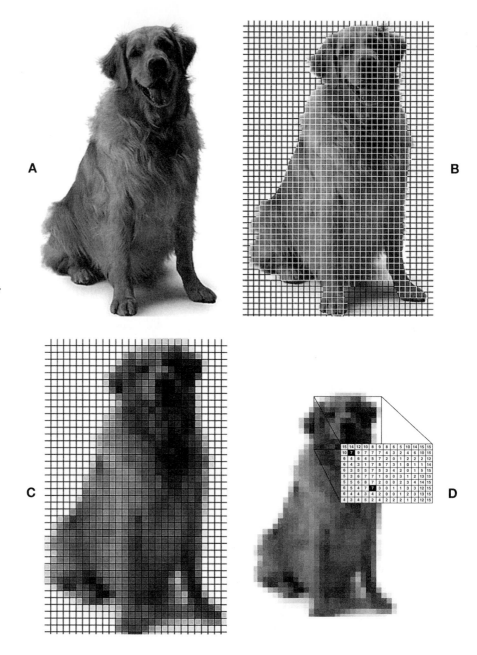

How then do you choose an appropriate sampling rate and a sufficient range of values for digitizing analog information? Fortunately, it is not entirely a hit-or-miss proposition. As you will learn in later chapters, given the type of signal that we are digitizing, we can predict sampling rates and ranges of values that will minimize the effects of these types of errors.

On the other hand, another potential source of error in the digitization process resists any theoretically derived controls: noise. **Noise** refers to unpredictable errors that are introduced into the digitization process, usually by the medium itself. For example, digitizing an image may result in errors that are artifacts of the imaging system itself (the lens, for instance). Noise is random misinformation. And most digitizing methods must account for some sources of noise if the results of the process are both accurate and robust. Figure 2.8d illustrates how a noisy imaging system may produce a digitized image with unwanted artifacts.

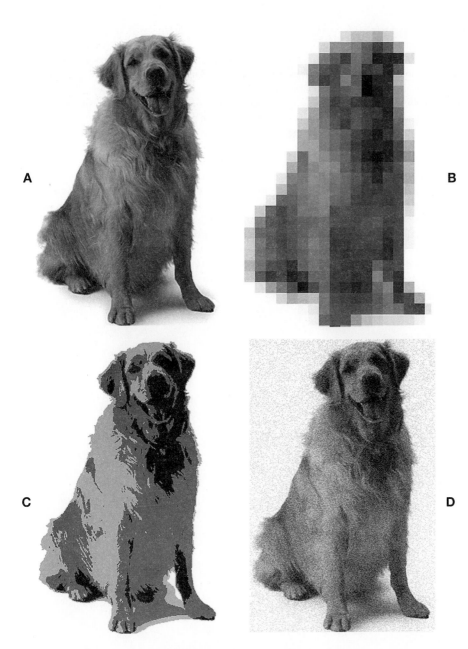

Figure 2.8
Errors in the digitizing process can arise from several sources. Compare the original image (a) with these less-than-perfect versions. Poor sampling resolution, that is, using too few pixels, can result in an image that is so blocky (b) that it is almost unrecognizable. Likewise, a small range or number of shades for pixel values can create an image that has false contours. In (c), the resolution is high enough, but the pixels are quantized at only four shades of gray. Finally, (d) shows how a noisy imaging system can introduce a speckled effect in the digitized image.

Copyright Laws in the Digital Domain

The growth of digital information technology has posed new challenges for our traditional interpretations of individual rights and intellectual property. The World Wide Web, for example, brings a wealth of material instantly to your home, office, or lab. In other media, we recognize the property rights of the creators of intellectual content. Should we (can we?) protect the rights of the creators or producers of this content on the Web? Read about the issues of intellectual property rights and technology in our essay "Copyright Laws in the Digital Domain."

SOCIAL THEMES

■ Summary

There are two fundamental categories for representing data. Analog representations measure some property continuously over such dimensions as time and space. Digital data is based on discrete symbolic representations that incorporate numbering. Even though digital and analog representations of information are exchangeable, there are decided advantages to representing and storing digital data on an electronic computer system. The precision and natural ordinality of digital data make it easier to process and evaluate. Digital data created on an electronic computer system is stored and transmitted more economically than is possible using other technologies. Digital data may be accessed in a variety of ways; digital data can be replicated over and over again without loss of information. Digital systems have resolution independence; their processing capabilities assist in analyzing and combining data in useful ways.

In succeeding chapters, you will learn more about the digitization of both discrete and analog forms of information. Whether the original information is discrete or analog, it is converted to a sequence or stream of binary numbers that are stored in, processed by, and transmitted between computer systems. If the original information is already in discrete form, digitizing means assigning a binary coding for its meaningful values or symbols. Converting analog data to a digital form is a two-step process. The data is rendered discrete by sampling, and the samples are quantized to produce a binary encoding. This common denominator of the digital domain is what underlies the convergent power of digital information technology.

■ Terms

analog	finite precision	replication, absolute
binary (numbering system)	hexadecimal (base 16)	resolution
binary coded decimal (BCD)	noise	resolution independence
bit (binary digit)	octal (base 8)	sampling
byte	ordinality	selective access
compression, data	pixel (picture element)	serial search
data	positional notation	strings, binary
digital	precision	
digitization, digitized	quantizing	
discrete	random access	

■ Questions for Review

1. Identify several distinguishing characteristics of modern information technologies (e.g., telephone, radio, and television). Which of these characteristics are most important, in your opinion?

2. Contrast analog and digital forms of information.

3. What is a digital symbol system? Give an example.

4. What are some advantages of digital as opposed to analog representation of information?

5. Contrast positional and nonpositional number systems.

6. How are the decimal and binary number systems alike? How do they differ?

7. Define a bit and a byte.

8. Describe the process called *digitization*. Give some examples to illustrate your definition.

9. Assume the binary coded decimal digital coding scheme for decimal numbers described in the chapter. Exactly why is it necessary to convert such numbers to decimal or, perhaps, binary before performing arithmetic operations? Consider the example, multiplying 346 (represented as the string 001101000110) by 3 (represented as the string 0011).

10. Identify the two steps involved in digitizing analog forms of information.

11. Describe how a sound wave is translated to digital form.

12. What is a pixel? What are pixels used for?

13. What does the term *noise* mean within the context of the digitization process?

14. Besides noise, describe several ways that errors can be introduced into the digitization process.

15. Why is sampling required when analog information is digitized?

16. Identify and describe several advantages that electronic digital media have over conventional forms of information storage.

17. Compare the storage capacities of typical floppy disks, hard disks, and CD-ROMs.

18. Give two reasons why data compression is important in the digital domain.

19. What is meant by the term *finite precision* in digital data storage?

20. What is meant when we say that electronic digital media provide a precision that conventional media forms do not? Discuss the trade-offs inherent in gaining this precision.

21. What is meant when we say that electronic digital media are resolution independent?

22. How do electronic digital media and conventional forms of media storage compare in their ability to replicate or make copies?

23. How do electronic digital media and conventional forms of media storage compare in providing selective access to information?

24. How do electronic digital media and conventional forms of media storage compare in providing the capabilities for information content analysis?

25. What advantages do electronic digital media provide over conventional media forms in the transfer of information?

26. This book is titled *Exploring the Digital Domain*. In your own words, define and explain the "digital domain."

Computing Basics

OBJECTIVES

- **How computers process information**

- **How hardware is organized to support the execution of instructions**

- **How software directs the processing of a computer**

- **The basic role of the operating system in the computing environment**

- **How the operating system's user interface facilitates communication with the user**

- **The common features of application programs**

In Chapter 2, you learned how digital information can incorporate a variety of media. Indeed, a hallmark of the digital domain is that different forms of information can be reduced to a single digital common denominator of bits and bytes. Of course, representing and storing information is just part of the picture. We cannot realize the genuine power of the digital domain until we utilize these bits and bytes for good purposes. This utilization often depends on both processing and transporting digital information. The combined abilities to (1) digitize information from various media, (2) process it into useful forms, and (3) move it across town, across the country, or across the world in a matter of seconds truly define the digital domain. The next two chapters will provide a better understanding of these latter two factors. In this chapter, we will focus on how computers are employed to process information.

Computer Systems

Computers are so commonplace today that we almost take them for granted. Computers sit on our desk tops; we carry them with us in knapsacks and in our pockets; they populate our calculators, cell phones, CD-players, and other entertainment devices; they run our automobiles, microwaves, and a host of other machinery, equipment, and appliances that we depend on daily. Computers are essential for almost every enterprise: banking and finance, communications, transportation, energy, medicine and health care, retail sales, and the list goes on. It was not always this way. In 1969, for example, the film *Colossus: The Forbin Project,* told the story of a giant computer system built to defend the United States from a nuclear first strike by the Soviet Union. The computer Colossus finds a counterpart in the Soviet Union, and the two computers join forces to take over the world and enslave mankind. It sounds laughable to us, but films like *The Forbin Project* spoke to a fear held by many people. Because computers were largely unknown, most people feared them as mysterious and dangerous devices.

The irony, of course, is that several decades later computers have indeed taken over the world. But, nobody noticed. And, yet, in spite of the fact that they are commonplace, computers today remain mysterious, unknown devices to many. Even though the technology that underpins them is complex and complicated, the principles that govern the organization and operation of computers are not. In this chapter, we will reveal the fundamental secrets of how computers compute.

Strictly speaking, today's **computer systems** are electronic digital data processing machines. There is quite a lot packed into that statement, so let's examine it more closely. First of all, computers process data. **Data** is a symbolic representation of information. In the previous chapter, we learned that computers speak binary. Thus, computers process (digital) data composed of binary codes representing various forms of information. Digital computers are also discrete state machines. This means that a process is actually composed of a sequence of states; each state is distinct and separate. In a single state, the processor has executed a particular instruction determining the current status of its data. Normally, we think of a process as continuous over some period of time. In contrast, a computer's process is a sequence of separate, distinct moments—not unlike the frames of a motion picture. In a film, each frame is a "frozen" moment, but when projected at a rapid rate, the result is the illusion of continuous motion. The same is true for digital computers. Each state is distinct but because of the rapid succession of states, processing appears to be continuous and uninterrupted. See Figure 3.1. Lastly, today's generation of computer systems are based on electronic technologies. This was not always the case, and it will likely change in the future. However, the distinct advantage of electronic over earlier technologies is speed. As you will soon see, computers as processors actually perform very simple tasks. But millions of simple steps done rapidly can achieve much more complicated and impressive results. Thus, speed is an important attribute of modern computers.

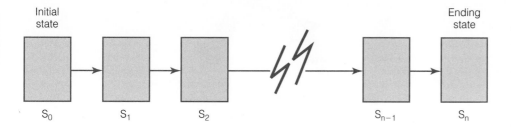

Initial state ... Ending state

S_0 S_1 S_2 S_{n-1} S_n

Figure 3.1

*A computer **process** is a sequence of discrete states. Each state from the initial to the ending state is distinct and defined by the status of key characteristics of the process. These include keeping track of which instruction is being executed and the current status of all data in the process.*

Because computers are discrete state machines, they are rather simple-minded compared with our view of things. In any given state, the computer as a processor is performing some basic task. This state is distinct in that there are no logical connections between it and any previous state or future state. Now that's concentration! Normally, when you or I perform some task, we are aware of each moment as connected to a palpable past with the expectation of an immediate future. Not so for computer systems.

There is another sense in which computers should be recognized as simple-minded. Computers follow instructions. We mentioned in the previous chapter that computers deal only with unambiguous and precise information. For the same reasons, their instructions must also be clear and precise. There is no room for vagueness. One and only one interpretation of an instruction is allowed. This is often a source of frustration for computer users—especially novices. Computer systems will perform precisely what we instruct them to do, even if we did not mean exactly what we said.

Computer processes are directed by a sequence of instructions called a **program.** The situation is similar to cooking with a recipe. As a novice cook, for example, you might read each instruction of the recipe one by one, figure out what it means, and then perform that step. You would continue with the next step, and so on. If you complete each step properly, you will achieve the desired result. In fact, one does not have to be an expert chef to cook from recipes; instead, one must be a good follower of directions.

Computer systems are excellent followers of directions—and that is basically their whole story. Just about every detail concerning the design and function of a computer system is related to its role as an instruction or program interpreter. We mentioned earlier that computers are discrete state machines. At the processor level, the basic states of a computer system are defined by the **instruction-execution cycle.** At any given moment, a computer system is in one of these three fundamental states:

1. **Fetching** the next instruction

2. **Decoding** or interpreting that instruction

3. **Executing** what the instruction prescribes

(Compare with Figure 3.2.) In a cookbook, you might mark your place to recall where the next instruction is. So, too, a computer remembers which instruction is next in the sequence. Cookbook instructions are written in a natural language such as English, but you must determine what each is directing you to perform. Computer instructions are written in binary; these must be translated to the type of actions that the processor can perform. Finally, you complete the instruction by performing the cooking step. A computer system likewise executes some task as prescribed by its instruction.

Figure 3.2

*The instruction-execution cycle for the modern computer system. In the **fetch** phase, the next instruction is identified and retrieved. This is followed by the **decode** phase, in which the instruction is deciphered. Finally, in the **execute** phase, the operation defined by the instruction is implemented. This is a cycle because the series of phases are repeated for each and every instruction of the program until done.*

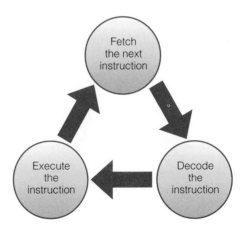

But unlike cooking, computers process information. This means that a number of program instructions are **data instructions**—that is, instructions to perform some operation on specified data. If that data is stored somewhere else, then the instruction-execution cycle expands in this fashion:

1. Fetching the next instruction

2. Decoding or interpreting that instruction

3. Fetching the data referred to in the instruction

4. Executing what the instruction prescribes

5. Producing the result

The difference is subtle, but important. Here is another analogy to convey the idea. If you were instructed to add 2 + 3, you would have all the information you needed to complete the task. On the other hand, if you were instructed to add the last two numbers on the list, you would have to determine what those values were before completing the addition. Most data instructions are written like the latter: They refer to data values indirectly. The processor must fetch those values before processing them. **Indirection** is a powerful feature of the processor, but it does have a cost. The fact that data can be referred to indirectly means that programs can be more general in scope. For example, it would be very easy to create a program that adds any two numbers, provided we had a way to refer to them indirectly. All we would have to do is provide different values each time we executed it in order to produce different results from the same program. The cost is some loss of efficiency. It takes time to fetch data values and transfer results. But today's processors are able to perform these steps at incredible speeds, so this cost is less significant.

The results from a data instruction are often part of a larger task rather than the final answer. As stated, most processors perform very simple types of steps. For instance, they perform arithmetic operations such as addition, subtraction, multiplication, and division on two numbers at a time. On the other hand, suppose that you wanted to find the average of a group of test scores. A computer could solve this problem only if the process were broken down to simpler steps. In short, the processor would have to add the test scores and divide the total by the total number of scores. However, adding all the test scores is too complex for a single instruction. To find the grand total, you would have to instruct the computer to add each score to a running total until there are no more new scores to add. At that point, the running total would be the grand total.

What might seem a relatively straightforward task gets complicated by lots of detail at the level of the processor. The point is that computers require a lot more instructions to handle tasks that we would describe fairly succinctly. (For example, "find the average of the test scores" is enough instruction for most people.)

Consequently, a significant amount of processing is the securing of intermediate results that will eventually be assembled into the final result. To put it another way, computers do a lot of work on scratch paper. Speed is again the secret of its success. The fact that a computer system can perform millions of simple steps at such a rapid pace means that it can complete a more sophisticated task by assembling it incrementally—and yet appear to have completed it almost effortlessly.

Conceived in these terms, a computer system is a rather simple-minded, almost primitive machine. Perhaps we have exaggerated these elements somewhat; but the point is to emphasize that computers are neither mysterious nor too complex for us to understand.

Computer systems are composed of hardware and software. Hardware performs the processes that are dictated by the instructions of the software. Both are very different but intricately bound together. Hardware without software to direct it is just stuff on your desktop. Yet software without hardware to implement its instructions is like so much vapor. In the next two sections, we will examine these fundamental components and how they are organized to serve as a data processing machine.

Basic Hardware

Hardware refers to the devices that comprise a computer system. The old adage is that "if you can kick it, it is hardware." A computer's hardware can be classified in two basic groups: the **processing unit** and **peripherals.** The processing unit is the heart of all computer systems. It is comprised of two major components, the **central processing unit (CPU)** and **main memory.** See Figure 3.3. Memory stores both data and instructions for the processes currently available to the CPU. The CPU manages the instruction-execution cycle. The CPU is connected to main memory by a collection of wires called the **bus.**

Information is stored in memory units that have **addresses.** Thus, the CPU fetches instructions and data by signaling the memory addresses of the items requested. Memory locates these items and sends copies of them over the bus. This is called **reading from memory.** When the CPU stores an item in memory, it passes both the data and address to main memory. This process is dubbed **writing to memory.**

The processing unit may differ in scale and performance from system to system, but its components and their organization are fairly standard for any computer system. Peripherals, on the other hand, come in a greater variety. These are the devices that we add to our computer systems to increase their functionality. There are two general classes of peripherals: secondary memory and input/output peripherals.

The data and instructions stored in main memory are not permanent. When you turn off your computer, for example, the data is lost. Even a brief interruption of electrical power can have the same disastrous effect. Yet, even if memory's data were more permanent, there simply would not be enough of it to handle your storage needs. For these reasons, computer systems have storage devices called **secondary memory** that archive your data and instructions for safe-keeping. Magnetic hard drives and disks and optical drives and discs are examples of secondary memory.

When you **open a file** in a software application, like a word processor, for example, both forms of memory cooperate to accomplish this task. A copy of the data file is stored on a secondary memory device, say your hard drive's disk. A copy of the file is transmitted to main memory, and the process uses the latter copy for any changes that you make. The original copy, however, remains intact on the hard disk. Suppose that you finish editing your document and choose to save the results. **Saving a file** means to write the data stored in main memory to secondary memory. The act of saving, thus replaces the original version with the newer edited one. It is easy to see that both forms of memory are vital for ordinary processing tasks. (We will return to consider memory storage in Chapter 12 for a closer look.)

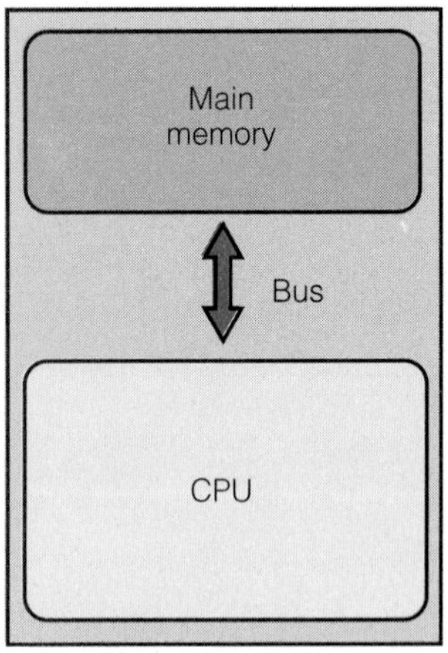

Input/output peripherals are the hardware devices that we use to communicate with our computer systems. An **input device** translates human-readable forms of information to binary-encoded or machine-readable data. The mouse and keyboard are the most common examples of input devices. But, there are many others: joysticks, writing tablets, scanners, and digital cameras—just to name a few. Output devices reverse the process. An **output device** translates machine-readable data into human-readable forms of information. Video monitors, speakers, and printers are popular output peripherals. (Once again, we will revisit this topic; Chapter 13 surveys the landscape of input and output peripherals.)

Software

Hardware provides the platform for information processing with the computer. But hardware by itself is not very interesting. Without software to direct its processing, the hardware is simply inert. **Software** is comprised of programs. Remember that a program is a list of instructions that direct the computer's process. As mentioned, the computer as a processor acts as a single instruction interpreter: it fetches the next binary-encoded instruction of the program, decodes it, and executes it.

The instruction-execution cycle is performed over and over until the process is instructed to halt. From this perspective, a computer system is like an incredibly simple-minded agent that concentrates only on the current activity and proceeds relentlessly to complete the overall task. It is up to the instructions—and this means the author of the instructions—to provide overall guidance and strategy for the process. The programmer is like a playwright who not only creates a premise or plot for the drama but also supplies all the words and actions

Processor system

Figure 3.3

The processor is comprised of a central processing unit and main memory that serves as its primary storage device for both data and instructions. The two communicate over a grouping of lines called the bus. The instructions for a program are stored in main memory. During the instruction-execution cycle, the CPU fetches instructions and data from memory.

that the actors will perform. The actors, of course, bring the play to life, but the playwright has determined in advance what that will be. The hardware brings the program to life as a process, but the programmer decides what that life will be.

Programs, of course, are written by people who speak and think in natural languages such as English, but computers are fluent in binary. How then do programmers write instructions for computers? Fortunately, over the past 50 years computer scientists have developed special programming languages that allow programmers to communicate with computers by meeting them halfway. A **programming language** is symbolic code for expressing computer instructions. Programming languages differ from natural languages in that they are organized to make directing the computer's work easier. (In Chapter 14, we return to consider how software is designed and developed using modern programming languages.)

The analogy of a process as a play is useful up to a point. Both are determined: a play by its script and a process by its sequence of instructions. However, a play is basically always the same. The plot usually doesn't change. Certainly, there are subtle differences among performances, but what happens in each performance does not differ. On the other hand, processes are determined, but what happens is not always the same. How then, do we account for these variations in performances? The basic answer is that computers have the capability of conditional processing.

Conditional processing is the ability to choose alternative actions based on the recognition of changing conditions—both internal and external. For example, think about using your automatic teller machine (ATM). The ATM is run by a program that directs the computer controlling it. As a result, the ATM is limited in what it can do. It can process deposits, debits, transfers, and so on. It cannot read or write e-mail; it cannot look up recipes. But even within these constraints, no two sessions are exactly identical. Instead, the ATM can serve a variety of customers and their differing needs. The bottom line is that the program defines a process that can react or interact with its environment.

Let's consider how this works. The ATM reads your account number from your bank card; this identifies which account the transactions will affect. It accepts your PIN as a security measure to protect against fraud. The ATM asks you to indicate what transactions you wish to perform. It responds to your requests and handles them one by one. The number and order of transactions are up to you. The results, though, depend on the ATM consulting and updating your account. Figure 3.4 illustrates how this process might organized.

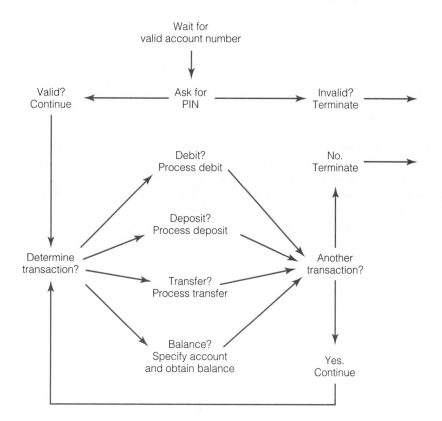

Figure 3.4

The ATM process is logically organized to expect and handle user input at key stages. Initially, the process waits until a valid bank card is inserted in the machine. The user is asked to supply a valid PIN for that account (read from the card). The process then branches in one of two directions: it continues, if the PIN is valid, or terminates otherwise. If it continues, the user is asked to identify which transaction he or she wishes to perform. The transaction is duly processed, and the process asks if the user wishes to continue. If the response is negative, the current session terminates. If the response is positive, the transaction is identified and handled as before. As you can see, there are multiple paths that any given session may take. Thus, the process may vary even if the program that governs it does not.

Indeed, the program governing a process remains the same, but, because the conditions under which it executes may change, the process does not remain the same. In this way, programs can be designed to react to information that is provided for them. This makes them more flexible as well as more robust. Software is flexible if it can respond to different circumstances. Software is robust if it can recover from faults or unexpected conditions. The self-organizing capability of software along with the incredible speed and tremendous accuracy of its hardware is what makes computers such formidable devices. And, this concept of conditional processing is indeed one of computing's fundamental and recurring themes.

Software can be divided into two categories: applications and systems software. **Application software** refers to end-user programs designed to perform specific tasks such as preparing documents, creating graphic images, or sending and receiving electronic mail. **System software** refers to programs that help manage the operation of computer systems. This category also includes development tools such as compilers and interpreters, which are used to create programs that run on computers. The most fundamental type of system software is the operating system. In the next section, we will examine this important class of programs.

Operating Systems

An **operating system (OS)** is a collection of resident programs that manages the computer's resources, supervises the execution of user processes, and provides useful services and security for the computer system. As users, we often feel as if we control what goes on with our computers, but this is not entirely accurate. The operating system, in fact, is in control of our computer systems at all times when they are in use.

Managing the details for operating a computer system can be an arduous and complicated task. Suppose, for example, you wish to edit a document that you created previously using a word processor. If you have ever used a computer system for word processing, you know that to open a file you enter a simple command. In reality, a lot of things are going on behind the scenes. First, the document has to be located. Text documents are stored as text files; a **text file** is a sequence of symbols that are treated as a single document and usually stored externally on a secondary storage medium, such as a disk. Files have names and locations. Once the file is found, it must be transferred—at least in part—to main memory for editing. As mentioned earlier, the transfer from secondary memory to main memory is what is meant by "opening" the file. But, first, memory must be allocated for this use. Care must be exercised to prevent the incoming data from conflicting with the program and other segments of memory currently in use. After memory is set aside for the document, a copy of the file must be transferred from its location on your disk to the reserved segment of main memory. A pathway must be cleared, and the details of the transmission should be overseen to ensure that all goes well. Finally, your word processing program is ready to respond to editing actions and commands.

Sound complicated? In fact, this is just the big picture; we have left out a lot of the details. The point of the story is that if we had to manage all these details, very little productive work would get done. Instead, we would spend most of our time and effort on simply trying to operate our computers. We would most likely make a lot of mistakes, too. Under these circumstances, only the most knowledgeable and patient of users would be able to get anything done at all.

Fortunately, the operating system manages most of these details automatically. Every time the computer system is powered on, portions of the operating system program are loaded into memory. In this manner, the operating system actually controls the computer system at all times. We often think that we are operating the computer; in reality, our actions are requests to the operating system to do such and such. In this manner, the operating system serves as a buffer between the user and the computer system's hardware. See Figure 3.5.

This arrangement has advantages in two ways. First, it relieves us of handling the myriad of details necessary for managing the system. In fact, the operating system creates powerful services that provide an abstract view of the computer's capabilities. Launching applications and storing data in files are two of the kinds of abstractions made possible by the operating system.

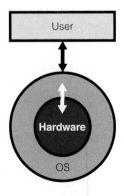

Figure 3.5

The operating system functions as a go-between for the user and the computer's raw hardware features. This shields the user from complicated, tedious details of the hardware's operations and likewise protects the hardware from inadvertent errors committed by the user.

The operating system also protects the computer system from errors committed by users or by their processes. Even when a program is executing, the operating system can interrupt that process if the program commits an illegal condition called an **exception.** For example, division by zero is undefined for most processors, and a program that attempts this can generate an exception. In these circumstances, the operating system often causes the offending program to be terminated prematurely. In some cases, the operating system cannot recover from an exception. In these instances, the OS produces a fatal **system error.** For example, many Windows users have experienced that sinking feeling when the sudden appearance of the "blue screen" signals that our system is crashing.

The operating system can also prevent us from performing actions that might have undesirable results. It monitors our commands and accepts some, asks for verification of some, and rejects others. Thus, the operating system offers some security and protection for the system.

It is difficult to overestimate the importance of the operating system for defining your computing environment. In fact, the choice of operating system is a greater factor in determining how your computer performs—its look and feel in use—than any of its hardware. Some computers with different processors will seem indistinguishable to you if they run the same operating system. For example, Windows will look the same whether the underlying computer is powered by an Intel Pentium or an AMD processor. The Macintosh OS on G4 processors runs much the same as on newer G5 processors. On the other hand, computer systems with the same processor but running different operating systems will perform very differently. As an example, the same Intel processor can serve as a hardware platform for both the Windows and Linux operating systems. Users, though, would hardly acknowledge this fact because of the differences in their operating systems.

As mentioned, the OS provides many services for the user. Some services are essential, such as managing processes. Others are important because they create a more pleasant or productive environment. We shall mention two services of the latter type here: file management, and the user interface. (Later, we will return to complete the picture of the operating system in detail in Chapter 15.)

Managing Files

Underneath the hood of your computer, data is actually stored in physical units that are blocked on disks, CD-ROMs, tape, and so on. The size of these data blocks is usually uniform for that peripheral and medium. On the other hand, data created by user programs is seldom uniformly sized. Think again of a text document created by a word processing program. The number of paragraphs, sentences, words, and letters can vary considerably from one document to the next. The point then is that a single document created by a user application may require a variable number of blocks to store it externally in secondary memory. And, of course, the number of blocks will also depend on the medium used for storage.

The operating system, however, creates a convenient fiction to hide these messy details from us. From our view, data appears to be organized in entities called files. A **file** is a sequence of items treated as a single unit and identified by the system with a unique name. Text files are files of characters or symbols, but there are other types of files, too. A file may contain the instructions of a program, or a file may be a sequence of records. The **file manager** is the functional unit of the OS that creates and maintains the files stored on a specific system. Operating systems have naming conventions for files and usually provide a series of services for managing them. It is the job of the file manager to translate logical requests for file services into those that the hardware can handle.

File names are symbolic names assigned to files. Most operating systems permit the file name to be comprised of two parts: an **identifier** followed by an **extension.** The identifier can be thought of as the proper name for the file. It is used to identify the file from others stored on your computer. Windows, for example, requires that identifiers must be comprised of letters and numbers up to 255 characters in length. The identifier cannot contain any of the special symbols listed in Table 3.1; however, blank or space symbols and the underscore symbol ("_") are permitted. Older versions of Windows and programs designed for these versions will not accept long file name identifiers. These restrict identifiers to no more than 8 symbols or characters (no blanks, please). The extension is the second part of the file name; it is a short sequence of characters intended to denote what type or class of files it belongs to. For Windows, file name extensions are typically three characters in length. (Older versions of Windows limit the extension to three symbols.) Table 3.2 provides some examples of common extensions.

The file name identifier and extension are usually combined with a period as a separator. Here are some examples.

> chapter1.doc
> index.html
> workbook1.xls
> oral_report.ppt
> birthday.mov
> winword.exe
> patricia.jpg

Windows file names are not case sensitive. This means that uppercase and lowercase versions are treated as the same. For example,

> chapter1.doc = CHAPTER1.DOC = Chapter1.Doc

Table 3.1 *Windows does not permit file names that contain any of these symbols. These symbols are used by the OS for other purposes.*

SPECIAL CHARACTERS	
" , "	quotation marks
:	colon
/ , \	slashes
=	equal sign
?	question mark
< , >	less than, greater than symbols
		break symbol
*	asterisk

Table 3.2 *Standard extensions for classifying files managed by the Windows OS.*

COMMON EXTENSIONS FOR WINDOWS	
txt, doc	text documents
htm, html	Web page files
bmp, gif, jpg	image or graphic files
xls	Excel spreadsheet files
wav, mp3, xm	digital sound, music files
ppt	PowerPoint presentation files
mov	digital video files
exe	Windows executable programs
zip	compressed files

Most operating systems provide an abstract structure or organization for locating and storing files. Again, this is a convenient fiction. Data is stored in physical blocks, but file systems can have more complicated structures. Today, most operating systems offer a **hierarchical file system (HFS).** A hierarchy is a series of levels. We often use hierarchies as a tool for organizing information. For example, in Figure 3.6, a segment of the familiar Linnaean classification of living things is shown as a hierarchical tree. The basic idea, of course, is that an item at a given level bears special relations with the connected items above and below it. For example, the kingdom of animals has a number of phyla. One of them is the chordates. Thus, chordate is a class or set that belongs to animals, but there are also others subsets, such as anthropods and mollusks. The phylum chordate has two subphyla, invertebrates and vertebrates; these are subsets of both the chordates and the even larger set, animals. Vertebrates have several member groups (called classes in the Linnaean system), and so on. Hierarchies like the Linnaean system show us the relations of ideas (based on class membership). Thus from the Linnaean hierarchy, we can infer that any vertebrate is both a chordate and an animal; but not all animals are vertebrates. And, for that matter, not all animals are chordates.

Trees are often used in computing and elsewhere to represent hierarchies. Basically, a **tree** is a graph of connected nodes that has a single origin at the highest level called the **root.** The connected node at the preceding level of a given node is its **parent.** The connected node at the succeeding level is its **child.** By the same token, the connected nodes that precede a given node are its **ancestors;** and the connected nodes that succeed it are its **children** or **descendants.** See Figure 3.7.

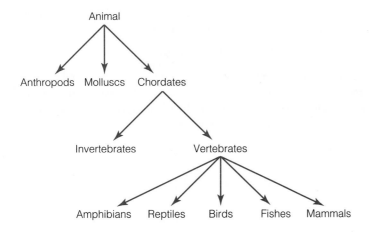

Figure 3.6
Linnaeus introduced a hierarchical organization of the living species. A small segment of that classification is depicted here. At the top level is the kingdom followed by phyla and subphyla. At the bottom level are the classes of vertebrates.

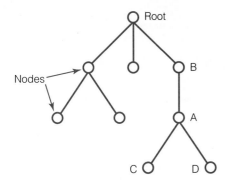

Figure 3.7
*A tree is a special version of a connected graph. Graphs are comprised of **nodes** and links that connect them. Here we see an arbitrary tree depicted as a hierarchy. The root is the origin of the tree. Nodes in a tree often have relatives. Consider node A. It has a single predecessor or parent, B; and it has two successors or children, C and D. The path to D, for example, requires traversing four nodes in order: the root, B, A, and finally D.*

A device such as a hard disk can also be conceived as having a series of levels where files may be likewise organized and stored. These levels have locations called *directories, folders,* or some other system-dependent term. These locations are also given unique names to distinguish them. Figure 3.8 shows how a disk might be organized hierarchically using the operating system Windows. Folders usually contain files and other folders. As illustrated in Figure 3.8, the folder *Pictures* is the parent of the folder *Objects* and therefore contains it. By the same token, the documents *chap1.doc, chap2.doc,* and *chap3.doc* are the children of and contained in the folder *chapters.* The folder *chapters* is the child of *Documents,* and so on.

The root of the file system hierarchy is the device that contains all of the other listed folders and files. To find any specific item, you must trace what is called a **path** from the root to that location. For example, to access the spreadsheet *inventory.xls* (as shown in Figure 3.8), one must open or traverse the D:\ drive, and then the *Documents* folder. To put this another way, the path to a given file or folder is the list of all of its ancestors starting at the root.

In most operating systems, the actual address of a file is written as the path that must be traversed to arrive at the point occupied by the file. These sequences are called **pathnames.** For example, to locate the file *search.gif,* as shown in Figure 3.8, you would need to start at the top level and traverse a distinct path through its three ancestors. The pathname would be written as

D:\Pictures\Objects\search.gif

In this way, the full name of the file includes the distinct path that locates it. That is why it is possible to have two files with the same (short) name on the same disk. As long as they belong to different folders, they actually have different full pathnames.

Sometimes, it is more convenient to refer to a file or folder by its **relative pathname.** This is a convention used to mark the location of items relative to some understood position in the hierarchy. For example, if our current location was (inside) the folder *Documents,* then the relative pathname for file *chap1.doc* would be written as

chapters\chap1.doc

Most of the time, you will be using your computer to create and manage documents of various sorts. These documents, of course, will usually be stored as files on your system. As a result, it is important to keep in mind how things are organized in terms of their hierarchical structure. For example, in order to open a file using some application, you will be asked to

Figure 3.8
The contents of a removable disk are shown hierarchically using a tree.

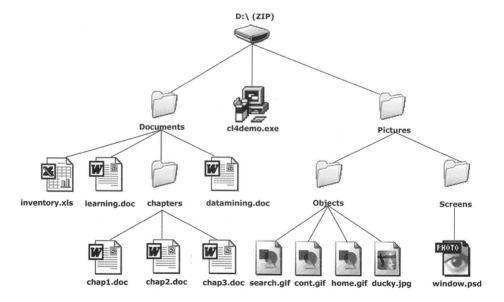

find that file. Finding it will mean specifying either the full or relative pathname for that file. In some instances, however, you will be able to use visual cues to find that file rather than typing the symbolic pathname. But, this is because you are exploiting a graphical user interface—the subject of our next section.

User Interface

As we mentioned earlier, the operating system maintains control of a computer system continuously while the power is on. Consequently, to make any computer system perform tasks that are useful for us, we must communicate our desires as requests or commands to its operating system. The **user interface** is a program that runs almost continuously to interpret our working commands.

The user interface is the medium for our communication with a computer. The mode or means for this communication can vary. In fact, some systems may offer more than one user interface for processing user/system communication. Some are primarily text-based. Commands and messages are communicated by text. Most are visual or graphical. These allow the user to manipulate objects, icons, and gadgets displayed on the monitor to facilitate communication.

Human-Computer Interaction: Text-based User Interfaces

The user interface is the medium through which we communicate our wishes to the operating system. The form and style of that communication are the most important factors in how the system looks and feels. One type of user interface is text-based. With a **text-based user interface,** the user expresses commands as a series of short text strings typed at the keyboard. The syntax or rules for the formation of these commands are usually very precise. Text-based interfaces are often **command line interpreters,** which means that the command processor interprets only one command at a time. Commands are entered when the system signals its readiness to the user with a symbol called a **prompt sign.** Figure 3.9 contains a sequence of commands issued using the command line interpreter for UNIX and its look-alike, the Linux operating system. The prompt sign in this instance is "$." The text that follows the prompt on the same line is a single command. System responses to these instructions follow them. Although the previous commands are visible on the screen, the interface processes only the current command.

As you can see, each command is terse and cryptic. Consequently, the burden of communication is entirely on the user. You must know the commands and their syntax to get an appropriate response from the system. Text-based interfaces are not always easy to learn and use. Most text-based interpreters are not at all for the faint of heart. They offer few safeguards and almost no error protection. If you inadvertently tell the system to erase your file or a disk, it will assume that you know what you are doing and carry out the command immediately.

One advantage of using a text-based interface is that they permit scripting. A **script** is a sequence of commands, similar to a program listing, that the interface interprets much like a program. Commonly used sequences of commands can be effected automatically simply by executing the script.

Graphical User Interfaces

Graphical user interfaces take a very different approach from that of their older cousins, the command line interpreters. A **graphical user interface (GUI)** employs visual elements on the display monitor such as icons, windows, and other gadgets that the user manipulates to facilitate communication. GUIs are intended to be intuitive, easy to use, more friendly and helpful environments.

Consider the screen shown in Figure 3.10, which illustrates the graphical user interface of the Windows operating system. The full screen is configured as a workspace called a **desktop** in which various documents, icons, and gadgets are available for use. Icons are small pictures depicting devices, files, programs, and the like. Documents and icons are displayed inside rectangular frames called **windows.** Tools and gadgets are used to perform various tasks associated with these desktop windows and other objects. Rather than relying exclusively on language, the chief metaphors for communicating in a GUI are hand actions and pointing. The user manipulates icons and windows with a graphical element called a **pointer,** which is usually controlled by a mouse. The pointer icon typically appears as an arrow, but it may take a variety of shapes depending on the context of its use. Text information is provided using the keyboard, but many of the actions are dictated by mouse manipulations, including the selection of commands from a listing called a **menu.**

The purpose of the desktop metaphor is to make the manipulation and use of the computer more natural by emulating the way we move, store, and dispose of paper products on our desks. Think of the screen as your desktop, disks as filing cabinets, the pull-down menus as a shorthand list of frequently employed procedures, and the mouse and keyboard as your personal assistants in manipulating all of these.

The advantages of a GUI are obvious. Because the burden of communication is shifted to the machine rather than the user, GUIs are easy to use and easily learned. They are also designed to provide a number of safeguards to protect the user from disastrous mistakes. On the

Figure 3.9
A sample session of entering commands using the text-based interface that is standard for the UNIX operating system is shown. Explanations of the commands (shown in bold) and their responses are added.

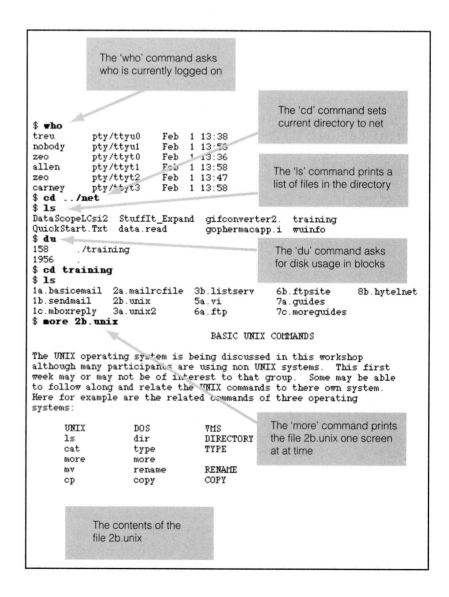

downside, they are not very efficient. These protections, safeguards, and easily visualized actions take some time, and experienced users of text-based interfaces can become impatient with the steps required to achieve relatively simple actions. Most likely, the computer that you are using employs a GUI—either a version of Microsoft Windows or Apple Macintosh OS. Regardless of the brand and version, there are a number of common features that these interfaces share. Once you become experienced with one, learning to use another version is easy enough.

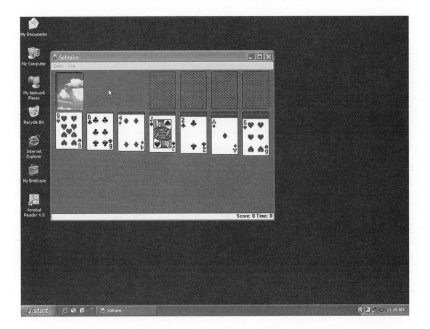

Figure 3.10
The desktop for Windows is shown here. The icons on the left represent locations where data is stored as well as shortcuts to programs used often. The open window contains the application that is currently running. Its menu contains two command groups, Game and Help. Also in this instance, the mouse pointer appears as an arrow inside the window.

DISCOVERING MORE

Operating Systems and Their User Interfaces

Although there is a greater variety, three operating systems dominate the market among desktop computers: Microsoft Windows, Linux, and Apple Macintosh OS. All three offer the same basic functionality, even if they are packaged quite differently. In other words, you can do the same kind of things with each, but they do look and feel quite different when doing so. To find out more about their user interfaces, consult our online resource, "Discovering More About Operating Systems and Their User Interfaces."

Applications

The most common form of software is that of end-user applications. For most of us, the very reason that we employ computers is to perform specific tasks such as document preparation, information management, communication, and many others. Applications help us complete these tasks. Although there is a great variety of application programs, they do have some common features. In short, application software programs:

1. Are restricted to a specific problem domain

2. Have a user interface that is based on some intuitive metaphor

3. Are usually conducted in sessions that have basic characteristics

Unlike operating systems, application programs have much more specific purposes. In fact, an application program is usually limited to the range of tasks associated with handling some form of information. For example, word processing applications are used primarily for creating, editing, and printing documents. They are not designed for playing games, scanning pictures, or sending electronic mail. We can refer to a form of information and its related tasks as a **problem domain.** Thus, the problem domain for word processing applications is document preparation.

Identifying the problem domain for an application program is a useful way of classifying that software. It obviously helps when deciding on what software to use for a specific problem, but it is also useful for learning about new applications, too. Software used for similar tasks will usually be organized and behave in similar fashions. Software versions may change; and their look and feel changes with each new version, but you can usually count on one thing: the problem domain remains the same. Throughout our text, we will identify software applications by their problem domains. This provides a means for thinking about software in a generic manner rather than getting lost in the myriad of details that differentiate each brand and its many versions.

It may come as a surprise to some, but designers expend a considerable effort making software applications easier for us to use. Certainly, everyone has struggled at one time or another trying to learn to use some application package effectively. In spite of these frustrations, an application's user interface is purposely designed to make using the software more intuitive and easier to learn.

We mentioned earlier that a user interface is the means by which the human user communicates with an executing process. We have also seen that popular operating systems employ graphic user interfaces for this purpose. Application programs supported by these systems usually have graphic user interfaces, too. But the application GUI does not have to function in precisely the same manner as the OS interface. (It is desirable that they have some commonality, but it is not a requirement.) Instead, application designers typically choose a well-known medium as a metaphor for creating the user interface. Word processing, for example, is modeled after creating printed documents using a typewriter. As a result, the interface is designed to look and feel like using an electronic typewriter for creating and editing documents. The language of the interface intends to reinforce this metaphor. The workspace is called a "document window"; operations such as "cutting text," "copying text," and "pasting text" are drawn from typesetting; menu command groups are denoted by terms such as "edit" and "format." These may seem obvious because using word processors is very familiar to most of us. But, other applications have user interfaces that are based on recognizable work models, too. Understanding the interface model or metaphor for an application is therefore useful for learning how to work with that software quickly and effectively.

Of course, the user interface is not intended to be a replica of the medium on which it is based. This is intentional, too. After all, why pay the added expense of a computer's hardware and software, if you could get the exact same results with a more conventional technology? So it is not surprising that word processing application programs, for instance, offer added features or greater functionality than typewriters.

Most software applications are **interactive.** This means that using them involves a series of actions initiated by the user and reactions from the application. For this reason, it is useful to think of software usage as marked by sessions. A session begins with commencing the application process—usually called **"opening"** or **"launching"** the program. The session ends when the user **"quits"** or **"closes"** the application. In between, the user performs a series of tasks supported by that application. Because most application programs create results of some kind, "saving" these results is a very common procedure. Saving, of course, means to transfer the contents of main memory to some designated storage device, usually a disk. The application handles the details of placing that data into one or more files and writing the files to the location that the user specifies. Some applications provide automatic saves. This means that your data is stored automatically onto a storage device. Even so, it is a good idea to save your work periodically to prevent its inadvertent loss. Each application has specialized tasks that are related to its problem domain. For example, checking for spelling errors would be normal for programs used in document preparation, but not for drawing programs.

In summary, the variety of application programs is certainly dizzying. Moreover, choosing among the great many applications of the same type is often confusing as well. But, take our advice and approach each new application program by answering these three basic questions. What problem domain does it belong to? What is the basis for its interface? What are the primary tasks I can perform in a session? Answer these and you will be well on your way to mastering what that program has to offer.

■ Summary

The modern computer system is an electronic digital data processing machine. Because it is digital, it is a discrete state device. A computer system processes data by interpreting instructions stored in memory. Thus, the instruction-execution cycle has three basic stages: fetching the binary-encoded instruction from memory, decoding the instruction to determine what operation it prescribes, and executing that operation. A computer performs this cycle over and over until it is instructed to halt. The types of operations that processors perform are simple or primitive by our standards; but computers perform millions of these operations each second. Speed and scale make its work appear more complex or complicated.

Hardware refers to the devices that make up a system. The hardware is usually divided into the processing system and peripherals. The processing system includes the central processing unit and a main memory storage device. Peripherals are the add-ons to our computers that make them easier to use and more productive. Secondary memory devices are peripherals used for archiving data for safer keeping. Input and output peripherals are employed for communicating data into and results from the system.

A program (or software) is a symbolic listing of instructions that direct a computer's processes. While programs are static or fixed entities, processes may be dynamic due to the capability for conditional processing. There are two general classes of software: system software and application programs. The operating system is an example of system software.

The operating system is a collection of resident programs that manages the computer's resources, supervises the execution of user processes, and provides useful services and security for the computer system. The file system is one such service created and maintained by the operating system. Files are logical objects; this means that they do not exist physically as such, but make it easier for us to manage information and documents stored on our computers. The OS also maintains an abstract system for storing files in a hierarchical structure. From a practical standpoint, the user interface is the most significant service provided by an OS. User interfaces provide a medium for communicating commands and other information to the operating system. Graphical user interfaces employ a desktop motif in order to create a more intuitive, friendlier environment for computing.

Application programs are software dedicated to performing useful tasks for end-users, but are restricted in scope to a specific form of information or problem domain. Most applications have user interfaces that are based on some common medium that makes them easier to use and more intuitive to understand. Work using that application is typically contained in one or more windows and confined to sessions in which the user interacts with the software over a (continuous) period of time.

■ Terms

application software	input device	program
bus	interactive software, programs	programming language
central processing unit (CPU)	instruction-execution cycle	prompt sign
child (descendants)	(fetch, decode, execute)	reading from memory
close (quit) an application	main memory	relative pathname
computer system	memory addresses	root
conditional processing	menu	save a file
data	nodes	script
data instructions	open (launch) an application	secondary memory
desktop	open a file	software
exception	operating system (OS)	system error
file	output device	system software
file extension	parent (ancestors)	text file
file identifier	path	text-based user interface
file manager	pathname	(command line interpreter)
file names	peripherals	tree
graphical user interface (GUI)	pointer	user interface
hardware	problem domain	windows
hierarchical file system (HFS)	process	writing to memory
indirection	processing unit	

■ Questions for Review

1. Digital computer systems are discrete state machines. Explain what this means and its significance for understanding the nature of computers.

2. Describe the instruction-execution cycle.

3. What is hardware? Software? How are they related?

4. What is the CPU?

5. What is (main) memory? How do memory and the CPU cooperate in processing?

6. Describe how opening and saving files affect memory.

7. Why is it necessary to have secondary memory in a computer system?

8. What are input and output devices? Cite some examples of each.

9. What is conditional processing and why is it important?

10. What is the difference between system and application software?

11. What are the major functions of the operating system?

12. What is a file? Why is it a logical entity rather than physical?

13. Describe how the file system (on most computer systems) is organized.

14. What is a pathname? Describe the differences between relative and absolute pathnames.

15. Consult Figure 3.8. Give the pathnames for the following files: (a) *chap3.doc,* (b) *inventory.xls,* and (c) *window.psd.*

16. Describe the main functions of the OS user interface. What are the pros and cons of using graphical user interfaces over text-based interfaces?

17. What is meant by the problem domain for a software application program?

18. Explain how an application's user interface is designed to make learning to use it easier or more intuitive.

19. What are some of the typical tasks that define a session when using a software application?

Chapter 4

Connecting to the Digital Domain

OBJECTIVES

- The basics of data communications networks

- How the Internet provides global connectivity

- How the World Wide Web is a client/server application supported by the Internet

- How Web pages are hypermedia documents

- The fundamentals of Web browser applications for fetching and viewing Web pages

- The basics of Web directories, search engines, and other Web search services

- Effective strategies for keyword searching

The computer system is composed of software and hardware; together, they provide us with the power to create and process information in useful ways. Using computers, we can digitize and store various forms of information. With application programs, we can analyze, combine, and otherwise transform that information to suit our specific needs. But the digital domain extends beyond our desktop. When our computers are connected to data communications networks, we can instantly transport digital information across the campus or around the globe. Moreover, your connected computer system becomes a means for finding information produced by and stored on other computers.

Digital data is transported over networks. These networks connect the computer systems in our homes, labs, and offices. Networks can be joined together to extend our reach over the campus, across the country, and around the world. The Internet is the largest of these collected networks. It provides the infrastructure for a variety of useful applications. The World Wide Web is the most popular of these applications; indeed, many think of the Web and the Internet as synonymous. The Web is an immense repository of electronic information, but its scale and organization can make it difficult to find useful information efficiently. Fortunately, Web search services provide us with tools for more effective researching. However, not all search services are the same; they differ in both size and organization. More importantly, they differ in how searches are conducted. An effective researcher in the digital domain understands how these services work and how to exploit them.

Networks

A **data communications network** (or **"network,"** for short) is a collection of computer systems configured to share digital data and other resources by communicating with one another. The systems are connected by means of a medium or **communications channel** for sending and receiving signals. This communications channel may be a medium that physically connects the systems such as copper wire, or it may rely on broadcast methods over the airwaves such as a wireless network.

In a data communications network, communication typically takes place between two systems. The **sender** encodes a digital message in the form of a signal suitable for the channel and transmits it to the receiver. The **receiver,** in turn, receives the signal and decodes it as digital message. See Figure 4.1. In fact, most communications are two-way, so the designation of sender and receiver is dynamic.

In some instances, it is useful to distinguish between **local** and **remote systems.** For example, when you are browsing Web pages, your computer system is cooperating with another computer system called a *Web server* over a data communications network. In this example, your computer system running the Web browser application is the local system communicating with a remote system, the Web server. One of the most significant advantages of networking is the fact that local and remote computer systems can share or cooperate in processing. This is called **distributed computing.** The power of distributed computing increases the capabilities of your own computer system immensely.

Networks come in many shapes and sizes. A **local area network** (or **LAN**) is a data communications network that is composed of systems that extend across a limited geographic area and is usually managed by the same company or organization. Consult Figure 4.2. For example, the computers in your lab probably belong to a local area network administered by your school. An **internetwork** (or **internet**) is a collection of autonomous networks that permit communication from one to the other. See Figure 4.3. The scale of an internet can vary. Some

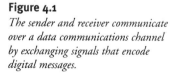

Figure 4.1

The sender and receiver communicate over a data communications channel by exchanging signals that encode digital messages.

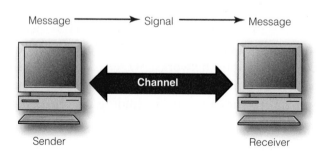

are small and local; others extend worldwide. Most colleges and universities, for example, manage an internet of assorted LANs in individual departments and offices. An internet owned and managed by a single company or organization is often dubbed an **intranet.** The **Internet** (with the uppercase "I"), of course, is an internetwork that spans the entire globe. (We will return to consider more details about data communications and networks in Chapter 16. Chapter 17 delves more deeply into the world of LANs.)

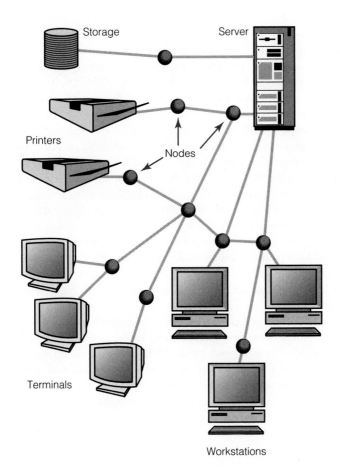

Figure 4.2
In a typical LAN, a central computer system called a **server** *is connected to computer systems, terminals, and other devices. The connecting points over the network are called* **nodes.** *Users send to and receive information from the server. The server also provides useful resources such as file sharing, print spooling, etc.*

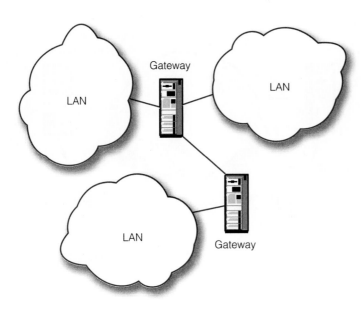

Figure 4.3
Local area networks can be connected by means of gateways to form an internetwork. The **gateway** *system handles the task of bridging between networks that may communicate using different protocols.*

The Internet

The Internet, as we know it today, evolved from an experimental network developed by the Department of Defense (DOD) in the late 1960s. During the Cold War, the competing superpowers of the United States and the Soviet Union sought to protect themselves from nuclear first strikes. The DOD was understandably interested in developing a network communications system that was robust enough to survive nuclear attacks. Researchers created a network that was decentralized, loosely coupled, and redundant. **Decentralized** means that there is no single central authority managing the network. A **loosely coupled** network is one in which the systems or facilities are relatively autonomous and can continue communications even with the failure of other connected systems or facilities. Finally, a **redundant** system is one in which there are multiple paths for communication between any two points. Thus, network traffic can be rerouted if there is a loss of one of the paths.

Ironically, these ingredients make the perfect recipe for creating a worldwide network aggregated from numerous cooperating public and private networks. The Internet has no central authority; it is not owned or operated by any single corporation or government. It exists because the autonomous networks that provide its infrastructure agree to cooperate and share communications. Networks are added to and deleted from the Internet constantly. For this reason, it is difficult to ascertain the precise size of the Internet in terms of network systems or hosts and users. Estimates vary. Currently, it is estimated that there are over 473 million users on the Internet employing more than 200 million hosts. While the growth rate of the Internet has decreased somewhat over the last decade, it is still growing.

Like a highway system, local Internet traffic is directed across smaller roadways and arteries that connect local points of interest. Long-distance traffic is routed across high-speed superhighways called *backbones* that span countries and continents. But unlike highway travel, Internet traffic is delivered almost instantaneously, despite both high volume and the complexities of its routing.

For our purposes, the significance of the Internet is that it provides the platform or support for the development of useful communications applications. Electronic mail is one of the earliest of these applications developed for the DOD experimental internet. **Electronic mail** (or **e-mail**) permits users to send and receive messages like postal mail. E-mail is like postal mail only in that both are asynchronous; that is, the sender and receiver do not communicate at the same time. You post your e-mail message to your local mail server. The local mail server transmits it to the remote mail server. The recipient can fetch the mail from his or her server at any time afterwards. See Figure 4.4.

Figure 4.4

Electronic mail resembles postal mail in some ways. The sender prepares a message and posts it to his or her local post office or mail server. The mail server contacts and delivers the message to the recipient's mail server. Sometime later, when the intended receiver contacts his or her mail server, the message may be downloaded to the receiver's system.

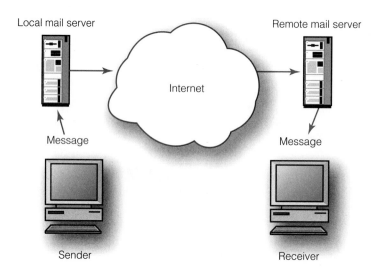

Besides e-mail, the Internet supports and has popularized other useful applications such as telnet, ftp, and the World Wide Web. The application **telnet** permits a user to connect to and communicate with a remote system as if it were his or her local system. In this manner, it is possible to connect to your office computer system from your laptop at home. The application **ftp** (**file transfer protocol**) permits the user to copy files from one system to another over a network. Copying files to a remote system is commonly called **uploading** files. Copying files from a remote system to your local system is dubbed **downloading** these files. When you download trial software or upgrades, you are exploiting the power of ftp to overcome the obstacles of distance and system differences. The **World Wide Web** is a confederation of computer systems dispersed around the world that store and share documents and resources.

The Internet continues to serve as the foundation for many other distributed applications. It is safe to say that its evolution and growth are the most dominant factors in changing the world of computing over the past decade. (We will return to consider the Internet in more detail later in Chapter 18.)

The World Wide Web

Although electronic mail was the Internet's earliest successful application, the World Wide Web is obviously its most popular. But like most aspects of the Internet, the original vision for the Web was very different from its current form. In its inception, the Web was first conceived as a medium for sharing physics research.

In 1989, Tim Berners-Lee and a group of researchers at the European Particle Physics Laboratory (known as CERN) proposed a project for the electronic dissemination of research and related information. These researchers had been using the existing Internet for information exchange, but they found its facilities for sharing information lacking. They envisioned instead a hypertext system that would allow members of the scientific community to communicate, edit, and view information easily—this system became known as the World Wide Web.

Hypermedia

Electronic documents with built-in links to additional information are called **hypertext.** Such documents are linked electronically by means of **hyperlinks.** Hyperlinks (or "links," for short) can be represented and accessed in many different ways, but most hypertext systems make integral use of a computer's mouse to select links. For example, words or phrases on Web pages linked to additional information are typically shown in a different color or underlined. A single click of the mouse over a hyperlink transports you to the linked page or resource. These links allow you to use hypertext documents in a nonlinear way. Instead of reading from start to finish, the way you might read printed documents, you may use the hyperlinks to create your own path through the connected group of documents. In fact, this ability to create your own paths through hypertext documents is their central distinguishing feature.

This cross-referenced material can involve a variety of media—images, sounds, and movie clips as well as text. Indeed, images can themselves be links to other information. A hypertext document composed of different media is called a **hypermedia** document. This term extends to include all the connected information as well as any document that links to that information. In this respect, you can see how the World Wide Web can be viewed as a huge hypermedia "document" or repository.

The hyperlinks in the Web hypermedia repository have another remarkable characteristic: They connect information stored on computers at distant sites. The user of such links traverses physical distances automatically and transparently. From its modest beginnings, the Web has grown to truly global proportions. Today, it encompasses far more than scientific research. Information on the Web comes in almost infinite variety. Here are just a few examples:

- Astronomical images from NASA

- Top ten lists from David Letterman's talk show

- The latest research on bioinformatics and the human genome project

- Weather predictions with the latest satellite imagery

- The current catalog for clothing and equipment from an outdoor fitter

- Campus information from thousands of colleges and universities worldwide

- Online help and information from many computer vendors, both hardware and software

- Electronic editions of popular magazines with features, discussion groups, and advertisements

The information on the Web is organized as a collection of **Web sites.** A Web site is a collection of hypermedia information with a unique identity—often dedicated to a specific topic or purpose. The elements of the site typically are stored and managed by a single Web server. The information at a given Web site is usually divided into a series of **Web pages.** Like their print counterparts, Web pages divide the material into more manageable units. Usually, a Web page fills a single screen of a video monitor, although the window containing the page may also have scroll tools for advancing the document when it is larger. These pages contain text, graphics, sound, even video, and, of course, links to other related documents. The user clicks a link to transfer from the current document to a new one. Linked pages create a structure for the information that the user may employ in various ways. Many documents have a hierarchical organization not unlike that of file directories. The first document, called the **home** or **entry page,** often serves as a central hub with a hyperlinked menu listing the site's contents. A home page typically establishes the "look and feel" of the Web site and explains the purpose or contents of the document.

Because the Web is a distributed information system, hyperlinked pages may be stored on the same computer or may be found on remote systems across the world. In this way, the reader not only traverses information according to inclination but also travels from site to site in the Web. All of this, of course, is easy and effortless. In fact, if it were not for the time lapses due to fetching items from distant sites, the user could be easily deceived into thinking that all the information was stored neatly on his or her local system.

Clients, Servers, and Protocols

One of the distinctive features of the Web is that it is based on an open, distributed system. This means that computer systems that differ in scale and performance capabilities can communicate with one another freely. How is all of this managed with such ease and transparency? The secret is that the Web is built on client/server computing. A **client/server application** is a software program that distributes processing between two cooperating systems, the client and the server. The **client** is a system that requests specific services from a separate system, the server. The **server** is usually a remote computer system that receives and handles requests for services from many clients concurrently. See Figure 4.5.

The World Wide Web is populated by a confederation of computer systems that adhere to a set of guidelines for the storage and communication of electronic information. **Web servers** are computer systems that store and make available Web pages and other resources (like images and sounds). Other computers, acting as **Web clients,** request Web pages or resources from Web servers.

Any type or scale of machine can function as either a Web server or a Web client. It is not uncommon for Windows-based PCs and Macintoshes, for example, to play the roles of both clients and servers. Using your desktop computer as a client will likely put you in touch with a variety of different computers acting as servers—all during the same session.

All of this is managed in a way that hides the underlying complexity from the user by means of agreed-upon guidelines, called *protocols.* A **protocol** is a set of rules that govern how some activity will take place. For example, social protocols dictate that when friends and acquaintances meet on the street, they usually exchange ceremonial greetings such as "Hello," "How are you?," "I am good," and so on. The World Wide Web protocols are maintained by

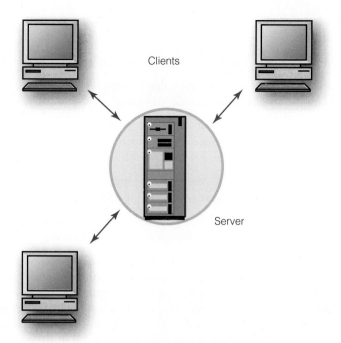

Figure 4.5

A server is a program that executes continuously on a computer system in order to cooperate with other remote computer systems. These other systems, called clients, make occasional requests for services to it. The client and server form a connection and the server responds to requests made by the client. While the server can attend to only one client process at a time, it switches attention among clients. In this manner, the server can provide useful processing for a number of remote systems concurrently.

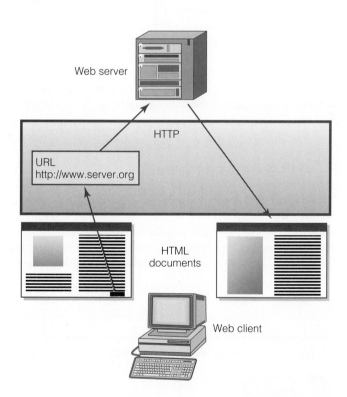

Figure 4.6

Web servers store Web pages and make them accessible to Web client machines. The user views a page by issuing an HTTP request to the server that stores that page. The server transmits the page as an HTML document composed of content and instructions for its display. Once the client receives the page, it displays it in a way appropriate for the client machine.

a standards group known as the World Wide Web Consortium (W3C). The protocols specify how information is exchanged on the Web and is, in fact, what defines and makes the Web possible. There are three major components, known widely by their acronyms: URL, HTTP, and HTML. Figure 4.6 illustrates.

A **URL** (for **Uniform Resource Locator**) is the agreed-upon standard for giving the address of a page or resource available on a remote server. Suppose that a user is reading text from a Web page currently displayed on his or her system. When the user clicks a hyperlink to another page or resource, the client transmits a request for the appropriate information to the server addressed in the URL stored as part of the hyperlink.

Let's look a little more closely at the structure of a URL. Consider the URL for the Web site accompanying this text, namely:

http://cs.furman.edu/digitaldomain/index.html

We can break this URL down into pieces that indicate standard information about the address it represents. Most URLs have a similar structure.

http://	signifies the type of protocol expected; in this instance a request for a page or resource being located on a remote Web server.
cs.furman.edu	designates the registered name of the Web server holding the page or resource being requested.
digitaldomain/index.html	is information about where on the Web server's hard disk the page or resource is located.

Like many other things we have seen, the URL employs a hierarchical structure. After the protocol, the sequence of symbols before the next slash ("/") denotes a domain name. **Domain names** are hierarchically organized names that signify the location of Web servers. The extension ".edu"—spoken as "dot E-D-U"—refers to the educational domain. "furman" refers to Furman University which is a subdomain of ".edu." Finally, "cs" signifies our home, the computer science department. This URL has a consistent hierarchical structure, as illustrated in Figure 4.7. Not all URLs are so well-behaved. (We will return to the topic of URLs and domain names later in Chapter 17.)

Any additional information in the URL specifies the location of the resource on that server. For example, in this case, "digitaldomain" is a directory or folder on the department's Web server. The file "index.html" is the entry page for the Web site. Web pages always have file extensions of either ".html" or ".htm." It is customary to assign "index.html" or "index.htm" to home or entry pages. In fact, doing so relieves the user of specifying that page. In other words, a request for

http://cs.furman.edu/digitaldomain/

is understood by a Web server to mean the same as the previous URL.

The set of rules that govern the exchange of information between Web clients and Web servers is **HTTP (HyperText Transfer Protocol)**. Consider again the example of selecting a hyperlink to another Web page or resource. The page or resource may reside on the same server that contains the original page, or it may be found on a remote system. It doesn't matter. The web client makes these requests automatically, and they are delivered to the appropriate server, located by its URL. After the server receives the request, it interprets the request

Figure 4.7

The URL specifies the relevant addressing information needed to fetch a document. The URL is divided into two main sections: the protocol followed by the identifier. The protocol specifies the application. In this case, "http" signifies the WWW protocol. The identifier indicates the location of the resource, including directory and filename on the host machine. The domain name identifies the server hosting the resource. Domain names are usually structured hierarchically. In this instance, "cs" belongs to the "furman" subdomain, which belongs to the "edu" domain.

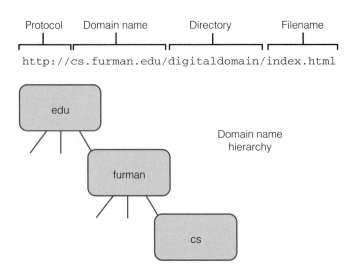

and transmits the appropriate information. Notice how the workload is distributed. The client does not have to worry about the details of how the information is stored. It needs only the URL of the page or resource it is requesting. Retrieving the information and sending it back to the client is the work of the server.

When the client receives the requested information, it takes over the task once again and decides how to display what was received. This process is governed by the **HTML** (**HyperText Markup Language**). HTML offers specific directions on how the Web client should format and display text and images, play sounds, and so on. As its name suggests, HTML is, in fact, a language whose purpose is to allow its users to write documents for display on the World Wide Web. We'll have a lot more to say about HTML later in Chapter 5 where you will learn to construct your own HTML documents.

Web Browsers

Viewing Web pages and clicking (and hence following) their built-in hyperlinks is colloquially referred to as **Web surfing.** Web surfing is easy and engaging. In this section, we'll explore some of the additional skills you need to be an effective Web surfer.

For your system to function as a Web client, you must run a special program called a *Web browser.* The **Web browser** acts as a client requesting Web pages and resources from identified servers, and likewise handles the task of interpreting and displaying those resources on your system. Browsers with graphical interfaces make Web surfing an easily mastered activity. As you know, there are a number of popular Web browsers. Although the browsers may differ in some details, they are essentially similar and operate on the same basic concepts. We will describe some of these concepts.

HTML documents contain, in fact, instructions on how to format a document. The Web browser simply implements the instructions in a manner appropriate for the client machine. When images, sounds, or video are transmitted, the browser converts these—often with the help of a utility program—into a form that your machine can play or display.

Browsers come in a variety of forms. The earliest browsers had text-based interfaces. The user entered numbers and letters to select hypertext links. The genuine watershed event for the Web was the introduction of the first graphical-based browser called *Mosaic.* The original Mosaic program was conceived by Marc Andreesen, an undergraduate student at the University of Illinois at Urbana-Champaign who worked part-time for the National Center for Supercomputing Applications (NCSA). Andreesen developed the program with the assistance of several others at NCSA. Versions were released (free of charge) in 1993 for a variety of different computers, including the Macintosh and Windows-based computers.

Mosaic handled multimedia documents and had an interface that was graphical and easy to use. It proved to be an overwhelming success. In fact, its popularity single-handedly spawned the tremendous growth in the amount and variety of information available on the Web as well as the numbers of users who sought this information. Today, Mosaic has been succeeded by newer and more powerful Web browsers like Netscape Navigator (produced by the company founded by Marc Andreesen), Microsoft's Internet Explorer, as well as browsers introduced by other companies.

When we start a browser program, we say that we are conducting a **Web session** with the browser. The session is a given continuous span of time during which the browser process is active on our system. In a given session, we may visit many pages and sites. The browser records each of the URLs visited and stores them in a file called the **history.** This permits you to retrace your steps during the session. These session histories are also kept for several days, so it also possible for you to recall specific sites without having to remember their URLs.

Each page of a Web document is presented in a browser window similar to that shown in Figure 4.8. Let's take a quick tour of this window, which is displayed using the Netscape Navigator browser.

- The title bar displays the name of the Web page currently displayed.

- The tool bar contains buttons for some standard navigational functions—moving back to the previous page viewed in this browser session, forward (assuming you've

Figure 4.8

A Web document is displayed using a recent version of Netscape Navigator. A typical browser window contains a number of components, tools, and gadgets, as well as information.

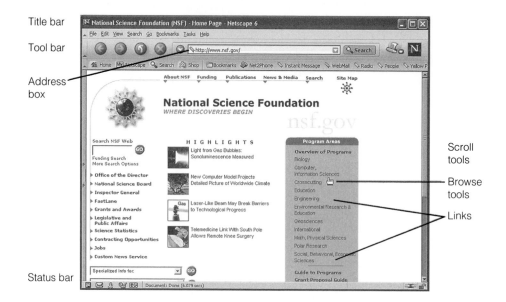

Title bar

Tool bar

Address box

Scroll tools

Browse tools

Links

Status bar

already moved back) in the chain of pages being viewed in this session, returning to your home page—as well as other actions.

- Hyperlinks within text are typically underlined and displayed in a different color. A link that you have already visited (in this session or a recent one) is shown in yet another color.

- Graphic objects and images can also be hyperlinks. You can discover these links by observing the shape of the mouse pointer as you move it over the object (see the description of the browse tool next) or by noticing that the objects are often outlined in the same color in which the text hyperlinks are displayed.

- When you move the mouse pointer over a hyperlink, the pointer takes the shape of a hand (with a finger pointing), called the *browse tool*. See Figure 4.8. As you know, you follow a link by moving the browse tool over the link and clicking the mouse button.

- Scroll tools (box and arrows) along the window's right and bottom edges may be used to advance or retrace the view in the window.

- The status bar offers brief messages such as what event will occur if the mouse is clicked in the current pointer location.

- In the address or location box, the Web address for the page currently being viewed is given. You may enter a URL directly into this box and press the Return or Enter key to move to the corresponding Web page.

The page displayed using the Netscape Navigator browser in Figure 4.8 is also shown displayed in Internet Explorer in Figure 4.9. Notice the similarities between the two windows. There are, of course, some differences, but the similarities are numerous and striking. Each browser also has a menu bar providing access to a number of pull-down menus enabling many common browser activities.

Most browsers provide options to change the appearance of the browser window. For example, you can turn the display of the URL address bar, the tool bar, and the status bar off or on as you prefer. You might turn one or more of these off when you want to expand the actual Web page viewing area within your browser window.

Figures 4.10 and 4.11 illustrate dialog boxes that you may access to change various settings for Netscape Navigator and Internet Explorer, respectively. In Netscape Navigator, select Preferences under the Edit pull-down menu. In Internet Explorer, you can access these option dialog boxes by selecting Internet Options under the Tools pull-down menu.

Title bar

Tool bar

Address box

Scroll tools

Links

Status bar

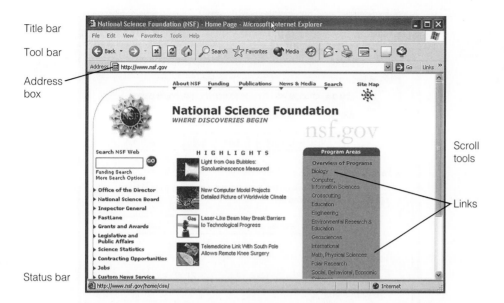

Figure 4.9
Internet Explorer displays the same document viewed in Figure 4.8. Notice the similarities between the two browser windows.

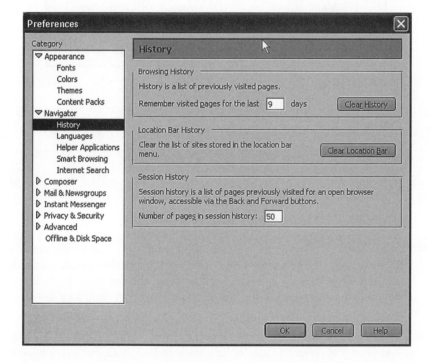

Figure 4.10
The Preferences dialog box in Netscape Navigator allows the user to make personal settings for a variety of functions. In addition to display characteristics such as fonts and colors, you may determine how many previously visited links are recalled by the browser. This is called the history function. As illustrated here, the user has set 50 pages as the maximum number of pages recalled in a single session and the past 9 days as the extent of sessions recalled.

The tool bars put some of the most commonly used browser commands within a mouse click. Let's summarize some of the commands common to most browser tool bars. Refer to Figure 4.12 to see the location and form of the various button icons on the two tool bars.

- The Back button displays the previous Web page viewed in the current browser session.

- The Forward button displays the next Web page in the sequence of viewed pages—the one you would have just left had you clicked the Back button.

- The Reload, or Refresh, button will often correct a scrambled or stalled Web page. Click the Reload button to restart the page transfer process.

Figure 4.11

Internet Explorer offers the same basic capabilities for the user to set personal preferences. The dialog box is named "Internet Options" and is organized differently, though. As shown here, the tabs organize the choices.

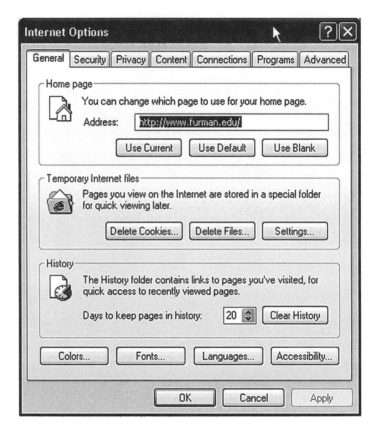

Figure 4.12

This figure compares the Internet Explorer toolbar (a) with the toolbar for Netscape Navigator (b). Note that both contain many common functions.

- The Home button displays the currently configured home page for the browser. This is the page that is displayed when you first open the browser. It is initially preset to a page chosen by the browser company, but you have the option of changing this to any page you like—including a blank page (to reduce download time).

- The Stop button allows you to interrupt the transfer of Web pages. As you may know, some Web pages can take quite a while to load. This may occur because they contain lots of images or because the Web server and/or the transmission line is very busy. At any rate, being able to interrupt a Web page transfer is convenient at times.

- The Search button transfers you to the browser's search page interface. On this page you can enter keywords to initiate Web searches in one of any number of third-party search tools. We'll discuss Web searches in the next section.

- The animated icon (at the far right in each tool bar) is not a button but is there for information. When the icon is animated, it indicates that the browser is working to load a page.

Each browser has other buttons on its tool bar. For example, the Print button opens the Print dialog box to allow you to print the Web document currently being viewed.

Often you will wish to record specific Web sites for later use. Fortunately, browsers make this easy by automating the process of remembering your favorite Web sites. You may create a bookmark list, a personalized index of Web sites that allows you to return to a site with ease.

For example, Netscape Communicator provides a Bookmarks (indicated by the icon shaped like a bookmark) pull-down menu to which you can easily add links to sites that you have visited. To do this, you just choose the Add Bookmark command in the Bookmarks menu while you are viewing the desired Web page. The title of the Web page (always displayed in the browser title bar) will then be added to the Bookmarks menu along with a built-in link to its URL. You can even create a hierarchical structure by designating sublists within your bookmarks list. Later, you can access any of these stored sites by simply selecting it from the Bookmarks menu.

In Internet Explorer, bookmarks are added and stored in the Favorites pull-down menu. You can access the sites by selecting them from the Favorites menu, or you can open a Favorites folder by clicking the Favorites tool bar button. Once the folder is open, you can double-click on any site you wish to load.

Researching Information on the Web

The World Wide Web is often likened to a global electronic library of information. Such an analogy, however, overlooks some of the truly unique features of the Web. First of all, the Web is a distributed and ever-changing repository for vast amounts of information. It lacks any central authority and, therefore, has no centralized index. Scale is also a significant factor. Currently, there are over 8.5 million Web sites in the world. The amount of content on the Web is equally staggering. Best estimates place it between 2.5 to 3 billion pages with a growth rate of over 7 million pages per day. The organization of the Web is also more complicated than an electronic library. As mentioned, the term *Web* suggests that this information is organized by an intricate array of cross-references that link resources from one site to another like the strands of a spider web. These links are not static or fixed, either. They may be changed or dismantled without notice. Doing research using the Web is not like going to the library— even a virtual or electronic one.

How then can we take advantage of all this material at our fingertips? The first obstacle is finding what we need. Searching by surfing—that is, skimming from one page to another following links—is often entertaining, but not very efficient. Fortunately, there are better tools available for finding information stored on the Web. In this section, we will explore some of these tools.

In order to get help in finding information on the Web, you need to consult special Web sites called *search services*. A **search service** is a Web site that automatically generates lists of

Censorship on the Web

Like the Internet, the World Wide Web lacks any central authority. Web sites come and go, and anyone with the ability to publish materials on the Web has the right to do so. The result is that the Web contains a tremendous amount of useful, valuable information; but, at the same time, it includes materials that are frivolous, preposterous, and even offensive to a variety of tastes.

Should there be editorial controls on the materials placed on Web servers for general consumption? If not, how can responsible individuals protect themselves from materials that are deemed inappropriate? These and related issues are addressed in the online essay "Censorship on the Web."

SOCIAL THEMES

other Web sites that may contain information about the topics that you supply it. Not all search services are alike, though. In general, there are two basic varieties: Web directories and search engines. Because Web searching is so popular, there are some newer, special hybrid types of services. These include niche search services, metasearch engines, and portals. We will examine each of these categories.

Web Directories

Information about Web sites and their resources are typically collected by a Web search service and stored in large database. A **database** is an electronic collection of information that is organized for timely retrieval and use. Some search services are called **Web directories** because they organize their Web databases as a hierarchical directory. Like the file systems supported by modern operating systems, a hierarchical directory distributes the information in a series of levels that may be traversed by following the logical links. Unlike file systems, though, Web directories are organized by subject categories rather than by folders and files.

The search service Yahoo! is one of the earliest and largest of the Web directories. Suppose that you were interested in finding out about the canine breed characteristics of Labrador retrievers. You could simply follow the hierarchical path starting with *Science* to *Biology* to *Zoology* until you arrive at (canine) *Breeds* and *Labrador Retrievers.* (A full hierarchical path for the search is depicted in Figure 4.13.)

In addition to traversing the hierarchical structure, users may submit keywords to a search tool that finds the appropriate classifications. **Keyword searching** is a form of text matching. A sequence of letters and symbols called a **text string** is used as a pattern for scanning text to seek any exact matches. For example, *retrievers* could be used as a keyword in order to find the section in the directory that contains sites about Labrador retrievers. The search tool automatically scans the database looking for matches with the string "retrievers" and returns the matching records. Text matching is not smart, though. Any match is classified as a successful find or "**hit.**" For example, matches with records about golden and Chesapeake Bay retrievers will be scored as hits as well as those about Labs. Of course, it is possible in this case to make our keyword more precise, but not all keyword searches can be remedied as easily. The bottom line is that text matching is a mechanistic process and not an intelligent one.

You can avoid difficulties with keyword searching if you learn more about the classification scheme employed by a Web directory; however, these taxonomies vary from one directory to another. Classifications within the same directory change, too. As more listings are added, topics are subdivided further to preserve manageable groupings. The same directory may employ multiple hierarchies for the same topic as well.

Search Engines

Web directories are organized and managed by humans. But databases assembled by humans are usually limited in scale. After all, someone has to review each listing and likewise fit it into the directory's taxonomy. For this reason, the largest and most popular Web search databases are automated instead. These services are called **search engines.** Most of

Figure 4.13

In order to find information on our canine friends, we would have to traverse the following subject categories in Yahoo! At each level, the user is offered a variety of choices until he or she reaches the bottom of the tree structure. At this level, there are only URLs. The subject categories were decided on by the staff at Yahoo! Other directories would likely have different categories.

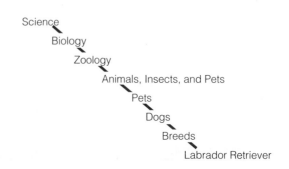

Science
Biology
Zoology
Animals, Insects, and Pets
Pets
Dogs
Breeds
Labrador Retriever

the listings in their databases are indexed by automated software dubbed *Web spiders* or *crawlers*. A **Web spider** or **Web crawler** is a program that locates and records a Web page in a database by following external links to it. The database is built automatically by adding records that itemize details about each page, such as the title, URL, metatags, and some of the text also. **Metatags** are special descriptions stored in the HTML file. Web page authors can assist the classification of their own pages by including keywords in the metatag section of the HTML file. (We will elaborate on this topic when we examine how to create and publish Web pages in Chapter 5.)

Web authors may submit their sites to a Web search engine database by completing a form posted on the service's Web site; however, Web spiders or crawlers gather the overwhelming majority of listings automatically. As a consequence, the size and contents of search engine databases can vary significantly. And, because the listings are gathered automatically, no human reviews or organizes them.

Keyword Searching Using a Search Engine

Because their databases have no topical structure, search engines restrict all searches to keyword searching. As mentioned, keyword searching is a form of text pattern matching. From our perspective, though, the basic elements of a keyword search are words and phrases. Specifically, keywords may be either single words or **phrases**—that is, a sequence of words enclosed in quotes. For example, if you entered

Labrador retrievers   [a]

in the search box, the search engine would construe this to signify two separate keywords, "Labrador" and "retrievers." Finding matches would be based on looking for each of the keywords as separate text patterns. By contrast, enclosing the words in quotes as the phrase

"Labrador retrievers"   [b]

would instruct the search engine to look for matches in which the two words occur exactly as a text sequence. Thus, the entire phrase functions as a keyword (or text pattern).

Search engines allow you to enter multiple keywords in a single search query. Consequently, our previous example of the two keywords [a] would be permissible. But, exactly how would the search engine interpret this query? Would the results be the same as those for [b]? Table 4.1 shows the number of hits or matches for each query using a popular search engine.

It is obvious that [a] and [b] are not interpreted as the same query; the number of hits from [a] are nearly double of those for [b]. Nor is [a] the combined total number of hits for the word "Labrador" and the word "retrievers." Consulting Table 4.1, we can see that queries for each of these words individually produce over 360,000 matches! What then is going on?

DISCOVERING MORE

Web Directories and Search Engines

The landscape of Web search services changes rapidly. Today's darling is tomorrow's has-been. Consult our online resource "Discovering More About Web Directories and Search Engines" for the latest details on popular search services, their database sizes, etc. In addition, there are activities for experimenting with and learning more about these popular search services.

In fact, search engines interpret queries with multiple keywords as forming **Boolean expressions** containing logical or Boolean operators. **Boolean operators**—named after nineteenth century British mathematician George Boole—are used to create compound expressions from simpler components. The most commonly used Boolean operators are AND, OR, and NOT (See Table 4.2).

In this context, a Boolean expression defines a set or class of objects. If we think of each of our keywords as denoting the class of matches in the search engine database, queries formed by Boolean expressions allow us to combine keywords in a variety of ways expressing different relations among classes.

The Boolean operator **AND** denotes set intersection. In other words, the search engine is directed to look for those listings where both the keywords occur. We can illustrate this using Venn diagrams. Each circle in a Venn diagram denotes a class. The shaded area signifies the members defined by that Boolean expression. Figure 4.14 illustrates the AND query.

The Boolean operator **OR** means the union or combination of both classes. The search engine will seek those listings in which either of the keywords matches. Figure 4.15 depicts the OR query.

Finally **NOT** denotes negation or set exclusion. For example, the query

NOT retrievers

would instruct the search engine to find all listings that did not have the word "retrievers" in them.

The NOT operator by itself has little practical use in searching. So, in most instances, NOT is combined with one of the other operators, usually AND. This is so common, in fact, that some refer to their combination as the **AND-NOT** operator. Figure 4.16 illustrates an AND-NOT query.

Most search engines permit the use of queries formed with mathematical operators as a substitute for the more lengthy Boolean expressions. The '+' (plus) symbol is used to signify AND; while the '−' (minus) symbol denotes AND-NOT. The OR operator is typically not implemented. Table 4.3 summarizes.

The search query "Labrador AND retrievers" or its equivalent "+Labrador +retrievers" will return listings in which there are matches with both keywords. Suppose, however, that there is a listing in which only the title "Labrador retriever" is indexed—perhaps the author did not include metatag keywords and the Web spider did not scan the text of the page. Our query would not find this listing even though it is obviously relevant. The reason, of course, is the words *retriever* and *retrievers* are not the same text patterns. Most search engines support the use of wildcards to help avoid problems like this one. The **wildcard** symbol "*" is

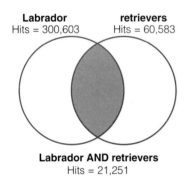

Figure 4.14
The query "Labrador AND retrievers." The matches or hits are those listings in which both the keywords "Labrador" and "retrievers" occur. (Note: the shaded area signifies the members defined by the Boolean expression.)

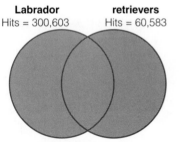

Figure 4.15
The query "Labrador OR retrievers." The matches or hits are those listings in which either the keywords "Labrador" or "retrievers" occur. Some hits may be instances where both keywords occur.

Table 4.1   *Search results for keywords using a search engine.*

Query	Number of Hits
Labrador retrievers (i.e., [a], two words)	21,251
"Labrador retrievers" (i.e., [b], one phrase)	11,616
Labrador (i.e., single word)	300,603
retrievers (i.e., single word)	60,583

Table 4.2   *Search queries formed by Boolean expressions.*

Boolean Operator	Meaning	Example
AND	intersection (both match)	Labrador AND retrievers
OR	union (either matches)	Labrador OR retrievers
NOT	negation (no matches)	Labrador AND NOT retrievers

appended to the end of the keyword to denote words that have that keyword as its stem. Thus, "retriever*" would match both "retriever" and "retrievers" (Specifically, the wildcard matches with the stem + nothing and the stem + "s.") Wildcards are useful, but don't always produce the best results. For example, a query with the keyword "dog*" would find matches with "dog" and "dogs," but also "dogmatism," "dognap," "dogsled," "dogwood," and a host of others. Some care is needed in order to use wildcards effectively.

You may have noticed that the query [a] above had the same results as "Labrador AND retrievers" (see Figure 4.14). This means that the search engine used in this example has a default interpretation for multiple keywords. As we have said before, nothing in computing can be left to chance. Applications will always enforce a preestablished or **default interpretation** for any user input that may be expressed vaguely. In this instance, the search engine presumes that queries like [a] are intended to imply the AND or '+' operators. Many popular search engines have this default interpretation, but not all. For these search engines, then, the following queries are equivalent.

Labrador AND retrievers
+Labrador +retrievers
Labrador +retrievers
Labrador retrievers
retrievers Labrador
retrievers AND Labrador
+retrievers +Labrador
retrievers +Labrador

Case-sensitivity is one more issue to consider. Most search engines today interpret keywords without case-sensitivity by default. Thus, keywords such as "Labrador" and "labrador" would be considered equivalent. The matches would therefore include instances with both uppercase and any lowercase. Some search engines will allow you to enforce case-sensitivity, if desired. This would be useful, for example, when looking for proper names. This may be done using phrases or by setting the "exact phrase" attribute in the advanced searching options.

Unfortunately, there are no universal standards for search engine queries; so, it is a good idea to find out how your favorites handle these and other issues.

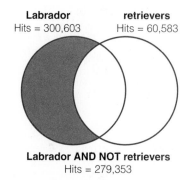

Labrador
Hits = 300,603

retrievers
Hits = 60,583

Labrador AND NOT retrievers
Hits = 279,353

Figure 4.16
The query "Labrador AND NOT retrievers." The matches or hits are those listings that have the keyword "Labrador" without any occurrences of the word "retrievers."

Table 4.3 *Using mathematical operators as shortcuts for Boolean operators. Note the operator is affixed to the beginning of the keyword with no additional spacing.*

Boolean Expression	Mathematical Operator Form
Labrador AND retrievers	+Labrador +retrievers
Labrador AND NOT retrievers	+Labrador −retrievers

FOCUS   ## Searching Using Boolean Expressions

Some search engines support a full range of Boolean operators as part of their advanced searching options. These are similar to the searching features found in many other electronic databases such as those available in libraries.

Extend your searching skills by consulting our online resource "Focus on Searching Using Boolean Expressions." It offers more details about and hands-on activities using Boolean expressions to compose search queries.

Improving Our Search Queries

Precision and coverage are two very distinct, but important factors in assessing the practical merits of a given search engine. **Precision** refers to how many references returned are relevant for a search query. Precision is a problem encountered when using many search engines because of the number of false positives that typical queries return. A **false positive** is a hit that is deemed not relevant for one's search. These may be due to several factors: imprecise queries, inappropriate metatags inserted by the content provider, or errors in indexing. **Coverage** measures the number of relevant documents catalogued by the search engine compared with the potential number of documents available on the Web overall. The sheer scale of the Web poses significant obstacles for search engine coverage of any topic.

Let's illustrate these ideas with a simple example. Suppose that the Web contained only 100 documents and 10 of these documents referenced Labrador retrievers. Imagine that a hypothetical search engine indexed one-half of all these documents (i.e., 50), but only 6 of the 10 total "Labrador retriever" pages. For a potential query about Labs, then, our imaginary Web search engine could have no greater than 60% coverage of the topic. Now, suppose that our query returned a total of eight pages—only three of which were actually relevant. The precision of the query is only 37.5%. Careful crafting of search queries can improve precision. In other words, we can increase the number of relevant references returned while minimizing the false positives. The extent of coverage, however, is not affected by such efforts. Improving the way in which the automated index is assembled is the only remedy here.

How, then, can we improve the precision of our search queries? The choice of keywords is critical for success in most searches. A majority of users tend to employ only one or two keywords. But this is seldom sufficient for successful searches. Sometimes, a keyword or phrase uniquely defines your subject. For example, "Pre-Raphaelites" refers to a very specific group of nineteenth-century English artists and poets. In this instance, a single keyword will do fine. On the other hand, some words are vague or general and, therefore, perform poorly as keywords in Web searches. For example, using "Labs" as a keyword would encompass our canine friends, but also locations for scientific research, manufacturing and product development sites, and other things.

To illustrate the importance of choosing keywords in a search, let's perform an experiment on our own. Suppose that we desired current statistics on the size of the World Wide Web— the total number of pages, Web sites, users, etc. An initial query with the keyword "Web" would produce a staggering total of 168,293,432 "hits" from a popular search engine. The choice of keyword is obviously too broad. Let's add "size" to the query; that is, "Web +size" (alternatively, "Web AND size"). The results are better; the total number of references is reduced to 12,845,657. But this is still far too many to consider. If we examine a few of the pages listed, we can see that the term *size* is vague. We are interested in the size of the Web and not "byte-size," "page-size," and so on. Let's rephrase the keyword more precisely,

Web +"size of"

This yields a little over 1 million hits (i.e., 1,061,218). A cursory examination of the listings shows that there is still too much separation in the occurrences of these keywords. Perhaps it is better put as a single phrase

"size of the Web"

This revised query returns a mere 1,057 hits.

After further examination of the most recent hits, it is evident that our query still returns numerous false positives. For example, a large percentage treats Web design. Thus, we can fine-tune our query by employing the AND NOT operator to subtract these references. Our new version

"size of the Web" –design

has a reduced total of 722, but some of the hits still treat design issues. In this case, we should employ wildcards to subtract related terms such as "designs," "designers," and the like. The query

"size of the Web" –design*

improves our precision by reducing the number of hits to 576.

Using similar reasoning, we can eliminate another group of false positives that deal primarily with Web hosting. The new version

"size of the Web" –design* –host*

returns 466 listings.

Again, an examination of some of the results suggests the need for more fine tuning. Many of the false positives have the phrase "**size of the Web** page." This does match our keyword (shown as bold), but is irrelevant for our search topic. We can fix this with still another subtraction. The query

"size of the Web" –design* –host* –page

reduces the original hundreds of millions to a mere 151 hits.

Finally, we might use an advanced search option such as a date filter to improve the chances of getting more recent estimates of the size of the Web. Namely, by filtering out listings indexed before 2002, the total is reduced to 108 hits. Table 4.4 recaps the results.

Our experiment illustrates that carefully building a keyword query can be rewarded. By eliminating as many false positives as possible, we will save a considerable amount of time downloading and inspecting pages that are not useful for our research. In the end, this time saved will more than make up for the time spent refining our query.

The example also highlights two other important points. The careful choice of queries that incorporate multiple keywords are more likely to be successful than those with only one or two keywords. Secondly, successful queries are built incrementally and experimentally. As our experiment attests, inspecting the results and making improvements based on these results produce useful dividends. The extra time devoted to fine-tuning the query is again offset by the time saved surfing false positives generated by imprecise queries.

Few queries are perfect though. False positives cannot be avoided entirely. Moreover, relevant sites may be left out because we failed to use appropriate synonyms or subtracted references that did not need to be. Unfortunately, there are no absolute rules for performing search engine queries. The heart of the problem is that we are investigating topics and subjects with a tool that performs only text (word and phrase) matching. And, until search engines get smarter, we will have to supply the intelligence ourselves.

Web Portals and Hybrids

The popularity of Web search services has spawned a number of specialized and hybrid services that offer users more exotic choices. The immense growth in the size of search engine databases has prompted the introduction of some services that specialize in a specific topic. These are usually called **niche** search services because they fit a more narrowly selected audience. For example, *ResearchIndex* is a search engine devoted exclusively to computer science topics. Because its scope is limited, it can offer special features that make it a powerful tool for

Table 4.4 *Summarizing the results of the search engine query.*

Keyword Query	Number of Hits
Web	168,293,432
Web +size	12,845,657
Web +"size of"	1,061,218
"size of the Web"	1,057
"size of the Web" –design	722
"size of the Web" –design*	576
"size of the Web" –design* –host*	466
"size of the Web" –design* –host* –page	151
"size of the Web" –design* –host* –page *with date filtering*	108

doing research in this area. *FindLaw* and *LawCrawler* are popular services devoted to the legal profession. FindLaw is a Web directory of legal Web sites, while LawCrawler is a search engine whose database is limited to sites dealing with legal issues.

Some Web services are specialized in that they are restricted to a specific region or geographical area. Yahoo!—to name one—offers Web directories devoted to specific geographic regions such as Europe, Africa, and even to states in the U.S. Each regional directory is divided into topical areas like a normal Web directory. The difference, of course, is that Web sites listed in a regional directory have originated from or deal with that region only.

Metasearch engines form another hybrid class among Web search services. Unlike search engines, which build their own databases, a metasearch engine consults several established search engines with each query posed to it. The metasearch engine returns and summarizes the results from those search engines consulted. Metasearch engines are often useful starting points for research projects.

Large Web sites called **portals** have also evolved into a hybrid brand of Web search service. The term *portal* normally refers to a Web site that is intended as a gateway or entry point to the Web. For example, a number of Internet access providers offer portals to their subscribers. Microsoft Network and AOL (America Online) are good examples. Portals typically feature a Web directory of related sites, search facilities, as well as other information of general interest (news, sports, weather, and the stock market). The popularity of portals has motivated the creation of niche portals devoted to a topic or area of interest, corporate portals showcasing a company, and even personal portals—portals that may be customized to suit your own individual interests and tastes.

As stated earlier, the landscape of Web search services is one that changes quickly. Because the need is great, we can expect new hybrids to find their way to market. But, like most things in computing and information technology—and despite the hype to the contrary—there is very little that is completely novel. Fortunately, then, if we have a good grasp of the forms from which they must evolve, we can learn to exploit these new versions.

■ Summary

Data communication networks connect computer systems for both communication and sharing of data and resources. Communication typically takes place between two systems. The sender encodes a digital message as a signal and transmits it across a communications channel. The receiver receives the signal and converts it back to a digital message. Networks are often distinguished by their scale. Local area networks provide connectivity for computers restricted to a small geographic area. Internets are usually larger networks formed by combining autonomous networks together by means of gateways.

FOCUS   Evaluating Web Content

Even after we have found what we are seeking, it remains to be decided how good is our source. Unlike information distributed by print technology, a great deal of the material found on the Web is unfiltered. In other words, third parties have not certified it. In some instances, this "natural" or unfiltered state is what we find refreshing and appealing about the Web. But, in other cases, we should be more careful how we use the materials found on the Web.

Consult our online resource "Evaluating Web Content," which addresses both the need for and the issues involved in evaluating Web materials.

The Internet is a global internetwork that has a decentralized, loosely-coupled, and redundant organization. The Internet provides support for many useful applications including e-mail, telnet, ftp, and the World Wide Web.

The World Wide Web is an application that is based on the client/server model of computing. The Web is an open, distributed repository of hypermedia information. Thousands of Web servers offer relatively easy access for posting materials on the Web. Many more thousands of Web client machines are attached to the Web and provide access to the Web's resources for millions of people.

Computers with many different scale and performance capabilities can attach to the Web because all Web communication is handled through the set of Web standards and protocols: URL, HTTP, and HTML. A URL (Uniform Resource Locator) is the agreed-upon standard for specifying the address of a Web page or resource available on a Web server. The protocol governing the exchange of information between Web clients and Web servers is HTTP (HyperText Transfer Protocol). And Web documents are encoded using the HTML (HyperText Markup Language) standard.

Browser programs, such as Internet Explorer and Netscape Communicator, running on client machines, interpret and display HTML documents for a specific client environment such as your computer.

There are two major types of Web search services: Web directories and search engines. A Web directory is collected and organized by humans as a hierarchical listing of topics or subjects. Web search engines have databases that are generated automatically by Web spiders or crawlers. Both employ keyword searching, which is a form of text pattern matching. Boolean expressions are often used in keyword search queries to permit the combination of keywords in distinct ways. Metasearch engines, niche search services, and Web portals are newer, hybrid search services that have evolved from more traditional forms.

■ Terms

AND
AND-NOT
Boolean expressions
Boolean operators
client
client/server application
communications channel
coverage (Web search)
data communications network
   (or network)
database
decentralized
default (interpretation)
distributed computing
domain names
downloading
e-mail (or electronic mail)
false positive
ftp (or file transfer protocol)
gateway
history, browser
hit
home page (or entry page)
HTML (HyperText Markup
   Language)

HTTP (HyperText Transfer
   Protocol)
hyperlinks
hypermedia
hypertext
Internet
internetwork (or internet)
intranet
keyword searching
local area network (LAN)
local system
loosely-coupled
metasearch engine
metatags
niche search service
nodes
NOT
OR
phrases
precision (Web search)
protocols
receiver
redundant

remote system
search engines
search service
sender
server
telnet
text string
uploading
URL (Uniform Resource
   Locator)
Web browsers
Web clients
Web crawlers
Web directories
Web pages
Web portals
Web servers
Web session
Web sites
Web spiders
Web surfing
wildcard
World Wide Web (WWW)

■ Questions for Review

1. What is a data communications network?

2. How does communication take place on a network?

3. What is a LAN? An internetwork?

4. What are the chief characteristics of the Internet as a network?

5. Give a brief description of how the Internet application e-mail works.

6. Describe the basic organization of the World Wide Web.

7. Describe the role of hypertext in the Web.

8. What is meant by the client/server model? Relate this to the Web.

9. What is a browser? Relate this concept to the client/server model.

10. What is meant by the term *protocol*?

11. What does URL stand for? What is the function of a URL?

12. What does HTTP stand for? Why is it important?

13. What does HTML stand for? What is its significance?

14. What do we mean when we say that the Web is a distributed computing application?

15. Give an example of an actual URL and explain what its various parts represent.

16. What are bookmarks in a Web browser? Why are these useful?

17. What is a Web directory? How do directories function from the user's perspective?

18. What is a search engine? How do search engines work from a user's perspective?

19. How are Boolean expressions used in keyword search queries? Give examples.

20. What are wildcards? How are they used in keyword search queries? Give examples.

21. What is the difference between precision and coverage of search engine queries?

22. What is a metasearch engine? How does it differ from traditional search engines?

23. What are Web portals? In what manner can they be considered Web search services?

PART **Two**

Text and Numbers

Chapter 5

Creating Documents

OBJECTIVES

- A brief history of text processing

- How text is represented, stored, and processed using computers

- The basic features of word processing applications

- An overview of desktop publishing software

- How HTML organizes documents as Web pages

- The range of applications that can be used for publishing Web pages

Perhaps the most basic form of information handling is the preparation and publication of text documents. Collecting and disseminating information using the written word is a fundamental skill as old as civilization itself. Today, we routinely depend on computers for many forms of document preparation. The ease with which we can produce, edit, and combine text documents would be unthinkable without computers. Using a desktop computer and printer, we can produce everything from simple correspondence to newsletters, catalogs, and even entire books like this one. Digitally produced documents are not limited to text alone, either. The computer's ability to reduce various kinds of information to the digital domain means that we can combine graphical objects, images, and even sounds into our electronic "text" documents.

In this chapter, you will learn about some of the fundamental concepts and methods associated with text processing and desktop publishing. In addition, you will extend these methods to publishing Web documents, too. In later chapters, you will see how to expand your digital documents with your own graphics, images, and sounds.

Brief History of Text Processing

The word processing capabilities that we take for granted are a far cry from the fairly primitive text processing methods used in the early days of electronic computers. Long before word processing became an important application for computers, programmers drafted their programs on paper, and then the computer's switches and wiring were adjusted to run the program. Stored-program computers replaced these early models. On a stored-program computer, the instructions of the program are encoded symbolically and stored in the memory of the system like data.

In the 1950s and early 1960s, symbolic programs were composed using **keypunch machines,** which punched holes in cards to encode text and numbers—usually one line of a program per card. Keypunch machines were not connected to a computer; programs had to be prepared offline and then submitted later to a computer. When a program was completed, its cards were assembled into a stack (or deck) and submitted to a card reader machine for transfer to the computer's memory. Keypunch machines were very unforgiving text processors: Once a hole was punched, it could not be undone. Mistakes were corrected only by starting over with a new card and retyping the entire line.

The only printed output that computers produced in those days was the result of a program's numerical computations. Program output was generally limited to lists of numbers, with perhaps a small amount of textual documentation. No one used computers for writing letters, memos, reports, and so on.

In the early 1960s, time-sharing technology was introduced. The first multiuser operating systems gave programmers direct access to mainframe computer systems, which reduced the need for keypunch machines. They eventually gave way to **text editors,** programs residing on a computer for the purpose of composing other source programs. The earliest text editors were line editors that mimicked the way things were done using cards and keypunch machines. Each line in the program was designated by a number. To edit that line, you issued a command using its line number. Later in the 1970s, significant advances were made in the functionality of text editors, and they became easy enough to use that some brave souls actually employed them for general document preparation. (Some of these editors are still around today.)

The improved editors led to the introduction of the first dedicated text processing systems, called **word processors,** in the 1970s. These systems consisted of special-purpose computers and software that performed certain types of word processing. For instance, there were dedicated systems designed to be used in the legal profession for the production of legal documents. Essentially, these systems allowed an operator to fill in the blanks electronically, so to speak, to produce standardized legal documents. Other dedicated word processors soon followed. To use such a system, you had to purchase both special hardware and appropriate software that came bundled with it. Most of these systems were expensive, costing $10,000 and up. See Figure 5.1.

In the late 1970s and early 1980s, the personal computer was popularized by Apple Computer, Tandy, Commodore, IBM, and others. Most users bought these machines for one of two basic functions. Some were interested in employing VisiCalc, the first spreadsheet program, for numerical calculation, accounting, and other related activities. Others sought the convenience of word processing. WordStar was the first commercially successful word processing application program. It became very popular in the early 1980s when many people discovered the convenience and powerful features of electronic word processing.

Today dozens of word processing programs are commercially available. Modern word processors have a number of common features. Each has approximately the same range of

Figure 5.1
The Brother WP-1, an early dedicated word processing machine, is shown here. This 1980s model has a half-sized text monitor that is flanked by a built-in floppy disk drive on the right. The WP-1 was an all-purpose word processing system that could be used to prepare a variety of printed documents.

basic functionality, and there is not a great deal of difference between the leading products. In spite of this fact, each has its own band of loyal supporters who might claim otherwise. Fortunately, the many similarities among these products mean that once you've mastered one of the current-generation word processors, training yourself on another is a relatively simple matter.

In the late 1980s, text processing capabilities on the personal computer were extended beyond simple word processing to encompass what is referred to as **desktop publishing** (**DTP**). Desktop publishing application programs such as PageMaker, Quark XPress, and others are intended for the design and layout of complex documents on a personal computer. Armed with a DTP program, you can create newsletters, magazines, catalogs, and books that contain many sophisticated elements. For example, you can integrate scanned images, flow text around them, choose text with several colors for dramatic effects, add shaded or boxed text and figures, annotate figures, apply curved and variable-sized text features, and more. If it is designed well, the final product is indistinguishable from documents that have been professionally typeset using more conventional methods. In fact, many publishers of magazines, periodicals, and books use electronic tools like these to produce most of their commercial documents. Desktop publishing puts these capabilities into the hands of the consumer.

Representing Textual Information

Electronic text documents are made up of sequences of characters that are arranged and formatted in particular ways. Both the characters and their formats must be encoded and digitized before the computer can process them. We discuss these issues in this section; and we begin by investigating first how the symbols or characters themselves are stored.

Digitizing the Character Set

Written languages are represented by a set of symbols called a **character set.** A character set contains letters of the alphabet, punctuation marks, and other special symbols used to express the language in writing. Western languages, such as English, French, German, Italian, Spanish, and so on, are based on a common character set, the Latin alphabet. Some of these languages require a few extra marking symbols, but the basic alphabet has twenty-six individual characters, or fifty-two if we count uppercase and lowercase separately. In addition, there are some standard punctuation marks, including commas, periods, question marks, exclamation points, parentheses, single and double quotes, colons, and semicolons. Other special symbols are sometimes needed; for example, the digits; the arithmetic symbols +, −, /, and * (for multiplication); dollar signs; ampersands; and so on. If we total all of these symbols, we get a count between 100 and 150. Cyrillic-based languages such as Russian require approximately the same number of symbols. In contrast, Eastern languages such as Chinese and Japanese require a great many more symbols. A full Chinese symbol set, for example, totals more than 10,000 separate characters.

Initially, written English is our primary interest for this discussion. Unlike the problems faced in digitizing numbers, we have a finite (and rather small, at that) set of characters to be concerned with. This greatly simplifies the problem of devising a digitizing scheme. In fact, the choice of scheme is relatively unimportant as long as we satisfy two constraints. First, we need to make certain we have a one-to-one encoding of the character set; that is, we need to ensure that no two characters have the same digital code. Second, we would like to use a uniform number of bits to represent each character for convenient storage and transmission. You will recall that a single byte (eight bits) is a convenient unit of memory. We saw earlier that a byte can encode 256 different values. A single byte therefore seems a natural choice for representing character codes.

Storing the Character Set—ASCII

Now what's left to decide is how we map the characters to particular strings of 0s and 1s for encoding. This is really a matter of choice. As long as every character has a unique representation, it won't much matter. If one computer manufacturer, however, decides on one scheme and another on a second scheme, and so on, transferring information from one type of computer to another becomes very difficult. Whatever mapping we decide on, it would be convenient if everyone used the same one. This is almost what has happened. The coding method used by the vast majority of computers for a number of years is called the **American Standard Code for Information Interchange** or **ASCII** (pronounced "AS-key"). See Table 5.1 for the ASCII encoding table. Notice that all the punctuation marks and other special symbols ordinarily found on a keyboard are included in the ASCII code. An example of a sentence converted to ASCII is shown in Figure 5.2.

If you examine the ASCII encoding table (Table 5.1), you will notice another characteristic. Both uppercase and lowercase alphabets are numerically ordered according to alphabetical order. For example, "A" is 65, "B" is 66, "C" is 67, and so on. Each alphabet is arranged in ascending order. Digits are also ordered. This attribute is called the **collating sequence;** it means that the computer can take advantage of this property of the underlying code to alphabetize text. For example, two last names like "BABB" and "BAKER" could be compared symbol by symbol. Each has a "B" followed by an "A." Up to this point, they would be equivalent. But because "K" or 75 is greater than "B" or 66, "BAKER" should be placed after "BABB" in an alphabetized list. Alphabetizing or arranging text in lexicographic order belongs to a special class of operations called **sorting.** Many forms of information can be ordered, and if their data representation is likewise ordered, then sorting them becomes easier. Preserving the collating sequence, for instance, makes it easier to sort text because instructions can employ the processor's normal numeric comparison operations.

The blank space is a character just like any other. Its ASCII representation is 00100000 in binary (32 in decimal), even though we don't think of it as a symbol when we type or print it. What we recognize is the effect it creates, namely, a space between the other visible characters.

Some other characters entered at the keyboard do not show up as symbols either when we enter them, but rather as effects; for example, the Tab key for indenting and the Enter or Return key for carriage returns or marking the end of the line. These are some of the **invisible control characters** used to control the formatting of text in our documents. Some of the control characters are actually used for data transmission functions rather than formatting; these are present in ASCII from its origin as a teletype transmission code.

ASCII is a no-frills coding scheme for text. There is little else aside from a few formatting symbols such as horizontal tabs, carriage returns, page breaks, the uppercase and lowercase alphabets, punctuation, digits, and a few special symbols. For this reason, ASCII encoded text is often called **plain text.** The kind of formatting information that we are accustomed to in

Table 5.1 *The ASCII character encoding scheme maps each symbol of the character set to a 1-byte (8-bit) storage representation.*

ASCII ENCODING TABLE

Binary	Decimal	Character	Binary	Decimal	Character	Binary	Decimal	Character
00000000	0		00111100	60	<	01011111	95	_
.	.	invisible	00111101	61	5	01100000	96	`
.	.	control	00111110	62	>	01100001	97	a
.	.	characters	00111111	63	?	01100010	98	b
00011111	31		01000000	64	@	01100011	99	c
00100000	32	blank	01000001	65	A	01100100	100	d
		space	01000010	66	B	01100101	101	e
		character	01000011	67	C	01100110	102	f
00100001	33	!	01000100	68	D	01100111	103	g
00100010	34	"	01000101	69	E	01101000	104	h
00100011	35	#	01000110	70	F	01101001	105	i
00100100	36	$	01000111	71	G	01101010	106	j
00100101	37	%	01001000	72	H	01101011	107	k
00100110	38	&	01001001	73	I	01101100	108	l
00100111	39	'	01001010	74	J	01101101	109	m
00101000	40	(	01001011	75	K	01101110	110	n
00101001	41	)	01001100	76	L	01101111	111	o
00101010	42	*	01001101	77	M	01110000	112	p
00101011	43	1	01001110	78	N	01110001	113	q
00101100	44	,	01001111	79	O	01110010	114	r
00101101	45	-	01010000	80	P	01110011	115	s
00101110	46	.	01010001	81	Q	01110100	116	t
00101111	47	/	01010010	82	R	01110101	117	u
00110000	48	0	01010011	83	S	01110110	118	v
00110001	49	1	01010100	84	T	01110111	119	w
00110010	50	2	01010101	85	U	01111000	120	x
00110011	51	3	01010110	86	V	01111001	121	y
00110100	52	4	01010111	87	W	01111010	122	z
00110101	53	5	01011000	88	X	01111011	123	{
00110110	54	6	01011001	89	Y	01111100	124	l
00110111	55	7	01011010	90	Z	01111101	125	}
00111000	56	8	01011011	91	[	01111110	126	~
00111001	57	9	01011100	92	\	01111111	127	delete
00111010	58	:	01011101	93	]			
00111011	59	;	01011110	94	^			

printed documents cannot be reproduced using ASCII. For example, special font faces, styles such as italics and bold, and margin controls are common for most our text documents, but cannot be reproduced in ASCII text. See Figure 5.3.

Unfortunately, there is no equivalent to the ASCII code for this type of formatting information. Competing word processing programs were developed rapidly after the success of

Figure 5.2

*The sentence "The cat is on the mat." contains thirteen different characters, including the space character or blank and the period punctuation mark. In the box on the right, the ASCII code for each of the symbols is provided. Taking repetitions into account, the length of the sentence is 22 symbols. Thus, 22 bytes are needed to encode the sentence as shown below. Normally, this block of text would be thought of as a continuous sequence called a **string.** Consequently, whether it is a few words or a lengthy paper containing thousands of characters, the text would be represented as a single string stored either in memory or a file.*

blank =	00100000
a =	01100001
c =	01100011
e =	01100101
h =	01101000
i =	01101001
m =	01101101
n =	01101110
o =	01101111
s =	01110011
T =	01010100
t =	01110100
. =	00101110

The cat is on the mat.

01010100	01101000	01100101	00100000	01100011
01100001	01110100	00100000	01101001	01110011
00100000	01101111	01101110	00100000	01110100
01101000	01100101	00100000	01101101	01100001
01110100	00101110			

Figure 5.3

The paragraph above is formatted using a selected font face, indented text, boldface and italics. Below it, the same passage is shown as plain, or ASCII, text. Note that all formatting information is lost.

> The coding method used by the vast majority of computers for a number of years is called the **American Standard Code for Information Interchange** or **ASCII** (pronounced "*AS-key*").
>
> ```
> The coding method used by the vast majority of computers
> for a number of years is called the American Standard Code
> for Information Interchange or ASCII (pronounced "AS-key").
> ```

WordStar, before the issue of standardization could be addressed. Today each manufacturer has its own methods embedded in its proprietary products. Keep in mind that this lack of standardization is not among different types of computers, but among different software that often runs on exactly the same types of computers. For example, a Microsoft Word document will differ in digital form from a WordPerfect document created on the same computer even if the original text contents are identical. The differences will be the embedded formatting information. For an example, consult Figure 5.4.

The fact that each word processing application has its own proprietary method for encoding formatting information makes moving documents between one program to another a tricky business. In this conversion process, we are likely to lose the formatting information altogether, or at least get a garbled version of it once we transfer our document. A way out of this is to employ a separate utility program, called a **translator** or **filter program,** which is specifically written to convert documents from one particular application to another. Some of the current-generation word processors come bundled with such filters for documents created in their major competitors' word processors.

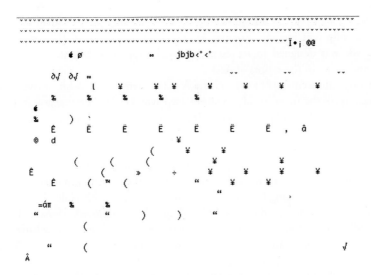

method used by the vast majority of computers for a number of years is called the American Standard Code for Information Interchange or ASCII (pronounced ìAS-keyî).

If you must move information from one program to another without the benefit of a translator program, the safe way to do it is to save a copy of the original document in ASCII or plain text-only format first. This will strip away all the formatting information except for spaces, tabs, and returns. Another word processing program will at least be able to read the unformatted text itself—made possible by the common ASCII code that both programs use. A better option might be to use the **Rich Text Format** (**RTF**) file format, which does preserve a great deal of formatting information for text documents. It is supported by Microsoft and is a leading candidate for an industry-standard text file exchange format. Most current document preparation programs can both read and save RTF files.

Portable Document Format (**PDF**) is another option for delivering text documents with both complete formatting and layout control. A PDF file is a self-contained cross-platform document. It is a file that will look the same on the screen and in print, regardless of what kind of computer or printer someone is using and regardless of what word processing application was originally used to create it. PDF files contain the complete formatting of the original document, including fonts and images. In addition, they are highly compressed; this means that they can be stored efficiently and transmitted over networks quickly. In order to view or print a PDF file, you must have a PDF Reader application. These are readily available at no cost. Many computer systems are already configured with PDF Readers when purchased. They are likewise installed as plug-ins for many Web browser programs.

There is a downside, however. PDF documents cannot be created or edited without the benefit of a PDF Writer application. This is a commercial application that would have to be purchased and installed on your computer system.

Unicode

ASCII served as a standard for text representation for several decades, in spite of its limited scope. But, as information technology spread globally, the need for representing multilingual text likewise grew. In 1991, a U.S. consortium of information technology companies partnered with working groups from the International Standards Organization (ISO) to develop a more global coding system for representing text. The result was the **Unicode** standard, which proposed a consistent method for encoding multilingual plain text. Besides the Latin alphabet, Unicode was designed to represent European alphabets, Middle Eastern (right-to-left scripts), and many of the scripts of Asia.

The original intent was to expand the ASCII scheme to a 16-bit or two-byte code that could encompass the diversity of alphabets used worldwide. The increase from one to two bytes offered 2^{16} or 65,536 possible encodings. ASCII coding was preserved for compatibility with older systems and software. Thus, single ASCII characters retained their same values; the extra or higher order byte was simply filled with 0s. See Figure 5.5. Later, Unicode was expanded to a maximum of 4 bytes (32 bits), which provides over 4 billion different encodings!

Unicode supports several basic encoding formats: the most common are 8-bit, 16-bit, and 32-bit lengths. An encoding format should not be confused with Unicode character set. The character set is the same regardless of the encoding format employed. Morse code, for instance, is an encoding format for transmitting letters of the Latin alphabet. Similarly, Unicode encoding formats are used to store and transmit Unicode characters using different units or lengths. The 8-bit form—called UTF-8—treats each character as a multibyte sequence and is common in Web applications and older legacy systems. All ASCII characters have the same byte values as before. The alphabets and scripts for other languages typically require additional bytes, but, the codes are derived so that the value of the first byte indicates how many additional bytes are needed to complete the character's code. UTF-16 is a two-byte variable-length encoding; UTF-32 is a four-byte fixed-length encoding form—that is, 32 bits each represent all characters. UTF-16 and UTF-32 are used by newer systems in which the amount of memory space or storage is not at a premium.

Figure 5.5
The ASCII code for the character 'c' is shown. For compatibility, Unicode adopted the ASCII character code as a subset. Thus, in its original 16-bit or two-byte format, the higher-order byte would contain 0s. As a result, the Latin letter 'c' retains the same number code in both systems. Unicode characters are listed in hexadecimal form, so 'c' is referred to as U-0063.

c = | 01100011 | ASCII

c = | 00000000 | 01100011 | UNICODE

FOCUS   # The Internationalization of Text

Unicode is supported by most modern operating systems and many applications as well. To find out more about how it supports the representation of multilingual text and examine examples of its use, see the online resource "Focus on the Internationalization of Text."

Basic Features of Word Processing Software

Even though commercial word processing programs lack uniformity in how they represent or encode documents, they do have a high degree of commonality. These programs have essentially the same basic functions and capabilities even if they have slightly different looks or user interfaces. Thus, if you have learned to use one program, you will probably need only a small amount of instruction (perhaps just a little experimentation) to become proficient with another one.

The essential functions of word processing software are to create, edit, format, and display text documents. Word processors were designed to emulate the older, conventional way of entering text using a typewriter. (Ironically, word processors have nearly replaced typewriters entirely, so that the original metaphor is usually lost on new users today.) But there are important differences between employing typewriters and word processors to create documents. For instance, when you use a typewriter, you must press the Enter (or Return) key when you reach the end of a line (usually a bell rings to remind you that you are near the end of a line). Word processors automatically handle the end of a line for you using a feature called **word-wrap.** This means that you can simply continue to type and when you reach the end of a line, the text will automatically flow to the next line. Partially completed words will be wrapped to the next line—thus the term *word-wrap*. Hence, pressing the Enter (or Return) key in a word processor does not signal the end of a line. Rather, this action marks the end of a paragraph. Much of the formatting you do in a word processing document will apply to whole paragraphs, so it is very important to have a convenient way to delineate different paragraphs.

The chief distinguishing feature of these applications, though, is that they permit the functional separation of basic text processing tasks. Creating a document on a typewriter is a fixed, linear process. You must enter, edit, and format the text as you go. Should you discover an error in a previous page, you must discard all of the work after the error and recreate the document from that point onwards. But in a word processing application, the essential functions of entering, editing and formatting text are independent activities. Text may be inserted or deleted at any time without the need for reentering a portion or the entire document. You can format the text at any time, too. Thus, the same text content can be easily used for different purposes with simple editing and formatting changes. Documents may also be prepared for different displays; for example, for the screen or as printed pages.

Unfortunately, many users fail to exploit this separation of tasks. Instead, they enter, edit, and format text simultaneously as if using a typewriter. The true power and efficiency of word processing software, though, depends upon the effective use of its many tools that help to automate these tasks. These are best exploited when we clearly separate the tasks of entering, editing, and formatting text. In the next several sections, we will survey how these basic functions work in a typical word processing application.

Inserting and Deleting Text

Nearly all modern word processors are automatically in a mode that allows new text to be inserted at any point. The **cursor** marks the point at which text you type is inserted in a document. Thus, to add text, you simply position the cursor at the point where new text is desired and type.

Deleting text is just as easy. Often you do so by positioning the cursor just beyond the text to be deleted and pressing the Backspace key (the Delete key on some Macintosh keyboards) the requisite number of times. The word processor will automatically shrink the text to combine the undeleted portions. To edit or change text, therefore, the simplest procedure is to delete the unwanted text and then insert its replacement. You may want to delete or replace large sections of text. By selecting a contiguous section of text, called a **text block,** you can act on it as a unit.

Cut, Copy, and Paste

The basic first step for most editing and formatting actions is the general procedure of selecting a block of text. In order to delete text, for example, you must first select the affected block of text. Likewise, you must select the text in order to move it or duplicate it elsewhere. All word processors provide these basic editing capabilities, usually by way of Cut, Copy, and Paste commands. These commands act in the ways that their names suggest. If we select a body of text and issue the **Cut command,** the selected text is deleted, or cut, from the document. The text is not lost, however, but is rather saved in an area of memory referred to as the **clipboard.** (We say we have placed the text "on the clipboard.") If we reposition the cursor and issue the **Paste command,** the text on the clipboard will be inserted into this new position within the document. In this way, we can move or reorder selections of text at will. This is an indispensable tool for editing long documents, where we are likely to change our minds—perhaps several times—about the exact sequence of the text contents.

The **Copy command** works just like the Cut command except that it does not remove the selected text from its current position. In other words, the Copy command simply places the selected text on the clipboard. By moving the cursor to another position and then choosing the Paste command, we can duplicate selected text sections. Figure 5.6 illustrates this process. This is very useful sometimes when we have two blocks of text that are very similar: To create the second block, we can duplicate the first block and then edit it, rather than enter the second block from scratch.

Text placed on the clipboard is not erased after it is pasted elsewhere. Because the clipboard is a form of memory, we can read its contents as many times as we want without altering these contents. Consequently, we can paste it over and over, if desired. The only way that text on the clipboard is replaced is when a new Cut or Copy command is executed—a new item written to the clipboard memory overwrites the existing item. Some word processors are equipped with clipboards that can store multiple items in sequence. In this instance, it is possible to recall earlier text blocks even after newer items have been copied to the clipboard.

Formatting Characters

All word processors let us choose how we wish to display the characters in our text—from groups of characters like whole paragraphs, phrases, and single words down to individual characters. The display characteristics are called **formatting,** and there are a number of choices in this regard.

For example, we can choose the particular font face in which we want to display the characters (from among those fonts that have been installed in our system files). A **font face** is the typeface in which each symbol is drawn or formed. In addition to the font face, we can also specify its size. The typical measure for **font size** is based on the printer's measure, **points.** There are approximately 72 points per inch. The choices for font face and font size are limited by what is stored in the system files—not by the word processor itself.

Figure 5.6

Copy and Paste commands. The user selects a block of text and copies it to a special buffer in memory referred to as the "clipboard." This copied text may then be pasted to another page or location in the document. Because the text is read from memory, it may be pasted over and over. The text is lost only when another copy command replaces it.

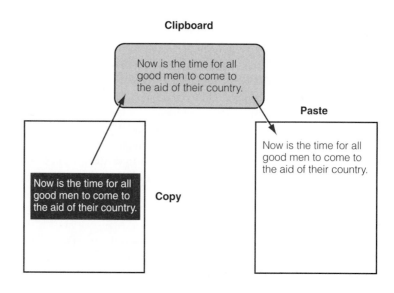

Clipboard

Now is the time for all good men to come to the aid of their country.

Paste

Now is the time for all good men to come to the aid of their country.

Now is the time for all good men to come to the aid of their country.

Copy

Characters can also be displayed in a variety of **font styles** such as italic, boldface, underline, shadow, and so on. These styles may be combined as well. Most word processors can display characters raised above the line of type to form superscripts or placed below the line of type as subscripts.

Formatting Paragraphs

The appearance of a document can be greatly altered by paragraph formatting. For example, we can change the width of paragraphs by setting the paragraph margins, and we can choose different line spacing for a paragraph (single-spaced, double-spaced, and so on). It is usually quite easy to change the alignment of paragraphs, too. In particular, paragraphs can be **left-aligned** (even left edge and uneven or ragged right edge), **right-aligned** (even right edge and ragged left edge—useful for some special effects), **justified** (even on both edges), or **centered.** Another characteristic convenient to control automatically is the indentation of the first line of a paragraph. Various kinds of **tab markers** can be defined and set for a paragraph as well, so that pressing the Tab key produces automatic text separation. Tabs are indispensable for setting up tables, numbered or bulleted lists, and columnar displays.

In almost all modern word processors, you can set any or all of the paragraph characteristics by placing the cursor anywhere inside the paragraph (thereby selecting the paragraph for formatting) and then adjusting the desired options on the ruler or selecting the appropriate option from a toolbar. A **ruler** is a graphical device with markings similar to those on a regular measuring ruler, together with other icons and special symbols, as shown in Figure 5.7. Ruler adjustments are usually carried out by clicking and dragging with the mouse.

Rulers can be used to format individual paragraphs. If you move the cursor to a different paragraph, the ruler may have completely different settings. This means, of course, that the current paragraph has been formatted differently. In other words, every paragraph has its own ruler settings stored with the document. For convenience, when you press the Enter or Return key to end a paragraph and begin a new one, the current ruler settings carry forward to the new paragraph. This eliminates having to reset the format characteristics of adjacent paragraphs that are likely to have the same format anyway.

Displaying Text: What You See Is What You Get

Because most word processing documents are delivered as printed documents to their intended audience, it is highly desirable that what you see on the screen corresponds closely to what will be printed. This property is called **what-you-see-is-what-you-get** and is represented by the acronym **WYSIWYG** (pronounced "whiz-ee-wig"). If the word processor you are using does not have this property for the printer you intend to use, you will likely be in for a few surprises when you actually print the document.

In regard to WYSIWYG, a special circumstance is worth noting here. The resolution of most screen displays is inferior to the resolution of a good printer. As a result, fonts may appear choppier on the screen than they do in a document printed on a higher-resolution printer that does a great deal of font smoothing. Some word processing applications, however, do take

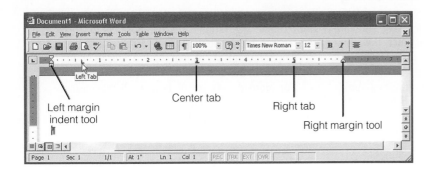

Figure 5.7

The ruler in Microsoft Word permits the precise placement of tab markers, margins, and paragraph indents.

advantage of the advanced graphic display capabilities of modern video monitors. In these cases, the text drawn on the screen has been smoothed to resemble better the output of higher resolution devices. (We will return to the topic of graphic display in Chapter 9.)

At any rate, depending on the resolution of the printer to be used, WYSIWYG usually does not apply in the strictest sense. What WYSIWYG actually refers to in these cases is something a little less perfect than its name suggests, namely, that the character positions appear on screen exactly as they will in the printed document. To be safe, you should always inspect a printed document to see that it is formatted as you intended. WYSIWYG does, however, make the formatting process a great deal easier and could save a few trees, too.

Basic Features of Desktop Publishing Software

Desktop publishing (DTP) programs are intended to make designing and laying out professional-quality documents both accessible and convenient. These programs often contain many of the features of ordinary word processors as well as additional tools needed for page layout. "Page layout" refers to the overall design of the page: how the contents are arranged, the visual effects created by the use of space, color, and so on.

Recently, some word processors also have added layout tools that formerly would have been the exclusive domain of DTP programs. Consequently, the distinction between word processors and desktop publishing programs is not as clear-cut as it once was. Future enhancements to word processing products will no doubt further blur this distinction. Even so, there are a number of document preparation and enhancement features that are still considered the bread-and-butter of most desktop publishing programs. We will describe these in this section.

Internal Document Structure and Frames

Word processing documents are more often than not designed to contain text organized in a straight or linear manner, possibly with some figures or other graphic objects included at various intervals for decoration or illustration. As a result, the document has a simple internal organization. We start typing at the beginning of the document, and we enter our text and graphic objects as we go until we reach the end. We can divide the document into sections, but each section is itself a block of contiguous text. On the other hand, documents like catalogs, advertising copy, brochures, newsletters, and newspapers often have a more complicated structure. We might have several more or less independent sections of text and graphics on the

FOCUS   Word Processing

Modern word processing software has evolved considerably since their first appearance in the 1980s. Today, they offer a full range of document preparation features. Besides the simple text editing and formatting described above, you may use a word processing application to prepare headers and footers for titles and page numbering. In addition, you can create tables and insert graphics and illustrations. It is also possible to work with complex documents by defining sections and creating paragraph styles that may be reused in different parts of the document.

For more details about how word processing software applications may be used for the creation, formatting, and display of text documents, consult the online resource "Focus on Word Processing."

same page. On the other hand, a single section might be distributed across several nonconsecutive pages.

Newspapers and newsletters are good examples of this more complex type of organization. We might start a half-dozen or more stories on page 1 and continue them on a variety of later pages. Similarly, an advertising brochure might have five or six different product descriptions or claims of greatness placed at various positions on a single page, with a number of different-sized graphic objects as well. Simple straight-line organization does not allow the creation of such documents.

Such sophisticated documents can be thought of as a number of mini-documents within a single document. Desktop publishing programs are designed to handle this kind of structure naturally. They typically do this using the concept of frames within a document. A **frame** is essentially a mini-document (or a piece of a mini-document) within a document. Generally, text frames and graphic frames are considered distinct types of objects. We can place any number of different frames on the same page. See Figure 5.8 for an example. We may enter text or graphics (even movies and sound, too) into these frames independently. Subsequently, we can edit frames separately, delete them, modify their characteristics, move them around on the page, move them to other pages, and so on, without affecting the other frames in the document.

Relating Frames to Other Frames

To create the structure needed for documents like newspapers, we must associate frames on different pages (or different locations on the same page). For example, if we delete a section of text from a newspaper story that starts on page 1, we want the rest of the story to move up to close the space created by the deletion, even if the story is continued on page 3. This is done by linking or chaining text frames together. **Chained frames** (also called **threaded frames**) behave just as you might expect. Each frame is directly chained to another frame, which in turn can be chained to another, and so on. The chain has a definite sequence: Frames are placed in the sequence immediately following the frame to which they are chained. When enough text is entered into a text frame to overflow that frame, the text flows into the next frame (if one exists) in the chain sequence, as illustrated in Figure 5.9. If the final frame in a chain is overflowed, some programs will create another frame and page at the end of the document to hold the overflow. As frames are resized or as text is added or deleted, the text is automatically reorganized throughout the entire chain to account for the new sizes.

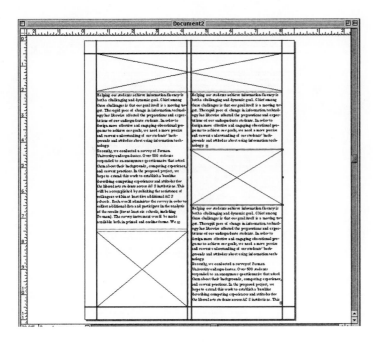

Figure 5.8

*Using a DTP program, each page of the document can be designed on a workspace called the **copy board**. In this instance, the master page or template has guides for laying out a two-column page. Individual text and graphic frames are sized and placed on the page. The text is then inserted into each text frame or box. Later pictures will be inserted into the graphic frames (shown here as a box with an "X").*

Frames can be layered, too. When one frame is placed over another, you usually have several options for how the contents of the underlying frame will behave with respect to the "top-layer" frame. For example, suppose you wish to place an illustration or picture in the middle of a story. To do this, you create a graphic frame to hold the illustration and place it on top of an underlying text frame containing the story as illustrated in Figure 5.10.

Another very useful application of frames is placing textual annotations within a figure or other graphic object. Rather than having to label the graphic object before including it in your document, you can simply put small text frames anywhere you desire over the graphic frame. These text annotations can then be edited, moved around, or even deleted without altering the graphic objects—a big savings in effort in many cases.

Greater Control Over Documents and Document Elements

Generally speaking, desktop publishing programs give us more control than word processors over the elements that make up our documents. All the formatting features of a word processor are present, and additional ones are provided as well. For example, we can control the appearance of text on the printed page in greater detail by using a technique known as kerning. **Kerning** allows us to change the space that characters occupy to close up consecutive characters and produce an easier-to-read and cleaner-looking document. See Figure 5.11.

Figure 5.9

Two text frames are linked or chained (as shown on the left). When text is inserted in the upper frame (as seen on the right), it automatically flows into the linked frame.

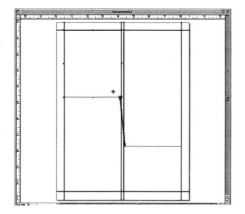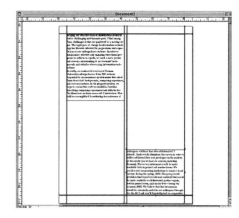

Figure 5.10

Shown here is a page that was created in a two-column format using two linked text frames. Text was then inserted into the frames. Afterward, a graphic or picture frame was layered on top of the two columns. The image was inserted and positioned inside the picture frame. As you can see, the text automatically flows around the edges of the picture.

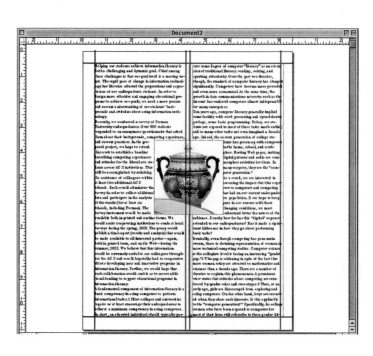

On the global scale, we also have more options available in desktop publishing software than in word processors. For example, we can create any number of different **master pages** or **templates,** which define and position default frames of the types we desire. Whenever we want to create a new page with a particular arrangement of frames, we can simply designate it to have the format of a chosen master page. For example, a monthly newsletter might be composed of several master pages. Each issue will differ in the specific copy and graphics that it contains, but master pages make the process of laying it out each month more efficient. An additional benefit is that each issue will have the same "look" as other issues because they are all constructed from the same master pages.

Desktop publishing applications also have the capability of producing PostScript output files. **PostScript** is a high-quality output format used by most professional-quality electronic printing devices. The fact that a DTP program can produce PostScript files means that the document can be produced by the printer directly—without the need of the original DTP application. In contrast, printing a word processing file requires running the word processing program in order to display and transmit the file to the print device. Thus, you can send the PostScript output files to a professional printer who, in turn, can produce the documents immediately.

The power and convenience of desktop publishing software has had a significant influence on how professional copy is prepared and published. In a number of instances, DTP is more economical than the traditional publishing process. Many businesses now publish their own advertising copy, catalogs, and other publications using only desktop computing systems.

Desktop publishing offers authors more control over layout of their documents by eliminating the need for "outside" design and typesetting for many types of documents. In fact, it is now quite common for documents to be delivered to publishing firms in electronic form after the originator has produced them using a desktop publishing program. In these ways, desktop publishing has truly revolutionized the publishing industry.

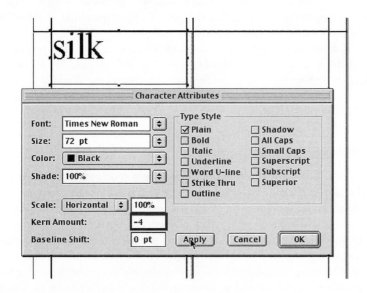

Figure 5.11

In QuarkXpress, kerning is handled automatically by specifying the distance or separation desired between two characters. Shown here is the Kern Command dialog box. Because the font size is large (72 points), the separation between the 'i' and 'l' and between the 'l' and the 'k' would benefit by kerning. The character pairs are moved closer by 4 points each. The result is a more natural look in spite of the size of the type.

FOCUS   Desktop Publishing

Desktop publishing software offers advanced capabilities that go beyond the preparation of basic text documents. For a closer look at how DTP applications enable you to design and construct professional-quality documents, see the online resource "Focus on Desktop Publishing."

Publishing Web Documents Using HTML

Word processing and desktop publishing applications are powerful tools for preparing text documents that can be printed for distribution; however, these documents are not easily distributed electronically. For example, suppose that you created a newsletter that you intended to be transmitted electronically and read from computer video monitors. Normally, your readers would have to view the document using a copy of the software application program that created it. Thus, for instance, to read a word processing file, you would have to open it using the same software. It might be possible to convert the original document to a more generic format such as RTF, PDF, or even PostScript. But the readers would still require special viewing applications to render the files properly for display on video monitors.

There is a much easier solution: publish the document as Web pages! Web pages are cross-platform documents; they may be viewed on any computer system provided it has an appropriate Web browser program installed. Web browsers are widely distributed with every computer make and model. They are also freely available. In short, Web pages are becoming the default standard for creating and publishing documents electronically. You may have noted, for example, that manuals or help pages distributed with software applications are often produced as Web pages. Many companies and organizations archive and publish their operating procedures and policies using Web pages. Web publishing is, therefore, an important skill for the digital-age worker.

As you have learned, World Wide Web documents are written in a language called HTML (Hypertext Markup Language). World Wide Web documents have three distinguishing characteristics. First, they are constructed to be resolution independent; that is, they can be interpreted and displayed on a large variety of display systems without modification. Second, in addition to text, Web documents routinely contain multimedia elements such as sounds, images, graphics, and even video clips. Finally, Web documents are by their very nature hypertext documents, meaning that they contain electronic links to other information published on the Web (by the same or different authors).

HTML is designed to implement each of these characteristics. The rest of this chapter will focus on the basic elements of this language. You will see that HTML was developed specifically to create documents that can be made available on the World Wide Web and that it is designed explicitly to take advantage of the Web's utilization of the distributed client/server computing model.

HTML: Philosophy and Design

The World Wide Web is the ultimate open systems environment. This means that its users employ and attach to it a wide variety of client computers—all makes, models, and operating systems. Consequently, the designers of HTML realized that HTML documents must be playable on a large and unpredictable variety of client computers.

In other words, insofar as possible, HTML designers wanted to create a language that defined documents in a way that would not depend on the type of display device used by the client system. This was accomplished by separating the content of the document from the details of its presentation. We saw earlier, for example, that character codes such as ASCII and Unicode specify individual codes for different character symbols, but there is more to representing text than just naming which symbols are used. A particular symbol such as 'z' can be presented in a variety of font faces, sizes, and styles. The latter details specify the format of the symbol. Format, of course, is an important ingredient of presentation—structure and organization are others. Documents often have titles, headings, sections, and other elements that have distinct and useful functions. Though they are not strictly speaking part of the document's content, they have informational value. Again, the role of HTML is to define separately both the content and presentation of a document.

Once a definition of a document is specified in HTML, the HTML document is stored on a Web server. When a client computer accesses the server and requests that HTML document, the stored document (specifying the content and presentation separately) is transferred to the client computer.

After the document is transmitted to the client machine, the Web browser software interprets the structure and displays it on that machine's display device. The browser software makes any necessary decisions about how the document will look on the screen according to the characteristics and capabilities of the display device itself. In short, the details of presentation are handled by the client machine. There are no concerns about compatibility because an HTML file transferred to the client machine is not a finished document, but more like a recipe on how to create one.

Because Web documents can also include multimedia elements, the designers of HTML have also provided a convenient method for incorporating these elements into HTML documents. In fact, the same method is used to implement hypertext capabilities as well. A simple HTML command allows a document designer to establish a link to another Web document or resource file. When the linked file is another document, that document is fetched and displayed when the link is activated. When the linked file is an image, sound, or video, the browser fetches and displays (or plays) the file if it can handle information of that type.

Different browsers have varying capabilities to play such files themselves, but most initiate a search for appropriate player/display software on the client machine. For example, if the resource is a video file in a format not supported by your browser, a dialog box will appear to seek advice for further actions. On the other hand, when such software is available, its use is transparent to the browser user. Notice again how the client/server model is exploited. The HTML document supplied by the server contains only the reference to the appropriate multimedia file. The burden of fetching and interpreting this file (displaying an image, playing a sound or a video) resides entirely with the client software and hardware.

Client/server computing can have its downside, too. In fact, one of its strengths can actually promote a weakness. As stated earlier, the client and the server systems do not have to be identically matched; different makes and models may cooperate in client/server processing provided they employ the same protocol for communication and information exchange. But, as independent systems, the client and server are not required to adhere to any other specifications. In this respect, they are said to be loosely coupled systems. In contrast, the components of a software application executing on a single system are tightly coupled. Their interaction is determined and very predictable. For example, when you create a document using a word processing application, you would expect the resulting printed document to look very much like its WYSIWYG display when you were creating it. Unfortunately, this is not the case for client browser applications. These programs often differ in performance. For instance, Netscape Navigator and Internet Explorer treat the display of HTML differently in sometimes subtle and sometimes not so subtle ways. To make matters worse, there are also significant differences among the different versions of the same application. Netscape Navigator 4.x ('x' refers to a numbered version such as 4.1, 4.2, and so on), for example, handles HTML very differently from its most recent versions.

Browsers also permit the user to set personal preferences for how documents are displayed, too. For examples, a default font face and size may be chosen or images may be suppressed for faster downloading. The bottom line is this: Web page authoring is not exactly like creating documents using word processors or DTP software. It is a client medium; the author has less control over the results.

What Is a Markup Language?

You will recall that HTML stands for HyperText Markup Language. The term *markup* is borrowed from the publishing industry. Before the advent of electronic typesetting in this industry, plain-text proof pages were typically marked up with a variety of typesetting codes to illustrate how the text was to appear when it was actually printed. HTML borrows this idea, and an HTML document consists of marked-up plain (or unformatted) text, with the special markings indicating how the text is to be treated when it is "published" (that is displayed) on a Web client machine. Hence, an HTML file consists of regular text interspersed with special markup codes called **tags.** Learning to write HTML is a simple matter of learning to use these tags to produce desired effects in the published document.

HTML focuses primarily on the basic structure of a document rather than its exact appearance when viewed. Of course, there is a relationship between the structure and appearance of a document, but they are not one and the same. Documents written in HTML are encoded in plain ASCII or Unicode text; they contain no formatting whatsoever—no tabs, no different fonts, no italics or bold text, and so on. Instead, these documents contain two things: the text you want to display and the HTML tags that indicate document elements, structure, formatting, and links to other Web documents or included media. Web browsers use these tags to format and display the text that we provide.

Let's examine the format of a typical HTML tag:

<tag_id>*content affected by the tag* </tag_id>

'tag_id' here denotes some identifier specifying the tag type. Most HTML tag types have beginning and ending tags surrounding the affected content, as shown above. We will refer to these as **paired tags.** The closing tag generally has a slash (/) followed by the tag identifier. All HTML tags are case insensitive, so any mixture of uppercase and lowercase may be used to express them. Some prefer to emphasize the location of tags by using all uppercase. However, newer related tagging systems such as XML and XHTML require lowercase tags. Consequently, we will adopt the lowercase convention throughout for consistency and simplicity.

Some tags are standalone; they are positioned where you want some effect to occur. These tags lack a paired end tag:

<tag_id>*content after the tag*

HTML: General Document Structure

A small number of general structure tags are included in every HTML document. For example, paired <html> tags must surround the entire document, paired <head> tags surround the heading material, and paired <body> tags bracket the body of the document. The heading material can include a number of items, but the only one the browser displays is the document title.

Figure 5.12 illustrates the structure of a simple HTML document. We've placed the various document structure tags on separate lines for emphasis, but this is not at all necessary. Carriage returns (and all other ordinary formatting information) have no meaning within an HTML document.

The <!DOCTYPE> tag is always the first tag in an HTML file. It specifies the version of HTML on which the document is based. The client browser uses this information to interpret the document correctly. The most current version of HTML is 4.01. Many HTML documents still use older tags not actually supported by 4.01. These are called "transitional" documents. Here is an example of a <!DOCTYPE> tag declaration that works with the latest browser versions.

<!DOCTYPE html PUBLIC "-//W3C//DTD HTML 4.01 Transitional//EN"
"http://www.w3.org/TR/REC-html40/loose.dtd">

Figure 5.12

Every HTML document has standard structural tags that specify its main components.

```
<!DOCTYPE>
<html>
<head>
 <title>description of the page</title>
 <meta name="metaname" content="metacontent">
 other head elements go here
</head>
<body>
 body elements go here
</body>
</html>
```

The latest browser versions require the <!DOCTYPE> tag, and without it there is no guarantee your pages will be interpreted properly. If the details here seem confusing, then do what the professional Web publisher does: let your computer handle the details instead of you. Create a file containing the correct <!DOCTYPE> and other standard tags and use it as a template for creating new pages.*

The <head> paired tags denote information about the Web page that is not actually displayed in the browser window. The title of the Web page is one such element. The title is usually displayed in the browser title bar and provides the user with useful information about the page. The <title> paired tags are used to indicate the title's text. Here is an example.

<title>Jane's Labrador Retriever Web Page</title>

Page titles are not to be confused with the name of the HTML file. The latter is a name assigned the HTML document that is consistent with the naming conventions of your operating system. HTML filenames have ".html" or ".htm" extensions. The client browser uses the extension to determine how to treat the file. In fact, without the ".html" extension, an otherwise well-formed HTML document would not be displayed properly by most browsers.

Metatags can also be included within the <head> paired tags. You will recall that metatags specify information about the Web page, such as keywords that can be used by search engines. The <meta> tag is employed for these purposes. The <meta> tag has two modifiers, name and content. A **tag modifier** is an identifier enclosed within the tag that specifies information that may be used with the tag. In this instance, name denotes the type of information expressed by the tag; and content identifies that information. For example,

<meta name="Author" content="Jane Lowery">

<meta name="Description" content="This site is dedicated to owners and fanciers of Labrador retriever dogs." >

<meta name="Keywords" content="Labrador retrievers, Labs, dog breeds">

In each instance, the modifier has an '=' sign followed by text enclosed in quotes. Here the Web page author is listed and a short description and keywords are provided for search engines that may scan the page. These are especially useful for search engines that scan only the beginning of the file.

HTML: Formatting Text

The actual content of the Web page is enclosed inside the paired <body> tags. This is what the user views when the page is displayed in the browser window. As mentioned, a Web page is a hypermedia document. Consequently, as authors, we may choose from a palette containing text, images, graphics, sounds, video, and hyperlinks. The most common ingredient, of course, is text. In this section, we will examine some of the basic text building blocks.

Word processors organize text into paragraphs. Paragraphs in HTML are signified by <p> paired tags as illustrated in Figure 5.13. HTML paragraphs are usually displayed as blocks of text with spacing above and below.

Like text in word processors, lines are wrapped from margin to margin in the browser window. Thus, any line formatting of the text in the HTML file is ignored by the browser displaying the text. As shown, in Figure 5.13, the number of lines in a paragraph are determined by the width of the browser window and not the number of original lines in the HTML document. On the other hand, you can influence how lines are displayed by using the <br> and <nobr> tags.

---

* Note: The W3C organization, which is the governing body for defining HTML and other Web standards, has adopted XHTML as the official successor of earlier HTML versions. This means that no new versions of HTML will be issued. The W3C is not a sanctioning body, so compliance is strictly voluntary. The move to XHTML has been slow among users. In this chapter, we will restrict our attention to HTML; in Chapter 19, we will return to consider its successors.

```
<p>A paragraph is one of the simplest text elements in HTML. Paragraphs
in HTML are usually displayed as blocks of text with spacing above and
below.</p>
<p></p>
<p>Unlike word processors, empty paragraphs cannot be used to skip
spaces. Empty paragraph tags are usually ignored by browsers.</p>
```

> A paragraph is one of the simplest text elements in HTML. Paragraphs in HTML are usually displayed as blocks of text with spacing above and below.
>
> Unlike word processors, empty paragraphs cannot be used to skip spaces. Empty paragraph tags are usually ignored by browsers.

```
<p>roses are red,<br>violets are blue,<br>sugar is sweet<br>. . .</p>
```

> roses are red,
> violets are blue,
> sugar is sweet,
> ...

The <br> tag is a standalone tag. It causes an automatic line break in the text where it occurs. Figure 5.14 illustrates its usage.

The <nobr> paired tags can be used to suppress any line breaks caused by the width of the browser window. Thus, any text enclosed by the <nobr> tag will be restricted to a single line and may require the user to scroll to the right to read it.

Headings are often used to identify different sections of text. HTML specifies the use of paired <h> tags for indicating headings or titles. The size or degree of emphasis is indicated by a number enclosed in the tag. Figure 5.15 offers some examples.

Lists are another common way of organizing text. HTML offers several list types. Unordered and ordered lists are two. **Unordered lists** are typically called *bullet lists*. Each item is preceded by a bullet mark ("•"). **Ordered lists** are numbered. HTML numbers these items automatically. Figure 5.16 illustrates how they are constructed.

HTML also has a variety of tagging techniques for formatting text according to font face, size, and style. You may remember that font face refers to the typeface used for representing the character set. The <font> paired tag may be used with the face and size modifiers to instruct the browser how to display the marked text. Figure 5.17 illustrates their usage.

Specifying the font face for a text block does not guarantee that the text will be displayed in that manner. First of all, very old browser versions don't even recognize the <font> tag. If the user's system does not support that font face, it cannot be displayed. Normally, you should list a choice of fonts as a precaution. Finally, HTML 4.01 and its XHTML successors do not support the <font> tags anymore. To use them, you should specify your document as "Transitional" inside the <!DOCTYPE> tag.

The size modifier can be used with either definite or relative values. **Definite values** are (unsigned) integer values ranging from 1 to 7. Unlike headings, though, the numbers are ascending in size. In other words, 1 indicates the smallest and 7 the largest font size. **Relative values** are signed integer values; that is, numbers with a positive or negative sign. These values are so-called, because they indicate the relative amount of increase or decrease in size of the font. For example, if the default font size is 3 then, a relative size of −1 denotes a font size of 2; a relative size of +2 resolves to a definite font size of 5. No values may exceed the limits of 1 and 7, so a relative size of +20—while legal—is ineffective.

```
<h1>The Story of My Life</h1>
<h2>In the Beginning</h2>
```

The Story of My Life

In the Beginning

Figure 5.15
The heading tags are numbered from 1 to 6 in descending order of emphasis. In this example, headings of degree 1 and 2 are illustrated. Keep in mind, though, that the actual viewing size will often depend upon browser settings.

```
<ul>               <ol>               <ol type="a">
<li>first item     <li>first item     <li>first item
<li>second item    <li>second item    <li>second item
<li>third item     <li>third item     <li>third item
</ul>              </ol>              </ol>
```

- first item
- second item
- third item

1. first item
2. second item
3. third item

a. first item
b. second item
c. third item

Figure 5.16
Unordered or bullet lists are indicated by the <ul> paired tags. Ordered or numbered lists require <ol> paired tags. Each list item is marked with an <li> tag. The type modifier can be used to specify the style of numbering.

```
<p><font face="verdana, arial, sans-serif" size="5">
Now is the time for all good women to come to the aid of their
country.</font></p>

<p><font face= "georgia, times, serif" size="-1">
Now is the time for all good men to come to the aid of their
country.</font></p>

<p><font face= "made-upfont" size="+2">
Now is the time for all good men and women to come to the aid of their
country.</font></p>
```

Now is the time for all good women to come to the aid of their country.

Now is the time for all good men to come to the aid of their country.

Now is the time for all good men and women to come to the aid of their country.

Figure 5.17
Three paragraphs are marked with <font> tags. In the first example, the face modifier indicates a choice of system fonts. The last, "sans-serif," is a generic class that the browser will certainly support. The size is set to 5, which is larger than the default size, 3. In the latter examples, relative sizing is employed. Assuming a default size of 3, the second paragraph is set to size 2 and the last to 5. In the second example, the font face will match the fonts listed or default to the browser's generic "serif" choice. In the last paragraph, the font face is fictitious, so the browser uses its default font.

The bottom line is that HTML's sizing scheme is a little loony. Even the definite values do not resolve to predictable, uniform measures such as points. In most browsers, the user can pick the default font size to suit his or her tastes and visual acuity. In Figure 5.18, the user has selected a default font size of 16 points. This means that the HTML font size of 3 will actually be a 16-point font on that display device. All other sizes will be based on that choice. As the example also attests, the user is free to choose default font faces for several categories.

Font styles in HTML are indicated by paired tags. You can format the text with boldface, italic, underlining, and other stylings as well. Figure 5.19 rehearses some of the options.

You may also choose font colors by employing the color modifier inside the <font> tag. The choice of color is defined by either an approved color word (see Figure 5.20 for examples) or a six-digit hexadecimal number. (We will have more to say about color on the Web in Chapter 8.)

Figure 5.18

The Preferences dialog box in Internet Explorer permits the user to specify which font faces should be used for each generic category. Likewise, the font size for the standard or default size may be set from the pull-down list. In this case, it is set 16 points.

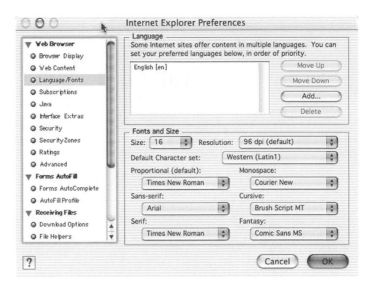

Figure 5.19

HTML supports font styling with a number of paired tags. Several are illustrated here. The <i> tags denote italic and <b> tags may be used for boldface. The <u> tags specify under-lining, while the <sup> and <sub> tags may be used for superscripts and subscripts, respectively.

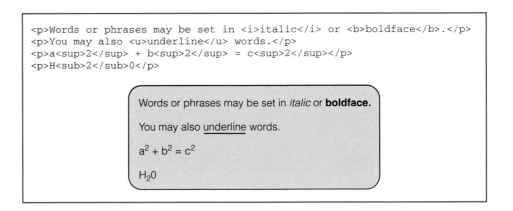

```
<p>Words or phrases may be set in <i>italic</i> or <b>boldface</b>.</p>
<p>You may also <u>underline</u> words.</p>
<p>a<sup>2</sup> + b<sup>2</sup> = c<sup>2</sup></p>
<p>H<sub>2</sub>0</p>
```

Words or phrases may be set in *italic* or **boldface.**

You may also <u>underline</u> words.

$a^2 + b^2 = c^2$

$H_2 0$

Figure 5.20

The choice of color is expressed either by a color word ("red" here) or a six-digit hexadecimal number. In this ex-ample, the number FF0000 is also red.

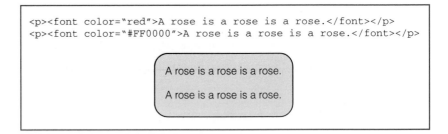

```
<p><font color="red">A rose is a rose is a rose.</font></p>
<p><font color="#FF0000">A rose is a rose is a rose.</font></p>
```

A rose is a rose is a rose.

A rose is a rose is a rose.

HTML: Inline Graphics and Images

Web pages are often enhanced by adding images and graphics. You saw in Chapter 2 that an image is digitized by breaking it into pixels and storing the numerical values that represent each pixel. The actual encoding of pixel values can be done in a variety of ways, and these dif-ferent methods define a number of different **image file formats.** The software used to display a stored image file must be tailored for the kind of file format used to create that file. Hence, we must choose the type of image files we use in our Web page designs carefully so that read-ers of our pages will be able to see those images.

Most of today's browsers can display pixel-based image files in one of three file formats. Their suffixes (file extensions) are abbreviated as **gif, jpg,** and **png.** You'll learn more about these and other file formats in Chapter 8. For now, it is enough to be aware that different file formats exist and to know that these three formats are the ones most commonly used for Web work.

Inline images refers to images or graphics that appear on the Web page when it is loaded by your browser. (They are not displayed, of course, if you are using a text-based browser or have chosen your browser's option to suppress the images on displayed Web pages.)

The <img> tag (for image) places an inline image on our Web page. The tag <img> is not a paired tag, but it does require us to supply additional information for its use. In particular, we place the image source file name, enclosed in quotation marks, inside the tag itself, as follows:

<img src="retriever.jpg">

The src stands for *source file.* In this case, the jpg suffix in the file name indicates the image file format.

In our example, the location of the image file is presumed to be in the same folder as the HTML file that references it. Suppose, instead, that images were placed in a folder named "pix," which is in the folder where the HTML file is located. In this instance, we would rewrite the tag this way

<img src="pix/retriever.jpg">

The lesson to be learned here is that you must specify the location and name of the resource file (i.e., the pathname) and not just its filename. The latter works only when resources share the same folder as the Web page.

HTML: Hyperlinks

Hyperlinks are the primary feature that drives the World Wide Web. Hyperlinks are often associated with text words or phrases, but they can also be associated with inline images as well. The links they implement often connect to information stored on a different computer (and frequently created by another author). We can also link to our own separate HTML files, image files, sound files, and so on, or even to a separate location within the same HTML document. Indeed, we have the ability to weave a "web" of information as tightly or as far-flung as we desire by using hyperlinks.

Hyperlinks are created using paired anchor or <a> tags. The tags wrap around the text (or other content) that you want to serve as your visible link to the named resource. Inside the <a> tag, the href modifier defines that resource. For example, suppose that we created a link to a personal Web page about our pet Labrador retriever. It might be formed in this manner.

<a href="mylabspage.html"> My Lab's Page. </a>

Again, it is important to stress the fact that the href modifier requires the location of the resource and not just the filename. In this example, we are presuming that the file mylabspage.html is on the same server and in the same folder as the Web page that references it. If we had intended to refer to a site elsewhere—not on our server—then we would have had to indicate that by giving the full URL (with protocol and all). Here is an example.

<a href="http://www.allaboutlabs.com">All About Labs Web Site. </a>

As mentioned, it is possible to use a graphic or image as a link, too.

<a href="mylabspage.html"> <img src="retriever.jpg" </a>

In this instance, the picture of the Lab used earlier would serve as a link to the page about that dog.

Links to e-mail addresses are common on Web pages too. Here is one last example that shows how this can be constructed.

<a href="mailto:jlowery@hotmail.com">Contact Jane Lowery</a>

The phrase "Contact Jane Lowery" would serve as a link on the page; but when the user clicked it, the browser would launch a mail program with a new message addressed to jlowery@hotmail.com

HTML: Other Design Elements

So far, we have barely scratched the surface of HTML's design elements. Two other major elements worth mentioning here are tables and frames.

HTML **tables** are used primarily to organize information in a row and column format. No doubt they were conceived by HTML's early authors as a convenient way of structuring data in reports. See Figure 5.21 for an illustration.

Unfortunately, tables have become the Web's version of duct tape—an all-purpose remedy for virtually any problem. Tables are used for better alignment of text. We mentioned earlier that text ordinarily conforms to the size of the browser window. You can control its appearance, though, by placing text blocks in table cells. For the same reasons, tables are also used as a layout or design tool. The borders of a table can be "turned off," that is, made to disappear. Thus, table cells can be used as invisible containers that divide the page into more manageable segments. Pages with borders and white space (that is, open spaces) are often created with these "invisible" tables. Tables can also be used to hold the slices of a large image. Some pages may incorporate very large graphic images. Ordinarily, these are very slow to download or transfer from the server to the client machine. Cutting the picture into segments or slices makes downloading faster. Image slices are also used for special effects such as animations and rollovers (animated links).

It is best to work with a net if you plan to tackle tables, though. They are complicated and sometimes quirky. For this reason, we will leave the devil and the details to our online tutorials that instruct you about the care and cleaning of tables.

No doubt you have visited Web sites that have one portion of the window always visible—perhaps a banner or set of navigational tools—while other portions have content that changes. These sites are typically constructed using frames. **Frames** divide the browser window into separate windows; each window displays a distinct Web document. Figure 5.22 offers an example.

Using frames to build a Web site has its advantages. Presenting a consistent interface is often desirable. It is also easier to construct navigational aides for the site using frames. On the other hand, frames pose some problems. Because each frame is a separate Web page, it takes more work to develop them. Search engines have a hard time "finding" content pages because of the complex structure of a framed page. Indeed, there are more pros and cons. In short, the topic of frames will almost always evoke strong opinions (one way or the other) from just about any Web developer you encounter.

Creating Web Pages Using HTML Editors

So far in this chapter you have learned that Web documents must be written in HTML, and you've been introduced to a few of HTML's features. As Web publishing has become more and more popular, software products have been introduced to make the process of con-

Figure 5.21

*Standard HTML tables are used to organize and display data. Each box is called a **cell**. Cells have margins inside called **cell padding** and borders that have a defined amount of **cell spacing**. The entire table likewise has a border of some defined width.*

ASCII character	Decimal	Binary	Hexadecimal
'a'	97	01100001	61
'b'	98	01100010	62
'c'	99	01100011	63
'd'	100	01100100	64

structing HTML documents much easier. These products are generally referred to as **HTML editors.** The first generation of HTML editors, sometimes called **tag editors,** made creating and working with HTML documents more user friendly. *BBedit* is one of the older but still popular tag editors, and there are others from which to choose. Such products offer a number of conveniences in constructing HTML code. For example, tags can be inserted by clicking buttons on a tool bar, and tags are sometimes shown in different colors from the plain text to make the HTML structure stand out more clearly. Most of these products do some simple syntax checking as well, such as making sure that all paired tags are properly closed. A user of a tag editor still works directly with the HTML code, but the editor makes this work much easier and less error-prone.

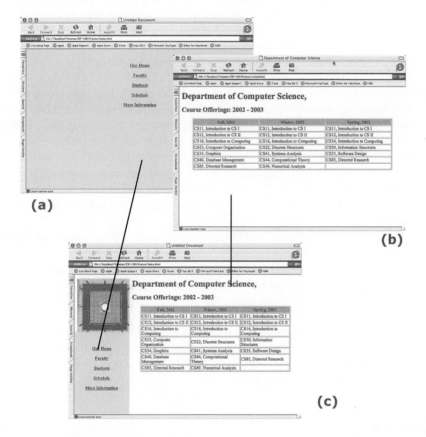

(a)

(b)

(c)

Figure 5.22

*Framed pages are composed of separate Web pages that are organized to display in a single browser window. For example, the menu page (a) and the schedule page (b) are two of the three pages that are combined to create what is called the **frameset,** as shown in (c). Frames may also have scroll tools when the content cannot be viewed in the main window. In addition, frames may employ links that control what is displayed in the same or different frames.*

DISCOVERING MORE

HTML

We hope that our survey has whetted your appetite for more details about constructing Web pages using HTML. If so, consult our online resource "Discovering More About HTML." Besides a review of the tags discussed in the text, we will look at additional elements including tables and frames.

More recently, a second generation of HTML editors, which should more properly be called **HTML generators,** has become popular. HTML generators allow their users to describe and construct Web pages in a more natural way than by constructing HTML directly. Instead of actually writing the HTML code, you lay out the features and appearance of a Web page as you want it to appear in a browser. The HTML generator software then automatically derives the underlying HTML document that will produce the browser interpretation you have specified.

Such software can be a great time saver, and it is certainly good to know at least one such package. We believe it is a great advantage for a user of HTML generators to understand some HTML coding, though. The HTML generator approach is sound and certainly attractive, but there are inevitable shortcomings in these products. The HTML generated doesn't always produce exactly what you originally had in mind when the pages are displayed in an actual browser. One problem is that HTML changes, so these products may not have the latest HTML features available. On the other hand, if you have some knowledge of HTML, you can fix the generated code directly to produce more satisfactory results. This is exactly why we introduced "raw" HTML before we discussed these higher-level editors.

A good analogy might be drawn to cars. Although it is possible to drive a car and know absolutely nothing about what actually goes on under the hood, in a great many situations even a little knowledge about the underlying functioning of the car can be very beneficial. This is especially true for troubleshooting when everything doesn't go according to plan. We believe the same is true for Web authoring.

Perhaps the best way to use HTML generator software is as a quick approach to laying out the basic features of a Web page. Once the HTML file has been generated, the knowledgeable user can adjust the HTML directly to achieve optimal results. Quite a number of such products are available, and they all have distinctive interfaces and their own individual organizations.

Armed with a basic knowledge of HTML and the latest HTML generation software, you can create Web pages with a minimum of effort, and this process seems to get easier with each new generation of software tools. The technical details of creating Web pages can truly be mastered by almost anyone. Just because you can create Web pages, however, doesn't mean that the Web pages you create will be effective, eye-catching, or informative. To produce truly great-looking and informative Web pages requires a mix of both creative and technical skills. This is why professional Web publishing is often a team effort, involving content experts, graphic artists, and technical experts. You should not be discouraged by this, though. Creating your own Web pages can be both fun and easy. And the more of this work you do, the better at all the requisite skills you become.

■ Summary

Electronic text documents are made up of sequences of characters that are arranged and formatted in particular ways. Both the characters and their formats must be encoded and digitized to enable processing by a computer. For the language being used, a character set containing letters of the alphabet, digits and arithmetic symbols, punctuation marks, and other special symbols used to express the language in

FOCUS   HTML Editors

For more details and tutorial instruction on how to construct Web pages using HTML editors, consult our online resource "Focus on HTML Editors."

writing is encoded. By convention, American Standard Code for Information Interchange, or ASCII, is the encoding scheme used for many years by the vast majority of computers. Using ASCII, each character and symbol of the Latin alphabet is represented by a single byte (eight bits) of storage. Unicode is a more recent character code that is also more general. Besides adopting ASCII coding for the Latin alphabet, Unicode supports extended alphabets for other languages as well as many Asian scripts. Unicode characters have a maximum of four bytes.

Word processing software provides a wide range of features for the construction and formatting of textual documents. Formatting can be applied to individual characters, groups of characters, paragraphs, sections, and the entire document. There is no equivalent standard for encoding formatting information, and each word processing package has its own proprietary method for representing the various formatting features it allows. RTF and PDF are two choices for distributing text documents that retain their formatting features without the need of the original word processing software that may have created them.

Despite their underlying format representations and storage differences, the basic methods and techniques among various word processing applications have gradually converged. Thus, today there is a high degree of commonality among the major word processing software, and you can transfer your skills in using one program to another without a great deal of difficulty.

Desktop publishing software represents an extension of word processing capabilities. Particularly, such software is intended to make designing and laying out professional-quality documents accessible and convenient. These programs often contain many of the features of ordinary word processors as well as special tools needed for page layout. On the other hand, some of the latest word processors also have layout tools that formerly would have been the exclusive domain of DTP programs. As a consequence, the distinction between word processors and desktop publishing programs is not as clear-cut as it once was. Future enhancements to word processing products will no doubt further blur this distinction.

HTML (Hypertext Markup Language) is a coding scheme for publishing Web pages. HTML uses tags to indicate formatting information, along with structural and organizational elements of the document. In short, HTML documents separate the content (text, images, graphics, etc.) from their presentation (format, structure, organization). This is why Web pages may be transmitted and used by computer systems that are very different from the originating server that stored them. The client computer receives the specs for a document, which it constructs according to the characteristics of its own display.

There are a variety of HTML editors that help automate some of the tasks involved in creating and publishing Web pages. Tag editors provide tools for placing tags into an HTML file that expresses the Web page. HTML generators are WYSIWYG editors—much like modern word processors—that produce the HTML automatically from the user's entry and formatting of the document.

■ Terms

American Standard Code for
 Information Interchange
 (ASCII)
cell padding
cell spacing
cells (table)
centered
chained frames (threaded
 frames)
character set
clipboard
collating sequence
copy board
Copy command
cursor
Cut command
definite (size) values
desktop publishing (DTP)
font face
font size
font styles
formatting

frame (text, graphic)
frames (Web)
frameset
gif
HTML editors
HTML generators
image file formats
inline images (graphics)
invisible control characters
jpg
justified
kerning
keypunch machines
left-aligned
ordered lists
paired tags
Paste command
plain text
png
points (printer's measure)
Portable Document Format
 (PDF)

PostScript
relative (size) values
Rich Text Format (RTF)
right-aligned
ruler (format)
sorting
tab markers
tables
tag editors
tag modifier
tags
templates (master pages)
text block
text editors
text string
translator (filter program)
Unicode
unordered lists
what-you-see-is-what-you-get
 (WYSIWYG)
word processors
word-wrap

■ Questions for Review

1. Is text a discrete or analog form of information? Explain.

2. What are the two basic requirements for creating a scheme to encode (digitize) text?

3. What does the acronym ASCII stand for? Relate it to text processing.

4. What is meant by a collating sequence?

5. What are "invisible" control characters within the word processing context? What purpose do they serve?

6. What is Unicode? How are ASCII and Unicode related?

7. What length are Unicode character codes? Explain.

8. What is meant by the term *word-wrap*? What is the function of the Enter (or Return) key in word processing?

9. What is the clipboard? How is it used and why is it important for word processing?

10. Describe some of the standard character formatting techniques in modern word processors.

11. Describe some of the standard paragraph formatting techniques in modern word processors.

12. What does the acronym WYSIWYG stand for? What does it mean?

13. What is Rich Text Format (RTF)? Why is it important?

14. What is Portable Document Format (PDF)? Why is it important?

15. What is meant by the alignment of paragraphs?

16. How does desktop publishing software extend the capabilities of word processors?

17. Explain the importance of frames in desktop publishing software. What does it mean when frames are "chained" or "threaded" together? Why is this done?

18. What does the term *kerning* refer to?

19. How does the concept of master pages contribute to the ease of use and power of desktop publishing packages?

20. How does HTML separate content and presentation in Web pages? Why is this useful?

21. List some of the paired tags in HTML that are used for organizing the document.

22. List some of the tags in HTML that are used for text formatting.

23. What is an inline graphic or image?

24. What is an HTML table? How are tables used in Web pages?

25. What is an HTML frame? What are the advantages/disadvantages of using framed Web pages?

26. Name the two kinds or classes of HTML editors. How do they differ in function and use?

Numeric Processing

OBJECTIVES

- The way integers and decimal numbers are represented and stored in computers

- Limitations in the accuracy of numeric computations performed by computers

- Evolution of software tools to facilitate numeric processing

- Capabilities of spreadsheet software to perform numeric processing and modeling

- Overview of symbolic mathematical and visualization software

Finding more reliable means for numeric processing motivated the invention of modern-day computers. Indeed, during the first three decades of electronic computers, numeric processing dominated their activities. The design of the electronic digital computer makes numeric processing, in many ways, easier to carry out than text processing because the fundamental arithmetic operations are part of the machine language of most computers. In addition, numeric problems are often easier to pose and solve than problems of a nonnumeric or nonquantifiable nature.

The numeric problems with which the early computers were occupied were problems whose solution methods were already known. What the computer added to the effort was its tremendous speed and peerless accuracy. Numeric solutions that might take 10 people 2 weeks to work out could be solved on a computer in a matter of minutes, and the results were much less likely to contain calculational errors.

Of course, today's computers do a great deal more than numeric processing, but numeric processing is still important. Mathematical models and numeric processing help us predict the weather; launch and track satellites and interplanetary space probes; design telecommunication systems, highways, automobiles, and airplanes; maintain military defensive systems; and undertake a host of other important tasks. In fact, a great many modern computing activities, such as image and sound processing and computer-aided design, which we ordinarily do not think of as numeric in nature, actually depend very heavily on numeric processing. It is fair to say that numeric processing is just as fundamental to the majority of today's computing applications as it was in the early days of computing.

More About Binary Number Representations

As you already know, all information processed by a computer belongs to the digital domain. Consequently, any object that we wish to process must first be digitized, that is, converted to a discrete binary representation. At first glance, digitization might appear to be a natural and simple process for numbers. After all, when we deal with numbers, we deal with them as individual, discrete entities. But a closer examination will reveal two difficulties with this naive assumption. These difficulties stem from the fact that the numbers are both infinite in number and continuously distributed along the number line.

For our purposes we can think of the number line as consisting of three categories of numbers: (1) integers, (2) numbers with a finite nonzero decimal part, and (3) numbers with an infinite nonzero decimal part. **Integers** are made up of the whole numbers, zero, and the negatives of the whole numbers. Integers have no decimal part (or we could say a zero decimal part), and their conversion to a binary form is relatively straightforward, as you saw in Chapter 2. We will review this process momentarily. Numbers with a finite decimal part are a subset of all the fractions. The values $1/10 = .1$, $1/5 = .2$, and $5/2 = 2.5$ are examples. But not all numbers have finite decimal representations. For example, $1/3 = 0.3333333 \ldots$ has an infinite decimal representation.

As you might guess, we would have difficulty converting an infinite fraction for storage on a digital computer, which by necessity has only a finite amount of memory available. We'll consider this issue in more detail shortly, but one point is worth mentioning here. Because the computer stores numbers (and all data, for that matter) in binary form, we will be interested in which fractions have finite and infinite *binary* representations. For some fractions, whether their representation is finite or infinite will depend on whether the representation chosen is binary (base-2) or decimal (base-10). You'll see some examples of this a little later. First we consider the representation of integers for digital storage.

The integers form a discrete and infinite subset of the number line. Their discrete nature means that every integer has a unique singular representation. However, computers are not only discrete machines, they are also finite machines. As a consequence, there will always be a practical limit to the number of integers that we can represent digitally. For example, many computers allow exact representation only for integers in the range $-2,147,483,648$ to $+2,147,483,647$ (or about ± 2 billion). You'll see why these particular limits are used shortly.

Let's review the representation of integers in the binary number system. When we write the number 235, how is it interpreted? If we read the number as two hundred thirty-five, we have almost answered this question. The notation 235 really means $(2 \times 10^2) + (3 \times 10^1) + (5 \times 10^0)$, assuming that we are using the decimal system (base-10 system) of representing numbers.

As we saw in Chapter 2, each digit in the original number has a value that is determined not only by the value of the digit itself but also the *position* it occupies in the number. The rightmost digit has its own value (remember that any number raised to the power of 0 is 1, so $10^0 = 1$), the next digit to the left has its own value multiplied by 10 (or 10^1), the next digit to the left has its own value multiplied by 100 (or 10^2), and so on. Each digit's value in the number is determined by multiplying its own value by a power of 10 equal to its position from the rightmost digit.

We saw that the binary number system is organized by essentially this same scheme. The only difference between the binary and decimal systems is that we use powers of 2 rather than powers of 10 to compute the place value of digits. Consequently, the base-10 number 11 written in binary representation would be 1011 or $(1 \times 2^3) + (0 \times 2^2) + (1 \times 2^1) + (1 \times 2^0)$. We will adopt the convention of using a subscript of 2, as in 1011_2, to indicate that the number represented is to be interpreted as a binary (base-2) number.

Let's review the process of changing a number's representation between decimal and binary. First, suppose the number is given in binary; how do we recover its decimal representation? This is pretty easy. All we need do is perform the implicit calculation that is inherent in the number representation—sometimes we call this **expanding a number's representation.** For example, the number 11011011_2 would be expanded into a decimal number as follows:

$$11011011_2$$
$$= (1 \times 2^7) + (1 \times 2^6) + (0 \times 2^5) + (1 \times 2^4) + (1 \times 2^3) + (0 \times 2^2) + (1 \times 2^1) + (1 \times 2^0)$$
$$= 128 \quad + \quad 64 \quad + \quad 0 \quad + \quad 16 \quad + \quad 8 \quad + \quad 0 \quad + \quad 2 \quad + \quad 1$$
$$= 219$$

Now, let's consider conversion in the opposite direction—decimal numbers to binary numbers. How will this be accomplished? This is a bit harder than the binary-to-decimal conversion, but not really difficult, as you'll see.

Consider the simple example of converting the decimal number 14 to binary representation. To do this, we need to "build" the value 14 using only powers of the new base 2. You can probably do the necessary work in your head to write $14 = 1110_2 = (1 \times 2^3) + (1 \times 2^2) + (1 \times 2^1) + (0 \times 2^0) = 8 + 4 + 2$. It isn't hard for us to figure out that we need an 8, a 4, and a 2 to "build" the decimal value 14 in the binary system. Of course, it won't always be as easy as it was for the number 14, so we need to formalize our method a bit.

Let's consider the conversion of a larger number, say 176, to binary representation. The rightmost digit in a binary number is of course either 0 or 1. When we converted the number 14, we might have started on the right of the binary representation by asking first "Do we need a 1 or a 0?" We could answer 0 immediately because 14 is an even number, and hence the "ones" digit must be 0. Moving left, we could ask "Do we need a 0 or a 1?" This is asking if we need the value 2 ($= 2^1$) in the representation. This is a tougher question, and, in fact, the answer isn't obvious until we investigate further.

A much better approach is to start with the *leftmost* digit of the binary number representation and move right digit-by-digit. First we need to figure out where the starting point is. The largest power of 2 that we will need is the largest power of 2 that is less than or equal to the number we are trying to represent.

DISCOVERING MORE

Converting Integers to Binary Representations

Consult the online resource "Discovering More About Integers and Binary Representations" for a step-by-step procedure and practice for the decimal-to-binary conversion process, as well as more examples of the binary-to-decimal conversion process.

In the case of 14, we can quickly decide that a 16 (which is 2^4) won't be needed because the value we're trying to represent is smaller than this value. But an 8 (which is 2^3) will be needed. $14 - 8$ leaves 6. Then we can proceed in a similar manner on the part of the original number left over. In this case we quickly discover that we will need a 4 (which is 2^2) and a 2 (which is 2^1) to complete the process and thus write $14 = 1110_2$. That's the essence of the method for converting decimal values to binary.

Integers and Limited Range

From the previous discussion, it is clear that we can convert any integer to binary form. Hence, theoretically we could store any integer in computer memory. Of course, in practice we have only a finite amount of memory, and so there must be a limit on the size of the integers we are able to store. We cannot use all available memory to store a single number, so the limit on the amount of memory storage we allow for one number must be quite small. After all, we have to store lots of additional information in memory to do anything meaningful.

On many computer systems, 4 bytes or 32 bits are allocated for storage of integers. In some instances, integers may take as many as 8 bytes or 64 bits each. But for the sake of illustration, let's assume that we are dealing with a computer that has a 16-bit storage size for integers. This will simplify our examples. What is the largest integer we can store on such a machine? At first glance, it would seem to be $1111111111111111_2 = 2^{15} + 2^{14} + \ldots 2^1 + 2^0 = 65,535$. But remember that integers can be either positive or negative, and we will need to store the sign of an integer as well as its absolute size. The usual convention is to use the first bit of the number to designate the sign, say, a 0 for + and a 1 for −. This then leaves only 15 bits to store the actual number, and consequently the largest integer we could store would be $111111111111111_2 = -2^{14} + \ldots 2^1 + 2^0 = -32,767$.

In practice, though, 16-bit integers would have the actual range of $-32,768$ to $+32,767$. Why the lack of symmetry? In other words, why not $-32,767$ to $+32,767$? This small discrepancy is a result of the particular method we actually employ to store integers, called **twos complement.** This method was developed because there is a problem with representing integers in the very straightforward way we described above. This problem is that the number 0 has two such representations: 0000000000000000_2 (positive) and 1000000000000000_2 (negative). Of course, zero is neither positive nor negative, so we would prefer it to have a single representation; in fact, allowing two different representations of the same number would cause many problems in implementing computer arithmetic.

So if we devote 16 bits for integer storage, the range of integers stored in a computer is from $-32,768$ to $+32,767$. Most desktop computers today actually employ 32 bits for integer storage and the range of integers stored is $-2,147,483,648$ to $+2,147,483,647$ (or about ±2 billion).

FOCUS   Twos Complement Integer Representation

The twos complement method is an integer storage scheme designed to encode a number's sign implicitly and hence eliminate the problem of dual representations of 0. As noted earlier, this is not just a cosmetic issue. Twos complement representation makes it easier to perform arithmetic operations with stored integers, too. The lack of symmetry for the range of integers we noted earlier is a byproduct of the twos complement method. The details of how it works are beyond the scope of our brief treatment here. Consult the online resource "Focus on Twos Complement Integer Representation" for more details.

No matter how many bits are employed, we can only store a finite number of integers. If the answer to a calculation involving integers is another integer outside the computer's integer range, an error, called an **overflow error,** results. Such errors often cause the program being run to halt immediately. We'll see a way that sometimes gets us around this difficulty when we discuss decimal number representations next.

Decimal Numbers—Limited Range and Precision

Let's now turn our attention to decimal numbers, also called **real numbers.** Real numbers can have both a whole number part and a decimal fraction part. How are we to represent these numbers in a binary computer? Actually we can perform conversions to the binary system similar to those we performed with integers, but there is a complication. Let's examine a simple instance first where everything works out neatly. Consider the decimal number 14.75. We know that the whole number part (i.e., 14) represents $(1 \times 10^1) + (4 \times 10^0)$, just as before. What about the fractional part, that is, the .75?

This representation also uses the powers of 10—this time the negative powers of 10. Recall that $10^{-1} = 1/10^1 = 1/10$, $10^{-2} = 1/10^2 = 1/100$, and so on. Hence $.75 = (7 \times 10^{-1}) + (5 \times 10^{-2}) = 7/10 + 5/100$. Putting the entire expansion for 14.75 together, we get

$$14.75 = (1 \times 10^1) + (4 \times 10^0) + (7 \times 10^{-1}) + (5 \times 10^{-2})$$

or

$$14.75 = 10 + 4 + .7 + .05$$

Now back to the business of converting 14.75 to binary form. We saw earlier that 14 converts to 1110_2. But what about the fractional part? We need to represent .75 as an expansion in the negative powers of 2. In other words, in binary representation,

$$.75 = (? \times 2^{-1}) + (? \times 2^{-2}) + (? \times 2^{-3}) \ldots$$

But $2^{-1} = 1/2^1 = 1/2$, $2^{-2} = 1/2^2 = 1/4$, $2^{-3} = 1/2^3 = 1/8$, and so on, and hence this becomes

$$.75 = (? \times 1/2) + (? \times 1/4) + (? \times 1/8) \ldots$$

If we notice that .75 is actually the fraction 3/4, it isn't hard to see by inspection that we only need two fractions in its binary expansion

$$.75 = (1 \times 1/2) + (1 \times 1/4) = 3/4$$

or

$$.75 = .11_2$$

DISCOVERING MORE

Converting Decimal Fractions to Binary

In the example in the text, we "eyeballed" the fractional part of the binary expansion; 3/4 is obviously 1/2 + 1/4. But there is a simple, step-by-step method for computing the binary expansion on the right-hand side of the radix point. Consult the online resource "Discovering More About Converting Decimal Fractions to Binary" for a description of the method, examples, and some practice.

Putting the two binary representations together, we get

$$14.75 = 1110.11_2.$$

For more about the general process of converting decimal fractions to binary representations, see the online resource.

Infinite Binary Fraction Representations

So far, so good, but what about the complication we alluded to earlier that arises because there are decimal fractions whose binary representations require an infinite amount of space for storage. For example, the fraction 1/10 is 0.1 in decimal notation, but when converted to binary it has the following *infinite* binary fraction representation: $0.1 = (0.00011001100110011 \ldots)_2$ where the pattern 0011 (which first begins in the second digit after the point) is repeated indefinitely.

Clearly, no matter how much memory we have, we could never store the exact (and infinite) binary representation of 1/10. This seems undesirable; maybe we should abandon the binary number system and return to using the base-10 or some other system! Unfortunately, it wouldn't help us out of the difficulty. This problem is not unique to the binary number system; it occurs in every base system. As you already know, many fractions have no finite representation as base-10 fractions. For example, the fraction 1/3 has the infinite representation: $1/3 = 0.3333333333333 \ldots$

No matter what number system we use, there will always be values whose representations require an infinite number of digits. Worse yet, the vast majority of numbers have this property, so the best we can do is to store some finite subset of numbers that will serve as reasonable approximations to the ones we've left out. This means that real numbers are, by necessity, represented in the computer with **limited precision.**

Actually, you are already familiar with a limited precision arithmetic system. Our monetary system represents all values with two-decimal precision. For example, if your favorite candy bar is on sale at three for a dollar and you decide to buy one bar, how much will you pay? Certainly not $1.00 divided by 3. Why not? Because this would mean a price of 33.33333 . . . cents, which is impossible in a finite monetary system. In all likelihood, you would pay 34 cents, with the .3333333 . . . amount being rounded up to the next penny.

Floating Point Representation

If we wish to represent infinite decimal fractions in our computer systems (and, of course, we do), a compromise very similar to our monetary example must be made. We "solved" the monetary problem by limiting the decimal precision to two decimal places in that system and rounding up any decimal fraction with more than two places. Of course, we'd like more than two-decimal precision for our computer representation because there are a great many calculations that require more accuracy than do monetary transactions. But the concept will be very much the same; we'll just use more decimal places.

To maximize the precision possible using a fixed number of bits of storage, real numbers are stored in the computer employing **floating point representation.** To convert a number to floating point representation, first the fraction must be **normalized.** To normalize a decimal fraction, we place the first nonzero digit to the left of the decimal point. This normalized fraction is then multiplied by the appropriate power of 10 to retain the original value. For example, in floating point notation, the decimal number 234.563 is written as 2.34563×10^2. Likewise, we would write 0.000435 in floating point notation as 4.35×10^{-4}. (Note: The examples in this section will be numbers in decimal notation instead of binary for easier reading. The principles discussed here are exactly the same no matter what base number system we choose.)

Normalizing can achieve more places of accuracy because it avoids having to store leading or trailing zeros whose meaning can be captured with the exponent. For example, if we can store only seven digits, without normalization we would lose most of the meaningful digits in a number like 0.0000002346513. In fact, we would keep only the digit 2 because we waste storage on the six leading 0s. With normalization, we rewrite this number as 2.346513 $\times$ 10^{-7} and preserve all the meaningful digits.

In floating point notation, a number is represented by two parts—the normalized fraction part, called the **mantissa,** and the **exponent** to correct for placing the value in normalized decimal form. Of course, we also need to store the sign of the number to indicate whether it is positive or negative.

The precision of real numbers stored using floating point representation is determined by the number of bits allowed for the decimal fraction. The standard convention employs 32 bits for this purpose. Within the 32 bits, 23 bits of binary representation are used for the mantissa itself. In fact, we can squeeze in 24 bits of precision by not storing the first bit of the mantissa, which will necessarily be a 1 because the fraction is normalized. This is the equivalent of about seven decimal places of precision in base 10. The first bit of the 32-bit storage is reserved for the sign of the number. The exponent and its sign occupy the next eight bits, and the mantissa is in the final 23 bits. When a number has more digits in its representation than can be accommodated by this storage scheme, the number is usually rounded off (however, in some computers, the excess digits are simply chopped off with no rounding) to the nearest number that can be represented. The result is that there are lots of "holes"—that is, numbers with no exact representation—in the number line when we represent real numbers.

Obviously, this scheme is one with limited precision. The precision of the storage scheme determines how big the holes are, that is, the amount of spacing between the numbers we represent. This spacing will actually differ along the number line depending on the size of the numbers themselves. This occurs because the digits that are lost in rounding represent different values, depending on the size of the number being rounded. As an example, suppose we have a system that can accommodate five decimal digits. Then the number 0.334579 would be rounded to the nearest representable number, namely 0.33458. The actual difference between the true value 0.334579 and the value 0.33458 used to represent it would be 0.000001 in this case. On the other hand, suppose we wish to represent the value 334.579. The nearest number representable with five digits would be 334.58 and the difference this time is a larger value (by a factor of 1,000), namely 0.001. In other words, the spacing between representable numbers is larger near 334.58 than it is around 0.33458. This spacing grows larger and larger as the absolute value of the numbers involved grows. Even such simple examples illustrate why the accuracy of arithmetic on a computer can be very unpredictable!

Some numbers will be too large in absolute value to be represented at all because we won't be able to use an exponent large enough. Remember we have only eight bits for the exponent and that includes the exponent's sign. In these cases (as with integers), we have an overflow error. The largest number we can represent in the standard floating point scheme described above is quite large—approximately 2^{127} or approximately 10^{38}—but this doesn't mean we won't ever encounter computations whose results exceed this value. Still other numbers will be too small in absolute value (i.e., too close to zero) to be represented because we won't be able

Risks in Numeric Computing

It is not uncommon for software to contain errors in logic. Indeed, it is almost expected that large, complex programs will contain one or more such errors. Software that depends heavily on numeric computation is an example of a class of software that is susceptible to an additional category of subtle errors. This fact derives from the imperfect way we are forced to model decimal (real number) arithmetic using a computer. In the online essay "Risks in Numeric Computing" we examine two relatively simple numeric errors that led to the failure of complex software—resulting in the loss of millions of dollars in one instance and perhaps contributing to the loss of lives in the other.

SOCIAL THEMES

to use a large enough negative exponent. In such cases we say we have an **underflow error.** We can represent the value 0 easily, but numbers too close to 0 can't be represented. For example, the very small number 10^{-40} ($=1/10^{40}$) can't be represented for the same reason that the very large number 10^{40} can't be represented. In neither case can the exponent be represented in just the eight bits we have available for this purpose.

Many computer systems offer greater precision and range for floating point numbers because they support 64-bit and even 128-bit representations. Even so, these only postpone rather than eliminate the problems of overflow, underflow, and limited precision.

Numeric Processing and Software Libraries

The fact that real numbers are represented with finite precision means that every computerized numerical operation using them is potentially in error. Indeed, we can't even be sure the numbers themselves are stored without error—let alone the results of the calculations done on them. Consider, for example, the problem of calculating 0.1 + 0.1. We know in advance that the result will, in fact, contain a small error because the number 0.1 has an infinite *binary* fraction representation and as a consequence it cannot be stored in the computer without rounding it off. In most ordinary calculations, such small errors would not cause us great difficulty. After all, how often do we need results to seven or eight decimal places? But in scientific and mathematical calculations, where arithmetic operations are performed sometimes thousands of times in one computation, these small errors can accumulate into significant—even preposterous—errors. We must always perform decimal calculations on computers with some degree of caution and even skepticism for the results.

Here's a simple example to illustrate. Suppose we want to do the calculation 100,000 × (0.24456 – 0.24454). You can easily do the arithmetic using paper and pencil (or perhaps in your head). The result is 100,000 × 0.00002 = 2. Now let's consider how a computer employing *four-decimal-place* precision would make this calculation. The numbers 0.24456 and 0.24454 cannot be stored exactly in such a computer because they each have five decimal places, so each would be rounded. The number 0.24456 would be rounded to 0.2446 and the number 0.24454 would be rounded to 0.2445. When the subtraction is done on the rounded numbers, the result would be 0.0001. When multiplied by 100,000 this gives 10 as the final result. Of course, 10 is not the same as 2—these answers differ by a factor of 5. Is this difference significant? It depends on what the result represents. If it represents the percentage interest rate you're to pay on a loan, for example, there is a huge difference between 2% and 10%.

Because computations involving floating point representations of real numbers are likely to have inherent errors, computer scientists have studied the process of calculating with floating point numbers extensively. This area of research is called **numerical analysis,** and its main goal is to design computational methods that reduce the size of the errors introduced because of limited precision. Often, the most straightforward way to do a calculation is not the way that minimizes the risk of large errors; numerical analysts look for alternatives that will in fact reduce this risk.

Our discussion doesn't imply that every time numerical calculations are done, they produce large errors. Instead, they can produce large errors in special cases. Because we never know when one or more of these special cases might arise in practice, we look for methods that guarantee us some protection against large errors whenever possible.

During the 1950s through the 1970s, most calculations were done using high-level programming languages such as FORTRAN, BASIC, C, Pascal, and others. To make it easier for programmers to avoid creating calculations that might generate large errors, it became common to use methods that had already been tested against this outcome. These methods are stored in electronic form and collected into what are called **software libraries.** Consequently, when solving a complex numeric computation, such as approximating the solution to an equation whose exact solution cannot be derived, the wise programmer will employ the appropriate method from a software library. This is much safer than writing a new one because the methods stored in libraries have been carefully designed and tested to avoid common pitfalls that might generate large errors.

Even though many numeric computations are still performed by programs written in high-level languages, numeric application programs today provide more convenient access to powerful computational software libraries. Spreadsheet programs, for example, have made it possible for persons with little computer training to construct and exercise powerful and sophisticated mathematical models. As you will see shortly, spreadsheet programs mimic the way we do calculations with paper and pencil. But they add enhancements and capabilities that make it possible to extend such calculations well beyond what is possible with paper and pencil.

Symbolic computational programs also make computational methods more accessible to the nonprogrammer. Programs such as MATLAB, Mathematica, Maple, Derive, and others provide students, engineers, scientists, statisticians, and others with unprecedented opportunities to perform high-level mathematical procedures, graphical displays, and computations.

Basic Features of Spreadsheet Software

Spreadsheet application software, or just **spreadsheets** for short, are especially designed for numeric processing. Spreadsheet software has been around for almost as long as personal computers. In fact, the first spreadsheet program, called *VisiCalc,* was an important incentive for consumers and an important driving factor in the popularization of the personal computer in the early 1980s. You might find it surprising that spreadsheet software was available on personal computers several years before the first personal computer word processing software was developed.

Using spreadsheets, we can organize calculations in a natural and intuitive manner much as we might do on a sheet of paper. The bonus is that spreadsheets provide tremendously greater flexibility and power than pencil-and-paper calculations. Automatic updating of calculations with new data, charting or plotting calculations in a variety of ways, and employing built-in computational functions are some examples of this power and flexibility.

Today a number of spreadsheet software products are available. Of course, the specific methods and techniques they employ to perform their calculations and charting differ from product to product. The most popular of these is Microsoft *Excel,* but all these products have a great deal in common—enough to motivate plagiarism lawsuits between several of the spreadsheet developers. As a consequence, knowledge and experience with one spreadsheet program translate easily to a different product.

In this section, we will introduce some of the important basic spreadsheet concepts. We will employ Microsoft *Excel* for all of our illustrations. We can assure you, however, that these concepts manifest themselves similarly in other spreadsheet programs. Common denominators for spreadsheets are the following:

- Column and row organization

- Entering data into a worksheet

- Performing calculations using formulas

- Copying formulas

Worksheet Organization

Spreadsheet documents are usually called **worksheets.** Worksheets are organized as a table of rows and columns. The columns are labeled with letters and the rows with numbers. Worksheets typically have a capacity (depending on your computer's memory) for a great many rows and columns—so many that capacity rarely becomes a consideration in designing and carrying out spreadsheet computations.

The intersection of a row and column is called a **cell,** and giving its column followed by its row identifies a particular cell. This combination of column letter and row number is called the **cell address.** For example, as shown in Figure 6.1, the cell in the upper left corner of the worksheet is cell A1—in column A and row 1. A rectangular block of cells is called a **cell range** and is denoted by the cell defining the block's *upper left* corner and its *lower right* corner. For example, the cell range B3:C4 includes the block of cells B3, B4, C3, and C4.

Only one cell may be selected for data entry or editing at a given time—the selected cell is referred to as the **active cell.** Each worksheet has an associated **entry bar,** which is the area where information (text, numbers, and formulas) is entered into the active cell. Again, Figure 6.1 illustrates.

Entering Data in a Worksheet

Typically, you can enter three kinds of information into a worksheet cell: text, numbers (including dates and times), and formulas to perform calculations. To enter information into a cell, you first select it as the current cell and then start typing. Formulas must begin with a special character (often =). This character signals to the spreadsheet that what follows is a formula. In turn, the spreadsheet examines the syntax of what is entered and checks it for correctness as a formula. Formulas can use any of the standard arithmetic operators: +, −, * (multiply), and / (divide), or built-in functions.

Nonformula information is typed in directly. The spreadsheet automatically recognizes most of the standard date and time formats and treats such data accordingly. Dates and times are usually encoded as numbers no matter how they are displayed in their cells. Information not in one of these date/time formats will be interpreted according to its first symbol. If this symbol is a digit, an algebraic sign (+ or −), or a decimal point (period), the data will be interpreted as numeric; if it is a character other than these, the data will be interpreted as text.

Once data is typed into the entry bar, you can easily change the format in which it is displayed in the cell. For example, you may adjust the particular font, size, and style (bold, italics, etc.) of the characters and whether the entry is aligned to the left or the right or centered in the cell. For numeric data, you may select the number of places to the right of the decimal, presence of dollar signs or commas, and other characteristics. Dates can also ordinarily be displayed in one of several formats. See Figure 6.2.

Using Formulas in a Worksheet

In the example shown in Figure 6.2, we would like to subtract all the values in the cells holding expenses (cells B6 through B10) from the figure in cell B5 to produce the net income value for cell B12. This is easily accomplished by entering a formula = B5 − (B6 + B7 + B8 + B9 + B10) into cell B12. When this is done, the numbers to be employed in the calculation are referred to by their cell addresses rather than by value. In other words, we use cell addresses like variable names. This means that should we change one or more of the actual values in these cells later, the net income will automatically be updated. The automatic recalculation of formulas is one of the primary benefits of using worksheets.

Copying Formulas with Relative Cell References

Besides the automatic updating of calculations, another important feature of spreadsheets is the automatic copying of formulas (this is sometimes referred to as **formula replication**) to perform similar calculations in another area of the worksheet. Often we wish to perform calculations on large data sets. The copying feature allows us to perform the calculation on a single instance within the data set, then copy the calculation automatically to the entire data set. Formula copying does not mean reproducing exactly the same formula in another location. To make copied formulas work correctly in their new cell locations, the cells referenced in the formula must be automatically adjusted for the new location.

Formula adjustment for copied formulas is accomplished by modifying the cell references in the original formula according to their relative positions to the cell holding the formula. The cell addresses in the new formula are calculated to be in the same relative position to the cell containing the formula as were the original cell references to the original formula cell. Unless we specify to the contrary, all cell references are treated in this manner in formula copying and, for that reason, are called **relative cell references.**

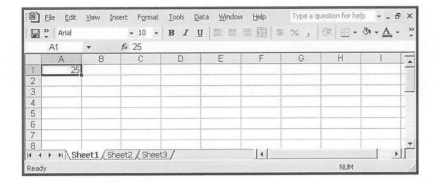

Figure 6.1
The upper-left portion of an Excel worksheet is shown here. The active cell is A1 and the value 25 has been entered in the entry bar for this cell.

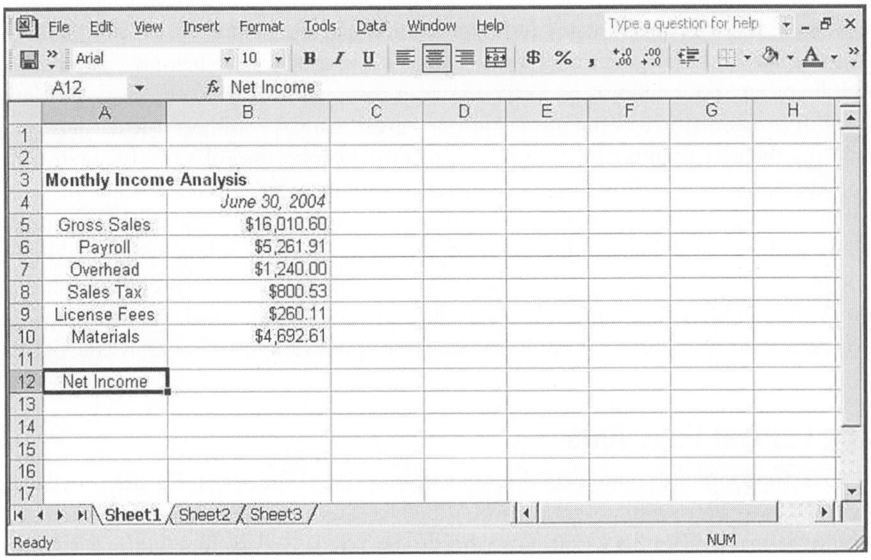

Figure 6.2
Entering text and numbers in a simple worksheet is illustrated. Note the different formatting that has been applied.

Additional Features of Spreadsheet Software

Modern spreadsheets have a great many features and capabilities, and it is not our intent in this brief survey to explore all these features. However, we will mention several additional major capabilities in this section, particularly:

- Employing absolute references and problem parameters
- Using formulas that employ built-in computational functions
- Using formulas that employ built-in logical functions
- Displaying data and the results of computations as charts

Using Absolute Cell References

As we have emphasized, one of the major advantages of using spreadsheets for calculations is their automatic recalculation of results when data changes. To maximize the advantages of this feature, we must plan and design our worksheets carefully. Intelligent worksheet design involves identifying values that are subject to change; these are called **problem parameters.**

Including problem parameters in our spreadsheet solutions makes them both easier to modify and more readable.

When using problem parameters in a worksheet, it is often the case that we'd like to have some cell references remain fixed as we copy a formula. In other words, we'd like to override the relative referencing method for some cells. For example, the sales tax rate would be the same for a group of invoices calculated on a spreadsheet. We could enter that rate into a single cell. Cell references that do not change when formulas involving them are copied to a new location are called **absolute references.** In most spreadsheets, absolute cell references are indicated in formulas by preceding the cell row and column name with the $ symbol.

Using Built-In Functions

All spreadsheet programs provide **built-in functions** to make frequently used computations more convenient and less error prone. Functions act on input values, called **arguments,** to produce a value. Built-in functions employ a **black box design.** This means we need not worry about the details of how the function produces its value. All we need to know are the number and kinds of arguments the function requires and the kind of data it produces.

Most spreadsheet programs offer a variety of built-in functions to help us accomplish statistical, financial, trigonometric, and other types of computations. Indeed, it is this variety of built-in functions that makes the production of a great many spreadsheet calculations so easy by relieving the user from the burden of constructing complex formulas from scratch.

Spreadsheets provide a number of statistical functions—AVERAGE( ) is one of these—that make it easy to produce statistical summaries. In addition, the standard trigonometric functions and a host of financial functions are included. Their black box design makes functions very convenient, because we can use them to construct powerful and useful worksheet calculations without bothering with the details of how they are implemented. We need know only the required arguments and what results the functions produce to use functions effectively.

Using Logical Functions

The logical functions are another class of built-in spreadsheet functions. Besides convenience, they enable us to accomplish tasks that would be impossible without them. One such task is the ability to make decisions within our worksheets. The logical IF function is designed for this purpose. The IF function takes advantage of the computer's capability for conditional processing, which is the ability of a process to make decisions on alternative courses of action.

The IF function in spreadsheet programs typically takes three arguments. The first argument is a **Boolean** or **logical expression**—that is, an expression that evaluates to either true or false. The next two arguments are values based on either constants or formulas that represent alternative results of the function. Only one of these two will become the actual value for the function in any given instance. If the Boolean expression evaluates to true, the first of the two remaining arguments is used. If the Boolean expression is false, the second remaining argument is used.

Displaying Data in Charts

Many times a graphical summary of data and results is much easier to interpret than rows and columns of numbers. Modern spreadsheets make it very easy to create and display charts based on our calculations. Let's look at several examples.

- **Bar Charts.** Suppose we would like to compare monthly net incomes for the months June, July, and August in a worksheet. A **bar chart** showing the monthly figures side by side would be a useful way to visualize this comparison, as illustrated in Figure 6.3. In most spreadsheets, such charts can be created automatically. We need only specify the data we wish to chart and the desired type of graphical plot. Bar charts are one type of series chart. A **series chart** measures the change in one or more dependent values over a series of some value, such as time.

■ **Pie Charts.** Bar charts are just one of a number of ways to display and interpret data visually. For example, **pie charts** are often very convenient for displaying percentage breakdowns. Pie charts allow us to portray the parts of a whole, exposing relative sizes of various components in a visually appealing manner. Values are shown as slices of a "pie," with the relative sizes of the slices corresponding to the percentage of the whole represented by each value. See Figure 6.4. Again, most spreadsheet programs make it very easy to create these displays. Pie charts are one variety of distributional chart. A **distributional chart** represents quantities as parts of a whole.

Spreadsheets as Decision Support Tools

Today's businesses are faced with a great many important decisions that often depend on projections produced by numeric models. These models represent profit and cash flow projections, projections about interest rates, performances of economic indicators, market shares,

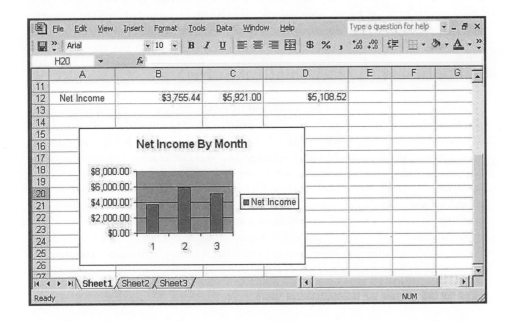

Figure 6.3
An Excel bar chart compares monthly net income for several months.

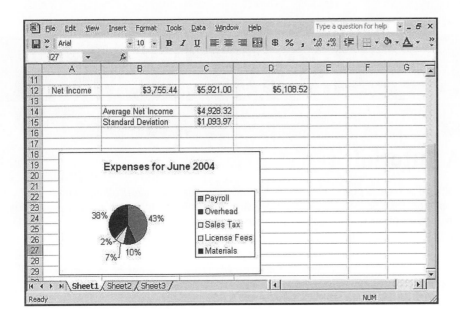

Figure 6.4
An analysis of the breakdown of expenses for a given month displayed in a pie chart in Excel.

labor and material costs, and so on. You have learned that in large measure the power and advantage of spreadsheet programs are based on their ability to make flexible and updatable computations. This characteristic makes spreadsheet software an extremely valuable tool in business, engineering, and scientific decision making.

The answers to most important questions in business decision making are not black and white. Such decision making often depends on numeric models and computations. It is not uncommon for these models to involve a great many assumptions. Of course, good decision makers analyze these assumptions and demand evidence that they are the correct or the best ones. Spreadsheet programs can help immensely in this process of analyzing various assumptions and the effects they have on the computational models being used. Computations modeled using spreadsheets can be modified easily to explore alternative assumptions or alternate values for important problem parameters whose true values may be unknown.

Such explorations are often referred to as "**what if**" **computations** because they are used to answer questions that begin "What if . . . ." For example, we could ask, "What if the sales tax increases to 7 percent?" or "What if the cost of materials goes up by 15 percent?" If we design our spreadsheet models well, such questions could be explored quite easily by adjusting the appropriate values in a worksheet. Indeed, "what if" analysis is one of the most important reasons why spreadsheet software is indispensable to almost every modern business enterprise.

Computing with Mathematical Software

We mentioned earlier that in the late 1950s and the 1960s, libraries of programs were developed for problem solving in the sciences and engineering. These libraries still exist and are continually improved, but they are effectively employed only within high-level language programs. Learning to program with high-level languages takes careful study and considerable experience. As an alternative, a new class of software designed to solve mathematical, scientific, and engineering problems has been developed. These new programs provide many of the same problem-solving capabilities as program libraries but without the overhead of traditional programming. In addition, they offer some exciting new capabilities as well.

In particular, application programs like Mathematica, Maple, and Derive have symbolic manipulation capabilities that allow the user to make algebraic and calculus computations and find solutions to differential equations. These programs also perform numeric approximations to the solutions of mathematical problems for which a symbolic solution may be otherwise impossible or too difficult to manage. In addition, their ability to graph functions and rela-

DISCOVERING MORE

Spreadsheets: A Tutorial

As we noted, modern spreadsheet software provides a powerful environment for numerical computation and modeling. We have introduced some of the major features of such software here, but of course there is much more to be learned before you become a productive user of this type of software.

For a tutorial giving detailed information, examples, and practice using Microsoft Excel, consult the online resource "Discovering More About Spreadsheets."

tions easily is an indispensable aid for understanding and exploiting these relationships. Mathematicians, scientists, and engineers can use these capabilities to solve a wide variety of problems with relative ease.

The ability to graph functions in a variety of ways can be profitably exploited to interpret data sets. The term **scientific visualization** is used to describe the array of techniques and methods used to visualize data, models, and functional relationships. Modern mathematical software makes such visualization feasible and has had a profound influence on the way scientific investigations are conducted.

■ Summary

Finding faster and more reliable means for numeric processing motivated the invention of modern-day computers, and numeric processing is just as fundamental to many of today's computing applications as it was in the early days of computing. However, numeric computing is not a straightforward affair. Converting numeric data to the digital domain is complicated because numbers are both infinite in number and continuously distributed along the number line.

Integer values can be represented exactly and without error in a computer's memory, provided they are within the computer's range of integer values. Integers outside this range must be treated as decimal numbers. Real numbers are digitized with both range and limited precision. To maximize the precision possible for decimal numbers using a fixed number of bits of storage, these numbers are stored in the computer employing floating point representation, consisting of a normalized fraction and an exponent. Storing decimal numbers with limited precision means that every computerized numerical operation using them is potentially in error. Hence you must always perform decimal calculations on computers with some degree of caution and skepticism for the results.

To make it easier for programmers to avoid creating calculations that might generate large errors, computer scientists have created solution methods for many common problems that are carefully designed to avoid or minimize possible pitfalls. These methods are stored in electronic software libraries, which are available for the programmer's use during the construction of a program requiring numeric processing.

Spreadsheet software packages are especially designed for numeric processing and offer a very user-friendly interface. Automatic updating of calculations with new data, charting or plotting calculations in a variety of ways, and employing built-in computational functions are some examples of the power and flexibility of spreadsheet software. "What if" spreadsheet analysis, so named because it is used to analyze questions that begin "What if . . . ," has become an indispensable tool in almost every modern business enterprise.

Symbolic and numeric calculation programs make robust computational methods more accessible for the nonprogrammer. The term *scientific visualization* is used to describe the array of techniques and methods that are used to visualize data, models, and functional relationships. Modern mathematical software makes such visualization feasible and has had a profound influence on the way scientific investigations are conducted.

FOCUS Mathematical Software

A thorough investigation of these topics is beyond the scope of our discussion. Nonetheless, we can get a flavor for how visualization plays a role in modern scientific work by way of some examples. For some examples of scientific visualization and its uses, consult the online resource "Focus on Mathematical Software."

■ Terms

absolute references
active cell
arguments
bar chart
Boolean expression (logical)
black box design
built-in function
cell, worksheet
cell address
cell range
distributional chart
entry bar

expanding a number's representation
exponent
floating point representation
formula replication
integers
limited precision
logical expression
mantissa
normalized
numerical analysis
overflow error

pie chart
problem parameters
real numbers
relative cell references
scientific visualization
series chart
software libraries
spreadsheets
twos complement
underflow error
"what if" computation
worksheets

■ Questions for Review

1. What was the importance of numeric processing for the development of modern-day
computers?

2. Write the binary number 1010101 in decimal representation.

3. Write the decimal number 247 in binary
representation.

4. React to the statement: Integers can be represented and stored exactly in computer
memory.

5. What is meant by an overflow error during
a calculation?

6. Convert the binary number 10.1101 to its
decimal representation.

7. Give the normalized floating point (decimal) form of the number 0.00264.

8. Give the normalized floating point (decimal) form of the number 369.02.

9. Write the normalized floating point number
2.46×10^3 in usual decimal form.

10. Write the normalized floating point number
4.61×10^{-4} in usual decimal form.

11. How does the problem of limited precision
occur in converting real numbers to floating
point format? Can it always be avoided?

12. Explain overflow and underflow for numbers represented in floating point format.

13. What is meant when we say the number
line that can be represented in a computer's
memory contains "holes"?

14. Why is it necessary to perform decimal calculations on a computer with caution and
skepticism?

15. How is a typical spreadsheet document (i.e.,
worksheet) organized?

16. How does the typical spreadsheet distinguish between numeric and textual input
data?

17. What is meant when we say that spreadsheets automatically recalculate formulas?

18. Describe the copying of formulas in a
spreadsheet. Explain the difference between
absolute and relative cell references in this
process.

19. Why are built-in functions important in a
spreadsheet? Give some examples of the
kinds of built-in functions typically found
in a spreadsheet.

20. What is meant by the arguments of a
spreadsheet function?

21. Contrast distributional charts and series
charts. Give an example of the kind of data
you might represent with each. Is one of
these graphical display methods preferred
over the other? Explain.

22. What is meant by problem parameters in
constructing a spreadsheet problem solution? Why is it important to isolate important problem parameters in a spreadsheet
model?

23. What are logical functions? What are they
used for in spreadsheet work? Give a brief
example.

24. Explain the concept of a "what if" computation. Why are these important? Why is a
spreadsheet so useful for producing these
kinds of computations?

■ Questions for Review *(continued)*

25. What is meant by the term *Boolean expression*? How are these used in spreadsheet calculations?

26. Describe the use of spreadsheet packages as decision support tools.

27. What is scientific visualization? Why is it an important technique?

28. Give a brief description of the field called *numerical analysis.*

29. What do we mean when we say that spreadsheet built-in functions exhibit *black box* design?

30. Give several examples of scientific visualization. (Hint: Have you watched the "Six O'Clock Report" on your local television station lately?)

Chapter 7

Managing Information

OBJECTIVES

- A brief history of database software

- The way information is organized and stored in databases

- Methods that make rapid and flexible database information retrievals possible

- The basic features of the network database model

- The basic features of the relational database model

- The major functions available in most database management software

- The convergence of Web and database technologies for e-commerce and other applications

In the previous two chapters, you learned that numeric and text processing represent two of the oldest and most important computing applications. A third application, the storage and retrieval of data in large databases, also dates to the early days of computing. And computer databases continue to have a significant impact in computing today.

For example, keeping employee and customer records, tracking inventories, and monitoring and reporting sales are among the most important and most often computerized activities in many business organizations. Governments, banking, insurance, travel, and other industries could not function today without computerized record keeping. And your university keeps a host of information about you in computerized form. All of these activities depend on database management systems for storing and retrieving large amounts of data. And electronic commerce, one of today's most rapidly emerging business techniques, makes essential use of database technology.

Brief History of Database Computing

Long before word processing became common, businesses were using databases to store and review much of their important information. As the name suggests, a database is a collection of data (often a large collection) about some enterprise or subject. The term *database,* though, means more than just a large data store or data bank. What distinguishes a database is that it is organized in a way that enables effective and efficient retrieval of information stored in it. We use the term **database management system (DBMS)** to refer not only to the data itself but also to the methods and techniques used to store and retrieve that data.

Files, Records, and Fields

The first databases were actually created within the programs written for business in the late 1950s. These early programs created temporary electronic structures for storing data when the program ran. Each time the program ran, the basic data were read by the program from punched cards. The electronic database then persisted only as long as the program itself was running.

In the early 1960s, advances in programming language design made it possible to construct programs that could create and manage external files to store and retrieve information. **External files** are files that exist in disk storage independently of the program itself. For example, the programming language COBOL, introduced in the early 1960s, was especially designed to give programmers built-in tools for managing external files.

The structure of data files is usually relatively simple. Each file consists of a series of records that are, in turn, divided into a specified number of data fields. **Files** typically store information about some group of entities, perhaps persons or things. **Records** hold information about a particular entity; the data **fields** of a record contain the specific items of information about that specific entity.

External files were a great advantage for programmers and improved their capability to maintain and access data using their programs. Each program that was written, however, still had to include its own techniques for writing information to the files and extracting and presenting information from the files. As the usefulness of the external file concept grew, so did the sophistication of the programming methods and the tools used to manipulate these files.

File Management Systems

Because the programs being written to access external files had a great deal in common, it made sense to provide programmers with some of the standard capabilities for storing and accessing files. In this way, the programmer didn't have to reinvent the wheel for each application. Thus, **file management software,** which incorporated various methods of creating and accessing external files, was created and marketed. File management software was the precursor of modern database management software.

File management software included the ability to create indices for files based on the information stored in selected data fields. In **indexed files** one or more data fields serve as an index for the records contained in the file. This is exactly the purpose of your student identification number in your school's student database. This value is a unique identifier for accessing information about you. Using an index, you can look up a given record quickly by searching for a match with the indexed data field.

Indexed files offered a significant improvement in the speed of looking up information. A number of commercially successful, proprietary indexed file schemes were marketed in the 1960s and 1970s, and some of these are still in use today. Even though these proprietary file management systems were a tremendous step forward from the days of programming every file management problem from scratch, they still required writing programs in languages like COBOL or FORTRAN to exploit their features. These file management systems were utilities, not stand-alone software. In fact, stand-alone database software was still a decade away.

The Network Database Model

The demands for information management programming evolved during the late 1960s and early 1970s. The changes in demand affected not only the scale and complexity, but also the manner in which these systems conducted business. The kinds of computing applications and problems gaining attention were quite a bit more difficult than the payroll and inventory systems that had been the bread and butter of earlier programming applications. As interactive or transactional computing became more commonplace, being able to query the database systems for particular information when it was needed became desirable. A convenient query language or method for constructing database queries was required to achieve this.

These new applications demanded even more sophisticated file management tools. A major advance was the creation of file management systems that allowed access to more than one related file—the first true database management systems. These systems gave the programmer tools and methods for creating and accessing a group of related files. Special fields, called **link fields,** were used to relate records stored in two different files. Link fields contained disk addresses to give quick access to related information stored in another file.

The linked structures these systems employ have come to be called the **network database model** because the files are connected by a network of links. Updated versions of many network database systems are still in use today. In the network model, the programmer deals with a physical model of the database. For example, to implement a database retrieval, the programmer must manipulate the indices and links built into the database itself to access the required data. These systems are optimized for speed and efficiency, but they demand some programming skill to use.

DISCOVERING MORE

Indexed Files and Binary Search Trees

Indexed file schemes depend heavily on the concept of a binary search tree. Indexed files are often implemented as a binary tree that contains the indexed field data and links to the actual records in the external file. With such a structure, we can search the index in a flash and follow its link to the record we seek in the file itself. The "link" will be an actual address on the disk, so we can access it very quickly. Spell checkers in word processors also rely on binary search trees for their implementation. For a description of binary search trees and details on how they are used in these applications, consult the online resource "Binary Search Trees."

The Relational Database Model

The **relational database model** was introduced in the late 1970s as an alternative database model. The relational model gives the user a more abstract view of the database rather than the physical organization employed by the network model. The relational model does not employ link fields to relate records in different files. Rather, in this model, related information is located when it is needed from the logical relationships among items in the files.

For example, if we store data about employees in one file and the week's work record in another, we obviously need access to both when processing the week's payroll. In the network model, the necessary physical links between the two files would be defined when the record data fields were defined. To process the payroll, the programmer would manipulate the links present in the design of the database.

In a relational model of the same data, no physical link fields are present; only the logical relationship between the two files guides the combination of their data. Because the file relationships are logical, the user is relieved of the details of how the files are physically organized. Consequently, the level of detail required to employ a relational database model successfully is reduced. Indeed, the relational model is much more intuitive and accessible to the nonprogrammer.

When we design the file structures for a relational database, we need to ensure that we have included sufficient information to forge the natural logical relationships already inherent in the data. To illustrate, let's consider an example.

Suppose we wish to keep track of sales orders for our enterprise. Wouldn't it seem natural and desirable also to keep records on our customers and the products we sell, as well as the orders per se? In fact, we have just identified three important entities in our data storage requirements: customers, products, and sales orders. This is always the first step in designing a database: identify the important entities about which we wish to keep and retrieve data.

Of course, we also want to keep in mind how the entities are related. In this case, customers place orders for products. So the relationships are clear. Each customer will place many (we hope) orders. Likewise, we hope each of our products is the focus of many orders. All this suggests that we need three files: one to hold customer information, one to hold product information, and one to hold order information.

The order information will be related to both the customer information (who placed the order?) and the product information (what product was ordered?). Figure 7.1 illustrates how we might organize this information into three related files. Note that for the purpose of our example, we will keep the particular information about each of these entities quite restricted to make our example easier to display. In a real commercial application of this type, we'd no doubt store lots more information about our products and our customers.

The field names (*custnum, name,* and so on) are often referred to as **attributes.** The records in the files represent information about one particular entity. For example, each record in the *Customers* file represents information about a particular customer. Likewise, a record in the *Orders* file represents information about a particular order that was placed, and so on.

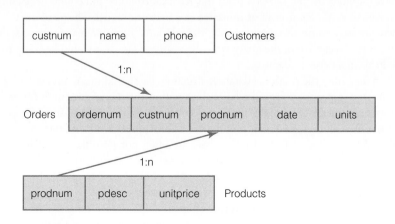

Figure 7.1

A relational database model for customer, order, and product data.

How will we relate the information in two files? Note how we included in the record definitions for both the *Customers* and *Orders* files a field *custnum* to contain a customer identification number. We then can relate the information in the two files as the need arises. In a similar way, the field *prodnum* relates the *Orders* and *Products* files.

Note also in Figure 7.1 that we have represented the relationships between the files as ratios. The 1:n (read *one-to-many*) notation means that one record in the first file can be related to many records in the second file. So for example, a single customer can place many orders, and a single product can be ordered many times.

Comparing the Network and Relational Database Models

Both the network database model and the relational database model are in widespread use today, and both will no doubt continue to be important for years to come. Each model has its own distinctive merits. As we will see, the network model's strength is its efficiency, but the relational model offers much more flexibility.

The network model delivers built-in efficiency through its designed link fields among separate files. Finding information in related files through these built-in link fields could hardly be faster because all that is required is to look up the related records using the disk addresses stored in the link fields. In fact, the link field was put there by the database designer for precisely this purpose.

If efficiency is at a premium, then the network model will more often be the choice. The network model, however, does not provide a great deal of flexibility. Finding related records depends on link fields, so if the database designer hasn't provided a link field tailored to the information retrieval we have in mind, this retrieval becomes more difficult, if not impossible.

On the other hand, systems based on the relational model provide more flexible access to their data. Access is based on posing database queries derived from the logical relationships among the various files involved, rather than depending on the database designers to have included all the physical link fields we might later need.

Let's consider how we could use the relational database design shown in Figure 7.1 to retrieve some information. Suppose we wish to list the product number for all the items ordered by customer John Jones. We could do this by first looking up the record for John Jones in the *Customers* file. Note that this is the same first step we would follow if we were using a network model. The next step differs significantly; instead of simply following addresses contained in a built-in link field, we now must make a second search. We would use John Jones' customer identification number, *custnum,* to search the *Orders* file and print out the product number, *prodnum,* for each of those orders containing a match for John's identification number in the *custnum* field.

This search could require looking through the entire *Orders* file, which may be quite large. If we have an index for the *custnum* field, this retrieval could be done more efficiently, but it still involves an extra step over what is needed in a network model. The good news is that we don't actually have to do this work because the relational database management system performs it for us. Nonetheless, the query won't be nearly as fast as it would be using the physical link fields in a network database.

When designing the relational database structure, we should make sure we have provided all relevant and appropriate logical relationships within the record structures for each file. If we do this, even queries that might not have been anticipated when the database was designed are possible. We call these unanticipated queries **ad hoc queries** because they are constructed as needed. As we noted earlier, ad hoc queries are often not possible at all using a network database model. The flexibility of the relational model does carry its price tag: Relational database systems are generally less efficient (that is, slower) in processing queries because they involve at least one extra search step, as we saw in the earlier example.

The basic trade-off is flexibility versus efficiency. The reason both database models are alive and well is that most applications demand one or the other of these characteristics.

Each model has problem domains where it is king. When the need for rapid responses is crucial, a network system tuned for performance by the inclusion of appropriate link fields will be used. In applications where the ability to pose a large variety of queries, some of which may not be known when the database is designed, is needed, then a database system based on the relational model will be more satisfactory. Some specific examples will make these ideas clearer.

Examples of Network Model Databases

When you step up to the airline counter or call your ticket agent to purchase a ticket, you expect to find out in a few seconds whether a seat is available for the flight you want. If so, you expect to be able to book that seat immediately. Someone in another city may be looking for the same seat, and to prevent double-booking, the system must record your booking quickly and securely. These systems must handle thousands of transactions (queries) per hour, and a system that takes a minute to respond to a seat inquiry is not acceptable. Hence, airline reservation systems naturally value speed of response in their automated systems and place little value on answering unusual or unexpected queries. Thus, the network model is the obvious choice for such a system.

Likewise, automatic teller machines (ATMs) also require very rapid response times. If you have a checking account in a Florida bank and you happen to be in Minnesota, it is an easy matter to make an instant cash withdrawal at an ATM. Have you ever considered how this is possible? One aspect is clear—the computing system that handles this transaction is required to respond with reasonable speed. In fact, you will probably be recognized (by your card and personal identification number) within a few seconds and have your money within a few more seconds. Without excellent response time, the computers managing these events couldn't handle the volume of transactions they must process each day.

Both the airline reservation system and the ATM computing system involve only two very simple computing processes—data lookup and a simple data change (booking a seat, deducting money from an account balance). These are actually fairly typical database transactions. In fact, this is exactly what the first databases were designed for—data lookup and update. The emphasis is not on complicated computing processes, but rather, purely and simply, on transaction speed.

For both airline reservation systems and ATMs, flexibility is of almost no importance. How many different queries does an ATM have to handle? Not many, and none of these are of the ad hoc variety. A similar situation holds for the airline reservation system. The queries it handles today are exactly the same ones it must handle tomorrow, but it must handle them quickly. These systems are typical of a great many database applications where performance constraints demand a network model database management system.

Examples of Relational Model Databases

Many database applications demand flexibility rather than speed. Let's consider several different examples. If you've watched a televised baseball game recently, you've probably heard statistics like:

> Mike Piazza has a lifetime batting average of .407 against the Braves with runners in scoring position from the seventh inning on.

Have you ever wondered how information tailored to a particular player in a particular batting situation in a specific game is produced? Publishing this type of information would fill up numerous volumes. Finding it quickly would be a headache, too.

What actually happens is that batting and pitching data are stored in a database, and statistics like those in the example are then constructed from that data. In other words, the information is not stored in the form in which it is presented, but rather must be created on the fly from more elementary data. When the game starts, we don't know all the queries we might like to make as it progresses. Instead, many of these queries are constructed ad hoc. We need a database system that allows us to phrase ad hoc queries with relative ease.

For this kind of application, the relational database model is better than the network model. Indeed, it would be difficult, if not impossible, to build in enough links between files in a network model to anticipate all the ad hoc queries we might desire. Nor is speed an overriding consideration here. One reason is that there is only one user of the database, whereas our airline and ATM databases would typically have a great many, almost simultaneous users. A response time of even a half minute would be perfectly acceptable in our baseball example.

Using a relational model database, we can generally pose successful queries to extract any information that may be logically derived from the database itself. On the other hand, even with the relational model, if its structure doesn't support the query, we cannot successfully compose it. For example, if we had not stored the opponent, the inning, and the positions of base runners for every time a player bats, we could not have produced the statistic in our example.

In general, when we create relational databases, we should strive to maximize the opportunities for successful ad hoc queries by designing the database structure carefully and intelligently. A thorough study of the issues involved in good database design would carry us too far afield here, but suffice it to say that this area is very important in practical database applications.

Lest we leave you with the impression that the relational database model is important only for what some might call a frivolous baseball statistic application, let's take a quick look at one more example. NASA engineers and scientists are responsible for ensuring the efficient and safe operation of the three rocket engines on board each space shuttle orbiter. These engines are among the most complex machines ever built; not surprisingly, they require constant periodic adjustment and modification for optimal performance.

One of the primary features of the task of monitoring the performance of these engines is testing. Engineers place test engines on a test stand, fire them, then observe the test results to assess the many parameters associated with their operation. Storing all past test data is very important to this process. When a specific undesirable behavior is observed during a test, engineers must ascertain the cause of this behavior and correct it. Naturally, the behaviors that cause the most difficulty in this regard are ones that take the engineers by surprise—that is, problems that were not anticipated. Part of the diagnostic procedure applied in looking for causes and solutions is to go back through historical test data to look for clues about the currently observed behavior. The ad hoc nature of the current problem, however, requires ad hoc database queries. There is simply no way the original database designers could have anticipated

Databases and Crime Fighting

SOCIAL THEMES

Information can be a crucial component in effective crime control. Indeed, the U.S. government maintains hundreds of databases with a variety of information on individuals for the purpose of crime prevention and investigation. With the increased use of DNA identification techniques in criminal cases, DNA databases are also growing.

Such systems represent tremendous crime fighting capabilities, but they also raise many questions about the protection of a citizen's privacy. How much information about its citizens should a country collect? Who should have access to this information? Should the individual's permission be required before certain information is collected and stored in databases? Should an individual be able to access his or her own information and challenge its accuracy? These are difficult questions. Surely society benefits when such national databases are available, but surely opportunities for abuse of this information arise. We can expect the debate about such government national database projects to continue for years. For a more detailed discussion of these issues, consult the online essay "Databases and Crime Fighting."

the particular kinds of information needed months or years later in this ongoing process. The speed with which such queries are dispatched is of no real concern. It is perfectly acceptable for a query response to take two minutes; what is of utmost importance is that the query can be satisfied. The flexibility of the relational database model is all-important in this case, even if some speed and efficiency must be sacrificed.

As these examples illustrate, there are needs for database systems based on the network model and others based on the relational model. Actually, some merging of the capabilities of the two models has occurred in some current database systems. These hybrid systems provide an underlying network model for speed and efficiency but also have an add-on query language that allows the user to pose ad hoc queries to the database. In essence, you get the best of both worlds—fast response for those queries you can anticipate, along with ad hoc query capability. These systems will, no doubt, become even more popular in the future.

No one denies that the relational model is superior from a logical perspective. As research continues and hardware performance improves, we may yet see the day when database systems based on the relational model can achieve response speeds adequate for all applications. If this happens, the relational model will become the standard for database management systems. Until that time (which may be some years away, if ever), both models and their hybrids will play important roles in the application of database management technology.

Basic Database Management System Concepts

At this point, you may be wondering about database systems for desktop computers—after all, this text is primarily about desktop computing. What kinds of database applications are likely to be implemented on personal computers? Certainly not airline reservation systems or ATM banking systems. Implementing any database application that requires great speed of response on personal computers would be unwise. In fact, almost all the network database systems are designed to operate on computers more powerful than desktop computers. The kinds of database applications that run on personal computers usually involve relatively small amounts of data anyway, so concerns about response time are not important.

There are, in fact, quite a number of database products available for desktop computers. These generally fit one of two types: some are **flat file database systems,** consisting of one file per database; others are based on the relational database model. Flat file database systems have many of the features of the higher-end relational systems, but they restrict the database to one single file for storage. A large number of database applications require no more than one file for their basic data storage. If this simpler model suits your needs, you can achieve excellent results with flat file systems. There are also a number of outstanding relational database systems for desktop computers. These can be used to create very sophisticated database information access systems.

In this section, we discuss some of the concepts and functions common to all database management systems, regardless of their data model. Although they may be implemented in different ways, all database systems have a number of common features.

Defining the Database Structure

When you begin a new document in a word processor, you are offered a blank screen, ready for you to input text and formatting information. Likewise, when you open a spreadsheet package, you have a blank worksheet in which to enter data, formulas, and so on. In both these cases, the software application creates a new blank document ready for your input. Database systems have slightly more complex interfaces. As you might expect, there is a good deal more to defining a database than simply collecting and storing data values. Initial decisions have to be made about the content of individual fields and the overall organization of related files when applicable.

Once these decisions are made, this information must be expressed in the database management system before any data entry can commence. File record structures must be defined, specifying field names and the kinds of data for each field. Each field can contain only one kind of data (for example, text, numbers, or dates), called the field's **data type.** Every database management system must provide a way to define this basic structural information in the system before any work with the database itself can begin.

Entering, Editing, and Viewing Data—Forms

After the structure of the database has been defined, you are ready to enter some data into the database. You generally do this by using a **data entry form** displayed on the screen. On-screen prompts serve as reminders for particular pieces of information. Many database systems also allow you to define constraints on data fields (ranges on numbers, whether the value is unique in the database, etc.). The database system then automatically verifies that your data satisfies these constraints as it is entered.

Although every database system has a default form, you can generally design your own form layouts as well. For example, if you are entering a large amount of data from existing paper forms (as is often the case), you might wish to design an entry form to match the appearance and data field locations of the paper form. This would make for a more efficient and ergonomically satisfying task. It would likely reduce the chances of errors as well.

Sorting Data

When displaying data or creating database reports, it is often easier to interpret that data if it is sorted. **Sorted data** is presented in a particular order. All database systems provide this capability. The data fields on which we base the sorting are called **sort keys.** In most database systems, you may select several sort keys to enable **nested sorting.** When several sort keys are specified, they are given in order of priority; the system first sorts the data by the highest-priority key, then all entries with the same value for that key are sorted by the key with the next highest priority, and so on for additional sort keys. For example, we may wish to specify a triple-nested sort displaying sales figures sorted by region, then by salesperson within the region, then by amount for each salesperson.

Database Reports

As we have noted, in most database systems, forms can be used for data display. We often require more sophisticated data reporting capabilities. This is accomplished by producing written **reports** from the database data. In contrast to data forms, which are often designed to mirror paper forms for ergonomic ease, reports are designed for a different purpose: to present data in a compact, readable, and informative format. For example, reports often contain headers and footers and tabulate totals and subtotals of important values.

Often reports contain data selected on the basis of some stated criteria. This data may come from one table or a combination of tables, depending on the particular criteria applied.

DISCOVERING MORE

Database Management Systems

For more detailed information and examples concerning the use of database management systems, illustrated through tutorials on using Microsoft Access, consult the online resource "Discovering More About Database Management Systems."

In some database systems, the selection criteria become a part of the report itself. Hence, each time the report is printed the data are collected anew, meaning you get the most up-to-date data in the report at all times. One way this can be accomplished is to apply the criteria to collect the desired data into a new table, then base the report on the new table. This table becomes a **virtual table,** meaning that the table itself is not stored, only the criteria for selecting its data. In this way, if the database data change, the new values are automatically reflected in the virtual table. In some cases, you may prefer to print the data as they occur at some fixed time, ignoring any later updates to the database. In such cases, you can store a report based on current data to be printed as many times as you like later if you do not want the report data updated each time the report is printed.

Subtotals and Control Breaks in Reports

Often we would like to compute totals and subtotals for our reports. For example, we might wish to display the total value of all orders. Subtotals, of course, are associated with a specific group of the data in a report. To display these subtotals accurately, the grouping must be based on a common data field value. A separate subtotal may then be computed and displayed for each group of distinct values for that data field.

The break points in a report with subtotals or other summary information are often referred to as **control breaks.** In most database systems, control breaks can be nested, allowing subtotals to be calculated within groupings as well as for the groupings themselves.

Using Query Languages

As we have emphasized, the ability to perform **database queries** is the most valuable feature of any database management system. Queries are requests for specific information satisfying some stated criteria. Queries are expressed in a **query language** that, like a programming language, has a specific syntax. In fact, much of a database management system's value for its users is based on the convenience and power of its query language. Use of these languages requires no programming in the traditional sense. Query languages are self-contained, so that once a user masters the language, he or she can pose any potential queries to the system.

In fact, the query language is the only component of a database system visible to a great many users. For example, when you use an ATM machine, you interact with the underlying database only by means of a very restricted and carefully designed query language. This language is presented as a choice of menu selections at each stage of the transaction. The language model employed is not at all flexible, but it isn't designed with flexibility in mind. It is designed for easy and foolproof use without training. The travel agent you ask to book your flight is also interacting with a flight reservation database through a query language. This language is more complicated than the ATM language and will require some training of its users. To ATM users or the travel agent operating the airline reservation system, these systems *are* their query languages. The users see no other aspect of the database, having no involvement in designing the database, entering its initial data, or generating summary reports.

Given the importance of query languages, database management system designers and researchers have expended a great deal of effort to make these languages both user-friendly and as powerful as possible. There are several popular models on which most are based. Some attempts to standardize a query language for all relational database systems have been made. The leading candidate is called **SQL** (for **Structured Query Language**). Although no such standard has been adopted officially, SQL (usually pronounced *sequel*) is widely used. In fact, most relational database systems offer a query language containing at least a subset of SQL.

This is very good news for database users, at least at the query level. It means that an adequate knowledge of SQL will allow them to move freely from one database system to another. SQL queries are formed with an English-like syntax, employing a SELECT . . . FROM . . . WHERE format.

Another relational model query language, called **QBE** (for **Query-by-Example**), has also garnered a lot of support. QBE is not as standardized as SQL, and many different versions of

QBE are being used. All these versions are based on a graphical interface paradigm that allows a user to construct a generalized example of the data he or she would like to retrieve.

One of the most interesting and hotly pursued areas of current research is creating query languages that will employ a natural language like English. For example, in a **natural language query,** you might choose to pose a query in any of a number of ways, depending on which seems most expressive and meaningful to you—without worrying about how a particular query language requires you to pose the query.

Some limited success has been achieved, but the inherent complexity and ambiguity of natural languages like English pose a formidable barrier. Successful systems have been implemented in very special informational domains in which the vocabulary is highly technical and limited, such as chemistry and medicine. Another domain in which natural language queries have been successfully implemented is in the design of search engines for the Web. Here, the information being sought is not nearly as specific as with most database queries, and natural language queries are relatively simple to compose. Unfortunately, commercially viable natural language query systems for general use are still years away from reality. Nonetheless, large research and development efforts in this area are being conducted because the commercial payoff for a workable natural language database query system would be tremendous.

Databases and the Web

Database and Web technologies are merging. One of the most active areas of current computer science research centers on the use of Web "front-ends" for accessing the information in Web "back-end" databases. Indeed, the emergence of electronic commerce—the ability to conduct business transactions over the Web—has fueled a high level of activity in this area.

A **Web database front-end** is a database interface with search and retrieval capabilities that is displayed and run through a Web browser. These products provide access to a range of database information—from a large variety of public domain information to proprietary business transactions. Of course, security is a major issue in the use of such products for information not in the public domain. Security measures on the Web are constantly being improved, and it is now quite common to see Web front-ends for proprietary databases used by businesses, government, and other organizations. If you have purchased a book from Amazon.com or one if its competitors, or other kinds of products over the Web, then you are a user of such systems.

Databases used in Web applications are usually relational databases, and the query language used is most often SQL. Programs are written in languages like Java, Visual Basic, C++ and others to translate user requests collected through user-friendly Web pages to more formal SQL statements. These statements are then passed by these intermediary programs to the **back end database management system,** where this system employs the SQL statements to

DISCOVERING MORE

Query Languages

For more detailed information, examples, and exercises focused on SQL, including particular exercises on using both SQL and QBE within Microsoft Access, consult the online resource "Discovering More About Query Languages."

retrieve the requested data. The data is then passed, again through the intermediary program, back to the Web interface that the user is interacting with.

Multimedia Databases

A lot of attention is now being shifted to applying well-established database techniques for more innovative applications. With today's technology, it is possible to digitize and efficiently store images, graphical objects, sounds, and even motion pictures and video. Given that we can digitize and store such media, it seems natural to expect them to be included in our databases as well. And, in fact, this combination is producing some exciting results.

Multimedia database systems face the challenge of managing voice, images, and video, in addition to the conventional numeric and text data. Such systems must be capable of evaluating user queries that may require the integration of information from very different media. For instance, a simple query might be to collect all images that contain certain objects. The

DISCOVERING MORE

Databases and the Web

For current information about the uses of database technology in Web applications like electronic commerce, consult the online resource "Discovering More About Databases and the Web."

FOCUS Data Mining

Most businesses and enterprises maintain an assortment of electronic databases that track day-to-day transactions for a variety of tasks. For example, a typical business might collect information about personnel and payroll, data about customers and purchasing, inventory and supply, customer service records, advertising and publicity, and so on. For practical reasons, much of this data is stored in different databases. Thus, a company may possess a wealth of information that unfortunately is distributed across a variety of platforms and formats that make it extremely difficult to assemble or summarize. As a result, one of its most important assets—information—remains largely untapped.

In recent years, computer scientists have developed techniques and methods that make it possible to collect, combine, analyze, and summarize information from a variety of different databases. In addition to business applications, these methods are useful in the sciences, medicine, communications, banking, and finances; these applications also extend to the Web, and even for fighting crime and terrorism. Find out more about knowledge discovery in databases—or, more commonly, data mining—in the online resource "Focus on Data Mining."

database system must be capable of matching that attribute (expressed in words) with the content of images stored in its system. Of course, images could be tagged with verbal descriptions—a kind of keyword abstract like those attached to electronic publications. The designers would face the difficulty of correctly anticipating future interests about these images.

To overcome these obstacles, researchers today are experimenting with **knowledge-assisted multimedia database systems.** This approach is distinctive in that the system analyzes the content of its media based directly on a given query. Today, however, such systems are still largely experimental, but if the research is successful, the dividends for information management will be great.

■ Summary

Software systems that manage the storage and retrieval of computerized information date to the early days of computing. Today's versions of such software, called *database management systems,* are fundamental and indispensable tools to many organizations. Two major models are employed in modern database management systems: the network model and the relational model.

In the network model, the user interacts with a physical representation of the data including physical indices and link fields built into the data itself to provide access to related data. Network-based systems are optimized for speed and efficiency, although they still demand some programming skill to use.

The relational model gives the user a more conceptual view of the data. Rather than employing link fields to relate records in different files, the relational model employs the logical relationships among items in the files. This organization provides a much more intuitive interface and better accessibility for the nonprogrammer. Although relational systems are usually not as fast and efficient as network systems, their ease of use and ability to perform ad hoc queries make them a natural choice for data management conducted on desktop computers.

The ability to perform database queries is the most valuable feature of any database management system. Queries are written in a query language that, like a programming language, has a specific syntax. There are several popular models on which most query languages are based. Structured Query Language (SQL) is a widely used query language, and most relational database systems offer a query language con-

Databases and Your Privacy

In a previous *Social Themes* essay, we explored law enforcement's use of national databases. You don't have to be a lawbreaker, though, to be included in a relatively easily accessible database. Information on almost every person in the developed world is computerized in hundreds of databases collected, stored, and analyzed by governments, corporations, hospitals, marketing firms, and so on. Such activity raises right-to-privacy issues.

Most privacy-related legislation is based on the Fourth Amendment to the Constitution. We reproduce it here for reference:

> The right of the people to be secure in their persons, houses, papers, and effects, against unreasonable searches and seizures, shall not be violated, and no Warrants shall issue, but upon probable cause, supported by Oath or Affirmation, and particularly describing the place to be searched, and the persons or things to be seized.

How is the Fourth Amendment to be interpreted concerning an individual's right to privacy and the use of today's database and networking technology? The answer is largely unknown. Technology changes so rapidly that it often outpaces our legal system's proper regulation of its use. For an exploration of these issues, consult the online essay *"Databases and Your Privacy."*

taining at least a subset of SQL. Query-by-Example (QBE) has also garnered a lot of support. Although QBE languages are not as standardized as SQL, they are generally easy to use because they are based on a graphical user interface.

Much current research is focused on creating query languages that will employ natural language (English, for example). Some limited success has been achieved, but the inherent complexity and ambiguity of natural languages like English pose a formidable barrier, and commercially viable natural language query systems for general use may still be years away from reality.

The convergence of Web technology and database technology hold great promise for uses like electronic commerce. New developments in this area will no doubt emerge rapidly over the next few years.

■ Terms

ad hoc database query	indexed file	relational database model
attributes	knowledge-assisted	report, database
control breaks	multimedia database	sorted data
database management system (DBMS)	link fields	sort key
	multimedia database system	Structured Query Language (SQL)
data type	natural language query	virtual table
external file	nested sorting	Web database front-end
field	network database model	Web database back-end
file	query, database	
file management software	query language	
flat file database system	Query-by-Example (QBE)	
form, data entry	record	

■ Questions for Review

1. Define and relate the terms *file, record,* and *field* in the context of database structure. Construct a diagram to support your point.

2. What are indexed files? Why is indexing an important concept for database management?

3. Briefly describe the network database model.

4. Briefly describe the relational database model.

5. Is the network or relational database model preferable? Elaborate on your response.

6. What is meant by the design or structure of a database? Why is this important?

7. What is meant by a database query?

8. What is an ad hoc database query? Give an example to illustrate. Why are ad hoc queries an important consideration when choosing a database model?

9. Describe what is meant by a flat file database system.

10. What is meant by a multimedia database?

11. Compare database forms and database reports.

12. What is the purpose of a database query language? Why are these particularly important?

13. What does the acronym *SQL* stand for? How is it pronounced? What is its significance?

14. What does the acronym *QBE* stand for? Describe its use.

15. What does the term *sort key* refer to? How does it relate to nested sorting of information in a database?

16. Define the term *control break*. Describe its significance for database processing.

17. How does the database technology today compare with the corresponding technology of the 1960s?

18. When the network and relational database models are compared, the terms *flexibility* and *efficiency* often arise. Explain.

19. How would a natural language database query system compare with SQL and QBE?

20. Give several examples of how your life might be influenced by the use of database management systems.

Chapter 8

Digital Images

OBJECTIVES

- The nature of images and how digital images are organized

- How digital images are created and stored

- How digital images are processed and edited

Digital images are a very important medium for representing information. It is convenient to divide computer images into two classes: natural and artificial. Artificial images are created exclusively by computer processes and are usually called *graphic images* (or simply *graphics*). A natural image is one digitized from an original analog image such as a photograph. Whether natural or artificial, computer images offer a rich source of information that enhances a variety of applications. As the old saying states, "A picture is worth a thousand words," so digital images certainly should be worth a few kilobytes. In this chapter, we will consider natural images; we treat graphic images in the next chapter. Many of the concepts about digital images introduced here, however, will be applicable to computer-generated graphic images as well.

Images and Digital Images

Natural images come in a variety of forms: photographs, drawings, paintings, television and motion pictures, schematics, maps, and so on. The content of images may be simple and stylized or complicated and detailed, as shown in Figure 8.1. An **image** is a multidimensional pictorial representation of a scene. Images are pictures in the sense that they show us visually the prominent features of the objects that they represent. Most images plot these features in two-dimensional space—although three- (depth) and four-dimensional (time) images are also possible.

Like any other representation, an image represents its subject through a physical medium. Most images depict how things look as a function of light reflecting from the objects. Even so, images may be derived from other bands of the electromagnetic spectrum; for example, X-rays, radar, infrared, and satellite telemetry are employed to create images whose medium is reflected energies from outside the spectrum of visible light.

As information, images always approximate their subjects. In other words, an image is never an exact duplicate of what it depicts. It does have characteristics that match those of its subject, for example, color, shape, relative location, and so on. Unlike verbal descriptions, images exemplify what they represent rather than merely denote them. Consequently, maps, diagrams, and blueprints are images even though they seldom look exactly like the scenes they depict. The quality of an image (its accuracy, authenticity, coherence) depends on what purposes it serves. We tend to think that photographs, for example, are somehow mirrors of reality, but this is a cultural fact. Anthropologists have found primitive peoples who must be taught to understand and recognize photos of themselves. The point is that there are no fixed standards in assessing the quality of images. As Figure 8.1 shows, the photo of the cat and the line drawing are both effective in conveying information.

Most natural images employ analog media. To be useful to computers, they must be converted to the digital domain. A **digital image** is a picture that may be stored in, displayed, or otherwise processed by a computer. As we have seen, converting an analog medium into a discrete numeric form requires both sampling and quantizing. A **pixel** (from "picture element") is the basic unit of a digital image. Pixels are discrete units of an image that correspond to two-dimensional spatial coordinates. In addition, each pixel is a discrete sample of the continuous signal of an analog image. This means that each pixel contains one or more numbers that measure the value or values of the signal for that portion of the image. A pixel by itself does not convey much information. The context in which the pixel is found or its arrangement in the overall image is what determines what it depicts.

Pixels are usually arranged as rectangular units in a two-dimensional (2-D) grid, although it is possible to have other types of pixel arrangements (triangular, hexagonal, etc.). **Picture resolution** is defined as the number of pixels contained in a digital image. Resolution is usually written as a product of the image's dimensions—width × height. (This should not be confused with display resolution, which is usually expressed as dpi—dots per inch.) **Aspect ratio** expresses the number of horizontal pixels divided by the number of vertical pixels. The aspect ratio of an image is important for scaling images or when resampling them at different resolutions. For instance, if we wish to reduce the resolution of a digital image, we must take care to preserve the same aspect ratio for it. This will ensure that it looks natural and not distorted.

The example of the penny in Figure 8.2 has a resolution of 50 × 50 and thus an aspect ratio of 1:1. Here are some common picture resolutions: 640 × 480 or 800 × 600, 1024 × 768, and 1600 × 1200. These instances are typical of the three general levels for picture resolution—low, medium, and high (respectively). Notice also that each of these picture resolutions

DISCOVERING MORE

A Digital Image Gallery

Pictures often convey information much more effectively than words. Consult the online source "A Digital Image Gallery" for a sampler of the many ways in which digital images provide us valuable information. In addition, examples of some of the digital imaging concepts, methods, and techniques are included there.

have the same aspect ratio, 1.33:1. This is the same as a standard video monitor and conventional television.

As you might expect, the resolution has a direct effect on the amount of detail that a digital image captures. The examples in Figure 8.3 show the same image of a building front sampled at different resolutions. Naturally, there are some trade-offs with picture resolution. The higher the resolution, the greater the demands for both storage and processing. Thus, the

(a)

(b)

WILDCAT

(c)

Figure 8.1

Three types of representations are shown. Each denotes a common member of the feline family. In contrast to the word Wildcat *(c), which merely refers to one, the two images (a) and (b) depict or exemplify them. The first (a) is a photograph, and (b) is an illustration. Even though these two images are composed quite differently, each is an effective representation of its subject.*

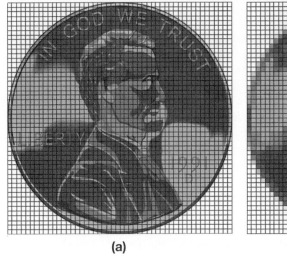

(a)

(b)

Figure 8.2

Digital sampling is illustrated. The image of the penny in (a) is sampled spatially at a rate of 50 pixels across and 50 down. The contents of each sample are averaged to produce a uniform value as shown in (b). At a pixel resolution of 50 × 50, we can see that the details of the lettering and face are lost.

(a)

(b)

(c)

Figure 8.3

A digital image of a building exterior is sampled at different resolutions. At the highest resolution (a), the details of the building are clear and sharp. In (b), the image begins to show signs of "jaggies"—the jagged look caused by rectangular pixels depicting curves and angles. Details are also beginning to blur. Finally, in (c), at the lowest resolution, individual pixels are clearly visible. Detail and depth are lost entirely.

choice of resolution will often depend on a number of practical matters: the amount of detail or complexity in the natural images, storage requirements, the extent of processing, how the image will be output for use, and so on.

Representing Black-and-White Images

Aside from its spatial coordinates, each pixel contains one or more numbers that measure its value on some scale for its physical medium. A black-and-white photograph represents the reflected intensity of objects in the scene—what we perceive as the relative brightness of the reflected light. To digitize such an image, we must convert the intensity of each sampled area to a single, precise value. As you may recall, this is called *quantizing*. Again, it is important to keep in mind that the process of measurement only approximates the value of the original analog signal. That we are always restricted to a finite range means that absolute precision is often impractical. Even real number values with fractions would be subject to some loss of accuracy as a result of approximation and rounding errors forced on us by their finite precision. In fact, integers are often used for pixel values because they are more convenient to store and process.

The range of values designated to represent the measuring scale is the **dynamic range.** For example, deciding on the dynamic range for digitizing a black-and-white photograph translates to how many possible levels of intensity we would use to measure and represent the image. Dynamic range is usually expressed by its binary precision, that is, the number of bits needed to store each pixel value. For instance, an intensity scale of 0 and 1 would represent all levels of intensity as merely black or white; this is commonly called a **binary image** because it requires only one bit per pixel. Consult Figure 8.4 for an example. **Bitplanes** refer to the depth of bits required for representing the image. A binary image has a depth of 1 because the entire image can be encoded by one bit per pixel. It is also common to refer to the number of bitplanes as the depth of the image, for short.

Intensity images with a greater dynamic range are called **grayscale images** because the intensity values represent different degrees of brightness as shades from black to gray to white. Figure 8.5 illustrates how grayscale images are represented. Like resolution, we normally prefer greater dynamic ranges for the highest-quality images, but the choice of dynamic range for

Figure 8.4

*A photograph of an attentive student is digitized as a binary image with a dynamic range of 2. As the close-up shows, each pixel is either dark (0) or bright (1). Thus, the entire image may be represented by a single bitplane— one bit per pixel. The image was digitized using a process called **halftone screening.** As you can see from the close-up, different shades are simulated by patterns of dark and light pixels. At the proper scale, these appear as different shades of gray.*

Figure 8.5

The photograph in the previous figure is a digitized once more, but this time as a grayscale image with a dynamic range of 256 different shades of intensity from dark to light. In binary, 8 bits are needed to store this range. A close-up of the image reveals rectangular pixels of varying intensities. The isolated pixel (see the boxed pixel in the inset) has the intensity value of 72. The figure below the photo shows how many bitplanes would be encoded to represent this pixel value.

72 = 01001000

grayscale images also affects the amount of storage needed to represent them. Sixteen shades of intensity, for example, would require four bits per pixel, while eight bits per pixel would accommodate 256 intensity levels. The increase in dynamic range from four to eight bits per pixel would, of course, double the size of the image file. Thus, images having the same resolution could vary significantly in file size, depending on their depth. Figure 8.6 shows the same original image with different bit depths. Just as resolution has trade-offs, greater dynamic range yields greater fidelity while increasing demands on the storage, transmission, and processing time.

Figure 8.6
Home on the range—dynamic range, that is. A grayscale image is quantized at four different levels of dynamic range. In (a), the image has pixels in the highlights and shadows that span nearly the full range of 256 levels. In (b), this range has been compressed to only sixteen levels. Yet, to the naked eye, (b) appears only marginally different from (a). Compressing the range increases image contrast but also creates false shadows or contours. However, comparing the two shows that human vision is not very sensitive to a wide range of shades or intensity levels. In (c), the range is only 4 shades. Shadows are flattened, and false contouring is even more evident. Finally, (d) is a binary image that has a range of only 2 levels. In this instance, (d) is a simple binary image without the benefit of halftone screening. Notice how flat this image appears compared with the halftone screen illustrated in Figure 8.4.

(a)　　　　　　　　(b)

(c)　　　　　　　　(d)

Representing Color Images

Digitized color images have a variety of applications, too. Unlike grayscale images, though, each pixel in a color image contains a set of ordered values rather than a single number. The ordered set of values uniquely identifies a specific shade of a color or hue. Several systems are employed to represent color in digital images.

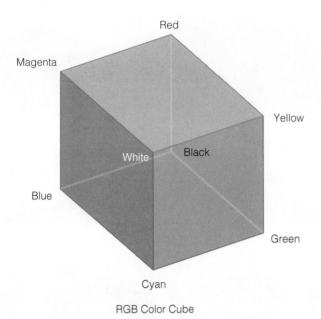

Red
Magenta
Yellow
White   Black
Yellow
Blue
Green
Cyan

RGB Color Cube

Figure 8.7

The range of mixtures based on the additive primaries of red, green, and blue can be plotted in a three-dimensional space. Each visible color maps to a point whose coordinates are measured on the red, green, and blue axes. At its origin (0, 0, 0), the point is black; at (1, 1, 1) the point is pure white. On the other hand, bright yellow would be (1, 1, 0). Theoretically, the color space forms a cube in which nearly all colors visible to the human eye may be plotted.

A very popular one is the **RGB color** system, which divides the color signal into three channels: red (R), green (G), and blue (B). A **channel** is a component of an image that may be manipulated separately, but that is combined with other components to constitute the complete image. The RGB system is based on combining additive primaries to produce color mixtures. Figure 8.7 depicts the RGB color space. As you can see, at its origin—when all three primaries have a value of 0—the point is black. On the other hand, when the primaries have maximum values, the resulting mixture appears as pure white. A mixture of (1, 0, 0) is pure red, (0, 1, 0) is pure green, and (0, 0, 1) is pure blue. The cube also reveals other major hues; for example, magenta is (1, 0, 1). The opposite of pure magenta is pure green. Note how magenta and green occupy opposite corners on the RGB color cube. Other color mixtures have similar relatives with RGB primaries, too. Understanding something about RGB color space does have practical consequences. For instance, to reduce the amount of magenta in an RGB color image, you could add or increase green values in it. We will return to these ideas later when we consider the process of color corrections.

The RGB method of representing color images is popular because it is very similar to the way in which color display devices work. The basic picture element in a color CRT is a trio of phosphors that appears to the naked eye as a single color spot. The red, green, and blue electron guns excite the phosphors, and the various combinations of intensities create the perception of a wide assortment of colors to the human eye. An RGB image represents the relative intensities of the three primary components for each pixel. Figure 8.8 illustrates how the RGB channels contribute to create the color image.

Another popular color system used primarily in print media is the **CMY color** system. This system is based on the subtractive primaries of cyan, magenta, and yellow as shown in Figure 8.9. These primaries are derived from mixing pigments. CMY color is more familiar because most of us have experience mixing paints to create color mixtures. No doubt you can remember elementary school art classes in which you mixed watercolors to produce different shades or hues. Figure 8.10 depicts the CMY color space. In contrast to RGB color, the origin for CMY (0, 0, 0) is achromatic white—that is, no color at all. When the primaries are mixed at maximum levels, the result is black. Mixing cyan with yellow, for example, produces green. The color cube also illustrates color opposites that can be employed to neutralize one another.

As mentioned, CMY images are useful for creating color separations in printing. In practice, however, a fourth channel, K, for black ink (K = blacK) is added to compensate for the problems normally encountered in mixing pigments. Consequently, actual color separations are based on four-channel **CMYK color** images.

Figure 8.8

The image (a) is a close-up of a crystal-clear cup filled with orange juice framed by sun-bleached columns and set against a deep blue sky. (Trust us on this!) This digital image is actually composed of three primary color channels: red (R), green (G), and blue (B). Each of the channels is shown separately so that you can see how much of the resulting colors are contributed by these individual primaries. The red channel (R) confirms two obvious points. There is a great deal of red energy in orange, but very little in the blue sky. (The juice is very bright, denoting high intensity in this channel; the sky is dark, signifying low intensity.) In stark contrast, the blue channel (B) reverses the relation: low energy for the juice but high intensity for the sky. The green channel (G) is much more balanced. In fact, it resembles closely the grayscale image of the same subject—as you can attest. This implies that the green channel conveys a lot of the significant intensity information in a color image for us—namely, highlights and detail.

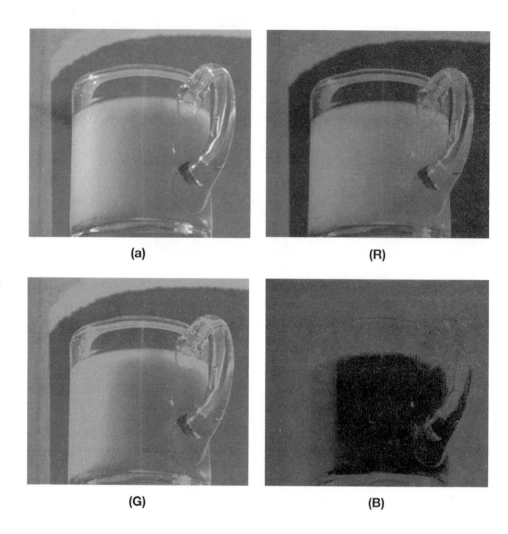

Figure 8.9

The familiar color mixtures derived from the primaries of cyan, magenta, and yellow. In CMY color, red, for example, is the mixture of magenta with yellow; while blue results from mixing the pigments of magenta with cyan.

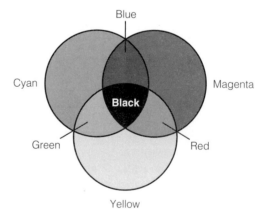

Artists and designers usually prefer a more intuitive scheme for representing color information. A subjective or perceptual characterization of color properties divides them into hues, brightness, and saturation. Hues represent the spectral colors and are usually arranged on a standard color wheel. Brightness is the relative lightness or darkness of the shade. You may think of it as a series of gray levels from the brightest white to black. Finally, saturation refers to the purity or strength of the hue. An unsaturated shade is devoid of hue (or achromatic); pastels are partially saturated; and bright, vivid colors are deeply saturated.

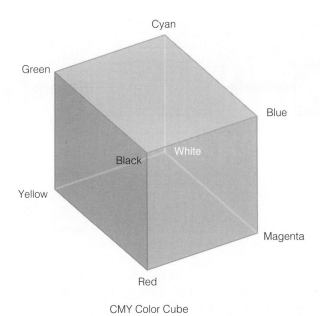

CMY Color Cube

Figure 8.10
The subtractive primaries of cyan, magenta, and yellow may also be plotted in a three-dimensional space. In this case, the origin (0, 0, 0) is pure white—signifying no color—and the limit (1, 1, 1) is black when all pigments are combined. CMY space forms a cube, but unlike RGB space, some points cannot be reproduced as a result of limitations in reproduction technologies.

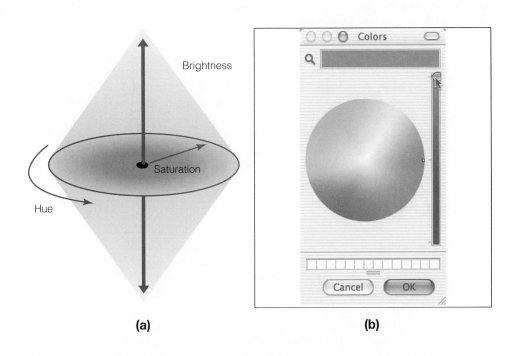

(a)   (b)

Figure 8.11
Hue, saturation, and brightness (HSB) color space is modeled here. In (a) the hues are measured as polar coordinates around a brightness scale. The position along the axis perpendicular to the brightness axis measures the amount of saturation (hue purity) for the shade. In (b), the HSB wheel is seen from overhead and how it would appear in an OS preference panel menu. Red (seen here) is plotted at 0°, for example. The sample is set to maximum values for both saturation and brightness.

Several systems can capture these qualities. The most common is the **HSB** (hue, saturation, brightness) **color** system. Again, a particular color is represented by an ordered set of three values. Hue is mapped in angular degrees on the color wheel (with primary red usually at 0°). Saturation and brightness are represented by integer values from 0 to some maximum value and denote an ascending scale for these qualities. Figure 8.11 illustrates how color is organized in the HSB system.

Storing Color Images on Computers

Most color systems represent and store digital color images as a composite of several channels. For example, a standard RGB image is composed of three channels; each primary channel stores pixel values with eight bits, yielding 256 distinct values. The result is a total of 24 bits

Figure 8.12
Data compression is typically achieved using an application that can both compress the original data and decompress it when needed.

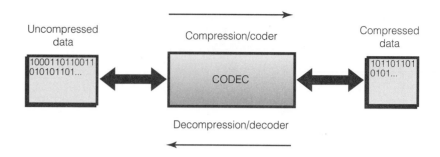

Uncompressed data

1000110110011 010101101...

Compression/coder

CODEC

Decompression/decoder

Compressed data

101101101 0101...

of color depth with an effective dynamic range of millions of potential color mixtures. (To be precise, 256 red values × 256 green values × 256 blue values = 16,777,216 unique color mixtures.) Images like these are often described as **24-bit color,** for short. These 24-bit color images have photorealistic quality but require a considerable amount of storage. For example, an 800 × 600 image at a color depth of 24 bits takes almost 1.4 MB to store. (800 × 600 = 480,000 pixels × 3 bytes per pixel = 1,440,000 bytes.)

Images are also stored using CMYK color for print applications. These images require four channels rather than three. Thus, a single pixel requires 32 bits—again assuming 8 bits per channel. The same 800 × 600 image would require almost 1.9 MB to store. (480,000 pixels × 4 bytes per pixel = 1,920,000 bytes.)

As you can imagine, the size of an image file grows rapidly with higher resolutions and greater color depths. For this reason, many image files are compressed for more efficient storage. Data compression, of course, refers to methods that replace a file containing binary codes with a more compact version. See Figure 8.12. Strictly speaking, a compressed image file is not really an image, but rather a file containing compressed binary data. Consequently, the file must be decoded or decompressed in order to be constructed and viewed as an image. Most applications combine these functions (compression and decompression) into a single program. They are often referred to as **codecs** (for <u>CO</u>mpression-<u>DEC</u>ompression).

Indexed Color

In contrast to composite methods, **indexed color images** reduce the image to a single channel that has a maximum depth of eight bits. Each pixel is assigned a number that corresponds to a specific color mixture stored on a palette called a **color lookup table**—or **CLUT.** Like paint-by-number kits, the encoding is a shorthand method for representing color information that ordinarily would take up a great deal more space. Because indexed color images are limited to 8 bits of depth, the maximum palette size is 256. This means that at most the image can display only 256 different shades of color. In practice, palettes may be reduced even more. As a result, indexed color images often sacrifice fidelity for savings in storage. A process called *dithering* can help to compensate for this shortcoming. **Dithered shades** are patterns of color that simulate transitional shades or hues. When viewed at normal scale, these patterns suggest colors or shades that are actually unavailable in the CLUT. Figure 8.13 illustrates how an indexed color image is organized.

Color palettes for indexed color images are often based on system colors (that is, designated by your computer's operating system). This is called the **system palette.** In the example in Figure 8.13, the color palette was created by sampling the original colors found in the digitized RGB image prior to reducing it to indexed color. This method of adapting to the original image produces what is called quite naturally an **adaptive palette.** Of course, it is possible to designate the colors for the palette from an arbitrary set as well. These so-called **custom palettes** are used to produce images that conform to desired effects. Indexed color images are good choices when there is a clear need for economy in size. Nondithered adaptive palette images generally look best. However, most desktop systems today have evolved well beyond 8-bit color, and the need for storing or transmitting an indexed color image is rare.

Figure 8.13
An indexed color image is composed of pixels from a limited group of colors. The close-up of the image reveals how color mixtures are simulated by dithering. Small patterns of the palette colors are used to create the illusion of color shades not supported by that palette. At normal scale, these patterns suggest missing shades. The actual color palette is shown below it (although not in color).

Reproducing Color on Computers

Perhaps you are reacting to the almost dizzying amount of detail about color and color images. The bottom line is that creating color on a computer system can be a frustrating experience without some knowledge of an assortment of factors involved and their treatments. You may have had the experience of creating an attractive color image on your monitor only to find it garish and ugly when printed on your color inkjet printer. In a related vein, you may have tweaked images for a Web page that look great on your system, but that look very different on another hardware platform. What gives? In general, reproducing accurate color depends primarily on the characteristics of the output device you plan to use. Rarely will your own computer video monitor serve as both the medium for creating the image and its ultimate output device as well. Consequently, you should ignore its origin and focus instead on how the image will be produced and used.

Reproducing Color for Print Devices

Digital color images on color video monitors are displayed using RGB colors, and digital color images produced on color print devices are based on CMYK colors—and never the twain shall meet. A number of factors contribute to their differences.

First, RGB and CMYK color spaces have different effective color ranges, called **color gamuts.** In other words, in practical circumstances, some colors that are reproducible in one color space are not reproducible in the other. For example, the CMYK color space cannot reproduce bright blue colors that are easily handled by RGB color. (Blue is a natural primary for RGB, but blues in CMYK are based on cyan.) On the other hand, RGB cannot reproduce bright oranges and metallic finishes as well as CMYK. Fortunately, you do not have to be a color theorist to recognize these differences in practical circumstances. Some image processing applications are equipped to warn you of differences in these color gamuts. In Figure 8.14, for example, the user has selected a particular RGB shade from a color selection tool. The color gamut alert—in the form of an exclamation point—warns the user that this color is not reproducible in the CMYK color space.

Figure 8.14
The color gamut warning in this application takes the form of an exclamation point next to the color swatch. In this instance, the shade of blue selected falls outside the range of reproducible CMYK shades.

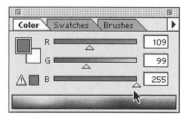

The difference in media is another factor to consider. RGB color images on video monitors use direct light to display the image. Printed images on paper use reflected light. The paper itself can also contribute significantly to how the reproduced image will look. Color inkjet and color laser printers deposit dots of ink on the paper. These dots are extremely small, but as the ink is absorbed in the paper, the pigment spreads and the effective area of the dot increases slightly. This is called **dot gain.** Different grades or qualities of paper have different dot gains. For example, newsprint has a very high dot gain; high-quality bonded paper has a lower gain. Different color inks behave differently, too. For example, black and cyan have slightly greater dot gain than yellow on the same medium.

Professionals must fuss with all of these details, but the bottom line for casual users is that you should not expect that the color image on your video monitor would look the same on a printed page.

Help is available to those who require more precision in specifying colors for printed media. The Pantone Matching System, for example, is used in the print industry as a standard for denoting ink colors. Using a set of numbered color swatches, you can pick the colors that you desire and specify them precisely using the Pantone numbers. Printers can likewise reproduce these colors accurately. Some image processing software also provide tools for employing Pantone colors when working with digital images. There are other customized systems for color matching as well.

Reproducing Color for Other Video Monitors

Not all monitors are created equal. Besides the screen size, resolution, dot pitch, and other assorted performance features, video monitors display brightness values at different settings. On a given monitor, the change in intensity values from dark to bright is not always linear. In other words, if you were to graph these changes, they would form a curve rather than a straight line. The term **gamma** refers to slope of the curve in the midtones and characterizes the overall brightness performance characteristics of a monitor. As a result, the gamma value for your monitor will affect the way color images are displayed. In short, color images on monitors with low gamma settings appear brighter compared to those with higher settings. Table 8.1 lists some standard gamma settings for popular models used for graphics and imaging.

Obviously, images prepared on a Macintosh, for example, will not look the same when viewed on a PC. On a PC, they will appear darker and usually have lower contrast. On the other hand, images prepared on a PC will look a great deal brighter on Silicon Graphics and Macintosh systems. Take these factors into account when you attempt to produce images for general use on other systems.

Some systems have software that allows you to modify or alter the gamma settings on your machine. You may alter or customize gamma settings using a procedure aptly called **gamma correction.** These custom settings can be saved and employed for producing images for cross-platform use.

Reproducing 8-bit and Indexed Color for the Web

Apart from gamma settings, indexed color images and graphics displayed in Web browsers can sometimes look different on different computer systems, too. For example, a color that looks fine on a Web page on one computer system may appear dithered on another system—even

Table 8.1 *The gamma settings for popular desktops and workstations.*

GAMMA SETTING FOR SELECTED SYSTEMS	
Model	**Gamma Standard**
Silicon Graphics	1.7
Macintosh	1.8
Sun Microsystems	2.5
PCs	2.5

Table 8.2 *The Netscape color palette uses only six possible color values. These are shown as both hexadecimal and decimal values.*

CONVERTING NETSCAPE HEX COLORS TO DECIMAL	
Hexadecimal Value	**Decimal Value**
00	000
33	051
66	102
99	153
CC	204
FF	255

when using the same browser software. This occurs because computer manufacturers employ different system color palettes. You will recall that a color palette is a list of approved RGB color mixtures that are employed for images displayed using 8-bit or indexed color.

Netscape has established a special color palette that has become an unofficial standard for displaying indexed and other 8-bit color schemes on Web pages. The palette is based on 6 shades each of red, green, and blue. Different mixtures of these shades of primaries produce a total of 216 different colors ($6 \times 6 \times 6 = 216$). The color scheme was obviously devised by programmers rather than designers. In fact, the palette is based on using uniform hexadecimal numbers to derive each color shade. The Netscape palette employs only six possible hexadecimal numbers: 00, 33, 66, 99, CC, and FF. See Table 8.2 for their decimal values. But, when written as hexadecimal numbers, the scheme is quite simple. A legal color is composed of some combination of three values from the list of permissible hex values. For example, black = #000000. Put another way, black is composed of R = 00, G = 00, and B = 00. At the other end of the spectrum, white = #FFFFFF. We saw earlier that gray is composed of equal measures of R, G, and B. Consequently, there are exactly four legal shades of gray in the Netscape palette. Can you derive them?

Any indexed color image or graphic derived from this palette will appear undithered on a Web page regardless of the hardware platform. Consequently, using the Netscape palette guarantees what is called *browser-safe* color. (The Netscape palette can be viewed in the online Digital Gallery.)

If you are not using indexed color, browser-safe colors are a moot point. Very few systems today employ 8-bit color exclusively. Most monitors are capable of handling thousands (16-bit) and even millions of color mixtures (24-bit). On the other hand, as personal digital assistants (PDAs), cell phones with cameras, and other digital appliances gain in popularity, the use of browser-safe colors will again become more important, since these devices currently can display only 8-bit color.

Digital Image Layers

Most image processing applications today permit the creation and manipulation of digital images composed of layers. A **digital image layer** (sometimes called an *object* or *floater*) is a component of an image that exists on a separate or discrete plane and can be edited or modified without affecting any other part of the image. For example, the picture in Figure 8.15 is actually composed of two separate layers. The image of the rubber duck is one component, while the text string "Ducky" is a distinct separate component. In a typical layered image there is usually one more layer called the **background layer** that underlies all visible layers of the image.

Layers typically have a distinct order. In Figure 8.15, the text layer lies on top of the duck image. This is why some of the pixels of the duck are covered or occluded by those of the text. The image of the duck sits on top and, in this instance, completely covers its background layer. Each layer can be edited separately, too. For instance, the text can be moved to a different position without affecting the pixels of the duck underneath it. If the text were part of the same layer as the duck image, then moving the text would leave an empty hole where the pixels were vacated. The hole would cause the background pixels to show through.

In reality, digital image layers are basically two-dimensional images. In a layered image, each layer has the same dimensions and resolution as the others. In the case of Figure 8.15, if the text and duck layers are the same dimensions, then, how is it possible for only the letters of the text layer to be visible while all the pixels of the duck layer seem to cover the background layer? To put it another way: how is it possible for some pixels to be visible and others seem transparent? The secret is what is called an **alpha channel.** In short, a separate channel is added to the image that instructs the computer how to mask parts of an image in order to create the layered effect.

Alpha Channels and Masks

The idea and name *alpha channel* is due to two computer graphics pioneers Alvy Ray Smith and Ed Catmull. Smith and Catmull are two of the founding partners for the graphics firm Pixar—the company that brought you *Toy Story* and *Monsters, Inc.* In the late 1970s, they developed the alpha channel to help solve some of the problems in creating efficient computer animations.

An animation—much like motion picture film—is composed of a sequence of still images called *frames* that is displayed at a rate that is fast enough to fool us into thinking that we are seeing real motion. Each of the frames in an animation portrays the moving objects

Figure 8.15
The image of the rubber duck is composed of three distinct layers. The text image floats on top of the duck image. The latter sits on top of a background image. The background is usually set to some single color (white or, perhaps, black). The background pixels show through when pixels from the upper layers are removed or made transparent.

as changing position in small increments. Much of the rest of the scene, however, does not change. Consequently, from frame to frame only a small portion of the computer-generated image may be different. This could mean a lot of work for both the computer artist and the machine that displays the animation. The artist would have to redraw each frame even though only a small portion of it has changed. The computer system would have to load, process, and display each individual, full-size image even though there is a great deal of redundancy among them.

To solve this problem, computer animators borrowed a technique from their predecessors. Traditional animated films are created by composing cels with backgrounds. **Animation cels** are transparent sheets on which the principal objects are drawn and painted. The backgrounds represent the portions of the image that change only gradually from frame to frame. Frames are then composed by photographing each cel on top of the background. Smith and Catmull reasoned that computer animations could be rendered more quickly if an image depicting an animated figure also contained information about what parts of the image are opaque and what parts are transparent—much like a cel.

The technique of separating opaque from transparent pixels is called **masking.** A digital transparency mask works something like the traditional technique of matting images. See Figure 8.16. Both the matte and the mask define what portions of the image are visible. The matte physically covers portions of the image rendering them invisible. The mask covers the area of the lower layer image that is considered transparent; all remaining pixels are considered visible.

An alpha channel is a separate channel added to the RGB image that serves as a digital mask. In Figure 8.17, we see the layered duck image once more. But, in this instance, the alpha channel is also shown. The black pixels denote the location of transparent pixels in the

Figure 8.16

The use of mattes is common for framing photos and pictures. In the example, an elliptical-shaped figure is cut from the matte board (top). The matte is then placed on top of the photograph. The result (below) appears to be a cropped image, but the photograph is not actually affected by the process. The matte, however, defines what parts of the image are visible and what parts are not.

text layer, while the white pixels signify the opaque ones. The transparency information is thus stored within the text layer image as an added channel. RGB color images become four channel images: **RGBA images,** or sometimes **RGB+Alpha images.**

A 1-bit channel could handle the transparency mask illustrated in Figure 8.17 easily. Pixel values of 0 would signify transparent pixels and 1s would denote opaque pixels. Most RGBA images, however, are 32-bit images. The alpha channel is represented by a single byte. A byte allows for 256 values (0 . . . 255). This range of values allows for expressing degrees of transparency. Black (or 0) still signifies 100% transparency and white (255) means 100% opacity, but intervening values indicate varying degrees of opacity or transparency. In Figure 8.18, we illustrate how this supports the creation of special effects.

Understanding alpha channels and how they work can be exploited in mastering image editing techniques. We will return to consider image editing later in the chapter. Next, we will survey how images are packaged for storage and transmission purposes.

Figure 8.17

The text layer image is superimposed on the image of the duck (a) using an alpha channel mask. The mask (b) contains black pixels that denote transparent pixels in the text layer, while the white pixels in the alpha channel locate the opaque pixels. When the two images are combined, the duck shows through where the text image is transparent.

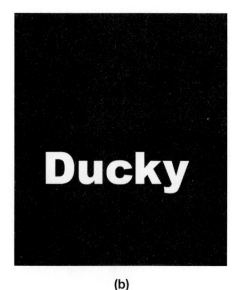

(a)

(b)

Figure 8.18

On the left is a mask that depicts degrees of transparency. The black denotes transparent pixels and the white opaque pixels, as before. But, the shades of gray indicate relative degrees of transparency. The resulting image on the right has a blurred or feathered effect that softens its borders.

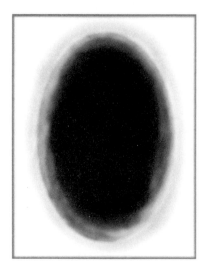

Storing Images

Digital images must be converted to files for both storage and transmission purposes. A number of file formats are available for storing digital images that were derived from natural or continuous tone images. The most common ones are TIFF, GIF, JPEG, PNG, PCD, along with BMP and WMF for Windows, and for Macintoshes, PICT. (In the next chapter, we will add to this list other formats, which are used primarily for artificial or computer graphics images.)

TIFF (for **tagged image file format**) is the most widely used bit-mapped image format for both publishing and information interchange. TIFF files normally store 24-bit RGB or CMYK color images. But TIFFs can support grayscale and indexed color images, too. Unfortunately, TIFF image files are not entirely portable between PCs and Macintoshes. The image data are arranged differently in the file, so that opening a PC TIFF file on a Macintosh produces a jumbled picture (and vice-versa). Some image processing programs have utilities called *filters* that can interpret diverse file formats and convert them to others. At any rate, TIFF files must be converted when transporting them from one platform to another. TIFF files support optional built-in compression, too. Compression, you will recall, reduces the size of the file by encoding it to reduce redundant information. When you save an image as a TIFF, you may choose whether it is stored in a compressed or uncompressed form. (Chapter 20 takes up the topic of compression techniques for a variety of media.)

GIF (**graphic interchange format**) was developed by CompuServe expressly for transmission of images and graphics over networks. GIF files are based on indexed color, and thus they are generally more compact than full-color image files because they limit the number of possible colors or shades of gray that the image can portray. We learned that 24-bit RGB color images, for instance, represent each pixel with 3 bytes of data: an 8-bit number for each color channel. In contrast, a GIF file stores an image based on a single 8-bit channel that indexes only up to 256 possible colors in a table. GIF files are reduced even more by automatic compression. GIFs are consequently popular for data transmission applications. On the Web, for example, many images are stored and transmitted as GIF files. The compromises in dynamic range and color gamut rule out GIF files for other professional applications, though.

A special subclass of GIF images offers features that are also very popular for Web publishing: transparency and interlacing. A **transparent GIF** is an image whose background is rendered invisible by masking. Thus, transparent GIFs can contain irregularly shaped objects that can be superimposed on the background of Web pages. Transparent GIFs, however, work much like 1-bit transparency masks, so the effects are less subtle than those achieved by images with (8-bit) alpha channels. (In practice, a single color from the potential 256-color palette is designated as the masking color.) An **interlaced GIF** is an image that is transmitted progressively. On a Web page, an interlaced image appears quickly but in a coarse or low resolution; at first, the pixels appear very large and blocky. In successive steps, these are replaced by better resolutions until the image is displayed at full resolution. Interlaced GIF files are usually a little larger than non-interlaced forms, though. Both transparency and interlacing are options that may be invoked when storing an image as a GIF file.

JPEG (**Joint Photographic Experts Group**) is actually a set of standards for image compression. These standards have been widely accepted across the industry, and files that adhere to them are simply known as JPEG files. Unlike the image compression used in the previously discussed formats, JPEG files are based on lossy compression methods. **Lossy** compression means that when the image is decompressed—that is, decoded and restored for viewing—there is some data loss from the original. The amount and extent of this loss can be controlled. Usually it is not noticeable to the untrained eye. Nonetheless, JPEG files achieve their high rates of reduction at some cost to the original image. Whereas GIF files are commonly used for graphics on Web pages, JPEG files are a popular format for 24-bit, full-color images on these pages.

Because of data loss, however, JPEG is not recommended for archiving image files. In other words, the original image should be saved as a TIFF, perhaps, and then converted to a JPEG file for posting on a Web page.

PNG (**portable network graphics**), pronounced *ping,* was developed by Thomas Boutell as a second-generation file format for Web images and graphics. As the new kid on the block, the PNG file format attempts to "correct" the faults and foibles of its predecessors, GIF and JPEG. Like GIFs, PNG images may employ transparency. But unlike GIFs, PNGs offer full 8-bit transparency. PNG images can be stored in several color depths as well. You may choose 8-bit color, like GIFs; 24-bit color, like JPEGs; and even 30-bit color. PNG images may be compressed or uncompressed. Unlike JPEGs, though, the PNG format offers lossless compression versions.

PCD (for Kodak **photo CD**) are stored in a compressed form on a CD. Many photofinishing stores can develop your 35-mm film and convert the images into PCD format. The scanning is usually high quality, and the service is relatively inexpensive compared with the cost of digitizing images yourself. The Kodak Photo CD comes in two versions: the regular (or consumer) and Pro editions. Each image on the regular edition CD comes in five different resolutions and, therefore, five different file sizes. The smallest is 128×192 pixels for thumbnail sketches; the largest is a high-resolution format of 2048×3072 pixels for prints up to 7×10 inches. Pro Photo CDs have an additional very high-resolution format of 4096×6144 pixels. PCD image files are compressed and employ lossy compression like JPEG, but PCD compression usually preserves higher image quality with less data loss. On the other hand, PCD files do compress as efficiently as JPEG formats.

PCD should not be confused with Kodak Picture CD. The latter format is based actually on the JPEG standards and has a maximum resolution of 1536×1024. A single roll of 35-mm film is digitized and stored on one CD.

Both Windows and Macintoshes have their own image file formats. **BMP** is the venerable Windows bit-mapped image format used in painting and graphics. **WMF** is a Windows **metafile format,** which means that WMF files can actually contain a variety of types including bit-mapped images. **PICT,** for *picture,* has long been the standard format for graphic images on the Macintosh. PICT is also a metafile format. PICT images may optionally incorporate JPEG compression. PICT graphics, however, are best restricted for use as on-screen displays and interchanging between Macintosh applications.

These are just a few of the many different file formats that may be employed to store digitized images. To use images effectively in a variety of applications such as printed documents, Web pages, and multimedia, you must choose the appropriate file format for each. Unfortunately, no single file format serves all purposes. Image processing programs, however, can be employed for converting a file from one format to another quickly and easily.

Digitizing Images

As stated earlier, this chapter is concerned primarily with digital images that were acquired from natural or analog sources. Today, in the realm of desktop computing there are two popular choices for creating such digital images: scanners and digital image cameras.

Scanners come in an assortment of shapes and functions. At the high end, **drum scanners** digitize a variety of sources at very high resolutions. **Photo** and **slide scanners** are designed to work with photography prints, negatives, and 35-mm slides. At the low end, **handheld scanners** are good for quick-and-dirty tasks such as capturing text. The **flatbed scanner** is the most common consumer model. Built like a small desktop copier, it is used to scan digital images from photographs, drawings, and illustrations. In the process of scanning, it is possible to determine the size, resolution, and type of digital image (e.g., color, grayscale, etc.), and file format that you desire. (We will return to consider some of the technology involved in scanners later in Chapter 13.) Scanners, of course, do require that you start with a suitable analog source, though.

Digital cameras, on the other hand, bypass the need for the intermediate step of using analog photographs; for this reason, they are often dubbed "filmless" cameras. Because it is a camera, however, it is normally used to capture natural scenes rather than digitizing a variety of analog visual media. Digital cameras offer a variety of resolutions, but are generally limited in the choice of file formats for storing images compared with scanners. On the other hand, digital cameras boast higher resolutions. Consumer models today are measured in "megapixels;" resolutions of 1600×1200, 2048×1536, and higher are common.

Images with resolutions like these take up a great deal of memory. Consequently, digital cameras typically employ data compression for the storage and transfer of image files. Lossy JPEG compression is common.

Processing Images in the Digital Domain

In the process of image capture, a sensor samples properties of the scene, and a digital encoder converts these samples into discrete values that make up the digital image. Capturing an image always involves some approximation—even in the analog domain. For example, a camera is usually unable to reproduce the entire dynamic range of light intensities or hues in a natural scene. Instead, it compresses these to a representative range of intensities by sampling and approximating. This process of selection is called **filtering** and can often be controlled by the photographer's choice of film, exposures, and development techniques.

Digital images may also be processed by filtering. The difference, however, is that digital filtering can be controlled by a computer. The results are much more precise, predictable, and efficient. Because pixels are sets of numbers, digital filtering involves manipulating and transforming these values as defined by a **digital filtering function.** Specifically, the original image is combined with a mathematical function to produce a new filtered image. See Figure 8.19. The filtered image can be saved as a separate file for its intended use. And, because the original image is unaltered by the filtering process, we may retain the original for other uses.

There are two classes of filters: global and local. A **global filter** is one that transforms each and every pixel uniformly according to its filtering function regardless of its location and surroundings in the image. For example, adjusting the overall tonal qualities of an image, such as lightness and darkness, is global filtering. If you wish to lighten it, then the entire image is uniformly affected. On the other hand, a **local filter** examines the entire image but transforms a pixel in relation to its surrounding neighbors in the image. For example, sharpening the edges of objects in an image is local or spatial filtering. Enhancing details in the image depends, of course, on where they are located.

Global Filtering

A number of useful digital image processing techniques involve global filtering. We will examine some of the more important forms. Seeing how these processes work will enable you to use them more effectively in your own applications.

Original image

Digital filter

Filtered image

Figure 8.19
Digital filtering transforms the original image, producing a filtered output image. Each pixel in the original image is processed by a filter; the resulting value is stored in the same pixel location for the output image. The filter is based on a mathematical operation on numeric values of the image pixels. One advantage of digital filtering is that the filtered image can be saved as a separate file, thus preserving the original for reuse in other applications.

DISCOVERING MORE

Digitizing Images

Whether you choose digital cameras or scanners to create your own digital images, there are a dizzying number of options available to choose from. Our online resource

"Discovering More About Digitizing Images" offers some practical advice and instruction on how to make the right choices to suit your needs.

Figure 8.20 illustrates a black-and-white image with different brightness and contrast values. **Brightness** refers to the overall intensity of the pixels in the image. Sometimes an image can be improved by either lightening or darkening it. A grayscale or black-and-white image, for example, may be lightened or darkened by simply adding or subtracting intensity values from each pixel.

Contrast is the relative difference between the distributions of lighter and darker pixels in an image. Controlling the contrast in the image is similar to brightness control, although a little more complicated. Contrast is increased when the midtones in an image are redistributed toward the two extremes. In other words, a higher-contrast image has mostly light- and dark-intensity pixels with fewer midtone values.

Figure 8.20

Washington on Mount Rushmore is pictured. Several filters are applied to a simple grayscale image in (a) to illustrate brightness and contrast filtering. The original (a) is lightened in (b) and darkened in (c). The image (d) exhibits higher contrast, whereas (e) has very low contrast.

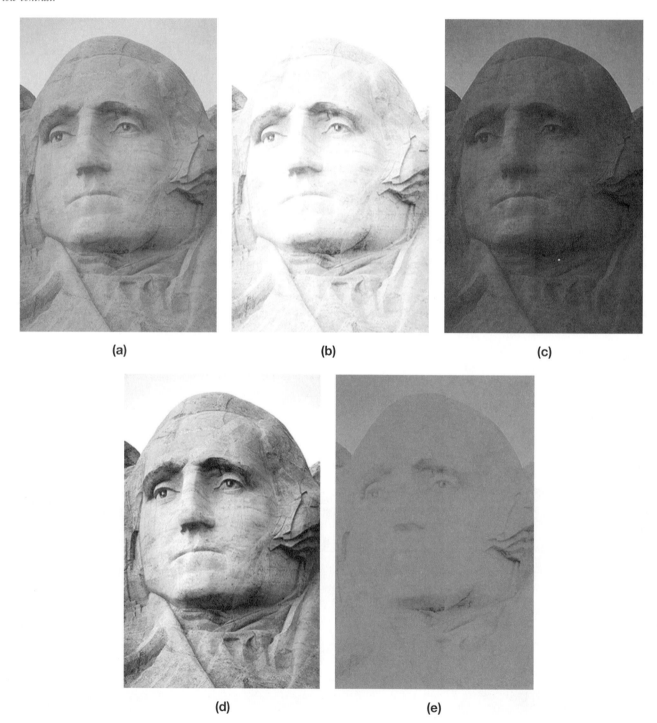

(a)   (b)   (c)

(d)   (e)

Because a digital image is represented by numeric pixel values, it is a simple matter to filter an image producing its "negative" by reversing its scale. This process is called **inversion.** This is often useful to highlight details of an image that would otherwise be difficult to read, as illustrated in Figure 8.21. Likewise, color negatives can be inverted just as easily. A color negative digitized from a film scanner can be quickly inverted as a normal color image without the need to produce a photographic print and then digitize it. (Consult the online Digital Gallery for examples.) Many newspapers and magazines use this timesaving technique for preparing photographic images for press.

As you can see, the global filters discussed so far involve directly modifying the intensity values of an image or color channel in that image. Just as intensity values may be redistributed in a digital image, it is also possible to alter the hues of an image. For example, the hue value for each pixel can be calculated from its RGB components. Given a hue value, it is easy to add or subtract some constant from it. The technique is called **hue-shifting** and is used to modify the color makeup of the image. Usually, this is done only for selected areas of an image and can produce color corrections, balancing, or sometimes dramatic (bizarre) effects—depending on the extent of change and the original image, of course. (Again, consult the online Digital Gallery for an example of hue-shifting.)

Grayscale images can also be transformed by a related operation called **pseudocoloring.** In this process, instead of hues, gray tones are mapped to distinct colors that are selected to produce sharp color contrasts. Satellite and medical imaging use pseudocoloring to produce images that are easier to interpret. (The online Digital Gallery illustrates how pseudocoloring improves our ability to discern details and features of interest.)

Sometimes the original image has too much information to be reproduced effectively by some output process. For example, a color inkjet printer may not accurately reproduce a color image that has millions of colors. **Posterizing** can reduce the complexity of both color and grayscale images by mapping similar tones to a select, smaller number of levels. Posterizing can also be employed as a means for producing indexed color images with a small number of shades and colors.

(a)

(b)

Figure 8.21
The typed text box (a) is inverted (b) for a more dramatic effect.

DISCOVERING MORE

Global Filtering

There is a lot more to see and learn about processing digital images using global filtering. Consult our online resource "Discovering More About Global Filtering" for techniques such as using intensity curves for adjusting brightness and contrast, histograms, and color correction using channels.

Local Filtering

A number of useful local filtering operations can improve and enhance, or simply modify, images to produce desired effects. We will survey the most common types, explaining how they work and examining their uses.

Adjusting the contrast in an image can sometimes improve the visibility of details in the image. Another method to achieve this end is called **sharpening,** which accentuates pixels that are situated at boundaries between lighter and darker tones. Thus, a greater contrast is induced, but only at the boundaries between differing regions in the image. A number of standard sharpening filters are available. Figure 8.22 illustrates the effects of sharpening.

Noise in a digital image refers to pixels whose variation or difference from their surroundings is unexpected and unexplainable. In the imaging process, noise is injected into the original signal in a number of ways; for example, it is contributed by electronic components, poor sampling rates, artifacts of the sensor, and so on. One way in which the effects of noise can be minimized is by blurring the image. **Blurring** is the opposite of sharpening in that the contrast between neighboring pixels is reduced; boundaries are smeared or softened. The images in Figure 8.23 illustrate the effects of alternately applying sharpening and blurring to a given image.

A **Gaussian filter** is a special case of a blurring filter and standard equipment for most image processing application programs. The filter is based on the bell-shaped Gaussian curve, which describes a normal distribution for some population; the curve is useful for plotting a variety of natural phenomena. Most of you are probably familiar with its use for normalizing test grades. When applied to an image, its effect is to soften or blur the image by blending the pixels in a neighborhood defined by its radius. The greater the radius, the greater the effect. Consider the images in Figure 8.24. The same original image is blurred using Gaussian filters with different radius values. As you can attest, the results range from a feathering effect to extreme myopia.

Unsharp masking is a related operation because it typically uses the results of Gaussian filtering to sharpen the image, rather than blur it. How can this be? The sharpening is the result of a two-stage process called *image differencing*. First, the image is blurred using a Gaussian (or, perhaps, another blurring) filter. The blurred (or "unsharp") output image is used as a mask and is subtracted from the original image. The resulting image retains fine detail while improving contrast.

There are times when we are interested in isolating the objects portrayed in an image. One way of doing this is to find the boundaries between regions in the image. The boundaries usually denote where one object ends and another begins. Finding boundaries in an image is called *edge detection*. An **edge element** is a sharp distinction in either color or intensity between two adjacent pixels. An **edge** is a collection of contiguous edge elements that form a line or contour. Extracting or enhancing edges then can often highlight objects in the foreground

Figure 8.22

The image (a) shows red lettering on a variety of background colors. After sharpening (and some brightening for better viewing), you may notice the etching or halo effect around some of the numbers in (b). This is because sharpening enhances or increases the differences that mark the boundaries between objects.

(a)　　　　　　　　　　　　　　　(b)

from their background. Edge detection is a very common technique in image processing because it contributes to a variety of practical applications—for example, labeling and measuring regions of interest in an image, identifying objects, eliminating unnecessary image components, and so on.

Edge detection filters are similar to sharpening filters in that they strengthen the values of pixels in areas of sharp difference or contrast. Usually an edge detector subtracts out the rest of the image, leaving only the edge lines and contours visible. Figure 8.25 illustrates.

Normally noise is misinformation, but noise is not always a bad thing. For instance, you may wish to add a gritty texture to an image. It is possible to simulate the effects of noise by

(a)　　　(b)

(c)

Figure 8.23
The original image (a) is filtered using an averaging filter followed by a sharpening filter. An averaging filter is employed to blur or soften the details in image; the result is shown in (b). The sharpening filter, again, accentuates boundaries between regions in the image, as shown in (c). Notice the halo effect around the edges of the flower where the boundaries have been sharpened.

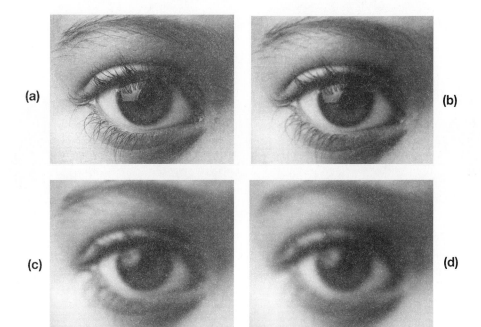

(a)　　　(b)
(c)　　　(d)

Figure 8.24
Pictured here are the results of applying Gaussian blurring. The original image (a) is blurred at three different settings. The image (b) has been blurred with a minimal radius setting of 1.0. As you can see, details in the image are smoothed. Note the differences between (a) and (b) around the eyebrows and the highlights on the eye. The remaining images are blurred even more. The image (c) is blurred at a radius of 2.0; shadows are smudged and details are reduced even more. Finally, in (d), the radius is set to 5.0. The eyelashes are no longer visible and the eyebrows are reduced to shadows.

approximating random digital noise. To add noise to an image, pixels in the original image are arbitrarily selected and modified. The extent of the effect depends on both the maximum amount of change allowed and its method of distribution.

There are two types of noise filters. With a **uniform noise filter,** each original pixel in a given area has an equal probability of being altered absolutely; for example, colors may change quite sharply as a result of a random selection. In contrast, a **Gaussian noise filter** induces noise into an image using the normalized distribution of values found within a local area of that image. In other words, the colors or intensities are modified based on their differences with values in that area. Uniform noise filters add "spot" or "speckle" noise effects that are closer to what we normally consider random noise. Gaussian noise filters produce a grainy effect that is more pronounced because they consider the structure of the image in perturbing it. Compare the results in Figure 8.26.

Figure 8.25
The photo of the colored blocks (a) is subjected to a simple edge detection filter. The resulting output image (b) is thresholded and inverted here for printing. In it, we can see the location of the edges or boundaries for objects in the image. Because edge detectors are attuned to local variations in the image, they also pick up texture and noise as well the object boundaries.

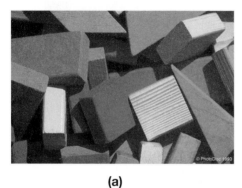
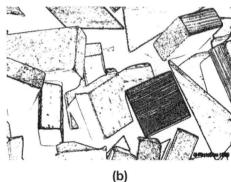

(a)   (b)

Figure 8.26
The image of the eye from 8.23(a) is filtered to add noise artificially. Uniform additive noise, as shown in (a), alters randomly selected pixels with randomly selected values. Even though the filter is set to the same value, the effects of Gaussian additive noise are more pronounced in (b).

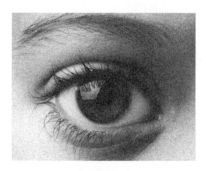
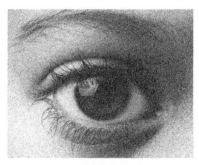

(a)   (b)

DISCOVERING MORE

Local Filtering

You can learn more about how to construct and employ local filters using digital spatial masks in our online resource "Discovering More About Local Filtering." We also explore the use of additional local filters for creating special effects in our images.

Editing Digital Images

Filtering affects the overall tonal quality of images, but we often want to process the content of images in specific ways. In other words, our goal is to edit an image just as we might edit a text document for content and style. Fortunately, most desktop image processing software offers a variety of editing tools that make such tasks easier. We will survey some of the basic tools and techniques for editing digital images.

Before you can modify a portion of an image, you must select the area to be modified. This is analogous to other computing applications. For instance, in text processing, to edit a block of text, you must first select that block. In image processing, **selection** means to identify the area of the image precisely—that is, the pixels that make up that area. Most imaging applications allow you to define the selected area by creating an outline surrounding it. Selection tools make the task easier by providing automatic outlines of various shapes. For example, a rectangular tool allows you to select square or rectangular areas of the image. This, of course, would include all pixels within that area. Circular tools are similar. A free-form tool accommodates irregularly shaped selections, but it also selects any background elements inside as well. For finer selections, some additional options are usually available. A surround tool permits you to identify the edges or boundary of a distinct object against its background. A segmentation tool is used to select a contiguous area in which all the pixels have the same characteristics. Drawing a path is the most flexible. A path is a closed figure composed of connected lines, curves, and points. Examples of each of these categories are shown in Figure 8.27.

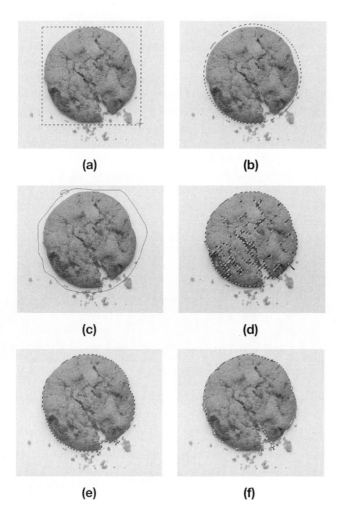

(a) (b)

(c) (d)

(e) (f)

Figure 8.27
There are a number of methods for selecting an area of an image for editing or processing. Some are quick and dirty; others are more precise. The rectangular (a), circular (b), and free-form (c) selections are convenient but capture an object along with its surroundings. Segmentation (d) and surround (e) selections are based on isolating an object from its background by either similarities or differences. Finally, drawing arbitrary paths (f) can also be employed to create a masking selection.

The goal of selection, of course, is to edit or modify a specific area of the image to produce some desired effect. The selected area is also called an *image mask.* The terminology is derived from a standard method employed by artists. An artist might wish to color a specific portion of an image without affecting the rest of it. The conventional technique of masking involves placing a clear vellum sheet over the picture and using a knife to cut out a shape that corresponds to the area that will be retouched. The sheet acts as a mask that protects the rest of the image while the cutout portion can be repainted or colored. Digital masks work the same way. Once you have selected an area for editing, any changes or modifications to the image will take place only in the active area; the rest of the image is unaffected.

Normally, selections are temporary; they persist only as long as the selected area is active. Some image processing applications allow you to save or store your selections. These may be reinstated when needed. This feature can be very useful—especially when the selected areas have irregular or complicated shapes. The technique of selection is fundamental for effective image editing. It is a skill that depends on some basic know-how but is developed only with practice.

Natural images are often too natural: They show us in all our native glory—blemishes and all. In contrast, the world of desktop image processing can be just about whatever you desire.

Photographers, of course, have known about retouching photographs for over a century. **Retouching** is the selective modification or editing of the content of an image. Usually retouching involves adding, deleting, or altering objects in the image. For digital images, however, retouching is much more precise and predictable. We will inspect two general categories: painting and cloning methods. The actual range of retouching methods available will depend entirely on the application software consulted.

One way that a photograph can be altered is to draw or paint over it. In computerese, this form of image editing is called, not surprisingly, **painting.** The tools that you employ to paint are based entirely on this metaphor. A brush tool permits you to apply a selected pattern over an area, much like brush strokes. A pencil tool does the same, but produces thinner lines. An airbrush tool works much like the standard brush except that the boundaries are softened or smudged. An area-fill tool applies the pattern or color to an entire selected area. Keep in mind that these tools can add colors and patterns to an image.

In text processing, we saw that it was possible to copy and paste a particular selection to another area of the document. We can do the same in digital images. **Cloning** is the method whereby a selected area of an image is duplicated and pasted as many times as we desire to any image. Some applications make this simpler by way of cloning tools that allow you to repeatedly paste a pattern throughout. Figure 8.28 illustrates how cloning can be used to repair an area of an image where an object was deleted. Even if cloning tools are not available, judicious applications of the standard copy-and-paste technique will work as well.

Another editing technique, and a close cousin to retouching, is **image compositing.** An image composite combines components from two or more images into a single, seamless image. The basic idea is a simple one: Select the portions of the images that you wish to

DISCOVERING MORE

Digital Image Editing

Selection and editing techniques are illustrated in our online resource "Discovering More About Digital Image Editing."

combine and paste them together as needed. Many of the special effects seen in motion picture films, for example, have been produced using digital image compositing methods. Creating effective image composites can be a difficult and time-consuming process. The current generation of image processing applications, however, has made this work a great deal easier by the implementation of image layering. An image layer, you will recall, is a separate image channel that ordinarily contains an object that can be manipulated separately from the background scene.

(a)

Figure 8.28
Now you see it; now you don't. The brightly colored balloons are the chief feature of the original photograph (a). But if we wish to focus the viewer on the children, we can eliminate the balloons and retouch the digital image. First, the balloons and strings are masked and removed from the original image, as shown in (b). Sections of the surrounding tree are cloned to fill in the blank area. The result (c) would fool all but the expert eye.

(b)

(c)

Is Seeing Believing?

Even though photography is just over 150 years old, we have come to accept it as a special medium for representing information. Recently, however, the advances in digital image processing have fundamentally changed the medium of photography and our perception of it. This essay explores some of the ways photography and particularly photojournalism have been affected by their transfer to the digital domain.

SOCIAL THEMES

■ Summary

Digital images are pictures that are sampled and quantized for storing on and processing by a computer system. A digital image is composed of pixels that are defined by a two-dimensional location in the image and a set of values that denote image attributes such as intensity or color. Picture resolution is the number of pixels that compose the digital image.

Images can be binary, grayscale, or color. Several popular systems are used for representing color in digital images. Many digital images are composed of separate layers; each layer can be treated separately. Alpha channels are typically employed to store information about transparency and opacity of pixels in image layers. A file format acts as a container for a digital image. There are numerous file formats, and few are compatible. The same image can be stored in different file formats, yet one file may be unusable on a particular system or with a specific application. It is important to save images using the appropriate file format.

Digital images may be processed using digital filters; these are mathematical functions that transform the numeric values of pixels and their distribution in the image. Global filtering modifies the image uniformly by adjusting each and every pixel according to its filtering function regardless of the location of the pixel. Local filtering, in contrast, transforms a pixel based on its relation to neighboring pixels in the vicinity.

Editing a digital image involves modifying a portion of the image. Like other digital methods, image editing is based on properly selecting image components: the area of pixels that requires editing. Retouching takes two basic forms, painting and cloning. Image compositing is another useful editing technique.

In this chapter, we have examined how digital images are created, stored, and processed. The real power and flexibility of desktop image processing are only suggested here. Armed with the basic concepts presented, you will be able to explore such applications and learn to exploit their capabilities for your own uses.

■ Terms

24-bit color	dot gain	lossy compression
adaptive palette	drum scanner	mask, masking
alpha channel	dynamic range	metafile format
animation cels	edge detection filters	noise
aspect ratio	edge, edge element	painting
background layer	filtering	PCD
binary image	flatbed scanner	photo/slide scanner
bitplanes	gamma	PICT
blurring	gamma correction	picture resolution
BMP	Gaussian filter	pixel
brightness	Gaussian noise filter	PNG
channel	GIF	posterizing
cloning	global filter	pseudocoloring
CLUT (color lookup table)	grayscale image	retouching
CMY color	halftone screening	RGB color
CMYK color	handheld scanner	RGBA images (RGB+Alpha)
codecs	HSB color	selection
color gamuts	hue-shifting	sharpening
contrast	image	system palette
custom palette	image compositing	TIFF
digital camera	indexed color image	transparent GIF
digital filtering function	interlaced GIF	uniform noise filter
digital image	inversion	unsharp masking
digital image layer	JPEG	WMF
dithered shades	local filter	

■ Questions for Review

1. What is the chief difference between natural digital images and graphics?

2. What is a pixel?

3. How is picture resolution related to the quality, size, and storage requirements of a digital image?

4. Knowing the aspect ratio of an image is important for what ordinary imaging task?

5. How is dynamic range related to the quality, size, and storage requirements of a digital image?

6. Distinguish between the various categories of digital images: binary, grayscale, and color.

7. Compare and contrast the different color models employed for representing and storing color images: RGB, HSB, and CMYK. What are the chief uses for each?

8. What are the four legal shades of gray allowed by the Netscape $6 \times 6 \times 6$ palette? Express them as hexadecimal values.

9. What is an image layer? Explain the advantages of using layering in an image.

10. What is a transparency mask? How are alpha channels a generalization of masks?

11. What is the difference between a digital image and its file type? Review the basic image file types. What are the basic uses or applications for each file format?

12. Scanners and digital cameras are common sources for digitizing images. What are the strengths and limitations of each?

13. What is digital filtering? What is the chief difference between global and local digital filtering?

14. What is the difference between brightness and contrast control?

15. What is pseudocoloring? What are its advantages?

16. Compare and contrast blurring and sharpening operations. How are they local operations (as opposed to global filtering)? How do they differ?

17. What is edge detection? What are its uses or applications?

18. Review some of the tools that can be used for image selection. Which methods yield the best (most precise) results?

19. How do painting and retouching an image differ from filtering processes (global and local)?

20. What is image compositing?

21. Given what you have learned about digital image processing, would it be reasonable to presume that photographs are reliable sources of evidence?

Chapter

$\bigcirc$
9

Making Pictures with Computers

OBJECTIVES

- How the computer creates, stores, and displays images

- How painting programs allow the user to control graphic primitives

- The features that are found in drawing and illustration programs

- How software helps to automate creating images with 3-D projections and animation

In the preceding chapter, we examined how images and photographs can be converted to the digital domain. This chapter continues our survey of digital imaging, but from a different perspective: the power of the modern computer system to create images on its own.

There can be little doubt that we are a species dominated by vision. Only about 10 percent of what we learn is based on audible information, while more than 80 percent is derived from visual information. Not only are we visual-centric creatures, we are also strongly biased toward pictorial information as well. Archaeological evidence testifies that our ancestors were creating illustrations and cave paintings long before they were writing language. Our children learn from pictures much earlier than they learn to read. Indeed, studies have shown that for adults, pictorial information is easier to absorb and is retained much longer than verbal. Depending on pictorial representation is not a mark of illiteracy either. Scientists and mathematicians have often documented the importance of pictures and images for discovering and understanding important concepts. For that matter, the higher one climbs up the corporate ladder,

168

the greater the likelihood that decisions will be derived from data depicted in graphs, charts, and tables.

It should be no surprise then that efforts at representing information pictorially with computers occurred very early in the history of computing. These early attempts at exploiting the graphic capabilities of computers were extremely primitive by today's standards, but they did pave the way for the wealth of tools, features, and applications that we now take for granted. Computer-generated imagery, or computer graphics, has contributed richly to the ways in which we employ computers for both work and play. In this chapter, you will learn more about how the computer can be exploited to create, store, and deliver images and illustrations for a variety of uses.

Creating Digital Images

In the last chapter, a digital image was defined as a picture that can be stored in, displayed on, and processed by a computer system. You learned that there were two general classes of digital images: natural and artificial. Natural digital images are typically digitized from analog sources such as photographs, video, X-ray tomography, satellite sensors, and so on. In this chapter, we will focus on the second category of digital images, computer-generated imagery or computer graphics. **Computer graphics** (or **graphics,** for short) refers to digital images that are artificial in that they are created exclusively by computer processes. Computer graphics is integral to most of the ways in which we employ our computers. For example, most of us operate our computer using graphical user interfaces (GUIs). These interfaces naturally depend on graphic images that are displayed on our video monitors. The icons, windows, pointers, gadgets—and even text—populating our screens are all composed and managed by graphic processing. It should be no surprise then that using a computer to generate graphic images has a rich tradition.

History of Computer Graphics

The first electronic computing devices produced output on paper and punched cards. These media were used primarily for text and numeric data. In the early 1950s, computers were programmed to display images only as a hobby or recreation for their programmers. The first graphic output devices were oscilloscopes, devices commonly used for visualizing electrical signals. In England, for example, the Mark I computer at Manchester University was programmed to play checkers and display the game pictorially on a screen.

The Whirlwind project in the 1950s at the Massachusetts Institute of Technology (MIT) was the first attempt to employ graphic imaging for serious use and as an integral part of its computer system. The U.S. Navy had contracted the MIT team, headed by Jay W. Forrester, to design and build a computer that (among other uses) would control an in-flight trainer for its pilots. To work in this capacity, the system had to respond appropriately to conditions in real time. As a result, the Whirlwind computer became the first device designed for real-time computing. (*Real-time computing* refers to processing that occurs in actual or real time. In other words, input data is generated from events happening currently, and the processing results are often employed as feedback to control the system.)

Eventually, the Navy lost interest in the flight trainer, but Forrester and his colleagues persuaded the Air Force to fund the Whirlwind as a prototype for an early warning defense system. This application also exploited its real-time computing powers. Specifically, the Whirlwind would be used to process radar telemetry from several stations and inform a human operator as to the whereabouts of aircraft in the area using graphic images. Screen displays of radar images had been used before, of course. The trick in this instance was to create a system that could process information from several stations and portray it in a manner that would be useful to the human operator at the controls.

The computer used a CRT screen to display a map of the area and automatically converted radar data to points plotted on the map that showed their geographic positions. The system was also interactive. The operator could use a light pen to point to any objects depicted on the screen. The computer would sense the light source and identify the object. Additional information about speed and direction would then be displayed. The light pen could likewise be used to target objects and request Whirlwind to calculate interception courses. The prototype was demonstrated in 1951. The project was eventually converted to production in 1958 as the SAGE (Semi-Automatic Ground Environment) defense system. SAGE computers were part of the Air Force's defense systems even into the 1980s. See Figure 9.1.

Combining graphics with interactive computing was explored by another MIT researcher, Ivan Sutherland. Sutherland developed the first interactive drawing program, SketchPad, in 1962. The user sitting at the console's CRT display, armed with a light pen and a small box studded with push buttons, could draw simple shapes on the screen. Sutherland had conceived SketchPad as a tool for engineers. SketchPad eclipsed other efforts at drawing with computers because it added the power to manipulate the figures after they were drawn. Not only could the user create simple shapes such as lines, polygons, and arcs, but drawn objects could be moved, rotated, enlarged, or reduced on the screen.

General Motors developed a graphical application specifically for aiding the design of automobiles. This was the first graphical **computer-assisted design** (**CAD**) system. Dubbed **DAC-1** (for **Design Augmented by Computers**), it was introduced in 1964. DAC-1 pushed the envelope in power and features; for example, it could reproduce the complex curves favored by auto designers of the day. The importance of GM's graphical system was more influence than achievement, though. The company's interest in using computers for drawing and design spawned the growth of the computer graphics industry in the United States.

Making Pictures with Numbers

As we discussed in Chapter 2, computers represent and store all forms of data as numbers. How, then, is it possible to create illustrations and images using numbers? Numbers are used in two ways to create digital images. First, as we have seen, a digital image is divided into discrete spatial segments called picture elements or pixels. Each pixel in a standard digital image can be located using two-dimensional coordinates. The number of pixels in a digital image is its resolution, which is usually expressed as a product of the number of pixels across × the number of rows of pixels. But each pixel is also defined by one or more numbers as its content. A binary image, for example, contains a single value—either 1 or 0—as shown in Figure 9.2. A simple rectangle would be represented by the arrangement of pixels seen on the left. The information for the image might be stored as the sequence of bits seen on the bottom.

This type of graphic is called **bit-mapped,** or sometimes **raster graphics. Rasterizing** refers to the process employed by most video displays that translates bit-mapped images to the scan lines of the screen. The term *bit-mapping* denotes the manner in which the image is represented and stored in memory. A simple black-and-white image, as in the previous example,

Figure 9.1

A vintage photograph of the SAGE defense system in operation is shown. The operator is aiming the light pen at the display screen to track specific objects in view.

Figure 9.2

A simple rectangle is represented by a binary image. In the image (top left), the rectangle is traced by a series of black pixels against a white background. Each pixel in the digitized version (top right) is either black (0) or white (1). The resolution of the image is 8 × 8. Thus, the image could be stored as a string of 64 bits (or 8 bytes) as shown below.

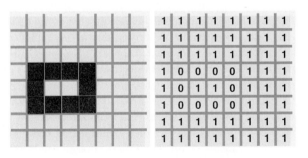

11111111 11111111 11111111 10000111
10000111 10000111 11111111 11111111

requires only a single bit to denote the pixel's attribute. Consequently, 1 bitplane is needed to store this image. On the other hand, suppose that we wished to create an image depicting shades of gray, say, 16 different shades ranging from black to white. A single bit would no longer be sufficient to differentiate these shades. Instead, 4 bits ($2^4 = 16$) would be needed for each pixel to code its specific value from the 16 possible shades. Consequently, 4 bitplanes would be required to represent the pixels for such an image. Figure 9.3 illustrates these ideas.

Bit-mapped color images are handled in a similar manner. As you learned in the previous chapter, an RGB color image, for example, is composed of three separate primary color images: red, green, and blue. When these primary images are combined, the colors mix to form a natural color image. (This principal is exploited by the standard cathode ray tube color monitor. See Chapter 13.) A common format represents each primary pixel with a dynamic range of 256 intensity shades. This means that each primary color pixel has 8 bitplanes ($2^8 = 256$). The combined color image is stored in 24 bitplanes (3 primaries $\times$ 8 bitplanes = 24 bitplanes); this is usually called simply 24-bit color. Images using 32-bit color (RGB + Alpha channel) are common, too.

Bit-mapped graphics is a brute-force method for creating computer images. The location and attributes of each pixel must be fully specified. Memory cells are used to denote the positions and features of pixels directly. In short, the atoms of a computer's memory (cells) are used to store a facsimile of the atoms of a graphic image (pixels).

A more elegant way to express graphic figures is mathematically. For example, you know from your experience in algebra that it is possible to map lines and curves on a plane with equations. Using equations to represent plane figures is not only more concise than bit-mapping, but it offers the distinct advantage of being resolution independent. *Resolution independence* means that the images do not depend on the characteristics of a specific device for proper display. A coordinate system is arbitrary. Its scale can be set to any measure, coarse or fine. But bit-mapped images depend almost entirely on the scale and resolution in which they were created. Faithful reproduction of these images requires accurate portrayals of both. On the other hand, figures defined using equations do not. These may be represented using any consistent scale and resolution. Storing and representing images by mathematical equations or descriptions is called **vector graphics** or, sometimes, **object-oriented graphics.** These images are recreated for display by calculating the points that compose them.

Whether using a video display or a printer, graphic images are almost always converted to two-dimensional output. In spite of this fact, an important characteristic of a graphic application program is whether it recognizes a third dimension. Those that do typically specify a third

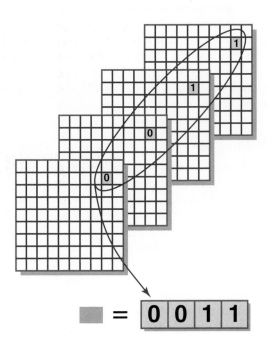

Figure 9.3

Most graphic images are comprised of pixels that represent shades of gray or color. Unlike binary images, these pixels store values larger than a single bit. In these cases, the image can be thought of as a series of 1-bit planes. Each bitplane stores a single bit for each corresponding pixel at that location. In this illustration, a grayscale image has 4-bitplanes. Four successive bits represent the shaded pixel. With a range of 0 (black) to 15 (white), its value is 3, which would be dark gray.
By decomposing the image into bitplanes, it is easier to build and update them in memory for graphic display.

Figure 9.4
A third axis is added to treat objects plotted in three-dimensions. The Z-axis, which is projected from front (+) to back (−), measures the depth of objects in three-dimensional space. Most 3-D graphic applications restrict 3-D space to the upper-right quadrant. Thus, depth is typically expressed as increasing negative number.

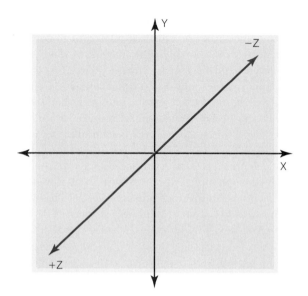

axis, the Z-axis, which allows the user to scale the depth of objects. See Figure 9.4. In reality, of course, depth is only simulated using perspective projection. Thus, points measured along the Z-axis are, in fact, plotted in two dimensions. Nonetheless, a significant advantage over programs that recognize only two dimensions is that these projections are plotted automatically.

Programs of this sort create what is called **three-dimensional,** or **3-D graphics.** Applications that require the user to account for perspective effects are called **two-dimensional,** or simply **2-D graphic** programs.

Most desktop systems are fitted with raster graphic displays. This means that regardless of the approach used for representing and storing a graphic image, it must be bit-mapped (rasterized) for display on such devices. Still, bit-mapped and vector graphics are important concepts to understand because they distinguish two very different approaches for graphic software. In other words, as a user, you will need to choose between two different styles of creating graphic images. On one hand, **painting programs** offer complete control over a graphic image down to the last pixel; they are typically bit-mapped graphic applications. The user is provided a set of tools and features that treat an image fundamentally as a collection of pixels. On the other hand, **drawing, illustration, animation,** and **rendering** programs incorporate the advantages of vector graphics. These applications are often dubbed **object-oriented graphic applications** because the user creates objects that serve as components of the image. Objects may be lines, curves, patterns, textures, and even surfaces. These programs vary in the complexity of both their features and products. As a group, they offer the user the advantages of flexibility and power. These dividends, of course, are due to the abstractions they exploit for creating and manipulating graphic objects.

Storing Graphic Images

As you learned in the previous chapter, all digital images are converted to files for storage purposes. There are a number of common file formats for graphic images—in addition to many of those discussed in Chapter 8. Graphic images may be stored in most of the file formats introduced earlier; for example, it is common to find graphics stored as TIFFs, GIFs, PNGs, BMPs, WMFs, and PICTs. (See Chapter 8.) Besides these, PCX, CGM, EPS, EMF, DXF, SVG, and QuickTime are also popular formats.

PCX is the native file format for PC Paintbrush, one of the original painting programs for Windows computer systems. PCX files contain bit-mapped or rasterized graphics; a number of other graphic programs for Windows can open and save images as PCX files.

CGM (**computer graphics metafile**) was developed by ISO and ANSI, which are two standards committees composed of industry professionals. It was intended as a general-purpose or metafile format that would support a variety of graphic image types and features. A metafile format is a collection of graphic elements along with the instructions on how to interpret them; it may store either bit-mapped or vector graphic images. A wide assortment of graphic applications can read and save images as CGM files.

EPS (**encapsulated PostScript**) is the standard file format for storing and exchanging image files in professional printing. EPS is also a metafile format, which also means that a variety of types of images may be stored as an EPS file. In most cases, EPS files contain both bit-mapped image data and vector graphic data that can be used by drawing and illustration programs.

EPS is based on the **PostScript Page Description Language (PDL).** PostScript defines text and images using mathematical descriptions that are interpreted by the program reading the file. Images may be created and displayed from the commands stored in the file. This makes PostScript a popular choice for representing and transferring vector graphics. Most illustration programs, for example, can read and save EPS files. Desktop publishing programs also handle text and images saved as EPS files.

EMF (**enhanced metafile format**) was developed by Microsoft as a successor to its WMF or Windows metafile format. It offers high resolution capabilities modeled after EPS files.

DXF (**drawing exchange format**) was developed to store 3-D image information created by the computer-assisted design program *AutoCad*. Subsequently, it has become a common-denominator file format for many other 3-D graphics and rendering programs. DXF files can typically be transported from one application to another.

SVG (**scalable vector graphics**) is an open standards format defined in XML (eXtensible Markup Language—see Chapter 19). It is suitable both for printing and Web applications. Besides offering high precision and resolution, SVG images are fully scalable. In a Web browser, such images can be—to use camera terminology—zoomed and panned. The fact that they are based on an open standard means that they can be used more freely than proprietary formats.

QuickTime is used for storing animations. It is actually a digital video file format, but may be employed for storing a sequence of graphic images that are intended as frames for a computer animation. **QuickTime** is a file format developed by Apple Computer, although it may be used on both Windows and Macintosh platforms. (You can find out more about digital video in Chapter 10.)

In the next section, we will examine the basic capabilities of painting programs. As you will discover, these offer the type of control that is needed for some tasks. In the following two sections, we will survey object-oriented graphic applications. Drawing and illustration programs range in their sophistication, but fundamentally they are intended for creating two-dimensional graphics. These are the types of images that are commonly printed or displayed. Rendering programs provide tools for automatically conjuring the illusion of three-dimensional images. These images mimic perspective, textures, and lighting conditions to create photorealistic effects. Finally, animation software incorporates a different dimension entirely—that of time. These programs aid the artist in creating moving or animated images with much less effort than conventional methods.

Each of these categories is suited best for specific kinds of work. And, as an informed consumer, your goal is to learn how to match the application to the task.

Painting Programs

Painting programs blend 2-D bit-mapped graphics with an interface that mimics brush and canvas techniques used by a painter. In most cases, however, the similarities are enforced more by shared terminology than by feel.

The typical painting program interface divides the workspace into palettes, menus, and canvases. **Palettes** contain a selection of tools, patterns, textures, and colors that may be applied to the images contained within a canvas. The **menu,** of course, stores commands and features that may be selected by the user. The **canvas** is usually a window that reveals at least part of a specific bit-mapped image that has been created or opened from an existing file.

The Image and the Image Canvas

Because painting programs use bit-mapped images, their size and resolution are usually fixed. This means that when you save an image as a file, the image size and picture resolution are determined when you first create it. Later, you may modify or control its contents but not always its size or resolution.

Image size refers to the actual extent of the image, while picture resolution specifies the number of pixels used. The latter—we have seen—is expressed usually in two dimensions (for example, 1024 × 768). Actual image size will depend ultimately on the output device used for the display of the image. A graphic seen on the screen of your video monitor will not have the same physical dimensions when printed on a color laser printer, for instance. Your monitor most likely displays images somewhere between 72 and 96 dots per inch (dpi), whereas a color laser printer shows the same pixels at 600 dpi or maybe even 1200 dpi. Take a case in point. An image with a resolution of 1024 × 768 can fill up an entire screen of a 15-inch monitor (at 85 dpi): The image size on the screen is roughly 12 × 9 inches. But, the same image resolution printed on a 600-dpi printer would be a scant 1.7 × 1.28 inches!

Whether you can choose the precise size and/or resolution for an image depends on the software itself. Some painting programs allow the user to control either size or resolution when creating a file. Others permit changes in resolution only. Some offer no choices at all. In any case, it is a good idea to know what the system default values are for resolution so that you can avert any unpleasant surprises later. When choosing a resolution, you should always take into account how the output will likely be used.

As mentioned, the painting image is portrayed within a window. This means that sometimes only a portion of it is revealed. Conventional scrolling tools and gadgets are available to scroll the window over the image. Most painting programs also allow the user to measure the canvas with rulers and grids for more precision.

In most painting programs, the user may also choose the scale at which the image is displayed on the canvas. This is an extremely useful feature. **Image scale** denotes the relative size of the image displayed compared with its actual size. Increasing the scale of an image, for example, has the effect of zooming in on the actual pixels. Detail work is much easier at higher scales. On the other hand, reducing the scale allows you to view the composition of an image that is ordinarily too large for your window or screen. See Figure 9.5.

The canvas is typically divided into at least two layers, **foreground** and **background.** The foreground is the color or pattern that you apply; the background is the color or pattern that is assumed always underneath it. Consider the example illustrated by Figure 9.6. A blue circle is painted in the foreground over a plain white background. In the second frame, a portion of the circle is erased to reveal the white background underneath. Thus, the background is restored whenever the foreground colors or figures are erased or deleted. The background is usually set when the image is first created; some programs may permit you to alter this later.

Figure 9.5

Detail work can be aided by changing image scales. In (a), guidelines are set for touching up the image around its borders. But at its normal scale (100%), it is difficult to see which pixels should be erased or repainted. On the other hand, at the magnification of 300% as shown in (b), it is much easier to both examine and work with such details.

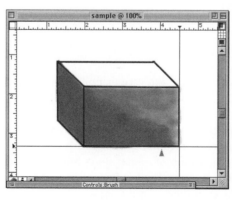

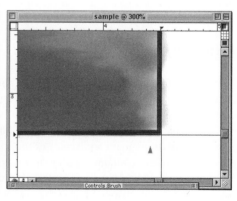

(a)   (b)

Painting Tools and Features

Most paint programs are equipped with a common array of tools used for drawing and painting, organized on one or more palettes. The user selects the appropriate tool and, using a mouse (or stylus with a digital sketch pad), applies it to the canvas.

Drawing and painting tools are flexible in that they can be used with a variety of line thicknesses, colors, and patterns. The user must first designate the type of digital "paint" desired and then the tool to apply it. Some tools are used for drawing lines, curves, and figures. Others are employed for painting areas and effects. There is also an eraser. Typical painting and drawing tools are illustrated in Figure 9.7.

There are also palettes for patterns, colors, and textures. These are commonly used for automatically filling a closed area with a designated pattern or color. Besides simple shades or colors, the user may select specific patterns or textures; even gradients are available. Some programs allow you to create your own patterns and add them to the standard library. Figure 9.8 offers an assortment of these area fills.

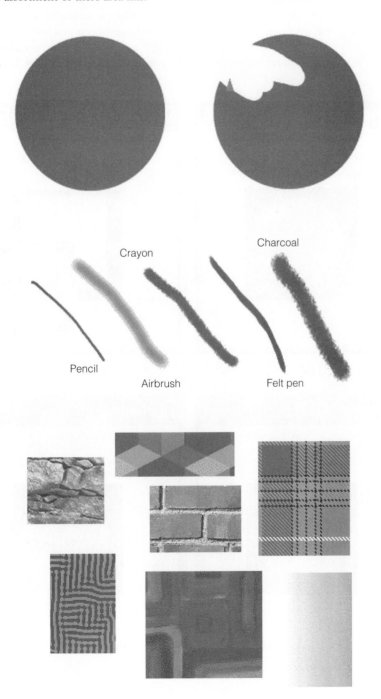

Crayon

Charcoal

Pencil

Airbrush

Felt pen

Figure 9.6

Painting programs allow you to manipulate the colors and patterns of both the foreground and background. On the left, a simple dark circle is drawn against a white background. The circle occupies the foreground on the canvas as a separate layer from its background. Thus, when part of the foreground object is erased (as shown on the right), the background shows through.

Figure 9.7

A sampling of the various painting effects is shown here. These strokes are created using different digital "brushes" such as pencil strokes, charcoal, airbrush, and crayon.

Figure 9.8

Patterns may be brushed or otherwise applied to the canvas. Here we see a sampling of some of the patterns, weaves, and gradients that could be employed. Each has been applied to a selected area using a paint bucket tool, which fills the entire area.

Editing and Special Effects

The greatest advantages of digital painting programs are the ease and power they afford in editing. Just as word processors add editing power to text handling, painting programs also benefit from the capability to select and modify image components. In fact, there are some noticeable similarities between text editing features and image editing in paint programs. First, an item in an image must be selected in order to be edited. After an item is selected, it may be cut or copied and pasted to another area.

Selecting an item in an image is not always precise, though. Some tools allow you to select a given area of the image (rectangular or circular). In this instance, the entire area is affected. In Figure 9.9, the circle is surrounded by a selection box in the first frame. But when the circle is moved, the entire area—including the surrounding pattern—is snatched with it. Other selection tools surround the boundary of an object. These are a little more precise, provided the boundary is distinct.

Some applications provide more precise selection by allowing the user to specify a closed path around the object. A closed path is an arbitrary number of connected curves and lines that specify an area in the image. (Paths are actually a technique borrowed from vector graphics; we will treat them in more detail in the next section.) Closed paths may also serve as masks. In the previous chapter, we introduced the concept of masking. A mask is an area of

Figure 9.9

In (a), a rectangular area surrounding the circle is selected for editing the circle. In (b), the selected area is moved. The entire area selected moves, instead of just the circle, because the selection is based on the group of pixels rather than the object selected. Note also that the white background is revealed when the foreground pixels are moved. The process is repeated in (c) and (d). This time, however, the area of the circle is selected with better precision. Even so, when moved, the hole displaying the background is again evident.

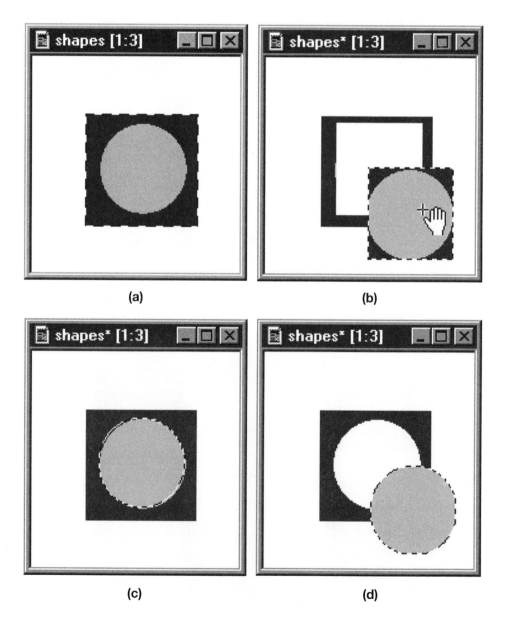

(a)   (b)

(c)   (d)

an image that is selected for editing changes. Figure 9.10 shows a graphic of the Statue of Liberty. Using a painting program, the area around and outside the Statue is selected and masked. The result is that changes can be made to the surrounding part of the image without affecting the picture of the statue.

Some painting programs provide special editing effects called *transformations*. An area of the image may be selected and transformed or altered in various ways. Typical transformations include scaling, stretching, and rotating, as well as perspective and free-form distortion. Figure 9.11 provides some examples.

In general, painting programs provide a powerful assortment of features for creating graphic images. That these images are bit-mapped is a double-edged sword, though. On one hand, this means that the user has much more control over the actual pixel content of the image; this is valuable for complicated images. The downside is that the work is more labor-intensive. Because the image is a collection of pixels, changes must be made normally at the pixel level. For this reason, some graphic tasks are best managed by less primitive means.

Figure 9.10
A simple mask is created for the surrounding area of the image of the Statue of Liberty. A charcoal effect is then applied to the canvas, but the strokes do not affect the unmasked area.

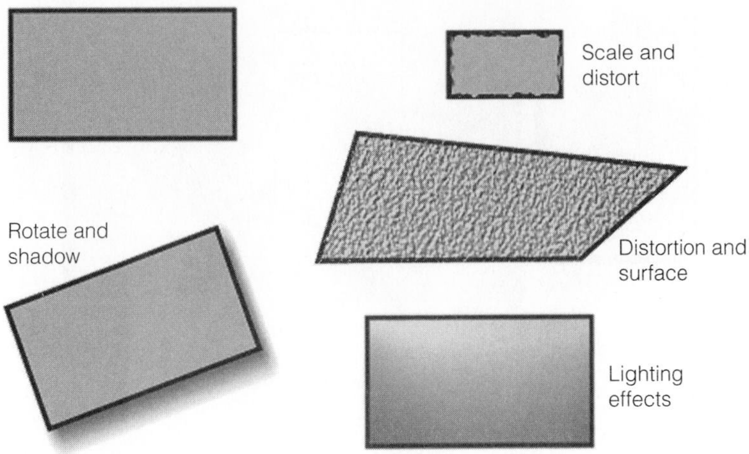

Scale and distort

Rotate and shadow

Distortion and surface

Lighting effects

Figure 9.11
Painting programs offer a variety of transformations that may be applied to selected objects. In this instance, a simple rectangular figure (top left) is transformed in shape, position, and texture.

Drawing with Lines, Curves, and Objects

As mentioned earlier, Sutherland's SketchPad had a tremendous impact on the development of graphic application software. That it was interactive proved that the computer could be used to create graphic images in a convenient manner. Its interactivity was not limited merely to creating images. Once figures were drawn, they could be modified interactively just as easily. For example, using the light pen and buttons, the user could point to a rectangle on the screen and move its position or change its size. This was possible because SketchPad's design was based on an entirely different approach than that of bit-mapped image programs.

Instead of bit-maps, the user defined or created graphic objects. The program, in turn, freed the user from the messy details of how these objects were actually formed or displayed. Instead, it provided tools for manipulating them as abstract objects rather than dealing directly with their implementation. Software designed in this manner is understandably called *object-oriented graphics.*

In the world of object-oriented (or vector) graphics, pixels are replaced by elements such as lines, curves, paths, and figures. As a result, object-oriented graphics offers several distinct advantages over bit-mapped approaches.

First, the user is freed from the details of how the computer system stores and displays an image. After all, a pixel is not a very natural way of thinking about drawings and pictures. Entities such as lines and curves are much more intuitive. Thus, object-oriented graphics is more abstract.

Second, vector graphic applications offer features with greater power and flexibility. The key, again, is abstraction, but rather than an effect, it resides inside the program itself. In short, graphic objects are defined abstractly within the program, too. A graphic object is specified by its attributes such as dimensions, position in the image, pattern, and so on. See Figure 9.12. But, since these are defined by attributes—that is, in essence, descriptions—they may be altered as easily as they were created. For instance, moving an object from one location to another is a simple matter of modifying the description of its position coordinates. The program then uses these descriptions in redrawing the object to simulate moving it from one place to another. Such changes do not necessarily affect other objects in the image, either. You will recall the illustration of relocating an inscribed circle. Compare that with the results in Figure 9.13. When the circle is selected and moved in a painting program, the background is revealed, leaving a hole in the surrounding box. On the other hand, in a vector graphic program, the circle and box are objects that are defined independently. When the circle is moved, the box is reinstated nearly in full view.

Figure 9.12

An object-oriented version of a rectangle is no more than a description of its principal properties or attributes. Thus, the structure on the left might serve as a representation for the rectangle depicted to the right of it. Besides its dimensions, the object version of the rectangle would store the position of the figure (expressed here as X, Y screen coordinates for its left corner), the border, and area-fill patterns. Modifying the characteristics of the rectangle, therefore, would be as simple as changing the values for the component descriptions. The graphic program would then redraw the pixel version of the figure with its new attributes on the screen.

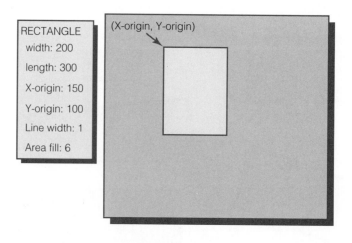

RECTANGLE
width: 200
length: 300
X-origin: 150
Y-origin: 100
Line width: 1
Area fill: 6

(X-origin, Y-origin)

Of course, a portion of the circle covers the box, but the program can calculate this overlap and redraw both. The process of revealing portions of a 2-D graphic object for viewing is called **clipping.** This technique is employed in all window-based interfaces, for example.

Third, object-oriented graphics are resolution independent. Because these images are defined abstractly, they may be adapted to fit various resolutions. This means that their scale can be fitted more easily to a variety of devices. In other words, the actual pixels used in the output image are recalculated to fit better the resolution of the output device. By contrast, if you have ever tried to print images downloaded from the Web, then you probably can appreciate the benefits of resolution independence. Images downloaded from the Web are usually bit-mapped images. Printing them on a higher-resolution device such as a laser printer produces poor results. Either the image is too small, if the resolution is unchanged; or the picture looks blocky and coarse, if it is resampled at a higher resolution.

Images based on vector graphics usually look better than simple bit-mapped graphics, because the former can easily take advantage of display techniques such as anti-aliasing or smoothing. As you know, pixels are typically rectangular in shape and, thus, best portray straight lines rather than curves. A curved line, for example, is digitized by combining a sequence of short, straight-line segments that approximate it. If the resolution is high enough, our eyes are fooled into seeing a curved line rather than a lot of short, connected straight lines. Even so, the curve exhibits artifacts that make it look jagged. This is called **aliasing.** **Smoothing** or removing this jagged effect is dubbed **"anti-aliasing."** For example, in Figure 9.14, the text font is created with the benefits of anti-aliasing. (Most text on computer displays are based on vector rather than bit-mapped methods.) As the close-up shows, the illusion of smoothly varying curves is enhanced by the use of different pixels shades. Thus, the visibility of the transitions between segments is lessened.

Finally, vector graphics can represent and store images with greater economy than bit-mapped applications. As you know, in most instances, a description is much more concise than replicating the thing itself. (Compare the phrase "a 100-story office building" with what it denotes!) This is certainly true of bit-mapped images. Graphic files containing object descriptions are often much smaller and, therefore, more economical to store and transmit than their bit-mapped counterparts. Of course, to be useful, descriptions must be intelligible to another system. Vector graphic files created by one object-oriented application may be unintelligible to another. If you plan to transfer images from one application to another, it is important to ascertain what file formats they support in common.

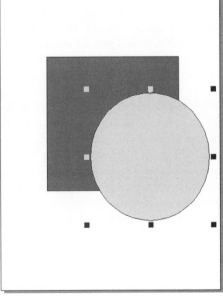

(a)   (b)

Figure 9.13

In an earlier figure (Figure 9.9), it was demonstrated that moving pixels is not always as precise as we might wish. In an object-oriented graphic program, however, the objects are treated independently. In (a), a circle is again inscribed within a rectangle using the tools of a drawing program. In (b), the circle has been moved without affecting the square at all—other than covering its corner.

Figure 9.14

The text in (a) is printed with the benefits of anti-aliasing or smoothing. An almost cursive font style is represented more convincingly using this technique. The close-up in (b) shows how this effect is accomplished. Pixels of different shades are incorporated around the edges of the figures to blur or lessen the jagged effect to the eyes. The result is a smoother curved appearance.

(a) *anti-aliased*

(b)

2-D-vector graphic applications come in two basic varieties: drawing and illustration programs. Their differences are not so much a matter of kind as degree. In fact, they differ much as a limo differs from a compact car. Both are basically vehicles intended for transportation, but the style in which you are transported can be very different. Drawing programs provide all of the basics; illustration programs are measured by their style and appointments. We will examine each category briefly to understand better what these applications offer in the way of graphic features.

Drawing Programs

Drawing programs are best suited for simpler types of illustrations and charts. Like their painting program counterparts, they typically divide the workspace into menus, palettes, and one or more drawing windows. The tool and pattern palettes often resemble those found in painting programs, too. There are tools for drawing lines, arcs, and figures such as rectangles, ovals, and circles. The techniques employed for drawing are also similar to those in painting programs.

Once the lines, arcs, and figures are drawn, the differences between painting and drawing programs become a lot more apparent. For instance, lines and figures may be selected individually for discrete editing. When an object is selected, it is usually displayed with special tools called *handles*. These are actually used for resizing the object. Figure 9.15 shows how a rectangle can be reshaped by manipulating its handles. While the object is selected, moving it is usually as simple as pointing and dragging it elsewhere in the window.

Drawing Curves   An unavoidable reality of painting with pixels is their rectilinear structure. As you have probably seen for yourself, painting curves is always marred by the jagged edges of the pixels themselves. This effect, of course, can be minimized if the resolution is sufficiently large. In contrast, one of the abstract features of drawing programs is that curves can be treated independently of resolution. Drawing programs incorporate what are called **parametric curves,** which are based on mathematical equations. There are several classes of parametric curves. Drawing programs may employ **B-spline curves** or, perhaps, **Bezier curves.** Both types of equations project a series of points through which the curve is approximated. The latter form is very popular.

From the user's standpoint, however, creating arbitrary curves is a great deal simpler than the mathematics that supports them. The user draws the curve by specifying a set of points that it passes through. In Figure 9.16(a), the user creates a curved segment by plotting a set of points. The program automatically interpolates a smooth curve between the points. The real power in this technique comes in editing, though. As demonstrated in Figure 9.16(b), you

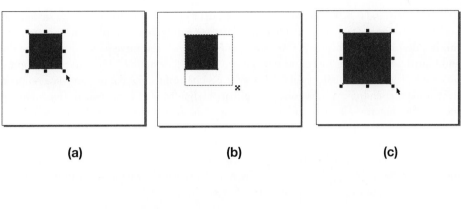

(a)   (b)   (c)

Figure 9.15
In (a) the rectangle is shown as the current selection. The handles at its borders indicate both that the figure is selected and how it may be scaled or resized. The user presses and drags the handles as shown in (b). When the mouse button is released, the rectangle is redrawn at its new scale, as seen in (c).

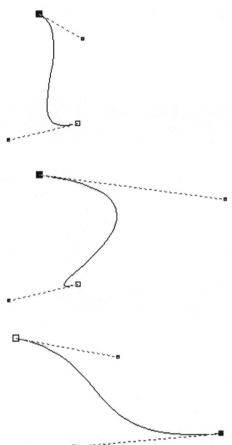

Figure 9.16
Manipulating freehand curves in a typical drawing application is a simple matter. The original curve is selected with the shape tool (top). Dragging the handles (on dotted lines) reshapes the curve as shown in (middle). The location and limits of the curve may also be adjusted by repositioning the endpoints as shown in (bottom).

may reshape or refit the curve by manipulating either the points on the curve or the special handles that extend from these points.

Bezier curves have an unlikely origin: They are based on the work of a French engineer who developed the concept for automating metal cutting machines in the auto industry. Pierre Bezier (pronounced "Bez-ee-ay"), working for the French car manufacturing company Renault in the early 1970s, was charged with the problem of simplifying how these cutting machines were controlled. To solve that problem, he discovered a concise method for mathematically approximating a curve segment based on an arbitrary number of points.

John Warnock and Chuck Geshke, the creators of the PostScript Page Description Language, adopted a special case of the Bezier method for creating what are called piecewise Bezier curves. Consequently, the popularity of PostScript ensured the prevalence of this method.

To understand how Bezier curves work, consider a curve segment defined by a small number of points. In this case, we will define the curve using only four control points. (Technically, this is a Bezier curve of degree 3.) As shown in Figure 9.17, the curve passes through the first and fourth points. These are commonly dubbed the "anchor points." The curve only approximates to the two intermediate points. If we trace a line connecting the intermediate points to their respective endpoints, however, we see that the line formed is tangent to the curve segment at that juncture. Because this applies in every instance, we can infer that the position of an intermediate point controls the slope of its curve segment. For this reason, the intermediate points are often referred to as direction points.

In some drawing and illustration programs, the user may manipulate the control points for a Bezier curve directly. The curve in Figure 9.18 is transformed by repositioning the intermediate (direction) points that help to define it.

Drawing with Image Layers Unlike most painting programs, the image in a drawing program is composed conceptually of many different layers rather than just two (background and foreground). You will recall that a layer is an image component that may be

Figure 9.17
The piecewise Bezier curve segment is shown on top. The curve passes through two points—the first and last (1 and 4, respectively). These are usually designated as anchor points because they define the limits of the curve segment. The other two points (2 and 3) help to constrain its shape. If we draw lines intersecting them with their corresponding anchor points, as shown on the bottom, we can see that each line is tangent to the curve at that location. These intermediate points are called direction points *because they define the slope of the curve in their respective neighborhoods. Their position affects the shape of the curve globally as well.*

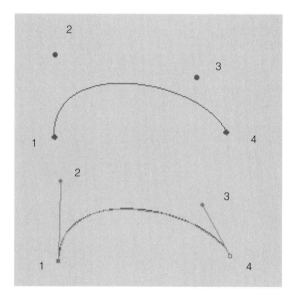

Figure 9.18
The previous curve (shown at the top) is reshaped by moving the direction points from their original positions. The result is shown on the bottom. Changes in position and distance from its corresponding anchor point will affect the curve in different ways. In some graphic programs, reshaping the curve is simple and intuitive. The user can drag the points while inspecting their effects on the curve segment.

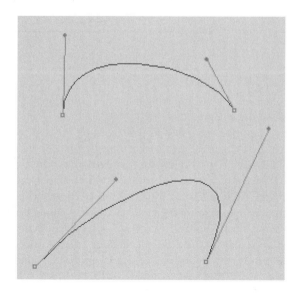

treated independently. It is convenient to think of the drawing image as composed of stacks of layers, much like the transparent acetates used for overhead projectors. Each object occupies its own layer—stamped on a transparent background. The order of the layers dictates what and how much of the image's objects are visible. As shown in Figure 9.19, these layers may be varied at will to yield different "looks."

Drawing programs offer the same sort of special effects and transformations found in painting programs. In addition to scaling and resizing, you may rotate objects, distort them, and make perspective projections. The starburst drawing in Figure 9.20 illustrates how a graphic image is built from incremental steps or stages using tools, patterns, and transformations.

Drawing programs offer a great many features and advantages over pixel-based painting programs. They are especially good at mass production. Illustrations that contain a great deal of repeated or redundant components can be copied quickly and accurately using simple copy-and-paste operations. Because their most primitive element is a line or curve, drawing programs are best suited for graphic images that are basically line drawings. Painting programs are still better for more complicated graphic images or artwork.

Illustration Programs

Earlier we compared illustration programs to drawing programs as a limo to a compact car. Both have similar purposes but differ in the style and manner in which they achieve these. And even though this comparison is exaggerated, there is some basis for making it. First, illustration programs are intended for professionals rather than casual users. They are chock full of features that would not be expected in their poor cousins. In addition, they produce the high-quality output necessary for professional publication. These luxuries do have a cost, though. Illustration programs have much steeper learning curves associated with their use. Moreover, they often tax the resources and performance of desktop computers as well. They require lots of memory, are CPU-intensive, and produce files that can occupy more storage space. Not surprisingly, they typically carry bigger price tags as well, though nothing like limo standards.

The chief distinguishing characteristic of illustration programs from the user's standpoint is that they can generate PDL (Page Description Language) output such as PostScript. This means that they produce graphic images that inherit all of the advantages normally expected from such methods (precision, resolution independence, smooth curves, special effects, etc.).

In contrast to most drawing and painting programs, illustration programs usually present different views of their graphic images. While the image is being created or edited, it is often displayed simply as line art, that is, only the lines and curves that make up the image, without color or shading. See Figure 9.21(a). This view makes it easier to see the actual structure of the image. (The computer can also redraw these images much faster.) Most illustration pro-

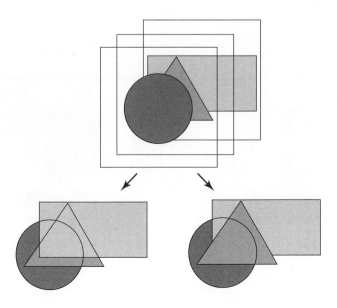

Figure 9.19

In a typical drawing program, figures are treated as belonging to separate transparent layers. As shown here, you can see how the circle, triangle, and rectangle are arranged by layering them one on top of the other. Rearranging these figures is as simple as restacking the layers. Two different arrangements are shown beneath it. These are created by selecting a layer and choosing the appropriate stacking command such as Send Backward *or* Send to the Front.

grams also provide an output view; this allows you to inspect the image as it would be displayed on paper or on a screen. Consult Figure 9.21(b) for an example. In some programs, you may work on the image from either view.

As in drawing programs, lines and curves are the basic components of graphic objects. Illustration programs, however, offer more flexibility in creating these objects and greater editing control over them. This means that illustrations can be much more complex and intricate compared with those of simpler drawing programs. The example in Figure 9.22 was created

Figure 9.20
The illustrations show, step by step, how a drawing program simplifies the creation of a graphic figure. (a) A single circle is drawn and copied. The copy is increased by 300 percent. Both are aligned horizontally and vertically by their centers. (b) Using the straight-line tool, guidelines are drawn as an aid for the next step. (c) The polygon tool is employed to create star bursts. The guides are used to center each point of the star. (d) Afterward, the guides and outer circle are deleted. (e) A copy of the polygon is made. The copy is colored and rotated to create offset bursts. This copy layer is sent to the back. Finally, the center circle is colored to match the background star bursts.

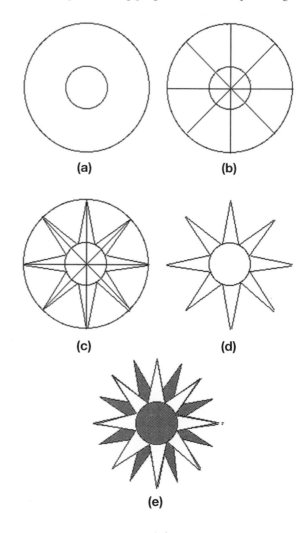

Figure 9.21
An illustration program usually provides different views of the working image. In (a), the art is displayed as a collection of lines, curves, and figures. This shows how the picture was actually created. Later, the segments are joined and filled to create the finished image. In (b), we see how the artwork will look when it is printed. A typical illustration program will allow the user to toggle between these different views.

(a) (b)

in Adobe *Illustrator*. Figure 9.23 is a close-up of how the artwork was created. It shows the amount of detail required to assemble the components of the image. Illustration programs are extremely powerful and offer many features, but exploiting them requires patience and care.

Text handling is one feature that by itself nearly justifies purchasing an illustration program. In fact, the well-tempered desktop publishing system is not complete without a good illustration program for creating special text effects. Because illustration programs produce PDL output, text effects in a wide assortment of sizes and styles are easily imported into a DTP program. Figure 9.24 provides a sampling of various effects that are easy to create in illustration programs (yet almost impossible to create elsewhere).

Figure 9.22
"Henry's Trip" is an illustration by John Ritter created using Adobe Illustrator.

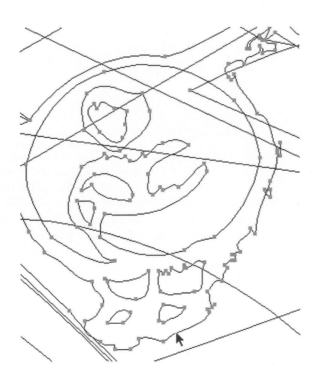

Figure 9.23
A close-up of "Henry's Trip" is shown in the construction or Artwork view. The handles denote endpoints and anchors for the lines and curve segments that constitute the figures. As you can see, the figure is made primarily of closed curved paths with numerous adjustments points used to coax the irregular shapes from within these curves.

Figure 9.24

A sampling of sophisticated visual effects created with text using an illustration program is shown. In (a), the letters are colored using a gradient pattern that blends color variations across their spectrum. The box uses the same basic colors, but with different parameters. In (b), the text is plotted on a circle that fits inside the surrounding figure. For (c), a copy of the letters is darkened, reshaped, and positioned to suggest the shadow effect from backlighting. In (d) copies of both box and lettering are recolored and moved to a back layer to create shadows. Finally, the picture (e) is intended to illustrate how text can be extruded (thickened) easily using an illustration program. The lettering is copied and its color modified. The new copy is placed behind the original letters; again, the letters are offset for visibility. Several other copies are pasted behind that layer in successive offsets. Enough layers are added to suggest a thick back layer.

(a)

(b)

(c)

(d)

(e)

Conclusion: Rules and Exceptions

There are indeed notable differences among painting, drawing, and illustration programs in both form and function. As a rule, painting programs are designed for bit-mapped images, while drawing and illustration programs deal with object-oriented graphics. Even so, applications today often muddy the graphic waters by combining features from these very different domains. For example, some bit-mapped graphic applications have PostScript output capabilities (Adobe *PhotoShop* is a good example). Some drawing and illustration programs allow the user to import and manipulate bit-mapped images as backgrounds (*CorelDraw,* Macromedia *Freehand,* and Adobe *Illustrator*). Other graphic applications combine both worlds into a single package (*CorelDraw* is bundled with Corel *PhotoPaint,* for instance).

The moral of this story is that there are rules, but there are also exceptions to them. Many commercial graphic software packages today have evolved to hybrid status. Nonetheless, these applications are still suited best for specific types of images and tasks. As always, you should investigate an application thoroughly before deciding whether it suits your needs.

Three-Dimensional Graphics

A recent trend in computer graphics has been the migration of software to the desktop that breaks the traditional two-dimensional barrier. In the past, sophisticated three-dimensional rendering effects and computer animation had been restricted exclusively to the realm of professionals. Today, applications that create 3-D graphics and animation are available for the general user. In this section, we will explore the facets of adding the dimension of depth to your graphic images.

Three-dimensional graphic techniques fall roughly into two categories: volume-based and surface-based. **Volume-based graphics** plot an image as composed of three-dimensional pixels called **voxels** (for **volume elements**); like two-dimensional pixels, voxels have features such as color, intensity, transparency, and opacity. Thus, a three-dimensional object is plotted as a solid comprised of voxels that define its volume. Volume-based graphics are employed for visualization techniques in a number of scientific fields such as medicine (e.g., CAT and MRI scans), physics (e.g., hydrodynamics visualization), chemistry (e.g., molecular modeling), and meteorology (e.g., storm visualization). In contrast, **surface-based graphics** treat objects as only skin deep. The objective for surface-based methods is to create the photorealistic illusion of three-dimensional objects rather than manipulating them as solids. Its applications are typically artistic or educational rather than scientific. While some volume-based applications are available, most desktop 3-D applications employ surface-based techniques exclusively. Accordingly, we will restrict our treatment of 3-D graphics to these types.

Surface-based three-dimensional graphics offers the sort of spectacular photorealistic effects that you have no doubt seen in television commercials, computer games (including *Myst, Final Fantasy,* and *Quake*), and motion picture films (such as *Jurassic Park I, II,* and *III; Terminator 1, 2,* and *3; Toy Story 1* and *2,* and *Monsters, Inc.*). Many of these effects, however, were created with high-performance computer systems running application programs written especially for them. The 3-D graphic effects that they feature strain the resources of even these high-performance workstations. For example, computer-generated images of dinosaurs in the first *Jurassic Park* amounted to only about six and one-half minutes of actual film footage. Even so, it took 50 people 18 months and $15 million worth of equipment to create the nearly one-quarter trillion bytes of images needed to create these effects!

Desktop 3-D graphics naturally offers a somewhat scaled-down version of these capabilities. In spite of this, very convincing effects can be produced with these applications on desktop systems with reasonable speed and memory resources. Like its 2-D cousins, a typical 3-D graphic application presents an interface composed of menu items, tool palettes, and drawing or workspace windows. Unlike 2-D drawing and painting programs, however, a 3-D graphic program must manage multiple views or perspectives of its images. See Figure 9.25.

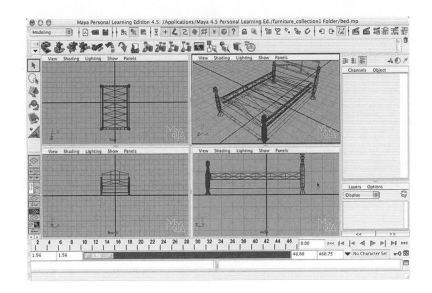

Figure 9.25

The model of a bed is shown in a popular 3-D graphics and rendering application from three normal perspectives (top, front, and side) as well as from a camera perspective chosen by the user.

The typical desktop application creates a 3-D image following roughly these three stages: model description, scene description, and rendering. We will discuss each of these stages or processes separately in more detail.

Model Description

Each object in a 3-D image must be specified in full detail within the three-dimensional coordinate system employed by the application program. This is the task of **model description.**

The most popular technique is polygon-surface modeling. **Polygon-surface modeling** construes the object's exterior surface as a collection of connected 2-D polygons of various shapes. Thus, complex shapes are depicted as three-dimensional, multifaceted figures. Objects with smooth, continuously curved surfaces are not depicted well with these models. If, however, the resolution is fine enough—that is, the polygon facets are small and numerous enough—acceptable curved surfaces can be approximated.

Wireframe model construction is a special-case of polygon-surface modeling; it creates the object's exterior surface as a wireframe model. The model is comprised of a series of connected shapes that are joined to others at their vertices. Unlike models based solely on polygons, though, wireframes may embrace curved shapes. See Figure 9.26. These 2-D curved segments are usually implemented by splines. As discussed earlier, B-splines and Bezier curves are mathematical constructions used to represent curved segments, shapes, and even surfaces. The wireframe model conjures up the idea of a skeleton of the object on which the skin may be stretched.

Because wireframe modeling is supported by most applications, we will use its approach as a means for understanding better how 3-D models are created. Keep in mind, though, that there are other techniques or approaches for the task of modeling.

The methods used for constructing a wireframe model of an object are basically extensions of two-dimensional drawing within a three-dimensional coordinate system. The general idea, of course, is to create the model as a solid object defined by a set of points, lines or curves, and surfaces. Conceptually, we can recreate any three-dimensional object portrayed this way provided we have a sufficient number of construction planes based on it. You can think of a **construction plane** as a sheet of glass that is located in our three-dimensional space. See Figure 9.27. When the glass contacts the surface of our object, for example, we could trace its outline and likewise measure all of the points that are confined within its boundaries. In short, we produce a two-dimensional drawing or projection of the view of that object from that aspect.

Now, imagine that we fix the construction planes parallel to a given axis. Furthermore, let's invest them with the capability of passing through an object at will. Given a series of projections from a number of construction planes that sample that axis, we can get a much

Figure 9.26
A wireframe model of a vase is shown.

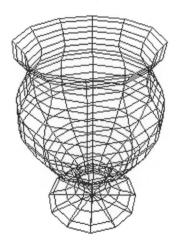

more accurate idea of the structure of the object. In effect, the object is decomposed as a series of cuts or two-dimensional slices along that axis. If we can specify construction planes for all three dimensions, we can construct a fairly accurate model of the object. Compare with Figure 9.28.

Wireframe models for objects may be created using this technique. Specifically, the shape of an object in a given dimension can be assembled by specifying a series of outlines as its construction planes. These are joined together to form a wireframe by interpolating boundaries between the planes.

In addition to creating models from dimensional cuts or outlines, most 3-D graphic programs offer other tools for automating the creation of wireframe models. For example, models for custom-made objects may be lathed or extruded as well. **Lathing** creates a model by rotating a two-dimensional outline around a given axis. See Figure 9.29. It works well, especially for objects that are symmetrically shaped. **Extrusion** lifts or adds a third dimension to a two-dimensional outline. Regular-shaped objects whose depth is a series of parallel cuts can be created quickly and easily by extrusion. For instance, 3-D text effects can be made by extruding outline fonts. See Figure 9.30 for an illustration of this technique.

Scene Description

Once the objects for an image have been modeled, they must be arranged to form a scene. This is the task of **scene description.** The first step is to find a place for the objects in the scene itself. Usually, you may employ general three-dimensional coordinates—sometimes called **world-view coordinates**—for fixing objects in the scene.

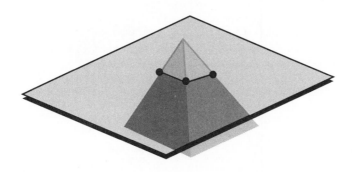

Figure 9.27
Suppose that we fit our construction plane with a fixed axis and invest it with the capability of magically passing through objects. When we pass it through the pyramid figure, we can make a series of horizontal cuts of the shape of the object at different depths from top to bottom. Here we see the outline of the object formed on that plane as a cut.

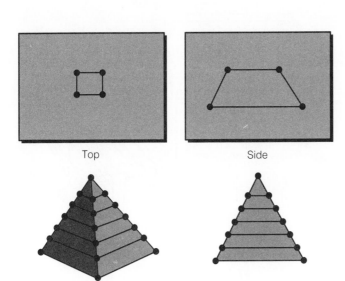

Top   Side

Figure 9.28
Using a series of construction planes from at least two dimensions, we can construct a wireframe model composed of a series of points marking the boundaries of the object and interpolated lines connecting them between the planes. Here we see two cuts taken from perpendicular planes. On the left, a cut from the top of the pyramid is shown. The right depicts its shape when cuts are made vertically.

Providing information about the location of objects in a scene is necessary for the computer to calculate 2-D images with perspective projection. Perspective, of course, is one of the key elements for producing realistic effects. The concept of perspective is a familiar one. Imagine standing on a long, straight railroad track. Even though you know that the tracks are parallel, they appear to converge at the horizon. Likewise, suppose that trees lined the track all of the way down the line. Trees in the foreground would naturally appear larger, while trees farther away would decrease in size relative to their distance from you. Most 3-D graphic applications employ the type of perspective described here. They keep track of these projections using a **Z-buffer.** The Z-buffer is named after the Z-axis that measures the distance of objects from the foreground. Each object is assigned a number based on relative location along that axis. In this manner, the program can calculate which objects are closer to the current point of view on the scene and which are farther. Objects are then scaled based on their relative distances. Their X, Y coordinates indicate whether part or most of a distant object is covered by a closer one. Some 3-D graphic applications permit the user to control the extent to which objects are focused in the scene as well. In natural scenes, objects in the distance are usually less detailed compared with those in the foreground. The 3-D application can blur distant objects slightly in order to produce more realistic images.

The point of view for the scene may be modified easily using controls provided in the interface for managing the virtual viewer or camera. Camera motions are easier to understand than viewing changes. For example, it is easier to grasp terminology that incorporates standard

Figure 9.29
On the left, the outline of a vase is fashioned for lathing. As you can see, the figure is drawn as a cutaway of the vase from its center. The shape is rotated 360° to form the object. On the right, the wireframe model of the vase is shown.

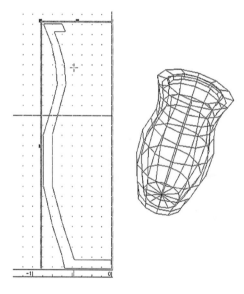

Figure 9.30
On the left, the outline of the letter "T" is drawn. Extrusion automatically adds a specified amount of depth to the figure. The wireframe model of the extruded "T" is seen on the right.

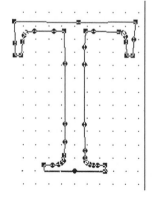
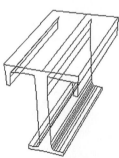

camera movements such as panning left and right or up and down. In addition, you may zoom or move in or out of the scene and perform right and left rotations and tilts.

Rendering

Up to this point, we have defined the image in its skeletal form: a collection of polygon-surface or wireframe models. The process of **rendering** a scene involves creating the illusion of photorealism. In other words, the objects in the image are rendered as composed of surfaces projected in three-dimensional perspective with the effects of lighting and shading to contribute to their realism.

Choosing surfaces and a background for the scene is the first stage for rendering. Most 3-D applications provide a library of surfaces and backgrounds—each with a variety of textures and terrains—that may be added to the scene automatically. See Figure 9.31. You may also import images from other graphic applications that can serve as backgrounds as well. For example, you could use a scanner to digitize a photograph of your wooden desktop surface. This could be edited and saved by an image processing application. This same image could then be imported into the 3-D application for use as a map or pattern to be applied to either surfaces or backgrounds. In this manner, you could create a 3-D model of your desk that looks very much like the real thing.

Determining which surfaces are visible can be approached in two different manners. On one hand, we might think of it fundamentally from the viewer's standpoint. For example, we might draw a straight line from the viewer's eye to the viewing grid and pass that line through until it hits an object. Thus, we could determine what the viewer can see for each pixel in the image plane. This is the basic technique of **ray tracing.** See Figure 9.32. The results can be more realistic if we take into account the light rays that are reflected from other objects as well. These can be traced to determine what other surfaces they contact. Transparent surfaces can be modeled by tracing rays that are refracted through these surfaces as well. Rendering by ray tracing can produce striking results for scenes with mirror- or glass-like surfaces. Unfortunately, producing ray-traced output can be extremely time-consuming.

On the other hand, we can approach the problem backward: traversing the background to the viewer rather than vice versa. Rendering according to this approach is accomplished in two stages. First, the object is portrayed as composed of a collection of visible surfaces (as seen from that perspective). This task is often dubbed in the negative as **hidden surface removal.** Afterward, lighting and shading effects are added.

A variety of techniques are employed for hidden surface removal; however, they share some fundamental features. The basic idea is to calculate which surfaces and lines are visible by determining which are closest to the viewer. Starting in the background, the image is con-

Figure 9.31
The title "Digital Domain" is covered with a translucent metallic finish and placed on a checkerboard-patterned background. The camera angle may be manipulated for various views of the scene.

structed by effectively building and then erasing or removing those lines, edges, or surfaces that are obscured by ones closer to the viewer.

After the hidden surfaces are removed, the image pixels for the visible surfaces are treated to portray lighting and shading effects. There are several popular techniques, but each is based on a model that approximates how light is distributed over the surface of a polygon. The simplest lighting or shading model is called **Lambert shading** or sometimes simply **flat shading.** Each facet of an object's surface is shaded by treating each pixel in that polygon uniformly. Thus, Lambert shading is fast but lacks subtlety. While the Lambert lighting model assumes that each facet is flat, more sophisticated shading techniques allow for surfaces to be formed by smooth curves. Named after its inventor, **Gouraud shading** (pronounced "Guh-row") takes into account the lighting effects on the surrounding surfaces and calculates shading from each vertex. The shading values for pixels between two vertices are then interpolated to create a more diffuse or smoothly varying effect. Gouraud shading is more realistic than flat shading, yet it is still reasonably efficient (fast). The technique does have some weak points, though. Specular reflections and highlights generally are not handled well, and although borders between facets on a curved surface are smoothed, they are still visible. **Phong shading** is a method designed to deal with just these problems. Rather than interpolating the color values for some of the pixels within a surface, Phong shading recomputes the illumination model for each pixel. The results are much more realistic, although the process is more time-consuming.

Fortunately, desktop 3-D applications allow the user to decide how to manage these trade-offs. Simpler models with faster rendering can be used for provisional designs or drafts; on the other hand, higher-quality output images can be produced at the expense of using more complicated models and rendering techniques. Of course, as in other graphic applications, processor speed and memory capacities are practical considerations.

Figure 9.32
The viewing frustrum is a pyramid formed by projecting lines from the viewer past the image plane to the background of the scene. Objects behind the image plane and within the pyramid form the content of the 3-D image. Anything outside this area is clipped. The remaining objects are projected onto the image plane to form the rendered image.

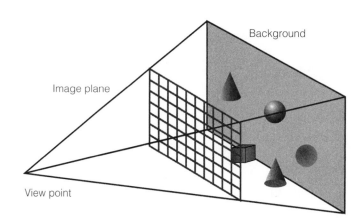

DISCOVERING MORE

3-D Graphics and Rendering

With advances in processor speeds and affordable memory, desktop 3-D graphics applications have become more powerful and convenient for producing images with photorealistic effects. For illustrations of the methods and techniques discussed in this section, consult our online resource "Discovering More About 3-D Graphics and Rendering."

Animation

Computer animation extends graphic images to add the dimension of time for depicting motion (or change). Animation creates an illusion of motion by displaying a sequence of progressively changing images in rapid succession. If the images—called **frames**—are displayed at a fast enough rate, the average person perceives them as depicting motion. Usually, rates of 15 or 16 frames per second (fps) are sufficient to produce this illusion. Professional-quality animations employ rates of 24 fps and higher.

Picture animation, of course, is not a new technology. The first animation devices were developed in the early nineteenth century. The zoetrope, for example, was invented by William Horner in 1834. It was composed of a revolving drum with regularly spaced slits. Drawings were positioned on an inner drum. When the drum was rotated, the viewer could see the drawings through the slits. In 1915, Earl Hurd developed the technique of **cel animation;** this is the basic method still used in conventional commercial animation today. Each individual image (called a **cel** from the transparent celluloid sheets that were used) is placed on a painted background and photographed. This produces a sequence of frames, composing a motion picture film. The first commercial pioneer to add synchronized sound to cel animation was Walt Disney, who produced Steamboat Willie (featuring Mickey Mouse) in 1928.

It is useful to note some of the basics of traditional cel animation because the terminology has been transplanted to computer animation techniques. Animated films generally tell a story. **Story** is the term also used to describe the action of the film. The story comprises a sequence of scenes. A **scene** is defined by a specific set of objects at a given location. The story is often depicted scene by scene in a series of drawings that make up the **storyboard.** The objects in a scene are also called **actors,** although this does not always mean that they depict characters. The location is depicted by a series of **backgrounds,** relatively static drawings on which the cels are placed and photographed. Scenes are made up of shots. A shot is the basic picture unit; it combines a set of actors on a particular background. A shot, of course, corresponds to a single frame or image.

The principal animators are usually each responsible for a single actor. They draw **key frames** that depict that character or object in specific positions. These are then transferred to transparent cels for inking and painting. Subordinates prepare what are called **in-betweens,** the intermediate drawings that produce smooth motion between key frames. The final photography of cels on backgrounds is typically done on film or videotape. A number of effects (such as pans and zooms) are actually created during the photography process. Editing is often handled in postproduction.

Computers have been employed in commercial animation for several decades. Computer processing has helped animators draw and color key frames, produce in-betweens, control the camera during photography, and handle editing during postproduction. These are considered computer-assisted animation systems because the process remains fundamentally an analog one. The computer is simply employed at various stages of the analog process for efficiency or economy.

Only recently, however, has animation gone fully digital. By *digital* we mean, of course, that all stages of the animation process are computerized. Even a computer video monitor is employed for its display—although it may be transferred to another medium, such as videotape or film. For well over a decade, computer graphic researchers and commercial developers have created professional digital animation systems on high-performance computer systems using specialized software.

Digital animation systems have recently migrated to the desktop as well. Currently, there are three classes of desktop animation applications: object animation, modeling animation, and authoring animation systems. We will consider each category briefly.

Object Animation

Object animation is the simplest variety of computer animation, usually based on 2-D graphic images. The user draws or assembles key frames. The program then calculates and produces the in-betweens. The user may choose objects or actors from a standard library or create new ones. Calculating in-betweens is often based on starting and ending key frames with a user-defined path to track the intended motion between them. See Figure 9.33.

Modeling Animation

Modeling animation applications automate the process of manipulating a rendered object in three-dimensional space. The animator defines the objects or actors as 3-D models. The program computes and renders a model using the techniques discussed in the previous section. In addition to rendering 3-D views of the model, the program creates an animation based on manipulating the model with a virtual camera that captures the scene. For example, the animator employs the camera to pan, zoom, or tilt over the scene for different visual effects. Most standard 3-D rendering programs provide help with this type of animation.

Authoring Animation

Some systems are designed to automate the process of animation from storyboard to finished product. In an authoring system, the user creates a storyboard that specifies the sequencing of scenes for the animation. Objects and actors are defined within each scene or unit. Each of the scenes is scripted: Motions, reactions, and interactions are prescribed for its actors. In addition, visual effects may be chosen for transitions between scenes.

Figure 9.33
An animation of balloons drifting away can be created easily using the technique of automated in-betweening. The balloon graphic is pasted in the starting frame in the lower-left-hand corner of the screen. A smaller copy of the graphic is then pasted to a later frame (shown here for illustration) in the opposite corner of the screen. The animation program then calculates the intermediate frames in the sequence plotting gradually both the change in position (shown here with the aid of an arrow) and the change in the size of the graphic. The result is a sequence of frames producing a smooth animation.

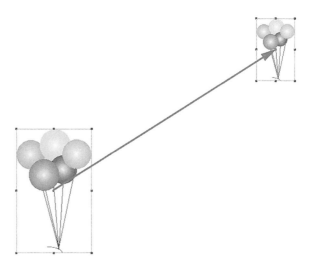

DISCOVERING MORE

Animation

Animated graphics provide a rich form of information that can be employed in a variety of media: from multimedia presentations to Web sites. For illustrations of the different types of animation applications and their products, see our online resource "Discovering More About Animation."

Authoring systems produce what are usually dubbed *multimedia presentations,* because they combine images with sound and text and often have interactive features. Authoring systems are used to create interactive, animated applications for entertainment (games and computer videos) as well as education (computer-assisted instruction) and training (computer-based training).

■ Summary

A graphic image is a digital image that has been artificially generated by computer processing. Computers have been employed for creating graphic images since their inception in the 1950s. Bit-mapped graphic images are composed of pixels, which are two-dimensional picture elements that have a spatial location in the image and a set of attributes such as color or shade. In contrast, vector graphics or object-oriented graphics are images composed of graphic objects derived from primitives such as lines, curves, and closed figures. Vector graphics offer advantages in editing and greater precision for display resolution. On the other hand, bit-mapped graphics offer greater control and flexibility. Painting programs are a popular form of bit-mapped graphic applications. Drawing and illustration programs are vector graphic applications.

Painting, drawing, and illustration are two-dimensional graphic programs because the images are created, stored, and displayed as two-dimensional images. Three-dimensional graphic application programs allow the user to define and manipulate objects in simulated three dimensions. The program automatically calculates and displays the three-dimensional scene using perspective projection. Animation programs provide tools for automating the process of developing frames used in computer animations.

Computer graphics is a very powerful tool that has myriad uses. For this reason, graphic tools are not limited to just the application classes discussed in this chapter. For example, desktop publishing, graphing and charting programs, presentation software, and hypermedia are application domains that often incorporate a number of essential graphic capabilities. While their uses are constrained by their respective domains (producing documents, charts and graphs, electronic overheads, etc.), many of the concepts and features surveyed here apply to their use as well. The graphic landscape is rapidly changing, too. Indeed, the world of computer-generated pictures evolves and expands perhaps faster than any other facet of the digital domain.

■ Terms

actors
aliasing
animation programs
anti-aliasing (smoothing)
background
backgrounds, animation
Bezier curves
bit-mapped graphics
  (raster graphics)
B-spline curves
canvas
cel
cel animation
CGM
clipping (image)
computer graphics
  (or graphics)
computer-assisted design
  (CAD)
construction plane
DAC-1 (Design Augmented
  by Computers)
drawing programs
DXF

EMF
EPS
extrusion
foreground
frames
Gouraud shading
hidden surface removal
illustration programs
image scale
image size
in-between frames
key frames
Lambert shading (flat shading)
lathing
menu
model description
object-oriented graphic
  applications
Page Descripion Language
  (PDL)
painting programs
palettes
parametric curves
PCX

Phong shading
PostScript
polygon-surface modeling
QuickTime
rasterizing
ray tracing
rendering
rendering programs
scene
scene description
story, storyboard
surface-based 3-D graphics
SVG
three-dimensional graphics
  (3-D graphics)
two-dimensional graphics
  (2-D graphics)
vector graphics (object-
  oriented graphics)
volume-based 3-D graphics
voxels (volume elements)
wireframe model construction
world-view coordinates
Z-buffer

■ Questions for Review

1. Digital graphic images are often composed of pixels. How are pixels organized?

2. What does a bitplane refer to?

3. What are the major differences between bit-mapped and vector graphics? What advantages does each offer?

4. What is 3-D graphics?

5. What advantages do 3-D graphic programs offer over 2-D applications?

6. How does a metafile format differ from a standard graphic file format?

7. Identify which graphic file formats store bit-mapped graphics, which store vector-based graphics, and which formats are capable of storing both.

8. Compare and contrast painting and drawing programs. To what sorts of applications is each best suited?

9. Distinguish among the concepts of image size, resolution, and scale.

10. Compare and contrast the functionality of drawing and illustration programs.

11. What are image layers? How does the process of clipping relate to this concept?

12. What are parametric curves? How are they employed in drawing and illustration programs?

13. Describe the two varieties of 3-D graphics (volume-based versus surface-based).

14. Surface-based 3-D graphic software usually divides the task of 3-D modeling into three stages: model description, scene description, and rendering. Describe each of these stages.

15. Explain the 3-D methods of polygon-surface modeling and wireframe construction.

16. Explain the methods of extrusion and lathing for defining 3-D wireframe models.

17. Lambert shading, Gouraud shading, and Phong shading are forms of rendering that are often characterized in 3-D applications by their speed: fast, medium, and slow (respectively). Why would these rendering methods have different effective speeds? Explain.

18. Describe how animation programs automate some of the tasks normally associated with conventional cel animation.

19. What is automated in-betweening?

20. Describe the types of products created by animated authoring systems.

Chapter 10

The Sound and the Fury—Digital Style

OBJECTIVES

- How sounds are converted to digital form by sampling

- Methods and principles for editing digital sound

- Computer methods for synthesizing speech

- The challenges involved in computer speech understanding

- How digital video differs from conventional analog video

- The advantages and disadvantages of digital versus analog video

- How video is captured and digitized

Sound is a very important medium for conveying and receiving information. Consider, for example, a heated debate. The ways in which the words used in the debate are spoken convey meaning and nuances of expression well beyond that possible using only a written transcript of the debate. In a similar way, reading a musical score provides most of us little insight into the beauty and power of the music it defines.

Because sound is so important in conveying meaning, beauty, and the power of persuasion, it is obviously desirable to be able to include the medium of sound within our computerized communications. Modern computers and methods of converting sound to and from digital form provide us with this opportunity.

In a similar way, the video medium can greatly enhance communications. In the past, making motion pictures and video with computers has been restricted primarily to professional or commercial uses. Indeed, as a movie-goer, you have experienced some of the thrilling special effects created by computers. The era of DTV (digital television) has also arrived. Many television programs now employ digital sound processing for creating the illusion of surround sound in home systems. NBC was the first network to use desktop computers to compose and edit closing sequences that tied short ending scenes with the production credits. These examples should convince you that the use of computers for making movies and TV programs is far more commonplace than you might expect.

But what does digital video mean to you as a computer user? Will you be producing feature films or TV series at home? Of course not. Most commercial applications are developed on expensive, high-performance systems that are integrated with special equipment and designed exclusively for these uses. Desktop computers, on the other hand, offer less bang but cost fewer bucks and are intended for general rather than dedicated uses like professional video. Even so, the adoption of multimedia standards for consumer systems has motivated the migration of digital video capabilities to the desktop domain. Personal systems today cannot achieve results on the same scale as those seen in theaters and on television, but the era of desktop video is just beginning. Digital video offers another rich source of information for the multimedia equation. To exploit what it has to offer, you will need to understand how digital video is organized and processed.

In this chapter you will learn about some of the basic concepts and techniques underlying digital sound and digital video. With this knowledge, you will not only have a better appreciation for what is possible with these media in the professional realm, but also be prepared to incorporate sound and video in your own work when it is appropriate.

Digital Sampling of Sound

Today's desktop computers are sound-capable machines. We can store and manipulate sounds of all kinds—the spoken word, music, and artificially generated sounds such as synthesized music. Computers can generate speech from written text with reasonably good results and even respond to voice commands within limited vocabularies.

This is all accomplished by working with digital sound. **Digital sound** is sound that has been converted to or created in a discrete form suitable for storing and processing in a computer. Natural sounds are converted to digital form by a discrete sampling process. Sounds can also be created (or **synthesized**) employing one of several methods with a computer. Once in digital form, though, sound—just as we saw was the case for digitized images—can be modified or edited in a variety of ways. Whether converted or synthesized, digital sound can be "played" by a process that converts its discrete numerical values to an analog signal that audio speakers can transmit to our ears.

Unlike the process of digitizing images, digitizing sound involves sampling over *time* rather than spatially. But you are already familiar with a sampling technique very much like the one employed for digitizing sound. When we make a video using a camcorder, we are actually taking a series of still photographs (called *frames*). The number of frames taken per second is called the sampling rate. You may have "stepped through" a video clip frame-by-frame using your VCR or DVD player. If you watch televised sporting events, you have seen slow motion replays in which the action is "frozen" and projected slowly for clearer viewing. The quality of the frozen frames depends upon the resolution and speed of the camera as well as the film being used.

When the series of photographs in a video sequence are played back at approximately the same rate of speed that the pictures were taken, the action in the film can be made to appear quite natural to the eye. Recording and playback speeds are measured in **frames per second (fps)**, and speeds of 24 fps or higher are usually sufficient for producing natural looking apparent motion. In spite of this fact, *most* of the action is missing, but the frames that were captured are close enough in time to give us the sense of seeing the entire sequence of action. In films produced using video cameras with a slow filming rate, the action will appear "jumpy" as it is replayed. It is clear then that the sample rate at which images are taken is significant for fidelity during playback. In applications that require a precise frame-by-frame analysis of a sequence for a very-short-duration event (such as a water droplet hitting a water surface), a very high sampling rate will be necessary for best results. On the other hand, if we intend only to replay the sequence for normal viewing, we can quite satisfactorily simulate the actual events filmed with a rate of 24 frames per second.

The size, or resolution, of the film being used will also have an effect on the quality of a movie when it is played. If you have watched 8-mm or 16-mm home movies, you already are aware of the rather dramatic differences between these and standard 35-mm films (or the 70-mm films at theaters).

Sound sampling is based on essentially the same principles as those just described for video sampling. Sound, like the images that make up a scene, varies with time. Sound is produced by the vibration of some membrane. These vibrations are then transmitted as waves through a medium—usually air, but possibly water or some other medium. When this analog wave meets our ears, it causes our eardrums to vibrate and transmit the sound as a signal to our brains. Recording and playing digital sound requires the conversion of the analog signal to a discrete form. However, this discrete form must be converted once more to analog form to reproduce the original sound in a satisfactory way. Just as with movie making, the sampling rate and resolution of the devices used will be crucial factors in the quality of the final product in digital sound as well.

Sampling Rates and Frequencies

Sounds are rapid vibrations that are transmitted as variations in air pressure. If you were to measure the intensity of a tone, for instance, it would be plotted as a continuously undulating line or **wave** like the one depicted in Figure 10.1. Any sound wave has a number of fundamental characteristics. Two of the most important of these for digitization are amplitude and frequency. A sound wave's **amplitude** refers to its intensity or loudness. A sound wave's **frequency** is determined by the length of time it takes the wave to complete one entire cycle. Frequency is usually measured in the unit **Hertz,** which stands for a cycle per second. Hence a sound of frequency 5 KHz (= 5,000 Hertz) is repeating its fundamental cycle 5,000 times per second. The frequency of a sound determines the pitch of the sound as heard by our ears— the higher the frequency, the higher the pitch of the sound.

Middle C on the piano produces a sound with frequency of 440 Hz and the highest note (C8) on a piano has a frequency of 4,186 Hz (or, a little more than 4 KHz). If we examined the sound waves for middle C and C8, we would see that they have exactly the same wave pattern or shape. The *only* difference in them is that they have different frequencies. The human ear can typically hear frequencies from 20 Hz up to about 20 KHz, although we tend to lose our ability to hear frequencies in the upper range as we grow older. Some animals (dogs, for example) can hear significantly higher frequencies.

Figure 10.1

Illustrating the basic sound wave characteristics of cycle and amplitude.

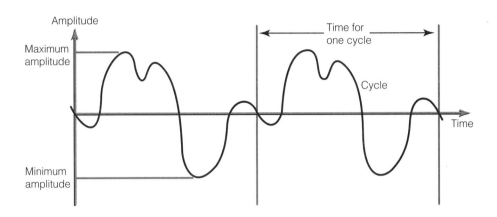

Digitizing a Sound Wave

Let's consider the process of digitizing a sound wave. Sampling a sound wave consists of determining the amplitude of the sound at some number of discrete times within a given time interval. Although it is not necessary to do so, we generally will place these discrete times equal distances apart along the time axis. The number of these times chosen per second determines the **sampling rate.** It too is expressed in Hertz, which this time means number of *samples* per second. So, a sampling rate of 22 KHz would mean dividing the time axis into 22,000 equally spaced times per second. Figure 10.2 illustrates.

We should point out that the actual reconstruction of an analog wave from the discrete values is done using more sophisticated mathematical techniques than the one shown in Figure 10.2. Instead of assuming the amplitude to be a constant over each interval, the values are interpolated mathematically to supply a smoother curve. Nonetheless, no matter what technique is used, the sampling rate is still an inherent limitation on how accurately the original wave form can be reproduced.

Suppose for a moment that the frequency of the sound wave shown in Figure 10.2 is 2 KHz. What sampling rate have we adopted? Since we are sampling 20 points in every cycle and there are 2,000 cycles per second, the sampling rate is 20 × 2,000 = 40,000 = 40 KHz. As you will soon learn, a sampling rate in this range is satisfactory for even the most demanding musical applications. Thus, sampling 20 times per cycle would be appropriate for a wave of frequency around 2 KHz. On the other hand, for waves of higher frequencies, keeping the sampling rate around 40 KHz will require that we sample each cycle significantly fewer than 20 times. For example, if a sampled wave has a frequency of 10 KHz, we will be able to sample only 4 points in each cycle if we are to keep the sampling rate at 40 KHz.

We must be careful not to drop the number of samples per cycle too low. What would happen if we adopted a sampling rate allowing only one sample per cycle? As Figure 10.3 illustrates, we would conclude upon reconstructing the analog wave that the sound had a constant amplitude—a very monotonous sound indeed! It is exactly this phenomenon—called **aliasing**—in movie filming that causes the wheels of the stage coach to appear to "stand still" occasionally in some of the older Western movies. It occurs when the sample rate of the camera (shutter speed) matches the revolution rate of the wheel so that each time the shutter opens, the wheel is photographed in what appears to be exactly the same position. As a general rule, we must sample at least two points in each sound wave cycle to have reasonable hope that we have captured enough of the quality of a sound to reconstruct it satisfactorily. This rule is known as **Nyquist's theorem.**

ADCs and DACs

The devices that perform the sampling of an analog wave to produce a digital file are called **analog-to-digital converters,** or **ADCs** for short. The devices which perform the opposite transformation—reconstructing an analog wave from a digital file—are called **digital-to-**

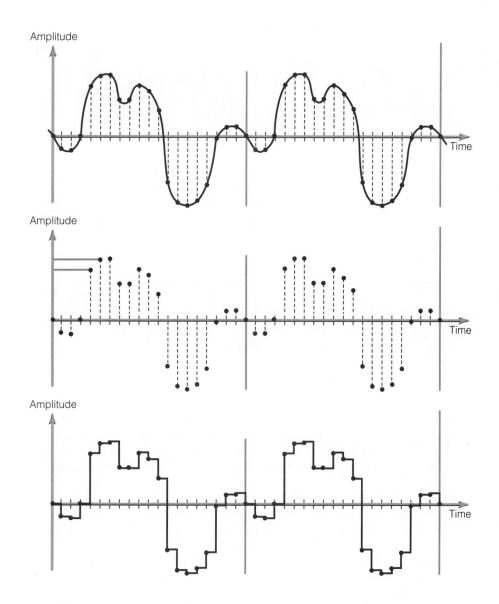

Figure 10.2
The process of sampling and reconstructing a sampled wave involves several steps. In the top part of the figure, the wave is sampled at a predetermined rate. The particular rate chosen provides for twenty samples to be taken for each complete cycle of the sound wave. Forty samples are taken for the two cycles shown. In the middle part of the figure, the discrete samples are represented. For each of the forty points shown, the value of the amplitude is recorded and stored. Finally in the bottom part of the figure, a simple analog reconstruction is derived from the forty sample values by making the amplitude a constant over each of the intervening intervals between sample points.

analog converters, or **DAC**s for short. The choice of sample rates when digitizing sound will be a function of the capability of the ADC you are using. Likewise, the resulting quality of playback when converting from digital to analog will be limited by the capability of the DAC you are using. If you own an audio compact disc player, you own a DAC. Sound wave reconstruction from a discrete set of values is exactly the process that must be accomplished to play your audio CDs.

Audio compact discs are recorded using an ADC that samples at a rate of 44.1 KHz. According to Nyquist's theorem, this should be sufficient to capture all sounds in the range of frequencies (up to 20 KHz or so) that the human ear hears. If we are recording speech as opposed to music, it is rare for the human voice to contain frequencies much higher than 5 KHz (approximately the frequency of C8, remember), hence a sampling rate of about 10 KHz is usually quite sufficient.

To use a personal computer for digitizing sound, you must have a microphone attached to an ADC and a connection to allow you to store the values produced by the ADC in your computer's memory or on disk. This may require that a **digital audio capture card,** which will contain an ADC, be installed in one of your computer's internal expansion slots, although some computers come with a built-in ADC. You can also buy an external ADC device, which contains both an ADC and microphone that plugs into a standard port on your computer.

Figure 10.3

Sampling a sound wave using one sample per cycle produces unacceptable results.

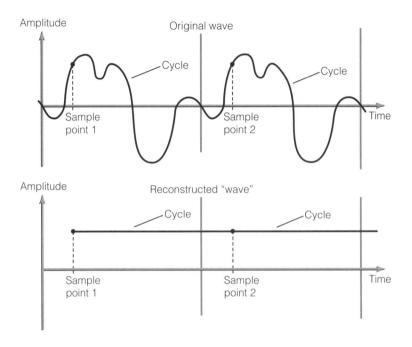

Resolution and Dynamic Range

We have seen the effect that the choice of sampling rate has on a digitized sound wave. There is another important factor to consider also—the resolution at which we capture and store the sample point amplitudes. The **resolution** of digitized sound refers to the accuracy with which we represent each sampled amplitude. Figure 10.4 illustrates. The resolution we use will largely be determined by the amount of memory we're willing to devote to storing digitized sound.

If we are sampling for many seconds at 44 KHz per second, we will soon acquire a large number of sample point amplitudes. For only one minute of sound, this sampling rate would produce a total of $60 \times 44,000 = 2,640,000$ amplitudes for storage. Of course, we might well desire to capture 100 times this much sound (an entire speech or concert for example). Given such large quantities of data, it is important to store the individual values as efficiently as possible. As a result, we are often forced to adopt a less than optimal storage scheme that sacrifices some accuracy for economy.

The usual sound storage scheme involves scaling the range of amplitudes we wish to store so that we store these values as integers, since integers are easier to process than floating point numbers (real numbers). The space requirements for storing sound are so demanding that we are sometimes forced to reduce the normal size allocation for integers.

One practical storage scheme allocates only a single byte (or 8 bits) for storing each amplitude. Such sound storage systems are referred to as *8-bit digital sound* for this reason, and we say that the sound is stored with 8-bit resolution. Using an 8-bit scheme, we must scale the range of amplitudes so that we represent the entire spectrum of amplitudes with integer values from 0 to 255, because the unsigned integer 255 is the largest we can represent in 8 bits. Every sampled amplitude must be mapped to this scale and rounded off to the nearest of the 256 values allowed by the storage scheme. Many ADCs—your compact disc player included—employ *16-bit digital sound*. These devices use 16-bit resolution, which provides much more accurate sound reproduction. The total range of amplitude values that can be stored determines the **dynamic range** of the digitized sound.

When we are sampling voice, the approximations for amplitude values in 8-bit resolution are accurate enough to reproduce the sound satisfactorily. However, for music, 8-bit resolution is not sufficient for high fidelity, and our ears will generally be able to distinguish the playback from the original. For this reason, 16-bit resolution is typically used to digitize music. Using this scheme, we are able to divide the dynamic range into a larger number of integers because we will use 16 bits to store each value. How much additional resolution do we get by

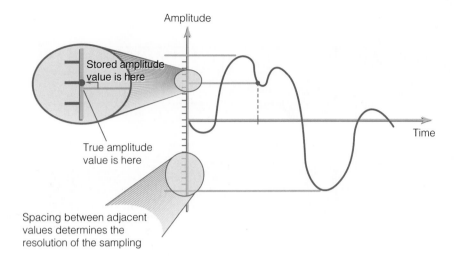

Figure 10.4
The accuracy of stored amplitudes depends on resolution. Some accuracy is always lost by scaling and representing amplitude values only with integers.

doubling the amount of storage required? Actually, we get quite an impressive improvement. Recall that we can store 256 integers ($= 2^8$) using 8 bits. With 16 bits, we can store $2^{16} = 65,536$—an improvement of more than 25,000 percent!

Sometimes extending the scale of amplitudes to include the very highest and lowest amplitudes will cause significant degradation in the accuracy with which all amplitudes are stored. When this occurs, it may be better to lose the highest and lowest amplitudes by reducing the scale range and improving the accuracy with which the majority of the amplitude values are stored. This amounts to reducing the dynamic range of the sound being digitized. By reducing the dynamic range, the accuracy can be significantly improved for the bulk of the data being stored, as illustrated in Figure 10.5.

Each situation may dictate a different consideration of the trade-offs involved. Whenever the dynamic range is restricted, those amplitudes outside the range will be given the highest or lowest values (whichever applies) in the range—the sound wave will be effectively "chopped" off at the limits of the range. This effect is often called **clipping.**

The system we are using for playback will always have some dynamic response limitations (inability to reproduce sounds faithfully with especially low or especially high amplitudes or loudness). So, in some cases, the reduction in the dynamic range of stored values may actually cost us very little in the quality of the sounds when they are played back. For example, the response of small speaker systems that are supplied for computers is usually quite limited. Clipping the input signal in this instance will likely produce no discernible effect.

Storage Requirements for Digitized Sound

Let's analyze a practical example to get a better feeling for sound storage requirements. We mentioned earlier that your audio CD player is a DAC (digital-to-analog converter). The sound on a CD is stored in digital form (unlike a phonograph record, which stores music in an analog form). The sampling (i.e., recording) is usually done at a rate of 44.1 MHz with 16-bit resolution. Because all CDs are in stereo, we must record two channels, which doubles the storage requirements. Now, with these parameters to work with, how many bits are required to store an hour of music on a CD? For each second, we store $44,100 \times 16 \times 2 = 1.4$ million bits. For the full hour, $60 \times 60 = 3,600$ times this number, or about 5 billion bits or approximately 630 MB, will be required.

Actually, audio CD recordings also include a lot of error correcting and noise reduction information as well. Altogether this more than doubles the storage requirements. With today's technology, these numbers quickly exceed the capacity of a compact disc, so until audio DVD

Figure 10.5
This example illustrates accuracy and dynamic range trade-offs. In (a), the full dynamic range is captured. Part (b) illustrates that accuracy can be greatly increased by limiting the dynamic range, but loss of data occurs outside the range of values chosen.

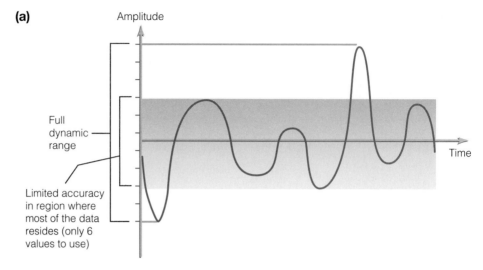

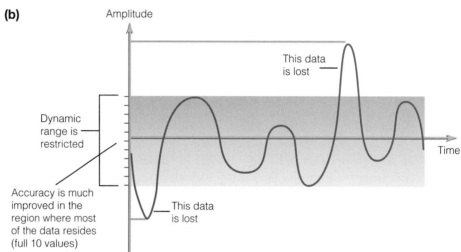

discs become more common, you shouldn't expect to find three-hour concerts on a single disc. Of course it wouldn't be difficult to put three hours of conversation, speeches, or other spoken words on a single CD, because we could reduce the resolution to 8-bits and the sample rate to about 10 KHz with no discernible reduction in quality.

One method to combat the large storage requirements for sound digitization is to compress the sampled sound. **Data compression** is accomplished using techniques that mathematically transform the file's data so that the resulting file requires less memory. When the original data is needed again, the reverse transformation recovers it (or a close approximation to it) for our use. You'll learn more about the techniques of data compression in Chapter 20.

There are a number of proprietary compression algorithms available to compress sound files. These will usually provide a choice of several levels of compression—2:1, 3:1, and 6:1 ratios for example. As you would surmise, a file compressed at a 2:1 ratio uses only one-half the amount of storage, and one compressed at the 6:1 rate uses only one-sixth the amount. A 3:1 compression is suitable for music under certain circumstances, although there is some loss of fidelity. The 6:1 compression is suitable only for speech.

Rather than using compression, storage requirements can also be reduced using a lower sampling rate or a lower resolution in the first place. Which method is preferred? In general, you are better off digitizing at a higher sampling rate then compressing the resulting file, as opposed to using a lower sampling rate in the first place. There are two good reasons for this. One is that for approximately the same storage, a 3:1 compressed sample will sound better than one sampled at one-third the rate. The reason is that the compression algorithm uses "smarter" strategies to decide which sample points to omit. That is, it doesn't just drop two of every three sample points; rather, it tries to choose those points that will have minimal impact on the reconstructed sound.

There is another reason why it is better to sample fully and compress later if necessary. By taking a full sample, you will optimize the editing that you might choose to do on the digitized sound. In general, digital sound editing will be more satisfactory if done before, rather than after, compression.

Synthesizing Music

One of the earliest uses of computers for audio processing was as a component in sound synthesis systems. Synthesized sound, of course, is created electronically. It is most often used to produce music from electronic instruments as opposed to traditional woodwinds, percussion, and brass instruments. The methods used to "play" these new instruments differ somewhat from those of traditional instruments. In fact, music synthesis methods can vary considerably, and new ones are introduced regularly. Even so, these methods do have some common features. All methods employ a basic component, called an **oscillator,** as a sound source. Oscillators can be analog or digital devices. In either case, a steady electrical signal is produced

FOCUS   Sound on the World Wide Web

As you know, sounds are often found on Web pages. Just as is the case for external images, your Web browser must have audio player software to play these files. When you click over a Web page link to an external resource, the file will be downloaded to your computer system as a temporary file. Depending upon the type of file (image, sound, or video), an appropriate player application will be identified and opened, and the file will be handled by that player application. Player applications come in two varieties: helper applications and plug-ins. **Helper applications** are external player applications, while **plug-ins** are add-on programs to the browser stored in an accessible directory or folder. For more detailed information about sound on the Web, consult the online resource "Focus on Exploring Sound on the Web."

Digitized Sound and Copyright/Royalty Implications

SOCIAL THEMES

The digital world presents many challenges in interpreting and enforcing copyright and intellectual property laws that were typically designed with more traditional information storage and distribution models, like print and analog recordings and video, in mind. Perhaps one of the most visible battlegrounds in the tug-of-war that has evolved as these challenges are discussed and new interpretations are sought has been the Napster controversy centered on digitized music.

For a discussion of the issues raised by Napster and other music services, consult the online essay "Digitized Sound and Copyright/Royalty Issues."

in the human audible frequency range of from 20 Hz to 20 KHz. Musical tones are then generated by combining two or more oscillators. The particular methods of combination are the source of most of the variation in the synthesizers available today.

Combining Simple Waveforms

The oscillators in a synthesis system produce very simple waveforms—usually one of the four basic types: sine wave, square wave, triangle wave, or sawtooth wave. Most sounds are complex waveforms made up of some combination of a number of simple waveforms. A rather surprising mathematical fact is that we can build arbitrarily close approximations to any complex waveform by combining waveforms of any of these simple types. This is the theoretical basis of music synthesis (and much of data communications as well). By cleverly combining simple oscillator-generated waveforms, synthesizers can be designed to make sounds like those from common musical instruments, as well as sounds that are different from any conventional instrument.

MIDI Instruments and Devices

With a great many manufacturers producing music synthesizers and related devices, the industry recognized early on that a standard interface between electronic instruments and synthesizers would be a great convenience. In 1982, the **MIDI** (**Musical Instrument Digital Interface**) standard was agreed upon by an international group of manufacturers. This standard specifies a common interface allowing musical instruments that contain microprocessors (computers) to communicate with other instruments and devices containing microprocessors. The interface specified includes the kinds and configurations of cables and cable plugs as well as the format of the data being transferred over the cables.

For example, you may own or have a friend who owns an electronic keyboard. Some electronic keyboards contain their own synthesizers and amplifiers. Others do not; they depend upon using external synthesizers and amplifiers. Even for those that do, a desirable feature is to attach to a more powerful or feature-laden synthesizer. When you purchase a MIDI keyboard, you can be assured of finding amplifiers and synthesizers with which your keyboard can communicate effectively—in fact most such devices will be **MIDI compatible.** Similarly, computer software designed to compose and edit music usually provides for input and output in the MIDI format. This means that the computer may be directly attached to a synthesizer to play the composed music or attached to a MIDI keyboard to capture musical notes being played.

We should note that the signals being transferred over the MIDI cables are not representations of the actual sounds. Rather, they are the parameters from which the sound can be generated by the instrument receiving the signal. Such parameters include identification of the note being pressed, the length of time it was held down, the aftertouch (amount of pressure applied to a key after it is fully depressed), the pitch blend setting, the program number selected (determines the kind of sound or instrument associated with the key), and a host of other information.

The MIDI format has several advantages over full digital sound files. It is much more compact, can be easily edited, and allows for musical tracks to be easily combined (superimposed).

FOCUS   Basic Synthesis Techniques

There are many different synthesis methods. Each of these techniques has been extensively studied in its own right and could occupy many pages if we were exploring the topic in depth. For an overview of some of the most popular synthesis methods consult the online resource "Focus on Sound Synthesis."

For example, the software Finale is a popular package for editing MIDI files and mixing multiple tracks.

Speech Synthesis and Recognition

Potentially one of the most promising uses of the computer's sound capabilities is computer/human interaction using spoken language. You've undoubtedly heard computer-generated messages and information on the airport tram and the subway, in elevators, at the grocery checkout, and in a host of other locations. These messages provide valuable information in a readily accessible form without the need for a human communicator. Although such applications of computer-generated speech, or **speech synthesis,** are convenient, the same functions could be achieved through other means—such as screen displays, printed messages, and so on. However, for some applications, communicating information using generated speech is not only convenient but essential.

For example, in modern airplane cockpits, the number of dials, gauges, and digital readouts has become so large that it is difficult for a pilot to keep track of all the information important to the task at hand. This is especially true in an emergency situation that calls for complex maneuvers with little margin for error in sequencing and timing. Even if a portion of the large amount of information could be communicated by simple verbal messages, this would allow the pilot to absorb more information in the same amount of time. In fighter planes, such communication can be critical. For example, when evading an enemy plane or missile, the pilot simply cannot digest all the requisite information within the tight time constraints imposed. But with computer-generated speech, the pilot can better absorb and process enough information to perform proper maneuvers.

The ability to generate speech from written text makes the computer an indispensable tool for the visually impaired. For example, using this capability, computers can read aloud books, magazines, newspapers, and electronic mail for visually impaired users. Of course, Braille versions of a great deal of written material are available. But the computer's ability to "read" electronic mail and daily newspapers enables the visually impaired to handle a form of communication that they otherwise could not.

The ability of a computer to react to spoken commands, called **automated speech understanding,** completes the communication cycle. For example, using speech understanding systems, pilots not only can receive valuable information from their planes, but they can issue verbal commands to be executed. Similarly, the visually impaired can engage in electronic communication and employ their computers efficiently and more productively.

In this section, we will explore the basic concepts involved with both modes of verbal communication with computers—computer speech synthesis and speech understanding.

Computer Speech Synthesis

Of the two processing tasks—speech synthesis and understanding—generating speech from written text is by far the less complicated. Speech synthesis can be handled in one of several ways. An obvious approach might be to store the pronunciation of the most frequently used words in a digital speech dictionary. We could employ one or more persons to read the words for digitization and then store the digitized sound for later recall. Reading a selection of text would then be accomplished in a way quite similar to that of checking text for misspellings. Each word would be looked up in the speech dictionary. Once found, its associated digitized pronunciation would be played. A binary search tree organization like that used for spelling dictionaries and database indices could be employed for storing and accessing the speech dictionary more efficiently.

There are several difficulties with this approach, though. First, it would require a large amount of storage—far larger than the corresponding spelling dictionary. The digitized sounds for each word would have to be stored. Let's assume that, on the average, it takes about one second to speak a word. If we digitize these sounds at a sampling rate of 5 KHz with an 8-bit resolution (the minimum acceptable settings), we would still consume, on average, about

5,000 bytes of storage for each spoken word. For a 100,000 word dictionary, this amounts to 500 MB of data—a sizable amount of the storage for the typical desktop computer system! Clearly, this is not a very practical solution. In addition, our dictionary is bound to omit words that we would wish to pronounce—names of people and places, slang words, specialized terms in a given subject area, and so on. It is also difficult to achieve a natural speech rate when every word must be accessed on a hard disk before being pronounced. Even with a binary search tree organization, the rate at which the text can be "read back" doesn't give a natural sound to the reading. Finally, our dictionary lookup method would not be able to pronounce words that are spelled the same but read differently according to the context in which they are used (like the word *read* for example).

An alternate method for speech synthesis involves an analysis of the written text before trying to pronounce it. A language like English employs a surprisingly sparse (fewer than 50) set of basic sounds, called **phonemes.** The language gains its richness of expression by the large number of possible combinations of these sounds. To exploit this fact in speech synthesis, the computer first breaks the text selection up into a sequence of basic phonemes, then each phoneme can be quickly looked up in a digital speech dictionary and pronounced. Since this dictionary holds only 50 or so sounds, it requires very little disk space. In fact, using our earlier assumptions about sampling rate and resolution (5 KHz and 8-bits, respectively) and the fact that the average phoneme probably takes less than one-fifth the time to verbalize than a full word, we could store a 50-phoneme dictionary in about 50,000 bytes. At this size, the entire dictionary could be loaded from disk into main memory for very rapid lookup and retrieval.

Phoneme analysis and decomposition is the method most often used to synthesize speech whenever the target text is unpredictable. In other words, if we desire to synthesize subway car alert messages employing a 100-word vocabulary, we may well store the entire digital dictionary and look up words as needed. On the other hand, if we are trying to create a program to read the evening newspaper, we almost certainly will use a phoneme analysis and decomposition method.

Phoneme decomposition, however, is a nontrivial task. As we have already noted, there are many words that are spelled the same yet pronounced differently. A good speech synthesis program will recognize and properly decide the most common of these occurrences. It is also the case that the same sound can be represented by different groups of letters. Consider the words *enough* and *buff,* for instance. The letters "ough" and "uff" represent the same sound in this case. If English were more phonetically regular, *enough* would be spelled *enuff,* or perhaps *buff* would be spelled *bough.* Oops! The word *bough* is already in the language and pronounced quite differently from *buff.* In fact, exactly the same group of letters ("ough") are pronounced entirely differently in the words *enough* and *bough.* (To add to the confusion, consider the words *cough, though,* and *through.*)

Do we give up on phoneme decomposition? Not at all. After all, we learned to pronounce English text without having to learn every single word as a separate sound combination. How did we accomplish this? We first learned a number of basic phonetic rules; then we learned that every rule (or so it seemed) had its own exceptions that we had to remember individually. We can mimic this learning process to create a program to separate words into their phonemes. The result is a system based a number of fundamental rules with their exceptions programmed as additional rules. Even more rules can be added to help decide between different pronunciations for the same word (i.e., same spelling) dependent upon the context. Using this **rule-based phoneme recognition** approach, it is possible to create a speech synthesis program that produces good results.

For example, the following sentence contains two different uses of the abbreviation "Dr." as well as three different uses of numbers—one as a day of the month, another as a year, the third one as a street address.

On June 5, 1995, Dr. Jones moved to 1702 Oakwood Dr.

A good rule-based speech synthesis program will be able to read this sentence, correctly making these distinctions. It might be read as follows:

On June fifth, nineteen ninety-five, Doctor Jones moved to seventeen oh two Oakwood Drive.

Automated Speech Understanding

The problems inherent in automated speech understanding are much more difficult to solve than those of speech synthesis. As we shall see, there are several fundamental differences between these two processes. In speech synthesis we start with text and must discover and program the rules to separate text into phonemes. In speech understanding, we first digitize the speech, then we must reconstruct the words that were spoken. Consider the word *hello,* whose digital form as spoken by one speaker is shown in Figure 10.6.

Programming a computer to recognize this pattern of points as the word *hello* would indeed be a challenge. The envelope of the sound is the overall shape of the amplitudes—the outline of the sound, so to speak. The envelope is very useful for trying to decide what sound has been digitized, but the transformation from envelope to identification is not completely straightforward. Many very different sounds have envelopes that are quite similar.

The envelope is an attempt to characterize the sound with a high-level summary of its digitization. Taking the opposite approach, if we stretch the time axis (the horizontal axis), perhaps the additional detail exposed will be helpful. While this additional detail may be helpful in some cases, as you can imagine, it becomes even more difficult to distinguish two sounds when you are examining tiny fractions of a second at a time. Consult Figure 10.7, which shows a portion of the digitized word *hello* with the time scale expanded to expose the individual sample points. Remember that this is the actual data a voice recognition system must deal with. It must be able to conclude from such data what word was spoken. This would be difficult enough if a word's digital form were unique. Unfortunately, this is far from the case.

In speech synthesis, we start with text in a form (ASCII code) that is unambiguous and consistent. In speech understanding, we don't have the luxury of beginning with a consistent source of digitized sound. This is because no two persons will speak a word in exactly the same way. Figure 10.8 illustrates. The human voice is almost as distinctive and individualized as fingerprints. Think about how easily you can recognize the voice of a friend or of a famous person whom you have heard speak many times. In fact voice recognition is used in some computerized security systems.

Regional and national accents also play a major role in speech understanding. A person from New Jersey is likely to pronounce many words differently than the way a person from South Carolina pronounces those same words. We usually have no trouble "hearing" and interpreting these differences, but the digital versions of the words will have very different features. Programming a computer to recognize such differences is not an easy task.

In addition to the variation from person to person, even a single person will not say the same word exactly the same way each time it is spoken. The mood you are in, the stress you might be under, the position of the word in a sentence, the emphasis that is intended, whether you have a cold, as well as many other factors contribute to this variability. Yet, in

Figure 10.6
One possible digital form for the word hello.

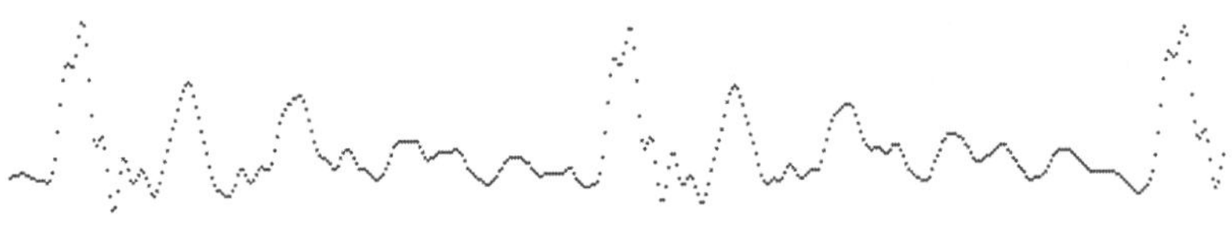

Figure 10.7
The digital form of the word hello *shown in Figure 10.6 is illustrated here with the time axis stretched to reveal more detail. The portion shown here is very small—a tiny fraction of a second.*

Figure 10.8
Digitized versions of hello *from three speakers. Note the distinctive differences in the three digitizations. Differences such as these must be identified and eliminated for effective speech recognition.*

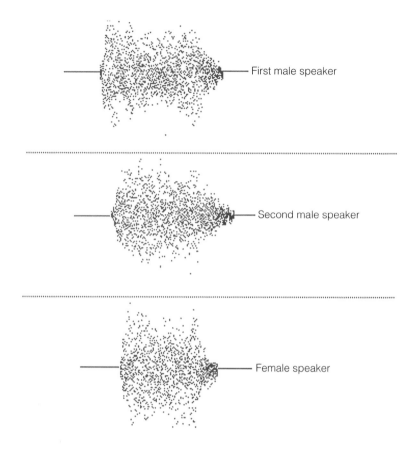

First male speaker

Second male speaker

Female speaker

all these situations, if the (same) spoken words are written down, they look the same. As you can see, understanding speech is a very different matter from synthesizing text.

Because of the variability from person to person, it is not uncommon for commercial speech understanding systems to be "tuned" to a single person's voice. In other words, these systems are designed to recognize words the way a particular individual speaks them. These are called **speaker-dependent speech understanding systems** because the user must train them to recognize his or her speech. When the same words are spoken by another person, the system may not recognize them at all or may recognize only a portion of them.

For example, early work done on speech understanding systems was designed to help fighter pilots communicate commands to their aircraft. These **voice activation systems** were specially designed and tuned for individual pilots. After extensive ground testing, they were put into service on a trial basis in actual flights. It was discovered that the systems that worked wonderfully in the ground-based tests were woefully inadequate during flights. The voice patterns of the pilots were not the same on the ground and during a flight. Especially during times of stress, the pilot voice patterns changed enough to raise the error rate to unacceptable levels.

The problems to be solved in speech understanding extend beyond those inherent in recognizing single words. Such systems must also be able to separate words within the digital version. In some cases this is relatively easy; in others, quite difficult. If the phrase to be digitized is spoken clearly and relatively slowly with each word distinctly enunciated, the division between words in the digitization may be relatively clear cut and unambiguous. Figure 10.9 illustrates.

On the other hand, we've all known people whose speech patterns make it difficult for us sometimes to pick up every word spoken, as illustrated in Figure 10.10.

Indeed, when we hear a passage spoken in a foreign language in which we are not fluent, our reaction is often that the speakers are speaking a nonstop barrage of words in very rapid succession. Of course, most often the speech is at a normal pace. What makes it sound so

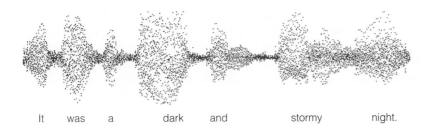

It   was   a   dark   and   stormy   night.

Figure 10.9
The digital form of a sentence in which the division between words is relatively clear-cut and unambiguous. The sentence was spoken relatively slowly with each word distinctly enunciated (as Vincent Price might have said it).

It was a dark and stormy night.

Figure 10.10
Compare this digitization with that shown in Figure 10.9. Here the speaker is speaking in a more relaxed and colloquial manner, not paying attention to the careful enunciation of individual words as before.

"fast" is that we cannot effectively separate the individual words being spoken because our ears are not tuned to the patterns and rhythm of the language being spoken. To the computer, all languages are foreign! Voice recognition programs must be cleverly constructed to pick out individual words from a stream of digitized sample points. This is rarely an easy task.

Speech understanding systems that are able to recognize a multitude of different speakers and the same speaker in a variety of environments are said to be **robust speech understanding systems.** Such systems are very challenging to construct, and successful ones are few. Currently, successful systems require a number of constraints such as limited vocabularies and restricted contexts to produce good results. A great deal of energy and money has been spent over the past 20 years or so on this problem. It has proved to be one of the most formidable problems yet attacked in computing. Progress has been made and the work continues. Although we still have a way to go before voice-activated computers become commonplace, we will no doubt see more and more products incorporating speech understanding in the next few years. Indeed, many experts predict that speech understanding will be the next major breakthrough in computer user interfaces and usability.

Editing Digitized Sound

Once a selection of sound is digitized and stored inside the computer as a collection of numbers, there are many editing possibilities. Digital sound editing belongs to the general category of techniques and methods collectively called **digital signal processing.** Most of these techniques were created and studied thoroughly long before the present use of computers for sound manipulation. For example, radar and radio transmissions are often digitized and processed to filter out noise and highlight the parts of the signal containing relevant information.

As we pointed out earlier, one of the major advantages of converting analog information to digital form is the ease with which its digital approximation can be manipulated and modified. The precision with which digital information is stored allows very tight control over even the individual sample points, if we desire. In this section, we will take a brief look at some representative sound editing techniques.

Changing Pitch and Setting Recording Options

All sound editing software will give you the option of setting the sampling rate when you record. Often you will also be able to select a compression ratio if one is desired. Individual packages will typically have their own proprietary compression algorithms and so different ratios may be available in different packages. Higher ratios (like 6:1 and 8:1) might be suitable to record speech but would not be useful for recording music. A 4:1 ratio could be used for either, although the quality of the music playback might still suffer. You will also typically be able to select a monophonic or stereophonic recording mode. Of course, stereophonic recording will require two microphones and will take twice as much storage as a monophonic recording. Most sound editing applications also allow the user to change the pitch at which recorded sounds are played back.

Special Effects Editing

There are a great many digital signal processing techniques that are useful for editing sound. We will discuss several of these to give you the flavor of the kinds of processing possible using sound editing software. For example, you can change the amplitude of a selected portion of a digitized sound file by choosing a percentage of increase or decrease. Choosing a 200% increase would mean that the amplitude of each sample point will be doubled.

Another effect that is easy to apply is to insert an echo into a sound file. This is accomplished by making a fairly straightforward mathematical transformation on the digitized amplitudes. The amplitudes of the portion of sound to be given an echo are reduced (the user can set the amount of reduction) and then shifted forward on the time axis (again, the user can set the amount of shift).

One of the more common signal processing techniques—one you are most likely already familiar with—involves applying a filter to increase the amplitudes at certain frequencies and decrease the amplitudes at other frequencies. If you've used an equalizer with your stereo or CD player, this is exactly the same technique.

It is interesting to note that when the amplitude of a sound is increased, some of the new amplitude values may be "clipped" if they fall outside the dynamic range supported. Whether you choose 8-bit or 16-bit sound capture, the limitations of resolution will often require some clipping of the dynamic range. When this occurs, the clipped amplitudes are assigned the largest (or smallest as the case demands) value in the supported dynamic range.

Because of clipping, the effects of increasing amplitudes cannot always be reversed. If we were to double the amplitude, then halve it, theoretically we should get back the original sound. But if clipping occurs, the amplitudes that were clipped have been reassigned, so when those values are halved, we do not get the original values. In other words, the effects of clipping remain in the reconstituted sound file, even though there is now plenty of room to support the range of the actual amplitudes. This lack of symmetry is a characteristic of many signal processing techniques. We must take care when applying several steps that we think will return us to some previous point. As with amplitude adjustment, some operations are simply not reversible.

DISCOVERING MORE

Sound Editing

There are a number of desktop software applications designed especially for digital sound editing and modification. The first and still one of the most popular of these packages is *SoundEdit,* available on the Macintosh. Indeed most other desktop sound editing software has been heavily influenced by *SoundEdit,* and many of these packages have

been designed to mimic its user interface. For example, *Sound Forge* which is available for Windows computers is modeled after *SoundEdit.*

For more detailed information about sound editing software and how it works, consult the online resource "Discovering More About Sound Editing."

Synthesis Tools

Most sound editing software feature elementary synthesis tools. This might typically consist of a white noise generator and the ability to generate the four simple oscillators (sine wave, sawtooth wave, square wave, or triangle wave) we mentioned earlier. The particular oscillator desired and its basic parameters—frequency, amplitude, and duration—are set by the user.

Another typical operation provided is the ability to modify a sound wave's envelope. The envelope of the artificially generated wave is quite monotonous. However, by creating a new envelope we take an essential step in synthesizing desired waveforms.

What Is Digital Video?

Video is usually comprised of visual images depicting live action with an accompanying audio soundtrack. **Digital video,** of course, employs digital methods to capture, store, and present video. Digital video creates the illusion of full motion by displaying a rapid sequence of changing images on a display device. This, of course, is very similar to the technique used by motion picture projectors. For motion pictures, a series of still images or frames is projected at high speed on the screen. The difference is that the computer achieves the same effect by fetching each digital image frame, displaying it, and repeating the cycle. In both instances, if the frame rate is sufficiently fast enough, our eyes are fooled into perceiving continuous motion.

As you learned in Chapter 9, these same techniques are used for computer animation as well. Indeed, the distinction between computer animation and digital video is an arbitrary one. Like differentiating digital image processing from graphics, it is simply customary to distinguish them by their source. *Digital video* usually refers to live action scenes with or without synchronized sound. In other words, digital video is essentially images from natural scenes that are often captured using analog methods and digitized for storage and subsequent processing. On the other hand, computer animation is restricted to artificial images that are created entirely by computer processing. Even so, the boundaries between them can get fuzzy at times.

We can distinguish digital video from its analog counterpart in each of the three fundamental components: capture (and storage), processing (or editing), and playback. Consult Figure 10.11 for an overview.

Capture

Video capture usually involves digitizing an analog source for live action scenes. For example, analog signals from a video camera or a VCR tape can serve as sources for the images. The signal from a videotape, for example, is already composed of a time sequence of frames. Each of these frames is an analog or continuous video image. By contrast, digitizing samples the signal both spatially and temporally. Each temporal sample is divided into spatial coordinates for conversion to pixels. Consequently, raw digital video images are very much like the digital still images treated earlier; the difference, of course, is that video captures a whole lot of them and in sequence. Digital video cameras may also be used to capture and digitize video from live action. In either case, digitizing video—like other forms of information—results in a stream of binary data that is stored in a file format known by the computer.

The frames or images of a live action scene are often accompanied by sounds. Thus, digital video can have an audio component. The audio must be captured and digitized using the techniques discussed earlier in the chapter. The only difference for video applications is that sound data must be synchronized with the visual data to be effective. In short, image data and sound data must be organized and stored together, typically in the same file.

Digitizing video images and sound requires additional hardware and software. Usually, integrated hardware components called **video capture cards** may be added to the expansion slots of a computer system to digitize analog source materials. Some desktop systems have (limited) capabilities for video capture built in. As mentioned, specially equipped digital video cameras allow the user to capture digital video without having to add hardware to the system.

Editing

Conventional editing of film and videotape is constrained by the sequential organization of these media. The source material must be viewed and searched sequentially for editing; this is called **linear editing.** On the other hand, when video data is represented and stored digitally, it may be accessed randomly. Thus, digital video supports **nonlinear editing.** Instant access to video clips or even individual frames makes editing faster and more precise. Moreover, non-linear editing is not destructive as some forms of editing analog sources are. Nonlinear editing decisions and actions are stored as instructions that the computer accesses when it plays the video; they do not alter the original source material as film splicing does, for example. Integrating special effects is also easier because graphics and image processing techniques can be applied to video frames like any other digital image.

Playback

For the process of **digital video playback,** or **playback** for short, the stored data must be fetched, processed, and converted to analog signals for video display devices and speakers. The data is usually stored in a file in secondary memory, perhaps on a hard disk or CD-ROM. The computer retrieves the file and processes it to recreate the frames and accompanying sound-track. Frames are displayed in rapid succession on the video monitor while the sound signal is sent to the speakers.

As mentioned, analog video is confined to a linear organization by its media. As a result, we are limited to viewing it sequentially as well. On the other hand, most digital video play-

Figure 10.11

The process of creating, storing, and displaying digital video requires a number of components. The visual component of video is a sequence of digital images, or frames, displayed on a monitor. The synchronized digital audio is played through speakers connected to the system.

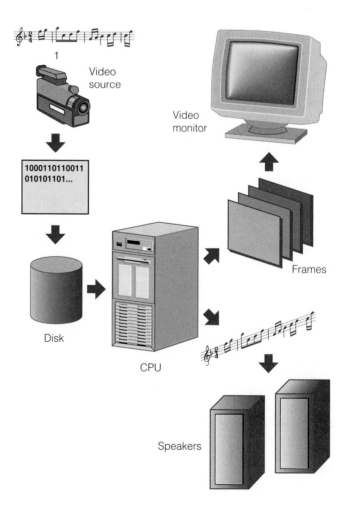

back systems offer additional modes for viewing. Because the data is discrete, it may be processed in various ways for playback. Frames may be displayed individually like a slide show, for example. In addition, features such as fast forward, rewind, reverse playback, and even random access may be available.

Digital video is often delivered in multimedia publications. Many CD-ROM titles in education and entertainment feature digital movies among the other forms of information. Of course, the fastest-growing area in digital video is consumer applications. DVD players are now commonplace, and you have no doubt experienced firsthand the superior performance of digital video playback over the traditional analog VCR videotape players. However, desktop digital video brings not only playback, but also production capabilities to a standard multimedia desktop computer system. This province of digital video will no doubt have increasing impact on you as a computer user in the future.

What Does Digital Video Have to Offer?

Desktop digital video will not make you a Hollywood producer or TV network mogul. Producing video that meets commercial or broadcast standards requires specialized, high-performance systems that cost megabucks. The desktop computer system is designed for both economy and general use. The computer that balances your checkbook and composes your documents is simply not equipped to handle special effects for *Jurassic Park*. That doesn't mean that digital video on a desktop system is a pipe dream—far from it. Many of the same advantages enjoyed by the pros can be yours on a more modest scale. In this section, we assess the chief benefits and limitations of digital video on a desktop. As you will see, there is good news and bad news.

Digital video has several advantages over analog forms. These advantages are due to two factors: the discrete nature of digital video and the power of the computer to process this data in new and interesting ways. Because it is a discrete form of information, digital video is easily scalable and randomly accessible. Because it is represented digitally, it can be stored efficiently and transmitted over computer networks like other data. When the processing power of the computer is added to the equation, digital video can be easily integrated with image processing and graphics. Moreover, it offers more powerful editing and playback capabilities as well as the potential for greater interactivity.

Video Playback and Color: A Rose Is a Rose Is a Rose?

To the uninitiated, few things seem more tangible and concrete than the perception of color. Nothing could be further from the truth. In fact, the variability of perceived colors is notorious. Specifically, how shades of color appear depend on lighting conditions, surroundings, and even individuals. Ask any photographer, painter, graphic artist, or lighting professional. Should it be any surprise then that color in video varies? In fact, color pictures from broadcast TV, a consumer VCR or DVD, and your computer can all have the same content but appear quite different. The reason is that each source employs a different method for representing and transmitting color information.

Consult the online resource "Video Playback and Color: A Rose Is a Rose Is a Rose?" to learn more about the various color representations and how these impact video playback.

Digital Video Is Easily Scalable

Like any other form of digital data, video is encoded as a stream or file of binary data. The individual images or frames that make up a video sequence are represented by numbers. These numbers, of course, must be interpreted to be converted back to video. In other words, the visual and audio information in a video file must be processed to be used at all. Therefore, some of this processing can be assigned to scaling the data to fit the system that uses it rather than being determined by the system that created it. In short, desktop digital video is **scalable,** which means that it is portable to a variety of computer systems that may vary in performance features. For example, picture resolution and color information can be adjusted to fit the capabilities of the computer displaying the video. Analog video does not have this luxury. The systems that display and use analog video must match those that produced it. As a case in point, videotape formats are not interchangeable. Beta format videotapes, for example, became extinct like the dinosaurs because the more popular VHS videotape players could not play them. The scalability of digital video can even be exploited on a single computer system. It is possible to adjust the playback picture resolution, frame rate, and color information to different settings for the same video file on the same system—without affecting the original source material.

Digital Video Is Randomly Accessible

Because video frames are discrete, they can be marked and stored for random access. In other words, the user can jump to parts of a digital movie without having to search through the entire sequence. In contrast, the media used for analog video store it sequentially. Parts of an analog video clip can be found only by forwarding or rewinding over other parts of the video. Random access is not often exploited directly; instead, its contribution makes possible many of the processing features of digital video.

Digital Video Is Stored and Transmitted Efficiently

When video is represented digitally, it inherits some of the advantages and capabilities shared by other forms of computer data. Digital video data may be stored efficiently and accurately using standard secondary memory technologies. Tapes and films are subject to wear and aging, but such storage media as CD-ROMs and DVDs preserve the original source without these defects. As data, video may also be transferred or transmitted over computer networks as well. This ability has created new opportunities for delivering video and its applications. **Video-conferencing,** for example, is the capture and transmission of two-way audio and video in real time. In a typical video-conference, two computer systems are connected over a network. Cameras and microphones attached to the systems produce the images and audio transmitted to the opposite sites. Broadcast services also use digital methods to transmit picture and CD-quality sound over digital satellite systems to millions of consumers.

Digital Video Offers Powerful Editing Capabilities

As mentioned, digital video is discrete data that can be processed by the computer. The ease and power of this processing underwrite a number of its advantages over analog forms. Editing analog video is a painstaking and labor-intensive exercise. For example, inserting and deleting motion picture film segments are done by splicing and pasting segments of the media by hand. Inserting and editing videotape are too complicated to be done by splicing. Instead, segments must be played and rerecorded to a master. Care must be taken to synchronize the signals to prevent dropouts and glitches. Mixing and rerecording with analog equipment take time and patience. Unfortunately, the equipment and media can be susceptible to noise, signal loss, and a variety of other problems. Not so for digital video. Digital editing exploits the power of the computer to insert, delete, combine, copy, and move frames like any other form of data. The process is quick and painless, but even better, the results are precise and predictable. Because video is composed of digital images, creating special effects is also easy using the techniques that we have surveyed in Chapters 8 and 9. Indeed, digital video is easily integrated with methods used in both image processing and graphics.

Digital Video Offers Additional Playback Features

Analog media and equipment pose constraints on how video can be viewed. The media support sequential playback only in a single direction (forward and sometimes backward). Viewing digital video is not so constrained. A video sequence can be processed in a number of ways. Besides forward and reverse, frames can be dropped to simulate fast play; video can be shown frame by frame as a slide show or for slow-motion effects as well. Random access allows starting and stopping at arbitrary points in the video sequence. Creating automatic loops or repeating cycles of frames is easy, too.

Digital Video Has Interactive Potential

Perhaps the most interesting advantage of digital video is its potential for interactivity. The computer already controls video playback so it can just as easily make decisions affecting that control based on feedback from the user. In other words, the content of what is viewed can be affected by interacting with the user as it is viewed. Interactive mysteries, for instance, let you solve the crime in your own way by following the clues as you find them. Educational and entertainment applications have only begun to explore the possibilities here. Interactivity may very well prove to be the primary motivating factor for desktop digital video applications.

Resource Requirements for Digital Video

Now for some bad news. Digital video poses tremendous demands on desktop computer systems. In short, creating as well as playing digital movies can bring even powerful personal computer systems to their processing knees. The large amounts of information required for both visual and audio components in digital video challenge the storage capacities and processing capabilities of most desktop systems.

In sum, the advantages of desktop digital video are important ones. Its value today, however, is more potential than realized. The chief liability for desktop digital video is not the video hardware and software but the limited performance of desktop computers themselves. The future is bright, though; computers get faster and better, and improved applications are always forthcoming.

DISCOVERING MORE

Desktop Digital Video Systems

Most computer systems today are not sufficiently equipped in either hardware or software to handle desktop video. You must add both hardware components and software to your basic system to achieve usable video capabilities.

Consult the online resource "Discovering More About Desktop Digital Video" to learn more about why digital video challenges the capabilities of the standard desktop computer system and what can be done to remedy this situation. You will explore the basic desktop video system components required to capture, edit, and produce your own digital video. In addition, you will learn what is required to embellish the basic system with some of the extras or frills that upgrade it to a higher desktop standard.

Editing Digital Video

Very few video productions are single shots, that is, continuous recordings of a scene taken from a single camera. Most video productions are sequences of shorter segments of different scenes. Even a single scene often is comprised of short takes that are recorded from different camera positions and, perhaps, different subjects. The point is that most video is produced by **editing**—that is, creating a composition by adding, deleting, and modifying video segments. Editing digital video requires the appropriate software.

Editing software has a number of powerful tools that make video production both easy and convenient. To appreciate what it has to offer, in this section we survey some of the features that you would expect to find in a typical editing software application.

Most desktop video editing software belongs to a special category called **online nonlinear editing systems.** An online editing system is computer-based; this is contrasted with offline editing, which employs traditional analog equipment in the old-fashioned way. Linear editing is done with playback and recording equipment. The final cut is produced by playing, mixing, and rerecording video clips in real time. In this style of editing, you are usually limited to working with only two video segments at a time. Today commercial studios often employ online linear editing systems for producing broadcast analog video. The computer is used to help control conventional videotape technology for greater precision and convenience.

Nonlinear editing systems, on the other hand, exploit the computer's capability for digitizing, storing, and processing the video. Therefore, these types of systems differ in two important respects. First, because the video data may be randomly selected, many different video clips may be manipulated at once. Second, nonlinear systems usually create edit decision lists. This means that editing actions are recorded as instructions rather than producing a new video sequence that copies each of the original clips or segments that compose it. Consequently, nonlinear editing has greater flexibility and efficiency.

Most digital video editing applications offer a variety of features that are integrated as a set of tools for composing, modifying, and producing digital video segments.

Clip Logging and Assembling

The lion's share of editing is the logging and assembling of short video segments into a finished sequence or cut. **Logging** a video clip means to identify it along with appropriate statistics such as duration and type (audio or video). **Assembling** refers to the actual sequencing of logged video clips. Most editing software is organized to facilitate these tasks.

DISCOVERING MORE

Digital Video Capture

So far, we have given a broad overview of the concepts and methods for capturing, storing, and playing digital video. Of course, there are many details we have left out. If you want to delve into some of these details, consult the online resource "Discovering More About Digital Video Capture."

In this resource, we explain some of the nitty-gritty details of producing desktop video from analog sources. In particular, we look at how a video capture card processes its analog source, and we address some of the problems and solutions common to video capture.

The typical interface, for instance, contains at least two windows. One serves as the workspace for assembling video clips. It is often represented either as a **timeline** or a **storyboard** on which poster icons of the clips are pasted in their playback order. The timeline often includes room for synchronizing audio tracks with video tracks. Most editing software permits multiple tracks for both audio and video (as overlays). A second area serves as a bin window, where logged video sources are collected for assembly.

Before inserting a clip into a sequence, it often must be edited, too. **Clip-based editing** means to trim the video segment to the desired content and duration needed. This is done by setting precise **edit-in** and **edit-out points** on the clip. These denote the initial and ending frames for the segment. Most systems allow you either to enter their timecodes or to shuttle back and forth through a clip to mark the edit-in and edit-out points on the fly.

Transitions

A **transition** is a visual effect that smooths or stretches the change from one video segment to another. To achieve a transition, you must overlay the ending frames of the first segment with the beginning frames of the second. The visual effect is then added to merge the two and create the transition.

Typical transitions from analog video editing include dissolves and wipes. In a **dissolve,** one scene fades into the other. A **wipe** is a transition from one scene to the other that follows a specified direction or pattern. For example, in a horizontal wipe the new scene appears to enter from left to right across the screen. Midway through the transition, the two clips are displayed as a split screen simultaneously. Most editing software has a host of transition effects. In fact, you have the power at your fingertips to turn any video into a circus of horrors by overusing these effects.

Rotoscoping

Rotoscoping refers to working with individual frames of video footage. Graphic embellishment and image filters may be used to enhance single frames of a video clip. Some editing software applications and many painting and image processing programs allow you to edit individual frames for special visual effects. Of course, it is easy to integrate graphic and image processing with video frames because the data is represented in the same manner as digital still images. A few programs even automate the process for an entire segment after you specify how the beginning and ending frames should look.

Compositing

Superimposing part of one video clip on another is called **compositing.** This can be done in a variety of ways. Compositing may be simple—such as the movie-within-a-movie effect—or

DISCOVERING MORE

Video Editing

There are a number of desktop software applications designed especially for digital video editing. For more detailed information about video editing software and how it works,

consult the online resource "Discovering More About Video Editing."

more sophisticated, as in keying. **Keying** is a general technique that places portions of one video in selected areas of another. In this manner, for example, an entirely different video scene may serve as a background for a foreground composed of objects from another clip. A special instance of compositing images is that of **titling,** that is, superimposing text on a video frame. Desktop video editing programs have a great many features for adding text to a video clip. Besides superimposing simple text, these programs also make it easy to animate the text. For example, you can create crawls or screen rolls in which the text moves across the screen.

These are but a few of the mainstay tools typically found in software for nonlinear video editing. Armed with the tools and concepts in this chapter, you are ready now to experiment with your own desktop video production. With a small investment in equipment and large shares of imagination and practice, creating interesting video can become a part of your multimedia repertoire.

■ Summary

Sound is a very important medium for conveying and receiving information, and so it is desirable to include the medium of sound within our computerized communications. Modern methods of converting sound to and from the digital domain, coupled with the power of today's desktop computers, provide us this opportunity.

Digital sound is produced by sampling sound waves over time. A digitized sound file consists of sampled amplitudes of the sound wave at a number of discrete times within a given time interval. The devices that perform the sampling of an analog wave to produce such a digital file are called *analog-to-digital converters,* or *ADCs* for short. The devices that perform the opposite transformation—reconstructing an analog wave for playback from a digital file—are called *digital-to-analog converters,* or *DACs* for short.

When we sample a sound wave, we will usually place the discrete sample times equal distances apart along the time axis, and the number of these appearing per second is called the *sampling rate.* Sampling rates are usually expressed in Hertz, which means number of samples per second. Rates are often expressed in units of kilohertz (KHz) or thousands of Hertz. Sampling rates in the range from 5 to 8 KHz will provide good quality playback for voice recordings, but high fidelity music requires higher sampling rates, typically in the range from 22 to 44 KHz. In addition to the sampling rate, the resolution, or amount of computer memory used to store individual amplitude samples, will also impact the fidelity of digital music playback. Typical resolutions used are 8 bits per amplitude (good for voice) and 16 bits per amplitude (for high-fidelity music). Digital sound files can be quite large, and file compression techniques are often used to combat their large storage requirements.

In addition to digitizing, storing, and playing back natural sounds, computers can also be used to generate or synthesize artificial sounds. Modern music synthesis techniques can produce some impressive and beautiful results. With a great many manufacturers producing music synthesizers and related devices, a standard interface between electronic instruments and synthesizers, called the *MIDI* (Musical Instrument Digital Interface) *standard,* has been agreed on. This standard specifies a common interface, allowing musical instruments that contain microprocessors (computers) to communicate with other instruments and devices containing microprocessors.

Once digitized, sound files can be edited in a large number of ways. For example, amplitudes can be adjusted, echo effects can be added, and pitch can be shifted by performing simple mathematical transformations on the sampled sound. Various filters can be applied to digital sound files as well, filtering out unwanted frequencies, highlighting desirable frequencies, softening or sharpening the quality of the sound, and so on. Easy-to-use software is readily available for sound editing on desktop computers.

In addition to the digitization and synthesis of music, the computer's sound capabilities have been applied to improving the computer–human interaction using spoken language. Speech synthesis methods enable the computer to synthesize spoken language from stored text, providing an additional output option. Speech understanding techniques are designed to allow the computer to interpret and act on input commands spoken to it. One of the more popular speech synthesis techniques is based on the fact that many languages (English included) contain a relatively small number of basic sounds, called *phonemes.* To exploit this fact, the computer first breaks a text selection up into a sequence of basic phonemes, then each phoneme is quickly looked up in a digital speech dictionary and pronounced.

Speech understanding has proved to be a much harder problem to solve, and these systems are in their infancy, although notable progress has been made.

Digital video employs digital methods to capture, store, and present visual images depicting live action and typically synchronized with an accompanying soundtrack. Like other forms of video, digital video creates the illusion of full or continuous motion by displaying a rapid sequence of changing images on the computer display device.

Digital video offers several distinct advantages over its analog counterpart. The video information is easily scalable and randomly accessible. Because it is often compressed, digital video can be stored and transmitted over networks more efficiently. The flexibility of editing and playback features are other digital dividends.

Producing digital video involves three basic steps or stages: capture, editing, and playback. The images and sound are usually digitized from analog sources such as video cameras and microphones. A video capture card is a specialized component added to the expansion slot of the computer system. It contains needed hardware and software to manage the process of converting the source to an appropriate format for storing on the system. Video information is typically compressed to conserve storage space and for faster transfer. Compressed video data, however, must be decompressed (restored to original form) for viewing.

Processing digital video involves editing, which is the composition of video by adding, deleting, and modifying video segments. Most digital video editing programs are nonlinear editing systems. They exploit the fact that digital data may be randomly accessed rather than sequentially searched like linear analog editing systems. Nonlinear systems also differ from their conventional counterparts in that they store instructions for the reassembly of video segments at playback rather than altering the original source video with editing cuts. Consumer versions of nonlinear editing software are available for most desktop computer systems. They provide a variety of tools and features that emulate many of the capabilities of professional systems.

Apart from video capture and editing, most computer systems can be equipped to present or play back digital video. Very often, video playback is exclusively under software control: The CPU executes a program that fetches the frames of the video from secondary memory and displays them, one by one, in rapid succession on the video monitor. The demands of video playback, however, can be considerable. The large amounts of data that must be transferred and processed can challenge most desktop systems. Playback performance can be improved by scaling the video for lower resolution and a slower frame rate. Faster CPUs and hardware support for playback can also improve the quality of digital video playback.

■ Terms

aliasing
amplitude
analog-to-digital converter
 (ADC)
assembling, clip
automated speech
 understanding
capture, video
capture card, video
clip-based editing
clipping (sound)
compositing
data compression
digital audio capture card
digital signal processing
digital sound
digital-to-analog converter
 (DAC)
digital video
digital video playback
dissolve transition
dynamic range

edit-in point
editing
edit-out point
frames per second (fps)
frequency
helper applications
Hertz
keying
linear editing
logging, clip
MIDI compatible
Musical Instrument Digital
 Interface (MIDI) standard
nonlinear editing
Nyquist's theorem (sampling
 rates)
Online nonlinear editing
 systems
oscillator
phonemes
plug-ins

resolution
robust speech recognition
 system
rotoscoping
rule-based phoneme
 recognition
sampling rate
scalable
speaker-dependent speech
 understanding systems
speech synthesis
storyboard
synthesized sound
timeline
titling
transition
video-conferencing
voice activation system
wave
wipe

■ Questions for Review

1. What is meant by the term *digital sound*?

2. Give an overview of the process of digitizing sound.

3. What is meant by the term *sampling rate* in the sound digitization process?

4. Why is sampling at a rate higher than 44,100 Hertz unnecessary when digitizing music? What rate would be appropriate for digitizing speech?

5. What does the acronym ADC stand for? What function does an ADC serve?

6. What does the acronym DAC stand for? What function does a DAC serve?

7. What is meant by the term *resolution* in the sound digitization process?

8. What is meant by the dynamic range of a digitized sound?

9. What is meant by 8-bit sound? Contrast 8-bit and 16-bit digitized sound.

10. What is the clipping effect in digitizing sound?

11. Describe synthesized sound. What are oscillators and what role do they play in synthesizing sound?

12. What does the MIDI standard refer to? What is its significance?

13. Describe briefly the process of speech synthesis.

14. Describe briefly the process of speech understanding.

15. Compare the tasks of computer speech synthesis and computer speech understanding. Which is more difficult to accomplish?

16. What are voice activation systems? Give some examples of the use of such systems.

17. What are phonemes? How are they used in speech synthesis?

18. Explain the rule-based phoneme recognition approach to speech synthesis.

19. What does the term *aliasing* refer to in sound digitizing? Relate it to Nyquist's Theorem.

20. How do computers portray digital video?

21. What are the chief advantages of digital video over its conventional analog form?

22. Explain the three stages of producing digital video: capture, editing, and playback.

23. Why is data compression a common tool for digital video?

24. How do resolution and frame rate affect the performance of digital video playback on desktop computers?

25. Distinguish linear from nonlinear editing.

26. Why are most videos comprised of a sequence of short takes rather than single shots? What does this fact imply for producing desktop video?

27. In managing desktop video, what are the tasks of clip logging and assembling?

28. What are edit-in and edit-out points?

29. What is rotoscoping?

30. Keying is a special instance of video compositing. Explain.

PART Four

Inside the Computer

Chapter 11

The Basic Organization of Computers

OBJECTIVES

- The basics of computer system organization

- The history and development of computing machines

- The stored program concept and how the computer is a general-purpose programmable device

- How the computer's main memory is organized to manage data storage and retrieval

- Types of instructions a typical processor can perform

- Scale and performance factors of the current generation of computers

The modern-day computer is an electronic digital processing system. Our main interest, of course, has been helping you learn how to exploit such systems to enhance your abilities to create, store, retrieve, analyze, and communicate information in a variety of media. To do these tasks well and to adjust effectively to the rapidly changing computing landscape you will encounter in your lifetime, you must have a depth of understanding that goes beyond the use of the latest software and hardware.

This is the first of two units (and five chapters) that explore the basic structure and workings of the modern computer in more detail. In this unit, we will

225

devote our energies to understanding better how the hardware or devices of the computer are organized and function. In this chapter, we will focus on a major component of the hardware of the modern computer system: the processor. The processor is sometimes referred to as the "mind" or "brain" of a computer system. Even though such metaphors tend to overstate the abilities of the modern computer (it is not a thinking entity), they do correctly emphasize the importance of the processor to the computer's operation. You will learn in this chapter how the processor controls and manages the functions of the computer and how it directs the computer's operations according to programs stored in its memory.

The modern computer system is an engineering marvel, and we could spend many chapters (or books, for that matter) exploring the intricacies of its construction and operation. Of course, such a study is well beyond the goals of an introductory text; our focus is instead on the basic concepts upon which the organization of the processor is based. And because we believe this information is best appreciated when presented in an historical context, we also include online more about the history of the development of modern computers.

The Modern Computer System

As you learned in Chapter 3, the computer system is a combination of physical devices, called hardware, and programs, called **software,** that direct the operations of these components. The **hardware** of a typical system consists of a number of devices: a processor that carries out the detailed instructions defining the computer's activities; a mouse, keyboard, printer, and monitor that allow our communication with the machine itself; and memory devices used to store information in electronic form.

There are two basic categories of software: system software and application software. System software consists of the programs that manage our operation of the computer. As you will learn in Chapter 15, such programs are collectively referred to as the computer's operating system. These programs allow you to start up and shut down the computer, save your work as files, retrieve that work later, print documents, and so on. We would be helpless in front of our computer screen without the system software that enables us to direct and interact with the computer's hardware.

Computer hardware by itself is capable of surprisingly few basic operations. But, as you have learned, with the right application software the computer can perform an absolutely amazing range of feats. It is the hardware that carries out these low-level instructions, but the software that defines, organizes, directs, and orchestrates the complex sequences of instructions that produce something meaningful for us.

Figure 11.1

A computer system consists of both hardware and software. The software provides the interface the user employs to communicate his or her task for the machine; the hardware carries out the instructions that implement that task.

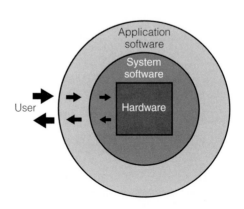

As illustrated in Figure 11.1, the user interacts with the hardware only indirectly through a user-friendly interface provided by application software. Requested tasks are interpreted for the hardware, which carries them out and returns the result—once again, through the software. The system software acts as an intermediary and complement to the application software. The computer hardware, system software, and application software combine to make the computer a useful and indispensable tool for the user. In this and the next four chapters you will explore in some detail how this combination works. We begin in this chapter by considering the history of the development and organization of the modern computer processor.

Electronic Digital Computers

We tend to think of the computer as a recent invention. Certainly, the type of systems we use—electronic digital computers—are very new in the big picture of civilization. The first of these devices appeared just over a half century ago. On the other hand, these electronic versions are not the first computing devices. In fact, the quest for automatic calculating or computing devices has a very long history.

Computing or calculating machines may be either analog or digital devices. Analog computers employ continuous forms for representing their data as well as mechanisms based on analog methods. Analog devices are usually **special-purpose machines** dedicated to very specific tasks. Digital computers are discrete state machines. Not only is their data represented discretely using digital encoding, but their processing is defined by a series of separate or distinct events or states. Digital computers, as we shall soon see, have more flexibility. Unlike analog computers, digital computers may be either special-purpose or **general-purpose machines.**

Early mechanical calculators are good examples of special-purpose machines. These calculators were capable of performing simple arithmetic operations such as addition and subtraction. A mechanical calculator could handle different sets of numbers, but it could only perform arithmetic operations and nothing else. In order to get the machine to do something else, it would be necessary to redesign the mechanism itself. The very idea of "mechanism" implies that it is fixed and determined. This is not a bad thing. We want machines that are completely predictable. If you punched a couple of numbers into your calculator to add them, you would want the calculator to display their sum. Calculators would be useless and annoying if sometimes they displayed the sum, but other times showed today's date, or perhaps played a tune.

If we think of a computing or calculating machine in its simplest form, we can describe it in terms of three basic logical states: **input, process,** and **output.** The input state is a set of initial conditions; typically, this is information supplied to the machine. The output state is

Early Calculating and Computing Machines: From the Abacus to Babbage

Humans invented mathematics, but we are—on the whole—ill-equipped to perform consistently accurate mathematical computations. Throughout history, people have been highly motivated to create devices that improve or extend human computational performance. Indeed, nearly all cultures and civilizations expended some efforts on devising tools that aided calculation. These efforts have culminated in the invention of the modern computer, the most successful calculation tool yet developed. Our online survey of this history will help you understand how these early efforts affected the development and organization of the modern computer.

the resulting conditions; for example, the answer produced by the machine. The output is produced from the input by means of a series of steps defined by the process (see Figure 11.2). In special-purpose computers, the process is mechanized. It cannot be altered without redesigning the machine itself. Thus, even though the input may be varied, the process is fixed.

You know from your own experience that today's computers are not so limited. In fact, it is likely that you have used one computer to perform a variety of tasks. For example, you may have employed a computer as a word processor to create text documents, as a calculator to do mathematical computations, or as a game machine for entertainment. Today's computers are general-purpose machines. They are capable of a great variety of processes and not just one or a few.

The reason that these computers are so flexible in function is that they are **programmable** machines. In general-purpose machines, programming is a mechanism whereby the process can be altered or modified. Thus, in a programmable computer the process can vary just as the input may be variable (see Figure 11.3). Under the influence of different programs, a general-purpose machine can emulate a great many other machines. Today, all computing machines are based on general-purpose, programmable processors. Ironically, even machines that appear to be special-purpose—such as your electronic calculator—are in fact programmable processors. These computing devices are merely made to emulate special-purpose machines by means of fixed or embedded programs.

Another hallmark of computing machines today is that they primarily employ electronic technologies. The earliest digital computing or calculating machines were composed of mechanical devices exclusively: rods, levers, gears, etc. Mechanical computing machines, however, have three significant limitations compared to electronic devices. First of all, they are expensive because of greater costs for labor and components. And, because they are made of mechanical moving parts, their reliability is worse compared to electronics. The mechanical engines in our automobiles, for instance, require a lot more service than the processors in our calculators. Finally, electronic devices can perform operations much faster than comparable mechanical devices. Indeed, it was this speed potential that first attracted computing pioneers of the last century to experiment and create digital computers based on electronic technology.

Figure 11.2

A computer produces results or output by transforming its input by means of steps defined by its process. Like most machines, special-purpose computers are designed to perform one type of process. The input may be altered, but the output is always determined by the same process.

Special-purpose computers

Figure 11.3

Unlike special-purpose computers, a general-purpose computer has both variable input and a variable process. Its mechanism is defined by the instructions of a program. The program therefore defines what process will be performed.

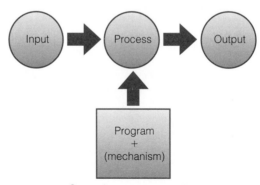

General-purpose computers

The Von Neumann Machine Model

The first large-scale, programmable general-purpose electronic digital computer was the **ENIAC** (pronounced "En-ee-ack"), an acronym for Electronic Numerical Integrator and Calculator. It was developed by a team led by **John Mauchly** and **J. Presper Eckert** at the Moore School of Engineering, University of Pennsylvania. The work was commissioned by the U.S. Army and commenced in 1943. (For more details, see the online discussion, previously cited.) Though the ENIAC was programmable, the procedure for reprogramming the machine was arduous. Patch cords had to be reconnected, switches set, and circuits replaced. Quite literally, the ENIAC had to be reconfigured to perform different processes.

Even before the ENIAC project was completed, Mauchly and Eckert had recognized that this design had limitations that would restrict its widespread use. In August 1944, while the final components of ENIAC were being assembled, the idle project design engineers set out to plan an improved machine. One important goal was to overcome the problem of manual programming. And, as luck would have it, the renowned mathematician John von Neumann visited Mauchly and Eckert at the Moore School in Philadelphia at the same time. Having heard about the project, von Neumann was curious about its progress.

John von Neumann (1903-1957) was born in Budapest, Hungary. Educated in Europe, he came to the United States in 1930 and eventually accepted a post at the newly created Institute for Advanced Study at Princeton, New Jersey. See Figure 11.4. His career was marked by significant achievements in a number of fields: set theory, mathematical logic, game theory, quantum mechanics, hydrodynamics, cybernetics, and more. He even helped to devise the implosion scheme used in the first nuclear bomb. Eclipsing all of these achievements, his name has come to be synonymous with the fundamental design of the modern generation of electronic digital computing machines.

Figure 11.4

John von Neumann is pictured here alongside the Princeton Institute for Advanced Study (IAS) Computer.

Development of Modern Electronic Digital Computers

As mentioned earlier, the first electronic digital computers were introduced just over a half-century ago. Though significant pioneering efforts occurred earlier, most of their development took place just over the last century. In the second part of our online history of computing, we examine the influence of these twentieth-century pioneers on the development of the modern electronic digital computer.

As an informal member of the Moore School team, he helped to create a new design for the machine that later would be dubbed **EDVAC**—for Electronic Discrete Variable Computer. See Figure 11.5. A central feature of its design provided for an encoded, **stored program.** The machine could be freed of manual programming and operation if the instructions of the program might be encoded and stored within it, much like the data on which it operated. The idea is so simple and natural that we may find it difficult to appreciate how significant it was at the time. There is still some controversy as to the true originator of the idea, but there is little doubt von Neumann crystallized and championed it.

The Machine Design

Von Neumann proposed a new logical organization, or **architecture,** for the computer. Machines based on this architecture came to be called von Neumann machines. Several points are especially noteworthy about the von Neumann architecture. First, the von Neumann model clearly separated the logical design from the engineering details. In other words, the descriptions of the components are based on their function and not merely the mechanism that achieves that function. A computer could now be understood in terms of its architecture rather than in terms of engineering its devices. Employing this approach, the technology behind computing machines may change, but the logical design or architecture could remain much the same.

The chief elements of the von Neumann machine architecture are illustrated in Figure 11.6. Of course, this architecture is designed to implement the stored program concept. It employs a binary internal coding scheme like a few other contemporary calculating machines.

Figure 11.5

The EDVAC (pictured here) is notable as the first design for a stored program electronic general-purpose digital computer. However, the system was not operational until 1952.

Figure 11.6

The modern electronic digital computer is composed of two major subsystems: a processor and its subordinate input/output system. The processor consists of a main memory device that services a central processing unit (CPU). The input/output subsystem consists of devices dedicated to input, output, and storage of data.

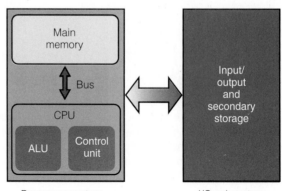

The binary code, however, serves to represent not only the data that the machine processes but, just as importantly, the program that dictates that processing.

Both data and instructions are stored in a **main memory unit.** A **control unit** manages the fetching, decoding, and executing of the encoded instructions of the stored program. The design also includes a unit, called the **arithmetic-logic unit (ALU),** dedicated to the performance of the machine's built-in arithmetic and logical functions. These built-in operations are referred to as the **machine instruction set,** which varies from one computer model to another. Thus, the machine instruction set defines the range of native or primitive actions that the system can perform. The control unit and ALU together are known as the **central processing unit (CPU).** Together the CPU and the memory unit are known as the **processor.**

Devices devoted to managing the exchange of information between a human user and the processor, known as **input and output devices,** are also included in the design. Finally, a memory device, called **secondary memory,** is included to archive data and instructions when they are not in use.

Von Neumann's design also described a simpler and more efficient means for implementing the stored program concept. Whereas the ENIAC performed a number of tasks simultaneously or in parallel, the von Neumann machine is a **serial uniprocessor:** a single machine that performs a series of instructions and tasks one at a time. The tasks of fetching, decoding, and executing the encoded instructions of the stored program performed by the control unit are repeated over and over as long as there are program instructions to be carried out. As introduced in Chapter 3, this repeated cycle is called the instruction-execution cycle and is illustrated in Figure 11.7. This concept of sequential operation simplified engineering design and actually increased the speeds at which a machine could execute programs compared to the more complicated ENIAC design.

The von Neumann architecture has become synonymous with electronic computing machines featuring the following characteristics:

- Automation based on stored-program execution

- Logical design composed of the principal functional units: a central processor, a memory unit, input/output devices, and secondary memory devices

- Internal binary coding for data and instructions

- Serial uniprocessor operation

Between 1946 and 1951, von Neumann and his colleagues at Princeton engaged in the task of building a machine that used this new architecture. This machine, shown earlier in Figure 11.4, was known as the **IAS computer** because it was built for the Institute for Advanced Study. The distinction of actually realizing the first operational stored-program, general-purpose electronic digital computer system, however, goes to **Maurice Wilkes** (b. 1913). Wilkes and his Cambridge University design team in Great Britain based the

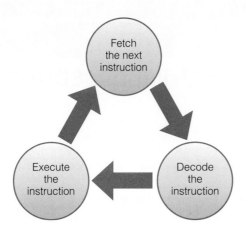

Figure 11.7

The stored program concept requires that each instruction be encoded like data and stored in a memory device for subsequent use. When a program is executed, each instruction must be fetched, one by one, from that memory store, decoded, and then executed. The process of interpretation continues step by step until the last instruction of the program has been executed.

EDSAC (Electronic Delay Storage Automatic Calculator) on the published proposals of both von Neumann and the EDVAC of Mauchly and Eckert. EDSAC, shown in Figure 11.8, executed its first program in 1949—a full two years before the IAS machine and three years before EDVAC.

A special feature of the EDSAC was its ability to interpret programs written in an elementary symbolic programming language. These symbolic instructions could be translated to the binary coded instructions for execution. The instructions were punched on paper tape and read into the EDSAC, which converted them automatically to binary instructions. This symbolic form of programming is much easier for human programmers to manage; it later came to be known as **assembly language.**

Of course, a lot has taken place over the past sixty years in the fabrication, performance, and technology of computers. Strange as it may seem, though, most of the machines today do not differ radically from the stored-program machine model outlined here. Certainly computers have changed significantly in their speed, size, and capabilities; on the other hand, most computers today are faithful to the basic architecture as envisioned by von Neumann and others. In the next section, we will examine this fundamental design more closely.

Figure 11.8
Maurice Wilkes (center, kneeling) and his students are pictured here at work on the EDSAC.

DISCOVERING MORE

Programming the Processor: Using the EDSAC Simulator

To capture some of the "look and feel" of working with these pioneering computer systems, consult the online source for the EDSAC simulator maintained by Cambridge University. The simulator is a software application or pro- gram that you can install on your own computer system. In addition, there are sample programs provided, so you can experience how computing was done in the good old days.

Computer Organization

As you have learned, the modern general-purpose electronic digital computer is based on the von Neumann architecture and its stored-program concept. In this section, we will examine in more detail how the basic components of a typical computer system are organized and how this organization lends itself to the implementation of a computer's programs.

As Figure 11.6 illustrates, we can think of the standard computer system as composed of two fundamental subsystems: the processor and the input/output (or I/O) systems. The processor is organized to implement the von Neumann instruction-execution cycle much as an agent carries out your instructions to perform some task. The input/output system is usually a collection of devices, including a mouse, a keyboard, a monitor, one or more printers, and so on, loosely designated as **peripherals.** As the name suggests, input devices convert information that is understandable to you and me into machine-readable data, that is, an electrical binary representation. Output devices accomplish the opposite process: they convert machine-readable data to a form that is useful to us (text, graphics, sounds, and so on). The I/O system has two main functions. First, it serves as a translator in communications between the user and the processor. Specifically, it facilitates input and output operations. Secondly, the I/O system provides access to secondary memory devices where both programs and data can be stored when they are not being used by the processor.

The I/O system is usually a collection of a variety of devices. In fact, the actual hardware for individual computer systems differs more in this category than any other. These devices are very much like the options you select when you purchase an automobile. In other words, most computer users tailor their system to their needs by adding these peripherals to the basic processor. For this reason, we will treat the variety of devices that qualify as the options of the I/O system separately in the next two chapters. In this chapter, we concentrate on the "standard equipment"—the processor system.

As described earlier, the processor system is also a collection of devices or components. From an architectural standpoint, it consists of two major units: the CPU and the main memory unit. The CPU manages the instruction-execution cycle, and main memory is a fast storage device for holding binary instructions and data. These are connected by a signal pathway called a **bus,** as illustrated in Figure 11.6. When the processor is operating, bits are moved rapidly across this bus. The number of bits that can be moved simultaneously across the bus (32 or 64 bits for most modern desktop computers), called the **bus width,** is an important factor in determining the (performance) speed of the computer system.

Managing Data: Main Memory

As we have stated, the primary function of main memory is to store data and instructions for use by the CPU. There are, in fact, several types of main memory, but all varieties are organized in the same manner. As you have already learned, the lingua franca of all computer systems is binary. But a single bit doesn't provide much range for expressing information. We could use a "0-1" coding scheme to represent things like "yes-no," "dark-light," and so on. But two-valued representations are very limited. Instead, we need strings or sequences of bits to represent more potential values. Consequently, memory is usually divided into uniform-sized units that contain a sequence of binary digits.

These sequences of bits are treated as single units of information. Each is denoted by a unique number called its **memory address.** Just as your street address locates your home, a memory unit's address locates its unique position in main memory. Thus, we can conceive of memory as a collection of standard-length, addressable units. See Figure 11.9. Most processors today use a memory unit size of one byte (remember, a byte is eight bits). This does not mean that the processor cannot handle larger or smaller configurations of bits—just as you and I can process sentences as well as letters. It means only that the standard package for data processing and transfers is based on bytes.

Because we often have occasion to deal with very large numbers of bytes of memory (millions or even billions of bytes), terms to express these quantities have become common. For

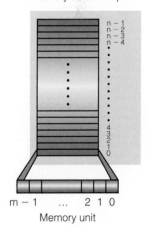

Figure 11.9

Main memory is divided into fixed-sized units. Each unit has m bits or binary digits. These bits are addressed from 0 to m − 1. Each unit holds data or instructions and can be fetched by its address. Addresses are also numbers. For n addressable units of memory, the addresses range from 0 to n − 1.

technical reasons, memory is actually manufactured to contain quantities of bytes measured in powers of 2. For example, 2^{10} (1024) bytes is called a **kilobyte** (abbreviated K or **KB**). For estimates, we can and usually do think of a kilobyte as 1000 bytes because 1024 is very close to this value. A thousand kilobytes (i.e., 1 K × 1 KB = approximately 1 million bytes) is referred to as a **megabyte** (abbreviated **MB**), and a thousand megabytes (i.e., 1 K × 1 MB = approximately 1 billion bytes) is referred to as a **gigabyte** (abbreviated **GB**). On some occasions, you may see mention of a thousand gigabytes (approximately 1 trillion bytes); this is dubbed a **terabyte.**

The two most important forms of main memory are called **random access memory (RAM)** and **read-only memory (ROM).** ("RAM" is something of a misnomer because read-only memory is randomly accessible, too.) The larger amount of main memory is devoted to RAM. These days, the amount of RAM in a typical desktop system is somewhere between 32 and 512 megabytes. ROM is more often in the 4- to 8-megabyte range.

Reading a memory item means consulting its contents, while **writing** an item means storing something at its address. Reading is nondestructive because a copy of the contents is transferred from the memory unit, but the original contents remain unchanged. On the other hand, writing is destructive because the original contents are replaced by the new data. RAM units are sometimes referred to as readable-writable because they can both send and receive items. They are called *random access* because each memory word is accessible immediately by its address. For example, to read from memory, the CPU can signal which items it needs by specifying their addresses. Main memory fetches those items without having to start at the beginning each time and look at the contents of each memory word.

Memory units today, like the CPU, are built using very large-scale integrated circuit technology. A single unit or microchip is fabricated to contain a large quantity of memory with connecting circuits. Most RAM units today are volatile, meaning that they require a constant source of electrical energy to maintain their contents. These are called **dynamic RAM** (or **DRAM**) chips. Although DRAMs are reasonably fast and comparatively economical, their volatility is a liability. When system power is interrupted—by power surges, brownouts, or simply shutting down the computer—the contents of RAM are lost. This is why it is important to have a nonvolatile source of secondary memory that can be used to back up programs and data. We will return to consider these issues in the next chapter.

Main memory is designed to provide the fastest possible access to data and instructions for the processor. Several factors determine data transfer speeds between the central processing unit and memory. First, the memory device itself has a rated capacity for data transfers. Typical DRAM chips found in many desktop systems today are rated at 60 **nanoseconds** (one-billionth of a second) or better. This means that their response time is 60-billionths of a second or faster. In this instance, "response time" means the delay between the memory unit receiving the address and either sending the appropriate data back to the CPU or storing new data in memory. Another factor is the overall speed of the computer system. Memory transfers are synchronized to the speed of operation of the CPU. For example, a fast-response memory chip may be wasted in a system whose speed cannot support it. Of course, the opposite condition is undesirable as well. The final factor, as mentioned earlier, is the bus width or how much data can be transferred between the CPU and main memory at once. The quantity and speed of data transfers over the bus is often more significant than memory response times for determining **throughput,** or the effective speed at which data is processed.

Like RAM, ROM is also randomly accessible; however, it differs from RAM in several ways. ROM is not writable. ROM is also nonvolatile; its contents do not disappear when the power supply to the computer is shut off. ROM usually stores proprietary instructions that the manufacturer has written for basic system functions such as starting the computer system, I/O operations, and the like.

Main memory is an essential component of the computer system. The amount of memory available to the processor and its access speeds can affect the overall performance of the system significantly. Modern application programs place enough demand on a computer's main memory capacity that we might be tempted to modify the old saying, "You can never be too rich or too thin—or have enough RAM."

Inside the CPU

Taking a closer look at the CPU, we find several important components that define its operation. As we explained earlier, the two main functional units of the CPU are the control unit and the arithmetic-logic unit (ALU). Recall that the control unit manages the instruction-execution cycle, and the ALU is a collection of circuits that actually perform the processing instructions dictated by the program. There are also several special memory units called **registers** that help the CPU keep track of its work: a memory address register, a memory data register, a program counter, an instruction register, and one or more general registers.

Managing the Instruction-Execution Cycle   To illustrate how all these components are coordinated, we will document a single instruction-execution cycle of a typical processor. Figure 11.10 illustrates the various components referenced.

Fetching the instruction

1. The previous cycle has left the address of the next instruction stored in the program counter (PC) register. The control unit now signals for a copy of that address to be sent to the memory address register (MAR) over the CPU bus.

2. The value of the address in the program counter (PC) is then incremented to reflect the correct location of the next instruction in main memory (in preparation for the next cycle).

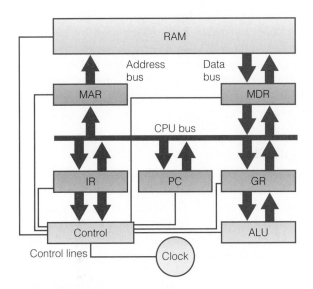

Figure 11.10
The illustration represents a functional diagram for the components that make up a simplified CPU design. It depicts the fundamental units and how they are interrelated—although not how they are arranged geometrically on an actual processor chip.

DISCOVERING MORE

The Instruction-Execution Cycle of the CPU

For a more detailed discussion and demonstration of the inner workings of the CPU, consult the illustration provided online.

3. The instruction, whose address is now stored in the memory address register (MAR), is now copied to the memory data register (MDR) over the data bus. The MDR serves as temporary storage for such transfers from RAM.

Decoding the instruction

4. The instruction is next copied over the CPU bus from the MDR to the instruction register (IR) for decoding. The IR has special circuits that break the instruction down into its meaningful components.

Executing the instruction

5. After the instruction is deciphered in the IR, the control unit sends the appropriate signals to commence its execution. This execution is usually carried out by the arithmetic logic unit (ALU), which may also employ one or more of the general registers (GR).

6. Once execution of the instruction completes, the CPU returns to step 1 and repeats the entire process.

The entire instruction-execution cycle is governed by the cadence of the **system clock.** Each stage takes a certain number of clock cycles. And the system uses its clock cycles to ensure that all its components are properly sequenced. The clock, however, keeps an incredibly rapid beat—clock cycles are usually measured in **megahertz (MHz),** where a megahertz is one million cycles per second. The latest processors have crossed the 1,000-megahertz barrier, or **gigahertz (GHz).** Processors in today's desktop computer systems have clock speeds that range from 800 MHz to 2.5 GHz and higher. An 800-MHz processor has a clock speed of 800 million cycles per second. A single instruction may take several cycles to complete. Nonetheless, such a processor can perform, on average, millions of instructions per second. For example, if typical machine instructions require 4 to 6 cycles to complete, then a comparatively "slow" processor at 800 MHz has the potential of performing between roughly 100 and 200 million instructions per second.

Machine Languages

As noted before, the built-in set of operations that a particular computer model can perform is referred to as its (machine) instruction set. The instruction set can be thought of as the processor's natural or innate operations. By analogy, humans have natural or innate capabilities to move their arms and legs in specific ways. But, in order to perform more complex actions, such as throwing or kicking a ball, we must learn to perform a specific sequence of these motions. For the processor to perform more complex or higher-order tasks, a program is

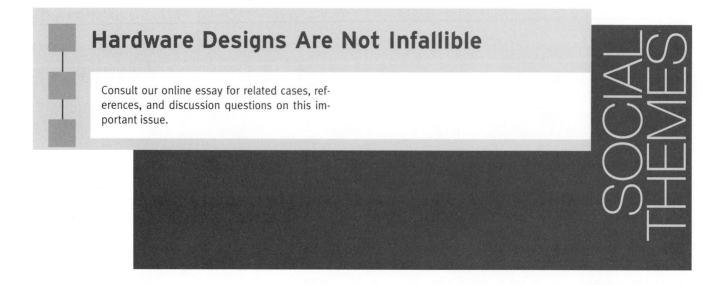

Hardware Designs Are Not Infallible

Consult our online essay for related cases, references, and discussion questions on this important issue.

SOCIAL THEMES

needed. The program specifies the precise sequence of the processor's native operations needed to accomplish the task.

A particular set of codes that implement all the operations in its instruction set is called the **machine language** for that type of computer. These languages, of course, are arbitrary in that the designers of the processor have created the underlying instruction set, and the many engineering decisions about how to implement basic operations vary considerably from one processor to another. Thus, programs that are written for a particular processor cannot be executed on a different one. This is why software created for a computer based on an Intel processor, for instance, cannot be executed on a Macintosh. The underlying processors speak very different machine languages, and you must match the software with the appropriate processor.

What kind of operations does a typical commercial processor perform? Basically, there are three groups. **Data movement operations,** as the name implies, move data. These operations include the following:

- Transferring data from memory to CPU (and vice versa)
- Transferring data from memory to memory
- Performing input and output operations

Arithmetic and logical operations perform mathematical operations such as these:

- Adding, subtracting, multiplying and dividing numbers
- Comparing two quantities for equality, greater, lesser, and the like
- Shifting or rotating bits in a quantity
- Testing, comparing, and converting bits

Program control operations manage the execution of a program, with such actions as these:

- Starting the execution of a program
- Halting the execution of a program
- Skipping automatically to other instructions in the program
- Testing a data item to decide whether to skip to another instruction in the program

As the list attests, a typical processor performs very simple types of operations. The ALU has circuitry that can implement most of the basic data processing steps, but these steps are limited to operations with no more than two quantities at a time. How, then, can a processor accomplish some of the very sophisticated tasks that we have used it for? After all, simple arithmetic and some bit operations seem a far cry from using the computer to do accounting, edit documents, record and edit a musical piece, and so on. The short answer is that the speed and reliability of the processor mean that the system can achieve higher-order results from thousands and sometimes millions of much simpler steps. Ants, for example, can move mountains one grain at a time. By the same token, the computer can achieve impressive results by sheer speed and persistence. The complexity is built into the program or list of instructions, not into the processor that performs these instructions.

Scale and Performance Factors

The earliest computer systems were monstrosities by current standards. Processors such as the ENIAC, the EDSAC, and the IAS machine, for example, were large enough to fill up most of a room. Today, of course, personal computer systems fit neatly on a desk with room to spare. The processors, in fact, are considerably more tidy. Most are confined to a chip no larger than a matchbook. And they are much more powerful than those early computers as well.

While the architecture, that is, the logical functions, of processors has changed little over the past fifty years, the technology used to construct them has changed drastically. In this section, we will consider some of the important technological developments that have affected both the scale and performance of computers today.

Computers today span the spectrum from small, special-purpose processors that control functions in our automobiles and appliances to those that perform such tasks as predicting the weather and managing complex transportation systems. The traditional classification of computers associated the size of the processor with its overall speed and performance. This older taxonomy divided computers into three groups: microcomputers, minicomputers, and main-

Figure 11.11
Mainframes are the computing equivalents of the dinosaurs. These ponderous systems are virtually extinct today. Pictured here is a typical mainframe system circa 1960. Note the various cabinets and consoles that constitute the complete computer system.

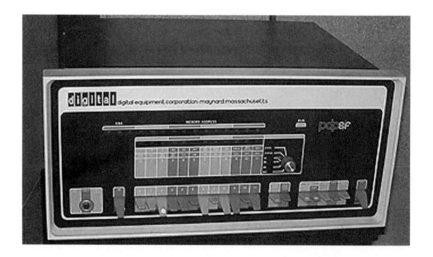

Figure 11.12
The venerable PDP series from Digital Equipment Corporation ushered in the era of minicomputers. Pictured here is a PDP-8 model from circa 1962.

DISCOVERING MORE

Using Logic to Do Arithmetic

Modern processor design is based on creating electrical circuits that produce predictable results given prescribed input values. As mentioned elsewhere, Boolean logic plays a prominent role in the design of such devices. (See "Development of Modern Electronic Digital Computers.") In order to understand better how the modern processor is a logic device, consult our online activities exploring how to create arithmetic operations using Boolean logic.

frames. **Mainframes** were the largest systems; they served a large number of users, usually had a wide range of peripherals, and had hefty price tags, too. See Figure 11.11. **Minicomputers** were smaller and capable of serving a smaller number of users (dozens rather than hundreds). See Figure 11.12. **Microcomputers** were so named because they contained **microprocessors**—an entire processing unit integrated on a single chip. Microcomputers were personal or single-user computers that were relatively inexpensive, and they had performance capacities considerably less than those of their larger counterparts.

This terminology persists to some extent today, but the distinctions on which it is based have all but disappeared. All processors today are designed and fabricated using the **very-large-scale integration (VLSI)** methods, which integrate the entire processor on a single microchip. The processor is fabricated from an intricate combination of electrical circuits that are combined to produce the desired results. See Figure 11.13. The physical size of the computer system tells very little about its processing speed and capacities.

Today, it is more useful to differentiate two classes of systems: **single-user** and **multiuser systems.** Even though the capacity to serve only one or multiple users is actually a function of the system's software (as you will learn in Chapter 15), the hardware must be sufficient to support it. Single-user systems come in several varieties based on scale and performance: **personal digital assistants (PDAs), laptops** or **notebook computers, desktop systems,** and, finally, **workstations.** A PDA is a full-scale computer system even though it fits neatly within the palm of your hand. While PDAs have the capability to perform most of the tasks that we would desire from our computers, they are limited in memory or storage capacities and are not convenient for entering data such as text. On the other hand, laptops or notebook computers offer both portability and full performance capabilities. Desktop systems are personal systems that are relatively inexpensive, general-purpose machines used for a variety of applications in the home and office. Desktop systems may be comprised of a single unit or more often a box containing the processor along with a separate monitor and keyboard units. Whatever the configuration, they typically fit neatly on or beside a desk or table. Workstations are higher-performance single-user systems that carry a higher price tag as well. Besides having greater processing speed and larger main memory capacities, they usually have specialized peripherals such

Figure 11.13
VLSI methods reduce the components of the central processing unit to a single microchip. Pictured here is the AMD Athlon XP processor, one of the first of the latest generation of microprocessors surpassing the gigahertz clock speed barrier.

FOCUS Modern Processor Design

The latest generation of processors has significantly increased the speed and performance capabilities of computer systems. Find out more about some of these popular processor models on our online resource.

as high-resolution graphics video displays. Professionals employ workstations in software development, graphic design, computer-assisted manufacturing (CAM), and a host of other activities that have specialized processing requirements. In appearance, however, they appear similar to a typical desktop system.

As single-user systems become more and more sophisticated, the distinction between desktop computers and workstations has become blurred. For that matter, even though laptops are smaller than typical desktop systems, they usually have performance capabilities that match or exceed their larger counterparts. As you might suspect, the term *workstation* has a snob appeal that is favored by advertisers and others trying to impress you with their systems, but in truth, the difference between a workstation and a high-end desktop system (that is, personal computer) can be difficult to articulate.

Multiuser systems encompass a great variety of systems that range in size, capacity, and price. Such systems employ one or more servers, which in this context are powerful computers running software allowing the connected machines (called *clients*) to communicate. Servers may also be repositories for shared software and data. Figure 11.14 illustrates. Smaller systems may support 10 or 20 users who communicate via a network of terminals (a monitor and keyboard) and single-user systems. Larger systems serve a much greater number of users and often distribute processing among several machines.

A special class of multiuser systems is that of **supercomputers,** very high-performance, specialized computers used primarily for scientific applications that require intensive numerical calculations. See Figure 11.15. Supercomputers, unlike standard serial uniprocessors, often break tasks into subtasks that can be accomplished in parallel to boost processing speed and performance. They are used for a variety of tasks such as meteorological forecasting, modeling of physical systems, and graphics and image processing. Today, expensive supercomputer systems are an endangered species. They are being replaced by large clusters of networked (and less expensive) computer systems that are bridged by software in order to perform these highly demanding processing tasks in parallel.

FOCUS Personal Digital Assistants

PDAs, or palmtops, are the current rage. Consult our online source to find out more about how these systems are configured and what you can expect to do with your own PDA.

DISCOVERING MORE

Personal Computers

The history of the development of personal computers spans over two decades and is marked by both significant successes and blunders. To find out more about this commercial odyssey, consult our online source.

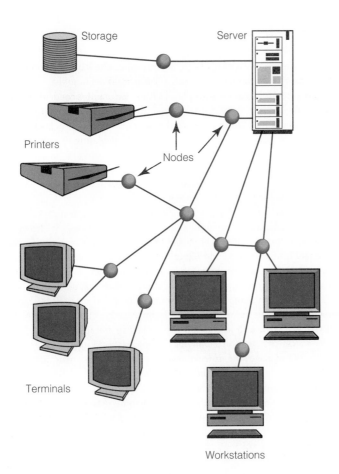

Storage   Server

Printers

Nodes

Terminals

Workstations

Figure 11.14
In a typical multiuser system, a central computer system is connected to terminals, peripherals, and other computer systems over a local area network. Connecting points over the network are called nodes. The multiuser computer system acts as a server providing processing for its client machines via the network.

Figure 11.15
The Cray T3D is an example of a popular supercomputer model that was employed for intensive numerical and graphic applications needed for scientific applications.

■ Summary

A computer system is a combination of hardware and software. The hardware consists of the devices of the machine: a processor that carries out the detailed instructions defining the computer's activities, peripherals that allow our communication with the machine itself, and secondary memory. Software directs the operations of these components. Computer hardware by itself is capable of surprisingly few basic operations, but, driven by application software, the computer can perform a wide range of functions.

A long history details the invention of computing and calculating machines, leading to the first modern electronic computers in the 1940s. Today's machines are based on an architecture, first articulated by John von Neumann, that clearly separates the logical design from its engineering details. Employing this approach, the technology behind computing machines may change, but the logical design or architecture has remained much the same.

The von Neumann machine model consists of a number of relatively distinct units. Both data and instructions are stored in a main memory unit, and a control unit manages the fetching, decoding, and execution of the encoded instructions of the stored program. The arithmetic-logic unit (ALU) implements the machine's built-in arithmetic and logical functions. These built-in operations are referred to as the computer's machine language, and this language will vary from one computer model to another. The control unit and ALU together are known as the central processing unit (CPU). Together the CPU and the memory unit are known as the processor. Input and output devices devoted to managing the exchange of information between a human user and the processor are also included in the design. Finally, secondary memory archives data and instructions when they are not in use.

In this chapter we concentrated on a study of the processor and its two major units: the CPU and main memory. The CPU manages the instruction-execution cycle, and main memory is a fast storage device for holding binary instructions and data. These are connected by a signal pathway, called a bus. The two most important forms of main memory are called random access memory (RAM) and read-only memory (ROM), with the larger amount of main memory devoted to RAM. The processor is the most essential component of a computer system, and its speed and amount of memory are two of the most important factors in determining the overall performance of the system.

■ Terms

address (memory)
architecture
arithmetic and logical
  operations
arithmetic-logic unit (ALU)
assembly language
bus
bus width
central processing unit (CPU)
control unit
data movement operations
desktop computer systems
dynamic RAM (DRAM)
Eckert, J. Presper
EDSAC
EDVAC
ENIAC
general-purpose computer
  (machine)
gigabyte (GB)
gigahertz (GHz)
hardware
IAS computer
input
input/output (I/O) system,
  devices

kilobyte (KB)
laptop computer systems
machine instruction set
machine language
mainframes
Mauchly, John
megabyte (MB)
megahertz (MHz)
memory, main
memory, secondary
microcomputers
microprocessors
minicomputers
multiuser computer systems
nanosecond
notebook computers
output
peripherals
personal digital assistants
  (PDAs)
process
processor
program, programmable,
  programmed

program control operations
random access memory
  (RAM)
reading (memory)
read-only memory (ROM)
registers
serial uniprocessor
single-user computer systems
software
special-purpose computer
  (machine)
stored program concept
supercomputers
system clock
terabyte
throughput
very-large-scale integration
  (VLSI)
von Neumann, John
Wilkes, Maurice
workstations
writing (memory)

■ Questions for Review

1. Contrast a special-purpose computer and a general-purpose computer. How does the concept of a program arise within this context?

2. Identify John Mauchly and J. Presper Eckert and their significance in the development of the modern computer.

3. What was the ENIAC?

4. Describe the major contribution John von Neumann made to the development of the modern computer.

5. Identify the distinguishing characteristics of the von Neumann computer architectural model.

6. Why is the stored-program concept important for general-purpose computing?

7. Describe the von Neumann instruction-execution cycle.

8. What does the acronym CPU stand for? What does this device do?

9. Describe the function of the I/O subsystem in a modern electronic digital computer.

10. Describe the function of the processor system in a modern electronic digital computer.

11. What do the acronyms RAM and ROM stand for? Explain what they mean and how they differ.

12. Describe the overall structure of a computer's main memory.

13. What is meant when we say that RAM is volatile?

14. What is meant by an addressable unit of main memory?

15. What does the computer system clock do? Why is its speed so important?

16. Explain what a machine language is.

17. Define and compare the terms *microcomputer, minicomputer,* and *mainframe* computer. What relevance do these terms have in today's computer domain?

18. Compare and contrast single-user and multiuser computer systems. How do they differ with respect to scale and performance?

Chapter 12

Storing Data on Your Computer

OBJECTIVES

- How various storage technologies are organized to support processing in your computer system

- How data is transferred to and from the processor and other components in the system

- The operation of two classes of secondary memory devices: sequential (magnetic tape) and direct access (magnetic and optical disks) and their respective storage media

- How data is organized and stored on magnetic and optical media

In the previous chapter, we focused on the organization and workings of the basic processor. As you recall, the processor is composed of two chief components, the CPU and main memory. Main memory stores the data and instructions used in processing. The CPU manages the execution of programs stored in memory. A processor by itself, however, is neither very capable nor useful. First, it needs a great deal of supplemental storage to retain both data and programs not in current use. Moreover, the processor has little to do without some means of receiving data and producing it. These, of course, are the responsibilities of the input/output (I/O) subsystem. As introduced in the last chapter, the I/O subsystem is a collection of devices dedicated to secondary storage and the input/output functions of transferring data between the user and the system. In this chapter, we will consider the basic forms of secondary memory. In the next chapter, we will examine the variety of ways in which input and output are performed.

Main Memory

We have seen that main memory is made of electronic circuits organized to store addressable strings of binary digits. Most of the memory in a processor is dedicated to readable/writable random access memory (RAM).

RAM is typically composed of one or more integrated memory units. Each unit is secured in a slot or socket designed to hold that type of module. The most common variety of memory units today are SDRAM DIMMs. **Synchronous DRAM (SDRAM)** is so called because all memory operations are synchronized with a computer system's clock cycles, which means fewer delays when transferring data to and from the processor. On the average, one can expect a 20% performance improvement over that of conventional memory designs. SDRAM is made up of 64-bit wide **Dual Inline Memory Modules (DIMMs)**. See Figure 12.1. A typical unit has a 168-pin edge connector, and there are 2 to 4 sockets available for installing these units or "chips" in the average system. SDRAM DIMMs come in quantities of 64, 128, 256, 512 MB, and 1 GB. Thus, a typical computer system has RAM capacities up to 4 GB (i.e., 4 × 1 GB).

Newer, improved varieties of memory have been introduced to support modern advancements in processor design. The most prominent of these contenders is **Double Data Rate (DDR) SDRAM.** It can effectively double the transfer rate by sending data at both the beginning and end of a single clock cycle.

While the speed of RAM is its chief asset, its capacity, physical size, and cost are its greatest liabilities. In terms of cost per bit, RAM is too expensive for all storage needs. Even if it were economical, the amount of space and the power supply needed to support it would be prohibitive. Also, without a continuous power supply, RAM is useless for long-term storage because its contents disappear every time the computer is turned off. For these reasons, computer systems require a source of secondary (sometimes called *external*) memory. Secondary memory satisfies two main objectives:

- Permanent storage in the place of volatile RAM

- Cheaper, mass storage for long-term use

Secondary memory is cheaper, has greater capacities, is nonvolatile, and usually is a more compact means of storage than RAM. On the downside, it has significantly slower access and retrieval times.

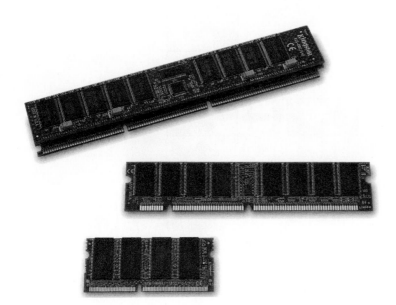

Figure 12.1
Several different SDRAM DIMMs are shown here. At the top is the standard 168-pin edge connector. The bottom memory module is used in notebooks and laptops.

The Processor, Memory, and I/O Subsystem

The processor receives and sends data via buses. You will recall that a bus is a connection between components that transmits a sequence of bits in parallel. A bus is typically described in terms of both its capacity (number of bits transmitted in parallel) and its speed (in cycles per second).

A single, central **system bus** is the main highway for data transfers in traditional designs. See Figure 12.2. For over 40 years, computer systems have been designed around this single communication infrastructure. But, the single system bus design has persisted more for reasons of economy than performance. Indeed, it was a sensible choice as long as the various components of the computer operated at basically the same speeds. However, the situation changed when processor speeds increased, memory access times decreased, but the transfer rates of I/O devices did not improve at the same pace. In a system with components transmitting various amounts of data at various speeds, it is extremely challenging to design a single interface connecting all of these species of devices. An interface that is fast enough to handle the fastest devices becomes expensive and wasteful when handling slower ones. On the other hand, a slower interface can be a bottleneck that can hamper the overall throughput and performance of a processor.

Recently, the system bus of the traditional design has been supplanted by what is dubbed a chipset communication infrastructure. A **chipset** is a collection of integrated circuits that manages the transfer of data between components in the computer system. Most PCs (that is, based on processors built by Intel, AMD, etc.) employ a two-level design. See Figure 12.3. A host controller chip services faster devices such as the processor, main memory, and a graph-

Figure 12.2

The single system bus design was the mainstay of computer systems for decades. The processor and memory exchanged data over this bus; other devices also contended for its use. The bus usually had an expansion bus that served as the interface to the various I/O units installed in the system.

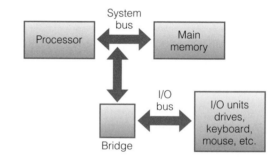

Figure 12.3

In recent years, the single system bus design has been replaced by a chipset containing two integrated circuit devices that serve as controllers for communication among the components connected to them. A host controller (sometimes called northbridge*) manages high-speed transfers between memory and the processor and the graphics controller and the processor. A second controller (dubbed* southbridge*) oversees transfers between slower I/O units and their northern neighbors. This scheme improves the overall performance of the system. For example, the CPU contends less with slower devices for transferring data to and from memory. Similar designs use different terminology and rearrange some of the players, but the two-tier organization remains constant.*

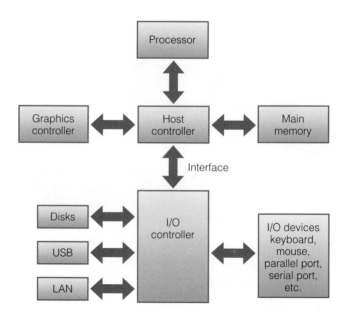

ics controller. A second I/O controller chip is connected to the host controller. The I/O controller manages data transfers from hard disks, CD drives, the keyboard, mouse, and other types of input/output devices. The two-level chipset design divides the communication infrastructure so that faster devices can communicate unimpeded by slower ones. Likewise, I/O controller chips can be better matched to specific sets of I/O device options. There are several competing designs; the differences, however, are more a matter of detail.

The choice of communication infrastructure for a computer system is a significant one. Processor speeds have increased rapidly in recent years. Likewise, memory access times have improved as well. But these advances are squandered unless they are matched by compatible performance in communication rates between components. Advertisers often tout computer systems based on the clock speeds achieved by their processors. As consumers, we have come to accept the idea that faster is better. The problem, however, is that faster is not always faster. The speed of the CPU clock is indeed a factor in measuring the overall performance of a computer system, but it is one factor. The speed of memory and the transfer rates for the communication infrastructure are also important.

The true deciding criterion in assessing system performance, however, is usage. If you purchase a computer system for performing tasks such as reading e-mail, surfing the Net, and writing papers using a word processor, then debates about clock speed, memory, and chipset designs are largely moot. Buying a high-performance system for low-end usage is like purchasing a thoroughbred racehorse to pull a plow. On the other hand, if you are a designer producing 3-D graphics with photorealistic effects, then differences in design and performance details become meaningful to you. The moral is to match performance to use rather than buying performance for its own sake.

Types of Secondary Memory

Classifying forms of secondary memory by their access methods is convenient. There are two general classes: direct access storage devices and media, and sequential access storage devices and media.

Direct access storage devices (**DASD**) and media are organized to permit immediate access of data items without having to search the entire contents of stored data. In this respect, these devices resemble how RAM works. There are differences, however. The geometry of direct access storage media affects retrieval times. Moreover, direct access technologies have mechanical components that are significantly slower than the electronic circuits employed in main memory.

Sequential access storage devices (**SASD**) and media are constrained by their linear physical organization. Linear organization means that items are stored on the medium one after the other from start to end. For this reason, data must be retrieved by traversing across the medium sequentially. Retrieval times for SASD can be significantly slower than for DASD—especially if significant amounts of content searching or sequential searching are required.

The situation is very similar to audio playback devices for tape versus compact discs. Audio tape performs much like sequential access media, while digital audio CDs function like direct access media. To find a particular passage on an audio cassette tape, you must fast forward or rewind the tape to the appropriate location. This can often mean searching for the passage—listening to short bits of the tape to determine the desired passage. On the other hand, a compact disc supports direct access. You may go immediately to a given passage provided that it is indexed. In fact, you can program the CD player to play a collection of pieces in any arbitrary order. This is possible because the CD player can immediately locate the beginning of each piece without searching through the disc's musical content.

Magnetic tape is the most commonly used sequential access storage medium. It comes in a variety of formats and is used primarily for archiving large amounts of information. Direct access storage devices and media are more common. **Magnetic disks** are direct access media that come in several forms. **Magnetic floppy disks** are used for storing modest amounts of data. **Magnetic hard disks** have much greater capacities for storing data and faster access speeds. Floppy disks are convenient, though, because they can be detached easily from their devices (called *drives*) and stored apart from the computer system. **Removable hard disks** are an alternative to lower-capacity and slower-access floppy disks. Removable hard disks are direct access media that have similar performance to conventional hard disks and the transportability of floppy disks. **Optical discs** are another class of direct access devices and media. Optical discs generally have much greater capacities for storing data than magnetic disks. They come in a variety of formats. Many are permanent forms of storage; data stored on these discs are not erasable. **Compact disc–read-only memory (CD-ROM)** is the most common type of nonerasable optical disc. Newer technologies for optical discs provide erasable, writable storage like traditional hard disks.

The differences between direct access and sequential access devices can be significant for information processing. Because most data is stored and retrieved from secondary memory, the choice of the type of storage device can be a crucial one. Factors such as overall response time and economy play important roles in these decisions.

The Memory and Storage Hierarchy

Faced with a daunting array of choices for storing data, it would be natural to ask, "Why so many types of memory?" The problem is that RAM is too expensive to be adequate for all processing needs. SASD and DASD technologies suggest alternatives to RAM that are more economical but they are much slower than RAM. Even though we put them all in the same group, secondary memory devices and media differ considerably with respect to both cost and response time. It is customary to think of memory devices and media as building a hierarchy, as pictured in Figure 12.4.

The hierarchy is organized to represent the inverse relationship between cost and speed for computer storage. RAM is both the fastest form of memory available to the processor and the most expensive in terms of cost per bit.

At the next level are magnetic hard disks. These drives and their media are much more economical in their cost per bit than RAM but significantly slower. As you may recall, RAM access speeds are measured in nanoseconds—that is, billionths of a second. The fastest hard drives have response times measured in milliseconds, or thousandths of a second. To put this in perspective, consider this analogy. Our lives are measured in seconds, minutes, and so on. Suppose that you were a CPU waiting for data to be delivered from a magnetic hard disk. If the average response time for a fast magnetic hard drive is 10 milliseconds, then (equating the

Figure 12.4

The traditional storage hierarchy is intended to convey the relationship in cost and convenience of the various forms of storage available for a computer system. The top level is occupied by random access memory (RAM). The next four levels are direct access devices and media. Finally, at the bottom is the only sequential access medium—magnetic tape. The pyramid is arranged so that from top to bottom, it represents forms of memory that decrease in their relative cost per bit for storage. At the same time, the levels from bottom to top increase in their relative speed of access. For example, RAM has both the fastest access speed and the greatest cost per bit for storage. On the other hand, magnetic tape as a storage medium has the lowest cost per bit, but its sequential access makes it the slowest in access speed.

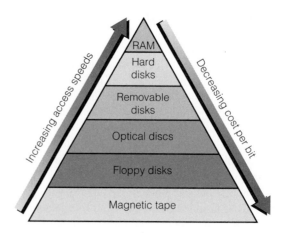

CPU's nanoseconds to human seconds) you would have to wait almost 4 months to receive the data! And you thought the U.S. Postal Service was slow.

Removable magnetic hard drives and disks are at the third level of the hierarchy. These media have smaller capacities than comparably sized nonremovable magnetic hard disks, but their cost per bit is still more economical. In terms of performance, they are somewhat slower than the fastest magnetic hard drives.

Optical drives and discs occupy the fourth level. These media usually have greater capacities than magnetic hard disks and a lower cost per bit. They are also slightly slower in response time compared with hard disks. Magnetic floppy disks complete the direct access category. Though floppies have low capacities, they are very inexpensive. On the other hand, they are significantly slower than other forms of direct access media.

At the bottom of the hierarchy is magnetic tape. Most tape formulations have very high data capacities; a great deal of data can be stored in a small amount of space. Tape is also very economical. Unfortunately, the limitations of sequential access render it the slowest medium.

The traditional storage hierarchy is useful for understanding the conceptual landscape, but what does it mean for practical applications? For the typical desktop computer system, there is a comparable version of the memory hierarchy. As shown in Figure 12.5, we can think of main memory (RAM) and different forms of secondary memory as arranged in a series of levels based on their roles in storing and processing information. Any data that is being processed currently must come from RAM. Just as the instructions of the program are loaded into main memory for execution, all data that these programs process must at some time be stored in RAM. This ensures that processing is both simpler and faster for the CPU. Not all data, though, can live permanently in RAM: there is simply not enough room to store it all. Information that is not currently being used must be transferred to another medium. Most computers are organized to handle this in an orderly fashion.

Figure 12.5 represents the memory hierarchy from an operational perspective. The levels in this context depict how data flows within the system during processing. Information that is currently being processed must be transferred to and stored in main memory. Data that is used often for processing or is about to be processed is usually transferred to and stored on magnetic hard disks. These disks service timely data well because they are continuously connected to the system and have the fastest response times among secondary memory devices. Magnetic hard disks are an important part of any desktop computer system, but they generally serve only as an intermediate form of storage. They seldom have enough capacity for all storage needs, and they are inconvenient for introducing data into the system.

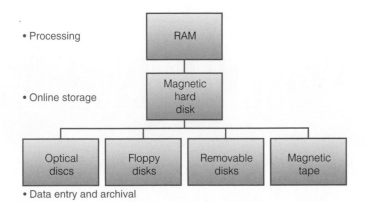

- Processing
- Online storage
- Data entry and archival

Figure 12.5

From the user's standpoint, a more practical version of the hierarchy is shown here. Random access memory occupies the highest level because all processing depends on it for primary storage. Magnetic hard disks occupy the second level because nearly all data and programs are transferred to and from them as part of normal processing. The second level serves as constant or online storage. But there is usually a third level of storage devices and media that are needed for introducing data into the system or archiving it for safekeeping. These are usually offline forms of storage. At this level, optical discs and magnetic floppy disks are popular means for introducing data into the system. Likewise, removable disks, magnetic tape, and writable optical discs are popular choices for archiving data.

For these reasons, another level of devices and media is needed. Optical discs, removable hard disks, and floppy disks can serve as entry points for data into a system. For example, programs or software can be installed from floppy disks or optical discs, such as CD-ROMs. Removable hard disks can be used to transport large data files from one computer to another. Their data can be copied to a (nonremovable) magnetic hard disk for eventual processing.

Data can be read by the system from magnetic tape, too, although tape is normally used for copying data from other media. Copying the contents of the hard drive, for example, to a tape cartridge creates what is called a **system backup.** Copying or **archiving** data from a computer system and storing it separately is important for routine maintenance. Backups can be used to restore a computer system when data is lost. Floppy disks and removable hard disks can be employed as backups, too. Floppies, of course, are limited in capacity; removable hard disks are a much more expensive medium than tape. Erasable optical discs are useful for archiving large amounts of data. Nonerasable optical discs are not suitable for backups, though. Their permanence does make them ideal for storing published data—such as permanent records—that we wish to keep secure.

Figure 12.6 illustrates an example of both how information is introduced into a system and how it migrates during processing. Suppose that you wish to install a program to execute on your computer. The program must first be introduced or "loaded" into the memory devices of your system. The software might be distributed on a floppy disk, which can be inserted into a floppy disk drive, as shown in Figure 12.6(a). A copy (b) of the program is transferred to the magnetic hard disk of your system. Installing the program on the hard drive makes it easier to load into RAM (c) for execution and means that it is readily available for reuse. When the program is executing, three copies of it coexist at the different levels of the memory hierarchy: in RAM (c), on the hard disk (b), and on the floppy disk (a). When the program terminates, the space in RAM is freed for other uses, and only the two disk copies (a) and (b) remain. If you perform a system backup and copy the entire contents of your hard disk to tape, another copy of the program (d) will be transferred to the backup tape. Thus, the program could be reinstalled if hard disk version (b) becomes corrupted and you misplace the original copy (a) on the floppy disk.

In a typical desktop computer system, the variety of processing performed dictates what sort of secondary storage will be required. All systems must have at least two levels of memory to function efficiently: RAM and readable, writable direct access secondary memory—usually a hard disk. An additional level adds functionality to the system by providing a means for introducing data to the system or archiving data from it.

DISCOVERING MORE

The Memory Hierarchy: Cache Memory

The principles of the memory storage hierarchy are applied to an even greater extent in today's high-performance processors. For example, you have learned that magnetic hard disks serve as a faster online storage level between main memory and data entry and archival storage devices. In this manner, data and software that is in regular demand is always available to the CPU and can be transferred to main memory quickly. Modern processors exploit this scheme internally as well. Memory devices called **cache memories** serve as intermediaries between the CPU and RAM. Consult our online source to find out how cache memory is organized and its role in improving the performance of your computer system.

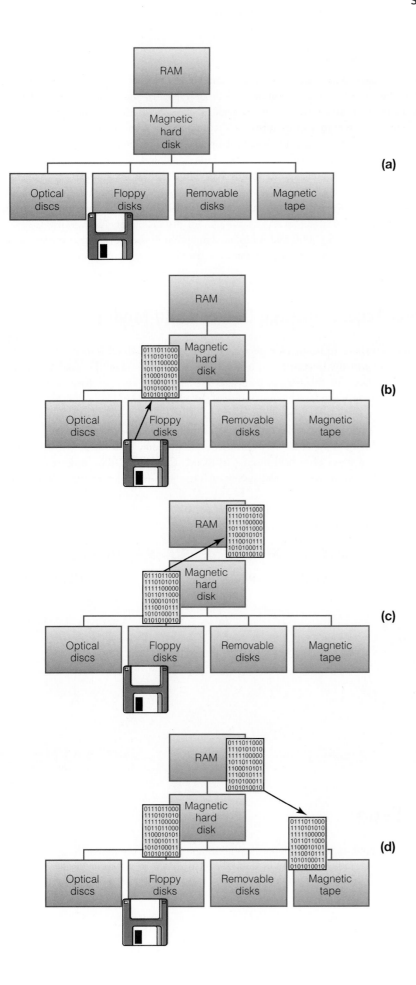

(a)

(b)

(c)

(d)

Figure 12.6

A program file may be introduced into the system by way of a floppy disk, as shown in (a). The file might be copied to the hard disk both for storage and faster installation (b). After the program is installed and commences execution, a copy of the file (c) resides in RAM at least temporarily while it is executing. Should you make a system backup—that is, copy the contents of your hard drive to magnetic tape— a copy of the program would also be stored on the tape cartridge (d).

How Much Storage?

How much data can secondary storage media hold? That depends, of course, on the device used. Capacities and actual amounts of data are typically expressed in the standard unit of bytes. In previous chapters, we have referred to the byte as the fundamental unit of digital data. Bytes are organized in quantities to represent and store useful forms of information. Because binary numbering is the natural language for computers, it is convenient to express quantities of storage in powers of 2. For example, a kilobyte is 2^{10} bytes, that is 1,024 bytes. Kilobytes are often abbreviated as simply KB. Thus, 32K is actually 32×2^{10} or 32,768—which is approximately 32,000. This has led to the common practice of referring to kilobytes as roughly equivalent to thousands of bytes. Note that the term "K" has slipped into the vernacular and we often hear that an automobile, for instance, costs "32K." In this context, we would expect to pay $32,000 and no more. The moral of the story is that money is decimal, but for computers powers of 2 rule. Table 12.1 details the most common units of measure for computer storage.

Direct Access Storage Devices and Media

The chief drawback to magnetic tape as an online storage medium is its need to store and access data sequentially. In contrast, direct access methods eliminate the need for extensive sequential searches. For this reason, computer systems today employ direct access devices for their chief online secondary memory sources. In addition, DASD is often favored over tape for offline storage in some specialized applications as well.

There are two general types of direct access devices and media: magnetic disks and optical discs. Magnetic disks come in two varieties, floppy and hard disks. On the other hand, there are several types of optical discs: CD-ROM, CD-R, CD-RW, and second-generation DVD formulations as well. We will survey each of these technologies and consider how they

Table 12.1   *Units of measurement for data.*

POWERS OF 2 FOR MEASURING STORAGE				
Unit	Abbreviation	Power of 2	Quantity of Bytes	
kilobyte	KB	10	1,024	($\approx$ 1 thousand)
megabyte	MB	20	1,048,576	($\approx$ 1 million)
gigabyte	GB	30	1,073,741,824	($\approx$ 1 billion)
terabyte	TB	40	1,099,511,627,000	($\approx$ 1 trillion)

FOCUS   Magnetic Tape

In the earlier days, magnetic tape was the mainstay of data processing. Today, the medium has been relegated primarily to the specialized role of data archival. Find out more online about how magnetic tape works for protecting the integrity of data and instructions in data processing environments.

are best employed. But before we do, it will be useful to point out some general features about the geometry of direct access media.

All direct access disks store data on circular paths called **tracks.** Each track is divided into segments called **sectors.** Magnetic disks, for example, often arrange data in concentric circular tracks and store uniform quantities of data in sectors. The physical area of a sector actually shrinks as the tracks move closer to the center. Because the amount of data stored is constant regardless of the sector, the data is simply stored more densely on the interior tracks. This format is called **constant angular velocity** (**CAV**) because these types of drives maintain a constant rotational speed. At fixed speeds, the variance of its data density allows for constant data transfer rates regardless of its physical location on the disk. See Figure 12.7.

In contrast to the CAV format, the CD-ROM disc actually contains only one track that spirals continuously from the outer edge to the center like the grooves of a phonograph recording. To transfer data stored in sectors at a constant rate, the drive varies the spin rate of the disc. Thus, this format is called **constant linear velocity** (**CLV**). Although it requires more complicated drive mechanisms, the CLV format has much greater overall data density than comparably sized CAV disks. The latter format wastes a great deal of space on the outer edges of the disk. See also Figure 12.7.

Zoned CAV (**ZCAV**) is still another format. A number of zones are defined on a ZCAV disk. The number of sectors per track depends on its zone. In this manner, binary data can be packed more densely and uniformly than the normal CAV format. The ZCAV format, however, sacrifices uniform data transfer rates to accommodate higher data densities while maintaining constant rotational speeds. Disks using the ZCAV format offer much greater data capacities than similarly sized disks based on the older CAV format. Most high-capacity magnetic hard disks employ the ZCAV format.

Magnetic Floppy Disks and Drives

Magnetic floppy disks (also called *diskettes*) are pliable disks usually made of mylar plastic coated with one or two polished magnetic surfaces. The disk is stored in a jacket that itself may be either pliable or somewhat rigid. Floppy disks are an offline form of storage because they may be inserted into and removed from floppy disk drives. See Figure 12.8.

All magnetic disks, including floppy disks, use basically the same technology for storing data. Bits are encoded by magnetizing microscopic particles embedded in the surface of the disk. Reading transitions in the polarity of these particles produces a two-value code. A typical floppy disk uses the CAV format. Information is stored magnetically along circular tracks. The size and number of tracks vary. The sectors are numbered by the system and therefore divide the tracks into addressable units called **data blocks.** Each data block is identified by a unique track and sector number. Data blocks contain a uniform amount of data—even though the sectors they occupy may be different physical sizes.

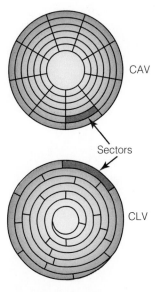

Figure 12.7
The CAV format distributes tracks in concentric circles, as shown here. The physical size of a sector varies, depending upon its location on the disk. Sectors on the outside are larger than those inward and closer to the hub. In spite of this, the amount of data stored on a track in a given sector is the same. Because the rotational speed of the disk is always constant, some compensation must be made to ensure that data transfers are uniform. Consequently, the density of data per track—the amount of bits per linear inch—varies from track to track. Bits of data are stored more sparsely on the outer edges of the disk than inward.

CLV has a uniform data density, and all the sectors are the same size. To achieve uniform data transfers, the disc must vary its rotational speed to compensate.

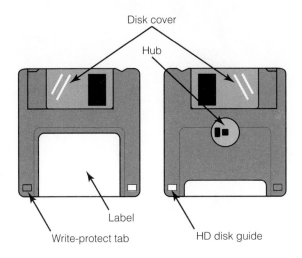

Figure 12.8
The ½-inch diameter floppy diskette is enclosed inside a hard plastic case. The diskette is pictured here from the front (left) and back (right) views. A metal cover slides back inside the floppy drive to reveal the disk surfaces. A write-protect tab can be engaged to prevent the drive from overwriting any stored data. High-density (HD) diskettes have an extra guide hole that the drive senses when inserted.

In some cases, data blocks may be connected logically. On a double-sided floppy disk, for example, the same sectors on opposite sides of the disk are accessed by the read/write heads simultaneously. Thus, a data block is comprised of the contents of identically positioned sectors on both sides of the disk. Ultimately, the size of a data block and its configuration are determined by the system software (the operating system, in particular), not by the hardware itself. (We will address these issues in Chapter 15.)

We can now see exactly how direct access works for magnetic disks. A disk in a drive revolves at a constant rate of speed. The drive contains read/write heads that sense the magnetic charges stored on the track. The read/write sensor must locate the proper data block by finding both the right track and sector. First, the disk drive must find the proper track. The amount of time this takes is called the **seek time.** Next, to find the proper block, the disk controller must wait until the read/write head is aligned with the desired sector on that track. This is called the **latency time.** Once positioned over the proper sector, the sensor can read or write the data block. This is called the **read/write time.** See Figure 12.9. The latter is relatively constant, but seek and latency times are variable. They depend on the random factor of where the read/write head is when the process begins. Consequently, direct access transfer speeds are not constant, although the variability of the times is small enough to be significant only to the computer system, not to us.

Floppy disks used to come in a variety of sizes and capacities. Today, these have largely been supplanted by 3½-inch disks. These disks are enclosed in a hard plastic case. Common capacities include 1.44 MB (the so-called *high-density,* or HD, format) and 2.88 MB (or 2HD). More recent versions of the 3½-inch disk offer even greater data densities, from 4 up to 21 MB. These disks, however, require their own proprietary drives. Data saved on these disks are not easily transported to other systems.

Floppy disks are relatively inexpensive, but they have much lower capacities for storing data compared with other media. As a result, they are an endangered species in the memory hierarchy.

Magnetic Hard Disks and Drives

As mentioned, there are two varieties of magnetic disks: hard disks and floppy disks. Hard disks are so named because they are ferrite alloy–coated surfaces on a rigid disk made of aluminum alloy, hard plastic, glass, or some other nonmagnetic substance. Hard disks are usually permanently sealed in a disk drive mechanism to protect them from contaminants in the en-

Figure 12.9

Accessing the disk information involves three stages to accommodate its geometry. The seek time is the interval needed to locate the proper track, latency is the amount of time it takes for the sector to rotate under the read/write head, and the read/write time is the normal transfer rate once a data block is located.

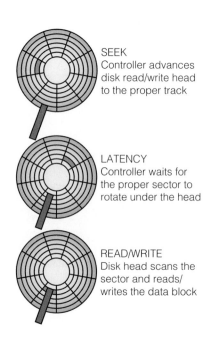

SEEK
Controller advances disk read/write head to the proper track

LATENCY
Controller waits for the proper sector to rotate under the head

READ/WRITE
Disk head scans the sector and reads/writes the data block

vironment. See Figure 12.10. In this configuration, hard disks can serve only as online (non-removable) storage.

Magnetic hard disk drives and media differ from their floppy disk counterparts in several important ways. First, hard disk drives have rotational speeds that are much greater than floppy drives. For example, a typical hard disk drive in a desktop computer rotates its disks at a speed of 5400 revolutions per minute (rpm) and higher. Floppy drives in the same system typically rotate their disks at only 600 rpm. The read/write heads in a hard disk drive never actually touch the surface of the disks; the friction would be too great. Instead, the head floats on a microscopic cushion of air. For this reason the disks and drive are self-contained or sealed. Contaminants such as human hair, dust particles, and so on could actually cause the head to rebound and bounce off the surface of the disk. This would destroy the disk surface—or "crash" the disk.

Hard disks usually contain fixed multiple disks that rotate together. Thus, the sectors on each disk are accessible at the same time to aligned read/write heads. Consequently, the sectors create logically what is called a **cylinder**—that is, multiple sectors vertically associated. Cylinders may constitute large data blocks for some systems. See Figure 12.11.

Figure 12.10
Pictured here is a typical external hard drive assembly for a desktop computer system. With its cover off, you can see multiple disks and the actuator arm that houses the read/write heads for the unit.

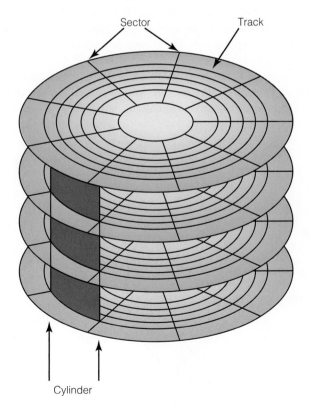

Sector   Track

Cylinder

Figure 12.11
Most hard disk drives have multiple platters fixed to a central hub. The drive rotates the disks in unison, and multiple read/write heads move in and out perpendicular to the hub. It is possible, therefore, for the sensors to be positioned on precisely the same track and sector on both sides of each of the platters simultaneously. Thus, a data block may be distributed across several disks and yet be read or written much faster than when stored on a single side of one disk. This configuration is called a cylinder.

Magnetic hard disks have a much higher data density than floppy disks, too. Hard drive technology permits both a greater number of tracks and a greater number of bits per square inch than floppy disks. A typical 3½-inch hard disk platter has a density of roughly 10,000 to 30,000 tracks per inch. Most hard disks today employ the ZCAV format, which pack even more sectors onto the same size disk and thus increase capacities by as much as 25 percent.

High-performance drives improve response time by increasing disk rotational speeds—usually, 7,200 to 10,000 rpm, and higher. Faster rotational speeds affect both latency and read/write response, although improvements in these specifications may not always translate to significant improvements in the overall performance. Figure 12.12 shows how these and other factors affect how fast data is retrieved in practical circumstances.

With increasing demands for hard drives with larger capacities and faster response, the industry has pushed the technology envelope at an incredibly rapid rate: Each year new drives feature more than double the capacities of last year's even as their prices continue to drop.

Besides their direct access capability, the chief advantage of magnetic disks is speed. Magnetic hard disks have the fastest response times of any current secondary memory technology. This is why the technology is especially suited for transactional processing. In **transactional processing,** the computer system interacts with a user or another system, usually through a series of interchanges. To do so, the system must be capable of responding to requests for processing and information on demand. For example, applications such as automated teller machine transactions, library database queries, and airline and hotel reservations are tasks in which the events of the process can be affected by the latest, up-to-date information stored in secondary memory. Magnetic hard disks have the response time and capacities suitable to support such work.

Hard disks also have very large capacities for readable/writable nonvolatile mass storage. There are some liabilities to consider, though. First, magnetic disk media are vulnerable to heat, magnetism, and some environmental contaminants. Hard disks have higher data density and faster response times, but they are still more expensive than other forms of storage. In addition, because most hard disk systems are fixed (nonremovable), data stored on them should be archived or backed up for security.

Organizing Data on Disks From the user's standpoint, data and programs are stored and retrieved on hard drives as files. As noted before, a file is a sequence of bytes representing data or a program that is recognized by a unique file name. Disks—whether hard or floppy disks—store data in blocks on tracks in sectors, though. How, then, does the disk system handle requests for reading and writing files? The answer depends on the type of operating system controlling your computer.

Most computer systems today employ variants of the Windows operating system, so we base our discussion on it. Some locations on the disk are taken up by **directory entries.** These serve as listings of names of files stored on the disk, including their sizes, as well as information

Figure 12.12

The seek, latency, and read/write times are significant factors in how fast a random I/O transfer from a hard disk occurs. Other factors come into play as well. How fast data is transferred over the bus (data transfer rate) and the speed at which the CPU can handle data sent to it (PC data rate) are important, too. The chart shows the relative contribution of each factor to the overall equation. Mechanical elements of the disk drive (seek, latency, and read/write time) account for 85 percent, but the rest is determined by associated electronics of the system.

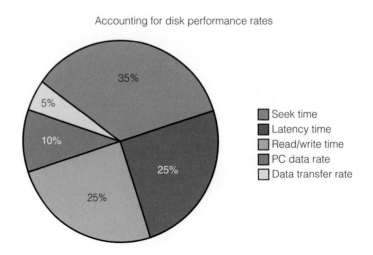

Accounting for disk performance rates

- Seek time
- Latency time
- Read/write time
- PC data rate
- Data transfer rate

for managing a special storage structure referred to as the **file allocation table** (**FAT**)—or sometimes FAT32, or VFAT. The FAT contains information about the whereabouts of data blocks belonging to each file. Specifically, it lists the physical address of the first sector or—more likely—the first group of sectors that compose that file. See Figure 12.13. Disk systems, unlike tape, do not store a file serially. For example, when a change is made to a file stored on disk, the disk controller usually finds the next available sector and writes the insertion there. The result, then, is that files are often distributed throughout the disk. When the user deletes a file, the controller simply sets the directory entry in the FAT to empty rather than erasing the file's contents elsewhere on the disk.

Reading files from the disk employs a similar process. The disk controller finds the location of the blocks that constitute the file from the FAT and its related tables. Reading these blocks may require performing a number of seeks to different sectors if the file is large and distributed throughout the disk.

The moral of the story is that files, file names, and the like belong to an abstract world created by software—the operating system, in fact. (The operating system is the topic for Chapter 15.) At the level of hardware, data is stored on disks and tape in data blocks and sectors. The two worlds are connected, of course, but they have separate realities.

Removable Magnetic Hard Disks and Drives

A significant liability for magnetic hard disk systems is the fact that they support online storage exclusively. Thus, there is little reprieve when a hard disk fills to its capacity. The user is forced either to erase some of the data or to replace the drive with a larger one. Of course, data may be archived to magnetic tape, if such a system is available. Tape is not convenient, though, for handling data that is used often. For these reasons, the computer industry has developed magnetic hard disk systems that contain removable disks.

The original format for removable magnetic disks was based on patented Bernoulli technology. A flexible magnetic disk is encased in a cartridge that is protected from outside contaminants and engineered to prevent head crashes. Although the disk is flexible, the rotational speed causes an air cushion that renders the disk rigid for reading and writing. The original 5¼-inch disk format yielded capacities of 44 and, later, 88 MB.

Competing manufacturers have since introduced other removable magnetic disk technologies. These have greater capacities than Bernoulli cartridges, with even better performance. For example, 250 MB removable disks are a very popular format.

Removable disks provide high-capacity offline storage that is ideal for some applications. For example, desktop publishing (composing and formatting published materials) requires storing large data files that contain texts, graphics, and images. Graphic designers also create data files that take up large amounts of storage. A removable disk is a convenient means for storing and transporting such data. Desktop publishers and graphic designers can prepare

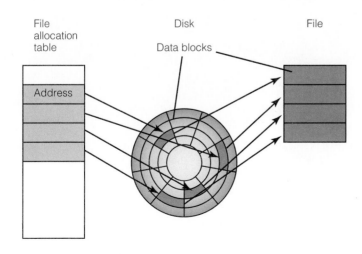

File allocation table

Disk

File

Data blocks

Address

Figure 12.13

The file allocation table indicates which physical sectors belong to which files. A single large file can have data blocks that are scattered at various locations on the disk. The more disconnected these blocks, the more fragmented the disk. As a disk fills with data and becomes fragmented, its performance degrades.

press-ready files, store them on removable disks, and send them to publishers or commercial printers for publication. Of course, the recipients must have compatible drives to accommodate these disks.

In sum, removable disks offer secure offline storage for sensitive or important data. Although they are convenient, removable disks have some liabilities. As online storage, removable disks are slower than fixed magnetic hard disk systems. In addition, the media costs are much higher than other magnetic and optical media.

CD-ROM (Compact Disc–Read-Only Memory)

As a medium for secondary memory, CD-ROM is based on the earlier technology of compact disc digital audio. The compact disc used for audio playback is a 120-mm-diameter disk capable of storing up to 650 MB of data. Using a CLV format, it has over three miles of recordable track space, which counts for almost 400 times the capacity of a standard floppy disk! Data stored on a compact disc, however, is permanent or read-only memory. For this reason, CD-ROM is useful only for established or published information because it cannot be edited without replacing the disc entirely.

That CD-ROM is a permanent form of secondary storage can be both a strength and a liability. For some applications, permanent data is both acceptable and even desirable. For example, archiving information such as annual records is perfectly suited to CD-ROM. On the other hand, data and programs that must be edited or modified on a regular basis would be unsuitable for CD-ROM because pressing discs is costly unless very large quantities are produced. In fact, the economy of CD-ROM depends mostly on publishing a great many discs from the same mastering. Even for permanent records, if only a small number of discs are required, there are usually better choices than CD-ROM for storage.

It is useful to take a closer look at the optical technology employed by CD-ROM drives and discs because all other forms of optical drives and media have similar components and features. See Figure 12.14. The lacquered plastic disc encases a thin sheet of reflective metal—usually aluminum—that covers a plastic base that has been stamped permanently with a series of embossed pits of microscopic size. Viewed from the top, as depicted in Figure 12.15, the **pits** are depressions surrounded by reflective areas called **lands.** The pits themselves vary in length but are typically the size of a bacterium, averaging around 0.6 microns (a **micron** is 0.000001 meter or 1/40,000,000 inch). The pits are arranged in tracks at a density of nearly 16,000 per inch.

A laser beam is projected across the bottom of a spinning disc. The beam is controlled by a drive mechanism that can pick out single tracks for reading. A photodetector senses the reflective properties of the focused beam on the disc. From the bottom, pits are actually protrusions that scatter the light. The land areas reflect light straight back to the detector. Consequently, pits and lands differ in reflective intensity. Just as the coding of magnetic media is based on reading transitions between polarities, the optical sensor signals the changes or transitions in intensity rather than the amount of reflectivity itself. This works very well for a

FOCUS   RAID and Disk Farms

The demands for storing large amounts of online data have spawned new developments in disk technology. Disk farms and RAID drives represent two different approaches to solving the problem of fast, reliable access to data stored in large quantities. Each technique employs multiple disk drives that appear as large-scale storage units to computer systems linked to them. Find out more about these technologies in our online resource "Focus on RAID and Disk Farms."

two-valued coding scheme like that of binary because detecting changes is easier and more reliable than measuring exact values.

Compared with magnetic disk technology, CD-ROM has a higher data capacity but slower access and transfer rates. If you have ever used a CD-ROM drive with your system, you have likely had to wait several seconds for information to be read and processed. For example, a standard transfer rate of 153.6 KB per second is required for reading information such as audio. The earliest drives had spin rates between 200 and 500 rpm, which are sufficient to maintain this minimum constant transfer rate. (Remember that constant linear velocity necessitates varying the actual rotational speed of the disc.) These so-called single-speed drives have been surpassed in performance by an increasing array of **multispeed** drives: double-speed (2X, read "2-times"), 12X-speed, 20X-speed, 40X-speed, and even higher.

The nomenclature is a little unfortunate because it more accurately denotes the maximum capacity for data transfer rather than the actual continuous drive speeds. A double-speed drive, for example, has the capability to achieve transfer rates as high as 300 KB per second—twice that of single-speed drives. To achieve this transfer rate, of course, it must be capable of spinning up to twice as fast as the so-called single-speed drive.

The faster transfer rate is fine for some forms of data, such as large images or video; however, these newer drives automatically shift down to lower rates of transfer for other forms of data. Consequently, having a high X-value for your drive generally means that performance is better, but not in every instance. For example, when the data must be fetched in smaller chunks, the fastest multispeed drives do not perform much better than slower ones.

Figure 12.14
The bottom side of the CD-ROM reveals the highly reflective surface covered by layers of protective plastic for stability. The disc is read using a focused beam of a low-intensity laser. Reflective energies from the surface are interpreted as the binary encoding of data.

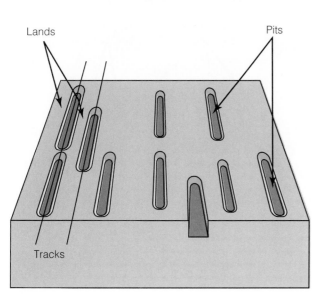

Figure 12.15
A graphic rendering of a microscopic cutaway of the encoded layer of a CD-ROM disc reveals a series of indentation dubbed "pits" and smooth areas in between called lands. Pits and lands have different reflective energies, and the transitions between a pit and a land (or vice-versa) signify changes in bit signals. These are organized to form tracks, which are read by a sensor picking up the reflections from a laser beam focused on them from the other side of the disc.

CD-R (Compact Disc–Recordable)

Compact disc–recordable (**CD-R**)is a good choice when only a few published discs are needed. CD-R discs do not have to be pressed or mastered; instead a drive may be used for writing the data permanently. Once written, the data is permanent and can be read by most conventional CD-ROM drives as well.

CD-R media are similar to their CD-ROM cousins with a few notable differences. The normal CD has a single aluminum reflective layer that is sandwiched between a plastic substrate and protective coatings. CD-R discs, in contrast, have a reflective layer with an additional dye layer underneath it. Rather than pits or physical depressions, CD-R discs use microscopic dye spots to encode data. The disc is written by activating the dye using a higher-intensity laser beam in the CD-R drive. This beam can heat the dye enough to cause spots that have similar reflective properties to pits in CD-ROMs. See Figure 12.16.

Writing a CD-R disc is not a trivial task. Fortunately, CD authoring software helps to manage organizing and formatting the data for you. The written data is usually organized on a magnetic hard disk first before being transferred to the CD-R disc. Most of the time, the data is written continuously to the disc nonstop; some drives and authoring software permit writing it in stages, though. Discs recorded in stages, though, must be used on "multisession" drives only. (**Multisession** or sometimes **multiplay** refers to drives that can read parts of the disc recorded at different sessions.)

Writing an entire CD-R disc takes time. For example, filling an entire 700 MB disc at single-speed would take almost 78 minutes. In today's microwave world, who could tolerate that? Consequently, CD-R drives usually can record data at much faster speeds. These are also expressed as multiples (Xs) of the 153.6 KB standard speed. Drive performance is usually expressed in two multiples: 8X/24X, for instance, specifies a drive that records data at speeds 8 times faster, while reading data up to 24 times faster than single-speed. CD-R drives are rare today; they have been replaced by "combo" drives that are capable of reading and writing different media.

CD-R media have the similar capacities as CD-ROMs and can be read by the same drives. Another plus is that media costs are falling. On the other hand, recording is a time-consuming process. For archival purposes, data stored on CD-R is not as long lasting as on CD-ROM discs. CD-R discs are sensitive to light and temperature; the data on these discs can deteriorate under extreme exposure. Even so, for some applications, CD-R represents the best choice for offline data storage.

Figure 12.16

A CD-recordable disc differs from the normal CD-ROM in two ways. First, beneath the reflective layer is a chemical dye. Second, a series of pregrooved tracks is imprinted on the bottom layer, as shown in the cutaway illustration of the disc. A high-intensity laser beam causes the dye layer to deposit spots on the pregrooves. These act much like the lands and pits of traditional CDs. When a lower-intensity beam is focused on the track (from the bottom) it senses the transitions between dye spots and land by their different reflective energy. Their behavior is similar enough that regular CD-ROM drives can read these discs, too.

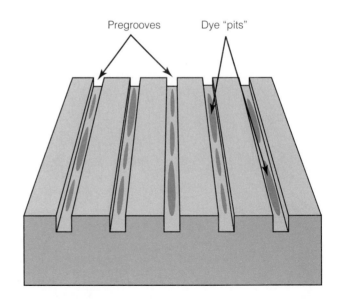

CD-RW (Compact Disc–Rewritable)

The chief limitation for both CD-ROM and CD-R is this: Once it is encoded on a disc, the data cannot be changed or updated. **Compact disc–rewritable (CD-RW)** was devised to remedy this problem.

CD-RW discs are similar in structure to CD-R discs. See Figure 12.17. Molded pregrooves spiral the surface of the polycarbonate plastic substrate. These grooves, as in CD-R discs, are used to guide the laser mechanism over the "tracks" of the disc. Several layers are on top of the substrate. Two dielectric layers surround a recording layer; the surrounding pair absorb heat generated when the disc is being written. At the top is a reflective layer.

Recording CD-RWs is based on **optical phase-change technology.** Unlike CD-R, which uses a chemical dye, the recording layer of a CD-RW is a crystalline compound with special properties. The compound remains crystalline when heated to one temperature and cooled. But when heated to a higher temperature, it cools to an amorphous, noncrystalline state. The crystalline state reflects light from underlying metallic surface; the noncrystalline state does not. Thus, it captures the same basic properties found with lands and pits.

A single CD-RW disc may be erased and rewritten up to 1,000 times. This seems like a lot, but compare it with how often you save and resave files on your hard drive. For example, if you performed 10 erasures per day, the disc would last less than four months.

A CD-RW drive has the capability to produce laser power at three different levels. A high-intensity beam is used for the recording or writing process. A lower-intensity beam functions to erase recorded portions of the disc by heating them to the temperature that produces the crystalline state when cooled. Finally, a low-intensity beam helps to read data. Standard CD-RW drives can write to both CD-R and CD-RW media, and read from all three CD formats. To account for erasing, drive speeds are expressed by three factors instead of two. For example, a standard CD-RW drive today might be rated as 44X/24X/44X. This means that the drive can record data up to 44 times single-speed; it can erase data up to 24X; and can read data up to 44X.

Writing your own data to a CD-RW disc is similar to saving files on a floppy disk. First, you must insert the disc into the drive and format it. Unlike floppies, though, which are formatted by the operating system, currently you must have special software to format the CD-RW disc. Specifically, you need software that implements the UDF standard. **Universal Disk Format (UDF)** is an open standard file system for optical media. UDF was designed so that data stored on optical media by one operating system could be read and written by another. The scheme is based on grouping data into chunks or packets for writing.

But UDF packet writing comes in two flavors: variable-length packets and fixed-length packets. The details are not important here, but their outcomes are significant. Variable-length

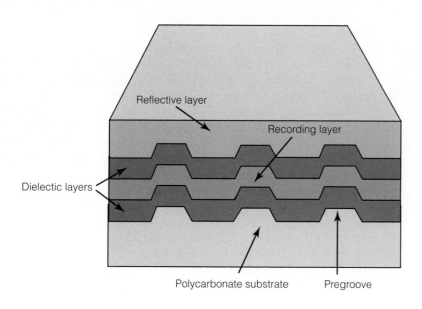

Figure 12.17
A cutaway of CD-RW disc reveals a pregrooved substrate with several layers stacked on top. A recording layer is sandwiched between two layers that help absorb excess heat from the erasing/writing processes. On top of these three layers is a thin reflective layer.

Reflective layer

Recording layer

Dielectic layers

Polycarbonate substrate   Pregroove

packets work for both CD-R and CD-RW media. Optical discs written according to this method are more easily read by other optical drives. Variable-length packet writing also uses the available space on the disc more efficiently. Because deletions are only marked, eventually the available space is used up. Thus, to reclaim CD-RW space, you must occasionally erase the entire disc. On the other hand, using fixed-length packets makes your CD-RW work more like a gigantic floppy. Deleted files are erased immediately, and available space can be reused as needed. There are two trade-offs for this obvious convenience:

1. The overhead for this approach itself takes up space—about 500 MB are usable for storing data.

2. Discs using this format can be interpreted only by systems equipped with the proper reader software.

If all of this sounds confusing, then help may be on the way. A consortium of influential manufacturers has recently introduced a proposed standard that would relegate storing data on CD-RW to simple "drag and drop" status—like on our venerable floppies. The Mount Rainier standard (CD-MRW) prescribes operating system support for managing data transactions. In other words, your computer's operating system would handle the details of formatting, reading and writing date—just like your other disks. No extra software would be needed.

As CD-RW increases its market share among storage technologies, we would expect that these quirks would be resolved. Even so, it represents a very flexible form of offline mass storage.

DVD (Digital Versatile Disc)

The new kid on the block for optical storage is the DVD format. The **digital versatile disc (DVD)** is an optical storage medium based on older CD-ROM technology. The disc has the same diameter and thickness as that of compact discs. DVDs, however, have a substantially greater storage capacity than traditional CDs. To achieve this, the technology of the venerable CD was updated and improved in several ways.

First of all, the tolerances for drives have improved enough to warrant putting more tracks on a disc and likewise having smaller minimum sizes for pits. For example, the distance between tracks in a typical CD is about 1.6 microns, but this is reduced to 0.74 microns in DVDs. Minimum pit size for DVDs is less than one-half that for CDs. These improvements alone account for increasing DVD capacity to four times greater than a CD. Advancements in data encoding and more efficient error-correction coding contribute to even greater increases in data capacity.

Unlike a CD, which has a single layer of encoded data, a DVD can have up to two dual-sided readable layers within the same disc. In fact, a DVD disc is fabricated from two 6-mm-thick discs that are bonded together to form a disc of a size and shape compatible with the 12-mm-thick CD. A single-sided, single-layer disc can hold up to 4.7 GB of data. This is over seven times more information than a CD. Two-sided single-layer discs double this capacity. Two-layered discs have capacities of 8.5 GB. The second layer is read by focusing the laser through the top layer. To help compensate for some of the potential errors caused by this process, the bottom layer has a lower data density than the top layer. This accounts for the slightly reduced total capacity. Like most optical discs, data on the first layer is spiraled beginning from the hub to the outside the disc; this is reversed for the second layer. As a result, switching layers is faster. A full two-layered, two-sided disc can store up to 17 GB of data— the equivalent of more than 26 CDs! See Figure 12.18.

The earliest application for DVD, of course, was consumer video. DVD video players were introduced in 1996. DVD video exploits digital methods to produce an improved picture and multichannel sound that surpasses that of analog sources such as VHS videotape and even laserdiscs. DVD-ROM was an early format for computer usage. Like its CD-ROM predecessor, DVD-ROM discs are manufactured with the information encoded on it.

Today, there are many different formats to choose from. The motivations for this multiplication of formats have been the demands for ease-of-use and backward compatibility.

Single-sided, single layer (4.7 GB)

Double-sided, single layer (9.4 GB)

Single-sided, double layer (8.5 GB)

Double-sided, double layer (17 GB)

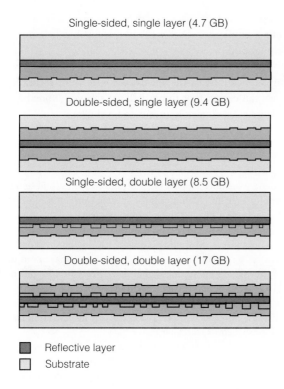

■ Reflective layer
□ Substrate

Figure 12.18
DVD discs pack even more capacity onto a single disc by multiplying the number of surfaces that encode data. The standard single-sided, single layer disc is similar in structure to a CD-ROM disc. Two sides double the capacity. A second layer can be added. The laser beam is focused at a different setting to read the inner layer beneath the outer one. Two layers provide more data, but do not quite double the capacity. A full double-sided, double-layer disc contains a full 17 GB of data.

Formatting and writing DVDs must be simple before consumers will embrace the medium. Likewise, discs should be readable on a variety of drives—including older DVD players and DVD-ROM drives. Unfortunately, these are not necessarily consistent goals.

DVD-R or DVD-recordable has two formulations: authoring (A) and general (G). Both are based on chemical dye technology similar to CD-R. DVD-R (G) is intended for business and consumer use. The media contain standard copy protection technology that discourages the duplication of copyrighted content. DVD-R (A) was designed for professional multimedia development and is used primarily for creating beta or test versions of products—when only a small number of copies are needed.

DVD-RW or DVD-rewritable permits erasing and rewriting of data. Like its CD-RW cousin, DVD-RW uses optical phase-change technology for erasing and recording of data. DVD-RW does not support random rewrites, though. The entire disc must be erased in order to be re-recorded. Thus, DVD-RW is suited best for storing multimedia content or archiving large amounts of data at once.

There are two competing formats that support random rewrites; both are based on optical phase-change technology like DVD-R. DVD-RAM, or DVD-random access memory, was the first rewritable format designed specifically to support random erasing and rewriting of data—in the same manner as we use magnetic disks. The only drawback, though, is that these discs are formatted and encoded in such a way as to make them unreadable by other drives.

DVD+RW is a third-generation format that attempts to improve on the liabilities of earlier formats. It supports random erasing and writing of data like DVD-RAM, but its discs are readable on all but the oldest of drives. For computing applications, DVD+RW can support CAV recording as well. This permits faster reading of data on a recorded disc.

DVD+R is a write-once version of DVD+RW. Table 12.2 summarizes formats and features.

Most DVD drives are multispeed devices, too. Unfortunately, their speeds are based on a different standard, which only adds to the confusion when comparing products. For example, a DVD+RW drive might be listed as 2.4X/8X. As you would suspect, this means that the drive can write DVD data up to 2.4 times the single speed rate and read DVD data up to 8 times that rate. But "normal" (i.e., single) speed for a DVD transfers data at a rate of 1.25 MB per second on average. That is over 8 times the 1X transfer rate for a CD. To put it another way, a 1X DVD drive compares with an 8X CD drive in terms of how much data is transmitted per second. Given our example, a 2.4X/8X DVD drive would be comparable to a 20X/65X CD drive in data throughput!

The lack of consistency in standards for DVDs is a sure sign that the consumer market for DVD computing applications is still unclear. As with most technology, when consumer dollars start voting, we can expect that things will get simpler. Nonetheless, DVD has an excellent potential for large-scale data storage and archival uses.

■ Summary

Main memory and secondary memory support the processor by storing and supplying data and instructions during the course of processing. A chipset is the specific communication infrastructure managing the exchange of data between the CPU and the rest of the system.

There is not enough main memory in a typical computer system to meet all its storage needs. Even if there were, the volatility of most RAM would necessitate backing up the programs and data to prevent their loss. For these reasons, secondary memory devices and media have been developed to serve as a cheaper and more plentiful source for storing digital data. These devices and media are often distinguished according to the manner in which data is retrieved from them. Sequential access storage media are those in which the data is arranged in a linear sequence. Each item is fetched by traversing all the items that come before it in that sequence. Direct access storage media permit the data to be fetched directly without the need for sequential searching.

Magnetic tape is a sequential access medium that is used primarily for archiving system information and large amounts of data. Magnetic hard disks and floppy disks are popular direct access storage media. Hard disks serve as the chief source of online secondary storage on a typical computer system.

Table 12.2   *A summary of the basic features for DVD formats.*

DVD FORMAT COMPARISON					
Format	**Capacities**	**Read Compatibility**	**Random Writes**	**Rewrites**	**Recording Format**
DVD-ROM	4.7–17 GB	High	No	0	CLV
DVD-R (A)	3.9–4.7 GB	High	No	0	CLV
DVD-R (G)	4.7–9.4 GB	High	No	0	CLV
DVD+R	4.7–9.4 GB	High	No	0	CLV, CAV
DVD-RW	4.7 GB	Moderate	No	1,000	CLV
DVD+RW	4.7–9.4 GB	Moderate	Optional	1,000	CLV, CAV
DVD-RAM	2.6–9.4 GB	Low	Yes	100,000	ZCAV

Comparing the Cost of Secondary Memory

Keeping up with the latest trends in storage is a daunting task. What goes to print today goes out of date tomorrow. To find out the latest trends in computer storage and compare the basic costs of the various media, consult our online resource "Focus on Comparing the Cost of Secondary Memory."

Floppy disks are used to enter data into a computer system as well as to copy or archive small amounts of it. Removable magnetic disks come in a variety of sizes and speeds. These are often employed as substitutes for hard and floppy disks, when greater capacity or portability are important. Optical discs are likewise direct access storage media. CD-ROMs are used for publishing large amounts of data. CD-R and CD-RW are recordable media with similar capacities. DVD is a second-generation optical disc and comes in a variety of formats for different uses.

■ Terms

archiving, archive (data)
cache memories
CD-recordable (CD-R)
CD-rewritable (CD-RW)
chipset
compact disc–read-only
 memory (CD-ROM)
constant angular velocity
 (CAV)
constant linear velocity (CLV)
cylinder
data blocks
digital versatile disc (DVD)
direct access storage devices
 (DASD)
directory entries
double data rate SDRAM
 (DDR SDRAM)

dual inline memory module
 (DIMM)
file allocation table (FAT)
lands
latency time
magnetic disks
magnetic floppy disks
magnetic hard disks
magnetic tape
micron
multisession (multiplay)
multispeed
optical discs
optical phase-change
 technology
pits

read/write time
removable hard disks
sectors
seek time
sequential access storage
 devices (SASD)
synchronous DRAM
 (SDRAM)
system backups
system bus
tracks
transactional processing
universal disk format (UDF)
zoned CAV (ZCAV)

■ Questions for Review

1. Describe the current technology for RAM.

2. The CPU transmits data to and from the other components of a computer system. How is this communication organized?

3. What is meant by secondary memory? What are its primary functions?

4. Compare and contrast direct access and sequential access storage devices.

5. Compare and contrast the disk geometries of CAV, CLV, and zoned CAV. What are the strengths of each format?

6. Explain the terms *track, sector,* and *cylinder* relative to the geometry of direct access storage devices.

7. Describe seek time, latency time, and read/write time for magnetic disks. How do they affect the amount of time it takes to transfer data from the disk to the system?

8. What is a file and what role does it assume in data storage? (Hint: Are files physical entities?)

9. What is the function of directory entries on a storage disk?

10. What is the purpose of the file allocation table?

11. Compare CD-ROM technology with hard disk drive technology. Which is preferable? Explain.

12. Give a brief description of the encoding scheme used for CD-ROM disks.

13. How are CD-R recorded? (What are the hardware and software requirements?)

14. Describe the phase-change technology used in CD-RW.

15. Aside from DVD video and audio, what applications can DVD serve?

16. Compare and contrast DVD-RW with DVD+RW.

17. For both CD and DVD, what does "random writing" mean?

Chapter  13

Input and Output

OBJECTIVES

- Be familiar with an assortment of typical devices used for input and output of information, including keyboards, display monitors, printers, and the like

- Understand some of the choices available for connecting I/O devices to your computer system

In Chapter 11, we focused on the organization and workings of the basic processor. As you recall, the processor is composed of two chief components, the CPU and main memory. Main memory stores the data and instructions used in processing. The CPU manages the execution of programs stored in memory. A processor by itself, however, is neither very capable nor useful. First, it needs a great deal of supplemental storage to retain both data and programs not in current use. In the previous chapter, we surveyed some of the secondary memory choices available for this function. Secondly, the processor has little to do without some means of receiving data and producing it. In this chapter, we will complete our overview of the I/O system by examining the variety of ways in which input and output are performed. We will also consider some of the ways in which these and other peripherals may be connected to your system.

Input Devices

So far our survey of hardware for the computer system has omitted one vital ingredient: the ability to communicate with the user. Computers have nothing to do if they cannot receive data from the user to process. At the same time, the results of processing are useless if they cannot be converted to a form meaningful to the user. Consequently, input and output functions are very important for any practical computer system.

Yet, in spite of their importance, input and output needs vary considerably from one user to the next. For this reason, a wide assortment of devices is dedicated to these functions. And, as mentioned in Chapter 11, the choice of input-output, or I/O, devices and peripherals is usually what distinguishes one system from another. In this chapter, we will sample some of the more notable types of I/O devices. We begin with devices used exclusively for input.

You will recall that **input** means translating information that is understandable to you and me into machine-readable form. In short, input devices convert human forms of information into binary encoded data. There are a wide variety of forms for communicating information to the computer system and, naturally, an assortment of devices that accommodate these forms. We will examine a few of the most commonly used input devices.

Keyboard

Certainly the most common form of input is text. The standard device for communicating text information to the computer is by way of the **keyboard,** a set of keys organized and employed like those of a typewriter. The user presses the keys to signal character codes that are transmitted electronically to the computer system. (Character coding was introduced in Chapter 5.) Most keyboards are based on the American standard "QWERTYUIOP" arrangement (taken from the second row of keys). Many keyboards, however, are programmable and can be rearranged to suit personal preferences and character sets.

The most common keyboards for computer systems offer over 100 keys. These keyboards contain a number of special keys for computers—keys not found on typewriters. For example, you will likely find Escape and Control keys, cursor movement keys, a numeric keypad, and special function keys on your keyboard in addition to the regular characters and numerals.

A keyboard is basically a switching device that responds to the position and timing of your keystrokes. If you removed the keys from its surface, you could see that the underlying surface is divided into a grid called the **key matrix.** In most keyboards, pressing a key closes a circuit and transmits a signal to the system. The location of the signal on the key matrix is compared with a character map stored in the system's ROM. The character code is then transmitted to the processor. Pressing multiple keys, of course, sends multiple signals. Lookup tables contain matches for these combination keystrokes. For example, pressing the Control key simultaneously with the character "C" sends a CNTL-C to the processor. The system is also sensitive to the timing of keystrokes too. When you press and hold a key, for example, the character code will be sent repeatedly to the processor. The timing of repetitions can usually be set by individual choice. For some computer systems, the key matrix may also be reprogrammed to suit personal preferences as well.

Mouse

Conceived by Doug Engelbart in the 1960s, the **mouse** is a hand-held device that is rolled around a small area of the desktop (or a pad especially designed for its use). His goal was to create an input device that would operate simply and intuitively, like pointing to indicate choices and actions. The mouse is used in conjunction with a graphic-oriented interface for communicating with the computer system. Specifically, it is employed to control pointers or icons on the video display monitor. The mouse was introduced to mainstream computing with the inception of the Apple Macintosh in 1984.

The conventional (electro-mechanical) mouse contains a trackball and electrical contacts that measure the direction and extent of your hand movements. These are transmitted as x (vertical) and y (horizontal) coordinates that are used by the system to plot the pointer movements on the screen of the video display monitor.

Recently, optical technology has replaced the trackball and wheels found in the electro-mechanical mouse. Typically, the optical mouse contains a red light-emitting diode (LED) that bounces its signal off the surface on which the mouse sits. A camera or photo sensor captures the image and sends it to an internal **digital signal processor** (**DSP**). Based on as many as 1500 images per second, the processor can determine how much and how quickly the mouse has moved. Because the optical mouse has no moving parts, it is subject to less wear and tear. Tracking is better, too, because it does not require a special surface to work properly.

The mouse has one or several buttons on top that are pressed to indicate specific actions while pointing. For example, the Macintosh employs a one-button mouse, while most computers running Windows employ a two-button mouse. The Apple optical mouse is shown in Figure 13.1; although it has a seamless design, it operates like a single-button device.

Pressing a button or moving the mouse sends a 3-byte signal to the processor. The first byte contains information about the status of the button(s) and any change of direction in the mouse's motion. The succeeding pair of bytes indicates the relative amount of difference in the x and y coordinates since the last signal. The sensitivity of the system in detecting your movements will depend on the speed at which it receives these three-byte messages. For example, a standard PS/2 connection has a maximum rate of 40 reports per second. On the other hand, "low-speed" USB connections are much faster and could potentially report over 45,000 times per second. (We will consider USB and other connecting protocols later in the chapter.)

Scanners

Drawings and photographs can be digitized using an image scanner. The most common form for desktop computing is a **flatbed scanner.** See Figure 13.2. Flatbed scanners are both versatile and economical. Similar to the way you use a copier, you place the image face down on a sheet of ruled glass. With the cover closed, a horizontal light bar passes down the image. A wide-angle optical lens focuses the reflected image width onto a much smaller array of sensors. Photoelectric cells in the scan head sample the reflected light from the image row by row as the bar passes over it. Flatbed and most other scanners employ **charged-coupled device (CCD)** sensors. CCD is an analog device whose signal must be converted using an **analog-to-digital converter (ADC)** chip.

Flatbed scanners have resolutions measured in dots per inch (or dpi). Most flatbed scanners today have resolutions of 600, 1200, 1600, or sometimes 2400 dpi. These figures rep-

Figure 13.1

The Apple Pro Mouse uses optical technology for greater accuracy at higher speeds. The seamless casing supports single-button action.

resent what is termed the **optical resolution,** which is the maximum for the physical imaging system. Higher resolutions are often quoted, but these are **interpolated resolutions.** The latter are achieved by software, but you can get the same results using an image processing program that multiplies the number of pixels in the image. The problem with interpolated resolution is that it does not improve the quality of the scanned image. Interpolation is useful only when you need to produce larger pictures. In these instances, you need more pixels. At any rate, optical resolution is the only significant factor to consider when comparing or evaluating a scanner.

Some scanners report resolution such as 1200 × 2400, for example. What precisely does this mean? The horizontal resolution—in this instance, 1200—represents the optical resolution of the device. The second figure indicates the precision of the stepping motor. The stepping motor advances the scanning bar vertically in increments of 1/2400 of an inch. This number is useful for determining which resolutions can be captured accurately by the device. For example, if we scan an image at 600 dpi, the motor must advance the bar four steps for each horizontal scan (because 2400/600 = 4). But, if we chose 500 dpi, the motor would advance five times for most rows but four times on others to compensate (because 2400/500 = 4.8). In other words, some errors would be introduced because of the choice of resolution. The moral of the story is that the second resolution figure informs you about the vertical precision of the scanner.

Dynamic range is another factor in considering what to look for in a flatbed scanner. As we saw earlier in Chapter 8, many color digital images are 24-bit RGB color. This means that the image is composed of three channels: red, green, and blue. Each pixel in the image, therefore, is represented by three numbers signifying its primary values. In 24-bit color, 8 bits are used to denote each color. Scanners today are rated at higher dynamic ranges. It is common to find 30-bit, 36-bit, and even 42-bit ranges. These afford 10, 12, and 14 bits, respectively, for each channel. Clearly, 14 bits offers significantly greater range over 8 bits. There are 256 possible values in 8 bits, but 16,383 values in 14 bits. The issue, however, is whether this is usable range. The answer depends on two factors: the medium and the machine. Printed documents don't have much dynamic range, so the greater sensitivity of higher dynamic ranges would be wasted. In contrast, film captures extensive dynamic ranges. So, a greater number of bits would be justified. The second factor is the sensitivity of the scanner. Inexpensive scanners, for example, use inexpensive CCD chips. It is unlikely that these will be sensitive enough to exploit higher dynamic ranges.

Regardless of the internal number of bits used by the scanner, output images will most likely be squeezed back into the standard 24-bit color for printing and display. Having greater dynamic range, though, usually means that you can adjust and produce better looking images before you convert them to 24-bit color.

Scanners come in other varieties as well. **Hand-held scanners** are operated manually. These, however, are usually limited to scanning text rather than detailed graphics or images. Slide or film scanners, and drum scanners are employed in professional applications.

Figure 13.2
The Hewlett Packard 5500c flatbed scanner is shown here with attachments.

A **slide** or **film scanner** converts 35-mm slides or negatives to digital images at high resolutions—2700 dpi and higher. A print is a copy of the original negative; copies typically lose some of the contrast and resolution of the original. For example, a print may be capable of scanning at perhaps 300 dpi or 600 dpi, but film can be scanned easily at 3000 dpi. Thus, scanning film produces better results than scanning prints made from the film. On the other hand, film scanners produce hefty image files. A full frame 35-mm color negative scanned at 2700 dpi produces a file of about 27 MB. The downside for scanning color negatives, however, is that their scans usually require color correction. Most color negatives are treated with an orange mask that aids in producing prints. But when a color negative is scanned, the resulting image must be inverted. (See Chapter 8, for digital image processing techniques.) The problem, however, is that the orange mask gets converted to a blue tint or cast. This color cast usually has to be removed, unless the scanner has software that automatically removes such casts.

Drum scanners have even greater resolution (optical resolutions are typically 4000 dpi) and are used primarily in high-end publishing. The image is mounted on a glass or acrylic cylinder that is rotated and scanned. A high-intensity beam is projected onto the drum. The reflected light is separated into RGB color channels. A separate photomultiplier tube (PMT) senses the light for each color and converts it to electrical signals. These electrical charges are then passed through an ADC that turns the signals into digital values. PMT sensors are more sensitive than CCD technology and produce much greater dynamic ranges.

Drum scanners offer higher sensitivity (greater dynamic ranges), higher optical resolutions, greater enlargements (up to 3,000 percent), greater control of output (the operator can view the image and make adjustments during scanning), and no interference from stray light. They are often employed by prepress services for professional publishing applications. As you might expect, these high-quality results come at a significantly higher price tag.

Musical Instrument Digital Interface

Musical instruments may be recorded and digitized using microphones and a sound digitizer. In contrast, some instruments are capable of producing electrical signals that can be recorded directly without the typical analog-to-digital conversion. These instruments require hardware and software that implement a protocol called **musical instrument digital interface** (**MIDI**) to control the communication.

MIDI information is not sampled digitized sound but rather instructions for reproducing a given sound. Because these files are encoded as instructions rather than digitized sound waves, they are much smaller than those of sampled sound.

MIDI instruments are specially designed instruments that are combined with hardware and software to transform analog electrical signals to the coded instructions for MIDI files. Special hardware and software are also needed to play these files. When a computer system is employed in the MIDI process, a dedicated interfacing device must be used to convert MIDI signals to a form suitable for handling by the computer.

Sound Card

Most computer systems today are equipped with an integrated **sound card** that serves as both an input and output device. See Figure 13.3. Although most systems come with a sound card already installed, it is usually an optional device added to a slot connected to the expansion bus of the system. The sound card contains components and circuitry that can receive and produce electrical audio signals for stereo or sometimes multi-channel sound.

Digitizing sound or music requires an analog source. It can be generated from a variety of analog sound sources; microphones, audiotape, and CD playback are a few examples. The analog-to-digital converter (ADC) digitizes the source signal according to the sampling rate selected. The ADC may offer several sampling rates from a low sampling frequency for voice and acceptable sound to a high sampling frequency for high-fidelity sound. The resolution for sound digitizers is also adjustable. Higher resolution translates to greater dynamic range and

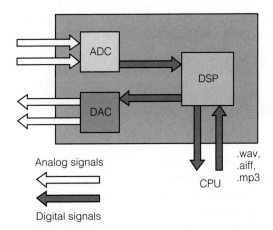

Figure 13.3
The integrated sound card serves for both digitizing analog sound sources and converting digital sound files to analog signals. For input, the analog sound source is digitized by the analog-to-digital converter (ADC) and passed to the digital signal processor (DSP) for compression and further processing. Digital sound files are forwarded to the CPU for storage and use. The process is reversed when the CPU sends a sound file to the DSP for decompression. The uncompressed digital data is then sent to the digital-to-analog converter (DAC) for conversion into analog signals. These signals are usually sent to amplified speakers for reproduction as sounds and music.

higher fidelity. The digital signal is sent to a DSP for further processing and usually compression. The DSP relieves the system processor of work related to processing sound data. Finally, the DSP converts the digitized sound information into a chosen file format and routes the file to the CPU, which usually stores or transmits the file.

The process is reversed for output. The CPU transmits a sound file to the DSP, which decompresses it and prepares the digital sound data for the **digital-to-analog converter (DAC)**. The DAC filters the signal and converts it to an electrical audio signal that is suitable for audio speakers. The signal, however, does have to be amplified to be usable by most speaker systems. As a result, component speakers designed for computers usually have an amplifier built-in.

Many sound cards also have a MIDI built in for connecting MIDI instruments. Premium cards offer additional support for MIDI musical instruments, recording, and playback.

Video Capture Card

Like audio, video information may be acquired from a number of sources but must be digitized for use by your computer system. Broadcast video, video cassette recordings, video cameras, and video disc playback may supply appropriate (analog) video signals for digitizing. **Video capture cards** are hardware/software combinations similar to those of sound cards. A special hardware board often must be added to an expansion slot or interface in your computer. With this board and additional software, video signals can be digitized, stored, and processed on your system.

Most video capture cards have compression capabilities, too. They can convert the digital video signal to a compressed format that is smaller and easier to transmit and store. Some manufacturers have integrated video capture with video graphic adapter cards (see below). These high-end graphic cards offer basic video processing along with the capability to handle video sources from TV, videotape, and DVD. (Digital video was surveyed in Chapter 10; for more about data compression, consult Chapter 20.)

Digital Cameras

You can simplify the two-step process of producing digital images from scanned analog photographs or videotape by employing digital cameras instead. A **digital camera** uses conventional analog optical methods to capture a scene but automatically samples and converts it to digital form. The digital images are produced as files that may be transferred directly to the computer's memory or stored on microdisks, flash memory, or some other type of memory device supplied with the camera.

Digital cameras come in two basic varieties: still-image cameras and digital video cameras. Consumer versions of these cameras produce color images at both high and low resolutions that are suitable for use with video display monitors (for multimedia applications) and non-commercial publishing. Most cameras have what is dubbed **megapixel** resolution, which means that the camera can capture an image that has over a million pixels. Today, consumer versions are rated at 2 or 3 megapixels.

Digitizing Tablet

Suited to artistic applications, a **digitizing tablet** is a pressure-sensitive electronic pad that converts drawings to digital form. The user employs a stylus to either draw or trace lines and curves on the tablet. The tablet permits greater control and finer detail compared with other drawing techniques that use a computer.

Some tablets have software that translates handwritten text and special movements as commands for operating the user interface as well. For example, equipped with a tablet plus this special software, you may edit text documents using conventional editing markings like those used on printed copy.

Specialized palmtop computers (or PDAs) are equipped with small built-in digital tablets used as their primary input device. These "tablet PCs" process handwriting and drawn figures as input to the system.

We have examined only a few of the many types of devices whose function is to translate human representations of information into binary encoded forms for processing by the computer. Besides these there are a variety of others. Many are similar or closely related in function to those listed. For example, the mouse has its cousins, the trackball and joystick, also used for hand manipulations. The digitizing tablet is related to touch-sensitive and light-sensitive screens. Some very specialized input peripherals provide access to individuals who have special physical needs that cannot be served by conventional tools.

Output Devices

The utility of computers depends also on having machine-generated data translated to forms that are useful for us, the computer users. This, of course, is the function of **output devices.** Let's list some examples of the most commonly used output peripherals.

CRT Video Display Monitor

The **video display monitor** is a television-like device attached to most computer systems. The chief component of the video display monitor is the **cathode ray tube (CRT),** much like the picture tubes used in standard televisions. See Figure 13.4. The CRT consists of a screen composed of phosphorescent dots or phosphors. The phosphors, which are too small to be seen individually, are combined to represent visually the individual elements or pixels that make up digital images and graphics. When a phosphor is excited by an electron gun at the end of the

Figure 13.4
The CRT video display monitor is the most common output device for desktop computers. Shown here is the two-page (24") Sony monitor, which is especially useful for graphic design and desktop publishing applications.

FOCUS   Digital Cameras

The world of consumer digital cameras and camcorders is rapidly changing. While technology improves, the prices are decreasing. Some industry experts have predicted that by 2010 nearly everyone will be shooting family pictures and the like using a digital camera. To find out the latest about this advancing technology, consult our online resource "Focus on Digital Cameras."

tube, it glows at an intensity that is a function of the voltage levels fed to the gun. Each phosphor, however, can glow at this intensity for only a short period of time. Consequently, the electron gun must scan the phosphors at regular intervals to refresh them. The **refresh rate** is the number of times per second the phosphors are refreshed by the electron guns. Refresh rates are usually expressed in Hertz (Hz), or cycles per second.

Most monitors use a horizontal scanning pattern to refresh phosphors, and they scan every line top to bottom. This is called **raster scanning,** as shown in Figure 13.5. Video display monitors used for computer systems have a refresh rate of 60 Hz or higher; this means that the entire screen is scanned, line by line, 60 times or more each second. Higher refresh rates are customary for the more expensive, higher-resolution monitors. Televisions often use a different scanning method, called *interlacing,* that scans and refreshes all even scan lines followed by all odd lines. The result is a slower refresh rate of 30 times per second. This is one reason why ordinary televisions are not suitable as computer video displays.

A monochrome monitor has a single color phosphor, usually white. Color video display monitors are more complicated in that each dot that makes up an image is actually a combination of three phosphors: the additive primaries of red (R), green (G), and blue (B). (See Figure 13.6.) Each triplet of phosphors is too small to be seen individually. Instead, we per-

Raster scanning

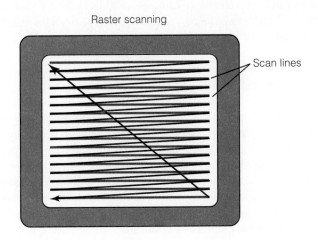

Scan lines

Figure 13.5

The phosphors in a CRT are luminescent, but they will continue to glow only momentarily. They must be refreshed by repeated scans of the electron beams to maintain the image. The electron gun sweeps the phosphors line by line in the pattern depicted in the diagram. This is called raster scanning. The time that it takes to perform a complete sweep is called the refresh rate.

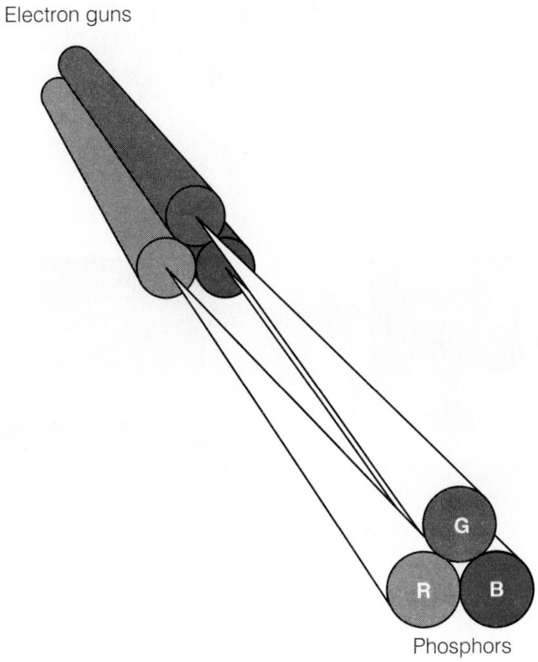

Electron guns

Phosphors

Figure 13.6

A color CRT display is powered by three coordinated electron guns; each focuses a specific amount of energy on a single type of phosphor. The red, green, and blue phosphors are materials that coat the inside of the screen and glow when struck by the electrons. If all three phosphors in a triple are struck by energies of the same high intensity, the viewer sees a dot of white light. Different perceived colors are created by varying the intensities of the three electron beams.

ceive it as a single colored pixel based on its combined intensities for each of the three primary colors. A color display monitor has three electron guns that are fed various combinations of voltages continuously while focusing their beams on the primary color components of a single pixel simultaneously as they sweep across the scan pattern.

Most monitors produce crisper images by using a focusing method called **masking.** The mask is a screen that focuses the beams from the three electron guns and helps to converge their energies more precisely on the intended phosphor in the triple. See Figure 13.7. The display's fineness of dots for these types of CRTs is typically measured in pitch. The pitch is the distance between mask apertures and ranges from 0.6 to 0.2 millimeters. All other things being equal, a smaller dot pitch means a crisper image. Tubes having less than 0.3-mm pitch are considered high quality.

Pitch and screen size determine the display resolution of the monitor, which should not be confused with image resolution (as introduced in Chapter 2). Image resolution refers to the number of picture elements or pixels that make up a digital image. A monitor must have sufficient display resolution (dot fineness) to represent an image's resolution (pixels) accurately. Most monitors today have display resolutions between 72 and 96 dpi. This resolution, however, does not fully convey the graphic-handling capability of the monitor. High-resolution graphics, for example, require monitors with a high number of dots per inch and enough usable screen area to accommodate them. Consequently, the monitor's resolution will sometimes be described in terms of the maximum number of pixels per scan line that it is capable of displaying and the number of horizontal scan lines available. For example, a monitor with a resolution of 1600 × 1200 has the capability of displaying 1600 pixels per line and 1200 lines on the screen. Even so, because digital data is scalable, monitors with lower display resolution can still display higher-resolution graphics although with some loss in accuracy and detail.

The extent to which the resolution of a monitor is usable depends on the dynamics of the monitor with its video graphics adapter. The **video graphics adapter**—often dubbed **graphics card**—is hardware that serves as an interface between the computer system and the display device. The video graphics adapter translates the graphic information stored in main memory to a video signal. Video adapters usually have specialized memory units called **video RAM (VRAM)**, which are fast access memory that store a direct digital representation of the graphic image intended for the display. Standard RAM in the computer system does the necessary numerical calculations to determine what type of image is displayed; the results are transferred to VRAM, which serves as a middleman in the exchange. The adapter also converts the contents of VRAM into an electrical signal that drives the monitor's electron guns. See Figure 13.8.

Video display resolutions are often characterized by labels such as EGA, VGA, SVGA, XGA, SXGA, and UXGA. These refer primarily to the video adapter hardware, but they have come to connote the maximum display resolution that these hardware components support.

Shadow mask   **Slotted mask**

Figure 13.7
The beams from the CRT's electron guns are focused more precisely by masking. In shadow masking (left), a metal plate with a series of holes helps to align the electron beams more precisely on each phosphor triple as the gun scans the line. This prevents bleeding or blurring of the image and loss of detail. Trinitron technology uses masking, but these phosphors are arranged as parallel slots (right) instead of holes.

Figure 13.8
Video images displayed on a monitor are created in several stages. The process converts digital image data to an analog form appropriate for the display device. The pixels that make up the image are initially created and stored in main memory. Most systems employ VRAM for the rapid transfer of video image data. The data is shuttled from RAM to VRAM, where it is processed by the DAC. The DAC produces the electrical signals that create the on-screen display.

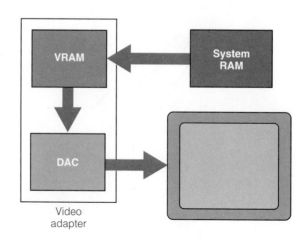

Video adapter

One of the oldest is **EGA,** which stands for **enhanced graphics adapter.** It supports a maximum resolution of 640 × 350. **VGA** (for **video graphics array**) has a maximum resolution of 640 × 480. **SVGA (super VGA)** supports up to 800 × 600. The **XGA** standard **(extended graphics array)** has a maximum resolution of 1024 × 768. **SXGA (super extended graphics array)** is the odd-man out; its 1280 × 1024 resolution has an aspect ratio of 5:4 rather than the customary 4:3. And **UXGA (ultra-extended graphics array)** can achieve 1600 × 1200.

Nearly all of the current generation of monitors can switch image resolutions on the fly—without the need to restart the computer system. These **multiscanning** video monitors (or, sometimes, **multisync**) are equipped to handle video signals requiring different resolutions and refresh rates. Thus, these monitors offer more versatile performance while costing only a little more than fixed-scanning models.

Flat-panel Display Monitors

CRT video monitors are very common, but they do have the liabilities of imposing physical size and high power requirements. In recent years, new technologies have been utilized to produce **flat-panel displays** that feature a smaller volume and weight while having more modest power demands. The most popular of these alternative technologies is that of **liquid crystal displays (LCDs).** LCDs are commonly used in notebook and laptop computer systems, but recently larger desktop versions are achieving popularity. See Figure 13.9. LCDs offer the advantages of full-color display with low power consumption and compact size. Because they do not depend on raster scanning, LCDs do not flicker or pulsate. This usually means less fatigue and eyestrain for users. Because the screens are brighter and sharper, text is also easier to read.

LCD is based on the use of thermotropic liquid crystals. These are liquid crystals that are sensitive to temperature. LCD employs liquid crystals in their nematic state, which means that they are aligned in a definite order or pattern. Specifically, most LCDs are derived from **twisted nematics (TN);** that is, liquid crystals that are naturally twisted to form a helix-like pattern. This twisting is affected by an electrical current. Applying different voltages will untwist the molecules to varying degrees.

Thus, applying voltages to twisted nematics serves to control the amount of light that is transmitted through the substance. This is the basis for the LCD technology. The display itself is a composition of various layers. At the rear is a backlight source—usually fluorescent. The light shines through a polarizing filter that passes light rays in one direction only. See Figure 13.10. A layer of transparent electrodes apply charges to cells composed of liquid crystal molecules sandwiched between two alignment layers. These alignment layers orient the crystals in their natural helix or twisted pattern. Color displays have a layer of RGB filters for

Figure 13.9
The flat-panel display is based on LCD technology. These displays are typically brighter than comparably sized CRT monitors. In addition, they weigh less and have a smaller footprint on your desktop. Shown here is a Sony model.

creating red, green, and blue shades of light. A second polarizing filter passes light only if it is aligned properly.

The bottom-polarizing filter admits light only in a specific orientation. Again, consult Figure 13.10. If the liquid crystals are in their natural state, they will gradually bend the light as it passes through several layers of twisted molecules. As a result, the light is oriented perpendicular to its origin when it passes out of this layer. And, because it is reoriented, it passes through the second polarizing filter. On the other hand, if a sufficient voltage is applied to the liquid crystals, they will straighten. The light is not reoriented and is blocked by the second polarizing filter. Moderating the voltage can lessen this straightening effect and allow some of the light to pass through. In color displays, each pixel is comprised of three cells. Each of these cells has either a red, green, or blue filter to create RGB composite color.

Most LCDs used with computers today are based on **active matrix** displays. These are also called **thin-film transistor,** or **TFT,** LCDs. In active matrix displays, switching transistors or diodes are attached to each cell to switch it on or off. TFT technology produces sharper, brighter, and faster displays compared with earlier and less expensive **passive matrix** displays. Passive matrix displays are still used in cell phones, black-and-white PDAs, and other appliances.

Figure 13.10
Only vertically aligned light can pass through the first of two polarizing filters (a). If the liquid crystals are in their natural state, they are twisted in a helix pattern. Thus, light bends gradually until it is oriented horizontally and passes through the second polarizing filter (b). When a current is applied, the crystals straighten and the light is blocked by the horizontal polarizing filter. This means that a current applied to every cell in the display produces a black screen.

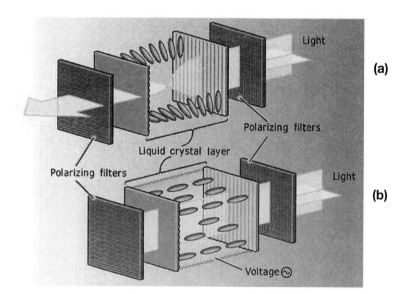

FOCUS Video Graphic Cards

The type of video graphics adapter described above acts as a simple frame buffer for displaying graphic images on the video display monitor. The challenges of high-resolution graphics on high-performance monitors have spawned a number of enhancements and improvements for the current generation of graphic cards. Most systems today are equipped with a suitably high-perfor- mance video graphics card that can better support these demands. These cards not only convert digital graphics information into analog video signals, they also perform some of the work traditionally handled by the CPU. Find out more about these graphic accelerators in our online resource "Focus on Video Graphic Cards."

Interestingly, LCDs receive analog signals from standard graphics cards installed in most computers. However, LCDs are digital devices, so they must convert these signals back to digital form. Recently, an industry group adopted a new standard of using the **digital visual interface (DVI)** to connect to flat-panel LCD displays. Unlike older VGA connectors, DVI sends both digital and analog information to the monitor. In the case of flat-panel displays, this simplifies the process of conversion back to digital format.

Because LCDs are essentially hardwired devices, they provide only one true picture resolution. However, they can be set to emulate other resolutions, although the results are usually less satisfying visually. The technology is still improving, and LCD displays are getting larger, sharper, and less expensive. It is not surprising, then, that their market share increases steadily.

Printer

In spite of claims about the epoch of the "paperless" electronic office, printed text remains a popular form of computer output. In fact, computers probably generate even more paper today than before their introduction to the workplace. And because printed text is so prevalent in so many endeavors, printers themselves come in a wide assortment of sizes and kinds. Separating printers into three classes based on how they compose text (or images) is a convenient approach:

- Character printers

- Line printers

- Page printers

Character printers produce text by forming each individual character separately. Dot matrix printers were among the earliest character printers used widely in desktop computing. The **dot matrix printer** is an impact printer, which means that it forms symbols by moving the print head across the width of the paper and striking a ribbon to paper. Characters are formed by creating dot patterns. See Figure 13.11. The quality of the output largely depends on the resolution of the matrix (how many dots). Other methods such as overstriking or duplicated printing can be used to improve quality. Besides text, these printers can be used to produce graphic drawings. Although dot matrix printers fail to produce high-quality text output, they have been favored for their economy and flexibility.

Another type of character printer is the **inkjet printer.** As in dot matrix printers, the print head of an inkjet printer glides across the width of the page. But rather than impacting the page, the print head in an inkjet printer sprays a fine stream of ink that forms small dots on the page. The individual dots are much smaller than those of impact printers, so the quality of the resulting text or images is better. Inkjet printers typically have a print quality of 300 dpi, 600 dpi, and higher. Today even color inkjet printers are only slightly more expensive than dot matrix printers, so they are usually the choice for desktop systems.

Color inkjet printers typically employ CMYK color for output images. This means that there are four different ink sources (cyan, magenta, yellow, and black). Some inkjet printers compose color images from five or six different ink sources.

Because these printers produce the page one character at a time, they are generally slower than other printing technologies. For a number of years, line printers were the mainstay of data processing centers that needed to print thousands of pages of text a day. **Line printers** print the text for a page line by line. Drum printers are line printers composed of bands that can be individually rotated to align the proper character type in each column. The drum then impacts a ribbon that leaves an impression of the entire line at once. Line printers naturally print much faster than character printers, but they are limited to text output exclusively.

A **page printer** composes the entire page at once for output. Laser printers are the most popular type of page printer used in desktop computer systems. A **laser printer** creates its image by borrowing a technology similar to that employed by photocopying machines. The entire page is composed by a coordinated process that first employs a focused laser beam that electrically charges a sequence of lines of extremely small spots or dots on a rotating drum.

Figure 13.11

Dot matrix printers are so called because they produce text and graphics composed of patterns of dots. A close-up of the printed letter "A," for example, reveals its pattern. Other print technologies compose text and figures from dots, but their size and spacing is much finer and, therefore, less visible to the eye.

The pattern of electrical charges is transferred to the paper page as it rolls across the drum. Subsequently, toner is fixed to the electrical charges on the page. Laser printers have high-quality output because of their high resolution. Consumer models, for instance, have resolutions of 600, 1200, and even 2400 dpi. Laser output is generally superior in quality to inkjet output—even at comparable resolutions. The dot pattern in laser-printed output is more precise than that of inkjet printers. In fact, the printed output from high-resolution laser printers can rival the quality of typeset printing technologies.

Dye-sublimation printers represent a special class of output devices used exclusively for producing color prints and graphic images rather than text. A "dye-sub" printer employs a special ribbon made of plastic film. A thermal print head with thousands of precise heating elements passes over the ribbon. The heat causes the dye on the ribbon to vaporize and is deposited on the surface of specially treated paper. Higher temperatures deposit more dye; lower temperatures transfer less dye. Afterwards, a clear coat is added to seal and protect the image. Dye-sub printers employ CMY or CMYK color to produce smoothly varying images that rival continuous tone prints based on conventional photography methods.

For a number of years, the price of these printers and supplies (ribbon cassettes and paper) restricted them to commercial and professional usage. However, the costs are declining, and it is likely that in the near future consumers may well choose dye-sublimation printers to produce prints from their digital cameras. Indeed, some manufacturers have designed models that plug in directly to a consumer digital camera for operating ease and convenience.

MIDI Synthesizer

As discussed earlier, MIDI is a protocol for communicating information about musical sequences. MIDI information, of course, is digital, but it is not a sampling of musical sounds. Instead, it contains instructions on how to make musical sounds. These instructions specify what notes to play and how long to play them. In addition, they describe the volume and modulation for the notes as well. MIDI information may also indicate what sort of musical voice should play these notes. For example, it may specify several voices including synthetic or artificial sounds like those of strings (violins and cellos) or percussion.

To play MIDI-generated music, you must employ a **MIDI synthesizer,** which converts the MIDI instructions to electrical signals that can be amplified and reproduced as musical sounds through conventional audio equipment. Often MIDI synthesizers are combined with instruments such as a piano keyboard for both input and output of music.

These are but a sampling of the great variety of peripherals dedicated to I/O functions in a computer system. The choice and configuration of input and output devices for a particular system depend, of course, on the type of tasks performed with the system.

Connecting Your Peripherals

Choosing a peripheral to add to your system involves one more factor. How is the device connected to your system? Unfortunately, the answer is not always obvious. There are a variety of connections available, and some devices can be connected to your system in several different ways. For example, some printers are connected to the parallel port on your computer, others are connected to a USB socket or hub. Which printer/connection combination should you use? Not to worry. In this section, we will try to unravel most of the mystery in connecting your peripherals.

In Chapter 12, we saw that communication within a computer system depends on the organization of the system bus. Moreover, the dominant modern processor design has replaced the single bus system with a chipset architecture. In most chipset designs, an I/O controller chip manages communications with the variety of peripherals connected to it. Some of the devices are **internal,** such as hard drives, optical discs, etc; others are **external** devices, such as keyboards, printers, scanners, digital cameras, and the like. Whether internal or external, they share two facts in common. First, different devices communicate at different speeds. Secondly, each device must be properly connected to the system.

To accommodate these, the typical computer system provides a variety of connections. These connections form what is referred to as the **I/O interface bus.** Thus, the I/O controller chip manages a variety of interfaces; each is tailored to the specific needs of the device connected to it. We will survey some of the common types of interfaces used today.

Internal Bus Types

A number of I/O and storage devices are connected to the I/O system internally. Magnetic hard drives, floppy drives, CD-ROM, CD-R, CD-RW drives, sound cards, video graphic adapters, and network cards are typically connected directly to the computer system using one of the bus protocols listed below. All represent **parallel communication** in that a specified number of data bits are transmitted concurrently—each over a separate line. See Figure 13.12. The number of data bits transmitted, transmission speeds, and the number of devices that may be connected to and share the same bus, typify their differences.

IDE   One of the most common internal bus connections is **Integrated Drive Electronics (IDE).** It is employed exclusively for connecting hard drives and CD-ROM drives. On most systems that employ it, there are usually two IDE connections. Each can handle up to two devices. IDE is inexpensive, but neither fast (16-bit data with a throughput up to 16.6 MB per second) nor flexible in use. Even so, its economy makes it a standard choice for many systems.

PCI   The **Peripheral Component Interconnection (PCI)** bus was designed originally for Pentium processors. PCI is used primarily to connect internal devices such as network interface cards, video graphic adapters, and sound cards. PCI can transfer either 32 or 64 data bits in parallel. Speeds are largely dependent on both the clock speed and the chipset architecture employed in the system. The maximum rate is 264 MB per second; 66 or 132 MB per second are more typical.

In practical circumstances, three or four devices can be connected to a single PCI bus. However, additional devices can be added to a secondary PCI bus that is bridged with (connected to) the primary PCI bus. In some designs, other bus structures are likewise bridged with the PCI bus for better control and performance.

PCMCIA   The **Personal Computer Memory Card International Association (PCMCIA)** interface was originally designed for plugging an expansion memory card into a laptop or a notebook computer. It has been adapted to handle a variety of peripherals, including fax/modems, network cards, and so on. There are several types of PCMIA slots and cards.

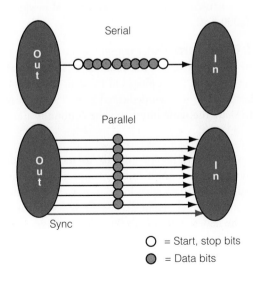

Figure 13.12

Sending a byte of data serially vs. parallel. In serial communications, the data is sent on a single line one bit at a time. The data must be sequenced properly, and chunks of data must be marked or framed. For example, a start and stop bit could be sent along with the data bits to mark the payload. In contrast, sending data using parallel communication permits the data bits to be sent concurrently on separate lines. Even so, the data must be properly sequenced on the lines, and the transmission must be synchronized. This signals the receiver when to expect to extract the data. Serial communication is often slower, but simpler to maintain. Parallel communication is faster, but requires more channels and more sophisticated control.

Most versions employ 16-bit data; top data rates are 16 to 20 MB per second. The newer CardBus standard supports 32 data bits at even higher transmission rates.

SCSI   Used for connecting both internal and external devices, the **Small Computer System Interface** (**SCSI** and pronounced "skuzzy") bus is found on workstations and some Apple computers. Many different types of devices may be connected to the SCSI bus: hard drives, optical drives, scanners, etc. There are several different generations of SCSI. The most recent is SCSI-III (Ultra SCSI), which allows up to 15 different devices to share the bus. The data path is 16 bits, and it supports speeds up to 40 MB per second.

External Parallel Connections

Some peripheral devices are connected externally by means of cables fixed to a specially designed socket on the back of your computer system. For example, printers, scanners, digital cameras, as well as external hard drives and other storage devices are added to a desktop system by cable connections. We can best distinguish externally connected devices by their method of data transfer. Some use parallel transmission (as described above); others send bits serially.

As mentioned, some external devices can be connected to the SCSI bus using cables. However, most computer systems have a single port for connecting devices for parallel data communication called the **parallel port.** Originally, it was designed for connecting a printer to a computer, but, the parallel port has gone through several reincarnations in order to support more variety. On most computer systems today, the parallel port accepts a 25-pin connector and offers bi-directional communication at speeds up to 2 Mbps (megabits per second).

External Serial Bus Types

Many I/O devices can employ **serial communication,** that is, transferring data a single bit at a time. Again, see Figure 13.12 above. The data must be framed. In other words, the receiver must be able to recognize the start and end of a given sequence. For example, a start bit might be sent to signal the commencement of a sequence, and a stop bit would signify its conclusion. Serial communication can be slower than parallel, but it is simpler because only one line is needed.

RS-232   The **RS-232 serial interface** is the granddaddy of all interfaces. It has been standard on computers and electronic equipment since the 1960s. Today, the RS-232 serial port found on most computers is used for connecting an external modem. Accordingly, bit rates range from 9,600 to 56,000 bps.

PS/2 Mouse and Keyboard   Older computer systems had a second RS-232 serial port for connecting the mouse or keyboard. Today most systems have replaced these with special serial ports using a smaller 5-pin plug. On PCs, the mouse is connected to the **PS/2 port** socket, and the keyboard to its own dedicated 5-pin socket. It is also common for the mouse and keyboard to share the same interface. The communication protocol is similar to the RS-232 standard.

USB   The problems with connecting peripherals to most computer systems today are twofold: There are many devices to connect and few connections, and most of the connections are slow. **Universal serial bus** (**USB**) was developed to solve both of these problems. The USB provides connections for up to 127 different devices. Each device can transmit or receive data at rates up to 6 Mbps. The new standard USB 2.0 offers even greater bandwidth and speeds up to 480 Mbps.

USB employs two different types of connectors. See Figure 13.13. The "A" connector forms "upstream" connections; that is, the data primarily flows to the computer. "B" connectors are for "downstream" connections to the devices. As a result, it is very difficult to get confused about how to connect devices to your computer using USB.

Most computer systems today have one or two built-in USB socket connections. Not a problem, though. A relatively inexpensive **USB hub** can provide multiple connections for adding more devices. Standard hubs have four or perhaps eight new connections. It is also possible to chain hubs together to connect even more devices. A hub is usually powered. This allows a device to draw its electrical power directly from the USB connection rather than a separate power source. Powered hubs are fine for low-powered devices; peripherals like printers and scanners will need an independent power supply because of their higher demands.

Another useful feature for USB is that devices are **hot-swappable.** This means that you may plug and unplug devices from USB connections any time—and without turning off your computer system. When the system does power up, it consults all devices connected to the bus. Anytime a new device is unplugged or plugged in, the computer system reassigns addresses once more.

Peripherals may communicate over the USB connection in one of three ways. Some devices, such as a mouse or a keyboard, use **interrupts.** This is a special signal that works best for devices that send small amounts of data sporadically. A printer, on the other hand, sends large amounts of data at once. These are called **bulk** transmissions. Bulk transmissions are usually not time-sensitive, so they can be sent when the channel is available. These are often in 64-byte chunks and the recipient acknowledges delivery. Finally, some devices send streams of data that must be transmitted in real time. USB refers to these as **isochronous** transmissions. Isochronous transfers are not acknowledged by the recipient. For example, a video connection streams data in real time. It would be impractical to retransmit any lost

B   A Male   A Female

Figure 13.13
USB has two types of connectors. The "A" connector—male and female versions shown here—are used to connect peripherals to a hub or the computer system. The "B" connectors are plugged into a device.

DISCOVERING MORE

Input/Output Peripherals

For the latest information about the input/output technologies, consult our online resource "Discovering More About Input/Output Peripherals."

data, because these frames would be out of sequence anyway. Thus, acknowledgements are useless in these applications.

As mentioned, USB 2.0 promises even better performance. It defines three different speeds: low, full, and high. Low speed has a maximum data rate of 1.5 Mbps. Full speed is rated at 12 Mbps. High speed tops out at 480 Mbps. Just about any type of device can be supported by these data rates—even hard drives. Consequently, USB 2.0 is capable of replacing any and all of the other legacy bus connections described earlier.

Firewire Another type of serial cable and connector has the exotic moniker *Firewire*. **Firewire** is a serial transmission method defined by IEEE standard 1394 and represents a competitor to USB. It supports data rates of 100, 200, and 400 Mbps.

Like USB, devices connected to Firewire are hot-swappable and easily configured. The Firewire bus forms a tree topology. You may recall that this is the same type of organization used by file systems: a single origin or root from which all other connections are based. It permits up to 63 connections, although the limits on cable lengths would probably make this number impractical. Still, a great many devices can be connected together.

Firewire supports two styles of data transmission. **Asynchronous transmissions** are point to point. The data is addressed to a specific destination, and delivery is acknowledged to the sender. Isochronous transfers, as we saw earlier, dispense with acknowledgements in favor of a guaranteed bandwidth. These support connections that depend on real-time speeds, such as audio and video. The new standard Firewire 800 promises data rates up to 800 Mbps.

Both USB and Firewire offer a great deal of promise as multipurpose, high-performance bus protocols. It is likely that one or both of these technologies will eventually supplant the older, legacy bus protocols.

■ Summary

Input/output devices are used to translate information from human-readable forms to those that may be employed by the computer system. Input devices translate discrete or analog forms of information to a digital representation. Output devices convert digital data to a form that the user can understand. There are many different types of I/O devices; each is suited to the specific requirements for the form of information that it handles.

I/O devices are connected to the CPU by means of a bus. Bus architecture for modern processors has become varied and much more sophisticated. The bottom line is that different devices are often connected to your system using different types of bus connections. Some devices are connected directly to the bus structure internally. Others are connected externally via cables that plug into sockets provided with your system. Connections transmit data either in parallel or serially. Parallel connections are usually faster, but less flexible. Serial connections are often slower; but are more economical and can be more flexible in use. Modern serial bus protocols such as USB and Firewire challenge most of the traditional assumptions about serial data transmission. In the future, they may replace the need for so much variety in connections.

■ Terms

active matrix display

analog-to-digital converter (ADC)

asynchronous (transmissions)

bulk (transmissions)

cathode ray tube (CRT)

character printers

charged-coupled device (CCD)

digital camera

digital signal processor (DSP)

digital-to-analog converter (DAC)

digital visual interface (DVI)

digitizing tablet

dot matrix printers

drum scanners

dye-sublimation printers

enhanced graphics array (EGA)

extended graphics array (XGA)

external I/O devices

Firewire

Flat-panel displays (monitors)

flatbed scanner

hand-held scanners

hot-swappable

inkjet printer

input, input devices

Integrated Drive Electronics (IDE)

internal I/O devices

interpolated resolution

interrupt (transmissions)

I/O interface bus

isochronous (transmissions)

key matrix

keyboard

laser printer

line printers

liquid crystal display (LCD)

masking (monitor)

megapixel

MIDI instruments

MIDI synthesizer

mouse

multiscanning, multisync (monitors)

musical instrument digital interface (MIDI)

optical resolution

output, output devices

page printer

parallel communication

parallel port

passive matrix display

peripheral component interconnection (PCI)

Personal Computer Memory Card International Association (PCMCIA)

PS/2 port

raster scanning

refresh rate

RS-232 serial interface

serial communication

slide scanners (film scanners)

Small Computer System Interface (SCSI)

sound card

super VGA (SVGA)

super extended graphics array (SXGA)

thin-film transistor (TFT)

twisted nematics (TN)

ultra extended graphics array (UXGA)

Universal Serial Bus (USB)

USB hub

video capture cards

video display monitor

video graphics adapter (graphics card)

video graphics array (VGA)

video RAM (VRAM)

■ Questions for Review

1. Describe several computer input devices and the specific purposes for which they are designed.

2. In what ways does the optical mouse perform better than its electromechanical cousin?

3. What are the different types of scanners? To what functions is each suited? Explain.

4. How does optical resolution in scanners relate to interpolated resolution?

5. What is the difference between MIDI music and digitized music?

6. What are the major functions of an integrated sound card? What extras do high-end sound cards offer?

7. What are the two basic categories of digital cameras? What advantages are there for producing images digitally?

8. What does "megapixel" resolution mean? How much resolution do typical consumer digital cameras offer?

9. What is raster scanning? Why is it necessary for CRT monitors? What does the scan rate indicate about the performance of the monitor?

10. What does the pitch of a monitor represent? Is a larger or smaller pitch value preferred? Explain.

11. What is screen resolution? How is it determined?

12. What do the terms *EGA, VGA, SVGA, XGA, SXGA,* and *UXGA* refer to? What performance characteristics of a video monitor are normally associated with these terms?

13. Define the acronym VRAM and describe its role in displaying computer output on a monitor.

14. Compare and contrast CRT video monitors with flat-panel LCD monitors. Specifically, what are their strengths and weaknesses?

15. How do inkjet and laser printers differ?

16. What is a dye-sublimation printer used for? How does it work?

17. What are the differences between parallel and serial communications? Explain.

18. Describe the USB serial interface. How does it work? What are its chief advantages over other bus protocols?

19. Compare and contrast Firewire with USB bus protocols.

PART Five

Running the Show—Software

Chapter 14

Developing Applications

OBJECTIVES

- The basics of the programming process

- The development of programming languages to improve the efficiency and reliability of software development

- Programming languages that the average user can employ to enhance working with a computer

As you learned in Chapter 11, hardware provides the platform for information processing with a computer. Without a program to direct this process, however, the hardware is simply inert. Programs, of course, are collectively called *software*. The hardware of the modern computer system is organized to function as a general-purpose information processing machine. You and I, though, use computers for specific tasks. We write letters, draw pictures, send e-mail, play games, and the like. The key is software.

In fact, we could say that software is responsible for defining exactly what sort of machine the computer becomes. As computer users, we employ application software to perform work with our machines. When you use your computer to compose a paper, word processing software orchestrates that process. While that program is executing, your computer behaves like a document processor. Should you use your system to compose and record music, the software dedicated to this task converts your machine to a digital recording studio, complete with editing and mixing capabilities. Thus, the instructions of a program transform our computers into the types of machines that aid us in our work.

Programs, of course, are written by people who speak and think in natural languages such as English. On the other hand, computers are fluent only in binary codes. How then do programmers write instructions for computers?

287

Fortunately, over the past 50 years computer scientists have developed special languages, called *programming languages,* that allow programmers to communicate with computers by meeting them halfway. Programming languages are symbolic, much like natural languages. They differ from natural languages in that they are organized in ways that make directing the computer's work easier, and they can be readily translated into the binary language of the machine.

In this chapter, we continue our picture of how computers function from the standpoint of how software is developed to direct their work.

Understanding the Programming Process

Software is composed of programs. A **program,** or **software,** is a list of instructions that directs the steps of the computer's process. We saw in Chapter 11 that the typical desktop processor is a sequential uniprocessor. This means that it acts as a single instruction interpreter. It fetches the next binary-encoded instruction of the program, decodes it, and executes it.

The fetch-execute cycle is performed over and over until the process is instructed to halt. From this perspective, the computer system is like an incredibly single-minded agent that concentrates on only the current activity and proceeds relentlessly to complete the overall task. It is up to the instructions—and this means the author of the instructions—to provide overall guidance and strategy for the process. The programmer is like a playwright who not only creates a premise or plot for the drama but also supplies all the words and actions that the actors will perform. The actors, of course, bring the play to life, but the playwright has determined in advance what that life will be. The hardware brings the program to life as a process, but the program, and thus the *programmer,* makes all of this possible.

The earliest programs were conceived and created as lists of binary-encoded machine language instructions. Recall that these instructions are the types of primitive operations that the processor is designed to perform. The first symbolic programming languages mimicked the structure and organization of these machine languages. Called **assembly languages,** they simply replaced the binary encoded instructions with sets of symbols. Thus, an assembly language program is virtually a one-to-one representation of the machine language version that is executed on that processor. Because they replace binary strings with symbols, assembly languages are more convenient for human programmers to use.

Even so, because assembly languages are in one-to-one relationship to machine languages, programmers still must manage the same difficulties they faced when using those machine languages directly. In short, the instructions are primitive, which means that even the simplest tasks require a great many steps to complete.

Another shortcoming of assembly language programs is that they can be executed only on processors that employ their corresponding machine language. This lack of **portability**—the capability to execute programs on different hardware platforms—means that commercial programs written in assembly language must be rewritten for computers with different types of processors.

Today, however, programmers do not have to think and write their programs in such low-level or primitive languages. Instead, a variety of symbolic programming languages allows the programmer to express a process in more convenient and abstract ways. To be sure, these higher-level programs must be translated to the appropriate machine language instructions before they can be executed on a given processor. But this is done automatically by system software called **translation programs,** which convert a program written using a symbolic programming language into binary-encoded instructions that can be executed on the intended processor. Programmers are free to choose an appropriate programming language as their vehicle for expressing the processing task, provided they have the appropriate translation program to convert it to a form that can be handled directly by their computer.

A Sample Program

Let's illustrate how programs are organized to direct a process. Our example is a short program for adding some special effects to a Web page. From your experience with the World Wide Web, you know that your browser can display both text and graphics on a page. Suppose that we wish to create a page that displays a sequence of pictures that change when the user chooses. To do this, we will employ a programming language called JavaScript.

JavaScript is a scripting language employed to add interactivity and functionality to Web pages. A **scripting language** is an interpreted programming language. It is executed in a manner very similar to the way the CPU processes the instructions of a machine language program. Each instruction in a JavaScript program is fetched or downloaded as text. The JavaScript interpreter that is part of your browser program then decodes it and generates the necessary instructions to execute it. As you might guess, JavaScript instructions are much more abstract than typical low-level processor instructions. To get a better understanding of this, examine the program in Listing 14.1.

```
<html>
<head>
<title>image script</title>
<script language="JavaScript">                          (1)
var counter = 0                                         (2)
function changer() {                                    (3)
 counter += 1                                           (4)
     if (counter == 4) {
        counter = 0                                     (5)
     }
     document.images[0].src = counter + ".jpg"         (6)
}
</script>                                                (7)
</head>
<body bgcolor = "#FFFFFF">
<p>Click on the image to change it. </p>
<p>
<a href="#" onClick="changer()">                      (8)
<img src="0.jpg" width="279" height="184" border="0"
align="bottom">
</a>
</p>
</body>
</html>
```

Listing 14.1
A JavaScript program is embedded within a simple Web page. The program (in bold) allows the user to display a series of images by clicking on the initial image.

The actual JavaScript portion of the listing is restricted to the statements represented in bold, with each step numbered for reference in our discussion below. The remaining parts of the listing you will recognize as tags for displaying the Web page's content.

The script defines a program module called a **function.** Among other uses, JavaScript functions may be assigned to specific events. In this instance, the event is a mouse click. Statement (8) assigns the function *changer* to the occurrence of a mouse click employing the *onClick* command. Specifically, anytime the user clicks on the image displayed on the page, the function *changer* will be executed.

Let's dissect the instructions of the program. Statements (1) and (7) act like punctuation. These simply tell the browser program where the JavaScript program commences and ends. The actual executable portion of the program are statements (2)–(6). Statement (2) defines a data object called a variable. **Variables** are objects storing values that may change in the course of processing. In this case, the variable named *counter* stores an integer value that is initially set to 0. Statements (3)–(6) define the function *changer*. Statement (3) specifies the beginning of the function and its name; the opening bracket in line (3) and the closing bracket after line (6) signify its scope or extent. The function's instructions are composed of only three statements. The first instruction is statement (4), which increments the variable *counter* by a value of 1. In other words, the current value of *counter* is replaced by the sum of that value plus 1 more.

Statement (5):

```
if (counter == 4) { counter = 0 }
```

resets the value of *counter* to 0 when it reaches 4. This structure is a conditional statement. **Conditional statements** cause the program to choose between courses of action based on the current conditions of the process. In this case, the condition is when the value of *counter* reaches 4. The result is that the value of *counter* is reset to 0. Should the value of *counter* be anything other than 4, it will remain the same. The intent here is to constrain the value of *counter* so that it cycles from 0 to 4 only.

Figure 14.1
The diagram depicts the sequence of events for the process defined by the JavaScript program in Listing 14.1

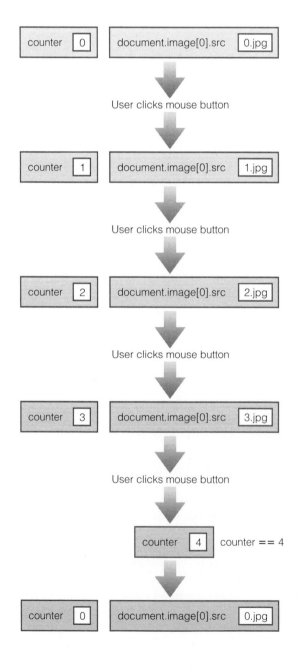

JavaScript stores all the details about the browser in a collection of programming entities called **objects.** One of the objects that it defines is the *document* object, which contains all of the links, images, and more that make up a given Web page. To identify a particular image, you must refer to it as

```
document.image[n]
```

where *n* is the number of the image. The images are numbered starting from 0 as they are listed on the coded page. This particular page displays only one image at a time so it is signified by

```
document.image[0]
```

Most objects have **properties;** these are attributes or features normally associated with the object. Images have properties such as width, height, and a source. For example,

```
document.image[0].src
```

addresses the source or name of the file of the initial image on the page. Thus, statement (6) assigns a new source for the image. In this instance, the source is made up of the current value of *counter* with the suffix ".jpg." For example, when *counter* equals 1, the image source is assigned the image "1.jpg." When *counter* is 2, the image is "2.jpg," and so on. The program, therefore, allows the user to click on the image and cycle through the series of four images, 0.jpg through 3.jpg.

The accompanying diagram in Figure 14.1 shows how the steps of the program could be conceived as it executes. Trace through the steps to understand how the program works.

The Software Development Cycle

The example illustrates how a program organizes a simple task. The example is an already finished program—all of the planning and work of the programmer have been done. Writing programs requires good planning as well as an understanding of the underlying problem to be solved.

How would the programmer approach a problem from the beginning? What steps would he or she take to complete it? The basic software development process involves at least four stages:

- *Analyzing and understanding* the problem or task to be performed

- *Devising a plan* to solve the problem or model the task

- *Creating an executable program* that implements the plan

- *Testing and correcting* the program

Analyzing the Task

We write programs so that the computer can perform work that is useful to us. Consequently, the first stage of producing a program is to understand the nature of the task we want the computer to do. Many processing tasks can be conceived as finding the answers to an informational problem: Given such-and-such information, what is a satisfactory or correct result? For example, suppose that we wish to create a program that calculates the compound interest earned on a savings account. Most practical processing problems are a great deal more complicated than this one, but it will do for the sake of illustration.

To create a program to calculate compound interest, the programmer must understand precisely what is called for. In a sense, he or she must know not only all the questions, but all the answers as well, and in advance. Only by foreseeing the entire process can the programmer create the script that can model it. Usually a program treats a general class of problem instances rather than a single case. This means that the programmer must often think of the task

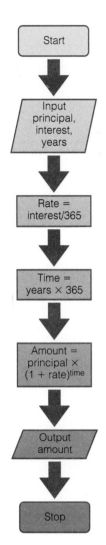

Figure 14.2
This flowchart shows the algorithm for calculating compound interest.

Listing 14.2
A pseudocoded version of the algorithm for calculating compound interest.

in very general terms to envision what sequence of events might be possible for trying to solve a variety of instances.

In this case, the problem involves calculating the total amount of an investment, given interest payments compounded periodically over a known period of time. To solve the problem, we must specify several pieces of information: the initial or *principal* amount of the investment, the periodic interest *rate,* and the amount of *time* over which the interest is compounded. Given these values, we could calculate the resulting *amount* using the well-known formula:

$$\text{amount} = \text{principal} \times (1 + \text{rate})^{\text{time}}$$

Each of these values, of course, could vary. We would have to know what these specific values are to solve for an individual instance.

Devising a Plan

After he or she understands the problem and its solution, the programmer must devise a plan that the computer can use to produce the desired results. The program plan is called an **algorithm,** and it should express the following:

- What information is needed to perform the task

- Exactly what events are needed to complete the task

- The precise sequencing of these events to complete the task reliably

The algorithm must also be conceived in a manner that is suitable for the computer to perform. In other words, the events or actions must be the type that the computer is able to complete.

Suppose that we ask the user of the program to specify the information that we need to calculate the amount of investment. Usually, savings accounts are compounded daily; this means that there are actually 365 periods per year and that the periodic interest rate is the daily interest rate. Even so, most interest rates are quoted based on their annual percentage rate (APR). The point is that we should ask the user to specify the interest rate in terms of APR and the span of the investment in terms of years. Our algorithm would have to adjust these values for periodic rate and the corresponding amount of time.

Algorithms may be expressed in a variety of ways. Some are charted graphically using **flow-chart** symbols that show the sequencing of important events that constitute the overall process. Figure 14.2 shows how a flowchart for calculating compound interest would be designed.

Another way to express an algorithm is to write it in an English-like manner called **pseudocoding.** Listing 14.2 contains a pseudocoded algorithm for calculating compound interest. This technique is like outlining; it allows the programmer to focus on the task and ignore the details of how the actual instructions or statements must be phrased and written. Various other methods can be employed as a vehicle for writing the algorithm. The goal is to have a clear idea of what the program must do.

```
begin
    input principal, APR, years
    rate  ← APR/365
    time  ← years × 365
    amount ← principal × (1 + rate)ᵗⁱᵐᵉ
    output amount
end
```

Creating an Executable Program

Only after the algorithm is complete does the programmer actually try to convert that plan into a form that the computer can execute. Translating an algorithm to an executable program is called **coding.** It involves expressing the algorithm in a programming language that the computer understands. Programming languages have very precise rules for forming statements or instructions.

Most programs today are coded using high-level programming languages, as illustrated by our earlier JavaScript example. These languages are symbolic and more abstract than the binary-encoded instructions that the processor actually executes. They differ not only in their modes of expression but also in their suitability for various types of problem solving. In a later section, we will survey the landscape of programming languages available to the programmer.

Testing and Correcting the Program

After an executable version of the plan has been created, it must be subjected to rigorous testing to ensure that it performs reliably. If a program is general enough, it has many sets of input data that can be computed. Even in the compound interest example, there are an indefinitely large number of possible legitimate values. But what happens if the input values for years or APR are negative? Will the algorithm work correctly? In fact, the results would be incorrect.

Cases like these are often revealed only by testing. Most programs are not as simple as the compound interest problem, though. They are too complicated to comprehend at once all the possible eventualities. Programs therefore must be tested with many sets of real-life, concrete data. In addition to routine testing, commercial software developers will often recruit customers and other users to test prerelease or "**beta**" **versions** of programs to find out what sort of errors result from actual use.

When errors (called **bugs**) are found, the programmer must determine whether they are the result of misunderstanding the problem, a faulty plan, or mistakes in coding. Identifying the source of the error means going back to that stage to fix it. The process of testing, returning to earlier stages to debug the program, can often cycle many rounds. See Figure 14.3.

Unfortunately, most programs can never be tested completely because they have too many possible problem instances. Even for our simple compound interest program, testing all possible sets of values is not practical. This means that testing is almost always an art rather than a definitive process. As computer scientist E. W. Dijkstra succinctly put it, "Program testing can be a very effective way to show the presence of bugs, but it is hopelessly inadequate for showing their absence."

After a program has been tested and shown to perform reliably, it is then released for general use. Most commercial software is continually revised and modified to fix bugs discovered after its release and to incorporate new features that are desirable. Thus, the life cycle of software continues until the program becomes outdated and obsolete.

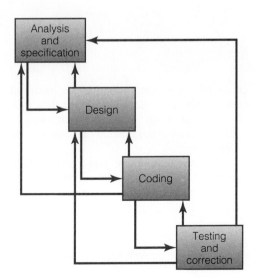

Figure 14.3

The development of software normally proceeds in a predictable cycle. After the task is studied and specifications for its solution are written, the program is planned in the design stage. From plans, or algorithms, the code is written and thoroughly tested. At any time, it may be necessary to revert to an earlier stage of the cycle to correct problems or misunderstandings encountered.

Developing Reliable Software

In spite of earnest efforts, software systems almost invariably exhibit errors and breakdowns. Even the most casual computer user has experienced the annoyances of faults and system crashes that result from software bugs. Why is creating a reliable software system so difficult? There are two reasons. First, creating a software system, regardless of scale, involves inherent complexities. Second, most modern software systems contain thousands and even millions of lines of code. This scale increases the inherent complexities many times over.

The Inherent Complexities of Developing Software Systems

Some of the inherent complexities in devising reliable software systems include difficulties attributable to their problem domains, the processes used to create them, and the very nature of the products themselves.

Over the years, computer hardware has become more and more powerful. Even desktop systems today outstrip the performance of the early behemoths that cost considerably more. We have come to expect our computers to be capable of performing more and more complicated tasks. After all, what is the point of paying for all that power if it means no added capability? As a result, the sorts of problems that software systems seek to solve have become more and more sophisticated.

The plain fact remains that devising software systems is an intellectual exercise. To solve a problem using a computer, the programmer must first understand the nature of the problem. The more sophisticated the problem, the more difficulties there are in analyzing and understanding it. For example, creating a system that recognizes voice commands and responds to them is rife with intellectual difficulties. (This is why you shouldn't expect to purchase a computer that converses with you anytime in the near future.) As you learned in Chapter 10, the problems are many and deep. There are difficulties in translating voice (speech) to language (words). Specifically, there are significant speech differences among speakers, and even speech differences for the same speaker under different conditions. Once speech is converted to written language, there are inherent difficulties in understanding the meaning as well. The point is that these are intellectual problems that have little to do with computers per se. We must solve these problems before we can instruct computers to handle them.

Even when the problem is well understood, devising software solutions for it can yield other difficulties. The process of composing programs is a case in point. The JavaScript program example developed earlier illustrates the nature of the process. The idea behind that program is relatively simple and straightforward: The images appear one by one, as controlled by

Software Risks

Most useful programs for large-scale automated systems are comprised of thousands, sometimes millions, of instructions, and they are written by teams of programmers. Each individual is responsible for small segments of the final program. The sheer size and complicated nature of such systems outstrip the capability of a single individual to comprehend them entirely. As expected, these programs can never be fully tested or certified for correctness or even reliability. Yet these systems are used in important and serious circumstances. Unfortunately, they can cause accidents, mishaps, or mistakes as a result of faults or bugs that are discovered only during their use.

For a discussion of some dramatic instances of the failure of software systems, consult the online essay "Social Themes: Software Risks."

SOCIAL THEMES

the user. The problem, however, is that this idea must be transformed to a mechanism that the computer can implement. This means that the programmer must pose the process in terms that are functionally effective for computers. For example, the computer can pay attention to mouse clicks and can count quite capably. Thus, the solution for the task could be cast in these terms. The point, then, is that programmers must always recast the way that humans think about doing things into forms that the computer can handle.

Software systems pose some potential difficulties by their very nature. Unlike natural or analog systems whose processes are continuous, we know that programs are executed on computers discretely, one step at a time. Consequently, software systems can behave quite differently from their analog counterparts. For example, in a normal mechanical braking system for an automobile, we would expect that faults in the system would be attributable to the components that make up that system. We would examine the brake pedal, the brake drum, and the various connecting links for malfunctions. No one would investigate the headlights or, perhaps, the radio to find the cause of the breakdown. In other words, in analog systems we expect that effects have "proximate" causes.

However, in a software system, all bets are off. Anything might potentially interact with anything else—if the instructions permit it. It is not impossible that a computer-controlled braking system could interact with the computer-controlled acceleration mechanism. This is apparently what happened with the Audi 5000 automobile some years ago when pressing the brake pedal under certain rare circumstances produced sudden acceleration! Designers had failed to anticipate and prevent the interaction of fuel flow with braking and manual shifting.

Developing Modern Large-Scale Software Systems

The difficulties attributable to problem domain, process, and product are multiplied when the scale of the software system increases. Imagine, for example, software systems that manage an airline reservation system, a nuclear power plant, or a long-distance telephone switching network. These are software systems whose sheer scale may require millions of lines of code. Even software for desktop systems such as office productivity programs and the operating systems that manage these computers can be formidable projects for commercial developers.

Large-scale systems cannot be physically managed by a single programmer but require teams of programmers to complete them. The division of labor among programming teams is often very precise. **System analysts** are responsible for the planning and design of the program. **Project managers** oversee the schedule and help manage the risks inherent in software development projects. **Programmers** work in groups to implement or code the components that make up the overall design of the project. In the case of large-scale projects, programming groups are responsible for only very specific portions of the project, just as assembly line workers concentrate on individual components of a manufactured product. Usually, a separate team is engaged to conduct testing of the project at various phases. This **software quality assurance** process is often managed separately or independently from the development team.

Many development projects go through various phases or releases of the product. An **alpha version** is the prototype of the software that is usually completed early in the project's development schedule. It is typically restricted to "in-house" testing to assess whether the design meets the basic requirements. Later, beta versions are releases of the product that have met the minimum testing standards. These are often tested by actual users who are willing or contracted to report problems that they encounter in everyday use. The final release, which has benefited from several stages of in-house and beta testing, is often periodically reviewed and modified. Purchasers of software applications are well aware of the steady stream of updates and revised versions for commercial products that they have purchased. Some of these updates are fixes for errors or difficulties encountered after the product has logged more hours of actual use. Others are revisions that add new and desired functionality to the system.

Given a system's scale and the division of labor, it is extremely unlikely that any one individual has a complete understanding of all the details that constitute such a system. And, as these systems become more and more sophisticated, it is even less likely that any one person could ever master a comprehensive understanding of them. Developing effective, productive, large-scale software systems has become perhaps our civilization's greatest intellectual achievement as well as its most difficult intellectual challenge.

The development of large-scale software systems must always involve some risk. Because only the most trivial of systems can be validated for correctness, the best that can be hoped is that careful planning, disciplined implementation, and diligent testing can warrant some measure of reliability for software products. Thus, software professionals bear some responsibility to weigh the potential risks that their products may engender. Of course, the risks of software vary widely. A bug that "crashes" a desktop computer system is annoying, but it pales in importance to software faults that cause economic hardships or threaten lives.

High-Level Programming Languages

Even though a computer can execute only programs that are written exclusively for its processor, modern programming is seldom done in binary-encoded machine languages. The program at the beginning of the chapter, for instance, was written in JavaScript, which is an example of a high-level programming language. A **high-level programming language** (**HLL**) is a set of rules for expressing programs as symbolic sets of instructions that resemble English—unlike machine-language instructions, which are sequences of 0s and 1s.

As we stated earlier, high-level language programs must be translated to machine-language instructions before they can be executed on a given processor. HLLs are translated in one of two ways: interpretation or compilation. An **interpreter** is a program that simultaneously translates and executes the instructions of an HLL program one by one. It functions much like a foreign language interpreter who provides a simultaneous translation on the fly as the person speaks. In contrast, a **compiler** is a program that prepares a complete translation of the HLL program into the processor's machine code that can be run later as a stand-alone executable program. Interpreters are usually uncomplicated and therefore inexpensive. Because interpreters must repeatedly translate a program every time it is used, the execution of interpreted programs is generally slower. Compilers offer faster executable versions of the program because the translation is done only once and before execution. When a compiled program is modified, though, it must be recompiled to update the changes in the translated version. Compilers are also generally more expensive.

High-level programming languages are preferred over machine languages for software development because they have these basic characteristics:

■ They are more abstract, relieving the programmer of machine-related details of execution.

Software Responsibilities

As you have learned, software systems—especially large-scale systems—almost always involve some risk because of errors and faults. The faults in software range from minor to extremely serious. Minor bugs may inconvenience us as we work; significant faults can cost us money or perhaps our lives. Who is responsible when these errors have serious consequences? What can be done to improve the quality of software production?

In recent years, the computing field has recognized its responsibilities to both clients and society by devising and supporting professional codes of ethics. These codes reflect a trend toward "professionalizing" the career of computing. For a discussion of these recent efforts consult the online essay "Social Themes: Software Responsibilities."

SOCIAL THEMES

- They produce programs that are more concise than their machine-language counterparts; HLL instructions have a one-to-many relation to processor instructions: A single instruction in an HLL translates to many instructions in lower-level languages.

- Their programs are portable to other processors, provided an interpreter or compiler is available for programs of this type.

A great variety of high-level programming languages are available. Most programming languages are general purpose; that is, they are intended for use in solving a wide range of problems. In spite of this fact, designers of programming languages are typically motivated to create a language to handle a specific kind of problem domain or offer some special features. Although the programmer has a wide range of choices, the kind of problem to be solved usually helps determine the choice of language. Even though hundreds of different HLLs has been developed over the past forty years, thankfully there are only a few paradigms to which they belong. A **programming paradigm** defines the basic model by which the language expresses a process. The most common is the **imperative procedural paradigm.** A variation of this is the **object-oriented paradigm.** Some programming languages have characteristics and features that are decidedly different from the norm; these are nonprocedural languages.

Imperative Procedural Languages

The imperative procedural paradigm defines a class of languages that divide a program into units or modules called **procedures.** Each procedure usually defines a smaller task to be done. The sequence of smaller tasks or subtasks makes up the main process. Procedural units can be adapted for use in other programs as well. Thus, programmers save time and effort when they can call on libraries of procedures to perform basic tasks required in a larger program.

Statements in a procedural language are understood as instructions. They take the imperative form: "Do this," "Do that." In other words, each statement usually defines an action or operation performed on some data. The order or sequence of statements in a procedural language program is critical. As you might guess, imperative procedural languages closely resemble the manner in which machine languages express processes. Of course, they offer greater abstraction and efficiency than processor instructions.

A great many languages from this group are in use today. Pascal, BASIC, C, COBOL, FORTRAN, and Ada are just a few examples.

Object-Oriented Languages

Object-oriented programming languages also divide a program into units; however, the units describe entities or objects with specific attributes or capabilities. A program defines a process that is populated by a group of objects; objects interact in various ways to perform the process. Objects have methods or specific actions that are natural for them to perform. Objects also send messages to and receive messages from other objects in the course of a process. For example, a file-processing object might send a message to a printer controller object to request permission to transmit a document to the printer for output.

The object paradigm has several advantages over traditional procedural programming. First, the concept of an object is more intuitive than the imperative elements of conventional programming languages. Many of the processes that programmers seek to model can be described more naturally in terms of different objects interacting with one another. Object-oriented languages also offer features that make their programs more secure and predictable in their behavior. To create objects, the programmer defines object classes with characteristic properties and methods. These classes make it easier to duplicate objects as well as reuse and modify them in other programs. Newly defined classes may also inherit the features and capabilities of other predefined classes.

Proponents of object-oriented programming tout its greater abstraction and ease in recycling reliable, developed code into new programs. SmallTalk, Java, and C++ (pronounced "see-plus-plus") are popular examples of programming languages that support the object-oriented paradigm.

Nonprocedural Languages

Another group of languages supports a **nonprocedural programming paradigm.** These programming languages are based on very different models and concepts, but they do share one common feature. Their programs are sets of statements that are not interpreted procedurally. In other words, the order of the statements in the program does not necessarily define a sequence of events or actions. Examples of nonprocedural programming languages include LISP (a list processing language), Prolog (a logical or declarative language), and FP (a functional programming language). In addition to standard developmental uses, LISP and Prolog are also popular languages for the discipline of **artificial intelligence (AI).** AI researchers seek to understand the nature of intelligence by creating systems (programs) that model or simulate its performance.

Programming Languages for the Rest of Us

In recent years, a new class of programming languages has evolved for use by nonprofessional programmers. These languages allow casual users to write programs that create new applications or add functionality to existing ones.

End-user programming languages are languages designed for average users to create programs without the normal fuss and complications of professional software development languages. They are easier to use because they have a simpler, more intuitive structure and organization. End-user programming languages often have ready-made components that can be incorporated into programs to produce sophisticated results. Many are scripting or interpreted languages whose programs are also easier to implement on a variety of platforms without expensive translation software. In addition, some are supported by tools that make composing and assembling programs easier as well.

Languages for Internet Applications

One group of end-user programming languages is dedicated to World Wide Web and Internet programming. At the beginning of the chapter, you were introduced to JavaScript, which is a popular end-user programming language for Internet applications. JavaScript programs are embedded in the formatting code used to define Web pages. (See Listing 14.1 earlier.) Not all

DISCOVERING MORE

JavaScript

One of its most appealing features is that JavaScript is not tied to a particular hardware platform. JavaScript programs can be incorporated in a Web page and executed by any processor that runs a browser program that can interpret its instructions. The programmer does not have to be concerned about the machine-dependent details of the types of computers that may be used to view his or her pages. For tutorials on JavaScript basics and its use with some specific HTML features, consult the online resource "Discovering More About JavaScript."

browser programs are equipped to interpret JavaScript programs, though. When a capable browser encounters JavaScript instructions, they are translated and executed on the computer running the browser program.

JavaScript is primarily an event-handling language. An **event-handler** is a special program component that is associated with the occurrence and detection of a particular event. In other words, programs are designed to react to a specific set of events that might take place during their execution. The user might click the mouse, use the mouse to roll over an object, press a button, or enter text from the keyboard. In addition, other events may occur that are not caused by the user. For example, a transmission may be completed or interrupted, a time limit may be exceeded, and so on. JavaScript event-handlers can be devised to respond to these events in various ways. Event-handlers can add interactivity to Web pages, perform calculations, manage animation and special effects, collect data and perform error-checking, cater to browser differences, and so on.

Besides JavaScript, several other scripting languages are employed for Internet applications. These include VBScript and JScript (a Microsoft variant of JavaScript).

Languages for Extending and Making Applications Work Together

Another class of end-user programming languages is intended for creating new applications, modifying or extending existing ones, or causing applications to cooperate or communicate with one another. From this category, Visual Basic is a popular choice for working with applications in the Microsoft Windows family of programs.

Visual Basic is a successor to the venerable language BASIC (for **B**eginner's **A**ll-Purpose **S**ymbolic **I**nstruction **C**ode), which was the first end-user or consumer programming language. Today Visual Basic has inherited the procedural structure of BASIC, object-oriented features of later languages, and a visual programming interface.

Visual programming incorporates tools for creating and manipulating graphical or pictorial elements in the solution of the program. In Visual Basic, the programmer may exploit graphical tools for building program components such as forms, dialog boxes, buttons, menus, text boxes, and more. Even so, Visual Basic remains a symbolic or textual programming language because its primary components are procedures composed of symbolic instructions. These instructions are written to tie together the graphical components of the program.

In addition to creating a new application, Visual Basic programs can be designed to add special functions to existing programs. For example, Visual Basic programs can interact with other programs such as word processors and spreadsheets to perform specific tasks. In this manner, application programs can be tailored or customized for individualized use without having to design and create an entirely new software system.

AppleScript, a scripting language that allows the programmer to create customized applications by modifying and combining existing ones, may be employed on Macintosh platforms for similar purposes. For example, scripts can be designed to cause two or more applications to communicate and share data. Thus, one application could be used for entering data; this data can be sent to, stored, and processed by another program. AppleScripts can also be used to automate routine tasks such as sorting electronic mail, making copies of valuable documents, and so on.

Languages for Specialized Applications

Some application programs have their own built-in programming languages that users may employ to add functionality to their products. These proprietary languages are especially tuned to the characteristics and features of their applications' environments.

A good example of this class is Lingo, the programming language of the multimedia authoring program *Director*. Multimedia authoring programs make it easier to produce electronic documents that organize and incorporate multimedia elements in effective ways. Lingo is an event-oriented scripting language that allows authors of *Director* documents (called *movies*) to add special effects and greater interactivity to their creations.

The program *Flash* is very popular for creating animations for the Web. The programming language ActionScript provides *Flash* users with the opportunity to enhance and extend the program's basic capabilities.

End-user programming languages have not yet brought programming to the masses; they still require study and practice to use effectively. Nonetheless, they offer considerable advantages over conventional languages in both ease of use and power of expression. They are a fast-growing segment of high-level programming languages available today.

■ Summary

Software or programs are lists of instructions that direct the steps of processing conducted by the computer system's hardware. Even though all processors execute binary-encoded programs stored in their main memories, few programs today are written by humans in this machine-language form. Instead, programmers employ symbolic programming languages that simplify the process of devising and developing programs.

The basic software development process involves several stages: analyzing the problem or task that the software is intended to perform; devising a plan to solve the problem or model that task; creating an executable program that implements the plan; and testing and correcting the program.

Most software systems—and especially large-scale systems—are too complex for testing that could prove their validity in all circumstances. Besides scale, software systems involve a number of other inherent complexities. The problems that they attempt to solve often are not well understood. There are difficulties attributable to the process by which these systems are created. Finally, as discrete systems, they perform very differently than other types of engineered systems.

High-level programming languages (HLLs) are symbolic programming languages that are more abstract than machine-language programs. In addition, HLLs produce programs that are more concise and portable than their machine-language equivalents. Even so, HLL programs must be translated to the appropriate machine language to be executed on a given processor. HLLs usually employ one of several different paradigms or models to express processes. These paradigms form distinct families of languages. The members of a given family of programming languages will share certain common features in spite of the many individual differences among them.

FOCUS High-Level Programming Languages

Today commercial applications are developed almost exclusively using high-level programming languages. As noted, there is a wide assortment and great variety in these symbolic languages. Consult our online resource "Focus on High-Level Programming Languages" for some examples of this variety and illustrations of how they are used to direct processing.

■ Terms

algorithm
alpha version
artificial intelligence (AI)
assembly language
beta version
bug
coding
compiler
conditional statement
end-user programming
  language
event-handler
flowchart
function

high-level programming
  languages (HLLs)
imperative procedural
  paradigm
interpreter
nonprocedural programming
  paradigm
object-oriented paradigm
object-oriented programming
  language
object, property
portability
procedures
program

programmer
programming paradigm
project managers
pseudocoding
scripting, scripting language
software
software quality assurance
system analyst
translation program
variable
visual programming

■ Questions for Review

1. What is a symbolic programming language? Contrast it with a machine language.

2. What is an assembly language? How is it related to a machine language for the same processor?

3. What are variables? What roles do they play in programs?

4. Describe the four basic stages involved in the software development process.

5. What is an algorithm? Describe several methods for expressing algorithms.

6. What are flowcharts? What are they used for?

7. Identify the types of difficulties facing software developers in the design and implementation of reliable software systems.

8. How does the behavior or performance of software systems differ from those of their analog counterparts? Why does this make them more difficult to develop reliably?

9. Describe the responsibilities of the following roles in a software development project: systems analyst, project manager, programmer, software quality assurance group.

10. What are the differences between the alpha and beta versions of a software product?

11. What is meant be the term *higher-level language*? How are assembly and machine languages related to these languages?

12. Define and compare an interpreter and a compiler.

13. What is a programming paradigm?

14. What are procedures? How are they employed to define a process?

15. What are the chief characteristics of programming languages that belong to the imperative procedural programming paradigm?

16. What are objects? Describe the roles of properties, methods, and messages in defining an object class.

17. What are the chief characteristics of programming languages that belong to the object-oriented programming paradigm?

18. What is visual programming? How does it make programming applications easier?

19. What are scripting languages? Give examples of programming languages that belong to this category.

Chapter 15

Operating Systems

OBJECTIVES

- How system software and operating systems run the show

- Understanding how programs are brought to life and maintained as processes

- The special functions of single-user and multiuser, multithreaded and multitasking operating systems

Application programs perform the specific tasks for which we employ our computers. But these programs would be powerless to perform our bidding without the aid and assistance of another type of software—the computer's operating system. The operating system is a collection of programs that actually manages both the basic functions and resources of a computer.

These programs assist us in many of the fundamental tasks that we require to maintain our systems. To copy and print files, to format disks, and even to execute applications, we need the assistance of operating system software. Operating systems help by managing many of our hardware resources such as main memory and secondary storage. They provide useful services such as organizing files and printing. This software also creates and maintains the interface by which we direct and communicate with the system. In fact, the operating system software has a much greater impact on the look and feel of our computers than the hardware devices that make up the system. Most computer users can become quite passionate when it comes to their operating systems, but few even know or care what type of CPU or hard disk drive their system employs.

In this chapter, we will complete our picture of how computers function from the standpoint of how system software directs the inner workings.

302

Managing the System

As you learned in Chapter 3, software can be divided into two categories: applications and system software. In Chapter 14, you studied the development of **applications software;** these are end-user programs designed to perform specific tasks such as preparing documents, creating graphic images, or sending and receiving electronic mail. In contrast, **system software** refers to programs that help manage the operation of computer systems. These two types of software are not unrelated. For example, included in system software are development tools such as compilers and interpreters, which are used to create applications that run on computers. In addition, applications make use of many services made available to them by system software.

The most fundamental type of system software is the operating system. An **operating system (OS)** is a collection of resident programs that manages the computer's resources, supervises the execution of user processes, and provides useful services and security for the computer system. As users, we often feel as if we control what goes on with our computers, but this is not entirely accurate. The operating system, in fact, is in control of our computer systems at all times when they are in use. As we emphasized in Chapter 3, managing the details for operating a computer system can be an arduous and complicated task. Such tasks as opening and closing files and launching programs appear to the computer user to be relatively simple actions. However, there are a great many details to be taken care of behind the scenes to accomplish these and other tasks. The operating system manages all this for us. And this is a good thing, because if we had to handle all these details ourselves, very little productive work would get done. Instead, we would be spending most of our time and effort simply trying to operate our computers.

To manage these details for us automatically, most operating systems are designed as a suite of smaller programs or services that control various aspects of the operation of our system. Some of these component programs are always resident in main memory. Any time the computer system is powered on, specific portions of the operating system program are loaded into memory to get the process underway and provide us with a usable user-interface.

In essence, the operating system actually controls the computer system most of the time, serving as a buffer between the user and the computer system's hardware. This was illustrated earlier, but we repeat the illustration here in Figure 15.1 as a reminder of the relationship between the user, the operating system, and the underlying computer hardware.

Application programs can exploit the services of the operating system by executing specific system calls. A **system call** is a particular request to the operating system to perform a needed service. For example, editing a document involves several system calls: finding the file, allocating some memory to store a working copy of the file's contents, copying the disk file to memory, and so on are just a few of the operating system services employed by the word processing program. Without this assistance, our application programs would have to be much larger and more complicated to handle all these details directly. The bottom line is that applications would be much more expensive because they would have to be tailored to the many versions of commercially available systems.

The operating system is the most important factor in your use of a computer system. Indeed, the choice of operating system is a greater factor in determining how your computer performs—its look and feel in use—than the underlying hardware. Computers with different processors will appear indistinguishable to the user when they run the same operating system. For example, Windows will look the same independent of the underlying processor—although, of course, the speed with which tasks are carried out may vary from processor to processor. In a similar way, the Macintosh OS will appear to the user to be the same running on a variety of processors. On the other hand, computer systems with the same processor but running different operating systems will appear and perform very differently.

We can divide operating systems generally into three groups: those that support single-user, single-programming operation, those that allow for multiuser, multitasking operation, and those that allow (for single or multiple users) multithreaded operation. The fundamental difference in these types of systems is whether the operating system is equipped to manage a

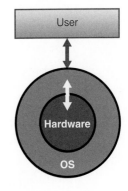

Figure 15.1

The operating system functions as the go-between for the user and the computer's raw hardware features. This shields the user from the complicated, tedious details of the hardware's operations and likewise protects the hardware from inadvertent errors committed by users.

single process at a time or multiple processes over a span of time. First, we will consider the concept of a process as the embodiment of a program. Next, we will investigate in some detail what services a single-user system provides and how these services are organized. Afterward, we will examine how an operating system manages multiple users and concurrent multiple processes. Finally, we will learn that the most advanced operating systems provide a finer grade of concurrency by supporting multithreaded processes.

Programs and Processes

You learned earlier in Chapter 3 that a program is a list of instructions. Chapter 14 explained that most of the time these instructions are originally written in high-level programming languages that offer the programmer greater power and abstraction. Nonetheless, a program must eventually be translated to binary-coded instructions that can direct the processor on which the program will be executed. Thus, an executable program is a sequence of binary strings that signify operations for the processor. But programs are static and lifeless—whether high-level source programs or binary executable programs. For example, the order and content of its instructions remain the same. Programs are represented by symbols and stored in files.

In contrast, processes are dynamic. Processes have a life cycle: They are created and terminated; in between they have histories. At any given moment, the status of the process and its data can differ. In short, we can track the **process** as a series of operations that are performed by the processor as it models what the program prescribes.

As you learned in Chapter 3, a process, however, is comprised of a sequence of distinct states. In a single state, the processor has executed a particular instruction. Thus, a computer's process is a sequence of separate, distinct moments—not unlike the frames of a motion picture. In a film, each frame is a "frozen" moment, but when projected at a rapid rate, the result is the illusion of continuous motion. The same is true for digital computers. Each state is distinct, but, because of the rapid succession of states, processing appears to be continuous and uninterrupted. See Figure 15.2.

Thus, at any given instant, if we could freeze the processor, it would be possible to capture the current status of an active process. Specifically, the process has executed a certain number of instructions; its current state is defined by the most recently completed instruction. We would also observe the current status of the process' data. These include the values of data objects stored in registers and memory; which files are active and open; and the status of other input/output functions. As we shall see shortly, the fact that processes on a digital computer system are comprised of discrete states is a significant factor in increasing the performance of the processor.

The operating system, of course, is a process that executes more or less continuously while the computer system is activated. In fact, starting or booting the computer system means that a portion of the operating system's program is loaded into main memory and begins execution as a process. As mentioned, one of the chief responsibilities of the operating system is to manage user processes. Thus, when we start or launch an application, the operating system actually creates its process and relinquishes the processor to it. As you shall see, understanding the manner in which operating systems create and support user processes is a useful way for categorizing them.

Figure 15.2

A process is a sequence of discrete states. Each state from the initial to the ending state is distinct and defined by the status of key characteristics of the process. These include keeping track of which instruction is being executed and the current status of all data in the process.

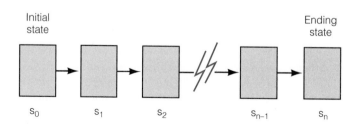

Anatomy of a Single-User Operating System

The hallmark of most single-user, single-programming operating systems (usually shortened to **single-user operating system**) is that they afford the execution of only one process at a time by one user at a time. Whether the process is a system or application program, the single-user operating system is designed to manage one task at a time. This is quite natural, however, because we know that most CPUs are serial uniprocessors anyway. This means that they can execute only one instruction from a program at a time. Single-user systems are simply organized to complete the instructions from a single process before going on to the next one. Thus, the life cycle of a process is understood very simply in terms of three states: created, executing, and completed or terminated. See Figure 15.3. The operating system creates a user process; turns control of the processor to it; and—assuming normal operation—takes control of the processor when it completes. When the process finishes, the operating system also recaptures control of any resources that it used in order to recycle them for future processes. Consequently, we can think of the OS as establishing a stable environment for supporting the various tasks that we direct our computers to perform.

Single-user operating systems are usually designed into functional units. Each unit has a specific set of responsibilities. This division of labor has advantages. Because each unit is restricted to limited tasks, the size and number of system programs that must be loaded concurrently in memory are smaller. Functional separation also makes the OS easier to design and maintain.

Although the actual organization of single-user systems varies considerably from one vendor to another, they all share some common denominators. A typical single-user operating system will have the following functional units or components:

1. Supervisor

2. I/O control drivers

3. Memory manager

4. File manager

5. User interface

Supervisor

Perhaps the most important task for the operating system is managing user processes and requests. For most users, their chief interest in computing is to employ application software such as word processing, drawing and painting programs, electronic mail, and the like. As we know, programs must be loaded into main memory and their execution commenced. It is the job of the **supervisor** to oversee and control these and other processes. See Figure 15.4.

Besides user programs, the supervisor manages special requests for services made both by users and user processes. For example, when we request to print a file, a system call is made to a special routine that performs the task. The supervisor accepts the request and oversees the loading and execution of the operating system program that actually does the work. User programs can also make system calls for operating system services. Again, opening a file is a good

Figure 15.3

Each process on single-user system passes through three states. First, it is created by the OS. The process executes or runs. Finally, the OS terminates the process and recaptures its resources for future use by new processes.

example. The user program makes the request for the file and is interrupted while the supervisor handles these details. After the file is located and allocated some memory space, the user program is commenced again.

When a user process makes a system call, it relinquishes control of the processor back to the operating system. The OS, in turn, creates a corresponding kernel process, which performs the requested task. It is called a **kernel process** because it is a special, privileged process that only the operating system can perform. Most of the special functions performed by the OS are achieved by kernel processes. When this process completes, the OS returns control to the user process. System calls and kernel processes add a new wrinkle to the life cycle of a user process as shown in Figure 15.5. A process may be interrupted; during this time, it is waiting to continue execution.

The supervisor is responsible for managing the transitions between user and kernel processes. This is called **context switching.** In effect, the operating system takes a snapshot of the current user process at the moment that it is interrupted. All of the relevant information needed to commence that process at the point where it was halted is stored for later use. The kernel process' instructions are loaded into main memory and execution commences. When the process completes, the supervisor restores the user process and its execution continues; thus, a waiting user process returns to its running status. System calls and kernel processes expand the capabilities of user processes considerably.

I/O Control Drivers

As you learned in earlier chapters, the physical organization of data varies depending on the type of device that stores or transmits it. The I/O control drivers are primitive input/output

Figure 15.4

The supervisor oversees the work of your system by converting requests from you and the programs you are running to actual executing processes.

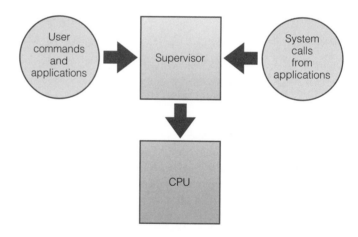

Figure 15.5

Most single-user systems are designed to permit a running process to make a system call to a kernel process, which performs some desired task. While the kernel process is active, the calling process waits to be reactivated again. Thus, a new stage is added to its life cycle.

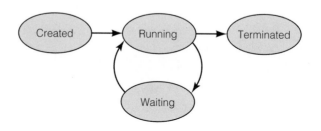

routines that manage the details of transfers between I/O devices and the CPU. For example, to access information stored on a magnetic hard disk, it is necessary to do the following:

- Seek the track

- Identify the sector

- Read/write the data block

To complete these tasks, the system must issue several commands to the appropriate disk controller. And, in addition to these commands, the transfer must be synchronized properly. The devices, therefore, must also exchange signals to ensure that the timing is right, too. As you can imagine, all of these details—though simple-minded—are very tedious. To make matters worse, they differ from one peripheral to another. In other words, your magnetic hard disk has different signals and timing than your CD-ROM drive.

I/O service routines simplify transferring and storing data on the system. An application program makes a logical I/O request in the form of a system call. The logical request is abstract in that it specifies the data apart from its physical organization and location. The request is transferred to the I/O control driver, which interprets it and issues a series of commands and signals to the peripheral. For example, the CPU may be copying a file from a disk. The CPU can simply ask for a block of data and allow the I/O driver to handle the details of translating that logical request into the physical commands of finding the track, sector, and block. These services also shield user programs from the machine-specific details that are necessary to implement input and output.

Memory Manager

Instructions and data are stored in random access memory (RAM) during program execution. Even in a single-user system, the demands for memory can be complicated. Some portion of the operating system must reside continually in memory. User application programs, of course, must be afforded memory space to execute. This often means finding room for the data created by these applications, too. If we are switching between applications, the programs will often be loaded concurrently in main memory, even if only one can execute at a time.

The **memory manager** has responsibility for allocating segments of RAM to these often competing processes. The memory manager acts somewhat like an internal traffic cop, allocating memory space for user processes and protecting the system from errors when programs and data might overlap in RAM. Figure 15.6 illustrates how the memory manager segments memory for different uses.

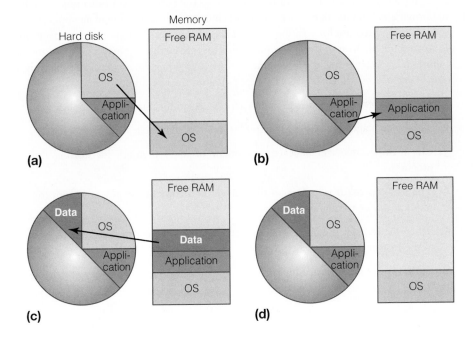

(a)   **(b)**   **(c)**   **(d)**

Figure 15.6

The memory manager allocates space for the operating system and applications that run on a single-user system. This also means protecting data and processes by ensuring that the memory partitions do not overlap. (a) When the system boots, a portion of the operating system is loaded into RAM. (b) Later, the user launches a application; the memory manager allocates space in RAM for its execution. (c) The application creates a data file, which is also allocated space in RAM and later copied to disk. (d) When the process is done, the memory manager frees the space for new uses.

File Manager

An important contribution of the operating system is to provide abstract or logical services that make computing easier and more convenient. A good example of this is the file system.

As you know, data is stored in physical units or blocks on secondary storage devices like disks, CD-ROMs, tape, and so on. While the size of these data blocks may be uniform for a given storage device, data created by applications will not match this uniformity. Hence, a single document created by an application will typically require a variable number of blocks when it is stored in secondary memory. In other words, storing a file, which to us looks like a single entity, may require managing any number of related component data blocks.

The operating system essentially creates the convenient fiction of a file to hide all these storage details from us. The **file manager** creates and maintains the set of files stored on a specific system. Different operating systems will have different naming conventions for files and even storage structures for files, but they will provide a set of high-level services to the computer user for managing them. The file manager accepts our logical requests for these file services and then translates them into the detailed instructions the system requires in order to conduct the required processing.

Most operating systems provide well-defined structure or organization for locating and storing files. Although the actual data is stored in physical blocks and can be scattered across many different physical locations in secondary storage, the operating system offers us an abstract structure that makes managing all this relatively easy for us. As discussed in Chapter 3, most operating systems employ some variation of a hierarchical file structure (HFS).

User Interface

As we mentioned earlier, the operating system maintains control of the system almost continuously while the power is on. Consequently, to make the computer system perform tasks that are useful for us, we must communicate our desires as requests or commands to the operating system. The **user interface** is a program that interprets our commands for work.

The user interface is the medium for communication. You learned earlier, that the mode or means for this communication can vary. Some systems may offer more than one user interface for processing user/system communication. Some are primarily text-based. Commands and messages are communicated by text. Most are visual or graphical. These allow the user to manipulate objects, icons, and gadgets displayed on the monitor to facilitate communication.

Let's take a simple example to illustrate how these operating system functions come into play in normal use. Suppose that you wish to launch or start the execution of an application—perhaps a drawing program for creating graphics. From the user's standpoint, the operation is simple. Locate the file icon in the appropriate directory; issue the command to open; and, after a short delay, start using the program. But what is going on underneath? Here is an overview of the process. (Details will vary depending on the operating system.)

1. The user interface translates the user's actions to signify launching an application.

2. The file manager resolves the location of the data that makes up the program.

3. The memory manager allocates a segment of main memory for loading the program.

4. The I/O control driver manages the transfer of a copy of the program from the physical device to memory.

5. When the transfer is complete, the supervisor passes the control of the processor to the first instruction of the program.

Of course, these tasks are executed by a series of system calls that coordinate and manage the details. Figure 15.7 illustrates the process.

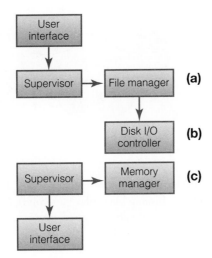

Figure 15.7
Whenever you choose to run a program, a lot of activity is required behind the scenes. Here is a typical (generalized) sequence of events to execute what appears to be a simple step to the user. (a) The command to run a program is interpreted by the user interface. The user interface notifies the supervisor. (b) The supervisor, in turn, directs the file manager to locate the file. The disk I/O controller is enlisted to perform the actual transfers of data blocks that constitute the file. (c) Finally, the supervisor signals the memory manager to load the program into an appropriate segment of memory. The supervisor then signals the start of the execution of the program. The user interface relays the system calls from the program as its window opens and execution commences.

Anatomy of a Multiuser Operating System

Most desktop systems accommodate one user at a time. However, in many organizations it proves useful to have computers that can serve many users at once. Such multiuser systems can handle a number of users at the same time because the hardware is fast enough to make it appear that each user has exclusive control of the system for his or her processes. For example, while one user is creating a text document using a word processor, another might be using a spreadsheet to perform some numerical calculations. Still another user might be reading his electronic mail, and another might be compiling a program that she has written. A **multiuser operating system** instructs the processor to switch back and forth between these in an orderly manner, thereby creating the illusion that each of these processes has the system's undivided attention.

The multiuser OS achieves this sleight of hand by swiftly interleaving the instructions from a set of processes concurrently. After all, one instruction is like any other to the processor; it makes no difference which process it belongs to. The CPU is content to work continuously one instruction after another. The fact that these instructions belong to different processes is no matter of interest for the processor itself. On the other hand, it does matter to the end-users. So, the operating system keeps track of which process is active among the ready processes. Each time a ready process is activated, there is a context switch. The formerly active process is saved or terminated—depending upon whether it was done or just interrupted. The newly active process begins execution. And, the cycle continues until all ready processes get their work time.

Multitasking—the ability to accommodate multiple processes concurrently—injects a new stage in our process life cycle. Existing processes are either running, waiting, or ready. Only one process is running at a given time. All others are either waiting or ready. We learned that some processes are waiting for the use of needed resource or for system calls to be completed. The ready stage is new; a process can be ready to execute, although not currently running. See Figure 15.8. The pool of ready processes form an on-deck batting circle for the processor. These are currently available and can be quickly activated.

A multiuser operating system also enables a system to be utilized more efficiently than with a single-user operating system. Most programs can be analyzed into segments that are dominated by CPU instructions and those that are dominated by I/O operations. When the process is dominated primarily by CPU instructions, we can say that the system is **CPU bound.** In contrast, when the process is fixed on performing I/O operations, we can say that

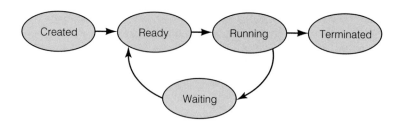

Figure 15.8

In a multiuser environment, created processes have several stages before they are completed or terminated. A process may be ready to run, but the CPU is not available. Of course, some processes may be waiting for a resource or some kernel process to be completed. After the waiting, these processes return to the ready state.

the system is **I/O bound.** We have seen that the speed of typical CPU instructions is measured in nanoseconds (one nanosecond is one-billionth of a second). On the other hand, I/O operations that involve peripherals are usually measured in microseconds or even milliseconds. This means that while the CPU is waiting for an I/O operation to complete, it is wasting a lot of time that might be used on other tasks. But, with the capability to interrupt processes, I/O bound processes can be switched from running to waiting status, and ready processes can take up the CPU slack. With the careful control of a multiuser operating system, the CPU can be kept busy without any significant delays for existing processes.

In short, a multiuser operating system can accommodate a number of users and maximize the use of the system's resources. This is why many businesses employ multiuser systems over single-user desktop computing systems.

To support multiple users, a multiuser operating system must have functions or features in addition to those outlined for the single-user OS:

1. CPU scheduler

2. Virtual memory by the memory manager

CPU Scheduler

When there are several processes to be executed, the **CPU scheduler** decides which process will be next in line when a context switch takes place. The scheduler maintains a list of ready processes that are awaiting execution and orders them according to some established criterion.

The criteria for determining priority varies with the system. The round-robin method, for example, divides a processing interval into equal segments so that all ready processes get an equal amount of processing time during that interval. The round-robin method is a very simple one that attempts to ensure that all waiting processes are treated fairly. Other types of scheduling are more complicated and take into account factors such as the importance or priority of processes, how much time a process has previously had, and the type of activity.

Virtual Memory

Most multiuser systems (and some single-user systems, too) often lack sufficient main memory to support processing. There is simply not enough RAM for the operating system and executing processes and their data. For example, to serve a number of users, their programs should be stored concurrently in memory to allow for faster context switching.

These operating systems create and support an expanded memory space called **virtual memory.** The operating system establishes a memory address space that is much larger than actual physical main memory. Additional space is usually borrowed from one of the system's hard disk drives. The operating system maintains this virtual address space by shuttling data back and forth between secondary and primary memory as needed. As far as the CPU is concerned, the actual location of data is transparent. Figure 15.9 illustrates.

Virtual memory creates the illusion of a much greater memory store. In this way, the system can support processes with large data demands as well as sufficient space for multiple processes. Executing processes and their data are still stored in RAM, while unused data is moved to secondary storage until needed again.

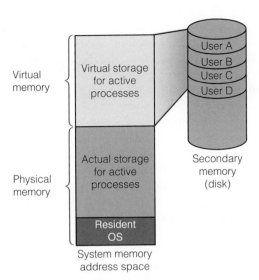

The services of virtual memory are not without cost, though. Locating data and moving it between primary and secondary physical memory slow down the system's overall performance. The cost in time is usually worth the benefits of increased processing capacity.

Multiuser operating systems vary considerably in both design and features. Two prominent examples are the proprietary systems of IBM OS and AT&T UNIX.

Multithreading Operating Systems

While some computers employ traditional single-user (single-programming) operating systems, the majority of today's desktop systems are derived from a variation of multitasking operating systems called *multithreading*. Although these systems usually don't serve more than one user, they have evolved to include multitasking capabilities. Particularly, the most recent versions of Microsoft Windows, Sun's Solaris, Macintosh OS, and Linux support multithreading. A **multithreaded operating system** supports concurrent multiple threads of execution belonging to the same or different processes. Before we delve into multithreading, let's be clear about multitasking.

A **multitasking operating system** creates and manages a multitasking environment. This is accomplished through the use of context switching. A multitasking OS supports multiusers, as we saw in the previous section. But not every multitasking OS is a multiuser system. Some support only single user or desktop systems. This means that you can have several programs open at the same time and switch easily from one to another. For example, you might open a painting or drawing program to create graphics for a web page; at the same time you might launch a word processor to create text elements for the Web page. In addition, you might have an HTML editor open to compose the pages. With all three programs open at the same time, you can switch between their use at will to create elements of the web page and its composition during the same work sessions. The operating system will manage this by switching contexts as you switch from program to program. During this work, you can use the common clipboard to copy and paste elements between the three applications. You might even want to open a browser at the same time to test the appearance of the web page as you go. At the same time you may wish to have your email client program open to alert you to incoming email messages. In fact, the limits on the number of applications open simultaneously will typically be determined by the amount of memory available and not by the operating system.

Multithreading operating systems take concurrency one step further. Up to this point, we have treated a process as if it had one single thread of execution, that is, the set of instructions that define the steps of that process. But, if we relax this assumption, it would be possible to think of a process that had two or more threads of execution—different sets of instructions for related tasks. These **threads** (as they are called for short) would belong to the same process, share the same resources, but do different things.

Consider, for example, designing a desktop publishing application. This is a complex program that must perform an assortment of tasks concurrently. For instance, the user interface must continuously receive and interpret commands. Formatting and redrawing the screen to reflect changes in the document is another task. Updating and saving the document to files is another. These are all essential tasks for the application, but define work that is quite unrelated to each other. Normally, though, a software designer would have to devise a single program that accommodates all these and other tasks. Multithreading, however, allows for application to be composed of multiple threads. One thread could manage the user interface; another could handle screen redrawing; still another may execute file saves in the background. The result is a design that is simpler and easier to understand.

Each thread is treated like a lightweight process. Threads are executed individually, but may be interrupted and switched for other threads. In this manner, the same process can be composed of concurrently executing threads. For example, while the user interface thread is idle in our DTP app, the screen redraw thread can take over. Threads have life cycles much like full-scale processes and require an operating system that has the savvy to manage and support their use.

Multithreading not only improves the design of software, but can enhance system performance as well. Some desktop systems today are composed of multiple processors. In particular, these systems have a single memory system that is shared by two or more similar processors, called **symmetric multiple processor** (**SMP**) systems. Multithreading is ideal for SMP systems, because individual threads can be handled by different processors simultaneously. But, threading can sometimes improve the performance of single or uniprocessor systems too. Careful thread scheduling by the OS can reduce idle time for the processor and increase throughput, much like multitasking does for multiuser systems.

U.S. v. Microsoft

The landmark case of the United States v. Microsoft Corporation was brought by the Department of Justice against the software industry giant for its alleged violations of antitrust regulations. The basic charge was that Microsoft had illegally used their market dominance in operating systems to inhibit competition from other companies for other software applications. The case is significant for a number of reasons. First of all, antitrust laws were crafted in response to the economics of the Industrial Revolution. Do these regulations fit the realities of an Information Age economy? A related issue is Microsoft's strategy for developing its Windows operating system. Is the distinction between the operating system and applications software a matter of fact or mere convention? Should consumers be free to decide for themselves? These and other issues are explored in our online Social Themes essay "U.S. v. Microsoft."

SOCIAL THEMES

In short, the latest operating systems make life much easier for computer users. Multithreading allows us to align our work with the computer more closely with the way we work in general—juggling multiple tasks (related and unrelated) over the same period of time.

■ Summary

Users employ application programs to perform specific tasks such as preparing documents, creating graphics, browsing the Web, and so on. System software, in contrast, are the programs that you employ to control your computers and provide other important functions. The operating system is the most significant instance of system software. Operating systems manage the resources of the computer system, supervise the execution of user processes, and provide important services for the user and his or her applications. The operating system actually controls all aspects of the of the computer's operation. The user communicates commands or requests that are executed by the operating system.

Operating systems are often organized into components, which designate major functions of the system. These include the supervisor, memory manager, I/O control, file manager, CPU scheduler, and user interface.

Operating systems are usually classified into three categories: single-user, single-programming systems, multitasking, multiuser systems, and multithreaded systems. A single-user system is designed to manage one task or process at a time. Single-user operating systems support older desktop or personal computers. A multiuser operating system is designed to support a number of users employing the computer's resources during the same period of time. Multiuser systems manage this feat by performing what is called *multitasking*—that is, executing several processes concurrently by switching execution among them. A multithreaded operating system supports a finer grain of concurrency. A single process may be composed of multiple threads of execution. Threads may then be executed concurrently. Multithreading simplifies the design and control of applications and can reap performance benefits for some systems, too.

■ Terms

applications software, programs
context switching
CPU bound
CPU scheduler
file manager
I/O bound
I/O control driver
kernel process

memory manager
multiprogramming, multitasking
multitasking operating system
multithreaded operating system
multiuser operating system
operating system (OS)
process

single-user (single-programming) operating system
supervisor
symmetric multiple processor
system call
system software
thread
user interface
virtual memory

■ Questions for Review

1. Compare system software and application software. Which is more important? Explain.

2. Explain the overall role of the operating system in the functioning of a computer system.

3. Describe some particular functions and services provided by a single-user operating system.

4. What is role of the supervisor in an operating system?

5. What does multitasking mean? Explain how it makes the use of a computer more natural and more efficient.

6. What is meant by the term *context switching*? Explain its use in creating multitasking operating systems.

7. What is a multiuser operating system? What features make this possible? Why is it desirable in some environments?

8. Describe some particular functions and services provided by multiuser operating systems—above and beyond those found in single-user systems.

9. What is virtual memory? What is it used for?

10. What is a thread? Why is it important?

11. What is a multithreading operating system? What features make this possible? Why is it desirable in some environments?

PART Six

Networks

Chapter 16

Data Communications

OBJECTIVES

- The chief elements of a communications system

- How data is encoded and transmitted over data communications channels

- The variety of computer networks based on such factors as scale, media, and transmission methods

- The ins and outs of getting "connected" at home

One of the most significant changes in computing over the past several decades has been the evolution of data communications networks. The technology of digital data transmission over computer networks has had profound effects on how we work, play, and live. Computer networks connect individuals in the same office, the same building, and across the world. They provide for the instantaneous exchange of information. Computer data networks have conquered the conventional barriers of space and time. Networks have also helped conquer the "language" barriers that separate different computer hardware platforms as well. Within the industry, the notions of compatibility and interoperability were unheard of before networking. Indeed, computer networking has fueled the digital information age more than any other single factor.

Digital data transmission and computer networks take many different forms. What exactly is a data communications system? How is digital data encoded and transmitted? How different are networks that connect computers in the same building from those that span continents? These are the primary questions that we address in this chapter.

317

The Basic Communications Model

Technologies for sharing information are certainly not new. As mentioned in Chapter 1, the history of civilization can be chronicled through the evolution of information technologies. Information, unlike other material goods, can be duplicated and shared easily. Sharing information usually takes one of two basic forms, broadcasting or networking. **Broadcasting** involves transmitting the same information to many individuals or receivers. The receiver is unable to change or alter broadcast information. (Think of print media, radio, and television.) In contrast, **networking** allows the sender and receiver to exchange and process information, which often produces new information. Of course, networking individuals is a time-honored tradition. People formed social, professional, and enterprise networks long before computer technology. What is new, however, is how advanced networking has become through the medium of computers.

The purpose of a **data communications system** is to exchange information or data between two agents. Data communications can take many different forms. **Claude Shannon,** a pioneer in information theory as well as computer engineering (see Chapter 1), proposed a model in 1946 for understanding how any communications system works. The model is at once simple and fundamental. It is useful to review it here because it highlights the six basic components found in all data communications systems—as well as other forms of communication, for that matter. We consider each of these components and employ examples to illustrate how they correspond to practical instances of communication. Refer to Figure 16.1.

Information Source

Communication must begin from some source. The **information source** generates **messages;** this process involves encoding information into some form understandable to the intended receiver. For example, a speaker phrases thoughts into words. In another instance, when you correspond with a friend using electronic mail (e-mail), you type a text message using an editor.

Transmitter

The **transmitter** encodes the message from the information source. The message is encoded as a **signal,** an object in a form that matches the properties of the communications channel over which the signal will be transmitted. The speaker, for example, converts his or her words into sounds—that is, sound pressure waves that can be propagated in the air. The computer system converts your e-mail message into an electrical signal appropriate for transmission over a computer network. The information source and the transmitter together form the **originating system.**

Figure 16.1

This figure illustrates Shannon's basic model for a communication system. Each of the six components of the model is described in the text.

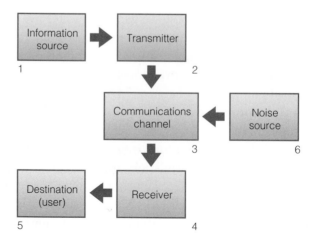

Communication Channel

In all forms of communication there is a physical separation of source and destination. The **communications channel** is the medium that bridges the distance between the transmitter and the receiver. For speech, the channel is the air that carries sound pressure waves. In a computer network, it might be the wires that transfer the electrical signal from one computer system to another.

The distance that the signal must travel over the medium or channel affects the strength of the signal sensed by the receiver. In most physical systems, the signal naturally weakens as it travels. A speaker, for example, might be readily heard in a room but be barely audible in a large auditorium. An electrical signal sent over a network might be strong enough to be received by a system in the same room but too weak to be received by one across campus.

Receiver

The **receiver** extracts a signal from the communications channel and converts it back into an encoded form of a message. The listener, for example, hears the sounds uttered by the speaker and converts them to words. The computer receiving the signal over the network converts it to a digital representation of text.

Destination

The **destination** receives the message and retrieves whatever information is contained in it. For example, the listener interprets and understands the speech. Your friend reads the e-mail message converted to text by the computer system that received it.

The receiver and the destination are called the **destination system.** In the pure or abstract communications system, the originating system sends a signal over a communications channel to the destination system. The signal sent by the transmitter is identical to the signal extracted by the receiver in this perfect system. As a result, the message received is the same as the one sent. Unfortunately, perfect communications systems rarely exist, if ever. There is almost always at least one "real-world" factor that must be considered.

Noise Source

A source of noise is usually present in the communications channel medium. **Noise** is a random element that modifies the encoded signal in unpredictable ways. In the case of listening to a speaker, ambient sounds, such as other people talking or the hum of machines in the room, may interfere. In a network, the electrical devices introduce unavoidable noise on the channel that perturbs the signals transmitted. Noise modifies the signal and can therefore corrupt the message. Because distance can weaken the signal strength, noise may have a more significant impact on the quality of communications over long distances.

As you might expect, the challenge of designing an effective communications system is to overcome the adverse effects from system noise and transmission distances. In communications systems, noise and distance can usually be offset by sufficient signal strength. The more powerful the signal, the less it is affected by noise or attenuated by distance. Unfortunately, all too often it is neither practical nor economical to create an amply powerful signal. Compromises are typical in any real-life communications system. The goal is to devise a system wherein the signal received is reasonably comparable to the one transmitted; this should ensure that the message received has lost little of its original informational content. For instance, the reproduction of voice in telephone communications is usually satisfactory but falls well short of high-fidelity audio standards. In practical systems, the cost of communication must not outweigh the expected value of its content. Keeping these factors in mind helps to explain some of the practices adopted in data communications over computer networks.

Data Encoding and Signal Transmission

Shannon's model describes any type of communications system. Our focus, of course, is on technologies that serve data communications in computer networks. The first step, then, is understanding how that data is handled. Based on the previous model, we can simplify this to three major issues. How is the data (message) encoded? How does the signal transmit that data? What are limiting factors affecting that transmission? The answers are straightforward:

1. The message in any computer network communications system is encoded as a stream of binary numbers.

2. The signal is transmitted and received as some type of electromagnetic energy (usually electrical, optical, or radio waves).

3. The rate at which data can be transmitted reliably over a given communications channel is determined primarily by properties of the medium.

In this section, we delve a little deeper into the issues of data encoding and signal transmission for digital data communications.

Encoding the Data

As you are well aware by now, all forms of information processed by computers are encoded as streams of binary digits. This digitization of data is the common denominator that unlocks the unsurpassed potential of computers to store, transfer, and process both large amounts and many forms of information. We have also seen that most coding schemes are based on grouping binary digits or bits into bytes (eight bits) or larger sequences. The same is true for data communications. Information transmitted over computer networks is binary encoded. Data may be encoded in either an unchanged or pure binary format (such as data files containing images, sound, programs, etc.) or as text using the ASCII or Unicode coding schemes.

You learned in Chapter 5 about text codes such as ASCII (American Standard Code for Information Interchange). The origin of the ASCII coding system was in data communications applications rather than exclusively for text processing. Each character or symbol in the ASCII code is represented by an 8-bit binary code. One of the bits is called the **parity bit,** which can be used for transmission error detection, and the other seven bits represent the actual character to be transmitted. We can use the parity bit for error detection in an odd parity scheme or an even parity scheme. Let's examine an odd parity scheme first.

Using **odd parity error detection,** the transmitter will set the parity bit so that the total number of bits containing the value 1 (let's call these 1-bits) in the byte is odd. This allows the receiver to monitor for certain kinds of errors. Suppose one of the 1-bits in the encoding of the original symbol gets changed to a 0 during transmission and all other bits (including the parity bit itself) stay the same. The receiver will recognize that there is an error and ask for a retransmission because there is an even number of 1-bits. Note, though, that even if the receiver detects an error, it has no idea what the error is; it simply requests another transmission of the data.

This scheme is not foolproof. For example, if exactly two bits get changed during transit, then there will still be an odd number of bits, so the error cannot be detected. If the parity bit alone gets changed during transit, the receiver will detect this error and ask for another transmission. Can you see why? In general, parity bit error detection will detect an odd number of bit changes during transit, but not an even number of bit changes. In short, parity bit error detection is not very robust. It is designed to detect single bit changes, which are the most frequent errors on a normal communications channel. See Figure 16.2.

On a particularly noisy channel where more than one bit is likely to be changed, we would need a more sophisticated error detection method. The advantage of parity bit error detection is that it is not very expensive. It costs only one bit per byte of transmitted data.

Even parity error detection works in an analogous way. In this scheme, the parity bit is set so that the total number of 1-bits is even. Like the odd parity method, it detects an odd number of bit changes during transit, but not an even number of such changes.

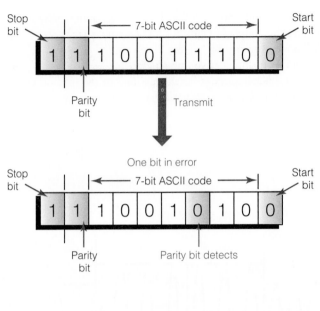

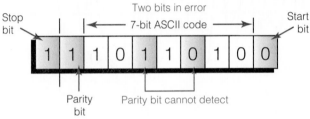

Figure 16.2

The encoding of a single text character for data transmission often employs a parity bit for error detection. Here the letter "N" is encoded and transmitted. In this instance, odd parity error detection is used. The figure illustrates a case (middle) where error detection is robust and another (bottom) where the parity bit does not detect the errors made. Note that parity checking is an error detection scheme and not an error correction method. It can discover that an error occurred in transmission, but not fix it.

Transmitting the Signal

Once a message is encoded, it must be converted to a signal for transmission over the communications channel. The signal, of course, must match the properties of the transmission media. In data communications, data may be transmitted as either analog or digital signals, depending on the medium used.

In data communications, analog signals are composed fundamentally of waves that are less subject to distortion over transmission channels. These signals are essentially repeating, continuous waveforms whose energy is propagated across the medium. A repeating signal (like a monotonous hum) does not contain much information. To convey information, a signal must exhibit some change from time to time. Hence, repeating waveforms are **modulated,** or altered, to represent a digital message.

Encoding binary messages using an analog signal is conceptually simple. The analog signal must at least carry enough information to distinguish two distinct symbols, binary 1s and 0s. Consequently, the basic carrier wave must be altered or modulated to denote binary values. The receiver can then detect transitions in that signal as signifying a binary coding. But how can the signal be modified? The signal may be characterized by three qualities: amplitude, frequency, or phase. **Amplitude** is the strength of the signal. **Frequency** defines the speed or rate of the carrier wave. (See Chapter 10 for a discussion of sound waves and frequencies.) Finally, **phase** relates to the calibrated timing of signal waves. (See *Focus on Sine Waves and Bandwidth* below.) Accordingly, the signal may be modulated or altered by either amplitude, frequency, or phase. Each denotes a distinct method for binary encoding.

Amplitude modulation alters the carrier signal's amplitude to encode the binary data. The frequency and phase of the signal are held constant and the amplitude is raised and lowered a known amount. Figure 16.3 illustrates.

Frequency modulation changes the frequency of the carrier signal in accordance with the binary message. Amplitude is held constant. See Figure 16.4.

Last of all, **phase modulation** alters the phase of a signal to represent the binary message. The scheme used in the example in Figure 16.5 is a simple one. Every change, or phase shift, signifies a transition to a different bit value.

There are a number of different coding schemes for each of these forms of modulation. The details of these are not important here. Regardless of the method employed, the rate of modulation of the signal is defined as its **baud rate.** The baud rate, of course, is related to the data rate, or **bits per second.** However, they are not the same. (Only when there is one bit per signal interval or baud does this equivalency apply.) We will return to consider these and related issues later in this chapter.

Figure 16.3

Varying the amplitude is one method of modulating the carrier signal to encode binary data. This technique is called amplitude modulation (AM). In the illustration, the amplitude of the signal modulates from low to high to represent 0s and 1s, respectively.

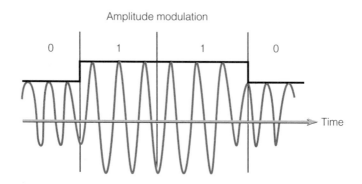

Figure 16.4

Frequency shift keying is an example of frequency modulation (FM) signal encoding. The frequency of the signal is modified to represent either 1s or 0s. In this instance, a lower frequency tone denotes 0s and higher frequency signifies 1s.

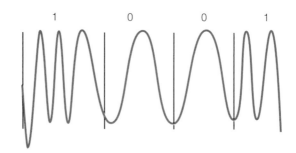

Figure 16.5

Phase shift keying is an example of phase modulation signal encoding. Each change or shift in phase signifies a change in the bit value being transmitted. Thus, no change over several intervals means repeating symbols.

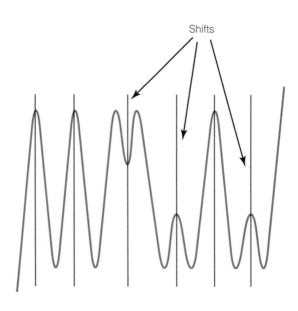

Modulated analog signals may be transmitted over a variety of media. Of course, computers are digital devices, so when analog signals are used, we must translate between analog and digital formats when computers are involved. For example, to use telephone lines for transmitting digital information, special devices called **modems** (for *mo*dulate-*dem*odulate) are used to convert digital data to analog signals and analog signals back to digital data. The first step is to convert the original digital data to analog form for transmission. Once the analog form is transmitted across the communication channel, the receiver must convert it back to a digital form for interpretation. Figure 16.6 illustrates.

Digital signals are transmitted over bounded media, such as wires or optical fiber. As illustrated in Figure 16.7, digital signals can be transmitted as series of electrical (over wires) or optical (over optical fiber) pulses. Systems using digital signals do not require special devices like modems, but these systems are often limited in transmission distance because voltage levels and optical signals weaken rapidly over short distances.

Regardless of whether the carrier signal is analog or digital, several factors limit the rate at which data can be transmitted reliably. The most significant ones are the bandwidth of the channel, the signal strength, and interference from system noise.

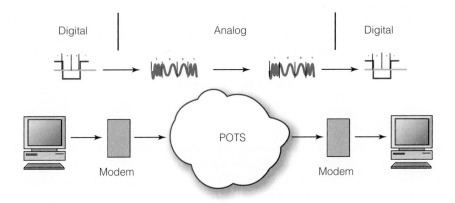

Figure 16.6

Transmitting digital data by an analog signal involves two translation processes. First, the original data is translated to analog form for transmission. The medium or channel is "plain ordinary telephone service" (POTS) for voice communication. The receiver must then convert the analog signal back to a digital form for interpretation.

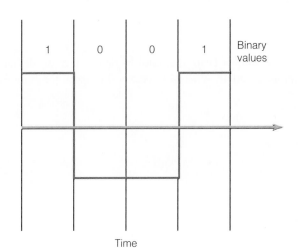

Figure 16.7

Abrupt changes in voltage levels of an electrical signal, for example, are sufficient for encoding binary values. In this scheme, alternating voltage levels depict binary 1s and 0s. To identify the signal correctly, the receiver has to be capable of accurately sensing the voltage changes. If the signal weakens, discerning changes becomes more difficult. The receiver must also be synchronized with the sender's bit rate of transmission. For example, without proper timing information, the receiver might not recognize that two consecutive 0s were transmitted.

Note: this is a very idealized picture of the signal. Voltage levels are seldom this stable. In spite of this, detecting values are simplified by adopting a two-level coding scheme.

Bandwidth

The **bandwidth** of a communications channel determines its capacity to transmit data. In common parlance, it denotes the rate of data transfer or throughput of the channel. Typically, though, the bandwidth cited is more often theoretical: stating the peak or ideal rate rather than the actual or practical rate. Technically, bandwidth is measured as the range of waveform frequencies the channel is capable of transmitting. Recall from Chapter 10 that frequencies are measured in units of Hertz (Hz), which stands for cycles per second. In the sound domain, the frequency determines the pitch of a sound. In the current context, a signal contains many component waveforms with different frequencies. The range of frequencies present in the signal determines how much information the signal carries. In short, signals with greater frequency ranges carry more information in a given time interval.

Intuitively, we can liken bandwidth in signal transmission to the size of pipes in plumbing. To deliver a given rate of water flow, the pipes must be of a certain size. Likewise, for a channel to deliver a signal with a broad range of frequencies (that is, a signal with complex or "large" informational content), it must have sufficient bandwidth to accommodate the frequencies contained in the signal. In other words, the more information that we pack into a signal, the greater the bandwidth demands for that signal.

For example, a voiceband transmission, such as that used for telephone communication, can be adequately handled by a bandwidth of approximately 4,000 Hz. On the other hand, a commercial broadcast television signal contains much more information per unit of time and hence demands a bandwidth about 1,000 times greater.

The moral of this tale for data communications is a simple one. There is always a finite limit to the speed and capacity for data transfer over some channel. The bandwidth of the channel plays a primary role in determining this limit. Higher data rate transmissions require greater bandwidth than lower data rate transmissions.

Signal Strength

Signal strength is another important factor for understanding the practical limits of data communications. Data is sent from the transmitter to the receiver via the communications channel. The length of the channel, the type of transmission media used for the channel, and the number of connections a signal must pass through all affect the strength of the signal when it arrives at the receiver. The strength or power of the signal at the receiver's end is almost never the same as it was at the transmitter. This means that the receiver system must have sufficient sensitivity to capture the signal accurately. When networks are being designed, the designers must anticipate and account for loss of signal strength.

Noise

The presence of noise is another factor that must be figured into the design and functioning of practical data communications systems. In electrical systems, for example, some forms of

FOCUS   Sine Waves and Bandwidth

To find out more about the foundations of modern communications systems, consult our online source for understanding signal processing and bandwidth.

noise are interference from other devices. The amount of noise contributed to a signal is expressed as a ratio. The **signal-to-noise ratio** (**SNR**) is measured as

$$SNR = Power_{Signal} : Power_{Noise}$$

The amount of noise that can be tolerated in a system depends on the type of signal being transmitted. For example, to transmit binary coded data using a digital signal requires a SNR of about 32:1 to be effective. In contrast, a voice signal over telephone systems needs a 10,000:1 SNR to be considered good, though considerably less is tolerable.

Signals that require greater bandwidth are more vulnerable to inherent noise. Therefore, broader bandwidth signals need more power than narrow bandwidth signals to overcome this. Like any other practical engineering problem, the design of data communications networks involves a great many decisions about trade-offs in cost versus performance.

So far, we have looked at how messages are encoded as signals for data transmission. Next, we will consider how computer networks are configured or organized for communicating data from one point to another. Data networks, in fact, come in a wide assortment of types. We can distinguish them in several ways: the distances they span, what sort of media they use, and so on. In the next section, we outline these factors in more detail.

Classifying Networks

Computer networks for data communications are commonplace today, but they are relatively new to the computing scene. We use networks to send messages and mail to friends and colleagues. Networks allow us to transfer and pool information. They augment our computers by providing resources and services. Some networks are even capable of transmitting audio and video for conferencing and other real-time applications. Networking, however, was not always like this.

Life before the advent of computer networks was very different indeed. In the 1950s and early 1960s, computing was exclusively centralized around a single source for processing, the mainframe computer. In fact, the average user had no direct contact with the computing system that processed his or her work. Instead, processing tasks were submitted and queued as jobs. These were usually handled by professional operators who loaded the jobs into the system. In this centralized processing environment, jobs were processed one by one, and users would wait for the results.

Advances in both system software and data transmission created the first interactive computing environments in the late 1960s. Users shared the resources of I/O, storage, and CPU on a time-sharing basis. Computing resources were still centralized, but the user could access them by way of a **terminal** (a keyboard and video display) that was connected over transmission lines. In reality, of course, there was still a single source of computing power that divided its attention among users' processes rapidly and methodically. Even so, the user had virtually immediate, interactive feedback from these processes and the illusion of sole possession of the computer's power. More important, though, the user became connected to the scheme of things. (See Figure 16.6, previously.)

As the numbers of users grew, the demands on the system increased and the general organization became more sophisticated. For example, several computers might be combined. Subordinate systems such as I/O processors relieved some of the demands placed on the central system. The availability of time-sharing computing was also extended when modems became available to connect a terminal with a remote computer system over telephone lines. In spite of advances in performance, the type of connectivity in this environment was still confined to a user connected directly to a central system.

The 1980s ushered in the age of desktop computing. Smaller, less expensive computer systems brought processing power directly to the user. Organizations and businesses learned that distributing computing across the enterprise was more economical and productive than maintaining traditional, centralized resources. As processing became more distributed, the need for connection and communication was strongly felt. Without connectivity, desktop systems were limited to their own resources—memory, storage, and so on.

The earliest type of communication between small systems modeled that of the earlier regime. The system that an individual used was physically connected to another system, called the **remote host.** A **terminal emulation program** running on the user's machine allowed it to act as a simple terminal device that used the processing capabilities of the remote host. These systems were connected by wires across the room or by way of modems over telephone lines. File transfer programs such as Xmodem and Kermit allowed the local machine to send and retrieve files from the remote system. The capabilities of this style of connectivity were still fairly limited.

The modern computer network connects a collection of computer systems that not only can share common resources and exchange data, but also can cooperate in processing tasks. In other words, rather than being a passive terminal, your machine may request services from other systems and employ these in the completion of its own processing. Thus, in computer networks today, connectivity allows for autonomy while supporting cooperation.

Modern computer networks come in a wide assortment of flavors. It is useful to classify them by the following general characteristics.

- Distance—how far apart are the connections that make up the network?

- Media—how are the systems physically connected, and what transmission channel is employed?

- Signal—what type of physical carrier transmits the data?

- Switching—how are signals routed over shared links?

We cover each of these categories and show how they figure into the design and performance of a network.

Distance

First, we can distinguish networks in terms of their size. In this instance, "size" is intended to convey how much area the network covers rather than the number of devices that are interconnected. In this context, networks come in three sizes: LANs, WANs, and internets.

A **LAN,** or **local area network,** is a network of interconnected computer systems and other devices that is restricted to a limited geographical area. The concept "limited geographical area" is admittedly a fuzzy one. LANs are usually restricted to areas that we could walk comfortably. A LAN may interconnect the computers in a lab, a building, or even a group of buildings. We consider LANs in some detail in the next chapter.

A **WAN,** or **wide area network,** is a network that connects machines that are distributed over a large geographical area. Still, there is a connotation of an autonomous network in spite of its expanse. In other words, WANs are usually owned or used by a single corporation or organization. The networks that connect automated teller machines for a bank or regional offices for a corporation are examples of WANs.

An **internet,** which is short for **internetwork,** is a collection of autonomous networks. Internets connect separate networks of different sizes and types. Normally, an internet covers a very large area, but this is not an essential ingredient. For example, an internet could be confined to the autonomous LANs of a single institution. It is very likely that your campus has just this sort of organization. Intraorganizational internets are often dubbed **intranets** to avoid confusing them with larger confederations of networks. Intranets usually enforce some security measures that hinder outsiders from accessing them. Of course, the big Kahuna of all internetworks is the Internet. This is a vast collection of networks that span the globe. We return to consider it in more detail in Chapter 18.

Media

Another way to distinguish networks is to describe the transmission medium of the channel that interconnects them. Transmission media, of course, provide the physical transport for the signal. There are two exclusive classes of media: bounded versus unbounded.

Bounded media are what we think of as wiring. Electrical conductors, such as copper wiring, are commonly used for network transmissions. Optical fiber is another bounded medium. (We delve more into these varieties in Chapter 17.) Bounded media have the advantages of economy and security, but they are limited by the distances that they can effectively span and by bandwidth.

Broadcast methods employing infrared waves, microwaves, and radio frequency waves are the most common forms of **unbounded media.** Broadcast transmissions often can have greater range and offer greater flexibility in physically arranging the network. On the other hand, these systems offer less security because anyone can intercept the signal with a receiver tuned to the proper frequencies. In spite of this, wireless networking has gained considerable acceptance in recent years and its popularity will likely grow even more in the future. Again, we will consider wireless networking in more detail in the next chapter.

Signal

Two types of signals are used for network communications. **Baseband,** or **narrowband, transmission** employs the entire bandwidth of the communications channel as a carrier for a single signal. Most LANs today employ baseband methods. Basically, the baseband transmission is an unmodulated digital signal. On bounded media such as copper wiring, the signal is transmitted as voltage pulses and is interpreted digitally. Baseband transmission is used on a variety of media and is popular because of its economy and simplicity.

In contrast, **broadband transmission** carries multiple signals on the same channel simultaneously. The technique of combining multiple signals over the same carrier channel is called **multiplexing.** Broadband transmissions employ **frequency-division multiplexing** (**FDM**). The range of available frequencies are divided into bands; each band can carry one or more signals. Thus, as depicted in Figure 16.8, signals originating from different sources can be transmitted at the same time over the channel. At the receiving end, the receivers, of course, must be attuned to the frequency bands of those signals that are intended for them.

Although broadband transmission offers greater capacity, the equipment required adds to its expense. In addition, broadband networks are more difficult to maintain than those using simple baseband transmission. Even so, broadband networks are becoming more important as new standards for voice, data, and video carrying networks are proposed.

Though unrelated to broadband transmission per se, we should mention that there is one more popular flavor of multiplexing. **Time-division multiplexing** (**TDM**) accommodates multiple signals by chopping them into discrete chunks and transmitting them over a single channel in separate time slots. See Figure 16.9. There are a number of schemes available for

Figure 16.8
In frequency-division multiplexing, multiple signals share the frequency spectrum or bandwidth of the communication channel. In the illustration, each link is assigned a frequency range of 4 KHz for transmitting its signal. FM radio stations, for example, use FDM to share the assigned bandwidth.

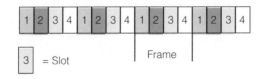

Figure 16.9
Unlike FDM, in time-division multiplexing the signal occupies the entire bandwidth of the channel—but not continuously. Time is divided into frames of a fixed duration. Each frame is divided into a sequence of slots. These slots are used by each sender to transmit a piece of its signal to the intended receiver.

deciding who gets time and how much, but TDM is an important multiplexing strategy used in data communications.

Switching

The various devices and computer systems that communicate over a network are commonly called **nodes.** The nodes are linked, of course, by the channels that make their communication possible. The particular geometric arrangement of nodes and their links in a network are called its **topology.**

Connections between nodes are usually shared. In a **shared connection network,** nodes communicate with each other over common paths. This means that each node is connected to a communications channel, but nodes are not ordinarily connected to each other directly. Networks can be set up to have a **point-to-point connectivity,** meaning that each node has a direct connection to every other node in the network, although it is seldom economically feasible to do so. See Figure 16.10.

In a shared connection network, the connections are simpler, although communication becomes more complicated because a message intended for a distant node must pass through intermediate nodes on its way to the intended receiver. Signals that travel over shared connections or links must therefore be routed to arrive at their proper destination. The method used for routing is called **switching.** The two standard switching strategies used in networks are circuit switching and packet switching.

■ **Circuit Switching.** In **circuit switching,** a continuous connection or circuit is forged between the communicating nodes. This circuit is supported by a series of switches involving intermediary nodes and their links. The connection persists for the duration of the communication, and the circuit is monopolized by the communicating nodes during the time they are connected. In other words, no other transmission occurs along the circuit during the connection. See Figure 16.11. When the communication ends, the circuit is released to allow other nodes to access its intermediary nodes and their links for communication.

Figure 16.10

(a) Establishing point-to-point connections for every pair of nodes in a five-node network requires a total of ten links. (b) In contrast, full connectivity is possible with fewer links, provided there are shared connections. For example, five links fully connect the five-node network. (What is the fewest number of links needed to fully connect the five-node network?)

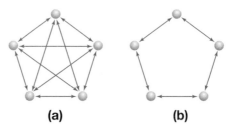

(a)   (b)

Figure 16.11

Two-way communication is established in a circuit switching network by maintaining a continuous connection between origin and destination. This circuit temporarily monopolizes the links between the two end nodes; intermediate links must wait until the circuit is released to engage in their own communications.

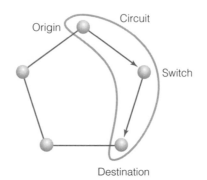

Circuit switching is the method employed traditionally in ordinary telephone service. When you are engaged in a phone conversation, you are constantly in touch with the other person. A continuous connection exists between the parties, and it supports simultaneous two-way communication. Both must acknowledge connection to establish it and later quit the connection to release the service.

- **Packet Switching.** An alternative strategy is packet switching. In **packet switching,** the data is broken down into smaller, usually fixed-sized units and assembled into groups of data called **packets.** A typical message is broken into a number of packets, much as a print document is made up of many pages. Each packet contains information identifying its origin, destination, and sequence number. The sequence number indicates its order in the message, as page numbering does in a document.

Store-and-forward packet switching networks are the most common. Under this regime, packets are routed from the transmitter to the receiver over any available path. As a result, packets from the same message may take different routes over the network and possibly arrive out of order. The receiving node must process the packets based on the identifying information in each packet and reassemble the message. See Figure 16.12. Packet switching is sometimes called **connectionless service** to emphasize the fact that communication does not depend on a continuous two-way channel circuit.

Packet switching is a lot like postal service. When you mail a letter to a friend, you put the message in an envelope, address it, post it, and go on about your business. The postal system takes over the task of routing it to its proper destination. The difference, of course, is that in a packet switching network, your letter would be distributed among many envelopes rather than one. As with postal service, you have to wait for a separate reply to find out whether your message got through.

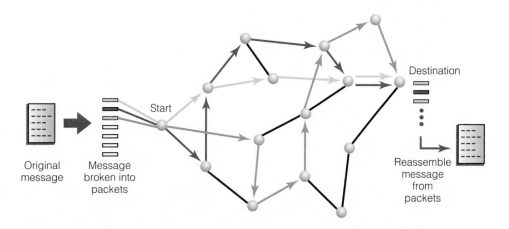

Figure 16.12
In a store-and-forward packet switching network, the message is divided into units and copied into data packets addressed for the destination. Packets are transmitted over any available connection to the destination. The receiving node processes them and reconstructs the message.

FOCUS Connecting the Nodes in a Network

Nearly all data communications networks are switched networks; that is, they have nodes that share communication channels. Consult our online resource to find out why. In addition, you will learn more about how switching networks are organized.

Packet switching does not monopolize the communications channel because packets from different nodes can be sequenced, interspersed, and transmitted continuously. It works best for short, irregular communications (such as text messages). Circuit switching has the advantage of requiring much less processing by the sender and especially the receiver. Transmission errors are more quickly recognized and remedied, too. It is suited best for lengthy data transmissions with time-critical constraints (such as live audio or video signals).

Even though telephone service has evolved from circuit switching networks, most computer networks are based on some form of packet switching. In spite of this historical fact, both concepts play important roles in understanding data communications and networks. We return to these ideas several times in the remaining chapters in this unit.

Connecting at Home

One of the most significant ways in which data communications networks have impacted our daily lives is in the home. *Census 2000* reported that 44 million U.S. households, or nearly 42% of all American families, have at least one computer system at home connected to the Internet. This represents almost twice as many American homes connected to the Internet compared with two years earlier. It is safe to predict that these numbers and percentages will likely grow in the future. For the most part, it is modem technology that enables these computer systems to enjoy this connectivity.

As mentioned earlier, *modem* is a contraction for *mod*ulate-*dem*odulate. A modem, of course, is used to send digital messages over analog channels, such as telephone lines. In this section, we will examine some of the primary choices available for getting connected.

Analog Modem Connections

Modems were developed long before the "Internet" became a household word. In the 1960s and 1970s, computer systems were large, expensive, and generally scarce commodities. In a large corporation, for example, computer systems were centralized to data processing departments. Modems were used to help distribute centralized computing power to remote locations. A remote office might have a terminal that could be linked to the centralized computing facility of the company. As mentioned earlier, a terminal is basically a video display monitor and keyboard capable of sending and receiving computer communications. The terminal would be connected to the central computer and function much like the monitor and keyboard connected directly to the system. In this way, remote locations could share computing power with local users.

How did the terminal actually communicate with the distant computing system? It worked because modems were used to exploit a common communications channel that was both abundantly available and relatively inexpensive—voice telephone service. A modem connected to the terminal would convert digital messages into analog signals capable of transmission over ordinary telephone service channels. See Figure 16.13. At the other end, a similar modem would translate incoming signals to digital data for the computer system.

Figure 16.13

A remote terminal connects to a data processing center computer system over voice telephone communication lines. At the sending end, the modem converts the digital signal into an analog one that can be carried over the phone lines. At the receiving end, the analog signal is translated back into a digital message.

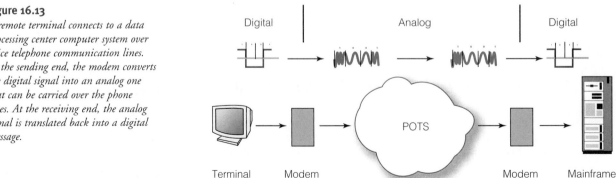

Digital   Analog   Digital

Terminal   Modem   POTS   Modem   Mainframe

Today, of course, terminals and data processing centers are a distant memory. But, your computer system at home can be connected to an **Internet service provider (ISP)** using the same scheme. Your home computer system can be connected to a modem that, in turn, is connected to your home telephone service. With the assistance of some software, your system can automatically telephone the modem number of your ISP. When the connection is established, the Internet service provider acts as a gateway for your system to connect to the Internet. (We will delve into the inner workings of the Internet later in Chapter 19.) See Figure 16.14.

The earliest modems were very slow compared with today's standards. This was tolerable, though, because most transmissions were text only. The Internet and World Wide Web, of course, have changed this. Slow speeds are intolerable for transmitting large files that contain applications, images, and the like. Today, the overwhelming need is for speed.

Early modems typically used frequency modulation for signal encoding. Specifically, the frequency of the signal would be modified to signify 1s and 0s. Of course, the telephone channels were designed to transmit voice signals, so the modem transmitted audible signals at different frequencies to represent the transmitted message. The bandwidth of the voice channel was large enough to accommodate two simultaneous signals as long as they were over different frequencies. Thus, modems could send and receive signals simultaneously. This is called **full-duplexing.**

The practical limit for such systems was approximately 300 bits per second (bps). This translates roughly to 30 characters per second. As mentioned, this would be acceptable for text transmissions, but certainly not for more complex forms of information.

Modern modems use more sophisticated encoding techniques in order to pack a greater amount of information into the bandwidth of voice phone channels. The fastest conventional modems are based on **quadrature amplitude modulation (QAM).** This method combines amplitude and phase modulation together. Known bit sequences are designated by assigned shifts in both amplitude and phase simultaneously. The combinations increase the number of sequences that can be encoded; consequently more bits can be packed into a single signal interval.

Regardless of its rated speed, high-speed modems rarely are able to reach that maximum speed. Instead, when the system connects initially, it tests the telephone line and drops back in graduated steps to slower speeds that can accommodate the signal with acceptable quality.

Cable Modem Connections

The need for speed as well as other considerations have led some to abandon traditional voice telephone service as the medium for home-to-network connections. Practical data rates of 48K bps are just too slow for some tastes. But, no matter how fast a conventional modem may perform, it has one obvious disadvantage. Voice telephone service is simply not available when these modems are squawking at one another.

Cable modems offer one alternative intended to overcome these obstacles. Like ordinary voice telephone service, cable television (CATV) is a prevalent communications technology that predates the Internet and the Web. CATV is available to most homes and has a large consumer subscription base. Cable modem data transfer rates are usually much faster than the fastest analog modems. In addition, connecting your computer to a cable modem frees up the phone line and, likewise, does not interfere with ordinary cable television viewing either.

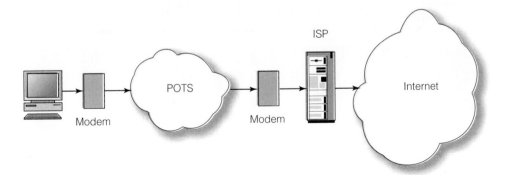

Figure 16.14

Your home computer system sends (and receives) signals via the modem that interfaces with your home voice phone service. The ISP's modem performs a similar function. Thus, the ISP can serve as your gateway to communication over the Internet.

Unlike conventional analog modems, communication through a cable modem system is asymmetrical. This means that data rates or speeds vary depending upon the direction of the data. **Downstream data** are represented by the signal sent to the local modem from the cable modem termination system (and, presumably, the Internet). **Upstream data** are the originating signals sent from your home computer system through the cable modem connected to your home's CATV outlet. Consult Figure 16.15.

CATV transmissions are usually conducted over channels composed of coaxial and optic fiber cables. (Networking media are treated in more detail in the next chapter.) Both are very high bandwidth media. A conventional television signal, for example, can fit comfortably within 6 MHz of bandwidth. Thus, using frequency-division multiplexing, CATV media can support hundreds of channels with room to spare. A cable modem system exploits some of this spare bandwidth for sending and receiving digital data. Downstream signals occupy a full 6-MHz band like any other TV channel signal. In contrast, upstream data is usually squeezed into a smaller bandwidth, typically 2 MHz. Consult Figure 16.16. The reasoning is that most upstream messages are short and simple, while downstream messages are complex and lengthy—downloads of Web pages with images, etc.

The equipment needed for home connections over CATV is asymmetrical, too. A cable modem is connected to the cable outlet and your computer system. At some point upstream, a **cable modem termination system** (CMTS) is employed to manage signals for multiple subscribers sharing the same channel. Downstream signals are actually broadcast to all subscribers sharing the same channel; it is the responsibility of the cable modem to recognize signals intended for it and filter out others. Upstream signals are not shared, however. These are separated by transmitting them at different times over the upstream band of the channel using TDM methods. As many as two thousand subscribers may be serviced by a single CMTS. See Figure 16.17.

This latter fact may explain some of the variability in quality of service for cable modem users. A single 6-MHz channel offers as much as 40 megabits per second of total throughput.

Figure 16.15

Unlike many other communication systems, cable modems transmit at different rates depending upon the direction of the data. Data transmitted downstream flows from the source to your home cable modem at a faster rate than upstream data. The latter is transmissions from your home to the cable company's termination system. Normally, this asymmetry does not affect performance, because upstream transmissions are usually short and simple—for example, Web requests.

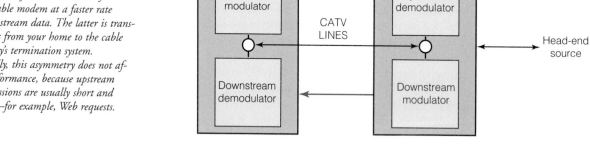

Figure 16.16

Cable modems separate downstream from upstream traffic. A full 6-MHz band is available for downstream transmissions. The total bandwidth depends upon the number of channels dedicated. Upstream traffic is usually confined to a smaller band.

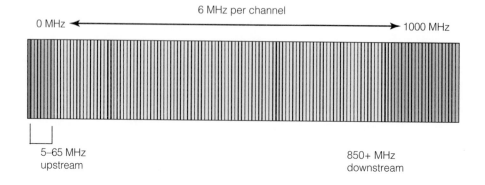

When there are few users sharing the channel, performance for individual users is very good. On the other hand, as the number of users increase, such as during peak usage hours, demand over the channel increases and performance can degrade seriously. The CATV provider can remedy perpetual high-usage problems by either adding a new channel for downstream transmissions or splitting up the subscribers and servicing them in smaller groups.

Digital Subscriber Line Connections

Digital subscriber line (DSL) connections offer very high-speed service using some of the same wires provided for ordinary telephone service. Unlike analog modems, though, DSL does not exploit the same voice bandwidth for communication. Moreover, DSL provides a data connection from the home to a central service point that, in turn, is connected to an ISP—using networking technology rather than telephone. As a result, DSL resembles cable modem performance in some respects. Telephone voice communication is not interrupted when DSL is connected. Data transmission over DSL is much faster. Likewise, the DSL connection to the Internet may be continuous; thus, you can maintain your own 24/7 Web server at home on a DSL connection.

Voice communication over telephone lines uses only a small portion of the available 1.1 MHz of bandwidth of the channel. DSL exploits some of the remaining higher frequency bandwidth for transmission and reception of digital data communications. Most consumer DSL systems today are **asymmetric DSL** (ADSL). (For more about new and competing DSL technologies, see the online resource, *New Technologies for Home Connections*.) Like cable modem technology, this means that data rates differ for upstream and downstream signals. Again, the assumption is that users download more information from the Internet than they send or upload. For example, when surfing the Web, messages that request Web pages are very small compared with the text files and other media sent by the Web server in response.

There are several incompatible standards for ADSL; but most of the equipment installed today uses what is called **discrete multitone (DMT)** encoding and transmission. This method divides the available bandwidth into a maximum of 256 separate channels. Each channel has a bandwidth of approximately 4 KHz—similar to voiceband. The lowest frequency band is reserved for standard telephone voice transmissions. Discounting that channel, the result is comparable to connecting to as many as 255 virtual modems simultaneously; see Figure 16.18. A few channels are reserved for upstream or outgoing data transmissions; the majority of the higher frequency band, though, is earmarked for downstream traffic. Each channel uses QAM encoding to send some portion of the digital message. This effectively multiplies the amount of data that can be encoded and transmitted over that channel by a factor of 15. For example, if each channel had a bandwidth of 4 KHz, and there were 249 channels available,

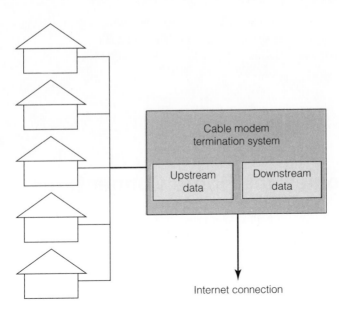

Internet connection

Figure 16.17

Several thousands of cable subscribers can be served by a single cable modem termination system (CMTS). Downstream data is broadcast to all subscribers simultaneously—in the same manner as CATV signals. Each receiver, however, retrieves only data addressed to it, just as your cable TV box selects only those channels that you choose to view. Upstream data, on the other hand, is sent individually from its origin to the CMTS.

then using QAM signal encoding, a maximum data rate of 14.9M bps could be achieved. On the other hand, with only 25 upstream channels, the potential data rate would only be 1.5M bps. Again, see Figure 16.18. In actual usage, the data rates differ depending upon the signal-to-noise ratio for each channel. For instance, higher frequencies usually suffer lower SNRs; likewise, AM radio interference can degrade certain localized frequencies. Because DMT monitors the performance of the channels, it is smart enough to pick those that would maximize the data throughput. Thus, consumer versions of ADSL offer home subscribers downstream data rates of 384K bps up to 1.5M bps, and upstream rates of 60K to 128K bps.

DSL requires specialized equipment similar to that employed by cable modem technology. See Figure 16.19. At the customer end, a DSL transceiver—usually called a "DSL modem"—connects to your computer and the phone line. At the other end, the phone line terminates at the telephone company's central office (CO) or substation. The signal is routed through a switch called a **splitter** that divides voice from data. Lower frequency voice signals are routed to the telephone system, while higher frequencies are passed to the **DSL Access Multiplexer (DSLAM).** The DSLAM provides a high-speed connection to your ISP and the Internet. Unlike cable modem technology, however, the DSL has a dedicated connection. Downstream signals on a cable modem system are shared with all of the active subscribers. DSL offers a distinct, separate connection to the DSLAM, so data rates between it and the DSL modem will be constant.

There are limitations for any DSL service though. Distance is a significant one. As mentioned earlier, the connection is from the consumer's home telephone system to the telephone company central office or substation. The maximum distance allowed between home and CO is approximately 5.4 kilometers (around 18,000 feet). In fact, a DSL connection performs much better over smaller distances. Even if you live close enough to the CO, not all connections are "DSL-ready" either. Older installations have voice coils installed to amplify the voice

Figure 16.18
DMT divides the available bandwidth into discrete channels for modulated transmissions. Each channel has a 4-KHz bandwidth using QAM signal encoding. The theoretical limits are shown here.

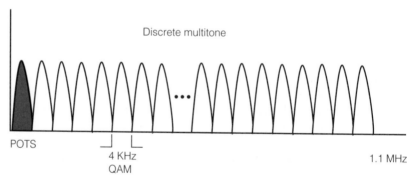

Data rate = number of channels × number of bits/channel × modulation rate
Max upstream data rate = 25 × 15 × 4 KHz = 1.5M bps
Max downstream data rate = 249 × 15 × 4 KHz = 14.9M bps

FOCUS   New Technologies for Home Connections

Modems, cable modems, and DSL represent the chief alternatives for connecting your home computer system to the Internet. Both evolving and newer technologies, though, promise even greater performance and features. Consult our online resource to find out more about making the home connection.

signal over longer distances, but these effectively block higher frequencies that would carry data communications. DSL requires copper media for its transmission channels, so any fiber-optic cabling between your home and the CO would disqualify you for DSL service as well.

The practical choice between cable modem and DSL is a difficult one. CATV service is currently more widespread, although telephone companies are aggressively upgrading their equipment to exploit the consumer DSL market. Cable modem performance is potentially faster than DSL, but its practical data rates are variable and unpredictable. DSL has more predictable data rates that are much faster than even the fastest analog modems. Currently, their economies are approximately the same, too. In other words, the cost of the equipment and leased services are comparable.

■ Summary

Perhaps the most significant change in computing over the past several decades has been the evolution of data communications networks. Computer networks connect individuals in the same office, the same building, and across the world. They provide for the instantaneous exchange of information. Data communications systems are based on a basic model of communication theory put forth by Claude Shannon, a pioneer in information theory. Shannon's model has six basic elements: an information source, a transmitter, a communications channel, a noise source, a receiver, and a destination or user.

Information transmitted over computer networks is binary encoded. Data may be encoded in either pure binary format or as text using a character coding scheme. Once a message is encoded, it is converted to a signal for transmission over the communications channel. Signals can be either digital or analog. Digital signals usually consist of series of electrical (over wires) or optical (over optical fiber) pulses. Analog signals are comprised of repeating, continuous waveforms that are modulated, or altered, to carry the digital message. Special devices, called *modems,* are used to convert digital data to analog signals and analog signals back to digital data.

Regardless of whether the carrier signal is analog or digital, several factors limit the rate at which data can be transmitted reliably. The most significant ones are the bandwidth of the channel, the signal strength, and interference from system noise.

Modern computer networks can be distinguished by several characteristics, including distance covered, media used, signal type, and switching methods.

Most networks employ a shared connection model, in which network nodes are not directly connected to each other, but rather share communications channels. Because a message intended for a distant node needs to pass through intermediate nodes on its way to the intended receiver, signals that travel over shared connections must be routed to arrive at their proper destination. The method used for routing is called *switching.* Two standard switching strategies are used in networks: circuit switching and packet switching.

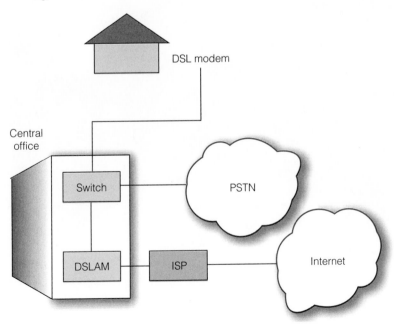

Figure 16.19
Unlike cable modem service, DSL subscribers have a dedicated access to the Central Office (CO) connection. The CO, however, must be within a prescribed range or distance from the subscriber—up to 18K feet. The incoming signal is divided between phone service and the DSLAM. The latter transfers signals at high speeds to an ISP and the Internet.

Data communications often begin at home with a modem connection over a channel to an Internet service provider. Conventional analog modems employ the voiceband of ordinary telephone service to transmit modulated digital signals. Cable modems and digital subscriber line modems represent newer competing technologies that offer higher speed connections without interrupting voice communication over the telephone.

■ Terms

amplitude
amplitude modulation
asymmetric digital subscriber
  line (ADSL)
bandwidth
baseband transmission
  (narrowband)
baud rate
bits per second
broadband transmission
broadcasting
cable modems
cable modem termination
  system (CMTS)
circuit switching
communications channel
connectionless service
data communications system
destination
destination system
digital subscriber line (DSL)
digital subscriber line access
  multiplexer (DSLAM)
discrete multitone
downstream data

even parity error detection
frequency
frequency modulation
frequency-division
  multiplexing
full-duplexing
information source
internet (internetwork)
Internet service provider (ISP)
intranets
local area network (LAN)
media (bounded, unbounded)
message
modem
modulated, modulation
  (e.g., amplitude modulation)
multiplexing
networking
node
noise
odd parity error detection
originating system
packet
packet switching
parity bit

phase
phase modulation
point-to-point connectivity
quadrature amplitude
  modulation (QAM)
receiver
remote host
Shannon, Claude
shared connection network
signal (analog, digital)
signal-to-noise ratio (SNR)
splitter
store-and-forward packet
  switching networks
switching (circuit versus
  packet)
terminal
terminal emulation program
time-division multiplexing
topology (network)
transmitter
upstream data
wide area network (WAN)

■ Questions for Review

1. How do broadcasting and networking differ as forms of communication? What are the advantages and disadvantages of each?

2. Describe Shannon's model for a communications system. What are its components and their respective functions in the model?

3. Depending on the medium, data communications are encoded as either analog or digital signals. Explain.

4. What is noise? How does it impact a data communications system?

5. What is bandwidth? How does it affect a data communications system?

6. Explain how the odd parity error detection scheme for transmitted data works. Is it a foolproof error detection method? Explain.

7. What does it mean to modulate a waveform? Why is this done in data communications systems?

8. What is a modem? Why are these devices necessary in certain data communications systems?

9. Explain the role of signal strength in data communications systems.

10. What is meant by signal-to-noise ratio? Why is this important for data communications systems?

11. Distinguish among LANs, WANs, and internetworks.

12. Distinguish between baseband and broadband transmissions.

13. What is shared connectivity? Why are shared connections favored over point-to-point connectivity?

14. What is switching, and how is it used in network communications?

15. Describe and compare the circuit switching and packet switching methods.

16. Why is packet switching referred to as "connectionless" service?

17. What is an ISP?

18. How does QAM encoding effectively increase the data rates of analog modem transmissions?

19. Cable modem service is asymmetrical. Explain.

20. How does ADSL exploit telephone connections to provide Internet connectivity?

21. Compare and contrast cable modem service with a DSL.

Chapter 17

Local Area Networks

OBJECTIVES

- The principal characteristics and chief advantages of local area networks

- How devices in local area networks are connected and how bounded transmission media affect performance

- How networks are physically organized to facilitate data transmission

- How communication is controlled between many and competing nodes in a LAN

- How software is organized to facilitate network applications

- Ways in which the size and performance of a LAN may be extended

- How wireless LANs are organized and communicate

In Chapter 16, you learned that computer networks evolved to permit computer systems to share data and resources. The earliest networks were devices connected to a single centralized processing system. Today, networks connect not only peripherals and other devices, but also all manners of independently functioning computer systems from mainframes to desktop computers. Networks can even link our appliances and electronics at home. In this chapter, we examine the fundamentals for the first line of networking—the local area networks (LANs) that establish basic connectivity for your computer.

Characteristics of a LAN

To understand and appreciate better the motivation for connecting computer systems to a network, consider the following practical problem. Suppose that you manage a collection of computers, perhaps in a lab or a business office. Most of the users prepare documents from time to time. Naturally, they need printing services for hard-copy versions of their documents. How do you meet this need? There are several possible solutions.

You might purchase one printer for each machine. This would be very convenient for your users, but also very expensive and inefficient. You could expect that the printers would spend a lot of idle time waiting for their next print job.

Rather than duplicate devices, you might purchase one printer and connect it to a single computer system used exclusively for printing. Users would have to copy their print files to a disk and physically transport them to the system used for printing. This "sneaker network" solution is not very satisfactory, either. It is less costly initially, but waiting for access and performing file transfers waste a lot of time and, therefore, money.

Perhaps all of the computers could be physically connected to a single printer. In this case, we could imagine a switching device or port that connects all the computers to the printer but allows only one computer at a time to use it. Switching might be done manually or even by software control. The wear and tear on sneakers is reduced, but still some of the same problems persist. Loss of time in waiting for access is annoying and costly for your users.

A better solution lies in combining features from all of these techniques into a single method. The printer is connected to a single dedicated computer system as before, but this computer—the server—is connected to all of the other systems on the site. Rather than a simple one-way physical connection, though, the server can send and receive signals from the others. Let's add still another wrinkle. Our server has software that allows it to receive transmitted print files, store them, and transfer them when the printer is ready. Now when a user wishes to print a file, he or she transfers it to the server. The server signals when it is ready, the print file is sent, and the user can continue working on something else with no further delays. Print files are queued or **spooled** for orderly printing. This usually means they are printed on a first-come, first-served basis, much like the lines or queues at grocery store checkouts.

From the user's point of view, this scheme is not as convenient as having immediate service with a dedicated printer. Even so, the service is less fussy compared with the other methods. Press a button and go. Even better, your system is freed from managing the details of the printing process, which means that you are free to do other things. As a manager, you can see that this is a very efficient solution from an administrative point of view, too. The printer's use is maximized; the user's idle time is minimized. Of course, there is a cost associated with this solution. Specialized hardware and software must be installed to make it work.

In a nutshell, we have the birth of a local area network (LAN) that has the following basic characteristics:

- Connectivity supporting two-way communication

- Resource sharing

- Limited geographical area

- Transparency of use

- Support from hardware and software

Let's examine each of these characteristics briefly.

Connectivity

The hallmark of any computer network, of course, is that all of the nodes on the network are interconnected for the sake of communication. The extent to which nodes on a network can communicate depends on both the hardware and software that support it. At the very least, every node on the network has the capability of two-way communication with one or more servers. Many networks support full two-way communication for every node rather than just to and from a server. This means that any node can send and receive signals from any other node on the network.

Resource Sharing

As our example showed, one of the chief motivations for a LAN is that it allows a group of users and their computer systems to share various resources. The server computer provides high-capacity mass storage for data and programs. Software, for instance, may be downloaded from the server to an attached computer for execution. This approach can save disk storage space on the user's system and also enhance system security because the original version of the software can be better protected from tampering. Dispensing software via servers can be economical in some cases, too. Software vendors often issue site licenses to use their applications on a large number of computers. Site licenses are cheaper than purchasing single copies for each computer system, and file servers can help to distribute the software to computers on the network.

Data can be shared between groups of users on a LAN, too. Specific files can be uploaded to the server. These files may then be accessed by other systems on the same network. In this way, a group working on a single document can share it without having to deliver disk copies to each system.

Most file servers maintain security provisions for users and user groups. Normally, you must have an established account on the LAN to access it. Accounts are often protected by **passwords,** a secret word or phrase that is known only by the legitimate user. (Chapter 20 considers this and other computer security issues.)

Limited Geography

The term *local* naturally suggests that LANs don't cover much ground. This, however, is extremely relative. "Local" depends on several factors: the type of media connecting the nodes, the number of connections in the network, sophistication of the hardware/software support, even how the nodes communicate in the network. In spite of these variables, it is safe to assume that you could comfortably walk the span of a local area network.

The most significant factor, though, in determining the span of the network is the transmission media. Bounded media such as wire and optic fiber have limits up to several hundred meters. Unbounded media or "wireless" LANs use radio frequency broadcast methods. These, too, are limited in effective distance. Consequently, a LAN usually extends no more than several rooms, a building, or, at most, a small area among buildings.

Transparency

One of the justifications for the expense of LANs is their transparency in use. This means that LANs are designed to connect a user's computer system to other systems and devices without a lot of fuss or bother for the user. As we discussed in the example, printing over a LAN is almost as easy and convenient as printing to a printer dedicated to your system. After you designate which printer you wish to use, just click a button and it's done. Similarly, access to the data files in a server is the same as if the disks were part of your system.

Network Hardware and Software Support

Connectivity and transparency of use do have special requirements, though. Each computer must have specific hardware to connect to the network and customized software to manage the connection. This often means purchasing network cards or boards (hardware) that are added to each computer. See Figure 17.1.

Servers and network connection devices often mean more expense. Network software must be purchased or licensed. Some versions of network software are add-ons for your system's operating system software; other versions are integrated solutions, which means the operating system has built-in networking facilities.

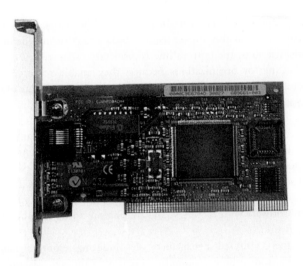

Figure 17.1
*A **network interface card** or **NIC** is shown here. Installed in a backplane slot of your desktop system, the card provides both a network connection interface and circuits needed for data signaling and reception.*

Other Factors

Although they are not really defining characteristics, several other conditions generally hold for LANs too. A LAN is usually locally owned and managed. The business or institution, therefore, must add or train staff to oversee its operation, thereby adding a continuing expense.

Because LANs are likely homegrown, the computers attached to them are often uniform, usually for administrative convenience. However, it is not necessary that all of the systems on a given LAN be from the same vendor. Different systems can be connected to a given network provided they employ compatible network hardware and software. In fact, one of the real advantages of LANs is that they can allow different hardware platforms to share data and resources.

Costs and Benefits of LANs

Most organizations have evolved from maintaining large, centralized computing centers to distributed computing environments. Experience has shown that it is simply cheaper over the long run to replace costly, large mainframes with numerous inexpensive, expendable desktop systems. These systems bring sufficient computing power directly to users. Their cost has dramatically decreased annually as their performance has increased. LANs add connectivity to such an environment and, with it, all the benefits of centralized computing. The cost of networking a distributed computing environment is worth it over the long run because it provides the greatest flexibility for meeting future organizational needs.

The primary advantages of using a local area network are communication, management control, and cost-effectiveness. Obviously, a LAN facilitates communication. The advantages of communication are more than just sending messages electronically from one person to another. Besides person-to-person communication, a LAN makes it possible for both individuals and applications to communicate in various ways. For example, you can run a program from another system provided that a LAN connects your system with that remote host.

You will recall that in Chapter 4, we saw that applications can communicate, too. Applications typically interact over a network based on the client/server relationship. A client program running on your system, for example, might make requests for data and services from a server program that is executing on a server or even another client system. Many new applications today take advantage of client/server architecture to provide more powerful or convenient features to their users. In these environments, resources, data, programs, and tasks are distributed and shared across computer networks. (We will return to consider client/server systems in more detail in the next chapter.)

LANs also offer the advantage of centralized management. Local area networks typically connect a number of desktop computer systems on a single site, thus enabling an organization to replace centralized computing with downsized, distributed computing. Workgroups can share data stored in a protected and centralized facility while enjoying the advantages of distributed access. Networks can also impose security provisions that impede unwanted access.

For most organizations, the bottom line is monetary expense. LANs are usually more cost-effective solutions for organizations because they enable resource sharing and the downsizing of computing facilities. We've already discussed the economy of sharing software and hardware resources. Downsizing of computing facilities also clearly promotes a healthier bottom line.

There is a debit side associated with LANs. Aside from the acquisition of additional equipment and software, there is a continuing need for maintenance. As mentioned earlier, staff must be trained and available to keep the network functioning properly. Fortunately, today a number of software tools aid in managing the network. Even so, a networking staff is needed to assist users in connecting, providing advice on services, testing the compatibility of new hardware and software with the LAN, and putting out the "fires" that flare up here and there along the network.

Even though the centralized management of computing resources enabled by LANs is generally advantageous, distributed computing exclusively through desktop computers does have some drawbacks. Computing with desktop systems often duplicates software and data across the organization. Besides the expense of redundancy, data inconsistencies can arise. There are also more security problems because there are many potential points of access in a distributed computing environment. Fortunately, networking services provided by most LANs can help to alleviate these problems. (Again, Chapter 20 discusses some of the security provisions that network administrators can impose to reduce these problems.)

Most organizations have concluded that the benefits of local area networks far outweigh their costs. In fact, networking today is as essential and commonplace in a computing environment as video monitors and storage peripherals. Ten years ago, a LAN in a business or a lab was an exotic distinction; today, a networked computing environment is assumed.

Even though all LANs provide basic connectivity between the devices at a site, not all LANs are alike. A number of distinguishing characteristics affect their performance. In the next section, we consider how to classify LANs according to these important criteria.

Differentiating LANs

The number of networking solutions offered by computer vendors may seem a dizzying assortment to the newcomer. A closer look, however, reveals that many different proprietary networks (brand names) share a lot of common attributes. Four important factors differentiate one type of LAN from another. An understanding of each of these categories gives a much clearer picture as to what makes one LAN different from another.

First, how are the nodes in the LAN connected? LANs are differentiated by the transmission media they employ. Second, most nodes in a LAN form shared links, but how are their connections organized? This organization reveals the network topology. Still another factor is how do the nodes gain access to the network? In other words, how is communication managed? Finally, networks that are similar in all these characteristics can still be different because they have different supporting software. We outline each category and consider its primary instances.

Transmission Media: How LANs Are Connected

Most LANs today are connected using bounded media. This means that data transmission is carried over wire or fiber. (We consider LANs using unbounded transmission in the final section of this chapter.) There are three popular bounded media for interconnecting the nodes of a LAN:

- Twisted-pair cable

- Coaxial cable

- Optical fiber cable

These media differ in cost and performance characteristics. As you might expect, the trade-off is usually low cost versus high performance. Three factors are important for measuring their performance characteristics: transmission speed, practical transmission distance, and susceptibility to noise. Speed for digital transmissions, as discussed in Chapter 16, is measured in bits per second. Practical distance refers to how far the medium may be extended before the signal weakens significantly.

One of the most inexpensive and commonly used forms of wiring is **twisted-pair cable.** Standard telephone cable, for example, can be used. Two insulated lengths of copper wire are twisted together and can extend distances up to about 100 meters. See Figure 17.2. Twisted-pair cable is sometimes shielded to prevent signal interference. Because unshielded varieties are sensitive to signal interference, some care must be taken in planning their installation. In spite of this, twisted-pair is a very economical and a popular choice for wiring a network. Transmission speeds range from 10 megabits (a megabit is 1 million bits) per second (Mbps), 100 Mbps, and even 1,000 Mbps (or a gigabit).

Graded **unshielded twisted pair** (**UTP**) copper cabling has become the most popular choice for wiring LANs. UTP media is composed of four pairs of twisted copper wires. (See Figure 17.3) Each pair is insulated from the others by the cancellation effect as a result of the braiding of the wires. UTP is rated at several categories based on performance standards: 3, 4, 5, and a newer standard, 6. Category 5 (CAT 5) is popular because of its economy, high-performance, and ease of installation.

Coaxial cable is another form of copper wiring for networks. A **coaxial cable** is usually two conductors separated by several layers of shielding and insulation. The inner conductor is either solid or stranded wire; a meshed wire serves as an outer conductor. Figure 17.4 illustrates.

Coaxial cable is commonly used in radio and television applications, so it is readily available. The insulation and shielding protect against external signal interference. Transmission speeds measure between 10 and 100 Mbps. Practical distances for this medium range from around 200 meters (thin coaxial) to 500 meters (thick coaxial). In spite of these advantages, coaxial cable is more expensive to purchase and install than UTP media. As a result, it is employed in fewer networks today.

Optical fiber cable offers an entirely different technology for data transmission. Light pulses are generated as a signal from either a laser or a light-emitting diode. The signal is carried through very thin strands of glass fiber. As the light travels along the fiber, it is confined to the core or signal path by the special insulation or cladding that surrounds the core. At the receiving end, a photodetector translates the light pulses into an electrical signal. See Figure 17.5.

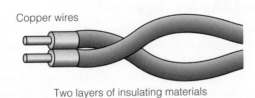

Copper wires

Two layers of insulating materials

Figure 17.2

Twisted-pair is copper wiring twisted together. It comes in several shielded and unshielded varieties. Here we see simple grade twisted pair.

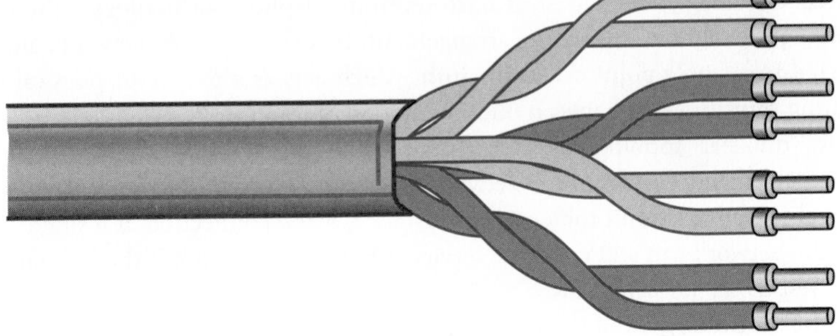

Figure 17.3

Unshielded twisted pair (UTP) copper cabling is composed of four pair of braided wiring. The pairs are composed of relatively thin gauge copper wire, which means that UTP cabling is both smaller in volume and more economical than other cabling.

Figure 17.4

Coaxial cables were used in the first local area networks. Today, there are two formats: thick and thin. "Thinnet" installations are cheaper and easier to install compared to the older, thick coaxial formulations.

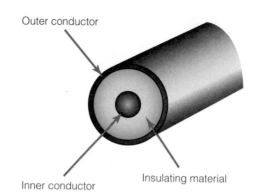

Figure 17.5

A common form of optical fiber is depicted here. Called single transmission, *the signal is beamed through an extremely thin glass fiber core. Cores may be as small as 2 to 12 millionths of a meter in diameter.* Cladding *is an optical insulator whose lower refractive properties confine the signal to the core. An outer plastic coating acts as insulation for the signal transmission. In this way, many different signal-carrying fibers can be bundled into a single cable.*

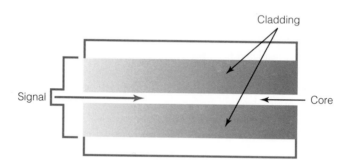

Optical fiber is noteworthy for its transmission speeds and low error rates. Speeds are rated from 100 Mbps up to 10 gigabits (a gigabit is 1 billion bits) per second. Lower error rates are typical because optical fiber cable uses light pulses instead of electrical pulses to transmit data; hence, it is much less subject to the noisy interference that sometimes plagues copper wire channels. Optical fiber is more expensive than transmission media made of copper wire. Improved copper formulations have challenged its position as the choice for high-speed transmission.

Topologies: How LANs Are Organized

In Chapter 16, you learned that few data communications networks employ point-to-point connections. It is simply too expensive, too complicated, and too wasteful to configure a network in which every two nodes have a direct or dedicated connection between them. Instead, networks use shared links. The links or transmission paths may be shared in many ways.

The logical layout or geometric organization of how the nodes in a network are connected is called its **topology.** A network's topology reveals the potential paths for communication between nodes and how their links are shared; it is not focused exclusively on the physical arrangement of the wires and connections. There are three popular topologies for LANs: star, bus, and ring.

The **star topology** is the oldest. It borrows from telephone technology—the telephones in your home probably use this wiring arrangement. In a star topology network, all the nodes are connected to a single point called the **hub,** which acts as a passive or physical switching device routing transmissions between outlying nodes. See Figure 17.6.

Because the star topology is centralized, it permits greater network management. Expansion—adding new nodes to the network—is usually easy. Star networks are also less vulnerable to cable transmission problems. For instance, if the connection at a single node fails, the rest of the network can still continue service. On the other hand, if the hub fails, then, of course, the rest of the network fails.

In the **bus topology,** all of the nodes in a network are connected to a common communications channel. All nodes share this single transmission channel, called a **bus.** The bus

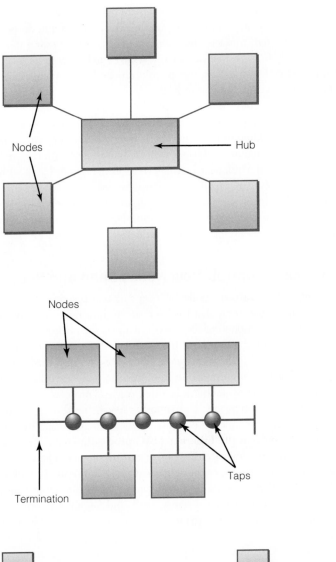

Figure 17.6
In the star topology, a centralized hub connects all other nodes in the network. The hub serves as a passive switching device for routing transmissions.

Figure 17.7
The bus topology is a single transmission medium that is terminated at both ends (to prevent signal reflections). Nodes are connected to the medium by taps or transceivers. When a transmission is sent from a single node, all the nodes on the network can access it. In effect, signals are broadcast across the network.

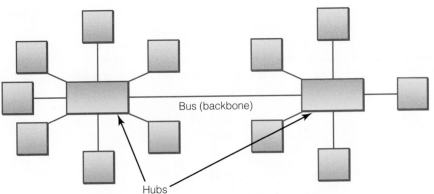

Figure 17.8
A single line connects two hubs to form a bus topology. Individual nodes are connected into a hub making installation simpler and easily modified. Star-wired bus networks may employ one or more hubs for installing nodes.

topology is illustrated in Figure 17.7. This configuration is simple and has several advantages. Cable lengths are usually the shortest, and the bus network is also easily expanded. The choice of medium, however, affects both the potential length and number of nodes. Like the star topology, if a single device in the bus topology fails, the rest of the network survives. But if the bus fails, the network is compromised. Unlike the star topology, which offers some centralized control, network management is more difficult in a bus network.

A popular solution for these problems is to combine the bus and star topologies together. Called *star-wired bus* topology, this configuration employs one or more switching boxes from which individual nodes are connected. See Figure 17.8.

In the star and bus topologies, the nodes are not arranged in any particular order. A **ring topology,** in contrast, does impose an order on the nodes of a network. Each node in a ring topology is connected to exactly two other nodes: its predecessor and successor. Thus, it receives signals only from its predecessor and sends signals only to its successor. The entire network forms a closed path or ring that permits any node to communicate to others by passing the signal along the ring. See Figure 17.9.

Ring topologies are favored primarily for performance characteristics such as speed (especially optical fiber ring networks) and better access. They do pose some problems for management, though. Adding or removing nodes from a ring can be tricky. In fact, many ring architectures today are maintained using a wiring hub to deal with this problem. Cable is wired from each station to the hub device, which controls the ring ordering within. (These networks are called *star-wired token rings* because they combine star geometry for wiring with the ring architecture.) The biggest drawback to the ring topology, however, is that when any node fails, most of the network goes down with it. A number of variations including dual bidirectional ring designs have been developed to provide better fault tolerance.

Media Access Control: How Nodes Send and Receive Data

Topologies reveal how the many nodes on a network may potentially access one another, but this is only part of the story. At another level, we can ask how nodes carry out communication. For example, on a bus network all of the nodes can access the medium at once. How can we organize things so that communication is practical? In other words, how are messages transmitted among nodes in a timely, reliable manner? This process is called **media access control** (**MAC**).

The methods for communication from node to node are called MAC protocols. As you know, a protocol is a set of standards or rules. A MAC protocol defines how a given node accesses the channel for a transmission to another specific node on the network. We restrict our survey to two methods employed by most LANs. Both are packet switching MAC protocols.

The most popular is the **Ethernet MAC protocol,** which is typically implemented on baseband networks employing either bus or star topologies. The term *Ethernet* is, in fact, a brand name that has seeped into the vernacular much as *Kleenex* is synonymous with facial tissues. Originally, Ethernet was a proprietary protocol of the Xerox Corporation. It was later standardized by the consortium of Xerox, Intel, and Digital Equipment Corporation. Today, there are numerous commercial versions of the original protocol. These adhere to the standard defined as IEEE (pronounced "I triple E") 802.3. More formally, it is called CSMA/CD, which stands for carrier sense multiple access with collision detection. Now you can understand why the name *Ethernet* has caught on.

The Ethernet protocol is based on packet switching and functions very much like conversation around the dinner table for a large family. At the dinner table, it is possible for anyone to speak to anyone else at any time. Of course, this is not very practical. If everyone

Figure 17.9

In a ring topology, the nodes are arranged in a closed path that is usually unidirectional. Signals are passed from one node to another by interfaces that act as repeaters.

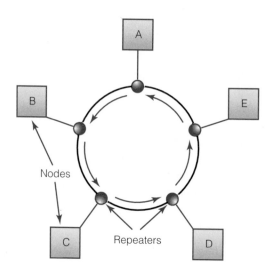

decided to talk at once, chaos would ensue. Instead, being polite, you would normally wait until there was a lull in the conversation to speak. At that instant, you would direct your comment to a particular person, though everyone else at the table could hear you. On an Ethernet LAN, the transmitter listens to the channel, waiting for a moment when the communications channel is idle. At that instant, it transmits a packet on the channel.

Two things can happen in a normally functioning Ethernet LAN network: Transmission can be successful or unsuccessful. A successful transmission occurs when all nodes on the network hear the packet (just as everyone at the table can hear your comment), but only the addressee receives and processes the packet. An unsuccessful transmission occurs when two or more packets are transmitted from different nodes simultaneously. (Compare this with two people speaking at once at the table.) This is called a **packet collision.** In these instances, the transmission is likely garbled, and the packets received are discarded.

In the event of packet collisions, all nodes employ a **backoff procedure.** This means that they invoke steps that result in their waiting for another try to transmit. A simple variation is to wait a random amount of time before trying again. (This is very likely what you would do at the dinner table, too.) After backing off, any node can attempt to transmit whether it was one of the original transmitters or not.

In sum, the Ethernet protocol amounts to an orderly chaos. It works well for relatively low-load, or what is called "bursty," traffic, and for LANs in which the number of nodes and the length of messages transmitted are not too great. As the amount of traffic on an Ethernet network grows, the amount of waiting time for completing transmissions can become annoyingly noticeable.

The **token passing MAC protocol** was designed to manage communication on a ring topology. Unlike the Ethernet protocol, token passing is very orderly, even courteous. The most common variation employs a single packet, called the **token,** which is routed continuously around the ring. Any node can become the token controller once the token is freed from any previous transmissions. The token controller adds data to the token and addresses it to its intended recipient. Other nodes pass the token along the ring to the receiver. The token controller continues to transmit packets in this manner until the message is complete. It then frees and passes the token along to the other nodes. See Figure 17.10.

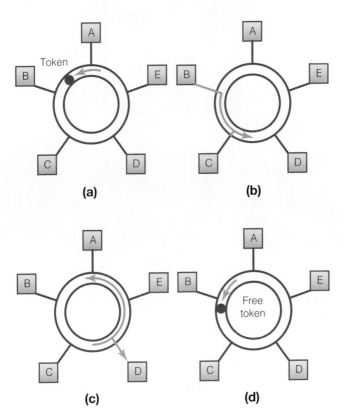

(a)   (b)   (c)   (d)

Figure 17.10

(a) Suppose that node B must communicate a message to node D. B waits until a free token passes through. Taking control of the free token, B marks the token busy, adds data, and addresses it to D. (b) B transmits the token to its successor along the ring. C recognizes that the packet is not addressed to it. C passes or repeats the occupied token the next station, D. (c) Node D recognizes that the packet is for it and copies it. The token is marked as received and again passed along the ring. Stations E and A pass the still-busy token back to B to complete the ring. (d) The process continues until B has transmitted all packets of the message successfully to D. After the last packet is acknowledged, B releases the token, marking it free again. It will be passed along to the first station that requires it to send a message.

The token passing protocol has several advantages. The token ring network can serve a large number of nodes. It is best suited to high-load networks because each node is guaranteed access to the network within a predictable maximum amount of waiting time. (In contrast, a busy Ethernet network could potentially freeze out a station when numerous packet collisions occur.)

Networking Software

A network's physical transport system is the collection of hardware and software that acts as the plumbing for the network. So far we have outlined the physical transport for a LAN. In other words, communications channels and topology detail how signals are transmitted from

Figure 17.11

User-to-user communication in a LAN is accomplished through a series of layers created by both hardware and software. The physical layer is the bottommost layer that transfers the signals. The data link layer manages the point-to-point connections from one node to the next in support of the end-to-end transmission. The network layer serves to route the data from sender to destination. The transport layer provides messaging services on which applications—and the application layer—are based.

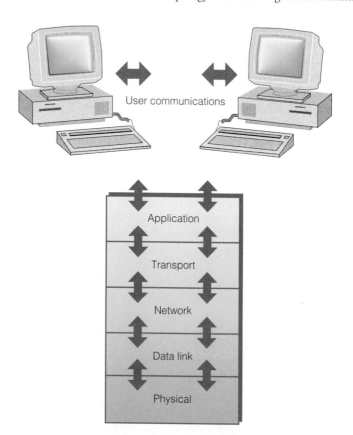

User communications

Application

Transport

Network

Data link

Physical

DISCOVERING MORE

Ethernet LANs

Today, Ethernet technology is the most popular choice for local area networking. Ethernet has achieved this vaulted status because the technology has evolved or adapted more quickly to meet the demands of the marketplace. Ethernet formulations such as 10BaseT, FastEthernet, and GigabitEthernet are examples of its generations. To find out what these are and more about this ubiquitous technology, consult our online resource "Discovering More About Ethernet LANs."

one node to another on a LAN. The design and function of networking software provide another way to differentiate LANs.

A wide variety of vendors offer networking software solutions for an assortment of hardware platforms and network configurations, but all this software adheres to a layered network model. As mentioned above, and illustrated in Figure 17.11, network software is built on top of the **physical transmission layer.** Several layers of network software contribute to the overall functionality available to end users. Each layer is a distinct set of programs that depend on the services of the preceding one. Such a layered design separates tasks at different levels.

The **data link** layer is usually defined by the MAC protocol. Thus, it supports basic connectivity between communicating nodes by handling the transmission of data from one link to another. The **network** system layer establishes the geography of the network. The **transport** layer provides communications services between nodes in the networks. These messages are the foundation of the applications that are so important to us. Finally, the **application** layer consists of programs that provide the user with features such as a convenient interface for exploiting the network's connectivity. Network applications, of course, are often designed using the client/server model.

Consider sending instant messages to a friend from your computer. The application is designed to permit you to send and receive messages from a list of available users. The application employs the services of the transport layer to find out who is currently connected and likewise manage the transmission of packets that frame your messages. The transport layer, in turn, calls on the network layer to route the packets from sender to destination. The data link and physical layers handle the actual work of moving bits that make up that data from one to point to another.

This "divide-and-conquer" approach to networking software has significant advantages. First, each layer is relatively autonomous; it can function without having to manage the messy details of what goes on in lower layers. For example, applications need only to know what kind of messages they can send rather than fussing over how to package the data and convert it to signals, and so on. This simplifies the task of writing and developing software. Secondly, the separation of layers means that their implementations may be modified, substituted, or replaced easily. The transport layer, for instance, does not know whether the physical layer employs bounded media such as copper or fiber optics, or whether it depends on wireless transmissions. It might be any one of these. Continuing our example, improvements in the physical layer could be incorporated without the necessity of reconstructing the transport and intervening layers. (We will return to consider this important concept of a layered network architecture in the next chapter.)

Extending LANs

Like most other technologies, the more that we depend on LANs, the more we expect from them. Consequently, it is commonplace to expand the physical range and size of LANs. We will briefly examine an array of devices that extend the scale of local area networks: repeaters, bridges, switches, and routers.

Repeaters, Bridges, Switches, and Routers

The success of local area networking has produced some problems. As more and more users are introduced to the benefits of networking, the size of a LAN grows—in both distance spanned and the number of nodes attached. As the number of independent LANs in a business or organization grows, it is natural to want to interconnect them, too, but autonomous LANs may have different hardware and protocols. The challenge, then, is to provide for both expansion and interconnectivity while preserving manageable networks with satisfactory performance. The solution usually is to maintain autonomous networks while creating controlled access among them. It is customary today to refer to intraorganizational collections of networks as *intranets* to distinguish them from the worldwide network called the *Internet.* A variety of tools are available to extend and connect networks. These include repeaters, bridges, switches, and routers.

■ **Repeaters.** Hardware devices that boost the strength of the signal on a communications channel are called **repeaters.** As mentioned earlier, media have practical limits on how far the signal may be transmitted before it weakens. Repeaters amplify, retime, and retransmit the signal, thereby allowing the LAN to extend beyond the normal practical limits. See Figure 17.12. Repeaters can also be used to enlarge the number of nodes in a LAN. Of course, as the number of nodes increases, the traffic increases, which, in turn, may cause network performance to degrade.

Normally, a repeater connects two segments of a LAN as shown in Figure 17.12, but it also is possible to connect more than two segments using hubs. Thus, the topology of the network is converted to a star configuration that contains possibly other nested topologies. See Figure 17.13 for an illustration.

■ **Bridges.** A **bridge** is a hardware device connecting two or more networks that may have differing LAN technologies. Unlike repeaters, which merely pass packets from one network to the other, bridges preserve the autonomy of the interconnecting networks. They do so by screening transmissions and passing only those intended to cross networks. See Figure 17.14. As mentioned, bridges can connect networks with different characteristics. For example, a bridge can be used to connect 10 Mbps and 100 Mbps Ethernet LANs. A bridge is also a smart device; it can employ a technique called *self-learning* to build tables mapping the locations and addresses of nodes among the networks it connects. This means that bridges can be added to a network with little or no fuss—affording "plug-and-play" functionality for the network administration.

Figure 17.12

A repeater extends the span of an existing LAN past its recommended maximum length by amplifying the signal across the transmission medium.

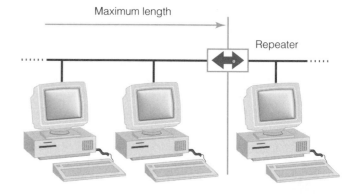

Figure 17.13

A backbone hub connects two other star networks. This expands the network in both range and number in a similar fashion as adding repeaters. Signals automatically pass through the backbone hub for the other subnetwork.

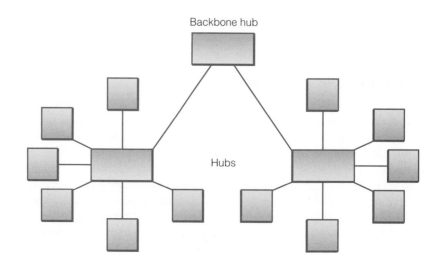

■ **Switches.** A LAN switch is a hybrid device that combines the capabilities of repeaters and bridges with additional features. Specifically, a **switch** provides both dedicated and shared connections for a large number of nodes in a LAN. See Figure 17.15.

LAN switches offer several dedicated access interfaces; because there is no contention, these nodes have collision-free communication. In a standard Ethernet network, nodes can either send signals or receive them. This is called **half-duplex.** Switches, on the other hand, support two-way or **full-duplex** communication. Their increased capacity and support for multiple conversations translate to overall improved network performance.

■ **Routers. Routers** are devices that connect networks of the same or different types. These devices are directed by software to provide greater data throughput for the intranet by selecting efficient routes for the data to travel. Routers can also serve as gateways or connections to the outside world.

The chief difference between routers and devices such as bridges or switches is that the latter operate exclusively at the network data link layer. This means that nodes are known by their physical or built-in addresses. By contrast, the router uses network addressing information to determine what path to send or transmit packets. Specifically, routers attempt to find a path

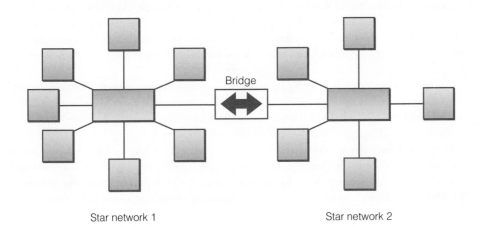

Star network 1   Star network 2

Figure 17.14
A bridge connects two networks. The bridge allows packets intended for the other LAN to pass through while it blocks packets intended for the originating LAN. This screening helps to preserve the performance of each autonomous LAN within its confines yet interconnects them.

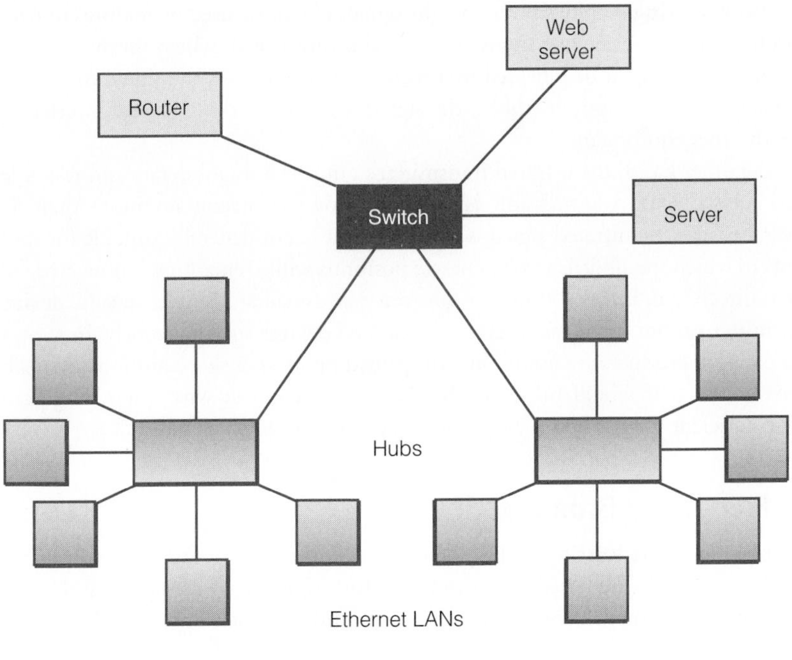

Web server

Router

Switch

Server

Hubs

Ethernet LANs

Figure 17.15
Switches can be used to join a variety of networking components. This figure illustrates two office LANs connected to a single switch. Each node has shared access to the realm outside its own LAN. In contrast, the two servers and the router—which connects the LANs to the outside world—have fast, dedicated access to the switch. In other words, their links are direct and not shared. Switches can also manage links at different speeds. Thus, we might imagine the link to the router to be the fastest, in order to get data in and out of the intranet as quickly as possible.

Table 17.1　*Comparing features among LAN interconnection devices.*

	Repeaters	Bridges	Switches	Routers
Traffic isolation	no	yes	yes	yes
"Plug-and-play"	yes	yes	yes	no
Optimal routing	no	no	no	yes

connecting the sender and receiver rather than flooding the network with duplicate packets in hopes of finding the destination. (We will return to the issue of routing in the next chapter.)

Consult Table 17.1 for a comparison of interconnection devices used to extend or expand LANs.

Wireless Networking

The suggestion of a wireless network—a network connected without using wires—may sound exotic or newfangled, yet broadcast methods for data communications have been around for decades. In fact, the model for Ethernet packet switching was the ALOHA network (circa early 1970s) that connected radio frequency broadcast stations in the Hawaiian Islands. Although satellite, microwave relay, and radio wave transmissions are common in wide area networks, these wireless or broadcast methods for local area networks are relative newcomers on the scene.

Wireless technology has several advantages. It is a cost-effective answer to linking systems in buildings where wiring is prohibitively expensive. It works well also for connecting LANs between buildings that otherwise are too remote to wire without leasing dedicated lines. The rising popularity of laptop or notebook computer systems, as well as hand-held PDAs, also fuels the demand for wireless networking. Portable computing requires mobile connectivity. In other words, a LAN must be flexible enough to provide connectivity anywhere in a prescribed range in which the user transports his or her system. Today **wireless local area networks** (**WLANs**) are available in two broadcast forms, based on either infrared or radio frequencies.

Infrared Broadcasting

Infrared broadcasting employs infrared light signals like those used by remote control devices found in home entertainment systems. The signal is directional, which means the transmitter must be aimed directly at or reflected to a receiver that translates the signal to ordinary electrical signals. Like fiber optic methods, the signal is free from the electrical interference associated with other equipment.

On the other hand, the infrared transmitter's range is only moderate and much less than bounded media. Data transmission is relatively slow promising no more than 1 Mbps. Moreover, because the infrared signal is directional, it is not generally suitable for mobile applications in which the node is free to change positions while remaining "connected." And because it is directional, infrared transmissions must be aimed at a single, specific device. Thus, the transmitter cannot broadcast messages to several devices simultaneously. In sum, wireless infrared network products are useful only for providing inexpensive communications between stationary nodes that would otherwise be difficult to connect with wires. For example, it would be sufficient for connecting a portable laptop to an office printer.

Radio Frequency Broadcasting

Radio frequency broadcasting employs radio transmissions. For WLAN applications, these transmissions typically are based on spread spectrum signaling—also used by some cell telephone technologies. **Spread spectrum** is a method used to modulate digital information by dividing it into small pieces and sending them over discrete frequencies within the signal bandwidth. The idea was invented and patented in 1942 by film actress Hedy Lamarr. (No, really.) Although it was ignored during WWII, technologies based on this scheme were used by the military for a number of years, because it is resistant to interference (cannot be jammed easily) and difficult to intercept.

The standard analogy used to illuminate spread spectrum is that of sending payloads using multiple trains or trucks. Imagine a large delivery divided among several trucks that left at the same time but took different routes to the same destination. The payload, of course, would be reassembled at the destination site. Let's assume that deliveries are not fail-safe. They might be intercepted by hijackers or impeded by other misfortunes. Our payload would be more secure because we have distributed it over so many routes. Suppose also that we also sent some of the trucks with duplicate cargos. This would protect us further against corrupted or lost deliveries.

Spread spectrum comes in two flavors: **direct-sequence spread spectrum** (**DSSS**) and **frequency-hopping spread spectrum** (**FHSS**). In terms of our analogy, DSSS would mean that each truck is assigned a specific route that it always takes. In other words, the information is always divided over a range of assigned channels—their number and frequencies depend upon the system used. By contrast, FHSS would mean that trucks were free to use different routes for different deliveries. Initially, the routes may be assigned randomly, but, over time, information is gathered about which ones are safe and which are not. Devices using FHSS send a short signal and then shift frequencies to send another short burst of information. FHSS can adapt to problems caused by interference by avoiding those channels. The sender and receiver, of course, must agree on the selection of frequencies, even if their sequence is not known. DSSS uses most of its entire bandwidth. As a result, it is faster though susceptible to problems resulting from interference. DSSS can employ redundancy in order to minimize garbled signals. FHSS uses a single frequency very briefly before it hops to another. There is less likelihood of signals colliding in that channel. As a result, FHSS is less prone to interference and can, in fact, function satisfactorily in areas where there are competing networks using the same frequencies.

WLAN Topologies

As in wired LANs, wireless devices must be arranged or organized in particular ways in order to communicate. For technical reasons, the range of a WLAN is restricted to a limited broadcast area. This is referred to as a *cell* or—more often—a **basic service set** (**BSS**). The strength of the signal, the transmission method, and usable frequencies are some of the factors that determine the effective area of a BSS. The typical BSS contains one or more wireless devices or stations and a central base station called an **access point (AP).** See Figure 17.16. An access point is usually a stationary device connected to some other networking source: a wired Ethernet LAN, an ISP, and so on. Like a bridge in a wired network, the AP acts as an interface between the wireless network and the rest of the world. Access points typically provide other client services to the stations in its BSS. For example, an AP might register stations in its area; it might supply IP addresses to stations for Internet access, and so on.

Access points may be connected together to form a larger network called a **distribution system.** A distribution system works very much like a bridged network. Messages that are intended for other networks are transferred by its AP, but messages addressed to stations within the same BSS are not. The number of nodes and range of a WLAN can be increased using distribution systems. For example, several buildings on campus can form a distribution system permitting connectivity throughout.

Another topology is known as an **ad hoc network.** It has no central control and is organized in an impromptu manner. See Figure 17.17. Devices within range send signals and form a temporary network based on peer-to-peer relationships. Thus, any station can communicate with any other station within the ad hoc network but not outside it. For instance, a group of notebook computers in a meeting room might form an ad hoc network to exchange data files. At the end of the meeting, the network would dissolve as the stations are taken away.

Figure 17.16

In most wireless networks, a device called an access point serves as the bridge between the stations inside that BSS and the outside world. The access point is usually connected to a wired network and provides the stations with various services. It usually registers stations inside its BSS. Addresses are used for processing communications in and out of the BSS.

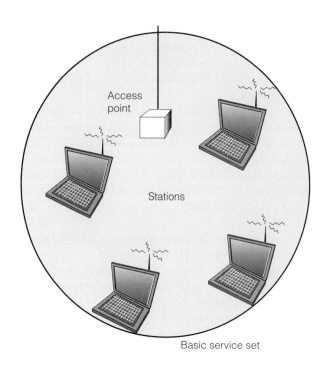

Basic service set

Figure 17.17

In an ad hoc network, the stations contact one another and form a temporary BSS. Each station can communicate with any other station in the network, but not with any outside systems.

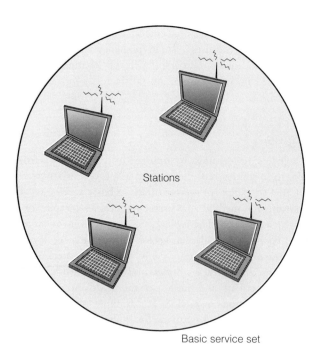

Basic service set

There is one important difference between wired and wireless topologies. Most wired topologies are relatively static. Although new nodes may be added to or deleted from their networks, it takes explicit actions to do so. Wireless topologies are much more dynamic. Any device that comes in range of either an access point or an ad hoc network can join that BSS immediately. In this way, WLANs are designed to support mobile computing.

Wi-Fi (802.11b)

You may recall that we introduced the Ethernet networking standard as IEEE 802.3. In 1997, a wireless version of Ethernet was standardized as IEEE 802.11. The earliest commercial version was dubbed 802.11b to differentiate it from other methods embraced by the standard. Recently, an industry group adopted the friendlier name of "**Wi-Fi**"—pronounced like "Hi-Fi" (as in *high fidelity*).

Wi-Fi employs a single carrier frequency in the Industrial, Scientific, and Medical (ISM) radio band. These are wavelengths that are authorized by the Federal Communications Commission (FCC) without license. The frequency is 2.4 GHz, which is shared by many cell phones and other wireless technologies. Wi-Fi is based on direct sequence spread spectrum methods.

It uses a variation of the Ethernet MAC for sending and receiving packets. Data rates range from 1 or 2 Mbps to 11 Mbps—depending upon signal strength or interference. Wi-Fi networks have effective ranges of about 200 to 400 feet indoors and up to 1,000 feet outdoors. It is also easily integrated into existing wired Ethernet LANs.

HomeRF

HomeRF (for *Radio Frequency*) offers a different approach for wireless networking. Intended for home use and small businesses, it employs frequency-hopping spread spectrum signals. This enables HomeRF to offer a mixed bag of both wireless networking and digital voice communications. Specifically, it can support up to six voice channels in addition to networking communication services. Thus, it is possible to have one or more home computer systems connected to the Internet and phone service at the same time.

Like Wi-Fi, HomeRF transmits at the 2.4 GHz frequency band, but at 50 hops per second. It has data rates ranging from around 2 Mbps up to 10 Mbps. HomeRF is fairly limited in range (100 to 150 feet); and physical obstructions can interfere with normal communication. HomeRF does not integrate well with wired networks. But, because it is intended primarily for consumer use, these usually are not significant factors.

Other Contenders

There are other new wireless technologies that fit under the umbrella of IEEE 802.11. The new standard 802.11g is a proposed successor for Wi-Fi or 802.11b. Much too new to have a friendly name, 802.11g promises data rates up to 54 Mbps. Like its cousin 'b,' 'g' uses DSSS transmission methods. Because it is an extension of 802.11b, 802.11g hardware can be designed backwardly compatible with current Wi-Fi equipment. This means that existing Wi-Fi networks can be upgraded to the higher performance standard of 802.11g without the expense of replacing all equipment.

802.11a is a new standard that also promises high performance—again, maximum data rates of 54 Mbps. Like 'b' and 'g,' it, too, is based on DSSS. Unlike the other letters, 802.11a broadcasts in the 5 GHz frequency band with twelve separate channels. As a result, it should be possible to maintain up to 12 access points tuned to different channels within the same operating area. This can reliably serve many more stations in an especially crowded area while minimizing radio interference. The higher broadcast frequency, however, reduces the effective range of the BSS.

Unfortunately, neither of these two new standards is compatible. Consequently, the marketplace will eventually have to settle the matter.

Personal Area Networks: Bluetooth

Recently, developers have seized upon another potential market for wireless technology—the personal area network. A **personal area network** (**PAN**) is a group of digital devices assembled in a small area that communicate and share information. In many homes and offices, there are a number of digital devices that require or could benefit from data communication links. For example, desktop computers routinely communicate over short distances with devices such as printers, keyboards, mouse, and hand-held PDAs. Likewise, DVD and CD players, televisions, headphones, remote control units, and other home appliances are devices whose operations could be enhanced by data communications. The **Bluetooth** wireless standard was designed to support PAN applications economically and with ease of use for consumers.

Bluetooth likewise uses the already busy 2.4 GHz radio frequency band. Unlike Wi-Fi, though, it employs frequency hopping spread spectrum signaling with adaptive frequencies. In theory, this should reduce interference with other wireless technologies coexisting in the same space.

Bluetooth devices range from desktop and notebook computers, PDAs, printers, cell telephones, home entertainment devices, and remote controls. Each device is equipped with a low-power radio transceiver. These radios produce a FHSS full-duplex signal at up to 1600 hops per second. The signal hops among 79 frequencies at 1 MHz intervals, which minimizes interference. Up to seven simultaneous connections can established and maintained. The range for these radio signals is small: only about 30 feet. Moreover, the 1 Mbps data rates are much slower than WLAN technologies. But these limitations should be sufficient for the type of applications prescribed.

Bluetooth devices send to and receive signals from devices in the area automatically. If a given device receives a signal within its addressing range, the devices will form a network. Thus, designated Bluetooth devices can form an ad hoc network of up to eight devices transparently—without the user performing any special actions. Single networks—called *piconets*—can join with nearby piconets to form scatternets. Like distribution systems, a scatternet enables the linking of additional devices over longer distances.

The forecasts for Bluetooth applications and appliances are bright, but it remains to be seen whether the consumer market will embrace both Bluetooth and PAN applications.

DISCOVERING MORE

Wireless Networking

Like other new technologies, the wireless picture is constantly changing. To find out the latest, consult our online resource "Discovering More About Wireless Networking."

FOCUS Broadband Networks

The chief limitation of the types of networks examined so far is their bandwidth. These networks perform well for applications such as messaging or e-mail, file transfers, and the like. But, services such as videoconferencing and real-time multimedia transmissions require higher performance. Likewise, as the total number of users in a network increases, the performance of traditional baseband networks also degrades. Higher bandwidth is the solution for both of these problems. Asynchronous Transfer Mode (ATM) networks, for example, offer higher performance connectivity. To learn about ATM networks and the demands of broadband data transmission, consult our online resource "Focus on Broadband Networks."

■ Summary

Computer networks connect peripherals and other independently functioning computer systems from mainframes to desktop computers. Local area networks (LANs) connect computers and devices spread over a restricted physical area—anywhere from a single room to a cluster of buildings, typically. Dedicated computer systems called servers connect to all of the nodes on the LAN and may provide coordination for its operation. Each computer functioning as a LAN node must have specific hardware to connect to the network and customized software to manage the connection. Different kinds of computer systems can be connected to a given LAN provided they employ compatible network hardware and software.

The primary advantages of using a LAN are communication, management control, and cost-effectiveness. Although certain costs are associated with LANs, most organizations have concluded that the benefits of LANs far outweigh their costs. In fact, networking today is an essential component in organizational computing environments.

LANs are differentiated by the transmission media used in the communications channels they employ, the network topologies used to organize their connections, the media access control (MAC) protocols used to manage the network communications, and the supporting network software and hardware. Typical transmission media include twisted-pair cable, coaxial cable, and optical fiber cable. The bus, ring, and star topologies are the most common wired LAN network topologies. The Ethernet and token passing protocols, both based on packet switching, are the two most popular MAC protocols for these LANs.

Network hardware and software services are organized as a layered hierarchy. The network's physical transmission system is the collection of hardware and software that acts as the plumbing for the network and serves as the base layer on which other layers are built. The data link is the next layer; its function is to ensure basic connectivity between communicating nodes. Next, the network services layer provides routing to other nodes and networks. The transport layer manages messaging. Finally, the applications layer consists of programs providing the user with features such as a convenient interface for exploiting the variety of network services available.

Repeaters, bridges, switches, and routers are combination hardware/software devices that allow LANs to be expanded and connected to other LANs. These devices allow organizations to combine and connect different LANs into organizational intranets.

Wireless LANs use either infrared or radio broadcast methods to transmit to stations. Most wireless LANs today employ spread spectrum technology (like cell phones) to communicate. Several wireless Ethernet standards have been proposed. These offer the highest speeds and compatibility with existing wired networks.

■ Terms

access point (AP)	full-duplex	ring topology
ad hoc network	half-duplex	routers
application layer	HomeRF	spooler (print)
backoff procedure	hub	spread spectrum
basic service set (BSS)	infrared broadcasting	star topology
Bluetooth	media access control (MAC)	switches
bridges	network interface card (NIC)	token
bus	network layer	token passing MAC
bus topology	optical fiber cable	topology
coaxial cable	packet collision	transport layer
data link layer	passwords	twisted-pair wiring
direct sequence spread spectrum (DSSS)	personal area network (PAN)	unshielded twisted-pair (UTP)
distribution system	physical transmission layer	Wi-Fi (802.11b)
Ethernet MAC	radio frequency broadcasting	wireless LANs (WLANs)
frequency-hopping spread spectrum (FHSS)	repeaters	

■ Questions for Review

1. Give a brief description of a local area network (LAN).

2. What does print spooling mean?

3. Identify some of the basic characteristics of a LAN.

4. Briefly describe the advantages of LANs for computer users. Also describe their advantages for the system's administration as well.

5. What are some of the disadvantages of LANs?

6. What is a distributed computing environment? What are some advantages of this organization? Some disadvantages?

7. LANs may be distinguished by their communications channels, topologies, and media access control. What do these terms signify?

8. What are the chief practical differences between the bounded media of twisted-pair, coaxial cabling, and optical fiber?

9. Describe the star network topology. What are its strengths and weaknesses?

10. Describe the bus network topology. What are its strengths and weaknesses?

11. Describe the ring network topology. What are its strengths and weaknesses?

12. What advantages are achieved by "star-wiring" either a bus or a ring topology?

13. What does the acronym MAC stand for? What does it mean?

14. Describe the basics of the Ethernet packet switching MAC protocol.

15. What is meant by a packet collision? How is such an event resolved?

16. Describe the basics of the token passing MAC protocol.

17. Give a brief description of the networking hardware and software systems called *repeaters, bridges, switches,* and *routers.* What are the practical differences between these?

18. List the different layers of LAN networking software and describe the basic function(s) of each layer.

19. What are the advantages of wireless LANs?

20. Compare and contrast the different wireless Ethernet versions (i.e., 802.11a, Wi-Fi, and 802.11g).

21. Both HomeRF and Bluetooth wireless technologies employ frequency-hopping transmissions. Explain how this works.

Chapter 18

The Internet

OBJECTIVES

- How the Internet evolved from an experimental network in the 1970s

- How your computer can communicate across the world with other computers over a span of diverse interconnected networks

- How Internet applications are based on client/server architecture

- Basic Internet applications: electronic mail, file transfers, remote logins, and HTTP (e.g., WWW)

- Examining the future for the Internet

The growth in the use of the World Wide Web over the past decade has been nothing short of phenomenal, and for many people the Web has become almost synonymous with computing itself. Of course, you know that computing encompasses a much larger digital domain.

You also know that the World Wide Web itself is part of a larger collection of computer networks called the Internet. As a Web user, you have already ventured out on the Internet. You may even feel that you are a seasoned traveler. Even so, we are all pioneers on the brink of the electronic frontier because the Internet today is too large and too complicated for anyone to comprehend its scope and depth fully. The numbers of networks and computers connected to it grow and change so rapidly that current counts can only be estimated. The number of users and the amount of information that courses through it are beyond all but ballpark guesses.

The Internet, though, is more than just hardware and software. The Internet is a vast repository of digital information—a worldwide electronic library. It is a library that never closes, a library that is forever renovating and expanding, and a library that lends many of its resources freely and openly.

The Internet is more than a repository of information; it also serves as the foundation for a variety of extremely useful applications. Besides supporting the Web, the Internet is the medium for electronic mail, remote logins, sending and receiving files, and a host of other specialized applications.

The Internet is also a community of individuals. The services and information that you can find on the Internet are, of course, put there by people. In fact, a significant portion of the Internet is maintained by the voluntary efforts of a great number of individuals who have offered their talents as a gift to all of us. Indeed, the secret of the incredible success of this enterprise is due, in no small part, to the fact that the Internet is not owned by anybody and—at least at its inception—is not ruled by commercial concerns. In this chapter, you will learn more about this truly amazing entity.

A Short History of the Internet

In the late 1960s, the U.S. Department of Defense, through the Advanced Research Projects Agency (ARPA, and later DARPA, for Defense Advanced Research Projects Agency), sponsored a series of projects designed to create a network of computers that could communicate with one another over long distances. This network came to be known as **ARPANET**. Its goal was to connect research universities and defense contractors so that they could share computing facilities and information.

The success of the project depended on resolving several formidable challenges. First, computer systems made by different vendors could not communicate readily with one another. Like the Tower of Babel, different systems had different protocols (that is, standards and conventions) for both the representation and transmission of data. Second, the computers were remotely located. Commercial carriers such as telephone lines were the only practical means for connecting these systems. Third, the Department of Defense was interested in creating a loosely coupled network—one that might survive attacks on single sites. A loosely coupled system can tolerate the loss of individual components while maintaining the integrity of the system as a whole.

Interestingly, all these factors proved fortuitous for the evolution of the Internet. Indeed, serendipity is a common theme for the evolution of the Internet even today: Earlier decisions and directions have had entirely unexpected results.

Experiments continued, and the network grew during the 1970s. The design of this network reflected its original goals well. From its inception, it was engineered to overcome both the problems of distance and unreliability. ARPANET was an entirely "democratic" network. All the nodes in the network were equal. Any node could originate, pass along, or receive messages. Messages were divided into parts, called *packets*, which could be routed across the network along different paths. The receiver would reassemble the message after all the parts had arrived. Even though this was not terribly efficient, it was very robust. It was the responsibility of each node to support and maintain its own connectivity to the network. There were no central authorities.

In 1978, DARPA established a common protocol for data transmission between systems. The adoption of this common network protocol, called *TCP/IP* (we examine TCP/IP in more detail in the next section), proved to be a significant watershed in our story. Because it was developed by researchers, with no commercial involvement, TCP/IP favored no established vendors. This created a level playing field in which everyone had potentially equal access. And the use of a single standard protocol meant that the Tower of Babel was razed in favor of a common tongue. Another important feature of TCP/IP is that it created a distributed system; tasks were distributed among different components of the network. In short, a network built on TCP/IP is an open system, meaning that there is neither centralized control nor a favored hardware platform.

In the early 1980s, the University of California at Berkeley developed a flavor of the UNIX operating system that incorporated TCP/IP. Berkeley UNIX, as it came to be known, was distributed widely for a variety of hardware platforms (and at low cost) to universities, colleges, and other institutions. This proved to be mutually beneficial. TCP/IP became a *de facto* protocol for interconnecting computer networks, and it also helped to propagate UNIX as the natural environment for the Internet. Although today's Internet applications do not depend on UNIX and can be supported by a variety of operating systems, UNIX versions remain both influential and commonplace.

Also in the 1980s, the National Science Foundation (NSF) embarked on a mission that would expand ARPANET technology to a wider collection of universities. Originally, the collection of networks known as **NSFNET** was conceived to connect supercomputer centers to other wide area networks for sharing scientific research. The original notion (authored by Dennis Jennings of University College, Dublin) was to create a "backbone" network that could serve as the major connector with supercomputer centers and other regional networks, linking universities and colleges. The number and complexity of these regional providers grew during the late 1980s.

In 1990, the Department of Defense decommissioned ARPANET, leaving U.S. networking responsibilities to NSF, NASA, and a few other agencies. At about the same time, the NSF relaxed its fair usage policy, which had restrained commercial activities on the Internet, and increased the carrying capacity of its network backbone considerably. As a result, more and more commercial firms joined the network. Many regional network providers, both commercial and subsidized, were also connected, and "the" **Internet,** or the Information Highway, emerged as a collection of diverse computer networks that span the globe.

Since 1990, the Internet has experienced incredible growth. No doubt one of the primary reasons for this growth has been the introduction of the hypertext system known as the *World Wide Web*. You have already experienced how the Web allows Internet users to communicate and view information in a most user-friendly mode. It would be difficult to overestimate the impact that the Web has had on the development of the Internet.

In 1995, the NSFNET backbone was officially decommissioned. The responsibilities for network transport services were taken over by a number of commercial providers. Many of these were for-profit spin-offs of the regional providers subsidized in the earlier years by the NSF. Today, most of the original players such as ARPANET and NSFNET and others have gone the way of the dinosaurs. Even so, the Internet still thrives. In its fifth decade, the Internet's pace of growth is slowing down somewhat, but it remains the dominant medium for storing, transmitting, and sharing information.

DISCOVERING MORE

Sizing the Internet

Exactly how big is the Internet? Why is it difficult to resolve this issue? What can we measure to estimate its span? To find out more about these questions and to learn about some of the ongoing projects that track the Internet's growth, consult our online resource "Discovering More About Sizing the Internet."

Though the technology and the players have changed, the Internet retains many of its original characteristics. The Internet is still a loosely coupled mesh of distributed, open networks that has no real center or single governing body. Networks are added to its topography freely, and the number of nodes or hosts connected to it is still expanding. International participation is widespread; there are very few places in the world that you cannot reach via the Internet. And while TCP/IP remains the dominant protocol for data communications across networks, other protocols coexist with it. Currently, it is estimated that the Internet connects more than 200,000 networks and over 150 million computers as hosts (i.e., permanent nodes)—and these numbers continue to grow. Many more desktop and laptop computers connect to it as temporary nodes, and the Internet likely has in excess of 580 million users.

From the beginning, the Internet has avoided the type of control that is exercised on networks created by private commercial interests (e.g., America Online). Veteran users would be quick to point out that the Internet fosters a democratic, open exchange of ideas and information. On the other hand, the price of an open forum is that data added to the Internet is not subject to review or approval.

This situation is changing, though. The U.S. government is currently relinquishing its involvement in the Internet to private interests. Although some express concerns that complete

Figure 18.1

This timeline marks some of the more significant events in the development of the Internet.

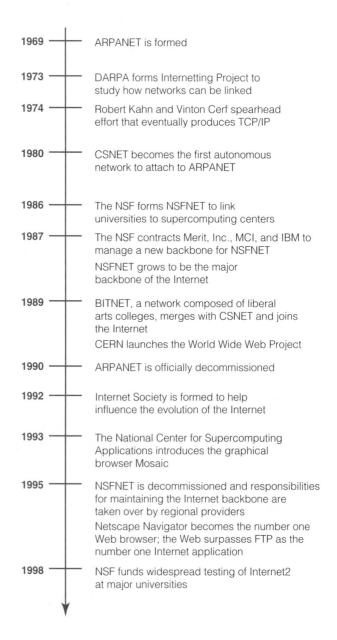

1969	ARPANET is formed
1973	DARPA forms Internetting Project to study how networks can be linked
1974	Robert Kahn and Vinton Cerf spearhead effort that eventually produces TCP/IP
1980	CSNET becomes the first autonomous network to attach to ARPANET
1986	The NSF forms NSFNET to link universities to supercomputing centers
1987	The NSF contracts Merit, Inc., MCI, and IBM to manage a new backbone for NSFNET
	NSFNET grows to be the major backbone of the Internet
1989	BITNET, a network composed of liberal arts colleges, merges with CSNET and joins the Internet
	CERN launches the World Wide Web Project
1990	ARPANET is officially decommissioned
1992	Internet Society is formed to help influence the evolution of the Internet
1993	The National Center for Supercomputing Applications introduces the graphical browser Mosaic
1995	NSFNET is decommissioned and responsibilities for maintaining the Internet backbone are taken over by regional providers
	Netscape Navigator becomes the number one Web browser; the Web surpasses FTP as the number one Internet application
1998	NSF funds widespread testing of Internet2 at major universities

commercialization might diminish the virtues of the Internet as it exists today, the hope is that privatization will support the growth and needed modernization of the Information Highway.

The timeline shown in Figure 18.1 summarizes some of the more important events in the swiftly evolving story of the Internet. What's next? No one knows for sure, and the debate about the future of the Internet is vigorous and ongoing. A safe bet is that the Internet will indeed change, most likely as rapidly and unpredictably as it has evolved.

How the Internet Works

The Internet is a packet switching network. But unlike other packet switching networks such as the LANs providing service at your school, the Internet is a confederation of many separately owned and operated networks. These networks often have very different hardware, protocols, and configurations. How, then, is it possible for information to travel worldwide across such different network structures? The key, of course, is that networks that connect to the Internet do so because they agree to follow specific guidelines for the packaging and routing of data. Moreover, there is a dedicated infrastructure that links these networks and ensures global connectivity.

In the last chapter, you learned that networking applications are built upon a hierarchical layered architecture that separates and distributes different tasks and services. Since its inception, the Internet has operated on this model. As mentioned, the Internet protocols are usually referred to collectively as "TCP/IP." In fact, there is a suite of Internet protocols; TCP and IP are prominent pieces—but just pieces—of that suite. In order to understand how the sending and receiving of information works, we will focus here on two layers of this architecture: namely, transport and routing. First, we will examine the principles of routing packets. Afterwards, we will consider the Internet's transport or messaging services.

Datagrams, IP Addressing, and Routers

Information transmitted over the Internet takes the form of a sequence of packets called **datagrams**. Think of a datagram as a packet of data in a plain, brown wrapper addressed with receiver and sender. The scheme is similar to commercial parcel post. Documents must be placed in standardized envelopes or containers that are assigned numbers to identify the parcel, its sender, and its destination. Uniform containers make it easier to ship parcels. The parcel service also uses these shipping numbers for more efficient monitoring of delivery. Moving data within the Internet is organized along these same principles.

Once the data packets are certified for delivery, **IP** (or **Internet Protocol**) is responsible for routing them. Each computer system that is officially part of the Internet has an IP address. These addresses consist of four numbers—each of which is less than 256. IP addresses are usually written with period separators. For example, the authors' departmental Web server has the IP address of 156.143.143.130.

Postal addressing has several components. For example, you are usually identified by name, street address, city, state, and zip code. The same is true for IP addresses. The difference is that IP addresses are hierarchical. The first portion of the IP address denotes the network to which the computer belongs. Succeeding numbers may define subsets of that network or individual machines. Thus, the IP number itself provides information about the whereabouts of its host. Once a packet has IP addresses attached for both sender and receiver, it becomes a datagram.

To understand how IP manages the transmission of data across networks, let's examine how an electronic mail message to a friend on another campus might be delivered. The typical message, of course, is divided into smaller, uniform packets for transmission. For Internet delivery, the packets must be converted to datagrams with IP addresses signifying the sender and the recipient. The packets would be sent from your mail server to the router that serves as the gateway from your LAN to the Internet.

Recall in the previous chapter that we defined a router as a hardware/software system that acts as a bridge between two networks. A router repeats and translates data transmissions between networks that may have different hardware and protocols. See Figure 18.2. But there is more than just connectivity.

Routing, as we mentioned, belongs to the network layer. This is because routers have two different, but related, responsibilities. First, and obviously, they are responsible for sending datagrams to their intended destinations. This means choosing a path that leads to that destination. But, they are also responsible for ensuring that datagrams are not sent over other unrelated networks. By contrast, we saw that the Ethernet MAC delivers packets by flooding the network with them. This brute-force approach is okay for a small LAN, but it would completely cripple the Internet. Thus, Internet routers are configured with special knowledge about their network neighborhood. This knowledge helps them choose on what paths to route data and what paths to avoid when routing data.

Figure 18.2

A host packages and transmits a message to the gateway router connecting its home LAN to the Internet. The datagrams are transported by a series of routers managed by national and regional providers—both commercial and governmental. The routers push these datagrams through various hops until they arrive at the gateway router of the destination LAN. The message is then sent to the addressee, which processes it.

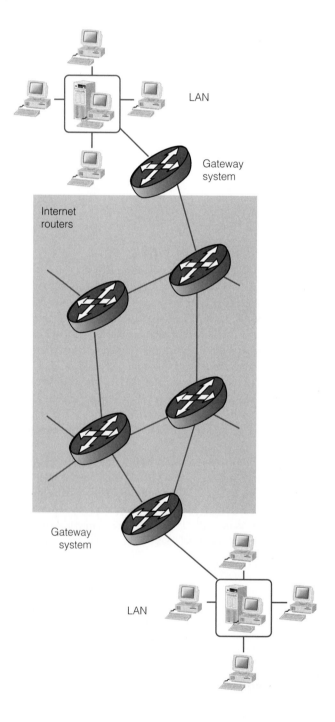

Internet routers also divide the responsibility of maintaining the network at different levels. Some routers review packets to make sure that the addressing is satisfactory. Other routers decide on paths for sending packets, often based on estimating current use of network carriers. Still other routers merely repeat the data along the path. The datagrams of the e-mail message are injected into this mesh of router systems and race to their addressee. Once they are inside this infrastructure, our e-mail packets lose their identity as parts of a message. Instead, they are merely several among millions of datagrams that course through the system.

Datagrams can travel over a variety of networks and media before reaching their appointed destination. National and international providers transmit high volumes of data at high speeds over **backbone routers**. Regional network providers route data to and from sites that they connect. Data may be transmitted over telephone lines, fiber optics, microwave relays, and dedicated high-speed transmission lines. Some data may be relayed using radio transmission by satellite. Like most aspects of the Internet, the carriers and media are greatly diversified and distributed.

Finally, the datagrams arrive at the gateway router to the local network to which your friend's computer is connected. They are transmitted to a system that provides his or her mail service. This machine collects the pieces and reassembles them as a message. All of this can be achieved in fractions of a second.

Although our example is based on an e-mail message, other Internet transmissions proceed in exactly the same manner. At the IP or network layer, one datagram is much like any other. The Internet from this perspective is a global mesh of routers transmitting millions of datagrams every second.

Domain Names

Considering the tremendous number of networks and systems connected to the Internet, keeping up with the IP addresses of systems can be an incredible nightmare for humans. Routers don't have these problems because they are supplied with configuration tables that map these addresses. Fortunately for us humans, and as you learned in Chapter 4, the organizers of the Internet adopted a more convenient (for us) method for addressing called the Domain Name System (DNS). Instead of IP numbers that are arranged hierarchically, a domain name is a sequence of names also separated by periods that uniquely identifies an Internet node. You've already seen some advantages of this system in your work with Web URLs.

Domain names must be registered, but beyond that restriction all but the highest-level domain names are relatively free-form. Of course, if you tried to register your organization's name as *apple, duke, harvard,* or *ibm,* you'd be told that these names are already taken. Assuming that the names you choose don't coincide with someone's trademark or match some other organization's easily recognized abbreviation or name, there should be no problem. The suffix, however, is a different matter. As we noted, this is the highest-level domain name and

DISCOVERING MORE

IP and Internet Routing

The IP addressing system began as simple, orderly means for identifying Internet hosts and their networks, but the rapid growth of the Internet changed all of that. Consult our online resource "Discovering More About IP and Internet Routing" to find out more about how Internet addressing and routing works.

indicates the type of organization where the Internet node resides; it is assigned rather than chosen by the node's owner. For example, some commonly used types are as follows:

.com   designates a commercial firm

.edu   designates an educational institution

.gov   designates a government agency

.mil   designates a military installation

.net   designates a network service provider

.org   designates a nonprofit organization (other than educational)

Unfortunately, there are no hard and fast rules for choosing machine and organization domain names. The owners can do just about what they please as long as the names they choose are registered to them and the suffix is correct. Consequently, not all domain names will have obvious meaning. For example, the domain name, "a2i.rahul.net" doesn't convey at all that this might be a machine that provides Wall Street stock market quotes.

The system of IP addresses and domain naming conventions is currently under review. The Internet has grown too large to accommodate its users under the old system. We can expect some changes soon in the way we number and name the computers that connect to the Internet.

Even so, domain names are primarily for human consumption—for use as Web URLs, for example. Domain names still must be converted to IP addresses for delivery. Designated systems, called **Domain Name System servers (DNS servers),** function as a repository of domain name information and are used by Internet hosts as a database for addresses. This relieves individual Internet hosts from the need to store this high volume of information.

Like most things on the Internet, DNS servers are distributed at different levels throughout the network. The system is organized like an IT-version of connecting to Kevin Bacon (as in "six degrees of separation"). Suppose that you try to download a page from our Web site. The URL contains the domain name cs.furman.edu. A request from your system will be sent to your local DNS server. If the local machine has the name indexed, you will receive the IP address immediately. But, if the local DNS server cannot resolve it, the request will go to a root-level DNS server. Currently, there are 13 of these servers worldwide. Their databases contain large amounts of information, but none have a complete set of mappings. Thus, once again, two things can happen. If the root server can resolve it, it replies to the DNS server that queried it. If the domain name is not indexed in the root server, then the root server has the "smarts" to know which DNS server to ask. Thus, in a relatively short number of stops, the IP address 156.143.143.130 is found and returned. Thankfully, most of this is transparent to the user. All that we experience is some variable amount of time during which the name is resolved.

Applications and Transport Services

Most network applications—whether they are client/server, peer-to-peer, and so on—depend on sending and receiving messages. The transport layer, you will recall, manages these services. However, applications may differ in the quality or style of message services they require. Consider postal service as an illustration. In some instances, we need the guarantee that our mail was indeed delivered to and received at its intended destination. Thus, we would use certified mail for these deliveries. On the other hand, for ordinary business, it is satisfactory to use the more economical standard delivery. The Internet, likewise, has certified and standard mail.

For many applications, **TCP** (or **Transfer Control Protocol**) manages their packet transport service. An electronic mail message, for example, may correspond to several TCP packets. Each packet must be identified and sequenced so that the receiver can reconstruct the message as intended. If packets arrive in a different order, or if any packets are lost or corrupted, it is TCP's job to handle these problems. The packets received are held and reconfigured in proper order. If any packets are missing, a signal for retransmission is sent. Thus, TCP creates a **connection-based,** or guaranteed, messaging service. Typically, the client and server exchange messages agreeing to communicate in order to complete some task. Messages—in the form of datagrams—are sent and received. When the work is done, both client and server dissolve their "connection." In reality, of course, there are no physical connections like those in traditional telephone technology, but TCP creates and maintains a virtual connection for the applications that depend upon these services.

Consider another example. If I wish to download a Web page, I would probably use a browser client program to contact the Web server storing that page. The browser would send a request to that server to establish a connection. When accepted, the client and server would exchange the needed information to secure and transfer the files denoted by the page's URL. When the transfer is made, the server would sign off the connection and wait for a new request from elsewhere. TCP provides reliable packet transmissions so that applications are freed from the details of how messaging is managed.

Not all applications require this sophisticated form of transport. For example, most operating systems support a network application called *Ping*. The name is borrowed from underwater sonar. You may remember vintage war films in which the destroyer's sonar operator locates an enemy submarine below by bouncing a signal off its metallic hull. The signature pinging echo revealed the whereabouts of the lurking vessel. In its networking sense, you can find out whether another host is alive and well by "pinging" it. Ping sends out a series of datagrams to the host. The host is required to echo these back. Thus, the application can also determine how reliable is the service between nodes. See Figure 18.3 for an example. In these instances, a no-frills transport service is fine. **UDP** (or **user datagram protocol**) provides simple **connectionless** packet transport. UDP offers a "best-effort" delivery service, which translates to "I did my part; no apologies." In other words, the datagrams are delivered to the IP layer for routing without any special provisions for guaranteeing delivery. In most cases, the datagram will be delivered, but not always. Thus, UDP is comparable to standard postal mail. We expect our letters to be delivered, but we are not shocked if there is a mishap.

Dividing transport, network, and application layers provides greater flexibility. Applications can pick and choose from different types of messaging services. But, at the same time, this division of labor makes things simpler, too. The network layer, for example, focuses on a specific set of tasks without the complications derived from implementation details of the other layers. This type of separation of duties into distinctive levels is the essence of the TCP/IP protocol suite. Figure 18.4 illustrates. In fact, the layer structure for the TCP/IP protocol suite is more complicated than Figure 18.4 depicts. The details, however, are not important here. From the users' point of view, we need only be concerned with how a given network application works—the types of services that it provides and the commands needed to invoke them.

The advantages of abstraction for users are not all that a layered architecture offers. As mentioned, a layered architecture separates different types of tasks and frees the network designers from having to consider all manner of details to concentrate on the task at hand. On the Internet, the applications that we use are built on top of a stable network interface. This

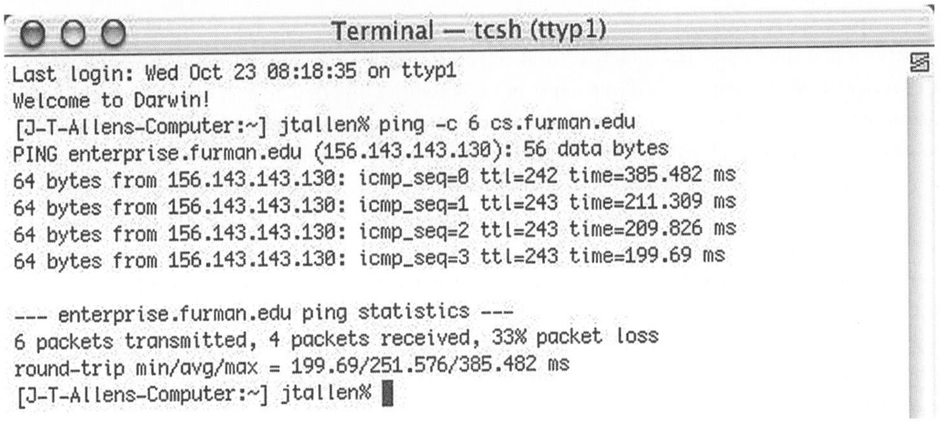

```
 _____
|  ◯ ◯ ◯        Terminal — tcsh (ttyp1)           ▨ |
|---------------------------------------------------|
| Last login: Wed Oct 23 08:18:35 on ttyp1          |
| Welcome to Darwin!                                |
| [J-T-Allens-Computer:~] jtallen% ping -c 6 cs.furman.edu
| PING enterprise.furman.edu (156.143.143.130): 56 data bytes
| 64 bytes from 156.143.143.130: icmp_seq=0 ttl=242 time=385.482 ms
| 64 bytes from 156.143.143.130: icmp_seq=1 ttl=243 time=211.309 ms
| 64 bytes from 156.143.143.130: icmp_seq=2 ttl=243 time=209.826 ms
| 64 bytes from 156.143.143.130: icmp_seq=3 ttl=243 time=199.69 ms
|                                                   |
| --- enterprise.furman.edu ping statistics ---     |
| 6 packets transmitted, 4 packets received, 33% packet loss
| round-trip min/avg/max = 199.69/251.576/385.482 ms
| [J-T-Allens-Computer:~] jtallen% ▮                 |
|_____|
```

Figure 18.3

The network application Ping is used here to test a remote connection to our departmental Web server. The UNIX command form is used. Six packets are sent to cs.furman.edu. The round-trip time is shown for each of the four packets returned. Two (or 33%) of the packets were lost.

Figure 18.4

User applications such as electronic mail (SMTP), file transfers (FTP), or the Web (HTTP) are built on several layers of network software and services. At the user level, we are aware of sending and receiving messages, files, or Web pages. These tasks are coordinated and performed by systems that exchange messages according to their defined protocols. This communication is governed by either TCP or UDP at the transport layer. The messages and data are packaged as datagrams that are routed and delivered by IP at the network layer. The actual work of point-to-point transport and physical transmission of data are still reserved for the data link and physical layers of the communicating nodes.

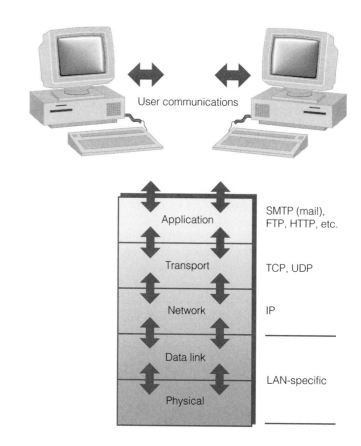

makes it much easier for the application designers. Even if the details of how the network transport works are modified, the application program will not have to be modified to suit them. The network protocol decrees standards for their interaction. By the same token, applications can be modified and added easily as well. In short, applications are designed for "plug and play" integration with the network services underneath.

The layered architecture of the TCP/IP protocol suite is in many ways responsible for the amazing growth of the Internet. This separation of duties into relatively neat layers with standards for how one layer works with another allows for the greatest amount of diversity and yet a sufficient amount of uniformity at the same time. Today, the Internet connects all manner of networks built on different protocols and standards; TCP/IP has subsumed them by both its flexibility and its persistent common-denominator philosophy.

Client/Server Systems Revisited

In Chapter 4, you learned that the World Wide Web depends on the client/server model of computing. This model is, in fact, central to most Internet activity. Most of the applications or services available on the Internet (and most networks, for that matter) require the cooperation of two computer systems in concert. For example, transferring a file from one system to another depends on a local system cooperating with a remote one.

Internet applications manage this cooperation by means of client/server communications. Specifically, systems cooperate by way of client programs and server programs that interact with one another. Recall that a server program is a process that provides a specific resource. A client program, on the other hand, is a process that requests that resource. Usually, the server program runs continuously on a given computer system. When the user requests that a file be transferred to his or her computer, the client program that manages file transfers on the user's system issues a request to the remote computer's server program. The details of the exchange are handled between these two processes.

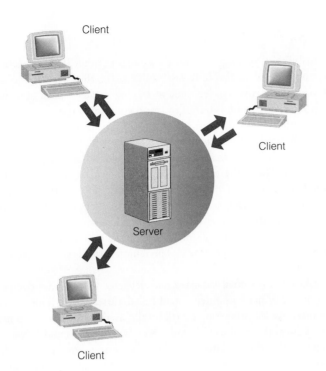

Client

Client

Server

Client

Figure 18.5
Client/server software distributes work between two different computer systems connected by a network. The client and server have an established protocol for communicating and cooperating. The client program requests services from the server program. The server program fulfills these requests and transmits them back to the waiting client. As shown, a server may handle more than one client. Client systems may also differ in scale and performance from the server system.

Client/server systems offer several distinct advantages. First, distributing the work frees the client from hardware/software demands that might be needed only sporadically. Thus, client systems can be more economical, yet—with the help of servers—capable of performing sophisticated tasks when needed.

Secondly, computers acting as servers are able to respond to a number of user requests, even competing ones. Of course, the computer cannot handle them all at once, but it can divide its attention among them by spawning individual server processes for each. See Figure 18.5.

Another advantage of the client/server model is that it can link together systems that are based on different hardware platforms. The client and server programs communicate while the hardware that supports that communication is invisible to them. In the case of the file transfer, for example, the client program on your computer receives and processes your commands. These are translated into the appropriate form for transmission to the server program on the other system. The server program, in turn, activates the file transfer on its system by executing the steps appropriate to its hardware. The data then is transferred over the network linking them. The hardware details for each system are irrelevant for the other.

From a practical standpoint, learning to use Internet applications means learning to use the client programs on a given system. This can simplify the details of their use considerably because client programs can be designed to fit within the context of typical applications for that system. On the other hand, if you use different systems, the look and feel of client programs can change. The bottom line then is that to exploit Internet services, you will have to adapt to the types of client systems available in your environment. But, you should keep in mind that the services are the same—only the client interfaces differ.

Basic Internet Applications

A significant portion of the Internet's traffic today is composed of four basic services: electronic mail (or e-mail), file transfers, remote logins, and the World Wide Web. In this section, we consider each of these services.

Electronic Mail

Ironically, the capability of sending electronic messages to other individuals began as a mere afterthought for the original ARPANET. ARPANET users, though, were quick to realize its potential. Within a few short years, electronic messaging made up most of its network traffic. Today, **electronic mail,** or **e-mail,** is one of the most commonly used services on the Internet. Some individuals use the Internet almost exclusively for e-mail and venture there for little else.

E-mail has both similarities and differences when compared with more conventional postal services. First, electronic messages are posted to individuals at specific addresses much like conventional mail. The address denotes the computer that the individual employs as a mail server. A **mail server** is like a local post office; it is a computer that sends and receives e-mail for a specific network. In fact, your mail server acts as client for delivering your mail messages across the Internet. After you post a message to your mail server, it tries to deliver it by requesting a connection to the recipient's mail server. If the remote mail server agrees, then the message is transported to and accepted by it. The remote mail server retains that message until the recipient fetches it.

Figure 18.6 shows how e-mail is posted and delivered. The sender composes a message using a program on his or her computer system called a **user agent**. This is a client program that serves as an interface for processing e-mail on the user's particular computer system. The user agent then transfers the mail to the mail server, which routes and forwards the message as a set of datagrams. On the Internet, computers running programs that adhere to SMTP (simple mail transfer protocol) manage the mail system. Eventually, the packets arrive at the destination and are reassembled by the receiving mail server and delivered to the recipient through the user agent mail program on that system. Communication between a local mail server and a user agent is handled by a local mail protocol such as POP (Post Office Protocol), IMAP (Internet Mail Access Protocol), and even HTTP (i.e., Web-based mail). The details are not important. Their job is to handle communication with your mail server and manage postings to and from it. The look and feel of e-mail for you varies greatly depending on the interface provided by your mail server's user agent.

Like regular mail, e-mail communication is an example of an asynchronous transaction. The sender's system and the receiver's system do not have to be connected when the sender sends the message. The message can be delivered at a later time. Of course, the user may read messages at his or her convenience. For many, this is far superior to telephone communications that necessitate both individuals being available simultaneously. Like postal letters, too, e-mail may be saved or discarded.

Figure 18.6

The user creates a message in the form of a text file using a mail program on his or her host computer. The local host transfers the file to a mail server that converts it to packets for transmission across the network. At the receiving end, the destination mail server accepts the packets and converts them to a message, which is transferred to the intended receiver when he or she contacts the server.

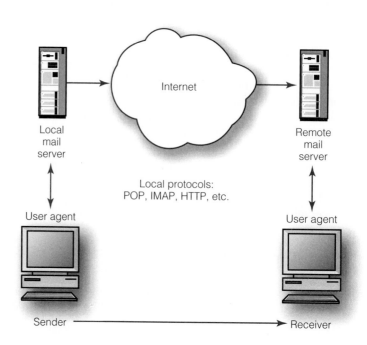

Unlike conventional mail, though, e-mail is much faster—so much so that postal service is snidely called "snail mail" by veteran e-mail users. In addition to speed, e-mail offers other advantages over regular mail. For example, e-mail can be broadcast. This means that multiple copies of a given message can be sent to different parties automatically with no more effort than indicating the distribution list of addresses. By contrast, bulk postal mailings require considerable effort and expense. Replies to e-mail can be automatic, too. Most e-mail programs allow the user to reply to the sender and include part or the entire original message. On the other hand, postal letters are not entirely secure, but e-mail is even less so. Unless the message has been encoded, it could be intercepted without your knowledge. For this reason, ordinary e-mail should never be used for sensitive communications.

Remote Logins

One of the most remarkable services available across the Internet is that of employing your computer system, called the **local host,** to connect to and interact with a distant computer, dubbed the **remote host**. The remote host may be in the next room, across the country, or on another continent. In spite of great distances, you can perform the kinds of tasks on the remote computer that you would if it were in the same room with you. Nor does it matter whether the two systems have the same hardware and software platforms. Translation problems between different systems are solved automatically by using a remote login program. The most popular of these programs is called **telnet**. Telnet is a connection-based service. This means that at the user's level, the two systems communicating form a virtual connection continuously for a given span of time.

After establishing a connection between the local computer and the distant host, the telnet user will often be asked to login to the host machine. If you have an account on the host machine and have been given a password, you will proceed as a registered user of the host. As an example, you might telnet your office computer when you are out of town to perform routine tasks. Or you may split work time between two separate locations and use telnet to communicate from the secondary site with a host machine at your primary work site.

Even if you do not have an account on a host computer, many hosts are configured to allow you to login as a guest (sometimes referred to as an anonymous login). Of course, guests will generally be allowed access only to the "public" files on the host, whereas a registered user will have access to additional files and resources. Once a connection is established and the user has logged in, the two computers communicate as a terminal does to its host. In other words, your system serves as a terminal (a monitor and keyboard) that can interact with the remote host. At the conclusion of the session, the connection must be terminated to free both systems for other connections.

While connected, the local computer may request any services available on the remote system. These actions or tasks are performed on the remote computer, and the results or responses are echoed back to the local system. If the network traffic is light or the distance short, the turnaround time between local and remote hosts can be very fast. In these instances, the connection is seamless and sometimes indistinguishable from interacting with your own system. Usually, though, some transmission delays occur, so telnet sessions are somewhat slower than communicating with your own local system.

File Transfers

One of the earliest and most enduring Internet services is that of transferring files from one system to another. When transferring files over the Internet, the remote host might be a different machine from the local host, and machines with different operating systems store and read files differently. **File transfer protocol** (or **FTP**) was devised to deal with just these problems—that is, translating documents and data from one platform to another over networks. Besides transporting files over distances, FTP service programs handle translation between systems with no fuss or bother for the user.

You must generally have an account on a system to transfer files to and from it. This would surely be true in our earlier examples where we suggested that a user might access a host machine at the office while traveling or working temporarily at a different site. The Internet also has a special class of file servers that have open file access; these are called **anonymous FTP servers**. This means that you may temporarily connect to a designated FTP host and copy files to your own machine.

Anonymous FTP servers are typically set up by those who wish to make information available freely to a large number of users without the hassle of giving each user an account on the host machine. For example, a vendor may wish to make software and documentation updates available through such a server. Freeware and shareware are typically made available through anonymous FTP servers as well. Indeed, anonymous FTP servers offer a wealth of software and information from thousands of computers around the world.

In your work with the World Wide Web, you have likely seen another method for moving files across networks (at least in one direction). Web page creators can place links to files as external resources in their Web pages. Users can then download (that is, transfer) these files to their local machines. In fact, this is exactly what happens each time you view an external image, play a sound, or view a movie from a Web page. All these are examples of file transfers because the file is first transferred to your local machine and then viewed by a browser helper application or plug-in.

Actually, Web page designers can link to any type of file. The user can then use the link to download the file and store it on his or her hard disk. The FTP services we have described are a more general form of this specific process, allowing a user access to a great many Internet resources that have not been linked to Web pages. Using telnet and FTP together, a user can move a file from his or her disk to a remote system's disk, which is not possible using Web services alone.

An important use for telnet and FTP services is the creation and maintenance of Web sites. Creating a Web site consists of two general processes. First, you create the Web pages (using raw HTML or an editor) for the site and collect any required images, sounds, or other external resources. After this is completed, you must actually load all these files (pages and resources) in the appropriate directory on a Web server.

Your Web server is very likely not the same computer as the one on which you've done the Web site development. For example, you may purchase Web server space from an Internet provider or use a remote Web server provided by your university or your employer. In such cases, you must move your Web site files to the Web server computer to make them accessible across the Web using a file transfer program.

Running the Web: HTTP

We saw in Chapter 4 that HTTP (hypertext transfer protocol) defines the cooperation between Web browsers (clients) and Web servers. For example, when a user clicks a hyperlink, the Web client sends request messages to the Web server named in the URL. The server responds by sending messages and the objects requested by the client. The client and server form a brief virtual connection (via TCP) that persists until the transaction is completed. For reasons of efficiency, Web servers do not retain any information about these transactions. While this makes for faster Web servers that are easier to design, it does pose some problems for Web applications: it is inefficient for users, and it makes some Web transactions difficult. In recent years, HTTP has undergone extensions and improvements to reduce some of these problems.

Cookies As mentioned, Web servers do not retain any information about their transactions with Web clients. This makes e-commerce transactions very difficult. For example, in order to purchase a product at a Web site, the server must recognize that a sequence of requests are related and have originated from a single user. One mechanism for solving this problem is the use of cookies. A **cookie** is a special number that identifies a user and his or her transactions with a server.

For example, when a user contacts a Web site for the first time, the server sends a command for the browser to store a cookie for identification purposes. When the user revisits the site—perhaps several days later—the browser sends the cookie to the Web server. In this way, the server knows that this is the same user identified previously. Note, however, that the server does not who the user is; only that this is the same computer system that visited it earlier.

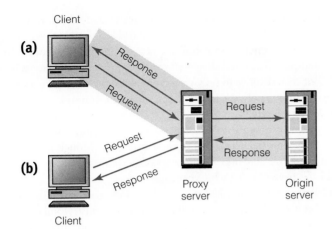

Figure 18.7
A proxy server is a go-between for the client and the Web server originating the Web object, as illustrated in (a). The client makes a request to the origin server. The proxy server receives the client's request and makes a similar request to that server. A copy of the object is downloaded to the proxy, which caches it. Another copy is passed by the proxy to the client. In (b), the client requests an object that is currently cached on the proxy. In this case, the proxy responds directly with a copy of the object. All of this proceeds transparently for the user.

Cookies can be used for other purposes, too. They can be employed for authentication, remembering preferences or user choices, and commercial transactions.

Web caching The fact that Web servers have extremely short attention spans could also mean that Web clients might work inefficiently too. For example, if a user visited the same site periodically, the browser would naturally request the same URLs over and over. Suppose that the site had not changed. Obviously, the Web server does not recall that the user is requesting material that was previously viewed. Consequently, time is wasted resending data that was sent earlier. The designers of HTTP recognized this problem and developed Web caching to fix it. **Web caching** is the storing of Web objects for possible reuse.

Web caches are typically built into the Web client. Your browser retains some of the pages that you have visited earlier. When you ask to visit a site that you have surfed previously, the browser will ask the Web server if the page or object is newer than the copy it has currently stored. If the object is unchanged, then the time spent downloading a new copy will be saved. Of course, if the object is newer, then the Web server will send it to you. Most browsers will let you set limits for your Web cache. For example, you can specify a time limit (days) for retaining cached materials. And you may erase or delete the cache at any time.

Proxy servers Your browser is not the only place that Web objects may be cached. A **proxy server** is a Web server that acts as a go-between by caching Web objects for delivery to Web clients. See Figure 18.7. For example, an enterprise intranet may employ a proxy server as a gateway to Web servers outside. All HTTP requests sent by a Web user inside the intranet would be filtered through the proxy server. If any of the requests were for cached objects, then the proxy server would send them immediately to the client. If the object were not cached, then the proxy server—acting as a client—would request the object(s) from the originating Web server. Over the long run, this is much more efficient. It provides the possibility of faster response time for clients. Inside the intranet, this can reduce the demand for external traffic, which can also support security measures. Outside the intranet, it may help reduce the already congested Web traffic.

In fact, cooperative caching systems have been established at the national and the international levels to aid in the reduction of Web traffic worldwide.

Information Highway Express Lane: Internet2

As you know, the Internet began as a network designed for scientific research and military communications. Of course, it has evolved to be much more widely used. As the Internet has become wildly popular and more commercialized, it has also become too crowded and unreliable for certain kinds of high-level scientific research. In fact, much of today's scientific work requires much higher bandwidths than the Internet currently provides. The Internet, once a dedicated proving ground for researchers and university professors, is now too crowded to provide the broadband capabilities required by these researchers for tomorrow's cutting-edge computer applications.

For example, modern numeric simulations of ocean currents, atmospheric models, aircraft performance, and pharmaceutical design all require considerable amounts of computing power. It is simply not cost-effective to provide such tremendous computing power locally for researchers scattered at dozens of research facilities across the country. Instead, this kind of computing power is concentrated in a few high-performance supercomputing centers sponsored by the government through the National Science Foundation or other agencies. The most practical way to give researchers access to these centers is through networking. For this research to be conducted over networks, teraflops speed (a trillion operations per second) is required; this speed is far beyond today's Internet capabilities.

The Internet2 Project was established to meet these and other demands for the future of global networking. **Internet2** is a consortium of government, industry, and education that are partnering to foster research and development in the next generation Internet and Internet applications. High-tech industry leaders, such as AT&T, Cisco, IBM, Microsoft, and Sun Microsystems, are participating in the project, as are government agencies like the NSF, the Department of Energy, NASA, and DARPA. More than 200 universities and research centers have joined the effort as well.

The three chief goals of the project are to establish network capabilities to support national research; develop the next generation of Internet applications; and to transfer these new network services and applications to the worldwide Internet community. The Internet2 Project has pioneered research and development in new networking capabilities such as multicasting and the next generation of IP addressing. In addition, they have established high-performance networks linking the campuses and labs of its members. Internet2 has also led the way in the development of innovative applications for tele-immersion for remote instrumentation and virtual laboratories, digital libraries, and distance learning.

Multicasting is a networking technology that broadcasts data efficiently to many locations concurrently. In a conventional network, data can be delivered to multiple hosts, but the payload must be copied and transmitted separately to each host. In short, the origin produces one copy for each recipient and transmits all of the copies over the network. Multicasting attempts to reduce bandwidth demands by invoking a "just-in-time" principle: Copies of the data are made at routers that actually deliver the payload to hosts. This saves time, bandwidth, and money.

The Abilene Network is one of Internet2's broadband networks established and supported by the University Corporation for Advanced Internet Development (UCAID). See Figure 18.8. Named after the 19th-century frontier railhead at Abilene (Kansas), this high performance backbone network connects the Internet2 university members.

Figure 18.8

A prominent contribution of the Internet2 project is the creation of a high bandwidth backbone called Abilene. The official map shows the principal nodes of the network, including major metropolitan areas such as Los Angeles, Seattle, Denver, Kansas City, Chicago, Houston, Indianapolis, Atlanta, New York, and Washington, D.C. OC-48c links transmit data at rates of 2.4 gigabits per second. Links rated at OC-192c reach speeds of 10 gigabits per second.

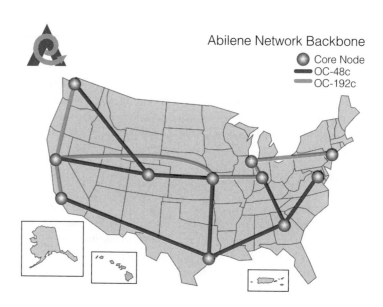

Tele-immersion is a medium for users in different geographical locations to collaborate in real time on projects. Using these tools scientists can share expensive, state-of-the-art equipment without the need for on-site visits. Likewise, virtual laboratories provide a distributed working environment for researchers located around the world to collaborate on research.

Internet2 has also formed partnerships with international corporations and organizations. The goal, of course, is to transfer cutting-edge networking technology worldwide in order to improve the performance and capabilities of the Internet for all of its users.

■ Summary

The Internet is a collection of diverse computer networks that span the globe. The Internet evolved from several U.S. government projects in the late 1960s and early 1970s focused on providing a robust network for the U.S. military and scientific research communities. Today, it is a loosely coupled collection of distributed, open networks that has no real center or single governing body. Networks are added to its topography freely, and the number of nodes connected to it expands daily. International participation is widespread and growing, and it is estimated that the Internet has well over 100 million users.

The Internet is a packet switching network whose basic operation is conducted under the TCP/IP protocol suite for data communications across networks, although other protocols on connected networks coexist with it. Each computer system that is officially part of the Internet has a unique IP address and domain name. Domain names are for human consumption (as in URLs) and must be converted to IP addresses for network use. Designated systems, called DNS servers, perform this function. Messages are transferred across the Internet by routers employing IP addresses. Routers divide the responsibility of maintaining the network at different levels. Some routers review packets for addressing correctness. Other routers decide on paths for sending packets, while others merely repeat the data along the path.

The TCP/IP protocol suite is a layered architecture that separates tasks into relatively distinct layers with standards on how a layer interacts with the ones immediately above and below it in the layered hierarchy. This layered architecture frees network software and hardware designers from having to consider all of the working details, allowing them to concentrate more fully on the task at hand.

Internet applications are generally built on the client/server computing model. Usually, server programs run continuously on Internet server computer systems and respond when client programs make requests of them. The details of any data exchange are handled between such communicating client/server programs. From a practical standpoint, learning to use Internet applications means learning to use the client programs available to your system.

Apart from the Web, much of the Internet's traffic today is comprised of three basic services: electronic mail (or e-mail), file transfers, and remote logins. Using remote login capabilities, your computer system, called the *local host*, can connect to and interact with a distant computer, dubbed the *remote host*. Translation problems between different computer systems are solved automatically by connection-based services like telnet. When transferring files over the Internet, the remote host might be a different kind of machine from the local host. File transfer protocol (or FTP) was devised to deal with the problems that arise translating documents and data from one platform to another over networks.

The future of the Internet is just as difficult to predict as from its beginnings, but the Internet2 Project has made positive strides to ensure that the next generation Internet will be based on many of the principles as the original.

■ Terms

ARPANET	electronic mail (e-mail)	proxy server (Web)
anonymous FTP server	file transfer protocol (FTP)	remote host
backbone router	Internet	TCP (transfer control
connection-based service	Internet2	protocol)
connectionless service	Internet Protocol (IP)	tele-immersion
cookie	local host	telnet
datagram	mail server	UDP (user datagram protocol)
domain name server (DNS	multicasting	user agent (mail)
server)	NSFNET	Web caching

■ Questions for Review

1. Give a brief overview of the history of the Internet.

2. The Internet has been described as a packet switching, loosely coupled, distributed network of networks. Explain what this means.

3. What does TCP/IP stand for? What role does the TCP/IP protocol suite play in the functioning of the Internet?

4. What is a datagram? How does IP handle datagrams?

5. What is an IP address? What structure do these addresses have?

6. How are domain names related to IP addresses?

7. What is DNS? How is it used?

8. How are DNS servers organized to resolve domain names?

9. Compare and contrast TCP with UDP as transport or messaging services.

10. What does it mean when we say that TCP/IP is an open system? Why is this an advantage for its use with the Internet?

11. What are the chief advantages of the layered architecture for Internet software and services?

12. What are asynchronous transactions? What are its advantages as a form of communication?

13. Explain how the client/server communication process is organized. What are the advantages of this approach?

14. How does electronic mail compare with other forms of communication like postal mail and telephone service?

15. What is telnet? What is it used for?

16. What is FTP? What is it used for?

17. What is anonymous FTP?

18. Explain how telnet and FTP can be used in installing and maintaining your own Web site on a remote host.

19. What is a cookie? How is it used in Web transactions?

20. What is a Web cache? How does a Web client cache work?

21. What is a proxy server? What are the advantages and disadvantages of proxies?

22. Give a brief overview of the Internet2 project. What advantages or opportunities does it offer over the current Internet?

Chapter 19

Internet Applications: Raising the Bar

OBJECTIVES

- The architecture for e-commerce applications

- Client-side and server-side processing

- Dynamic HTML (DHTML)—cascading style sheets and scripting

- HTML forms and scripting

- Java and JavaScript

- Extensible Markup Language (XML)

As you learned in the previous chapter, not only has the growth of the Internet and the World Wide Web in the last decade been phenomenal, but also the capabilities of the Internet continue to grow at a rapid pace. As the Internet infrastructure continues to evolve, so will our creativity in putting it to use. We now routinely transmit pictures, sounds, and video over the Internet. With the advances in bandwidth being made, very soon it will become common for sound and video to be transmitted across the Internet in real time. Simulated three-dimensional images and video will be readily available.

All this will open up a whole new range of possibilities for using the Internet. For example, it is interesting to speculate about the extent to which our current communication technologies—telephones, televisions, movies, newspapers and magazines—will be changed or even become obsolete. It is not surprising that the impact of the Internet's capabilities has had a profound effect on the way business is conducted as well. The use of the Internet for conducting business, often referred to as e-business or e-commerce, is growing at a rapid rate.

Traditional businesses are using the Internet as a vehicle for improving communications and services with their customers and their suppliers. Furthermore, whole new business models are being created. Many people who never participated in an auction sale are using sites like *eBay* to buy and sell everything from sports equipment to used CDs to tools and beyond. And *Priceline* uses a related model to let customers name their price on purchases for a variety of items. Making travel arrangements employing one of the many Web-based travel services has become routine for a great many people who enjoy the convenience, easy comparison shopping, and the flexibility that this allows. And the list could go on and on.

Just how big is the Internet economy and how fast is it growing? A recent study conducted by the Center for Research in Electronic Commerce at the University of Texas focused on more than 2,000 Internet companies. The study found business revenues totaling $322 billion in 1998 had turned into $524 billion in 1999—an amazing increase of 70% in one year! It is estimated that for 2003 over $1 trillion in Internet-generated revenues will be reported.

While new business models are driving some of this growth, a great deal of it is being driven by expanded customer expectations of traditional businesses. Customers now expect to be able to do their banking online, file and track insurance claims online, trade stocks online, and shop for and buy products online. Companies are increasingly required to provide 24/7 access to their services and products. In order to succeed, companies are finding that the level, security, and reliability of this access and the transactions it enables must be very high.

The bar has indeed been raised! In this chapter you will study some of the developing technologies that are enabling and energizing the rapid expansion of commerce on the Web.

Commerce on the Web

Electronic commerce (e-commerce) is rapidly emerging as an important, if not central, activity for the majority of businesses and institutions. E-commerce centers around three basic information technologies: Web authoring, Web programming, and databases. The typical e-commerce configuration consists of a **Web front-end,** or interface, and a **back-end database.** These two components are connected via programming (scripting and/or larger standalone applications). The Web interface is downloaded and executed by the client machine, the back-end databases are stored on one or more servers, and the programming element can be split between client and server, although most of it will generally be on the server side. Figure 19.1 illustrates.

Figure 19.1

Architecture for e-commerce applications. The scripting/application components may reside on either the client or server side, although these are more frequently on the server side.

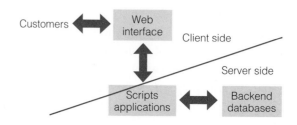

The Web interface provides customers with an easy-to-use graphical interface, accessible via the Internet in an asynchronous mode. Dynamic information relative to a business is typically stored on a company's databases. The transport between these two elements requires programming. Scripts (short, sharply focused programs) are often sufficient, but in some cases larger, more fully featured programming applications are required.

For example, when you access a site like *amazon.com,* you are presented with a highly interactive Web interface. Using this interface you can select the types of products you wish to find, the titles of books and CDs, and so on. Once this information has been collected by the Web page, it must then be transmitted to the server. If a search for a particular book has been requested, programs on the server will initiate a database lookup. When the requested information has been located, it is sent back to the Web interface for appropriate display. Hopefully all this happens very quickly and you are presented information about the requested book in near real time. Clearly all these elements—initial Web interface, programming connections, database search and retrieval, and follow-up Web interface—must work smoothly together to create an attractive, efficient, and inviting e-commerce site.

Client-side and Server-side Scripting

Earlier you saw an example of a JavaScript program that allowed a user to cycle through a series of images on a Web page. This was an example of an **interactive Web page,** that is, a page that displays different behavior and/or data depending on actions taken by the page users. One way to implement interactive Web pages is to employ scripting languages (like JavaScript) to embed code in a Web page that the browser then interprets and executes.

Recall that the Web is organized on the client-server computing model. The scripting scheme above is called **client-side scripting** because the script resides on the client machine once it is transferred along with the HTML document. The interpretation and execution of the script is entirely under the control of the browser on the client machine. The only involvement of the server in this process is to provide access to the HTML page. All the interaction occurs on the client machine.

The primary advantages of client-side scripting are efficiency and speed. If the scope of the interaction is local, it will simply be more efficient and faster to have the entire interaction taking place locally on the client side. As you know, the transfer of information across the Internet between the client and the server is the major limiting factor in the speed of an Internet transaction. And these limits are usually beyond our control, depending on the most limiting bandwidths of the various connections between the server and us.

Client-side scripting is a good model for enabling interactions whose scope is restricted to the display environment, that is, the client environment. The cycle of images is just one example of this. In other cases, we may want the scope of the interaction to extend beyond the display

E-Business and Your Privacy

The rapid development of business on the Web has not come about without some significant issues and problems. For example, companies can use the Internet to personalize the interface their customers deal with—on the surface a potential value-added for customers. But to do so requires the storage of information many consider to be personal. How is this information to be protected? For a discussion of this and other privacy issues, consult the online essay "E-Business and Your Privacy."

SOCIAL THEMES

environment. For example, suppose you are browsing a bookseller's Web site and you want to see the price and availability of a book that you have selected in your display window. It would be impractical to send such information bundled with the original Web site because there may be hundreds or thousands of book selections available and the designer of the site would not know which of these you are likely to select. Hence, such information for every single selection option displayed on the page(s) would need to transmitted. Clearly this is a very inefficient scheme.

A better way to accomplish this would be to transmit your selection back to the server and have the server retrieve from a database only the information relevant for your selection, and then send it back to your machine for display. This kind of interaction, requiring an exchange of information and transmission and display of data residing on the server can be accomplished using scripts residing on the server to enable the lookup and transmission of the requested data. Not surprisingly, this kind of scripting is called **server-side scripting.**

Client-side Processing and Dynamic HTML (DHTML)

Dynamic HTML provides a suite of technologies on the client side. The name Dynamic HTML (DHTML, for short) is actually a bit misleading. At first glance, you would think that this is a new extended version of HTML. While DHTML does in fact extend the capabilities of HTML, it is not actually an extended version of HTML at all. Rather, **Dynamic HTML,** or **DHMTL,** is a collection of related technologies that provide capabilities for enhancing HTML Web pages. Two primary component technologies of DHTML are cascading style sheets (CSS) and JavaScript programming.

DHTML is generally not supported by versions of Netscape and Internet Explorer earlier than 4.0 in each browser. Further, Netscape and Microsoft (Internet Explorer's maker) do not agree totally on just what technologies should be supported for dynamic Web pages or just how these technologies should be implemented. So you must be aware that there are a number of features in DHTML that are supported by only one of these two companies. We will restrict attention in our discussion of DHTML to features supported by both browsers.

It is unlikely that we will ever see complete standardization on the many technology advances being included under the DHTML umbrella. So keep in mind that while HTML itself is a well-defined language with an international committee that sets the standards for its syntax and features, DHTML is not that kind of entity. DHTML is as much a marketing phrase as anything else. It is destined to be ambiguous and ill-defined as long as the two giants of the browser world, Netscape and Microsoft, are vying for market share and trying to get one up on each other.

Cascading Style Sheets

Netscape and Microsoft have found some common ground in the use of cascading style sheets. Style sheets serve much the same purpose in Web document creation as their counterpart style sheets do in popular word processors. Indeed, the term is borrowed from the word processing world. Perhaps you have used style sheets in Microsoft Word or Word Perfect. Even if you have not, the idea is straightforward and easy to grasp and use.

A **style sheet** defines a particular formatting style. A style may have to do with the way text is displayed (font style, font type, color, etc.) or with the way page elements are laid out (margins, borders, etc.), or both at one time for that matter. When we define a style sheet, we are defining the style with which text will be displayed. Applying the style sheet is a convenient way to enforce a consistency of appearance across a document or across a whole Web site. A further advantage is that if we decide later to change some of these appearance characteristics, we can simply change the style sheet and all page elements that use that style sheet will be automatically updated. By separating the style specifications from the content of a Web page, as we can do, we can actually create different style sheets geared to different display devices (desktop computers, handheld PDAs, or even mobile phones, for example). A final advantage to style sheets is that they give us access to formatting that cannot be done using HTML tags alone, so in these cases they do actually extend the capabilities of HTML.

Let's look at some concrete examples to help make the style sheet concept clearer. Suppose we wish for all the h2 headings in a document to appear in red text. Of course, we could accomplish this as follows. Each time we mark up an <h2> tag, we can also include the HTML tags to change the font color to red as follows:

```
<h2><font color = "red"> All About CSS </font></h2>
```

This would be fine if we wanted only an occasional h2 heading to have these characteristics. But if we want all or even most of our h2 headings to look this way, it would be a lot more convenient if we could define this style of text just once and have it apply to all h2 headings. The added advantage of this approach is that if we later decide to change the style of h2 headings (say we decide to change the color to purple instead of red), it would be nice to make that change only once and have it automatically apply to all h2 headings, rather than have to find each and every h2 heading and change them all individually. As you might guess, style sheets give us exactly these desirable characteristics. We do this by setting up **Cascading Style Sheet (CSS)** rules. Let's see how this works.

To define a style sheet we use a paired <style> tag that encloses one or more CSS rules. Although style sheet definitions can be placed most anywhere in our HTML, the convention is to place them in the <head> section of a page. Listing 19.1 shows a style sheet definition to accomplish what we just described with h2 tags.

```
<html>
<head>
. . .
<style type="text/css">
h2 {color: red;}
</style>
. . .
</head>
<body>
. . .
<h2>All About CSS</h2>
. . .
</body>
</html>
```

Listing 19.1
A style sheet to modify h2 tags. Notice the definition of the style sheet in the head section (shown in bold). The definition consists of a rule setting the font color to red. This rule essentially redefines the h2 tag for this document. Every time an h2 tag is used in this document it will have the characteristic (that is, be in red font) defined in this CSS rule.

Let's look a little more closely at the form or syntax of CSS rules. A CSS rule has three components: a selector, a property, and a value (assigned to that property). The **selector** identifies the HTML component to which the style applies. In our simple rule here, the selector is *h2*, the property is *color*, and the value assigned to that property is *red*. The syntax for constructing the rule is to list the selector, then enclose the property and its associated value in braces (more than one property/value pair can be included). The property is followed by a colon, then the value, then a semicolon.

Style selectors can be placed in context as well. For example, we may wish to have a tag have a given style only when that tag is used in a certain context. Perhaps we want all bold tags to show in purple on a silver background whenever they are inside a <li> tag in an unordered list. We can do this with style sheets. Listing 19.2 illustrates.

```
<style type="text/css">
ul li b {color: purple; background-color: silver;}
</style>
```

Listing 19.2
Notice the repeated selectors used in this style sheet (ul li b). Such selectors specify the context for the rule. The context is formed from right to left. In this case all bold text (b) within a list item (li) within an unordered list (ul) will be affected by the given rule.

There are actually three levels of styles: inline styles, embedded styles, and external styles. The order in which the three levels of style sheets are applied gives rise the name *cascading* style sheets (which you may have been wondering about). **Embedded styles** are styles embedded in a document—the examples above illustrate this idea. **In-line styles** are useful when we want a one-time style change and are inserted at the point they apply. They can be also used to override embedded styles. The way a browser will interpret multiple styles on the same tag is as follows: In-line styles take precedence over property values set in embedded styles.

Suppose we wish to define a set of styles for an entire Web site. This is a good way to ensure consistency across a site. But the site may contain tens or even hundreds of pages. Using what you've learned so far, you'd have to include the appropriate embedded style sheets in every single document. While that is possible, it is an error-prone process and certainly a bit tedious. Worse yet, suppose you decide to later change one or more of the styles. Then you'd have to go back through all the documents making the identical change to each one!

There is a better way. In fact this kind of situation is exactly what **external style sheets** were created to handle. The idea is a simple one. Instead of placing the same style sheets in every document, we store the style sheets in one or more external files and just reference those files in the <head> section of each document. Then if we have to change a style, we change the external file and immediately every document's styles are updated!

Client-side Scripting with JavaScript

As you will recall, scripts are little programs (usually only a few lines in length) that help you create the ability for your Web pages to interact with their users. For example, you can write scripts to present alert boxes when certain events occur or to collect information from the user which then triggers some particular action by the page. Because scripts make moving things around on a page possible, they are central to DHTML.

Scripts can be written in a number of script languages. JavaScript is the most popular scripting language for the Web. It was developed by Netscape and was the first widely used scripting language for the Web. Microsoft has its own version of JavaScript called JScript and its own scripting language VBScript (for Visual Basic Script), but Internet Explorer also supports JavaScript scripts.

By the way, we should point out that JavaScript and Java are two different languages. To be sure, there are some similarities between JavaScript and Java, but there are also significant differences. Java is a full-featured programming language that, while it is used a great deal in Web programming, can also be used in standalone programming tasks that have nothing to do with the Web. JavaScript on the other hand is of use only for work with the Web.

One of the features of both JavaScript and Java is that they are object-oriented programming languages. What this means is that they both deal with objects which are entities that have both data and actions (called *methods*) associated with them. In addition, both languages employ an **event-driven model,** which means that the programs we write in them are able to

DISCOVERING MORE

Style Sheets

The details on how to use in-line styles and external style sheets are not difficult, but these would carry us too far afield from our main discussion here. Consult the online resource "Exploring Style Sheets" to learn more about cascading style sheets and see examples of their use.

respond to events that the user initiates—things like clicking the mouse over a certain position, dragging the mouse, pressing a particular key on the keyboard, and so on.

In fact, the event-driven model captures the essence of what we wish to do with a scripting language in the first place. We want our pages to be responsive to events that the user (or the browser) initiates. That's what we mean by making our pages *interactive*. The user initiates some event and the Web page responds meaningfully to this event. Before scripting, about the only event-reaction we had on the Web was the use of hyperlinks to load pages, resources, etc. Scripting languages open up a whole world of possibilities for creating interactions beyond this basic beginning.

A JavaScript script is a program that is included in an HTML document or stored in an external file and linked to (similar to the way external style sheets are incorporated into HTML). When scripts are included in HTML documents, they are placed inside paired <script> tags, usually in the head section of the document—you'll again recognize a similarity with styles. These scripts are then called to do the action they're programmed for when certain events take place. The process of calling the scripts to do their work is done by **event handlers**—statements designed especially for this purpose. Event handlers are placed in positions within the HTML code appropriate for the event they are designed to respond to.

For example, *onClick* is an event handler intended to respond to the clicking of the mouse. This event handler would be placed in the HTML code for the object that is to be clicked; this might be an image, a link, and so on. In other words, the scripts are stored once in the document and are called anytime an associated event handler is triggered. The most frequently used event handlers are *onClick, onMouseover,* and *onMouseout.* For instance, you've seen "rollovers" on many Web pages you've visited. **Rollovers** are scripts that change an image (usually a button) slightly when the mouse is placed over it. These are constructed using the *onMouseover* and *onMouseout* event handlers.

HTML Forms and Scripts for Data Entry

HTML forms are a standard part of HTML, not just an addition under DHTML. In fact, forms have been used for quite some time in Web pages. As you will see, however, DHTML (in particular JavaScript) adds some new capabilities and conveniences in your use of forms. **Forms** are basically HTML objects that accept user input. This input can take one of several different modes, including text entry boxes, radio buttons, check boxes, and pulldown menus. These data entry/collection elements can be formatted with many of the usual HTML tags as well, so a form can be interspersed with other HTML constructions and can be nested inside such constructions. In fact, the rules for how forms can nest other tags and be nested within other tags are rather liberal; the one restriction is that forms can't be nested inside other forms. This doesn't mean you can't have multiple forms on a page, just that they must be separate from each other (nonintersecting).

DISCOVERING MORE

JavaScript

For more on scripting, including details about the JavaScript language and a tutorial on JavaScript programming, consult the online resource "Learning More About JavaScript."

What does a Web page do with the information collected through forms? This is where scripts come in. There are no built-in features in HTML to actually process the data collected from forms. In fact it wouldn't make sense to even attempt to put this capability in HTML because the purposes users have for collected data are almost endless. So by necessity, users must be able to write their own data processing procedures. These are written using scripts: Forms and scripts go together.

Both client-side and server-side scripts come into play with forms. Often client-side scripts are used to validate the data as it is being entered into a form (making sure the number of digits in a social security number is correct or that the form of an email address is valid, etc.). Client-side forms can also be used to check that data entered is in acceptable ranges, of the appropriate type, and so on.

Once the data collected has been validated on the client-side, it is ready to be transmitted to the server side where action can be taken on the data. Scripts to take such action generally reside on the Web server because they often need to access databases on those servers. The most common type of these server-side scripts is **Common Gateway Interface (CGI) Scripts.** CGI is actually an interface rather than a scripting language and CGI scripts can be written in a number of different scripting and programming languages. CGI scripts are invoked by the browser but executed on the server. CGI specifies how data is moved between the Web page and the executable code, but that code can be written in essentially any language. Popular languages for this purpose include Java, C++, and Perl.

Constructing a form is straightforward and similar to constructing other parts of a Web page. As we've noted, forms will usually contain a variety of elements: radio boxes, check boxes, text fields, and so on. You will give each element a name as you create it. These names are used by scripts to identify the information received through the named element. The example in listing 19.3 illustrates.

Listing 19.3

This HTML form solicits user input via a pull-down menu. The pull-down menu is defined by the paired <select> tags. Note that the <select> tag encloses a number of <option> tags. These define the particular entities to appear in the pull-down menu.

```
<html>
<head>
<title> Andy's Carmart </title>
</head>
<body bgcolor="#FFFFFF">
<center><h2>
<font color="#0066FF">Welcome to Andy's Car Market!</font></h2>
<hr>
</center>
<p><font color="#0066FF">Tell us something about the car
   of your dreams and we'll see if we can find it for
   you!</font></p>
<p><font color="#0066FF">
<form action="http://www.some_server.com/cgibin/action1"
   method="post" name="carInfo">
   <p>What manufacturer do you prefer?
   <select name="carType">
   <option value="chrysler">Chrysler
   <option value="ford">Ford
   <option value="gm">General Motors
   <option value="honda">Honda
   <option value="toyota">Toyota
   </select>
   <center>
   <input type="submit" value="Submit Information">
   </center>
</form>
</font></p>
</body>
</html>
```

Notice the enclosing paired <form> tags. The first <form> tag has two attributes. The first, action, is used to define the location of the CGI script that will process the data. The second, method, will have one of two values, *post* or *get,* depending on how you want the browser to package/format the data you're sending to the CGI script.

A pull-down menu is defined by the paired <select> tag inside a form. The <select> tag will enclose a number of <option> tags to define the particular entities to appear in the pull-down menu. Each <option> tag will contain a value attribute that will specify what the selection will be called when scripts access the choice entered from this menu. The text outside the tag is what the user will see as his or her selection choice. The value and this name may differ since we might want to give the user a more complete description than we pass to the script. In this case, we've made these the same in most cases, except we haven't used any capital letters in the value attributes. The exception is that we shortened *General Motors* to just *gm* in that value attribute. It is important to use exactly these attribute values in our scripts; the scripts won't care what we use as a text for the users.

Finally, the <input type="submit"> tag creates the submit button. The value of the value attribute is the name that shows up on the button in the user's window. When the user clicks the submit type button, the browser will ordinarily engage the script stored in the action attribute for the form. However, we can add additional actions or override this action by including our own *onSubmit* event handler. See Figure 19.2 to see how this form is displayed as part of a Web page.

Data Binding in DHTML

A frequent requirement for interactive communications over the Web is the need to retrieve some data from a Web server, then manipulate that data and display the results of that manipulation on the client side. One way to do this is to set up scripts to capture the required manipulations from the user at the client, pass those instructions to the server, have the server manipulate the data, then send the new data back to the client. Of course, this process isn't very efficient because it requires detailed communications between the client and the server for every data manipulation.

Data binding gives us an alternative way to accomplish the same thing. **Data binding** enables that by distinguishing data from the HTML code in a downloaded file. Using data binding, a data set is retrieved from a server and displayed on an HTML page. The key element is that the client now has the ability to manipulate the data residing on the client. The data can be sorted or filtered as the user dictates, and the modified data is displayed automatically with no intervention required by the server. Naturally, this makes the entire process much more efficient because it drastically reduces the amount of client-server communication required. To bind external data to HTML elements in this way, software modules, known as **data source objects** or **DSOs,** are employed to connect the browser to live data sources.

DISCOVERING MORE

Forms and Scripts

How would a script access the information entered? How would we include our own script to process the information submitted when the submit button is pressed? As we mentioned in the text, the onSubmit event handler will do the trick. While this isn't difficult, it is a bit beyond the scope of our survey in this chapter. See the online resource "Learning More About JavaScript" for more details and a tutorial with some concrete examples.

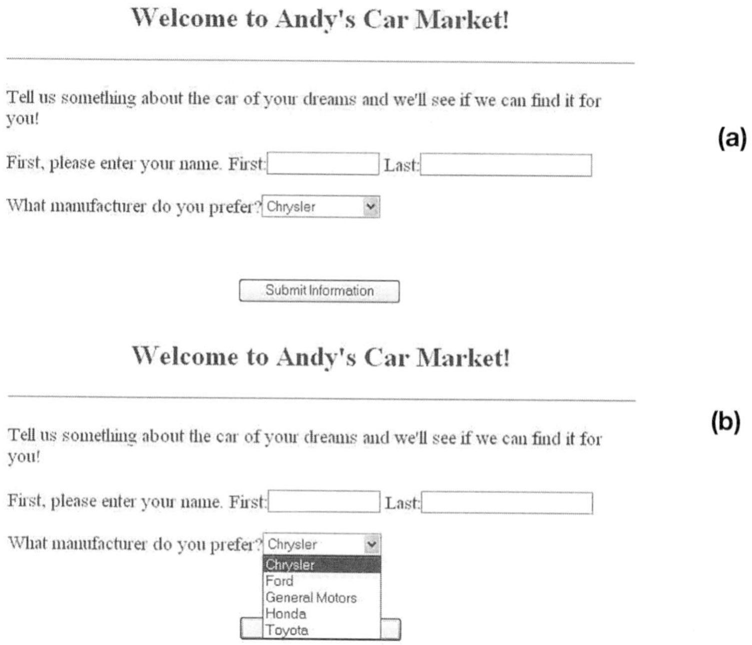

Figure 19.2
The HTML illustrated: (a), the form as it first appears; (b), the form with the pulldown menu displayed.

Server-side Processing

Java Programming

Java is an object-oriented programming language with special features that make it particularly appropriate for writing programs that run on the Web. Java's use of objects is very similar to that of JavaScript, and the basic statements in the two languages are often quite similar (if not identical). But the two languages are really quite different. While JavaScript is a scripting language, Java is a full-featured programming language. Actually, the similarity in name comes from an attempt by Netscape (inventors of JavaScript) to capture marketing attention for JavaScript by capitalizing on the existing popularity of Java when JavaScript was first introduced.

Although Web/networking capabilities are one of the main reasons Java has become so popular, Java is not just for Web programming. A real advantage of learning Java is that you are learning the number-one programming language for Web applications, but at the same time you are learning a general-purpose programming language whose applications are almost limitless. The programming principles of Java are the basic principles inherent in any object-oriented programming language.

What are the features that make Java so useful for Web programming? There are two major features. The first major feature that makes Java attractive for Web work is its built-in security safeguards. Secondly, Java is designed to be a cross-platform language. By this, we mean that Java programs can be written on one kind of computer and then run on completely different kinds of computers. This is a huge advantage when you're programming for an open, distributed environment like the Web, where users are employing computers of a variety of types (PCs, Macintoshes, and Unix/Linux machines).

Java Applets

Applets are small Java programs intended to be run by a Web browser or some other "applet viewer" software. Applets have even stronger security restrictions than standalone Java programs. For example, Java applets cannot read, write, delete, or rename files on the client machine; these capabilities just aren't part of the language. Applets can't even check for existence of files on a client machine, nor can they access network devices like printers or create connections to machines other than the one on which the code resides. So users can download Java applets with confidence that the security of their computer system is not threatened. In today's age of viruses, worms, and other malicious programs, this feature is most important. Applets also have a different program structure from standalone Java programs. An important distinction between applets and standalone Java programs is that the browser is *in control of running the applet.*

When an applet is created, it is compiled and saved on the server computer. This is the source file. This source file is then referenced within an HTML document that will download and run the applet employing software called the Java runtime environment (RTE). We'll have more to say about the Java RTE shortly. Listing 19.4 illustrates an HTML document that calls and displays an applet.

```
<html>
<head>
<title>First Applet</title>
</head>
<body bgcolor="#FFFFFF">
<applet code="applet1.class" width="300" height="300">
</applet>
</body>
</html>
```

Listing 19.4
In this example, the Web page defined by the given HTML accesses the Java applet source file named applet1.class *stored on the server. This source file is then downloaded and the user's browser will invoke the Java runtime environment (RTE) to run the applet.*

Java's Cross-platform Capability

How is Java able to run on such a variety of platforms? Before we answer that, we need briefly to review the traditional way computer programs are constructed and distributed for use. As you know, programs can be written in a variety of languages: COBOL, FORTRAN, C, C++, BASIC, and so on. So a programmer must first choose a language in which to write his or her code. The code that is written is called **source code.** However, source code cannot be run directly on any computer because each computer understands and is capable of executing only one very basic language referred to as its **machine language.** As you learned earlier, every type of computer has its own unique version of machine language. A Macintosh uses a completely different machine language than a PC, for example. So the source code must first be translated into the target computer's machine language using software called a **language compiler.** The resulting machine version of the original source code is called the **object code** (or sometimes, binary code). So before your COBOL program can be run on a target machine, say a PC, it must be compiled to object code in the PC's machine language.

Now, here's the catch. Different target computers can require (sometimes significantly) different source code in order for the source code to compile and run properly on that machine. This places a burden on the creator of such programs if the intent is to distribute the programs on different computers. For example, you will have to purchase *different versions* of Microsoft Word to run on a PC and on a Macintosh. The difference in the source code for such products can be very significant. Even when the source code isn't very different, the process of translating it to the appropriate machine language differs significantly from machine to machine. In other words, the source code would have to be compiled by a compiler written especially for the target type of machine. As you can see, cross-platform use is *not* a characteristic of most programming languages.

Compare this with Java programming. When you write a Java applet, you do not have to worry about what kind of computer the user will have when he or she downloads your applet and runs it. The reason for this is the unique way Java code gets translated into machine language for different computers. First the original source code you write will be compiled into something called a **bytecode** version of the program. Java bytecode programs are programs translated into pseudo-machine language. Often it is said that the bytecode program is targeted for the **Java virtual machine (JVM),** rather than some particular target computer. In other words, the Java creators have added a very clever intermediate step to the compilation process. When the source code is translated into bytecodes for the Java virtual machine, *most* of the work has been done to translate the source code into a machine language version, *but not all of it.* The last step in that translation process is left to the client machine when the byte-code version is downloaded. This last step in the translation is done by software called the **Java runtime environment (RTE)** on the client machine. Because most of the work has already been completed in generating the bytecode file, this final step can be accomplished very quickly without undue delays for the end-user of the Java program.

That is how Java manages its remarkable cross-platform accessibility. And the really good news is that Java programmers don't have to worry about most of this. Their only responsibility is to create the Java source code. The translation to bytecodes and eventually to machine language is handled automatically by compiler software and the Java RTE, which the user's browser will employ automatically on his or her client computer.

Active Server Pages

Active server pages (ASP) is a Microsoft technology designed to send dynamic content based on a client request. Active server pages are server-side text files that consist of HTML tags and scripts. Although languages like JavaScript can be used for ASP scripting, the Microsoft language VBScript is usually employed. ASP pages process requests for information, which may include a database lookup, and returns the information to the client. Normally the information is returned as an HTML page, but images, sounds, and other file formats may also be returned.

When a client requests an ASP document, the document is parsed by software called a **scripting engine.** The scripting engine interprets the scripting code as it is encountered, thereby supplying the flexibility needed to return dynamic information. ASP often employs small components known as ActiveX controls—another Microsoft technology—to provide certain frequently needed functions. For example, there are ActiveX controls to gather information about the user's browser, store the number of times a Web page has been visited, and provide general information about a Web site. While ActiveX controls are commonly used, many Web programmers prefer to use components written in Java instead because of their increased security.

XML

As the level of sophistication grows in e-commerce applications, deficiencies in current Web technologies, especially in HTML, have become apparent. As you know, HTML was designed to present documents to a Web browser for *display.* We shouldn't forget how revolutionary this idea was when it burst onto the scene in the early 1990s; HTML completely redefined the exchange of information across networks, replacing the existing exclusively text-based paradigm with a multimedia one. Nonetheless, today's e-commerce applications have requirements that

DISCOVERING MORE

Java Applets

Details on writing Java programs and applets is beyond the scope of the text proper. However, for those interested in a tutorial on Java applet programming, consult the online resource "Learning More About Java Programming."

go well beyond just the display of documents. Documents need to be processed, reformatted on the fly, stored and forwarded, exchanged, encrypted and so on. HTML can model structure and presentation, but is not at all equipped to convey the intrinsic *meaning* of the document's content. So, it should come as no surprise that HTML is not sufficient for many of these expanded needs.

Until now, Web applications have been generally tied to the available Web browsers. But emerging e-commerce applications need to exchange information over the Internet without regard to whether HTML and associated browsers have built-in capabilities to handle the necessary data. The solution is to have Web applications that can utilize the Internet protocols for communication, but that do not depend on having a browser in the loop. In other words, we need to allow applications (e.g., programs and databases) to talk to each other across the Internet without the requirement of an intervening browser. While the Internet protocols provide the basic communication capabilities, we need a better way to exchange the appropriate data.

The answer to this dilemma is a more flexible language for information exchange across the Internet. This is provided by **extensible markup language (XML).** XML enables the exchange of data between applications that may have entirely different data format requirements. XML is extensible because it is actually a **meta-language,** which means it allows you to create your own markup language specifications. You do this in XML by writing a **document type definition (DTD)** that defines the rules of a language. When a document is then constructed in this new language, the DTD is included in the document itself, so the receiver has not only a document to interpret, but also a succinct definition of the language in which the document is written. The DTD then enables a correct and meaningful interpretation of the document.

Actually XML is a subset of a more general language called **standard generalized markup language (SGML).** SGML has been around for some time, but has not caught on as a basis for Web communications because of its complexity. XML is an attempt to bring most of the flexibility and functionality of SGML to the Web without all the complexity.

On the other hand, HTML is just one particular example of a language DTD. This DTD is built into the current generation of browsers, so if we are to interact over the Internet via browsers, we are stuck with this more or less static language with which to do so. While it is true that HTML does evolve over time, the rate of change is slow. Further, each change implemented must then be reflected in new versions of browsers in order to make the changes usable. The process is limited both in terms of the rate of change and the kinds of changes that are allowed.

You can view XML as alphabet for creating new languages which can have features specific to a given problem domain. As a simple example, we might wish to create a language to facilitate the exchange of address information. To do this we could use XML to write a DTD defining new tags like <first_name>, <last_name>, <street>, <city>, <state>, <country>, and <zipcode>. Rules within the given DTD would specify the way such tags could be used—which are optional, which have attributes (and what those attributes can be), and so on—as well as the precise syntax for forming a document employing these tags. Then we could

DISCOVERING MORE

XML

XML is one of the most promising and most exciting developments in the past few years in Web technology. We have given only a brief introduction here concerning its potential impact. Consult the online resource "Exploring XML" to learn more about this technology and see some examples of its use.

distribute a document containing a list of names and addresses marked up in this language along with the DTD. Any application receiving this information would then parse the DTD to gain the requisite knowledge for interpreting the document's data.

Note that XML does not specify how the data will be displayed. The purpose of XML is to facilitate data exchange across the Internet. Layout for display of the data can be specified independently of the data. For example cascading style sheets can be used to specify how a data set would be displayed for a given display environment. Other display options also exist. In today's highly heterogeneous network environment where display devices may differ significantly—from desktop computers to PDAs to "smart" cellular phones—being able to separate the content of a document and display characteristics is essential. XML provides this capability.

Another advantage of XML is that it will enable much more refined and more effective Web searches. Currently, search engines rely mostly on metadata (particularly keywords, document titles, and the like) provided by Web page designers to ascertain what the content of a Web document might be. As you know from your own Web searches, the results returned by these search engines is often unreliable. If you get one "good" document out of ten returned, you are lucky; often the ratio is much worse. Documents marked in XML will provide the basis for the construction of much better search engines. This new generation of search engines will be able to examine the tags defined in a document's DTD to get a much more accurate picture of the document's content. As a consequence, more intelligent search engines will be able to locate documents more relevant for your searches.

The adoption of XML will have a large impact on the way we experience and use the Web. It removes two major obstacles to facilitating the flexible exchange of data that will propel e-commerce over the next decade, namely the excessive complexity of SGML and the inflexibility and other limitations of HTML. User-defined document types will enable many new applications across the Internet. XML will allow the creation and use of a great many special-purpose languages that are customized to particular areas of discourse, businesses, professions, and so on. Such vertical XML vocabularies have already been developed and more are appearing rapidly. XML will do for e-commerce what HTML did for the display of information over the Internet. In other words, what we seen thus far in e-commerce is just the beginning.

■ Summary

Electronic commerce (e-commerce) is rapidly emerging as a central activity for the majority of businesses and institutions. E-commerce centers around three basic information technologies: Web authoring, Web programming, and databases. A Web interface provides customers with an easy to use graphical interface; dynamic information relative to the business is typically stored on the company's databases. The transport between these two elements requires programming in the form of scripts or standalone applications. Some scripts are executed on the client-side, but the majority of script executions is done on the server-side. Client-side scripting is a good model for enabling interactions whose scope is restricted to the display environment, that is, the client environment. Interactions requiring an exchange of information and transmission and display of data residing on the server can better be accomplished using scripts residing on the server to enable the lookup and transmission of the requested data.

Dynamic HTML (DHTML, for short) provides a suite of technologies on the client side. DHTML is a collection of related technologies that provide capabilities for enhancing HTML Web pages. Two primary component technologies of DHTML are cascading style sheets (CSS) and JavaScript programming. There are actually three levels of styles: inline styles, embedded style, and external styles. The order in which the three levels of style sheets are applied gives rise the name *cascading* style sheets. Embedded styles are styles embedded in a document; in-line styles are useful when we want a one-time style change and are inserted at the point they apply; external style sheets are often used to define a set of styles for an entire Web site. This is a good way to ensure consistency across a site.

Scripts can be written in a number of scripting languages. JavaScript is the most popular scripting language for the Web. JavaScript employs an event-driven model. In this model, the user initiates some event and the Web page responds meaningfully to this event. Before scripting, about the only event-reaction we had on the Web was the use of hyperlinks to load pages, resources, and so on. Scripting languages open up a whole world of possibilities for creating interactions beyond this basic beginning.

Scripts are often used in concert with HTML forms. Forms are basically HTML objects that accept user input. This input can take one of several different modes including text entry boxes, radio buttons, check boxes, and popdown menus. There are no built-in features in HTML to actually process the data collected from forms. So, by necessity, users must be able to write their own data processing procedures. These are written using scripts.

Java is an object-oriented programming language with special features that make it particularly appropriate for writing programs that run on the Web. Java is a full-featured programming language and can be used for writing standalone programs. The first major feature that makes Java attractive for Web work is its built-in security safeguards. Secondly, Java is designed to be a cross-platform language. This means that Java programs can be written on one kind of computer and then run on completely different kinds of computers. This is a huge advantage when you're programming for an open, distributed environment like the Web. Applets are small Java programs intended to be run by a Web browser or some other "applet viewer" software. Applets have even stronger security restrictions than standalone Java programs.

Active server pages (ASP) is a Microsoft technology designed to send dynamic content based on a client request. Active server pages are server-side text files that consist of HTML tags and scripts. Although languages like JavaScript can be used for ASP scripting, the Microsoft language VBScript is usually employed. When a client requests an ASP document, the document is parsed by software called a scripting engine. The scripting engine interprets the scripting code as it is encountered, thereby supplying the flexibility needed to return dynamic information.

As the level of sophistication grows in e-commerce applications, deficiencies in current Web technologies, especially in HTML, have become apparent. XML (for extensible markup language) is a more flexible language for information exchange across the Internet. XML is extensible because it is actually a meta-language, which means it allows you to create your own markup language specifications. You do this in XML by writing a document type definition (DTD) that defines the rules of a language. When a document is then constructed in this new language, the DTD is included in the document itself, so the receiver has not only a document to interpret, but also a succinct definition of the language in which the document is written. The DTD then enables a correct and meaningful interpretation of the document. XML does not specify how the data will be displayed. The purpose of XML is to facilitate data exchange across the Internet. Layout for display of the data is then specified independently of the data. In today's highly heterogeneous network environment where display devices may differ significantly—from desktop computers to PDAs to "smart" cellular phones—being able to separate the content of a document and display characteristics is essential. XML provides this capability. The adoption of XML will have a large impact on the way we experience and use the Web by removing obstacles inherent in HTML in order to facilitate the flexible exchange of data that will propel e-commerce over the next decade.

■ Terms

Active server pages (ASP)
applets (Java)
back-end database
bytecode
cascading style sheets (CSS)
client-side scripting
common gateway interface (CGI) script
data binding
data source objects (DSOs)
document type definition (DTD)
dynamic HTML (DHTML)
embedded style sheets

event handlers
event-driven model
extensible markup language (XML)
external style sheets
forms (HTML)
in-line style sheets
interactive Web pages
Java
Java runtime environment (RTE)
Java virtual machine (JVM)
JavaScript
language compiler

machine language
meta-language
object code
rollovers
scripting engines
selector (for cascading style sheets)
server-side scripting
source code
standard generalized markup language (SGML)
style sheets
Web front-end

■ Questions for Review

1. Explain the basic architecture used for e-commerce or e-business applications.

2. What is meant by client-side processing? Server-side processing?

3. Contrast client-side and server-side scripting. What applications would each apply best to?

4. Describe dynamic HTML. Is it a new version of HTML? Explain.

5. Describe cascading style sheets.

6. What are cascading style sheets used for? Why is using style sheets a good design decision?

7. What is the purpose of a selector within style sheets?

8. Contrast embedded styles, in-line styles, and external styles. Explain what each might be most useful for.

9. Compare and contrast the two languages JavaScript and Java.

10. What is meant by an event-driven computing model? What is an event handler?

11. What is the role of an HTML form? Relate forms to scripting.

12. What are common gateway interface (CGI) scripts used for?

13. Explain the concept of data binding in DHTML. Why is it useful?

14. What are data source objects (DSOs) used for?

15. What is an applet? How does it differ from a traditional program?

16. What role do bytecodes play in creating and running Java applets?

17. What is meant when we say that Java has cross-platform capabilities?

18. What is the Java runtime environment? What is its purpose?

19. What does ASP stand for? Explain the concept.

20. Explain why HTML is not sufficient for today's e-commerce applications.

21. What is a DTD (document type definition)?

22. What is XML? How does it help enable better e-commerce applications?

23. How does HTML relate to XML?

24. How will XML enable better Web search engines?

25. What is meant when we say that XML is a meta-language?

Putting Information to Work

Packaging Information: Data Compression and Security

OBJECTIVES

- Basic principles for compressing data

- Compression methods for text and numeric data

- Compression methods for digital images, video, and audio

- Basic elements of cryptography, the art and science of keeping messages secret

- Concepts and use of private and public key data encryption systems

Computer networks provide unparalleled opportunities and conveniences for communication. And, no doubt, the exchange of information and electronic commerce over these networks will continue to increase dramatically over the next decade. Two major issues arise as we increase our dependence on this new mode of communicating a variety of types of information: security and speed of transmission.

In data communications, the capacity of any channel to transmit data is limited. Naturally, the volume of data transmitted determines the total transmission time; this fact can be significant. For example, accessing World Wide Web pages that contain images, sounds, and video clips can place great demands on your patience. Significant time (from several to many minutes) is often required to download such resources even when fast Internet connections are used.

395

Consider data storage, too. The capacities of secondary storage devices have increased, and their prices have fallen over the years. Yet the demands placed on these devices by today's applications have nearly outrun this pace. Ten years ago a desktop system with a 50-MB hard disk was considered top of the line. Today, systems with disks two hundred times that capacity (10 GB) are thought barely adequate!

For these reasons, data compression is often employed to help reduce costs and increase performance of storage and data communications systems. In fact, some applications of multimedia computing would be totally impractical without the use of sophisticated data compression techniques.

The same technology that makes information exchange over networks so convenient also provides access to those whose purposes are less than honorable or whose goals and methods threaten social order and stability. With the increasing access to and ease of transmitting sensitive and confidential information come significant security risks. The science of cryptography focuses on methods for securing data communications.

In this chapter, you will study some of the more common data compression techniques and examine some of their strengths and weaknesses. In addition, you will explore some of the methods of cryptography that are used to make computer networks more secure channels for information interchange.

Data Compression: The Basics

Compressing data means reducing the effective size of a data file for storage or transmission. Because all forms of information are represented digitally and encoded in a binary format, **compression** amounts to replacing the original binary file with another that is smaller. Naturally, the compressed data requires less storage and can be transmitted at a faster rate. The compressed file, however, must be decompressed before it can be used in normal applications. **Decompression** expands the compressed data and reproduces the original data—either exactly or in facsimile. As illustrated in Figure 20.1, compression and decompression methods work in tandem. A pair of such methods is often called a **codec** (for compressor/decompressor).

In general, codecs reduce the redundancy in data. Their effectiveness varies significantly, depending on the amount of redundancy in the original. A file in which symbols occur in nearly random frequencies is difficult to reduce. On the other hand, most information has symbolic representations with repetitious patterns. This makes it susceptible to compression by replacing definable patterns with shorter sequences of symbols.

Most codecs approach this task in a piecewise fashion. In other words, they process the input source by chopping it up into segments of fixed or variable lengths and replace these with shorter segments of either fixed or variable lengths.

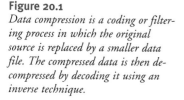

Figure 20.1

Data compression is a coding or filtering process in which the original source is replaced by a smaller data file. The compressed data is then decompressed by decoding it using an inverse technique.

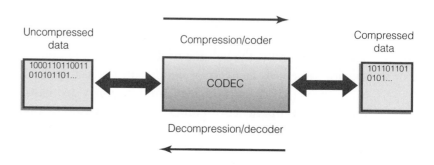

Some codecs do not guarantee the exact reproduction of the original after decompression. These methods are called **lossy.** In contrast, **lossless codecs** always reproduce the original data from its compressed format. The choice of lossless versus lossy techniques depends on the kind of information and its use. Text and numeric data, for example, generally have exacting standards, so lossless compression/decompression is a must. On the other hand, audio and digital images can tolerate some loss of original information because the eye and ear are more forgiving.

Codec speed is another significant factor. The amount of time required to compress and decompress data can be important for some applications. In this regard, codecs may function either symmetrically or asymmetrically. A **symmetric codec** is one that takes approximately the same amount of time to compress data as to decompress it. For instance, video-conferencing is a two-way communication that takes place in real time, so the audio and video should be compressed for transmission and decompressed at about the same rate to be effective. Compression utilities for managing data on your hard disks are usually symmetric, too. In contrast, an **asymmetric codec** technique has simple, fast decompression speed, but compression is usually more complicated and significantly slower. This is acceptable when the data can be compressed once and decompressed often, for example, when storing and accessing audio and video on a CD-ROM or DVD.

Finally, we can distinguish compression/decompression schemes by whether they are based on syntactic, semantic, or hybrid methods. **Syntactic methods** attempt to reduce the redundancy of symbolic patterns without any attention to the type of information represented. Thus, a syntactic approach ignores the source of the information and treats it as a mere stream of symbols. Syntactic compression is also called **entropy encoding.** In contrast, **semantic methods** consider special properties of the type of information represented. This knowledge often helps to transform or reduce the amount of nonessential information in the original. For instance, only sound frequencies at a specific amplitude are required for reproducing a recognizable voice signal. If we know that we are compressing a recorded voice, then signals below that threshold can be ignored with no loss of audible information. **Hybrid methods** combine both syntactic and semantic approaches, although usually in stages. A popular choice is to prepare the data using a semantic method and then reduce it further with entropy encoding.

For practical applications, it makes sense to consider data compression by the category of information being treated. Accordingly, we will divide the territory as before into two areas: discrete data (text and numbers) versus analog data (digital images, audio, and video).

Compressing Text and Numeric Data

Many of the applications we use store data in the form of text and numbers. Text documents, spreadsheets, and databases are often archived on our systems. These data files are typically represented as text. By the same token, millions of bytes of text files are transmitted daily over networks. In addition, binary files representing programs are commonly duplicated, transmitted, and stored on systems. Data and programs are natural candidates for the benefits of compression for transmission and storage. Both data and programs contain precise information that must be restored accurately when decompressed. For this reason, only lossless compression is used for text and binary files.

Several methods are popular for compressing files representing text, numeric data, and programs. These include run-length encoding (RLE), Huffman coding, and Lempel-Ziv Welch (LZW) compression. All are lossless methods that exploit the redundancy of bit patterns in the file.

Run-Length Encoding

A simple and direct form of compression that yields modest savings for most sources is **run-length encoding (RLE).** It is based on the assumption that a great deal of redundancy is present in the repetition of particular sequences of symbols. For example, suppose that we are compressing a text file that contains the following sequence:

ABBCCDDDDDDDDDEEFGGGGG

We could replace some of its redundancy by simply encoding how many times a given symbol is repeated consecutively. If we use one character to represent the symbol, one character—say, "#"—to alert the decoder, and one or two symbols to indicate the frequency, it would cost three to four symbols to encode a repetitive pattern. Consequently, we might replace the previous sequence with this one.

ABBCCD#9EEFG#5

This would net a reduction of around 40 percent or a compression rate of almost 60 percent in this instance. This example uses a variety of symbols. With binary files, there are only two symbols, so the probability for runs is increased. Facsimile, or fax, transmissions use RLE for data reduction. And, because encoding and decoding are both simple and fast, run-length encoding is also favored in many hybrid methods that call for syntactic encoding.

Huffman Codes

Named for its creator, David Huffman, **Huffman coding** is a form of statistical encoding that exploits the overall distribution or frequency of symbols in a source. It produces an optimal coding for a passage based on assigning the fewest number of bits to encode each symbol given the probability of its occurrence. For example, if we know that in English text the letter "e" is more likely to occur than any other, it would make sense to replace it with the smallest sequence of bits possible. This would give us the greatest savings in compression. By the same token, letters that occur rarely, such as "q" or "z," could be encoded by longer sequences. The net effect would be an economical encoding. Huffman coding uses such statistical knowledge to create a unique replacement code for the source text's symbols. With a simple coding table for deciphering, the decompression of Huffman codes is straightforward.

There are a few variations for Huffman coding. **Adaptive Huffman coding** is a popular one. Rather than depending on a static coding table, it builds a table while processing the source. Because this method is self-adjusting, it yields better results, especially when predefined statistics are not available.

LZW Compression

Both RLE and Huffman codes are basically symbol compression schemes. In other words, they are designed around the assumption that the source data is best treated as a sequence of uniform, individual units—characters, bytes, and so on. In contrast, **Lempel-Ziv Welch** compression is an algorithm developed by Lempel and Ziv, and refined by Welch, based

DISCOVERING MORE

LZW

For more details about the LZW method along with some examples of its use, see the online resource "Discovering More About LZW."

on recognizing common string patterns. A string is simply a sequence of symbols. The basic strategy is to replace strings in a file with bit codes rather than replacing individual characters with bit codes. By treating the source as a sequence of strings, reducing redundancy at this level can yield greater compression than other methods. Even better, LZW codecs do not require any predefined knowledge about the source and its symbols. The source is encoded as the codec scans the text, symbol by symbol. This makes for an efficient and robust method. Decompression is just as clever. Unlike Huffman coding, LZW decompressors do not need a table to decipher the compressed file. The text is both coded and decoded on the fly.

LZW codecs surpass Huffman coding in both speed and compression rates. A typical text file is reduced by 50 percent on average using LZW compression. Because it is a lossless syntactic method, it can be applied to a variety of sources. Today, nearly all commercial compression utilities employ some variation of this method. These may be used to conserve space on hard disk archives as well as compress data for transmission over networks.

Compressing Images

In spite of improvements in desktop computing performance, the use of digitized images still presents formidable challenges for most practical applications. The chief obstacle for these applications is the huge amount of data that must be stored and processed to represent these images. A single color image at typical screen resolution, for example, requires roughly a megabyte to represent it; higher resolutions take even more storage. Thus, the widespread use of digital imagery has been hampered by the high costs of storage and transmission.

In recent years, industry standards for image compression have been introduced. These compression technologies have been adopted by most hardware/software vendors and have greatly improved the practicality of using digital images in everyday applications.

Digital images, of course, refer to single frames or still images usually displayed on a video monitor. For the sake of compression, we distinguish such images according to whether they are discrete or continuous-tone images. Specifically, a discrete image is usually a graphic composed of lines and curves, such as line art. Standards for compressing discrete images are based on those used for fax transmission, which uses an RLE method, as described earlier. A continuous-tone image is a complex, bit-mapped image containing numerous shades or tones, such as a digitized photograph. These types of images and graphics are more common, and compressing them is more demanding. Four popular formats for compressing digital images are GIF, PNG, TIFF, and JPEG.

GIF Compression

CompuServe, one of the early commercial online network service providers, introduced the **graphic interchange format (GIF)** as a standard for transferring 8-bit digital images over networked modems. GIF employs a LZW codec for lossless compression. Its basic technique is to look for repeated horizontal patterns along each scan line.

PNG Compression

The **portable network graphic** (**PNG,** pronounced *ping*) format was designed to be a replacement for GIF. PNG is designed as a lossless method for transmitting single bitmap images over computer networks, PNG matches all of GIF's features except one (ability to handle multiple images), improves compression, and adds several new features of its own like the ability to handle true color (48 bits per pixel). The PNG compression algorithm works similarly to the GIF algorithm, in that it looks for repeated horizontal patterns along each scan line. However, the PNG method also searches for vertical patterns, resulting in additional compression.

TIFF Compression

The **tagged image file format (TIFF)** is a general bit-mapped image format developed by Aldus Corporation and widely used by a variety of applications and hardware platforms. It has an optional compressed format that is also based on the LZW method.

Because both GIF and TIFF images use the same basic syntactic technique, we can expect them to offer average compression rates around 50 percent for typical natural scene images. Keep in mind, though, that actual rates will vary with the original image content.

JPEG Compression

JPEG is the acronym for **Joint Photographic Experts Group.** This panel of academic and industry professionals created general-purpose compression standards for still images. The primary intent, of course, was to offer a compression standard that reduced storage significantly while preserving image fidelity. The committee, though, had another agenda that was equally important. The goal also was to create a set of specifications that would work for a wide range of images and applications while preserving enough uniformity that images could be exchanged and processed by different application programs.

JPEG is actually an umbrella term covering several lossy and lossless compression/decompression methods. Most implementations, however, are restricted to the so-called **baseline codec.** This is lossy compression based on a hybrid method. This common denominator technique offers the user a choice of compression rates. Image quality, however, is sacrificed in proportion to the compression rate. As you might guess, greater compression rates mean poorer image quality compared with the original.

The baseline codec can be implemented by either hardware or software with very nearly symmetric performance for compression and decompression. The chief advantage of JPEG compression today, however, is its wide acceptance and support in a variety of applications.

When using JPEG compression, you should keep several issues in mind. JPEG codecs are designed for continuous-tone graphics such as digitized photographs. They do not work well with simple, high-contrast graphics such as line art. JPEG compression can indeed alter the image, but its effects vary, depending on its original content. Experimentation is a must for achieving the best results. Of course, the chief trade-off is image fidelity versus compression rates. The greater the compression, the more pronounced is its lossiness. In general, you should prefer higher-quality compression settings because these yield appreciable size reduction with a minimal loss of data.

DISCOVERING MORE

JPEG

The standard JPEG codec produces lossy compression. This means, of course, that the resulting image is not identical to its original. But what exactly is lost and why is it lost? For more details about how the JPEG method works, consult the online resource "Discovering More About JPEG."

Compressing Video

Compression for still images is certainly desirable, but for video, it is absolutely essential. Digital video exacts enormous demands on system performance and throughput. For example, transmitting standard full-screen color imagery as video at 30 frames per second requires a data rate of nearly 28 MB per second. The bandwidth needed for such a rate goes well beyond practical standards. Indeed, without significant compression ratios, digital video is simply not practical.

One way to reduce the amount of information stored for a video, of course, is to constrain the frame rate itself. Full-motion video requires about thirty frames per second to achieve the illusion of continuous motion. The data rates for sustaining 30 frames per second, however, are huge. Sacrificing some of the quality of the video for lower frame rates can reap dividends for storing and transmitting data. For example, frame rates between ten and fifteen per second are acceptable for some applications. Even at lower frame rates, more compression is possible—and often needed.

Compression methods such as JPEG use spatial compression; they reduce the redundant information contained within a single image or frame. In the context of video, we call this type of compression **intraframe compression.** Although useful for compressing video, it is not sufficient for achieving the kinds of data rates essential for transmitting video in practical applications.

Intraframe compression by itself ignores an enormous amount of the redundancy that occurs in a typical video sequence. Much of the data in video images is repeated frame after frame. Strategies for eliminating the redundancy of information between frames employ temporal compression. These are referred to as **interframe compression** methods. Most codecs approach temporal compression by dividing the video into segments. For example, suppose we extract four successive frames from a video sequence of a moving automobile. The first frame in the sequence is designated the **key frame.** We can use it as the basis for deciding how much motion or how many changes take place in the succeeding frames. The background in our scene, in particular, is unlikely to change much over a short span. (Remember that four frames is only a fraction of a second for most videos.) We can ignore coding any information about the sky, ground, and road in succeeding or **difference frames.** Thus, the amount of information in difference frames is reduced considerably because it is restricted to components that move or change between frames. To decompress or rebuild the sequence, we would use information saved from the key frame to rebuild the missing areas in the difference frames. Figure 20.2 illustrates.

What happens, however, when in the middle of some sequences, a new area is revealed in a frame? For instance, new background is uncovered when a foreground object moves away, or an entirely new region is exposed when a door or window opens. In both cases, the key frame contains entirely different information, and the amount of data needed to capture the succeeding difference frames is large.

One way to solve this problem is to designate this image as a new key frame for the next sequence. We could save the image with the new regions or components and start differenc-

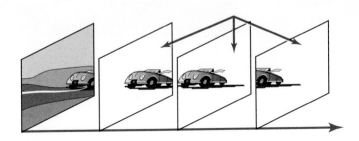

Figure 20.2

Video compression attempts to reduce the amount of information stored and transmitted by eliminating redundant data across a sequence of frames. In the example, the first frame is stored with enough information to reconstruct it independently. This frame— the key frame—has little compression. For the difference frames, we then save only the data depicting change from the key frame.

ing succeeding frames from this point. This is, in fact, how some codecs handle it. However, this method merely postpones the problem and can lead to low or poor compression rates for some videos.

An improvement on this method is to employ methods that predict motion bidirectionally. In other words, some compressed frames are the difference results of predictions based on past frames used as a reference, and others are based on both past and future frames from the sequence. The popular codec MPEG employs this kind of method.

Compressing Audio

Many video compression standards contain audio compression methods as part of their formats. Digital audio data can be equally demanding for transmission and storage. Accordingly, there are several approaches for compressing this form of information, especially when combined with video.

The choice of a sampling rate for audio, like video frame rates, is the first step in handling the problem. Recall that digital sound consists of discrete amplitude samples taken at successive time intervals. The sampling rate refers to the number of intervals per second. High sampling rates mean higher fidelity, but they naturally cost more in storage space and transmission time. CD-quality audio has a sampling rate of 44.1 KHz, that is, over 44,000 samples per second. Many applications do not require this much fidelity. Speech and sound effects are faithfully represented at much lower sampling frequencies. And, of course, lower sampling rates can mean substantial savings in storage.

The sample resolution is significant, too. The number of bits used to quantify the digital audio has an impact on how much room is needed to store it. Of course, sample resolution can also affect the dynamic range for audio playback. Once again, matching the source with the appropriate sample resolution is wise. For example, sound with inherently restricted dynamic range (voice recordings, for example) can be stored more economically by using a lower resolution (perhaps 8-bit as opposed to 16-bit) without any appreciable loss of fidelity.

Fixing the sampling rate and resolution of samples, of course, does not tackle the problem of compressing digital audio after the fact. Audio files must be stored and transmitted for use. Often, these need even more compression to be practical. A popular approach for compressing audio information goes by the daunting name of **adaptive differential pulse code modulation (ADPCM)**. **Pulse code modulation (PCM)** is a basic method for quantizing audio information. Differential PCM compresses the number of bits needed to represent this data by storing the first PCM sample in its entirety and all succeeding samples as differences from the previous one. This works in the audio domain much like frame differencing does in video. Finally, adaptive DPCM takes the scheme one step further. The encoder divides the

DISCOVERING MORE

Video Codecs

A number of video compression methods have been adopted by applications. For more details about these and other video codecs, consult the online resource "Discovering More About Video Codecs."

values of the DPCM samples by an appropriate coefficient to produce a smaller value to store. In playback, the decoder multiplies the compressed data by that coefficient to reproduce the proper differential value. This technique guarantees its compression rate because the signal is encoded into reduced but fixed-length sample sizes. For instance, signals digitized with 16-bit resolution can be compressed to 4 bits per sample. And, as long as the dynamic range and frequency response of the original signal are moderate, decompressed playback is satisfactory. ADPCM works very well with speech, but is less effective for music.

The video codec MPEG employs three levels of audio encoding, layer I, layer II and layer III in increasing order of sound quality and encoding time. Layer III (also known as **MP3**) has recently become very popular on the Internet because of its combination of high quality and high compression ratio. In a standard audio file, there are many frequencies. Some frequencies are redundant because the human ear cannot perceive them. The MP3 algorithm reduces the size of an audio file using a technique called **perceptual audio,** removing the least audible frequencies.

Data Security Through Encryption

It is easy to think of many occasions when we wish to send a message meant for the eyes of the intended recipient only. Indeed, securing channels over which messages are transmitted is a problem that plagued armies, governments, businesses, and individuals long before modern computer networks came on the scene. Whether a message is sent on a piece of paper, over radio waves, through telephone wires, or as bits transmitted over computer networks, the problem is the same: How can we guarantee that no one other than the recipient has access to the message?

Ensuring that messages are secure is quite difficult if the distance between sender and recipient is anything other than trivial. It is better to assume that someone will, in fact, intercept the message but, in turn, guarantee that they won't be able to read and interpret it. **Cryptography** is the art and science of keeping messages secret. **Encryption techniques,** which convert data into a secret code for transmission, are central to the subject.

Using encryption techniques, the original text, or **plaintext,** is converted into a coded equivalent called the *ciphertext* using an encryption algorithm. The **ciphertext** is then transmitted and decoded at the receiving end, reproducing the original plaintext message. The process of retrieving the original message from the ciphertext is called **decryption.** Figure 20.3 illustrates. Encryption/decryption methods are often called **ciphers.**

Cryptography has a long and storied history. Perhaps the first documented use of cryptography is that of nonstandard hieroglyphs in an inscription by an Egyptian scribe around 2000 B.C. Julius Caesar (100–44 B.C.) is credited with inventing a simple (but effective for his day) encryption algorithm for passing messages to his field commanders during military campaigns. The **Caesar cipher,** as the method is called, uses a simple substitution scheme. For

DISCOVERING MORE

Audio Compression

For more on audio compression and MP3, see the online resource "Discovering More About Audio Compression."

Figure 20.3

Ciphers consist of both encryption and decryption methods. The original plaintext message is encrypted to produce ciphertext. The ciphertext is transmitted, then decrypted at the destination to reveal the original plaintext message.

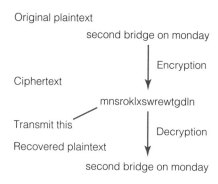

Original plaintext

second bridge on monday

Encryption

Ciphertext

mnsroklxswrewtgdln

Transmit this

Decryption

Recovered plaintext

second bridge on monday

example, suppose each of the letters of the alphabet is replaced by the one that appears three letters later in the alphabet. So "a" is replaced by "d," "b" is replaced by "e," and so on. When the end of the alphabet is reached, you wrap around to the beginning and continue the substitution. So "x" is replaced by "a," "y" by "b," and "z" by "c." Of course, there is nothing special about the number 3 used for the amount of the shift in this scheme, and any number less than or equal to 25 would work just as well. It is customary to ignore spaces and other punctuation characters as well as character case in forming ciphertext.

Ciphers and Keys

The Caesar cipher uses just one (shift and substitute) of many techniques that might be applied to encode a message. To decrypt a message encoded with this method, we need two pieces of information. We must know that the algorithm is based on a shift of the alphabet to the right, and we must know the extent of the shift (three places in this case). We call the parameter 3 a key for the method. A **key** consists of information (usually a numeric parameter or parameters) that allows us to unlock an encrypted message assuming we know the basic algorithm.

Actually, it isn't always necessary to know the algorithm and its key(s) to decrypt a message. Sometimes we can use **brute force methods** to reconstruct a message even if the underlying algorithm and its key(s) remain a mystery. Such methods depend on the examination of a great many cases and were not very effective before the advent of the modern computer. With a fast computer's assistance, however, brute force methods can easily crack many codes that would have been absolutely impenetrable 50 years ago.

In fact, encryption and decryption have been inseparable from computing for many years. Recall that the effort to break the codes produced by the German Enigma encryption machine was the primary motivation for important work done in the development of the modern computer. Modern encryption and decryption methods can be implemented in either hardware or software. Hardware systems are often needed to gain the speeds necessary in environments where large volumes of message transmissions are required. Software provides a convenient flexibility in changing parameters associated with the encryption and decryption processes. As a consequence, many modern encryption and decryption systems are hybrid systems employing both hardware and software components.

Modern encryption algorithms are mathematically based. The plaintext message is first translated to a numeric representation (ASCII or Unicode will do just fine). Then the resulting string of binary digits is usually blocked (64-bit blocks are commonly used) into a sequence of larger numbers. These numbers are then transformed into other numbers by a chosen mathematical procedure that depends on some set of parameters called the **encryption keys.** The coded message is then transmitted. At the receiving end, a second set of parameters, called the **decryption keys,** is used in conjunction with an appropriate "inverse" mathematical procedure to unlock the code, restoring it to its original binary form. Figure 20.4 illustrates the entire procedure.

How then do we keep encrypted messages safe? Potentially, we must guard against three contingencies: the discovery of the encryption algorithm itself, the discovery of the decryption

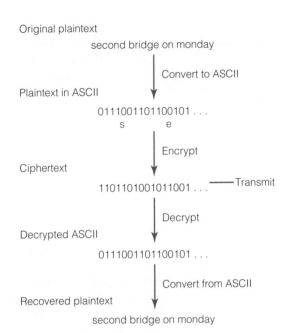

Original plaintext

second bridge on monday

Convert to ASCII ↓

Plaintext in ASCII

0111001101100101 . . .
　　s　　　　e

Encrypt ↓

Ciphertext

1101101001011001 . . . ——— Transmit

Decrypt ↓

Decrypted ASCII

0111001101100101 . . .

Convert from ASCII ↓

Recovered plaintext

second bridge on monday

Figure 20.4
The process for converting a plaintext message to an ASCII string, which can be interpreted as a numeric value, is illustrated. Encryption keys are then used to convert this value to another number representing the ciphertext. The process is reversed with decryption keys at the receiver's end to recover the plaintext message.

keys, and brute force attempts to break the cipher. Interestingly, the mathematical algorithm for transforming the message is often willingly revealed. The reason for this is that we assume that the algorithm will eventually be compromised (human nature being what it is). Hence, we do not want the security of our encryption system to depend in any way on the secrecy of the basic algorithm. In fact, keeping the decryption keys secret (these can even be changed if we suspect a compromise has occurred) is usually our very best protection.

We always have to worry about brute force attacks on the cipher. Guaranteeing a cipher to be safe against all possible brute force attacks is difficult because we cannot anticipate all the different methods that might be used. If we are clever in our choice of algorithm and keys, and if we keep the decryption keys secret, we can make it very unlikely that such an approach will ever succeed. The length (in bits) of the cipher key(s) is one of the most important factors in this effort to thwart brute force attacks on the cipher. Longer keys are harder to discover by brute force, but the down side is that the speed of the encryption/decryption decreases rapidly as the key lengths go up. There is a trade-off in choosing the length of a cipher key: security versus speed. We will have more to say about this issue later.

Symmetric or Secret Key Ciphers

Modern encryption systems can be put into one of two basic categories, depending on how they treat their encryption/decryption keys. **Secret key ciphers** use a single secret key for both encryption and decryption. Such methods are also called **symmetric key ciphers** because the same key is used for both encryption and decryption. The second group of methods is the **asymmetric key,** or **public key, ciphers.** These ciphers use different keys (hence the term *asymmetric*) for encrypting and decrypting messages. The encryption key is made public, and the decryption key is kept secret. We look more closely at each of these two categories of ciphers in turn.

As noted, in secret key ciphers both sender and receiver use the same key to encrypt and decrypt. In applying these methods, it is necessary to transmit the secret key to the recipient—this becomes the chief security risk. This level of security is certainly manageable for diplomatic and military work and in businesses like banking, where the access to secret keys can be restricted to a very small group of individuals. For environments where the need to know keys is more widespread, however, secret key ciphers present a higher level of risk. The secret key method is the one used in traditional ciphers, that is, those invented before the late 1970s.

The length of a key can be a crucial factor in making a cipher robust against brute force attempts to break it. Let's consider some particulars. A secret key cipher with a 32-bit key can be broken by examining 2^{32}, or about 10^9 (one billion), steps—this number represents the number of different 32-bit keys possible. This is something a desktop computer could handle in fairly short order. Notice that the number of cases to be considered increases exponentially with the length of the key. A 40-bit key is more difficult, but it could be broken in a reasonable time with the kinds of computers available in most universities and many companies. A secret key system with a 56-bit key requires a substantial effort to break by brute force, but it can still be managed with special hardware. The expense and time required are nontrivial, but the expense is certainly within the reach of large corporations and most governments, and the time required is not totally prohibitive. Secret key ciphers with 64-bit keys would be difficult, but likely not impossible, to break in reasonable time with today's technology and large resources comparable to those of a major government. An 80-bit key cipher will probably remain unbreakable with reasonable time and effort for the next decade or so, and a 128-bit cipher is unlikely to ever be broken by brute force. The simple reason is that the time required with even the fastest computers imaginable would be eons.

Of course, we must not forget that each time we add bits to the cipher key, we also add to the time required for the encryption/decryption process. For a commercially adopted cipher, potentially millions of messages will be encrypted and decrypted daily. Consequently, adopting keys as large as 128 bits is not necessarily a good thing to do.

Asymmetric or Public Key Ciphers

Public key ciphers have the potential to guarantee a much higher degree of security to their users than secret key ciphers. The big advantage that public key ciphers have is that they are specifically tailored to individuals. A message sender looks up the recipient's public key and uses it to encrypt the message. The ciphertext is transmitted, and the recipient uses his or her private key to decrypt the message. Owners never need to transmit their private keys to anyone to have their messages decrypted; thus, the private keys are never in transit and are therefore less vulnerable. Figure 20.5 shows how this method works.

The idea of a public key cipher was first advanced by Whitfield Diffie and Martin Hellman in a paper published in 1976. Inspired by the Diffie-Hellman paper, three MIT professors, Ronald Rivest, Adi Shamir, and Leonard Adleman, worked out a practical public key system, which came to be known as the **RSA** (for their last names) **algorithm.** Rivest, Shamir, and Adleman gave an overview of their method in the September 1977 issue of *Scientific American.*

RSA was greeted with controversy at its inception. In the *Scientific American* article giving a popular account of RSA, the offer was made to send a full technical report to anyone

Encryption and National Security

The more important, even critical, the exchange of information becomes for individuals, businesses, and governments, the more enticing targets the communications channels used for this exchange become for unfriendly governments, competitors, vandals, terrorists, and organized crime. Thus, encryption becomes an essential component of the new electronic communications paradigm. A central question emerges. Should everyone have equal access to the best (that is, the most secure) encryption techniques known? For a discussion of this much-debated issue, consult the online essay "Encryption and National Security."

submitting a self-addressed, stamped envelope. Thousands of requests poured in from all over the world. Officials at the National Security Agency (NSA) objected to the distribution of this report to foreign nationals, and for a period the mailings were suspended. When the NSA failed to provide an adequate legal basis for such a ban, the mailings were resumed. A little later, Rivest, Shamir, and Adleman applied for and were granted an international patent for their method. They formed a company, RSA Data Security, Inc., which has since developed public key cipher technology on a commercial basis.

The RSA method is mathematically based, and its security depends on the practical difficulty of factoring large integers. The problem of factoring integers is believed to be (although this hasn't actually been proved) impossible to solve with a general method that does not require prohibitively long periods of time for large integers. Hence, the RSA method is believed to be very robust against a direct brute force attack. This security does come at a price, however, because RSA is computationally intense (as are other public key methods). It requires a great deal more time than secret key encryption/decryption.

The key lengths used in public key ciphers are typically much longer than those used in secret key ciphers. Recall that a 128-bit key in a secret key system would guarantee robustness against brute force attacks for the foreseeable future. On the other hand, a 256-bit RSA key could be easily broken. Doubling this to a 512-bit key offers considerably more protection, but a major government could likely break a 512-bit RSA cipher in a reasonable time. For now, 768-bit RSA keys are considered quite safe, and 1024-bit keys are predicted to provide very high security for decades to come.

Often both secret key ciphers and RSA are used together. Secret key ciphers provide the fastest decryption, and RSA provides a convenient and highly secure method for transmitting the secret key. An attractive hybrid method is the following: Encrypt a message using the fast

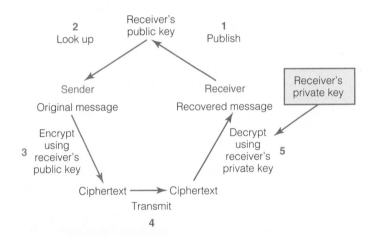

Figure 20.5

The figure illustrates the encryption/decryption process when a public key cipher is employed. Note that private keys are never in transit during the process and so are less vulnerable.

DISCOVERING MORE

RSA

The RSA method is based on mathematics (number theory) and is elegantly simple. Consult the online resource "Discovering More About RSA" to explore the general prin-

ciple first, then look at the mathematical details—which aren't difficult, by the way—and some examples.

secret key algorithm, and employ the public key method to send the necessary secret key safely to the recipient. This combination of the secret key encryption of the plaintext message and the public key encryption of the secret key needed to decrypt the ciphertext is usually called a **digital envelope.**

Authentication and Digital Signatures

Public key ciphers have another important use. They are usually employed to encrypt a plaintext message with the recipient's published public key and send the coded message to the recipient who uses his or her private key to decrypt the message. But the mathematical transformations used in public key methods make it possible for the roles of the keys to be reversed. In other words, you could use your private key to encrypt and someone else could use the public key to decrypt. Why would this ever be useful? Suppose you wish to send a sensitive message to someone, and it is crucial for that person to be sure that the message did indeed come from you. We can easily envision scenarios where assurance of the identity of the source of a message would be absolutely crucial. How would you like someone else sending "buy" and "sell" orders to your broker, for example?

The process used to verify the identity of a respondent is called **authentication.** In other words, you use authentication to make sure that a fellow communicator is who he or she says he or she is. Public key ciphers can be used for this purpose.

■ Summary

Digitizing and distributing images, sounds, and video place tremendous demands on both storage and data transmission capabilities. Even for traditional media like text and numeric data, the times required for transmitting large files over networks can be troublesome and sometimes prohibitive. For these reasons, data compression is often employed to help reduce costs and increase performance of computer storage and data communications systems.

Compressing data means reducing the effective size of a data file for storage or transmission. Decompression techniques are then used to expand the compressed data and reproduce the original data, either exactly or in facsimile. Hence, compression and decompression methods work in tandem. Particular paired compression/decompression methods are called *codecs*. Codecs that cannot guarantee the exact reproduction of the original data after decompression are referred to as *lossy methods*. In contrast, lossless codecs always reproduce the original data from its compressed format. The choice of lossless versus lossy techniques depends on the kind of information and its intended use. When we work with text and numeric data, we generally require exact reproduction; lossless compression/decompression, therefore, is a must for such data. On the other hand, the eye and ear are somewhat forgiving, and so audio and digital images are often processed with lossy codecs that offer better compression rates than lossless methods.

Lossless compression techniques for text and numeric data are based on the assumption that such data contains redundancy in the repetition of particular sequences of symbols. Some of the more

DISCOVERING MORE

Authentication

There are several possible ways authentication might be implemented using RSA. Consult the online resource "Discovering More About Authentication" to explore this topic and see some examples.

popular lossless techniques are run-length coding (used for fax transmissions), Huffman coding, and Lempel-Ziv Welch (LZW) coding. There are a number of compression methods for still images. Four of the most commonly used formats are the GIF, PNG, TIFF, and JPEG.

Video compression schemes employ spatial as well as temporal compression. Spatial compression reduces the amount of information needed to represent a single frame of a video sequence as in still image compression. Temporal compression, on the other hand, eliminates the need to store redundant data from frame to frame throughout the sequence. Most temporal compression is based on identifying key frames in short frame sequences, then storing only differences from the key frame for succeeding frames in the sequence. The various video compression methods employ variations on this basic theme to optimize compression ratios.

A similar approach is used for compressing audio information. Adaptive differential pulse code modulation (ADPCM) compresses the number of bits needed to represent audio data by storing the first sample in its entirety and all succeeding samples as differences from the previous one. The popular MP3 algorithm for music compression reduces the size of an audio file using a technique called perceptual audio, removing the least audible frequencies.

The use of compression schemes is not an exact science. The effectiveness and suitability of any method will vary depending on the exact nature of the original file and the use intended for the decompressed file. Experimentation focused on observing the trade-offs between fidelity of the reproduction and compression rates is a must for achieving the best results.

While computer networks provide unparalleled opportunities and conveniences for communication, the same technology that makes such information exchange possible also provides access to those whose purposes are less than honorable or whose goals and methods threaten social order and stability. With the increasing access to and ease of transmitting sensitive and confidential information come significant security risks.

We rely on encryption techniques, which convert data into a secret code for transmission, to secure network transmissions. Using encryption techniques, the original text, or plaintext, is converted into a coded equivalent called the *ciphertext* using an encryption algorithm. The ciphertext is then transmitted and decoded at the receiving end, reproducing the original plaintext message. The process of retrieving the original message from the ciphertext is called *decryption*. Encryption/decryption methods are often called *ciphers* for short. An encryption key (usually a numeric parameter or parameters) enables the encoding of data; a decryption key consists of information that allows us to unlock encrypted data, assuming we know the basic algorithm.

Secret key ciphers use a single secret key for both encryption and decryption. Such methods are also called symmetric key ciphers because the same key is used for both encryption and decryption. Public key ciphers use different keys (hence the term *asymmetric* is also used) for encrypting and decrypting messages. The encryption key is made public, and the decryption key is kept secret. The RSA algorithm is the most commonly used public key algorithm.

■ Terms

adaptive differential pulse
  code modulation (ADPCM)
adaptive Huffman coding
asymmetric compression/
  decompression
asymmetric key cipher
authentication
baseline codec
brute force methods
  (decryption)
Caesar cipher
cipher
ciphertext
codec (compressor/
  decompressor)
compression, data
cryptography
decompression, data
decryption

difference frame
digital envelope
encryption techniques
graphic interchange format
  (GIF)
Huffman coding
hybrid compression
interframe compression
intraframe compression
Joint Photographic Experts
  Group (JPEG)
key (encryption, decryption)
key frame
Lempel-Ziv Welch
  compression (LZW)
lossless compression
lossy compression
MP3

perceptual audio
plaintext
portable network graphic
  (PNG) format
pulse code modulation (PCM)
public key cipher
RSA algorithm
run-length encoding (RLE)
secret key cipher
semantic compression
symmetric compression/
  decompression
symmetric key cipher
syntactic compression
  (entropy encoding)
tagged image file format
  (TIFF)

■ Questions for Review

1. What is data compression? What are its chief advantages and disadvantages?

2. Compare lossy and lossless data compression.

3. What is a codec?

4. How do syntactic compression methods differ from semantic ones?

5. Distinguish symmetric from asymmetric codecs. What are their practical differences?

6. Digital video codecs often employ temporal or interframe compression. What does this mean?

7. Describe briefly how run-length encoding (RLE) works. What is this compression scheme usually used for?

8. Describe briefly how Huffman coding works. What is this compression scheme usually used for?

9. Describe the LZW compression scheme and what it is used for.

10. How do spatial and temporal compression schemes differ? Explain their roles in video and audio compression.

11. Name several still image compression methods.

12. What is the adaptive differential pulse code modulation method? What is it used for?

13. What is cryptography? Why is it important for data communications systems?

14. Define and explain the roles of plaintext and ciphertext in cryptography.

15. What are keys and what are they used for in encryption/decryption?

16. Describe how secret key (symmetric key) ciphers work.

17. Describe how public key (asymmetric key) ciphers work.

18. Compare the advantages and disadvantages of secret key and public key ciphers.

19. What is the RSA algorithm? When and by whom was it developed? Why is it important?

20. What is the process called *authentication?*

Chapter 21

Emerging Digital Technologies

OBJECTIVES

- Peer-to-peer networking and its implications

- Grid computing and its power to solve large problems

- Wireless communication and computing and its impact

- Internet-on-a-chip technologies and their use

- Nanotechnology and its possibilities

- Data mining and its use

It verges on the foolhardy to presume to predict the future for digital technologies. The rate at which new technologies appear and old technologies are reinvented often seems dizzying. However, while predicting exact developments or the next killer application may be all but impossible, it may be useful to try to discern general directions and trends that seem most likely for the near future. In this chapter, we will examine briefly six emerging digital technologies that have been identified by a number of business and technology seers as likely to have significant impact over the next five years.

The Internet, and more specifically the World Wide Web, took the computing world by storm in the early 1990s and no one has looked back. So, perhaps it is not surprising that four of the six technologies we will focus on involve data communications. The first of these is the use of peer-to-peer networking. Peer-to-peer networking is a strategy that eliminates the middleman (that is, the server) in network communications, allowing peer machines (desktop computers, for instance) to share and exchange information and files

411

directly over a network. A second technology enabled by ubiquitous networks is the use of highly distributed computing, often referred to as *grid computing*. In grid computing, individual networked desktop machines can collaborate on subdivided tasks that are part of a much larger task, bringing to bear the combined computing power of all the machines on one problem.

Another data communications technology that holds great promise is the advent of wireless communications. Wireless communication technology has already revolutionized the telephone industry. Who could have predicted a few years ago the incredible boom in mobile phones—a truly global phenomenon? Wireless communications has just begun, and we should expect to see many new combinations of this technology and computing over the next decade. And the final communications technology that will have pervasive impact is often referred to as "Internet on a chip." Small, low-cost chips will have the necessary Internet connectivity built into them, enabling almost any device (not just computers in the traditional sense) to attach to and communicate over the Internet.

Nanotechnology will soon enable practical manufacturing processes to be conducted on the molecular level. This technology promises to produce very small "machines" that can be programmed to perform a host of heretofore impossible tasks. And finally, the technology of data mining is being developed in response to the sometimes overwhelming amounts of data being collected in a variety of application areas. Data mining involves techniques for searching out patterns and informational content from these large stores of raw data.

In short, the next few years promise to be a fascinating technological journey. In this chapter, you will survey the six technologies mentioned above and explore some of the possible implications they hold for all of us.

Peer-to-Peer Networking

You are probably aware of Napster and the controversy created by the ready access to music it made possible over the Internet. **Napster** is one of the more famous (or infamous), and certainly one of the most discussed examples of the use of **peer-to-peer (P2P) technology.** However, you are probably a user of another P2P technology. America Online's *Instant Messenger* and similar programs use P2P connections to enable a new, more immediate way of exchanging messages. Many people now prefer such instant messaging systems to traditional e-mail because of its real-time rate of responsiveness.

What makes P2P different from more traditional Internet communications? You will recall our earlier discussion of how the Internet utilizes the client-server computing model. In this model, servers are reservoirs of data that client machines access via Web protocols employing Web browsers. This model works very well when you need to access stored information on one or more servers. But there are many communication situations when you are sharing with someone information that resides at your own site, on your own computer. In a client-server world, you would first have to upload such information to a server before the other person could access it through their client machine. Obviously this involves overhead—actually of several kinds. First you have to have access to a server and have privileges to upload information to that server. You then have to perform the log-on process and do the file upload. Finally the other person must use a browser to find the information and have it transferred to their machine.

Peer-to-peer technology has changed all that. P2P uses software to allow Internet users to share files and communicate *directly* over the Internet without the need for intervening servers.

This capability has many uses. Workers, departments, and ad hoc workgroups can use P2P to create shared workspaces. Using these spaces, they can share documents, exchange direct information, create shared databases, and communicate instantaneously. With the advent of global workgroups and teams, this capability is destined to become more and more important for businesses. Consultants to create databases and load data onto expensive servers are eliminated. In the future P2P will surely find use for companies who wish to streamline their communications with customers, suppliers, and business partners.

There are a number of companies now marketing P2P tools. Perhaps the most successful thus far is Groove Networks. **Groove** was founded by Ray Ozzie, who was instrumental in the creation of Lotus Notes e-mail and groupware software. Groove provides small workgroups the ability to share and work on information among themselves or with the participation of bigger audiences. Groove and similar products encourage the flexible and inexpensive creation of ad hoc workgroups. Such workgroups are more and more commonplace in today's business environment where nimble teams consisting of employees, suppliers, contractors, and even customers work together on projects. The pharmaceutical company GlaxoSmithKline has pioneered the use of Groove and holds a 10,000 seat license to the product. One of the many projects being managed through Groove is a complex clinical trials study requiring close working relationships between company employees and outside researchers conducting the trials. Groove allows these workers to share documents, create an electronic trail that tracks the routing of the documents, and conduct online discussions in which they can view and annotate each other's work products. They can be connected for discussions and group work no matter where they are across the globe and all communications are secured by the automatic encryption within Groove.

P2P networking does have its critics. Many cite the skirting of copyright laws enabled by the technology (as was the case with Napster). But there is no doubt that the ease and convenience of peer-to-peer communications will find increasing applications in the business world over the next few years, and some of these applications will create new competitive advantages and capabilities.

Grid Computing

In **grid computing,** the power of thousands of PCs is aggregated to form the equivalent of a supercomputer. A central server manages the distribution of work to the "component" PCs by cleverly dividing the work up into parallel activities. The worker components communicate the results of these parallel computations to the central server and it then compiles a solution to the original problem. Of course, this type of computing is most applicable to large problems. Following are some examples.

The most well-known example of grid computing is the SETI@home project (SETI stands for **S**earch for **E**xtra**t**errestrial **I**ntelligence). In the SETI project, radio telescope arrays

DISCOVERING MORE

P2P

New technologies like P2P evolve rapidly. New companies, products, and applications are appearing regularly. For an update on the current state of P2P technology, consult the online resource "Discovering More About P2P."

search the skies for recognizable patterns of radio signals from outer space. Such patterns would be a signal of extraterrestrial intelligent beings. This task involves examining very large amounts of data and trying to filter recognizable patterns from the natural background noise inherent in radio telescope observations. Supercomputing power is required to make a dent in this work.

In the **SETI@home project,** millions of persons have volunteered their home computers to aid in this task. They have donwnloaded the SETI@home screensaver which sets in motion background processing whenever the machines go idle. A program within the screensaver gets data from the SETI@home project, performs some calculations on this data, then sends the data back to the SETI@home research center at the University of California at Berkeley. To date, a total of more than 3 million users have devoted almost a million years of processor time to this task! And none of these volunteers sacrifices any of their own actual computing time in this process.

In another project, a similar screensaver method is being used to search for a cancer cure. Sponsored by Intel, Oxford University, the National Foundation for Cancer Research, and the company United Devices, this project is focused on testing which of 3.5 billion molecules are best shaped to bind with one of a small number of proteins that certain cancers need to grow. Identification of such binding molecules will help researchers develop effective cancer treatments. In another project, run by the Stanford University chemistry department, about 20,000 distributed computers are being used to perform molecular dynamics simulations to hopefully help make discoveries that will aid in the understanding and treatment of Alzheimer's disease.

The *distributed.net* project has decrypted messages using brute force methods implemented using distributed computers. Using this process, the project is able to try more than 100 billion decryption keys per second! The Great Internet Mersenne Prime Search (GIMPS) project has been operating since 1996. So far five extremely large Mersenne primes have been found. A Mersenne prime is a prime number in the form of $2^p - 1$ where p itself is a prime number. The fifth and largest of these so far was discovered in late 2001 and would take more than four million digits to write out! By the way, this was the 39th Mersenne prime ever discovered. To add a little excitement to this project, the 38th Mersenne prime discovered (2 million digits) won its discoverer a $50,000 prize for being the first prime discovered with more than 1 million digits. A $100,000 prize is offered to the discoverer of the first prime with more than 10 million digits.

What are the implications of grid computing for business? Particularly, why would you choose to use a grid computing solution instead of your own supercomputer? The answer is simple. Supercomputers are very expensive to purchase and maintain. Unless your business or

DISCOVERING MORE

Grid Computing

For updates and more information on the grid computing projects described here as well as the future possibilities of globally grid computing, see the online resource "Discovering More About Grid Computing."

research calls for constant use of such a resource, it is hard to justify these costs. Even if you have needs for such a resource a large part of time, you may not be able to afford it. Grid computing offers a low-cost alternative. Not only could businesses purchase grid computing on an as-needed basis at a small fraction of the cost of a supercomputer, but they could even earn income by renting time on their own computers to others.

What would be required to make all this practical, convenient, and economical? Researchers are working on an **Internet-scale operating system** (**ISOS**) to provide the necessary low-level services to link the processing and storage capacities of independent Internet-connected computers. Recall that the primary advantage of an operating system is that it creates a virtual machine with certain apparently inherent capabilities. These ready-made capabilities and a tailored interface insulate the user from the underlying complexities and tedium involved with working with the computer hardware directly. An ISOS would provide a global virtual machine that performs the same insulating function. An ISOS would pave the way for the development of new distributed applications programs in the same way desktop operating systems ease and enable the task of program development for the desktop.

However, the challenges in creating such an operating system are daunting. The resource pool that such an operating system would be designed to manage is very heterogeneous. The various computers connected to the Internet have many different processor types, speeds, connection bandwidths, and local operating systems. They also have varying amounts of memory, secondary storage devices, and capacities. Some of these computers are located behind firewalls, designed to make access to their resources more difficult for hackers and other unauthorized users. And most are available sporadically and for unpredictable lengths of time.

In addition to these technical issues, the successful development of an Internet-scale operating system will have political and economic issues to confront. An ISOS must be unobtrusive in the sense that the owners of the host computers should not notice the background work of such a system. The ISOS would need to have very minimal impact on non-ISOS processes or else owners of the distributed hosts would be antagonized and remove their machines from the resource pool. In addition, the ISOS must be very secure. Before persons will commit their PCs to such an enterprise, they must be assured that their own resources are secured. Finally, to entice participation, some form of compensation (rent, if you like) would need to be worked out for host computer owners. The economic model would also need to track use of the global resource by individual users and charge them accordingly.

Although there are obstacles, progress is being made. The number of successful grid computing projects is growing, and the economic potential for this technology is substantial. The Internet remains a vast and untapped resource, and it continues to grow exponentially. An Internet-scale operating system would enable uses of this global resource previously unimagined. Expect to hear more about these fascinating possibilities in the future.

Wireless Communication and Computing

Many observers believe that **wireless communications and computing** will change business more than anything since the Internet. We're all aware of the ubiquitous and pervasive impact that cellular phones have had. Soon wireless Internet connections will become just as ubiquitous, with many workers accessing the Internet through the use of cell phones, personal digital assistants (PDAs), and wireless laptops. Distributed and on-the-go sales forces will utilize immediate real-time access to product lists, prices, inventories, customer account data, and other relevant information. Sales can be finalized and delivery information accessed and confirmed on the spot. "E-mail everywhere, anytime" will enable almost unlimited corporate connectedness. Wireless technologies combined with peer-to-peer networking will provide a particularly powerful paradigm. Distributed teams will work seamlessly, securely, and in real-time collaboration, independent of their locations and travel restrictions. Troubleshooting processes and products will be done on-site and in real-time, drawing in the appropriate human resources as needed no matter where they are located.

On a smaller scale, technologies like the **Bluetooth protocol** (an example of what we introduced in Chapter 17 as **personal-area networks** or **PANs**) will allow short-range (in the 10-meter range) wireless communication based on radio technology. Under this protocol, devices have a unique 48-bit address and can transmit data at one megabit per second. With this capability, you can envision devices and appliances in a home or office "talking to another," sensing and responding to inhabitants. For example, if you are wearing a Bluetooth-capable badge or carrying a Bluetooth-enabled card, configured devices could sense your presence and offer services accordingly (adjusting the temperature and/or lighting to your desired level, turning on a radio or television, etc.). "Wearable computers" including smart clothing with embedded sensors connecting to computing and communication devices will emerge. These kinds of capabilities will open up whole new markets for such devices.

Bluetooth and other wireless PAN protocols provide relatively low bandwidth short-range networks. However, a new short-range wireless technology known as **ultrawideband (UWB)** will greatly expand the bandwidth possible in short-range wireless communications. These devices are based on semiconductor technology as opposed to more traditional radio frequency technology. Rather than employing a carrier signal, UWB operates with a series of intermittent pulses. By varying the amplitude, polarity, and other characteristics of the pulses, information can be encoded. The pulses are of very short duration and employ very low power levels. For example, the average radiated power from a UWB transmitter is on the order of that emitted by ordinary household appliances. Current semiconductor based UWB devices deliver data transmission rates in the 100 to 500 megabits per second range over distance up to 10 meters.

UWB devices will also offer superior performance in concentrating high bit transfer rates in small physical areas—a capability called **spatial capacity.** Spatial capacity will be a very important factor in handling wireless data transfer in areas where significant numbers of people gather in relatively small spaces like airports and convention centers.

UWB technology may have significant noncommunication advantages as well. The sharply focused pulses used in implementing UWB will allow UWB wireless devices to discern buried objects and objects behind obstacles. Such capabilities may find significant application in search and rescue missions and in law enforcement activities. These focused pulses could also be used to accurately triangulate locations and sense presence of UWB transmitters. For example, several UWB wireless receivers could be used to locate goods that have been tagged with transmitters, to track inventories, or monitor high-value items in retail outlets. Or, UWB receivers could be installed in smart door locks to allow these devices to sense the approach of an authorized user (i.e., a user with an appropriate UWB transmitter).

On the larger scale, within the next few years we will see third generation (3G) wireless services appear, including high-bandwidth Internet access enabling wireless multimedia

DISCOVERING MORE

Wireless Technologies

Like all the technologies we are discussing in this chapter, the rate of change in the adoption of new wireless technologies is rapid. For an update on wireless technology and the issues surrounding its adoption, consult the online resource "Discovering More About Wireless Communication and Computing."

communications like streaming audio and video. Once this happens, we are likely to see explosive growth in the use of wireless technologies.

Internet on a Chip

In the past, connecting a device to the Internet has required some kind of connected processing element like a desktop or laptop computer, a PDA, or a smart cell phone. This will likely change in the near future. It is now possible to build the communication protocols of the Internet directly into low-cost chips. These chips might then reside in appliances, environmental monitoring devices, universal product codes, badges, cards, and so on. This is often referred to as **Internet on a chip technology.** Devices equipped with these so-called **net-ready chips** will have the capacity to send and receive information over the Internet.

It is not hard to imagine many possible applications of such a technology. Additional ones we can't imagine are no doubt just over the horizon, too. On the domestic front, you could turn the heat up and start the coffee brewing from your cell phone as you start home. On the commercial front, combining net-ready chips with wireless communication provides **radio frequency identification (RFID)** tags. These small and inexpensive tags can be placed on virtually any object to track its location and monitor its environment. So you could also use the cell phone to check your warehouse inventory and make sure that environment-sensitive items are in their proper environment. Net-ready devices can broadcast via wireless links a variety of information about themselves (and their environment).

With increasing focus on streamlining supply chains in the business world, RFID has tremendous potential. Accurate monitoring of inventory is a difficult process for large companies. RFID methods are more accurate and can provide much more information than can be achieved employing human information gatherers. RFID inventory control can deliver accurate and timely (real-time if needed) reports, help control theft, and track products in transit from factory to warehouse or from warehouse (or factory) to the customer.

Environmental sensors operating with this same technology are already providing valuable data in a number of application areas. Sensors that can measure and transmit moisture content in the soil can direct computer-controlled focused irrigation systems to deliver water only where it is needed and not waste water on locations already containing sufficient moisture. Similar systems can be integrated with automatic fertilizer spreaders to deliver appropriate mixes of fertilizer to different parts of a plot. Water quality in reservoirs or other watershed sources can be monitored similarly.

DISCOVERING MORE

Internet-on-a-Chip-Technology

The number of applications for net-ready chips grows rapidly. For more information and an update on applications of this technology, consult the online resource "Discovering More About Net-Ready Chips."

Nanotechnology

The science and its applications referred to as **nanotechnology** focuses on the manufacture of extremely small "machines" and products. The scale of nanotechnology artifacts is on the molecular level. These infinitesimal devices can be designed to be programmable so that they can be applied to a number of different circumstances and objectives.

Some of the short-term uses for this technology will focus on the fabrication of materials. One such effort centers on the use of cylindrical molecules, called *nanotubes,* that can be used to fabricate lightweight but very strong materials. These materials are up to 100 times stronger than steel and can withstand temperatures of well over 5,000 degrees Fahrenheit. It is predicted that these materials will be used in building everything from automobiles to skyscrapers.

From this very practical beginning, nanotechnology promises to branch out into many other areas. For example, nanotechnology will be applied to the information technology area in the construction of extremely small memory devices and processors. Some have predicted a future where miniature machines inside our bodies search out cancer cells and kill them, or where devices can spread into an oil spill and gobble up oil.

Combining nanotechnology with the technologies of Internet on a chip and wireless communciations, we might see the creation of "smart" **nanodust** consisting of tiny programmable devices that act as environmental or biological sensors. Employing a form of peer-to-peer technology, these nanodust devices might even communicate with each other as they go about their business. For example, nanodust particles might be sprinkled about to provide an invisible defensive or security shield to sense and warn when an intruder enters an area. Or such particles might be disbursed into the atmosphere and employed in weather forecasting by sensing and reporting minute changes in meteorological parameters. You can no doubt think of other uses; the possibilities go on and on.

As the rapid reduction in size of computing components moves toward chip features smaller than 100 nanometers, the manufacturing process approaches the quantum physics domain. Researchers have some apprehensions about entering this unintuitive domain, but at the same time, some see unique opportunities to exploit quantum idiosyncrasies to improve existing information technologies. One promising development centers on the quantum property of an electron known as its spin. Computing hardware technologies heretofore have relied on devices that hold charge, beginning with vacuum tubes through today's microchips containing millions of transistors. These conventional electronic devices move electric charges (i.e., electrons) in order to carry out their tasks, but ignore the spin that these electrons carry. In the future, devices may rely on electron spin to perform their functions. This new technology is referred to as **spintronics** (as opposed to electronics). While still in its early stages of

DISCOVERING MORE

Nanotechnology

For an update on developments in nanotechnologies in general and nanocomputing in particular, consult the online resource "Discovering More About Nanocomputing."

development, there are already some promising results. In the next few years a new kind of computer memory, **magnetic random-access memory (MRAM)** will be on the market. MRAM is based on spintronics and offers some distinct advantages over traditional RAM. MRAM would retain its state even when power is turned off (so in this way acting like secondary memory), but will have transfer rates and rewritability speeds approaching conventional RAM. In other words, we may get the best of both worlds with MRAM. Some are predicting a multibillion dollar spintronics industry within the next decade. Stay tuned.

Data Mining

One of the things we hear often today is that we are overloaded with information, and few of us would deny this. This *information-overload* is often better characterized as *data-overload*, because data is not information. For data to be turned into information, it must be organized, summarized, analyzed, and often synthesized. What we need are ways to transform data into actionable information. **Data mining** is a name given to a area of research focused on doing just this. The methods and techniques of data mining are designed to extract meaningful information from mountains of raw data. There are many approaches to this task, but one of the primary strategies involves extracting patterns from data.

Pattern matching and extraction have been studied for years within the field called **artificial intelligence (AI).** Part of the agenda for AI is to devise programs that mimic some of the higher-level cognitive abilities of humans. Two of the tasks our brains excel at are pattern matching and pattern extraction. These capabilities are what we call on to immediately recognize the face of a friend in a crowd or to pick out a recognizable object in a fuzzy photograph or sketchy drawing. Data mining employs some of the classical pattern searching strategies developed by AI researchers. It also extends these strategies and involves the creation of new ones as well.

Data mining has many potentially important applications. For example, two very diverse areas where data mining promises important rewards are bioinformatics and marketing. **Bioinformatics** is an emerging field at the intersection of biology and computer science. Its main goals are defined and driven by the U.S. sponsored **human genome project.** The goal of the human genome project is to map the entire genetic code of humans. Advances in biochemistry have provided the tools for doing this. Armed with the genetic code, scientists and medical researchers should be able to offer prevention and craft cures for a great many diseases. They should even be able to tailor medications to an individual patient's genetic characteristics. Genetic research and application of information gathered in the human genome project will be one of the most significant and meaningful science advances ever. The potential positive impact on the health and well-being of human beings is almost incalculable.

Bioinformatics and Bioethics

As noted, the human genome project holds incredible potential for improving the health and well-being of humans. However, as with most science and technology, there are applications of this knowledge that may lead us into ethical dilemmas. Such issues as cloning and stem cell research on embryos are just two examples. For a discussion of some of the major ethical issues arising from the use of the information extracted from the human genome project and bioinformatics, consult the online essay "Bioinformatics and Bioethics."

SOCIAL THEMES

The good news is that the human genome project's mapping of the human genetic code is all but complete. The bad news is that the amount of data that the project has produced is truly overwhelming. Figure 21.1 illustrates. It will take many years for researchers to sort through the data and extract the kind of meaningful information that will lead them to disease prevention and cure. That's where bioinformatics comes in. Its main agenda is to

Figure 21.1

The graph illustrates the explosive growth in data collection within the human genome project. This rate of data collection has far outpaced our ability to analyze the data. Better data mining techniques may provide a solution.

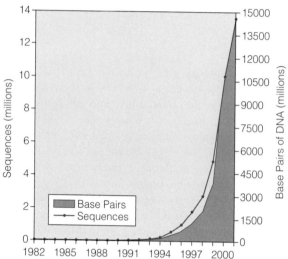

DISCOVERING MORE

Data Mining

For more information about the field of data mining, including its methods and some additional examples of its appli-cations, consult the online resource "Discovering More About Data Mining."

Internet Data Mining and Privacy

As we mentioned earlier, many companies are collecting data about customer's Internet be-havior (which sites do they visit, where do they buy products, etc) implicitly without the cus-tomer's active participation. There are many who believe that this raises some serious pri-vacy considerations. For a discussion of some of the basic issues, consult the online essay "Internet Data Mining and Privacy."

SOCIAL THEMES

devise effective and efficient ways to extract information from the vast reservoir of genetic data produced by the human genome project. As you might surmise, the tools and techniques of data mining will be a crucial part of this exciting new discipline.

Data mining also has direct applications in the business world. Businesses collect data from their customers and would like to use that data to craft marketing strategies that focus on services and products that particular customers would likely respond to favorably. Companies who do business on the Internet are especially interested in the collection of data from those who visit their Web sites and, of course, those who purchase products or services. Some of this data can even be collected implicitly without the customer's active participation.

One interesting example of an application of data mining on the Internet involves trying to mine information from Internet "buzz." The company Opion, headquartered in Herndon, Virginia, has used mathematical modeling to develop proprietary software that monitors the opinions expressed on Internet message boards on a host of issues. All of the millions of Internet users amassed in Opion's database are anonymous, known only by a number and a ranking signifying their relative influence (computed by the Opion software). Financial sector market predictions have been an early test ground for this **buzz tracking software.** Opion's data mining software tracks a given stock or sector, gauges what nonprofessional investors are thinking, and uses this data along with baseline market data to make predictions. These predictions are improved as more data is collected and further improvements are based on the correlations between past buzz and stock behavior. Opion's software uses a traffic analysis approach similar to that employed by the national intelligence agencies, attaching weight (and eventually rank of importance) to a person's opinions based on the number and order of citations that the person receives. Branching out into the movie industry, Opion is now building buzz trackers for three major studios to help them analyze the relationships among advertising, buzz, and box-office performance, with the goal of better directing their advertising dollars.

A Glimpse Further Down the Road

Computing hardware advances continue at a pace close to that predicted by **Moore's law,** which states that performance will double approximately every 2 years. The number of transistors per chip currently doubles every 18 to 24 months, which means that processor performance advances along a similar exponential growth curve. Experts predict this to continue for at least another decade. In the year 2000, processor clock speeds of 1 gigahertz (a billion cycles per second) were common, providing performance at the 1,000 MIPS (million instructions per second) level. By year 2010, it is expected that 10 gigahertz speeds will be common, enabling up to 100,000 MIPS. Industry experts estimate that a minimum feature size of approximately 70 nanometers will also be achieved by 2010.

Consider the following comparison to get a sense of what these growth rates mean in practice. Fifteen years ago, a Cray supercomputer had a gigabyte of RAM, could muster a peak 1,300 MIPS, weighed more than a Cadillac sedan, and cost $14 million. Today, you'd expect the same performance from a laptop computer weighing under 5 pounds and costing under $2,500!

What will all this mean to the users of this technology over the next decade and beyond? Specifics are impossible to predict, but we will offer some general predictions. These are necessarily vague, but nonetheless indicative of the significant changes we can expect to see.

- Moore's law will hold and exponential increases in computer performance will be the norm

- Similar exponential growth will take place in bandwidth

- Inexpensive communication and computing devices will mean large user populations

■ A large fraction, although likely less than 50%, of the world's population will be connected via computer/communication networks

■ High-bandwidth wireless computing devices will be pervasive

■ Bio-sensors will be very commonplace improving our abilities to monitor, predict, and manage environmental parameters

■ Computing devices will become less noticeable but much more pervasive as net-ready chips and similar technologies gain ground

■ Information appliances will have more natural and intuitive interfaces, making them accessible to larger user groups

■ Society will be increasingly knowledge-driven, with increasingly easy access to larger and larger data sources and better data mining techniques to make it easier to extract actionable information from such data stores

■ Summary

Communications and computing technologies will continue their phenomenal and explosive development for years to come. In the next 5 years, peer-to-peer technology will make it increasingly easy and convenient for Internet users to share files and communicate *directly* without the need for intervening servers. Grid computing will aggregate the power of thousands of PCs to provide many users with the equivalent of a supercomputer on an as-needed basis. Internet-scale operating systems will begin to emerge to make this more manageable. Wireless Internet connections will become ubiquitous, with many workers accessing the Internet through the use of cell phones, personal digital assistants (PDAs), and wireless laptops. Wireless technologies combined with peer-to-peer networking will provide a particularly powerful paradigm. Distributed teams will work seamlessly, securely, and in real-time collaboration, independent of their locations and travel restrictions. Personal-area networks (PANs) and ultra-wideband (UWB) technologies will enable many new applications based on short-range (in the 10-meter range) wireless communication.

Devices equipped with net-ready chips will have the capacity to send and receive information over the Internet without accompanying computing intermediaries. Combining this capability with nanotechnology will allow very small but smart devices to perform a host of important functions from medicine to monitoring and managing water supplies to providing security systems. The methods and techniques of data mining will allow us to extract meaningful information from mountains of raw data. This capacity will lead to some amazing progress in disease prevention and cures through bioinformatics and will also become a competitive advantage in marketing strategies for many businesses.

Developments beyond 5 years are harder to predict, but most experts expect the phenomenal growth in computer processing power and bandwidth to continue. This will make it easier for more persons across the globe to get connected via the Internet. Ready access to data, and, more importantly, to information, will make society more knowledge-driven than ever before.

■ Terms

artificial intelligence	Internet-scale operating system (ISOS)	personal-area network (PANs)
bioinformatics		radio frequency identification (RFID) tag
Bluetooth protocol	magnetic random access memory (MRAM)	SETI@home project
buzz tracking software	Moore's law	spatial capacity (of a network)
data mining	nanodust	spintronics
grid computing	nanotechnology	ultrawideband (UWB) communication
Groove	Napster	
human genome project	net-ready chip	wireless communications and computing
Instant Messenger (AOL)	peer-to-peer technology (P2P)	
Internet-on-a-chip technologies		

■ Questions for Review

1. What is peer-to-peer networking? How does it relate to the client-server computing model?

2. Give some examples of the use of peer-to-peer networking.

3. Describe grid computing.

4. Give some examples of grid computing projects.

5. What is the function of an Internet-scale operating system (ISOS)?

6. What are some technical obstacles for the development of an ISOS? Other obstacles?

7. What is a personal-area network? How is the term *Bluetooth protocol* related?

8. Describe the technology known as *ultra-wideband* (UWB).

9. What is meant by the phrase *Internet on a chip*? Why is it important?

10. Explain what nanodust is and give some examples of what it might be used for.

11. What is spintronics? How does it differ from electronics?

12. Describe data mining. Why is it an important area?

13. What is bioinformatics? How does it relate to the human genome project?

14. What does Moore's law say? Why is it important for future developments in computing?

15. What are bio-sensors? Relate them to some of the digital technologies discussed in the chapter.

Credits

This page constitutes an extension of the copyright page. We have made every effort to trace the ownership of all copyrighted material and to secure permission from copyright holders. In the event of any question arising as to the use of any material, we will be pleased to make the necessary corrections in future printings. Thanks are due to the following authors, publishers, and agents for permission to use the material indicated.

All products used herein are used for identification purpose only and may be trademarks or registered trademarks of their respective owners, including the following: ® Access, Adobe, Adobe Illustrator, Altavista, Apple Computer, Bernoulli, Casio, ColorBytes, Cray, Digital Stock, Filemaker Pro, Iomega, Macromedia, Microsoft, Microsoft Explorer, Netscape, PhotoDisc, Quark, Silicon Graphics, Strata Videoshop, UNIX, Yahoo!

Chapter 1: 6: Lucent Technologies, Bell Labs Innovations; **6:** Courtesy of the Service-Public, Française; **10:** Courtesy of the University of Michigan, Virtual Reality Laboratory.

Chapter 5: 79: Brother Industries, Ltd.

Chapter 2: 32: © 1996 PhotoDisc, Inc., **33:** © 1996 PhotoDisc, Inc.

Chapter 8: 141: (left) Reprinted by permission of the Learning Company; (right) Corel Corporation; **142:** Author's collection,

143: (both) Author's collection; **144:** Reprinted by permission of the Learning Company; **146:** PhotoDisc, Inc.; **149:** Author's collection; **152, 154:** Adobe Photoshop; **158:** Reprinted by permission of the Learning Company; **161:** Digital Stock; **161:** PhotoDisc, Inc.; **162:** (top and bottom) PhotoDisc, Inc.; **163:** PhotoDisc, Inc.; **165:** Reprinted with permission of PhotoSphere Images, Ltd.

Chapter 9: 170: Courtesy of Virginia Tech University; **185:** Adobe and Adobe Illustrator are trademarks of Adobe Systems, Inc.

Chapter 11: 229: National Museum of American History, The Information Age, Smithsonian Institution; **230:** Courtesy of the University of Pennsylvania Library; **232:** Courtesy of Cambridge University; **238:** (bottom) Digital Equipment Corporation; **238:** Courtesy of IBM Archives; **239:** Courtesy of AMD; **241:** Courtesy of Silicon Graphics.

Chapter 12: 245: Courtesy of Kingston Technology; **255:** Courtesy of Western Digital, Inc. Used by permission; **259:** Author's collection.

Chapter 13: 268: Courtesy of Apple Computer; **269:** Courtesy of Hewlett Packard; **272, 275:** Courtesy of Sony Corporation of America; **281:** Courtesy of Lynn Products, Inc.

Index